Praise for Gary Gruber

"Dr. Gruber is recognized as the leading expert on stand▮   have been lauded throughout the country. His personal presen▮   s enthusiasm' like an epidemic with his audiences."

—*PBS*

"[When you want the solution to the problem] tap the super genius, Gary Gruber."

—*Washington Post*

"His methods make the questions seem amazingly simple to solve."

—*Library Journal*

"I thank you and my 15-year old son (high school jr.) thanks you."

—Ted Koppel, ABC News, *Nightline*

"The work that Gary Gruber does should be given to every student and every teacher."
—Dr. Shirley Thornton, Former Deputy Superintendent, California State Department of Education

"By learning Dr. Gruber's strategies, a student can increase his(her) IQ to do well on any exam."

—*Teen Magazine*

"Gruber is the Dear Abby of testing."

—*Detroit News*

"I hope Dr. Gruber's work reaches many more students. I know that they will find his suggestions priceless."

—Julie Martin, *Phoenix Gazette*

"[The Gruber book] is the only commercial book that I've seen that would actually help a test-taker."

—David Owen, *Washington Post*

"With the use of Gruber's special techniques, students can raise their test scores significantly and increase their general learning ability."

—*Courier Journal*

"Gruber clearly demonstrates his concepts in this valuable resource for students facing the SAT or any standardized test."

—James Scholtz, *Booklist*

"Gary Gruber is the Guru of College Testing Programs."

—*The Light*, San Antonio, Texas

"This [Gruber] is the man who knows the ins and outs of testing."

—Bob Lee, *Bob Lee Magazine*,
KSL Radio, Salt Lake City, Utah

"I was glad to see the focus . . . is on developing critical thinking skills, which are helpful in all walks of life, not just for taking tests."

—Alan Ginsburg, Acting Director,
Planning and Evaluation Service,
US. Dept. of Education, Washington, DC

GRUBER'S COMPLETE ACT

GUIDE 2019-2020

8th
Edition

Also Available from Gary Gruber and Skyhorse Publishing

Gruber's Complete SAT Guide 2019-2020
Gruber's Complete GRE Guide 2019-2020
Gruber's Essential Guide to Test Taking: Grades 3-5
Gruber's Essential Guide to Test Taking: Grades 6-9
Gruber's Word Master for Standardized Tests

GRUBER'S COMPLETE ACT® GUIDE 2019-2020

8th Edition

Gary R. Gruber, Ph.D.

Skyhorse Publishing, Inc.

Copyright © 2019 by Gary R. Gruber

All Rights Reserved. No part of this book may be reproduced in any manner without the express written consent of the publisher, except in the case of brief excerpts in critical reviews or articles. All inquiries should be addressed to Skyhorse Publishing, 306 West 37th Street, 11th Floor, New York, NY 10018.

ACT® is a trademark registered by ACT, Inc., which is not affiliated with, and does not endorse, this product.

Skyhorse Publishing books may be purchased in bulk at special discounts for sales promotion, corporate gifts, fund-raising, or educational purposes. Special editions can also be created to specifications. For details, contact the Special Sales Department, Skyhorse Publishing, 306 West 37th Street, 11th Floor, New York, NY 10018 or info@ skyhorsepublishing.com.

Skyhorse® and Skyhorse Publishing® are registered trademarks of Skyhorse Publishing, Inc.®, a Delaware corporation.

Visit our website at www.skyhorsepublishing.com.

10 9 8 7 6 5 4 3 2 1

Library of Congress Cataloging-in-Publication Data is available on file.

Cover design by Daniel Brount

Print ISBN: 978-1-5107-5420-1
Ebook ISBN: 978-1-5107-5421-8

Printed in the United States of America

To the millions of students who have successfully used my books to markedly increase their scores and get into the college of their choice.

And to all of the students who seek to achieve and excel in both school and life, and to the parents and teachers who encourage their children in the path of curiosity, critical thinking, and joyful passion for life and learning.

Gary R. Gruber, Ph.D.

Contents

ACKNOWLEDGMENTS

The author gratefully acknowledges sources for reading and English passages quoted or adapted within. All original sources have been attributed wherever determinable. Readers who identify additional sources are invited to contact the publisher at the address below so that additional sources may be acknowledged in future printings:

Skyhorse Publishing, Inc.
306 W. 37th St., #11
New York, NY 10018

The following passages are reprinted with permission:

Pages 97–98: Arthur Whimbey, "Teaching Sequential Thought: The Cognitive-Skills Approach." *The Phi Delta Kappan* 59, no. 4 (December 1977), pp 255–259. Reprinted with permission of Phi Delta Kappa International, www.pdkintl.org. All rights reserved.

Page 110: Milton Lomask, "When Congress Tried to Rule." *American Heritage* 11, no. 1 (December 1959). Reprinted by permission.

Page 423: Christopher Lehmann-Haupt, "Books of the Times." *The New York Times*, May 29, 1974. Reprinted by permission.

Page 606: Food web for the temperate deciduous forest, Parenting the Next Generation, available at http://www.vtaide.com/png/index.htm. Courtesy of Alan S. L. Wong.

Introduction

IMPORTANT NOTE ABOUT THIS BOOK AND ITS AUTHOR

This book is the most up-to-date and complete guide to the current ACT. Every exam is patterned after the ACT, and *all* the strategies and techniques deal with the ACT. The ACT incorporates all the Gruber Critical-Thinking Strategies.

This book was written by Dr. Gary Gruber, the leading authority on testing and test preparation, who knows more than anyone else in the test-prep market exactly what is being tested in standardized tests such as the ACT. In fact, the procedures to answer the ACT questions rely more heavily on the Gruber Critical-Thinking Strategies than ever before, and this is the only book that has the exact thinking strategies you need to use to maximize your ACT score. Gruber's test preparation books are used by the nation's school districts more than any other books.

Dr. Gruber has published more than 40 books with major publishers on test-taking and critical-thinking methods, with more than 7 million copies sold. He has also authored more than 1,000 articles on his work in scholarly journals and nationally syndicated newspapers, has appeared on numerous television and radio shows, and has been interviewed by hundreds of magazines and newspapers. He has developed major programs for school districts and for city and state educational agencies for improving and restructuring curriculum, increasing learning ability and test scores, increasing motivation, developing a passion for learning and problem solving, and decreasing the student dropout rate. For example, PBS (the Public Broadcasting Service) chose Dr. Gruber to train the nation's teachers on how to prepare students for college entrance tests through a national satellite teleconference and videotape. His results have been lauded by people throughout the country from all walks of life.

Dr. Gruber is recognized nationally as the leading expert on standardized tests. It is said that no one in the nation is better at assessing the thinking patterns of how a person answers questions and providing the mechanism to improve faulty thinking approaches.

Gruber's unique methods have been and are being used by the nation's learning centers, by international publications, textbooks, and teaching aids, by school districts throughout the country, in homes and workplaces across the nation, and by a host of other entities.

His goal and mission is to get people's potential realized and the nation "impassioned" with learning and problem solving, so that they don't merely try to get a fast, uncritical answer, but actually enjoy and look forward to solving problems and learning.

For more information on Gruber courses and additional Gruber products, visit www.drgarygruber.com.

Important: Many books do not reflect the current ACT questions. Don't practice with questions that misrepresent the actual questions on the ACT. For example, the math questions created by the test makers are oriented toward allowing you to solve many problems without a calculator as fast as you could with one, and some can be solved faster without a calculator. This book reflects the ACT more accurately than any other commercial book, and the strategies contained in it are exactly those you need to use on the ACT. It is said that only Dr. Gruber has the expertise and ability to provide you with the tools needed for success on the exam far better than any competitor! Don't trust your future to less than the best material.

THE AUTHOR HAS SOMETHING IMPORTANT TO TELL YOU ABOUT HOW TO RAISE YOUR ACT SCORE

What Are Critical-Thinking Skills?

First of all, I believe that intelligence can be taught. Intelligence, simply defined, is the aptitude or ability to reason things out. I am convinced that *you can learn to think logically* and figure things out better and faster, *particularly in regard to ACT questions*. But someone must give you the tools. Let us call these tools *strategies*. And that's what Critical-Thinking Skills are all about—*strategies*.

Learn the Strategies to Get More Points

The Strategy Section (beginning on page 39) will sharpen your reasoning ability so that you can increase your score dramatically on each part of the ACT.

These Critical-Thinking Skills—Part 3's 5 General Strategies and 28 Easy-to-Learn Strategies (including 19 Math Strategies and 9 Reading Strategies)—are used throughout this book. The Explanatory Answers for the 3 Practice Tests in Part 10 direct you to those strategies that may be used to answer specific types of ACT questions. The strategies in Part 3 of this book are usable for more than 90 percent of the questions that will appear on the Math and Reading portions of your ACT. It is obvious, then, that your *learning* and *using* the 33 easy-to-understand strategies in this book will very likely raise your ACT score substantially.

Study the Brief Review of English Grammar

Here (Part 7) you will find the most important grammar rules. If you wish to go into more detail, study the Complete ACT Grammar and Usage Refresher (Part 8).

Study the Mini Math Refresher

If you believe you are weak in basic math skills, study the Mini Math Refresher (Part 5). The material in this section is keyed to the Complete ACT Math Refresher (Part 6) for more thorough instruction.

Take the 101 Most Important Math Questions Test

To see what your weak basic math skills are, take the 101 Most Important Math Questions test (Part 2) and look at the solutions. The questions are keyed to the Complete ACT Math Refresher (Part 6) so you can further brush up on your weak areas for any questions you missed.

The Explanatory Answers to Questions Are Keyed to Specific Strategies and Basic Skills

The Explanatory Answers to the practice tests in this book are far from skimpy—unlike those of other ACT books. Our detailed answers will direct you to the strategy that will help you to arrive at a correct answer quickly. In addition, the math solutions in the book refer directly to the Complete ACT Math Refresher section, particularly useful in case your math skills are rusty.

Lift That ACT Score

By using the material in this book—that is, by taking the tests, learning the specific strategies, and refreshing your basic skills—you should increase your ACT score substantially.

QUESTIONS ASKED
ABOUT THE ACT

What Is on the ACT?

The ACT is divided into four parts with an optional Written Essay as a fifth part.

1. The ACT English Test

Seventy-five questions in 45 minutes test standard written English (punctuation, grammar and usage, and sentence structure), development (organization, focus, and cohesion), and rhetorical skills (strategy, organization, and style). Spelling, vocabulary, and rote memory of rules of grammar are not tested. The test consists of five passages, each accompanied by a set of multiple-choice questions. Four scores are reported: a total test score on all 75 questions, along with subscores in three reporting categories: Production of Writing (29%–32%), Knowledge of Language (13%–19%), and Conventions of Standard English (51%–56%). If you spend 1½ minutes skimming through each passage, you will have about 30 seconds to answer each question.

2. The ACT Math Test

Sixty questions in 60 minutes test mathematical skills taken in courses up to grade 12. Nine scores are reported: an overall score for all 60 questions plus scores in eight reporting categories: Preparing for Higher Mathematics (57%–60%)—including subscores in Number and Quantity (7%–10%), Algebra (12%–15%), Functions (12%–15%), Geometry (12%–15%), and Statistics and Probability (8%–12%)—as well as Integrating Essential Skills (40%–43%) and Modeling (>25%).

3. The ACT Reading Test

Forty questions in 35 minutes test your reading comprehension skills. The test comprises four passages, each preceded by a headline that indicates the type of material (e.g., prose fiction, humanities, social studies, natural science). There will be three long prose passages and one passage consisting of two short pieces of prose; in the latter case, some questions may ask you to compare the paired readings. Four scores are reported: an overall score for all 40 questions plus three subscores in Key Ideas and Details (55%–60%), Craft and Structure (25%–30%), and Integration of Knowledge and Ideas (13%–18%). If you spend 2 to 3 minutes reading through each passage, you will have about 35 seconds to answer each question.

4. The ACT Science Test

Forty questions in 35 minutes measure the interpretation, analysis, evaluation, reasoning, and problem-solving skills associated with the natural sciences. The test includes several sets of scientific data and information, each followed multiple-choice questions. Questions test your understanding of the features of, and concepts related to, the information provided (e.g., in graphs, tables, text) as well as your ability to draw conclusions based on that information. Sometimes you will need to draw on your own knowledge based on common high school courses such as biology. Four scores are reported: an overall score based on the 40 questions, plus three subscores: Interpretation of Data (40%–45%), Scientific Investigation (20%–30%), and Evaluation of Models, Inferences, and Experimental Results (25%–35%). Note that you are *not* permitted to use a calculator on the science test. If you spend about 2 minutes reading each passage, then you will have about 30 seconds to answer each question. You may want to spend less time in first reading the passage or looking at the data and refer back to the information when looking at the questions.

5. The ACT Writing Test (Optional)

If you elected to take this 40-minute test, it will not affect your other scores or your composite score. You will be presented with an issue (prompt) and three perspectives on that issue, and you will be asked to

(1) analyze those perspectives, (2) express your own perspective, and (3) relate your perspective to the ones provided in the prompt. The viewpoint you express in your essay will not affect your score. You will receive a composite Writing score of 2–12 plus four "domain" scores: Ideas and Analysis, Development and Support, Organization, and Language Use and Conventions. The image of your essay will be given to your high school and the colleges to which the ACT test scores are reported.

How Long Will the Test Last?

The total time of the four multiple-choice tests will be 2 hours and 55 minutes. There will be a 10- to 15-minute break between tests 2 and 3. Allow 5 hours total (including breaks). If you are taking the Writing Test, you will be given an additional hour.

ACT vs. SAT: How Should I Decide Which Test to Take?

College applicants are often required to take either the ACT or the SAT, depending on the college to which they apply. Check first with the schools you are applying to and find out which test they prefer.

Depending on the school, you may have a choice of whether to take the ACT or the SAT. The correlation between the questions on the ACT and those on the SAT happens to be very high—if you score well on one, you will likely score about as well on the other. They cover a lot of the same material. Both exams test grammar, math, and critical reading skills. However, the ACT includes a whole section on scientific data interpretation (the SAT has a few similar questions in its Math section); fortunately, you don't have to have a scientific background to excel on the ACT.

The ACT is more *memory*-oriented, while the SAT is more *strategy*-oriented. If you memorize quickly and retain facts well under pressure, I recommend the ACT. If you are more prone to strategizing or you like puzzles, I would take the SAT.

What Verbal/Grammar Background Must I Have?

The reading comprehension parts of the test are at the 10th- to 12th-grade level, but strategies presented in this book will help you even if you are at a lower grade level.

What Math Background Must I Have?

The math part will test number/quantity (7%–10% of questions), algebra (12%–15%), functions (12%–15%), geometry (12%–15%), and statistics/probablilty (8%–12%). However, if you use common sense and learn the strategies and thinking skills presented in this book, you don't need to take full courses in these areas. Many of the strategies in this book will help you quickly solve the problems on the test.

What Science Background Must I Have?

The ACT website states that "some of the questions require that the students have discipline-specific content knowledge (e.g., knowledge specific to an introductory high school biology course), but science content is always assessed in concert with science skills and practices." For the most part you simply need to know how to interpret and analyze data presented in these areas.

What Percentage of ACT Study Time Should I Spend Learning Vocabulary Words?

Students should spend perhaps 4 hours at most. To build your word recognition quickly, learn the "Hot Prefixes and Roots" list (page 128).

Should I Take an Administered Actual ACT for Practice?

Yes, but only if you will learn from your mistakes by recognizing the strategies you should have used on your exam. Taking the ACT merely for its own sake is a waste of time and may in fact reinforce bad methods and habits. For some National testing dates, if you take the exam at a National test center you may, for an additional fee, obtain a copy of the test questions, your answers, a list of correct answers, and scoring instructions. To learn more, visit the ACT website at www.act.org.

Should I Be Familiar with the Directions to the Various Items on the ACT before Taking the ACT?

Make sure you are completely familiar with the directions to each of the item types (English, Reading, Math, Science, and Writing). See General Strategy 2, page 40, and for updated information visit the ACT website at www.act.org.

It's Three Days Until the ACT. What Can I Do to Prepare?

Make sure you are completely familiar with the structure of the test, the basic math skills needed, and the basic verbal (including grammar) skills. Take a few practice tests and refresh your understanding of the strategies used to answer the questions.

What Should I Do to Prepare on Friday Night—Cram? Watch TV? Relax?

The ACT exam is given on a Saturday. On Friday night, I would just refresh my knowledge of the structure of the test, some strategies, and some basic skills (verbal, grammar, or math). You want to keep the thinking process going so it is continual right up to the exam. Don't overdo it; just keep it somewhat continuous. This will also relieve some anxiety so you don't feel you are forgetting things before the exam.

What Should I Bring to the Exam on the Test Date?

You should bring the following items with you to the test, and nothing else:

- your paper ticket for the exam
- a few sharpened #2 pencils with erasers
- a photo ID such as a driver license or school ID
- a calculator permitted by the current rules; visit www.actstudent.org
- a watch with no alarm, to pace yourself

Can I Use a Calculator on the Math Portion of the Test?

Students can use a four-function, scientific, or graphing calculator. Note, though, that it is possible to solve every question without the use of a calculator. An updated list of which calculators can be used on the test can be found at the ACT website, www.act.org.

Is Guessing Advisable?

There is no penalty for wrong answers, so you should always guess if you can't answer the question.

The Test Is Given in One Booklet. Can I Skip Between Sections?

No, you cannot skip between the sections. You have to work on one section until the time is called. If you get caught skipping sections or going back to an earlier section, then you risk being asked to leave the exam.

Should I Answer All Easy Questions First and Save Difficult Ones for Last?

I would answer the questions as they are presented to you, but if you find you are spending more than 30 seconds on a question and not getting anywhere, go to the next question. You may, however, find that the more difficult questions are actually easy for you because you have learned the strategies in this book.

Should I Use Scrap Paper to Write on and to Do Calculations?

Scrap paper is prohibited in the test center, but you can use your test booklet (not your answer sheet) to draw or write on. Many of my strategies expect you to label diagrams, draw and extend lines, circle important words and sentences, etc., so feel free to write anything in your booklet. The booklets aren't graded; only the answer sheets are. See General Strategy 4, page 41.

What Is the Most Challenging Type of Question on the Exam and How Do I Attack It?

Many questions, especially at the end of a section on the test, can be challenging. You should always attack challenging questions by using a specific strategy or strategies and common sense.

What Are the Most Crucial Strategies?

All specific verbal and math strategies are crucial, including the general test-taking strategies described on pages 40–41, regarding guessing, writing and drawing in your test booklet, and being familiar with question-type directions. The key reading strategy is to know the four general types of questions that are asked in reading—main idea, inference, specific details, and tone or mood. Important math strategies include the translations strategy—words into numbers, drawing of lines, etc.

How Is the Test Scored?

Each test (English, Math, Reading, and Science) will have a scale score from 1 to 36. A composite score will be the total scale score from all four tests, divided by four. There will also be subscores as described before.

Can I Take the Test More than Once? Will All My Scores Be Reported to the Schools to Which I'm Applying? How Will My Scores Be Used?

Check with the schools to which you are applying to see how they use the reported scores—whether they average them, whether they take the highest, etc. Ask each school whether it sees unreported scores. If so, find out how the individual school deals with single and multiple unreported scores.

How Do Other Exams Compare with the ACT? Can I Use the Strategies and Examples in This Book for Them?

Many other exams are like the ACT, so the strategies here are definitely useful when taking them. The ACT is less strategy-oriented and more memory-oriented than the SAT, but the strategies in this book will certainly be useful. If you are taking the SAT, however, you should get the book that deals directly with the SAT: *Gruber's Complete SAT Guide 2019-2020*, 21st edition.

How Does the Gruber Preparation Method Differ from Other Programs and Guides?

Many other ACT programs try to use quick-fix methods or subscribe to memorization. These quick-fix methods can be detrimental to effective preparation because the ACT designers constantly change questions to prevent "gimmick" approaches. Rote memorization methods do not enable you to answer a variety of questions that appear in the ACT exam. In more than thirty years of writing preparation books for standardized tests such as the SAT and ACT, Dr. Gruber has developed and honed the critical-thinking skills and strategies that are based on all standardized tests' construction. So, while his method immediately improves your performance on the ACT, it also provides you with the confidence to tackle problems in all areas of study for the rest of your life. Remarkably, he enables you to look at a problem or question without panic, extract something curious or useful from it, and move to the next step and finally to a solution, without rushing into a wrong answer or being lured into a wrong choice. It has been said that test taking through his methodology becomes enjoyable rather than painful.

WHAT ARE
CRITICAL-THINKING SKILLS?

Critical-Thinking Skills are general skills for finding the most creative and effective way of solving a problem or evaluating a situation. The most effective way of solving a problem is to extract some piece of information or observe something curious from the problem, and then use one or more of the specific strategies or Critical-Thinking Skills—together with basic skills or information you already know—to get to the next step in the problem. This next step will catapult you toward a solution with further use of the specific strategies or thinking skills.

1. **Extract or observe something curious.**

2. **Use specific strategies together with basic skills.**

These specific strategies will enable you to "process" think rather than just be concerned with the end result; the latter usually produces a fast, rushed, and wrong answer. The Gruber strategies have been shown to make test takers more comfortable with problem solving and to make the process enjoyable. The skills will last a lifetime, and you will develop a passion for problem solving. These Critical-Thinking Skills show that conventional "drill and practice" is a waste of time unless the practice is based on these generic thinking skills.

Here's a simple example of how these Critical-Thinking Skills can be used in a math problem:

Which is greater, $7\frac{1}{7} \times 8\frac{1}{8} \times 6\frac{1}{6}$ or $8\frac{1}{8} \times 6\frac{1}{6} \times 7$?

Long and tedious way: Multiply $7\frac{1}{7} \times 8\frac{1}{8} \times 6\frac{1}{6}$ and compare it with $8\frac{1}{8} \times 6\frac{1}{6} \times 7$.

Error in doing the problem the "long way": You don't have to *calculate;* you just have to *compare,* so you need a *strategy* for *comparing* two quantities.

Critical-Thinking way:

1. *Observe:* Each expression contains $8\frac{1}{8}$ and $6\frac{1}{6}$.

2. *Use strategy:* Since both $8\frac{1}{8}$ and $6\frac{1}{6}$ are just weighting factors, like the same quantities on both sides of a balance scale, just *cancel* them from both multiplied quantities above.

   You are then left comparing $7\frac{1}{7}$ with 7, so the first quantity, $7\frac{1}{7}$, is greater. Thus $7\frac{1}{7} \times 8\frac{1}{8} \times 6\frac{1}{6}$ is greater than $8\frac{1}{8} \times 6\frac{1}{6} \times 7$.

Here's a simple example of how Critical-Thinking Skills can be used for a verbal problem:

If you see a word such as *delude* in a sentence or in a reading passage, you can assume that the word *delude* is negative and probably means "taking away from something" or "distracting," since the prefix *de-* means "away from" and thus has a negative connotation. Although you may not get the exact meaning of the word (in this case the meaning is to "deceive" or "mislead"), you can see how the word may be used in the context of the sentence in which it appears, and thus get the flavor or feeling of the sentence or paragraph.

Notice that the Critical-Thinking approach gives you a fail-safe and exact path to the solution without superficially trying to solve the problem or merely guessing at it. This book contains all the Critical-Thinking Strategies you need to know for the ACT test.

Dr. Gruber has researched hundreds of ACT tests (thousands of ACT questions) and documented 33 Critical-Thinking Strategies (all found in this book) common to every test. These strategies can be used for any math, reading, or logical reasoning problem.

In short, you can learn how to solve a specific problem and thus find how to answer that problem, or you can learn a powerful strategy that will enable you to answer hundreds of problems.

A 4-HOUR STUDY PROGRAM
FOR THE ACT

For those who have only a few hours to spend in ACT preparation, I have designed a *minimum* study program to get you by. It tells you the basic math skills you need to know, the reading practice you need, and the most important strategies to focus on, from the many in this book.

General

Study General Strategies, pages 40–41.

Critical Reading

Study Reading Comprehension Strategies 1 and 2 (first three questions for each strategy), pages 102–106.

Math

Study the Mini Math Refresher beginning on page 137.

Study the introduction to the 28 Easy-to-Learn Strategies on pages 42–43.

Study the following Math Strategies (first three questions for each strategy):

Strategy 2, page 46

Strategy 4, page 54

Strategy 5, page 57

Strategy 8, page 64

Strategy 12, page 72

Strategy 13, page 74

Strategy 14, page 76

Strategy 17, page 84

Strategy 18, page 87

You may want to take the World's Shortest Practice Test for the ACT Exam on page 1. If you have time, take Practice Test 1, starting on page 394. Check your answers with the Explanatory Answers starting on page 453, and look again at the strategies and basic skills that apply to the questions you missed.

English Test/Writing Test

Look through the material in Part 7, "A Brief Review of English Grammar," and (if you are taking the ACT Writing Test) Part 9, "The ACT Writing Test."

Science Test

Look through Part 4, "The ACT Science Test," beginning on page 133.

LONGER-RANGE STUDY PROGRAM AND HELPFUL STEPS FOR USING THIS BOOK

1. Learn the 5 General Strategies on pages 40–41.

2. Take Practice Test 1 on page 394 and score yourself according to the instructions.

3. For those problems or questions that you answered incorrectly or were uncertain of, see the Explanatory Answers, beginning on page 453, and make sure that you learn the strategies keyed to the questions. For complete strategy development, it is a good idea to study all the strategies in Part 3, "Strategy Section," beginning on page 39, and learn how to do all the problems and questions within each strategy.

4. If you are weak in basic math skills, take "The 101 Most Important Math Questions" test in Part 2, beginning on page 13, and follow the directions for diagnosis.

5. To see if you are making use of the strategies you've learned, turn to Part 1 and take "The World's Shortest Practice Test for the ACT Exam," beginning on page 1, and follow the directions for diagnosis.

For Math-Area Basic Skills Help

6. For the basic math skills keyed to the questions, study Part 6, the "Complete ACT Math Refresher," beginning on page 147, or for a quicker review look at Part 5, the "Mini Math Refresher," beginning on page 137.

For Writing Help/Grammar Help

7. Look through Part 9, "The ACT Writing Test," beginning on page 367. You may wish to refresh your grammar ability by looking through "A Brief Review of English Grammar" (Part 7), beginning on page 293, and the "Complete ACT Grammar and Usage Refresher" (Part 8), starting on page 303.

Science

8. For the ACT Science Test, look through Part 4, which starts on page 133.

Now

9. Take the remaining three ACT Practice Tests beginning on page 391, score yourself, and compare your answers with the Explanatory Answers. Always refer to the associated strategies and basic skills for questions you answered incorrectly or were not sure how to do.

QUESTIONS RECENTLY ASKED OF DR. GRUBER IN INTERVIEWS

How Did You Get Started in Test Prep? Do You Still Personally Train Students?

When I was in fifth grade, I scored 90 (below average) on an IQ test. My father, who was a high school teacher at the time, was concerned, so he was able to get me an IQ test, hoping I could study it and increase my score. However, when I looked at the test, I was so fascinated with what the questions were trying to assess, I started to figure out what strategies and thinking could have been used for the questions and saw interesting patterns for what the test maker was trying to test.

I increased my IQ to 126 and then to 150. The initial experience of scoring so low on my first IQ test and being branded as "dull minded" actually sparked my fascination and research with standardized tests. I was determined to help all other students obtain my knowledge and experience so they would be able to reach their full potential, as I had. So I constantly write books, newspaper and magazine articles and columns, and software, and I personally teach students and teachers.

What Is the "Gruber Method" and How Does It Differ from Other Test Prep Methods?

The unique aspect of my method is that I provide a mechanism and process whereby students internalize the use of the strategies and thinking skills I've developed and honed over thirty years. The method reinforces those strategies and skills so that students can answer questions on the ACT or SAT without panic or brain-racking. This is actually a fun process. The Gruber Method focuses on the students' patterns of thinking and how each student should best answer the questions. I have even developed a nationally syndicated test—the only one of its kind—that actually tracks a student's thinking approach to the ACT (and SAT) and directs the student to the exact strategies necessary for him or her to learn. Instead of just learning how to solve one problem at a time, if you learn a Gruber strategy you can use it to solve thousands of problems.

What Advice Can You Give to Students Suffering from Test Anxiety?

I find that when students learn specific strategies, they see how a strategy can be used for a multitude of questions. And when they see a question on an actual ACT that uses the strategy, it reinforces their self-confidence and reduces their sense of panic. Students can also treat the ACT as a game by using my strategic approaches, and this also reduces their anxiety.

Should Students Take the ACT or the SAT?

The correlation happens to be very high for both tests, so if you score well on one, you will score similarly on the other. The material is about the same; for example, there is grammar on both tests. Math is about the same, except the ACT is less strategically oriented. There is reading on both tests, and those sections test about the same things. However, on the ACT there is a whole section on scientific data interpretation (the SAT has some questions on this topic in the math section). And the ACT is more memory-oriented than the SAT. If you are more prone to using memory, I would take the ACT. If you are more prone to strategizing or if you like puzzles, I would take the SAT. In any event, I would check with the schools to which you're applying to find out which test they prefer.

What Is the Single Most Important Piece of Advice You Can Give to Students Taking the ACT or SAT?

Learn some specific strategies, which can be found in my books. This will let you think mechanically without racking your brain. When answering the questions, don't concentrate on or panic about finding the answer. Try to extract something in the question that is curious and/or will lead you to the next step in the question. Through this, you will process the question, enabling you to reach an answer.

What Is the Single Most Important Piece of Advice You Can Give to Tutors Teaching the ACT or SAT?

Make sure you learn the strategies. Teach students those strategies by using many different questions that employ each strategy, so students will see variations on how each particular strategy is used.

What Recommendations Can You Give to Tutors Who Want to Use Your Books in Their Test-Prep Programs?

Read "A 4-Hour Study Program for the ACT" on page xxiii. You can use the information there to create a program for teaching students. Always try to reinforce the strategic approach in which students hone and internalize strategies so they can use them for multitudes of questions.

Apparently, Very Few People Know the Answer to This Important Question: When Should Students Take the SAT or ACT?

Students should find out from the school to which they are applying the preferred test dates for the ACT or SAT that they need to register for. However, students who want to take the ACT or SAT for practice should take it only on the test dates for "disclosed" exams—which means that the test answers and the students' answers are given back to them. For the ACT, check www.act.org. For the SAT, check out the College Board's website, www.collegeboard.org. After getting the test and the results for each question back, students can learn from their mistakes by going through the questions they got wrong and then working on the strategies and basic skills they could have used to solve those questions.

PART 1

The World's Shortest Practice Test for the ACT Exam

20 Questions to Approximate Your ACT Score

And the Exact Strategies You Need to Improve Your Score

Although it shouldn't take you more than approximately 40 seconds to answer each question, you may take this test untimed and still get a fairly accurate prediction of your ACT score.

The top schools require ACT scores of around 27. Following is a test that can determine if you have the goods—and it won't take you more than 20 minutes.

Note: In the actual ACT test, the Math Section has 5 choices, and all the other sections (English, Reading, and Science) have 4 choices.

ANSWER SHEET

Complete Mark ● **Examples of Incomplete Marks** ⊙ ⊗ ⊖ ◔ ◍ ◖ ◐ ◯

ENGLISH

	A	B	C	D			A	B	C	D
1	○	○	○	○		4	○	○	○	○
2	○	○	○	○		5	○	○	○	○
3	○	○	○	○						

MATHEMATICS

	A	B	C	D	E			A	B	C	D	E
1	○	○	○	○	○		4	○	○	○	○	○
2	○	○	○	○	○		5	○	○	○	○	○
3	○	○	○	○	○							

READING

	A	B	C	D			A	B	C	D
1	○	○	○	○		4	○	○	○	○
2	○	○	○	○		5	○	○	○	○
3	○	○	○	○						

SCIENCE

	A	B	C	D			A	B	C	D
1	○	○	○	○		4	○	○	○	○
2	○	○	○	○		5	○	○	○	○
3	○	○	○	○						

ENGLISH TEST

4 Minutes

Questions 1–5 are based on the following passage.

This passage is from Rachel Carson's The Sea Around Us, *1950.*

(1) Sometimes the meaning of glowing water is ominous. (2) <u>On</u> the Pacific Coast of North America, it may mean that the sea is filled with . . . a minute plant that contains a poison of strange and terrible virulence (3)<u>—about four days</u> after this minute plant comes to dominate the coastal plankton, some of the fishes and shellfish in the vicinity become toxic. (4) This is because in (5) <u>their</u> normal feeding, they have strained the poisonous plankton out of the water.

Questions

1. Which sentence could appear as the sentence preceding the first sentence of this passage?

   (A) The sea has many interesting attributes.
   (B) The Pacific coastline is frightening.
   (C) Ships sometimes take southern routes to avoid bad weather conditions.
   (D) There are strange plants in the sea.

2. (A) NO CHANGE
   (B) Off
   (C) Apart from
   (D) Not from

3. (A) NO CHANGE
   (B) . About four days
   (C) ; about four days
   (D) , about four days

4. At this point the author is considering adding the following true statement right before the last sentence: "The fishes and shellfish die soon after." Should the author make this addition here?

   (A) No, because this destroys the connection between the last sentence and the preceding one.
   (B) No, because there is too much of a leap from "toxicity" to "death."
   (C) Yes, because it follows that if fish are toxic they will soon die.
   (D) Yes, because this qualifies the last sentence and puts it in its right place.

5. (A) NO CHANGE
   (B) they're
   (C) its
   (D) it's

MATHEMATICS TEST

6 Minutes

1. Given the functions $f(x) = \sqrt{x + 1}$ and $g(x) = 6x + a$, in the xy-coordinate plane, $y = f[g(x)]$ passes through the point (3,5). What is the value of a?

   (A) 6
   (B) −6
   (C) 18
   (D) −18
   (E) $6 + 4\sqrt{7}$

2. If a and b are consecutive integers such that $a > b$, then:

   (A) a is even
   (B) b is even
   (C) $a - b$ is even
   (D) $a^2 - b^2$ is even
   (E) $a^2 + b^2$ is odd

3. What is the distance between the parallel sides of the isosceles trapezoid shown below if the parallel sides are 6 feet and 10 feet and the nonparallel sides are both 4 feet?

   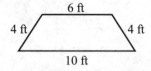

   (A) 2
   (B) $2\sqrt{2}$
   (C) $2\sqrt{3}$
   (D) $3\sqrt{2}$
   (E) $3\sqrt{3}$

4. In the triangle shown below, with sides 4, 5, and 6, what is cos x?

   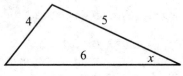

   (A) $\frac{6}{5}$

   (B) $\frac{2}{3}$

   (C) $\frac{3}{4}$

   (D) $\frac{4}{5}$

   (E) $\frac{3}{\sqrt{6}}$

5. Three students are in an honors class. Each student scores 85% on a test. The teacher of the class would like to bring up the average class score to 90%. She lets one of the students retake the test. What is the score the student must make on the retake test in order to bring the average class score to 90%?

   (A) 90%
   (B) 92%
   (C) 96%
   (D) 98%
   (E) 100%

READING TEST

5 Minutes

Questions 1–5 are based on the following passage, *A Contrast between Homeschooling and Classroom Schooling.*

Homeschooling is becoming more and more desirable because children do not have the burden of traveling to school and becoming exposed to other children's sickness and everything else that goes with being in a
5   crowded room. There is also the individual attention that the parent or tutor can give the student, which creates a better and more efficient learning environment. Many educators believe that as standards become more and more flexible, homeschooling may in fact be
10 the norm of the future.

However, in many studies, it has been shown that students benefit in a classroom setting, since the interaction and dialogue with other students creates a stimulating learning environment. The more students
15 who are in a class, the more diversity within the group and the more varied the feedback. With a good teacher and facilitator, a classroom can be very beneficial for the student's cognitive development. So there are advantages and disadvantages in the different methods
20 of schooling. Further studies should be carried out to determine the pros and cons to each method.

Questions

1. In homeschooling, the optimal condition for an effective learning environment is based on

    (A) the closeness of a parent and child
    (B) the reduction of travel time
    (C) a one-to-one learning experience
    (D) the sanitary conditions in the learning environment

2. Which of the following is not addressed by the author's discussion of classroom schooling?

    (A) The advantage of classroom learning with the student interacting and sharing ideas with other students.

    (B) The student's being exposed to multicultural approaches to the learning experience.
    (C) The greater number of students in the classroom leading to more feedback for each student.
    (D) The positive relationship between the different types of students and learning.

3. Which criterion is the same in homeschooling and regular classroom schooling?

    (A) the health conditions
    (B) the feedback from other students
    (C) the diversity of the students
    (D) the learning experience

4. Which of the following adjustments would make an ideal environment for learning, according to what is addressed?

    (A) In homeschooling, the student could travel on weekends to cultural areas.
    (B) In school, the teacher could occasionally work with students on an individual basis.
    (C) In homeschooling, the student could be exposed to interaction with other students on a regular basis.
    (D) The student can spend one-half of his educational time in school and one-half of his educational time at home.

5. Which statement would the author of this passage agree with?

    (A) Homeschooling provides much more of a learning experience than classroom schooling.
    (B) Classroom schooling provides much more of a learning experience than homeschooling.
    (C) Neither homeschooling nor classroom schooling is effective in learning.
    (D) It is not known which is more effective—classroom schooling or homeschooling.

SCIENCE TEST

5 Minutes

The definition of *density* is *mass divided by volume.* That is,

$$\text{density} = \frac{\text{mass}}{\text{volume}}$$

Table 1 contains the phases and densities, expressed in grams per cubic centimeter $\left(\frac{g}{cm^3}\right)$, of a variety of pure substances at a temperature of 25° C and at a pressure of 1 atmosphere.

Table 1

Substance	Phase	Density $\left(\frac{g}{cm^3}\right)$
Arsenic	solid	5.73
Glucose	solid	1.56
Iron	solid	7.86
Lead	solid	11.34
Zinc	solid	7.14
Ethanol	liquid	0.79
Ethyl ether	liquid	0.71
Glycerol	liquid	1.26
Mercury	liquid	13.59
Freon-12	gas	0.00495
Krypton	gas	0.00343
Methane	gas	0.00065

Figure 1

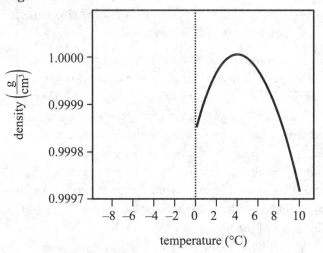

Figure 1 describes how the density of liquid water changes with temperature.

Figure 2

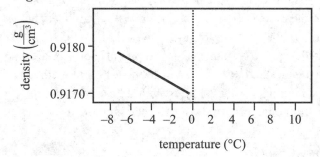

Figure 2 shows how the density of solid water changes with temperature.

Figures adapted from John C. Kotz and Keith F. Purcell, *Chemistry & Chemical Reactivity*, 1987.

Questions

1. As the temperature of liquid water increases from 0° C to 10° C, the density

   (A) can be more than $1.0 \frac{g}{cm^3}$

   (B) increases, then decreases
   (C) increases only
   (D) decreases, then increases

2. A chemist concludes that the mass of 1 cm³ of any liquid is greater than the mass of 2 cm³ of any gas. Which liquid and gas from Table 1 support this conclusion?

   (A) Mercury, methane only
   (B) Mercury, Freon-12 only
   (C) All of the liquids and gases
   (D) None of the liquids and gases

3. As water increases in temperature from solid through liquid, its density

   (A) first decreases, then increases, then decreases
   (B) first increases, then decreases
   (C) decreases only
   (D) increases only

4. At 25° C, equal amounts of ethanol, glycerol, and water of density $0.9971 \frac{g}{cm^3}$ are poured into a cylindrical flask. Layers of each compound form in the flask. Which of the following represents the order from highest level to lowest level of the compounds in the flask, according to Table 1?

   (A) Ethanol
       Glycerol
       Water
   (B) Ethanol
       Water
       Glycerol
   (C) Glycerol
       Water
       Ethanol
   (D) Glycerol
       Ethanol
       Water

5. Referring to Figure 1, at 4° C, 200 grams of water would completely fill a container of what volume?

   (A) 100 cm³
   (B) 200 cm³
   (C) 300 cm³
   (D) 400 cm³

ANSWERS

English Test

1. A
2. B
3. B
4. A
5. A

Reading Test

1. C
2. B
3. D
4. C
5. D

Mathematics Test

1. A
2. E
3. C
4. C
5. E

Science Test

1. B
2. C
3. A
4. B
5. B

SCORING

Your Score Here:	Translates to This Score on the Actual ACT:			
Number of Correct Answers for Each Part	Math ACT	English ACT	Reading ACT	Science ACT
1	16–25	7–12	10–13	10–13
2	26–31	13–19	14–19	14–19
3	32–33	20–25	20–26	20–26
4	34–35	26–34	27–33	27–33
5	36	35–36	34–36	34–36

EXPLANATORY ANSWERS

With Important Strategies

English Test

1. Choice A is correct. In a passage, we start generally, then discuss specifics. Choice B is incorrect. We are discussing the sea, not the Pacific coastline. Choice C is incorrect. There is no direct connection between this sentence and the first sentence in the passage. Choice D is incorrect. Plants are discussed later in the passage, so the first sentence about plants would not be appropriate here.

   Strategy: Know How to Connect Sentences in a Passage.

2. Choice B is correct. We are talking about something away from, or "off," the Pacific coast. Choice A is incorrect. We are not talking about something on the coast—we are talking about something in the water *off* the coast. Choice C is incorrect. We are not contrasting the coast and the sea, so we do not use the word *apart*. Choice D is incorrect. "Not from" does not make sense here, since we eventually talk about the sea.

   Strategy: Know How to Use Appropriate Words to Describe Something.

3. Choice B is correct. We need a new sentence here, because something new is discussed. Choice A is incorrect. The dash is not appropriate since the part is not directly linked to the preceding part—a new idea is discussed. Choice C is incorrect. The semicolon is not appropriate since a new idea is discussed here. Choice D is incorrect. The comma would create a run-on sentence.

   Strategy: Know How to Use Punctuation to Link Parts of the Passage.

4. Choice A is correct. We need to maintain a connection here—when it says the fish become toxic, we need another sentence immediately following this one explaining why they become toxic. Choice B is incorrect. There is not too much of a leap from "toxicity" to "death." Choice C is incorrect. This may be so, but inserting the sentence would destroy a connection, as described before. Choice D is incorrect. This is not true since a connection would be destroyed between the last sentence and the one preceding.

   Strategy: Know When and How to Make Connections by Using Another Sentence.

5. Choice A is correct. Since we mean more than one, we use *their*. Choice B is incorrect. *They're* means "they are," which does not make sense. Choice C is incorrect. Since we are referring to more than one, we do not use *its*. Choice D is incorrect. *It's* means "It is," which does not make sense.

   Strategy: Know What to Use When We Are Talking about Quantity.

Mathematics Test

1. Choice A is correct. Since $y = f[g(x)]$ and $g(x) = 6x + a$, $y = f(6x + a)$. But $f(x) = \sqrt{x + 1}$, so $y = f(6x + a) = \sqrt{6x + a + 1}$. If $y = f[g(x)]$ passes through $(3,5)$, then $5 = f[6(3) + a] = \sqrt{6(3) + a + 1} = \sqrt{18 + a + 1} = \sqrt{19 + a}$. Thus $5 = \sqrt{19 + a}$. Square both sides: $25 = 19 + a$; $a = 6$.

2. Choice E is correct.

   Math Strategy 8: When Each Choice Must Be Tested, Start with the Last Choice and Work Backward

   Math Strategy 4: Remember Classic Expressions

   Method I:

   You could try integers for a and b like $a = 4$ and $b = 3$ (making sure that $a > b$). Then you would test out the choices using Math Strategy 8. So for Choice E, $4^2 + 3^2 = 16 + 9 = 25$, which is odd. You may want to try another set of numbers like $a = 3$ and $b = 2$. So you would get for Choice E, $3^2 + 2^2 = 13$. You would be on safe ground to choose E, but frankly I wouldn't bet my life on it! You could perhaps go on to Choice D, trying $a = 4$ and $b = 3$. You get $4^2 - 3^2 = 7$. So Choice D is ruled out. Go to Choice C: $a - b = 4 - 3 = 1$. Choice C is ruled out. Now go to Choice B: $b = 3$ so Choice B is ruled out. Now for Choice A: a is even if $a = 4$. But of course a could have been 3 and b could have been 2, so Choice A would be ruled out and only Choice E remains (which is the correct one).

But let's look at a much more powerful and general method:

Method II:

Since a and b are consecutive integers, with $a > b$, then $a = b + 1$. So using Math Strategy 8 (Choice E), we have, substituting $a = b + 1$ for a, and using Math Strategy 4, $(x + y)^2 = x^2 + 2xy + y^2$, where $b = x$ and $1 = y$, we get $a^2 + b^2 = (b + 1)^2 + b^2 = b^2 + 2b + 1 + b^2 = 2b^2 + 2b + 1$.

Now we factor out the common 2 and get $a^2 + b^2 = 2(b^2 + b) + 1$.

Since $2(b^2 + b)$ is even (an integer multiplied by 2), when added to 1, you get an odd integer. Therefore, Choice E is correct.

Method III:

Here's a method to use if you are familiar with properties of integers. For Choice E we have $a^2 + b^2$ is odd. Now suppose a is odd. Then b must be even, since b is 1 less than a. Thus a^2 is odd and b^2 is even. $a^2 + b^2 = $ odd + even = odd.

Suppose, though, that a is even. Then b is odd, since b is 1 less than a. Then a^2 is even and b^2 is odd. So $a^2 + b^2$ is odd. Thus Choice E is correct.

3. Choice C is correct.

Math Strategy 14: Draw or Extend Lines to Make a Problem Easier

Math Strategy 3: Know How to Find Unknown Quantities from Known Quantities

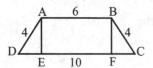

You can see that $AE = BF$. Also you can see that $AB = EF = 6$. Using Math Strategy 3, we get $DC - AB = DE + FC$. Since $DC = 10$ and $AB = 6$, $DC - AB = DE + FC = 4$. But because of the symmetry of the isosceles trapezoid, $DE = FC$, so $DE = FC = 2$.

Now by the Pythagorean theorem, $AD^2 = DE^2 + AE^2$, so
$16 = 4 + AE^2$
$12 = AE^2$

$\sqrt{12} = AE; \sqrt{4 \times 3} = AE; \sqrt{4} \times \sqrt{3} = 2 \times \sqrt{3} = AE$.

4. Choice C is correct.

Math Strategy 14: Draw or Extend Lines to Make a Problem Easier

Math Strategy 4: Remember Classic Expressions

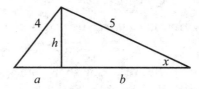

Draw a perpendicular line to the base.

Using the Pythagorean theorem,

$$a^2 + h^2 = 4^2 \qquad \boxed{1}$$
$$b^2 + h^2 = 5^2 \qquad \boxed{2}$$

Subtracting $\boxed{1}$ from $\boxed{2}$: $b^2 - a^2 = 5^2 - 4^2 = 9$

Using Math Strategy 4:

$b^2 - a^2 = (b + a)(b - a) = 9$. But $b + a = 6$ (given), so $6 \times (b - a) = 9$; $b - a = \dfrac{9}{6} = \dfrac{3}{2}$. Since $b + a = 6$ and $b - a = \dfrac{3}{2}$, adding equations, $2b = 6 + \dfrac{3}{2} = \dfrac{15}{2}$, $b = \dfrac{15}{4}$. Thus $\cos x = \dfrac{b}{5} = \dfrac{15}{20} = \dfrac{3}{4}$.

5. Choice E is correct.

Math Strategy 5: Know How to Manipulate Averages

Know what "average" means:

$\dfrac{(85 + 85 + x)}{3} = 90$. Multiply by 3 to get rid of the fraction. $85 + 85 + x = 270$; $170 + x = 270$; $x = 100$.

Reading Test

1. Choice C is correct. Watch for *key phrases*. See lines 5–8: "individual attention . . . which creates a . . . more efficient learning environment." What is in all other choices may sound right because they are all mentioned, but an effective learning environment is not based upon them.

2. Choice B is correct. Choice A is addressed in lines 13–14. Choice C is addressed in line 16 ("varied the feedback"), and Choice D is addressed in line 15 ("diversity"). But for Choice B, multicultural ways are *not* mentioned, as students could all be of one culture.

3. Choice D is correct. The criterion that appears in both passages is the learning experience. See the second sentence (lines 5–8) and lines 11–14. The other choices are incorrect because the criterion presented in each choice is not present in both homeschooling and classroom schooling.

4. Choice C is correct. What is missing in homeschooling is the interaction with other students, as stated in lines 11–14. Thus interaction with students on a regular basis would fill the void. Note in Choice B, the "occasional" work may not be adequate. In Choice D, for students spending one-half of their time at home and one-half in school, it may be difficult and awkward to coordinate or relate what is taught or developed at home and what is taught or developed at school. Choice A is incorrect because traveling to cultural areas on weekends would not really create much more of an ideal environment for learning.

5. Choice D is correct. See the last sentence (lines 20–21).

Science Test

1. Choice B is correct. As you can see from Figure 1, the graph first goes up, then reaches a high point at density $1.0 \frac{g}{cm^3}$, then goes down. Choice A is incorrect because the high point of the graph is at $1.0 \frac{g}{cm^3}$.

2. Choice C is correct. In Table 1, the mass of 2 cm^3 of Freon-12, krypton, and methane are, respectively, 0.00495×2, 0.00343×2, and 0.00065×2. You can see that these are all less than 0.10. This is less than the mass of 1 cm^3 of ethanol, ethyl ether, glycerol, and mercury, which are, respectively, 0.79, 0.71, 1.26, and 13.59. Thus, all of the liquids and gases support the chemist's conclusion.

3. Choice A is correct. In Figure 2, we see that in water's solid form, as the temperature increases from −8 to 0° C, the density decreases from 0.9180 to 0.9170. In Figure 1, in water's liquid form, as the temperature increases from 0° to 10° C, the density increases to 1.0, then decreases. Choice B is incorrect. Don't just look at Figure 1—that is just based on liquid water. Choice C is incorrect. Don't just look at Figure 2—that is just based on solid water.

4. Choice B is correct. The greater the density, the further down in the flask the compound will be. According to Table 1, the density of ethanol is 0.79; of glycerol, 1.26; and the density of water is given as 0.9971. Thus, the configuration in Choice B fits the criterion.

5. Choice B is correct. According to Figure 1, at 4° C, the density of liquid water is approximately $1.0000 \frac{g}{cm^3}$. So 200 grams would occupy 200 cm^3.

PART 2

The 101 Most Important Math Questions You Need to Know How to Solve

Take This Test to Determine Your Basic (as Contrasted with Strategic) Math Weaknesses

Diagnosis and Corrective Measures Follow Test

ANSWER SHEET

A. Fractions

1. _____
2. _____
3. _____
4. _____
5. _____

B. Even–Odd Relationships

6. _____
7. _____
8. _____
9. _____
10. _____
11. _____
12. _____

C. Factors

13. _____
14. _____
15. _____
16. _____
17. _____
18. _____
19. _____
20. _____
21. _____

D. Exponents

22. _____
23. _____
24. _____
25. _____
26. _____
27. _____
28. _____
29. _____
30. _____
31. _____
32. _____

E. Percentages

33. _____
34. _____
35. _____

F. Equations

36. _____
37. _____
38. _____
39. _____
40. _____

G. Angles

41. _____
42. _____
43. _____
44. _____

H. Parallel Lines

45. _____
46. _____
47. _____
48. _____
49. _____
50. _____
51. _____

I. Triangles

52. _____
53. _____
54. _____
55. _____
56. _____
57. _____
58. _____
59. _____
60. _____
61. _____
62. _____
63. _____
64. _____
65. _____

J. Circles

66. _____
67. _____
68. _____
69. _____
70. _____

K. Other Figures

71. _____
72. _____
73. _____

74. _____
75. _____
76. _____
77. _____
78. _____
79. _____
80. _____

L. Number Lines

81. _____
82. _____

M. Coordinates

83. _____
84. _____
85. _____
86. _____

N. Inequalities

87. _____
88. _____
89. _____
90. _____
91. _____
92. _____

O. Averages

93. _____
94. _____

P. Shortcuts

95. _____
96. _____
97. _____
98. _____
99. _____
100. _____
101. _____

101 MATH QUESTIONS TEST

Following are the 101 most important math questions you should know how to solve. After you take the test, check to see whether your answers are the same as those described, and whether or not you answered the question in the way described. After a solution, there is usually (where appropriate) a rule or generalization of the math concept just used in the solution to the particular problem. Make sure that you understand this generalization or rule, as it will apply to many other questions. Remember that these are the most important basic math questions you need to know how to solve. Make sure that you understand *all of them* before taking any standardized math test such as the ACT.

IN THIS DIAGNOSTIC TEST, DO NOT GUESS AT ANY ANSWER! IF YOU DON'T KNOW THE ANSWER LEAVE IT BLANK.

A. Fractions

1. $\dfrac{\dfrac{a}{b}}{c} =$

   (A) $\dfrac{ab}{c}$

   (B) $\dfrac{ac}{b}$

   (C) $\dfrac{a}{bc}$

   (D) abc

   (E) none of these

2. $\dfrac{1}{\dfrac{1}{y}} =$

   (A) y

   (B) y^2

   (C) $\dfrac{1}{y}$

   (D) infinity

   (E) none of these

3. $\dfrac{\dfrac{a}{b}}{c} =$

   (A) $\dfrac{a}{bc}$

   (B) $\dfrac{ac}{b}$

   (C) $\dfrac{ab}{c}$

   (D) abc

   (E) none of these

4. $\dfrac{\dfrac{1}{x}}{y} =$

   (A) xy

   (B) $\dfrac{x}{y}$

   (C) $\dfrac{y}{x}$

   (D) $\left(\dfrac{x}{y}\right)^2$

   (E) none of these

5. $\dfrac{\dfrac{a}{b}}{\dfrac{b}{a}} =$

   (A) $\dfrac{b^2}{a^2}$

   (B) $\dfrac{a^2}{b^2}$

   (C) 1

   (D) $\dfrac{a}{b}$

   (E) none of these

B. Even–Odd Relationships

6. ODD INTEGER $\times$ ODD INTEGER =

   (A) odd integer only
   (B) even integer only
   (C) even or odd integer

7. ODD INTEGER + or − ODD INTEGER =

   (A) odd integer only
   (B) even integer only
   (C) even or odd integer

8. EVEN INTEGER $\times$ EVEN INTEGER =

   (A) odd integer only
   (B) even integer only
   (C) even or odd integer

9. EVEN INTEGER + or − EVEN INTEGER =

   (A) odd integer only
   (B) even integer only
   (C) even or odd integer

10. (ODD INTEGER)$^{\text{ODD POWER}}$ =

    (A) odd integer only
    (B) even integer only
    (C) even or odd integer

11. (EVEN INTEGER)$^{\text{EVEN POWER}}$ =

    (A) odd integer only
    (B) even integer only
    (C) even or odd integer

12. (EVEN INTEGER)$^{\text{ODD POWER}}$ =

    (A) odd integer only
    (B) even integer only
    (C) even or odd integer

C. Factors

13. $(x + 3)(x + 2) =$

    (A) $x^2 + 5x + 6$
    (B) $x^2 + 6x + 5$
    (C) $x^2 + x + 6$
    (D) $2x + 5$
    (E) none of these

14. $(x + 3)(x - 2) =$

    (A) $x^2 - x + 6$
    (B) $x^2 + x + 5$
    (C) $x^2 + x - 6$
    (D) $2x + 1$
    (E) none of these

15. $(x - 3)(y - 2) =$

    (A) $xy - 5y + 6$
    (B) $xy - 2x - 3y + 6$
    (C) $x + y + 6$
    (D) $xy - 3y + 2x + 6$
    (E) none of these

16. $(a + b)(b + c) =$

    (A) $ab + b^2 + bc$
    (B) $a + b^2 + c$
    (C) $a^2 + b^2 + ca$
    (D) $ab + ac + b^2 + bc$
    (E) none of these

17. $(a + b)(a - b) =$

    (A) $a^2 + 2ba - b^2$
    (B) $a^2 - 2ba - b^2$
    (C) $a^2 - b^2$
    (D) 0
    (E) none of these

18. $(a + b)^2 =$

    (A) $a^2 + 2ab + b^2$
    (B) $a^2 + b^2$
    (C) $a^2 + b^2 + ab$
    (D) $2a + 2b$
    (E) none of these

19. $-(a - b) =$

    (A) $a - b$
    (B) $-a - b$
    (C) $a + b$
    (D) $b - a$
    (E) none of these

20. $a(b + c) =$

    (A) $ab + ac$
    (B) $ab + c$
    (C) abc
    (D) $ab + bc$
    (E) none of these

21. $-a(b - c) =$

    (A) $ab - ac$
    (B) $-ab - ac$
    (C) $ac - ab$
    (D) $ab + ac$
    (E) none of these

D. Exponents

22. $10^5 =$

    (A) 1,000
    (B) 10,000
    (C) 100,000
    (D) 1,000,000
    (E) none of these

23. $107076.5 = 1.070765 \times$

    (A) 10^4
    (B) 10^5
    (C) 10^6
    (D) 10^7
    (E) none of these

24. $a^2 \times a^5 =$

    (A) a^{10}
    (B) a^7
    (C) a^3
    (D) $(2a)^{10}$
    (E) none of these

25. $(ab)^7 =$

    (A) ab^7
    (B) a^7b
    (C) a^7b^7
    (D) $a^{14}b^{14}$
    (E) none of these

26. $\left(\dfrac{a}{c}\right)^8 =$

    (A) $\dfrac{a^8}{c^8}$

    (B) $\dfrac{a^8}{c}$

    (C) $\dfrac{a}{c^8}$

    (D) $\dfrac{a^7}{c}$

    (E) none of these

27. $a^4 \times b^4 =$

    (A) $(ab)^4$
    (B) $(ab)^8$
    (C) $(ab)^{16}$
    (D) $(ab)^{12}$
    (E) none of these

28. $a^{-3} \times b^5 =$

    (A) $\dfrac{b^5}{a^3}$

    (B) $(ab)^2$

(C) $(ab)^{-15}$

(D) $\dfrac{a^3}{b^5}$

(E) none of these

29. $(a^3)^5 =$

    (A) a^8
    (B) a^2
    (C) a^{15}
    (D) a^{243}
    (E) none of these

30. $2a^{-3} =$

    (A) $\dfrac{2}{a^3}$

    (B) $2a^3$
    (C) $2\sqrt[3]{a}$
    (D) a^{-6}
    (E) none of these

31. $2a^m \times \dfrac{1}{3}a^{-n} =$

    (A) $\dfrac{2}{3}a^{m+n}$

    (B) $\dfrac{2a^m}{3a^n}$

    (C) $\dfrac{2}{3}a^{-mn}$

    (D) $-\dfrac{2}{3}a^{-mn}$

    (E) none of these

32. $3^2 + 3^{-2} + 4^1 + 6^0 =$

    (A) $8\dfrac{1}{9}$

    (B) $12\dfrac{1}{9}$

    (C) $13\dfrac{1}{9}$

    (D) $14\dfrac{1}{9}$

    (E) none of these

E. Percentages

33. 15% of 200 =

    (A) 3
    (B) 30
    (C) 300
    (D) 3,000
    (E) none of these

34. What is 3% of 5?

    (A) $\frac{5}{3}$

    (B) 15

    (C) $\frac{3}{20}$

    (D) $\frac{3}{5}$

    (E) none of these

35. What percent of 3 is 6?

    (A) 50

    (B) 20

    (C) 200

    (D) $\frac{1}{2}$

    (E) none of these

F. Equations

36. If $y^2 = 16$, then $y =$

    (A) +4 only

    (B) −4 only

    (C) ±4

    (D) ±8

    (E) none of these

37. If $x - y = 10$, then $y =$

    (A) $x - 10$

    (B) $10 + x$

    (C) $10 - x$

    (D) 10

    (E) none of these

38. What is the value of x if $x + 4y = 7$ and $x - 4y = 8$?

    (A) 15

    (B) $\frac{15}{2}$

    (C) 7

    (D) $\frac{7}{2}$

    (E) none of these

39. What is the value of x and y if $x - 2y = 2$ and $2x + y = 4$?

    (A) $x = 2, y = 0$

    (B) $x = 0, y = -2$

    (C) $x = -1, y = 2$

    (D) $x = 0, y = 2$

    (E) none of these

40. If $\frac{x}{5} = \frac{7}{12}$, then $x =$

    (A) $2\frac{11}{12}$

    (B) $\frac{12}{35}$

    (C) $\frac{7}{60}$

    (D) $\frac{60}{7}$

    (E) none of these

G. Angles

Questions 41–42 refer to the diagram below:

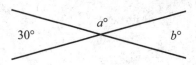

41. $a =$

    (A) 30

    (B) 150

    (C) 45

    (D) 90

    (E) none of these

42. $b =$

    (A) 30

    (B) 150

    (C) 45

    (D) 90

    (E) none of these

Question 43 refers to the diagram below:

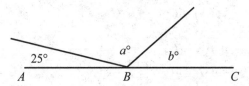

ABC is a straight angle.

43. $a + b =$

    (A) 155

    (B) 165

    (C) 180

    (D) 145

    (E) none of these

44. What is the value of $a + b + c + d + e + f + g + h$ in this diagram?

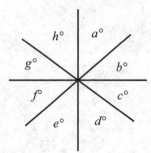

(A) 180
(B) 240
(C) 360
(D) 540
(E) none of these

H. Parallel Lines

Questions 45–51 refer to the diagram below:

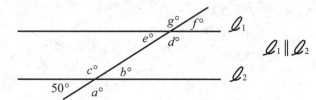

45. $a =$

(A) 50
(B) 130
(C) 100
(D) 40
(E) none of these

46. $b =$

(A) 50
(B) 130
(C) 100
(D) 40
(E) none of these

47. $c =$

(A) 50
(B) 130
(C) 100
(D) 40
(E) none of these

48. $d =$

(A) 50
(B) 130
(C) 100
(D) 40
(E) none of these

49. $e =$

(A) 50
(B) 130
(C) 100
(D) 40
(E) none of these

50. $f =$

(A) 50
(B) 130
(C) 100
(D) 40
(E) none of these

51. $g =$

(A) 50
(B) 130
(C) 100
(D) 40
(E) none of these

I. Triangles

(*Note*: Figures are not drawn to scale.)

52. $a =$

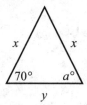

(A) 70°
(B) 40°
(C) $\dfrac{xy}{70°}$
(D) cannot be determined
(E) none of these

53. $x =$

(A) 3

(B) $\dfrac{50}{3}$

(C) $3\sqrt{2}$

(D) cannot be determined

(E) none of these

54. Which is a possible value for a?

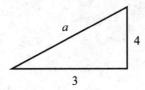

(A) 1

(B) 6

(C) 10

(D) 7

(E) 8

55. In the triangle below, $x =$

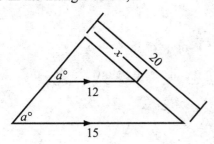

(A) 12

(B) 16

(C) 15

(D) 10

(E) none of these

56. In the triangle below, if $B > A$, then

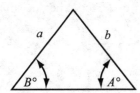

(A) $b = a$

(B) $b > a$

(C) $b < a$

(D) a relation between b and a cannot be determined

(E) none of these

57. In the triangle below, if $b < a$, then

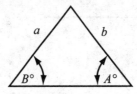

(A) $B > A$

(B) $B = A$

(C) $B < A$

(D) a relation between B and A cannot be determined

(E) none of these

58. In the triangle below, $x =$

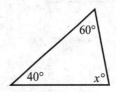

(A) 100

(B) 80

(C) 90

(D) 45

(E) none of these

59. In the triangle below, $x =$

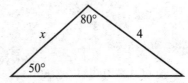

(A) $4\sqrt{2}$

(B) 8

(C) 4

(D) a number between 1 and 4

(E) none of these

60. In the diagram below, $x =$

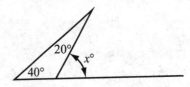

(A) 40

(B) 20

(C) 60

(D) 80

(E) none of these

61. In the right triangle below, $x =$

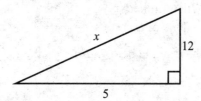

(A) 17
(B) 13
(C) 15
(D) $12\sqrt{2}$
(E) none of these

Questions 62–63 refer to the diagram below:

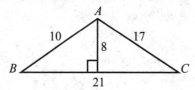

62. The perimeter of the triangle ABC is

(A) 16
(B) 48
(C) 168
(D) 84
(E) none of these

63. The area of triangle ABC is

(A) 170
(B) 85
(C) 168
(D) 84
(E) none of these

Questions 64–65 refer to the diagram below:

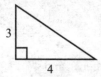

64. The area of the triangle is

(A) 6
(B) 7
(C) 12
(D) any number between 5 and 7
(E) none of these

65. The perimeter of the triangle is

(A) 7
(B) 12
(C) 15
(D) any number between 7 and 12
(E) none of these

J. Circles

Questions 66–67 refer to the diagram below:

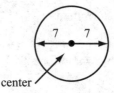

66. The area of the circle is

(A) 49
(B) 49π
(C) 14π
(D) 196π
(E) none of these

67. The circumference of the circle is

(A) 14π
(B) 7π
(C) 49π
(D) 14
(E) none of these

68. In the diagram below, $x =$

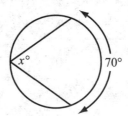

(A) 70°
(B) 35°
(C) 90°
(D) a number that cannot be determined
(E) none of these

69. In the diagram below, $x =$

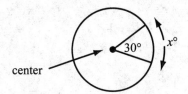

(A) 30°
(B) 60°
(C) 90°
(D) a number that cannot be determined
(E) none of these

70. In the diagram below, $y =$

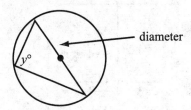

(A) 145°
(B) 60°
(C) 90°
(D) a number that cannot be determined
(E) none of these

K. Other Figures

(*Note*: Figures are not drawn to scale.)

Questions 71–72 refer to the diagram below:

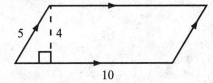

71. The area of the figure is

(A) 15
(B) 20
(C) 40
(D) 50
(E) none of these

72. The perimeter of the figure is

(A) 15
(B) 30
(C) 40
(D) 50
(E) none of these

Questions 73–75 refer to the figure below:

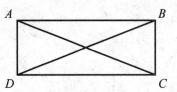

ABCD is a rectangle.

73. What is *BC* if *AD* = 6?

(A) 4
(B) 6
(C) 8
(D) 10
(E) 12

74. What is *DC* if *AB* = 8?

(A) 4
(B) 6
(C) 8
(D) 10
(E) 12

75. What is *DB* if *AC* = 10?

(A) 4
(B) 6
(C) 8
(D) 10
(E) 12

Questions 76–77 refer to the diagram below:

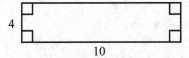

76. The area of the figure is

(A) 14
(B) 40
(C) 80
(D) 28
(E) none of these

77. The perimeter of the figure is

(A) 14
(B) 28
(C) 36
(D) 40
(E) none of these

Questions 78–79 refer to the figure below:

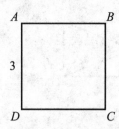

ABCD is a square; *AD* = 3.

78. What is the area of the square?

(A) 9
(B) 12
(C) 16
(D) 20
(E) none of these

79. What is the perimeter of the square?

(A) 9
(B) 12
(C) 16
(D) 20
(E) none of these

80. The volume of the rectangular solid below is

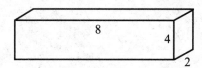

(A) 48
(B) 64
(C) 128
(D) 72
(E) none of these

L. Number Lines

Questions 81–82 refer to the diagram below:

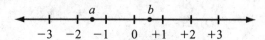

81. Which best defines the range in values of *b*?

(A) $-2 < b < 1$
(B) $0 < b < 2$
(C) $0 < b < 1$
(D) $-3 < b < 3$
(E) $0 < b$

82. Which best defines the range in values of *a*?

(A) $-2 < a$
(B) $-2 < a < -1$
(C) $-2 < a < 0$
(D) $a < -1$
(E) $-3 < a < 0$

M. Coordinates

Questions 83–85 refer to the diagram below:

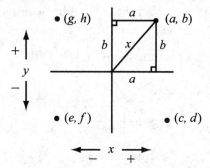

83. How many of the variables *a, b, c, d, e, f, g, h* are positive?

(A) 1
(B) 2
(C) 3
(D) 4
(E) 5

84. How many of the variables *a, b, c, d, e, f, g, h* are negative?

(A) 1
(B) 2
(C) 3
(D) 4
(E) 5

85. If *a* = 3, *b* = 4, what is *x*?

(A) 3
(B) 4
(C) 5
(D) 6
(E) none of these

86. What is the slope of the line below?

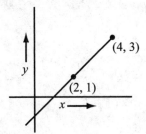

(A) −1
(B) 0
(C) +1
(D) +2
(E) +3

N. Inequalities

Note: Any variable can be positive or negative or 0.

87. If $x > y$, then $4x > 4y$

(A) always
(B) sometimes
(C) never

88. If $x + y > z$, then $y > z − x$

(A) always
(B) sometimes
(C) never

89. If $−4 < −x$, then $4 > x$

(A) always
(B) sometimes
(C) never

90. If $m > n,$ where q is any number, then $qm > qn$

(A) always
(B) sometimes
(C) never

91. If $x > y$ and $p > q$, then $x + p > y + q$

(A) always
(B) sometimes
(C) never

92. If $x > y$ and $p > q$, then $xp > qy$

(A) always
(B) sometimes
(C) never

O. Averages

93. What is the average of 30, 40, and 80?

(A) 150
(B) 75
(C) 50
(D) 45
(E) none of these

94. What is the average speed in mph of a car traveling 40 miles in 4 hours?

(A) 160
(B) 10
(C) 120
(D) 30
(E) none of these

P. Shortcuts

95. Which is greater?
(*Don't calculate a common denominator!*)

$$\frac{7}{16} \text{ or } \frac{3}{7}$$

(A) $\frac{7}{16}$

(B) $\frac{3}{7}$

(C) They are equal.
(D) A relationship cannot be determined.

96. $\frac{7}{12} + \frac{3}{5} =$

(A) $1\frac{11}{60}$

(B) $1\frac{13}{60}$

(C) $1\frac{15}{60}$

(D) $\frac{10}{17}$

(E) none of these

97. $\frac{7}{12} − \frac{3}{5} =$

(A) $−\frac{1}{60}$

(B) $−\frac{3}{60}$

(C) $−1\frac{11}{60}$

(D) $\frac{4}{7}$

(E) none of these

98. $\dfrac{4}{250} =$

(*Don't divide 250 into 4!*)

(A) 0.016
(B) 0.04
(C) 0.004
(D) 0.025
(E) none of these

99. What is *c* if

$$200 = \frac{a + b + c}{2} \text{ and } 80 = \frac{a + b}{3}?$$

(A) 160
(B) 140
(C) 120
(D) 100
(E) none of these

100. What is the value of $95 \times 75 - 95 \times 74$?
(*Don't multiply* 95×75 *or* $95 \times 74!$)

(A) 65
(B) 75
(C) 85
(D) 95
(E) none of these

101. Find the value of

$$\frac{140 \times 15}{5 \times 7}$$

(*Don't multiply* $140 \times 15!$)

(A) 20
(B) 40
(C) 60
(D) 90
(E) none of these

ANSWERS, DIAGNOSIS, SOLUTIONS, GENERALIZATIONS, AND RULES

Answers

A. Fractions
1. B
2. A
3. A
4. C
5. B

B. Even–Odd Relationships
6. A
7. B
8. B
9. B
10. A
11. B
12. B

C. Factors
13. A
14. C
15. B
16. D
17. C
18. A
19. D
20. A
21. C

D. Exponents
22. C
23. B
24. B
25. C
26. A
27. A
28. A
29. C
30. A
31. B
32. D

E. Percentages
33. B
34. C
35. C

F. Equations
36. C
37. A
38. B
39. A
40. A

G. Angles
41. B
42. A
43. A
44. C

H. Parallel Lines
45. B
46. A
47. B
48. B
49. A
50. A
51. B

I. Triangles
52. A
53. A
54. B
55. B
56. B
57. C
58. B
59. C
60. C
61. B
62. B
63. D
64. A
65. B

J. Circles
66. B
67. A
68. B
69. A
70. C

K. Other Figures
71. C
72. B
73. B
74. C
75. D
76. B
77. B
78. A
79. B
80. B

L. Number Lines
81. C
82. B

M. Coordinates
83. D
84. D
85. C
86. C

N. Inequalities
87. A
88. A
89. A
90. B
91. A
92. B

O. Averages
93. C
94. B

P. Shortcuts
95. A
96. A
97. A
98. A
99. A
100. D
101. C

Basic Math Skills Diagnosis

Math Area	Total Questions	Study These Answers (see answer key, p. 27)	Pages in Text for Review	Complete Math Refresher Numbers (starting on p. 147)
A. Fractions	5	1–5	29	101–112, 123–129
B. Even–Odd Relationships	7	6–12	29	603–606
C. Factors	9	13–21	29–30	409
D. Exponents	11	22–32	30	429–430
E. Percentages	3	33–35	31	106, 107, 114
F. Equations	5	36–40	31	406–409
G. Angles	4	41–44	32	500–503
H. Parallel Lines	7	45–51	32	504
I. Triangles	14	52–65	32–35	306–308, 505–516
J. Circles	5	66–70	35	310–311, 524–529
K. Other Figures	10	71–80	36	303–305, 309, 312–316, 517–523
L. Number Lines	2	81–82	37	410a
M. Coordinates	4	83–86	37	410b–418
N. Inequalities	6	87–92	37–38	419–428
O. Averages	2	93–94	38	601
P. Shortcuts	7	95–101	38	128, 609

Solutions, Generalizations, and Rules

A. Fractions

1. (B)

$$\frac{a}{\frac{b}{c}} = a \times \frac{c}{b} = \boxed{\frac{ac}{b}}$$

c → *Invert to multiply*

Alternate way:

$$\frac{a}{\frac{b}{c}} = \frac{a}{\frac{b}{c}} \times \frac{c}{c} = \frac{ac}{\frac{b}{\cancel{c}} \times \cancel{c}} = \boxed{\frac{ac}{b}}$$

2. (A)

$$\frac{1}{\frac{1}{y}} = 1 \times \frac{y}{1} = \boxed{y}$$

y → *Invert to multiply*

3. (A)

$$\frac{\frac{a}{b}}{c} = \frac{\frac{a}{b}}{c} \times \frac{b}{b} = \frac{a}{cb} = \boxed{\frac{a}{bc}}$$

→ *Multiply by $\frac{b}{b}$*

4. (C)

$$\frac{1}{\frac{x}{y}} = 1 \times \frac{y}{x} = \boxed{\frac{y}{x}}$$

y → *Invert to multiply*

5. (B)

$$\frac{\frac{a}{b}}{\frac{b}{a}} = \frac{a}{b} \times \frac{a}{b} = \boxed{\frac{a^2}{b^2}}$$

a → *Invert to multiply*

Alternate way:

$$\frac{\frac{a}{b}}{\frac{b}{a}} = \frac{\frac{a}{b} \times a}{\frac{b}{a} \times a} = \frac{\frac{a^2}{b}}{\frac{b}{\cancel{a}}\cancel{a}} = \frac{\frac{a^2}{b}}{b} = \frac{\frac{a^2}{\cancel{b}} \times \cancel{b}}{b \times b} = \boxed{\frac{a^2}{b^2}}$$

B. Even–Odd Relationships

6. (A) ODD × ODD = $\boxed{\text{ODD ONLY}}$

   $3 \times 3 = 9; 5 \times 5 = 25$

7. (B) ODD + or − ODD = $\boxed{\text{EVEN ONLY}}$

   $5 + 3 = 8; 5 - 3 = 2$

8. (B) EVEN × EVEN = $\boxed{\text{EVEN ONLY}}$

   $2 \times 2 = 4; 4 \times 2 = 8$

9. (B) EVEN + or − EVEN = $\boxed{\text{EVEN ONLY}}$

   $6 + 2 = 8; 10 - 4 = 6$

10. (A) $(\text{ODD})^{\text{ODD}}$ = $\boxed{\text{ODD ONLY}}$

    $3^3 = 3 \times 3 \times 3 = 27$ (odd)

    $1^{27} = 1$ (odd)

11. (B) $(\text{EVEN})^{\text{EVEN}}$ = $\boxed{\text{EVEN ONLY}}$

    $2^2 = 4$ (even); $4^2 = 16$ (even)

12. (B) $(\text{EVEN})^{\text{ODD}}$ = $\boxed{\text{EVEN ONLY}}$

    $2^3 = 2 \times 2 \times 2 = 8$ (even)

    $4^1 = 4$ (even)

C. Factors

13. (A) $(x + 3)(x + 2) = x^2 \ldots$

    $(x + 3)(x + 2) = x^2 + 2x + 3x \ldots$

    $(x + 3)(x + 2) = x^2 + 2x + 3x + 6$

    $(x + 3)(x + 2) = \boxed{x^2 + 5x + 6}$

14. (C) $(x + 3)(x - 2) = x^2 \ldots$

    $(x + 3)(x - 2) = x^2 - 2x + 3x \ldots$

    $(x + 3)(x - 2) = x^2 - 2x + 3x - 6$

    $(x + 3)(x - 2) = \boxed{x^2 + x - 6}$

15. (B) $(x - 3)(y - 2) = xy \ldots$

$(x - 3)(y - 2) = xy - 2x - 3y \ldots$

$(x - 3)(y - 2) = \boxed{xy - 2x - 3y + 6}$

16. (D) $(a + b)(b + c) = ab \ldots$

$(a + b)(b + c) = ab + ac + b^2 \ldots$

$(a + b)(b + c) = \boxed{ab + ac + b^2 + bc}$

17. (C) $(a + b)(a - b) =$

$(a + b)(a - b) = a^2 \ldots$

$(a + b)(a - b) = a^2 - ab + ba \ldots$

$(a + b)(a - b) = a^2 - ab + ba - b^2$

$(a + b)(a - b) = a^2 - \cancel{ab} + \cancel{ba} - b^2$

$(a + b)(a - b) = \boxed{a^2 - b^2}$ ***Memorize***

18. (A) $(a + b)^2 = (a + b)(a + b)$

$(a + b)(a + b) = a^2 \ldots$

$(a + b)(a + b) = a^2 + ab + ba \ldots$

$(a + b)(a + b) = a^2 + ab + ba + b^2$

$(a + b)^2 = \boxed{a^2 + 2ab + b^2}$ ***Memorize***

19. (D) $-(a - b) = -a - (-b)$

$-(a - b) = -a + b$

$-(a - b) = \boxed{b - a}$ ***Memorize***

20. (A) $a(b + c) =$

$a(b + c) = \boxed{ab + ac}$

21. (C) $-a(b - c) =$

$-a(b - c) = -ab - a(-c)$

$= -ab + ac = \boxed{ac - ab}$

D. Exponents

22. (C) $10^5 = \boxed{100{,}000}$

 └ write 5 zeros

23. (B) $107076.5 = 1\,0\,7\,0\,7\,6\,.\,5$

$\quad\quad\quad\quad\quad\quad\quad\quad {}_{5\ 4\ 3\ 2\ 1}$

$= 1.070765 \times \boxed{10^5}$

24. (B) $a^2 \times a^5 = \boxed{a^7}$

Add exponents

$a^m \times a^n = a^{m+n}$

25. (C) $(ab)^7 = \boxed{a^7 b^7}$

$(ab)^m = a^m b^m$

26. (A) $\left(\dfrac{a}{c}\right)^8 = \boxed{\dfrac{a^8}{c^8}}$

$\left(\dfrac{a}{c}\right)^m = \dfrac{a^m}{c^m}$

27. (A) $a^4 \times b^4 = \boxed{(ab)^4}$

$a^m \times b^m = (ab)^m$

28. (A) $a^{-3} \times b^5 = \boxed{\dfrac{b^5}{a^3}}$

$a^{-m} \times b^n = \dfrac{b^n}{a^m}$

29. (C) $(a^3)^5 = \boxed{a^{15}}$

Multiply exponents

$(a^m)^n = a^{mn}$

30. (A) $2a^{-3} = \boxed{\dfrac{2}{a^3}}$

$ax^{-b} = \dfrac{a}{x^b}$

since $a^{-n} = \dfrac{1}{a^n}$

31. (B) $2a^m \times \dfrac{1}{3}a^{-n} = \dfrac{2}{3}a^m a^{-n}$

$\quad\quad\quad\quad\quad\quad = \dfrac{2}{3}a^{m-n} \text{ or } \boxed{\dfrac{2a^m}{3a^n}}$

32. (D) $3^2 + 3^{-2} + 4^1 + 6^0 =$

$3^2 = 3 \times 3 = 9$

$3^{-2} = \dfrac{1}{3^2} = \dfrac{1}{9}$

$4^1 = 4$ (any number to 1 power = that number)

$6^0 = 1$ (any number to 0 power = 1)

$3^2 + 3^{-2} + 4^1 + 6^0 = 9 + \dfrac{1}{9} + 4 + 1 = \boxed{14\dfrac{1}{9}}$

E. Percentages

Translate: is → =

of → × (times)

percent (%) → $\dfrac{}{100}$

what → x (or y, etc.)

33. (B) 15 % of 200 =

   ↓ ↓   ↓ ↓ ↓

$15\dfrac{}{100} \times 200 =$

$\dfrac{15}{100} \times 200 =$

$\dfrac{15}{100} \times 200 = \boxed{30}$

34. (C) What is 3 % of 5?

  ↓ ↓ ↓ ↓   ↓ ↓

$x = 3\dfrac{}{100} \times 5$

$x = \dfrac{3}{100} \times 5$

$x = \dfrac{15}{100} = \boxed{\dfrac{3}{20}}$

35. (C) What percent of 3 is 6?

  ↓   ↓   ↓ ↓ ↓ ↓

$x \quad \dfrac{}{100} \quad \times 3 = 6$

$\dfrac{x}{100} \times 3 = 6$

$\dfrac{3x}{100} = 6$

$3x = 600$

$x = \boxed{200}$

F. Equations

36. (C) $\quad y^2 = 16$

$\sqrt{y^2} = \pm\sqrt{16}$

$y = \boxed{\pm 4}$

37. (A) $x - y = 10$

Add y:

$x - y + y = 10 + y$

$x = 10 + y$

Subtract 10:

$x - 10 = 10 - 10 + y$

$\boxed{x - 10} = y$

38. (B) Add equations:

$x + 4y = 7$

$x - 4y = 8$

$\overline{2x + 4y - 4y = 15}$

$2x = 15$

$x = \boxed{\dfrac{15}{2}}$

39. (A) $x - 2y = 2$ $\boxed{1}$

$2x + y = 4$ $\boxed{2}$

Multiply $\boxed{1}$ by 2:

$2(x - 2y) = 2(2)$

We get:

$2x - 4y = 4$ $\boxed{3}$

Subtract $\boxed{2}$ from $\boxed{3}$:

$2x - 4y = 4$

$-\,(2x + \ y = 4)$

$\overline{0 - 5y = 0}$

$\boxed{y = 0}$ $\boxed{4}$

Substitute $\boxed{4}$ into either $\boxed{1}$ or $\boxed{2}$:

In $\boxed{1}$:

$x - 2y = 2$

$x - 2(0) = 2$

$\boxed{x = 2}$

40. (A) $\dfrac{x}{5} = \dfrac{7}{12}$

Here's how to find x:

Cross-multiply x:

$\left(\dfrac{x}{5} = \dfrac{7}{12}\right)$

$12x = 35$

Divide by 12:

$\dfrac{12x}{12} = \dfrac{35}{12}$

$x = \dfrac{35}{12} = \boxed{2\dfrac{11}{12}}$

G. Angles

Questions 41–42 refer to the diagram.

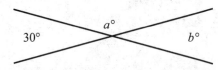

41. (B) $a°$ and 30° are *supplementary* angles (they add up to 180°).
So $a + 30 = 180$; $a =$ 150 .

42. (A) $b°$ and 30° are *vertical* angles (vertical angles are equal).
So $b =$ 30 .

43. (A) $a°$, $b°$, and 25° make up a *straight* angle, which is 180°.

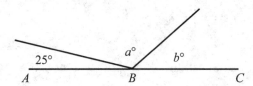

ABC is a straight angle.
$a + b + 25 = 180$
$a + b = 180 - 25$
$a + b =$ 155

44. (C) The sum of the angles in the diagram is 360° , the number of degrees around the circumference of a circle.

H. Parallel Lines

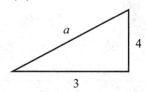

$\ell_1 \parallel \ell_2$

45. (B) $a + 50 = 180$
$a =$ 130

46. (A) $b =$ 50 (vertical angles)

47. (B) $c = a$ (vertical angles)
= 130

48. (B) $d = c$ (alternate interior angles are equal)
= 130

49. (A) $e = b$ (alternate interior angles)
= 50

50. (A) $f = e$ (vertical angles)
= 50

51. (B) $g = d$ (vertical angles)
= 130

I. Triangles

(*Note*: Figures are not drawn to scale.)

52. (A)

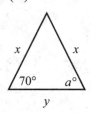

If two sides are equal, base angles are equal. Thus a = 70° .

53. (A)

If base angles are equal, then sides are equal, so $x = 3$.

54. (B)

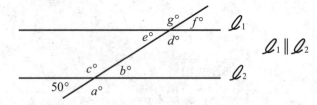

The sum of two sides must be *greater* than the third side. Try choices:
(A) $1 + 3 = 4$: (A) is not possible.
(B) $3 + 4 > 6$; $6 + 3 > 4$;
$4 + 6 > 3$: OK.
(C) $3 + 4 \ngtr 10$: (C) is not possible.
(D) $3 + 4 = 7$: (D) is not possible.
(E) $3 + 4 \ngtr 8$: (E) is not possible.

55. (B) Using similar triangles, write a *proportion* with x.

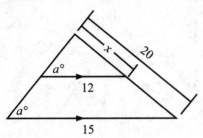

$$\frac{x}{20} = \frac{12}{15}$$
$$15x = 12 \times 20$$
$$x = \frac{12 \times 20}{15}$$
$$x = \frac{4 \times 3 \times 5 \times 4}{5 \times 3}$$
$$x = \frac{4 \times \cancel{3} \times \cancel{5} \times 4}{\cancel{5} \times \cancel{3}} = \boxed{16}$$

In general:

$$\frac{m}{n} = \frac{q}{p} = \frac{r}{r+s}$$

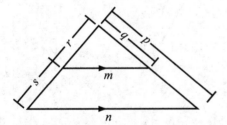

56. (B) The greater angle lies opposite the greater side and vice versa.

If $B > A$, $\boxed{b > a}$

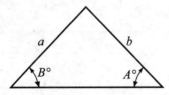

57. (C) The greater side lies opposite the greater angle and vice versa.

If $b < a$, then $\boxed{B < A}$

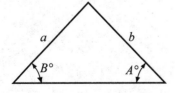

58. (B) Sum of angles of triangle = 180°.

So $40 + 60 + x = 180$
$$100 + x = 180$$
$$x = \boxed{80}$$

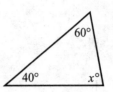

59. (C)

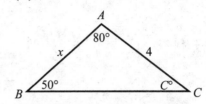

First calculate $\angle C$. Call it y.

$80 + 50 + y = 180$ (sum of angles = 180°)

$y = 50$

Since $\angle C = y = 50$ and $\angle B = 50$, side $AB =$ side AC.

$AB = x = \boxed{4}$

60. (C) $x° = 20° + 40°$ (sum of *remote* interior angles = exterior angle).

$x = \boxed{60}$

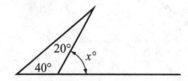

In general,

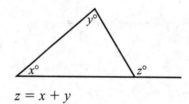

$z = x + y$

61. (B)

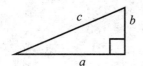

In right Δ, $a^2 + b^2 = c^2$
So for

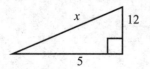

$5^2 + 12^2 = x^2$
$25 + 144 = x^2$
$169 = x^2$
$\sqrt{169} = x$
$13 = x$

Note: Specific right triangles you should memorize; use multiples to generate other triangles.

Example of multiples:

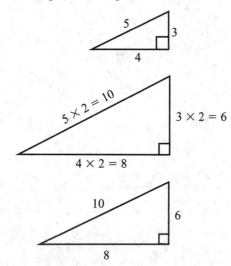

Memorize the following standard triangles (not drawn to scale):

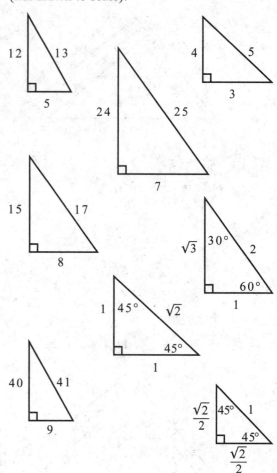

62. (B) Perimeter = sum of sides
$10 + 17 + 21 = 48$

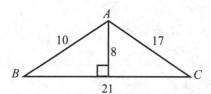

63. (D)

Area of $\Delta = \frac{1}{2}bh$

Area of $\Delta = \frac{1}{2}(21)(8) = 84$

64. (A) Area of any triangle $= \frac{1}{2}$base $\times$ height

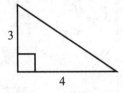

Here 4 is base and 3 is height.

So area $= \frac{1}{2}(4 \times 3) = \frac{1}{2}(12) = \boxed{6}$.

65. (B)

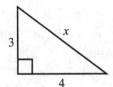

To find perimeter, we need to find the sum of the sides. The sum of the sides is $3 + 4 + x$.

We need to find x. From the solution in Question 61, we should realize that we have a 3–4–5 right triangle, so $x = 5$.

The perimeter is then $3 + 4 + 5 = \boxed{12}$.

Note that you could have found x by using the Pythagorean theorem:

$3^2 + 4^2 = x^2$; $9 + 16 = x^2$; $25 = x^2$; $\sqrt{25} = x$; $5 = x$

J. Circles

Questions 66–67 refer to the figure below.

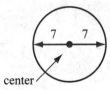

66. (B) Area $= \pi r^2 = \pi(7)^2$
$\qquad = \boxed{49\pi}$

67. (A) Circumference $= 2\pi r = 2\pi(7)$
$\qquad = \boxed{14\pi}$

68. (B) Inscribed angle $= \frac{1}{2}$arc

$x° = \frac{1}{2}(70°)$

$\quad = \boxed{35°}$

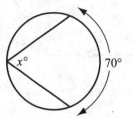

69. (A) Central angle $=$ arc
$\boxed{30°} = x°$

Note: The *total* number of degrees around the circumference is 360°. So a central angle of 30°, like the one below, cuts $\frac{30}{360} = \frac{1}{12}$ the circumference.

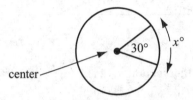

70. (C) The diameter cuts a 180° arc on the circle, so an inscribed angle

$y = \frac{1}{2}$arc $= \frac{1}{2}(180°) = \boxed{90°}$.

Here is a good thing to remember:
Any inscribed angle whose triangle base is a diameter is 90°.

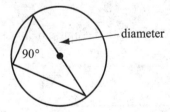

K. Other Figures

Questions 71–72 refer to the figure below.

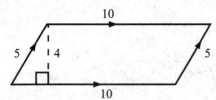

71. (C) Area of parallelogram = base × height = (10)(4) = 40

72. (B) Perimeter = sum of sides = 5 + 5 + 10 + 10 = 30

Questions 73–75 refer to the figure below.

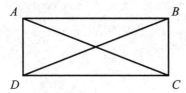

ABCD is a rectangle.

73. (B) In a rectangle (as in a parallelogram), opposite sides are equal.

    So $AD = BC =$ 6.

74. (C) In a rectangle (as in a parallelogram), opposite sides are equal.

    So $DC = AB =$ 8.

75. (D) In a rectangle (but not in a parallelogram), the diagonals are equal.

    So $DB = AC =$ 10.

Questions 76–77 refer to the figure below.

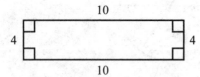

76. (B) Area of rectangle = length × width
    = 4 × 10 = 40.

77. (B) Perimeter = sum of sides = 4 + 4 + 10 + 10 = 28.

Questions 78–79 refer to the figure below.

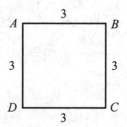

78. (A) Area of a square with side x is x^2. (All sides of a square are equal.) So length = width. Since $x = 3$, $x^2 =$ 9.

79. (B) Perimeter of a square is the sum of all sides of the square. Since all sides are equal, if one side is x, perimeter = $4x$.

    $x = 3$, so $4x =$ 12.

80. (B) Volume of rectangular solid shown below = $a \times b \times c$.

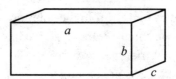

So for:

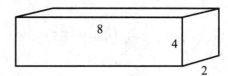

$a = 8$, $b = 4$, $c = 2$
and $a \times b \times c = 8 \times 4 \times 2 =$ 64.

Note: Volume of cube shown below = $a \times a \times a = a^3$

L. Number Lines

Questions 80–81 refer to the diagram below.

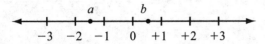

81. (C) b is between 0 and +1

so $0 < b < 1$.

82. (B) a is between −2 and −1

so $-2 < a < -1$.

M. Coordinates

Questions 83–85 refer to the diagram below.

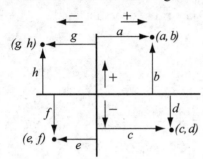

Horizontal right = +
Horizontal left = −
Vertical up   = +
Vertical down   = −

83. (D) a, b, c, h positive (4 letters)

84. (D) d, e, f, g negative (4 letters)

85. (C)

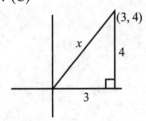

Remember the 3–4–5 right triangle. $x = 5$
You can also use the Pythagorean theorem:
$3^2 + 4^2 = x^2$; $9 + 16 = x^2$; $x^2 = 25$; $x = 5$

86. (C)

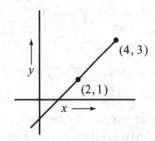

The slope of a line $y = mx + b$ is m. If two points (x_1, y_1) and (x_2, y_2) are on the line, then the slope is

$$\frac{y_2 - y_1}{x_2 - x_1} = m.$$

Here $x_1 = 2, y_1 = 1, x_2 = 4, y_2 = 3$.

So $\frac{y_2 - y_1}{x_2 - x_1} = \frac{3 - 1}{4 - 2} = \frac{2}{2} = 1$.

N. Inequalities

87. (A) You can multiply an inequality by a positive number and retain the same inequality:

$x > y$

$4x > 4y$ ALWAYS

88. (A) You can subtract the same number from both sides of an inequality and retain the same inequality:

$$x + y > z$$
$$x + y - x > z - x$$
$$y > z - x$$ ALWAYS

89. (A) If you multiply an inequality by −1, you *reverse* the original inequality sign:

$$-4 < -x$$
$$-(-4 < -x)$$
$$+4 > +x$$ ALWAYS

90. (B) If $m > n$,

$qm > qn$ if q is *positive*
$qm < qn$ if q is *negative*
$qm = qn$ if q is *zero*

So, $qm > qn$ SOMETIMES

91. (A) You can always add inequality relations to get the same inequality relation:

$$x > y$$
$$\underline{+\ p > q}$$
$$x + p > y + q \quad \boxed{\text{ALWAYS}}$$

92. (B) You can't always multiply inequality relations to get the same inequality relation. The answer is $\boxed{\text{SOMETIMES}}$. For example:

$$3 > 2 \qquad\qquad 3 > 2$$
$$\underline{\times\ -2 > -3} \qquad \underline{\times\ 2 > 1}$$
$$-6 \not> -6 \qquad\qquad 6 > 2$$

However, if x, y, p, q are positive, then if $x > y$ and $p > q$, $xp > yq$.

O. Averages

93. (C) Average of 30, 40, and 80 =

$$\frac{30 + 40 + 80}{3} = \boxed{50}$$

Average of $x + y + z + t + \ldots$

$$= \frac{x + y + z + t + \ldots}{\text{number of items}}$$

94. (B) Average speed $= \dfrac{\text{total distance}}{\text{total time}}$

Distance = 40 miles, Time = 4 hours

Average speed $= \dfrac{40 \text{ miles}}{4 \text{ hours}}$

$= \boxed{10 \text{ miles per hour}}$

P. Shortcuts

95. (A) Don't get a common denominator if you can do something easier:

$$\left(\frac{7}{16} \xrightarrow{\text{multiply}} \frac{3}{7} \right)$$

$$49 \qquad\qquad 48$$

$$49 \quad > \quad 48$$

so $\dfrac{7}{16} \quad > \quad \dfrac{3}{7}$

96. (A)

$$\frac{7}{12} \xrightarrow[\text{multiply}]{+} \frac{3}{5} = \frac{7 \times 5 + 3 \times 12}{12 \times 5}$$

$$= \frac{35 + 36}{60}$$

$$= \frac{71}{60} = \boxed{1\frac{11}{60}}$$

97. (A)

$$\frac{7}{12} \xrightarrow[\text{multiply}]{-} \frac{3}{5} = \frac{7 \times 5 - 3 \times 12}{12 \times 5}$$

$$= \frac{35 - 36}{60}$$

$$= \boxed{-\frac{1}{60}}$$

98. (A) Don't divide by 250! Multiply both numerator and denominator by 4:

$$\frac{4}{250} \times \frac{4}{4} = \frac{16}{1,000} = \boxed{0.016}$$

99. (A) Get rid of denominators!

$$200 = \frac{a + b + c}{2} \qquad\qquad \boxed{1}$$

Multiply $\boxed{1}$ by 2:
$$200 \times 2 = a + b + c \qquad\qquad \boxed{2}$$

$$80 = \frac{a + b}{3} \qquad\qquad \boxed{3}$$

Multiply $\boxed{3}$ by 3:
$$80 \times 3 = a + b \qquad\qquad \boxed{4}$$

Now subtract $\boxed{4}$ from $\boxed{2}$:
$$200 \times 2 - 80 \times 3 = a + b + c - (a + b)$$
$$= \not{a} + \not{b} + c - \not{a} - \not{b}$$
$$400 - 240 = c$$
$$\boxed{160} = c$$

100. (D) Don't multiply 95×75 or 95×74!

Factor *common* 95:

$$95 \times 75 - 95 \times 74 = 95(75 - 74)$$
$$= 95(1)$$
$$= \boxed{95}$$

101. (C) $\dfrac{140 \times 15}{5 \times 7}$

Don't multiply 140×15 if you can first *reduce*.

$$\frac{\overset{20}{\cancel{140}} \times 15}{5 \times \cancel{7}} = \frac{20 \times 15}{5}$$
$$\underset{1}{}$$

Further reduce:

$$\frac{20 \times \overset{3}{\cancel{15}}}{\underset{1}{\cancel{5}}} = \boxed{60}$$

PART 3

Strategy Section

Using Critical-Thinking Skills to Score High on the ACT

5 GENERAL STRATEGIES

General Strategies for Taking the ACT Examination

Before studying the 28 specific strategies for the Math and Reading questions, you will find it useful to review the following 5 General Strategies for taking the ACT examination.

General Strategy 1

Don't Rush into Getting an Answer without Thinking

Be Careful if Your Answer Comes Too Easily, Especially if the Question Is Toward the End of the Section

Beware of Choice A if You Get the Answer Fast or without Really Thinking

Everybody panics when taking an exam like the ACT. And what happens is that they rush into getting answers. That's okay, except that you have to think carefully. If a problem looks too easy, beware! Especially beware of the Choice A answer. It's usually a "lure" choice for those who rush into getting an answer without critically thinking about it. Here's an example:

Below is a picture of a digital clock. The clock shows that the time is 6:06. Consider all the times on the clock where the hour is the same as the minute, as in the clock shown below. Another such "double" time would be 8:08 or 9:09. What is the smallest time period between any two such doubles?

6:06

(A) 61 minutes
(B) 60 minutes
(C) 58 minutes
(D) 50 minutes
(E) 49 minutes

Did you subtract 7:07 from 8:08 and get 1 hour and 1 minute (61 minutes)? If you did you probably chose Choice A: the *lure choice*. Think—do you really believe that the test maker would give you such an easy question? The fact that you figured it out so easily and saw that Choice A was your answer should make you think twice. The thing you have to realize is that there is another possibility: 12:12 to 1:01 gives 49 minutes, and so Choice E is correct.

So, in summary, if you get the answer fast and without doing much thinking, and it's a Choice A answer, think again. You may have fallen for the Choice A lure.

Note: Choice A is often a "lure choice" for those who quickly get an answer without doing any real thinking. However, you should certainly realize that Choice A answers can occur, especially if there is no "lure choice."

General Strategy 2

Know and Learn the Directions to the Question Types before You Take the Actual Test

Never Spend Time Reading Directions during the Test or Doing Sample Questions That Don't Count

All ACT tests are standardized. For example, all the English Test questions have the same directions from test to test, as do the Math Test, etc. So it's a good idea to learn these sets of directions and familiarize yourself with the types of questions early in the game before you take your actual ACT.

Here's an example of a set of ACT directions for the English Test.

English Test

45 minutes—75 Questions

Directions:

In the five passages that follow, certain words and phrases are underlined and numbered. In the right-hand column, you will find alternatives for the underlined part. In most cases, you are to choose the one that best expresses the idea, makes the statement appropriate for standard written English, or is worded most consistently with the style and tone of the passage as a whole. If you think the original version is best, choose "NO CHANGE." In some cases, you will find in the right-hand column a question about the underlined part. You are to choose the best answer to the question.

You will also find questions about a section of the passage, or about the passage as a whole. These questions do not refer to an underlined portion of the passage, but rather are identified by a number or numbers in a box.

For each question, choose the alternative you consider best and fill in the corresponding oval on your answer document. Read each passage through once before you begin to answer the questions that accompany it. For many of the questions, you must read several sentences beyond the question to determine the answer. Be sure that you have read far enough ahead each time you choose an alternative.

If on your actual test you spend time reading these directions and/or answering the sample question, you will waste valuable time.

As you go through this book, you will become familiar with all the question types so that you won't have to read their directions on the actual test.

General Strategy   3

Do Not Leave an Answer Blank

There is no penalty for guessing, so make sure you answer every question, even if you have to "blindly" guess. Strategies in this book, however, should greatly reduce your need for guessing.

General Strategy   4

Write As Much As You Want in Your Test Booklet

Test Booklets Aren't Graded—So Use Them as You Would Scrap Paper

Many students are afraid to mark up their test booklets. But the booklets are not graded! Make any marks you want. In fact, some of the strategies demand that you extend or draw lines in geometry questions or label diagrams, circle incorrect answers, etc. That's why when I see computer programs that show only the questions on a screen and prevent the student from marking a diagram or circling an answer, I realize that such programs prevent the student from using many powerful strategies. *So write all you want in your test booklet—use your test paper as you would scrap paper.*

General Strategy   5

Use Your Own Coding System to Tell You Which Questions to Return To

If You Have Extra Time after Completing a Test Section, You'll Know Exactly Which Questions Need More Attention

When you are sure that you have answered a question correctly, mark your question paper with ✓. For questions you are not sure of but for which you have eliminated some of the choices, use **?**. For questions that you're not sure of at all or for which you have not been able to eliminate any choices, use **??**. This will give you a bird's-eye view of what questions you should return to if you have time left after completing a particular test section.

28 EASY-TO-LEARN STRATEGIES

19 Math Strategies + 9 Reading Strategies

Critical thinking is the ability to think clearly in order to solve problems and answer questions of all types—ACT questions, for example, both Math and Reading!

Educators who are deeply involved in research on Critical-Thinking Skills tell us that such skills are straightforward, practical, teachable, and learnable.

The 19 Math Strategies and 9 Reading Strategies in this section are Critical-Thinking Skills. These strategies have the potential to raise your ACT scores dramatically.

Note: On the Math Questions in the ACT, each question will have 5 choices, whereas in the English, Reading, and Science sections each question has only 4 choices.

Be sure to learn and use the strategies that follow!

How to Learn the Strategies

1. For each strategy, look at the heading describing the strategy.

2. Try to answer the first example without looking at the explanatory answer.

3. Then look at the explanatory answer and, if you got the right answer, see if the method described will enable you to solve the question in a better way with a faster approach.

4. Then try each of the next example(s) without looking at the explanatory answer(s).

5. Use the same procedure as in (3) for each of the example(s).

The Math Strategies start on page 44, and the Reading Strategies start on page 102. However, before you start the Math Strategies, it would be wise for you to look at the *Important Note on the Allowed Use of Calculators on the ACT*.

Important Note on the Allowed Use of Calculators on the ACT

Although the use of calculators on the Math ACT will be allowed, using a calculator may sometimes be more tedious when in fact you can use another problem-solving method or shortcut. So you must be selective on when and when not to use a calculator on the test.

Here's an example of when a calculator should *not* be used:

$$\frac{2}{5} \times \frac{5}{6} \times \frac{6}{7} \times \frac{7}{8} \times \frac{8}{9} \times \frac{9}{10} \times \frac{10}{11} =$$

(A) $\frac{9}{11}$

(B) $\frac{2}{11}$

(C) $\frac{11}{36}$

(D) $\frac{10}{21}$

(E) $\frac{244}{360}$

Here the use of a calculator may take some time. However, if you use the strategy of canceling numerators and denominators (Math Strategy 1, Example 3 on page 45) as shown,

Cancel numerators/denominators:

$$\frac{2}{\cancel{5}} \times \frac{\cancel{5}}{\cancel{6}} \times \frac{\cancel{6}}{\cancel{7}} \times \frac{\cancel{7}}{\cancel{8}} \times \frac{\cancel{8}}{\cancel{9}} \times \frac{\cancel{9}}{\cancel{10}} \times \frac{\cancel{10}}{11} = \frac{2}{11}$$

you can see that the answer comes easily as $\frac{2}{11}$.

Here's an example of when using a calculator may get you the solution *as fast as* using a strategy without the calculator:

25 percent of 16 is equivalent to $\frac{1}{2}$ of what number?

(A) 2

(B) 4

(C) 8

(D) 16

(E) 32

Using a calculator, you'd use Math Strategy 2 (page 46) (translating *of* to *times* and *is* to *equals*), first calculating 25 percent of 16 to get **4**. Then you'd say 4 = half of what number and you'd find that number to be **8**.

Without using a calculator, you'd still use Math Strategy 2 (the translation strategy), but you could write 25 percent as $\frac{1}{4}$, so you'd figure out that $\frac{1}{4} \times 16$ is **4**. Then you'd call the number you want to find *x*, and say $4 = \frac{1}{2}(x)$. You'd find $x = 8$.

Note that both methods, with and without a calculator, are about equally efficient; however, the technique in the second method can be used for many more problems and hones more thinking skills.

Key Way of Solving Math Equations on the ACT

So many people ask me, "How do I solve problems in math—what's the way to really solve a problem, especially on a test, and especially on the ACT?" I recently looked at some actual ACT questions and wanted to see how fast I could solve them and what approach I was taking that others may not take.

Here's what I can tell you:

You first need the basic skills, like knowing what an odd number is or how to multiply numbers with exponents. All this, of course, can be found in the Math Refreshers part of this book. But what is really critical is knowing *what to do first in the problem*. What to *extract* from the problem that will *lead you to the next steps* that will finally lead you to a solution. And you want to do all this without wracking your brain. (This can be found in more detail in Math Strategy 17, page 84.)

Here are two examples from actual ACT tests:

Which of the following equations expresses *c* in terms of *a* for all real numbers *a*, *b*, and *c*, such that $a^3 = b$ and $b^2 = c$?

(F) $c = a^6$
(G) $c = a^5$
(H) $c = 2a^3$
(J) $c = \frac{1}{2}a$
(K) $c = a$

You have to know what is being asked and spot what you need to work with.

The question says "express *c* in terms of *a*." So you should immediately think that you cannot have "*b*" in the answer, just *c* and *a*. So when you see "such that $a^3 = b$ and $b^2 = c$," you want to get rid of the *b*. How do you do this? You substitute (a basic skill) $b = a^3$ into $b^2 = c$. That is, replace in $b^2 = c$, a^3 for *b*.

You get: $(a^3)^2 = c$ or $a^6 = c$. (Choice F).

Here's another actual ACT question:

A certain perfect square has exactly 4 digits (that is, it is an integer between 1,000 and 9,999). The positive square root of the perfect square must have how many digits?

(A) 1
(B) 2
(C) 3
(D) 4
(E) cannot be determined from the given information

What should you do first? You need to get an idea of the range of numbers you need to work with. To see a range, look for the lowest quantity and the greatest quantity. Everything in between is the range.

Work with what's given. The lowest number given is 1,000 and the highest number is 9,999. So ask yourself what number times itself gives you about 1,000. I'd say 30; $30 \times 30 = 900$. So some number a little more than 30 when multiplied by itself gives you 1,000 or perhaps a little more than 1,000. Now ask yourself, what number times itself gives you 9,999 or a little less than 9,999. I'd say a little less than 100 since $100 \times 100 = 10,000$. That number would be 99 or a little less. Thus you get a range in numbers from 31 to 99, all of which are two-digit numbers. Thus Choice B is correct.

19 MATH STRATEGIES

Using Critical-Thinking Skills in Math Questions

Note: Some of the examples here are harder than the actual ACT questions in order to help you become really good at solving the ACT questions. Note that unlike the other sections of the ACT test, the Math Section has 5 choices, not 4.

Math Strategy   1

Cancel Quantities to Make the Problem Simpler

Cancel numbers or expressions that appear on both sides of an equation; cancel same numerators and denominators. But make sure that you don't divide by 0 in what you're doing! You will save precious time by using this strategy. You won't have to make any long calculations.

Example 1

If $P \times \dfrac{11}{14} = \dfrac{11}{14} \times \dfrac{8}{9}$, then $P =$

  (A) $\dfrac{8}{9}$

  (B) $\dfrac{9}{8}$

  (C) 8

  (D) 11

  (E) 14

Choice A is correct. Do not multiply $\dfrac{11}{14} \times \dfrac{8}{9}$!

Cancel the common $\dfrac{11}{14}$:

$$P \times \dfrac{\cancel{11}}{\cancel{14}} = \dfrac{\cancel{11}}{\cancel{14}} \times \dfrac{8}{9}$$

$$P = \dfrac{8}{9} \ (Answer)$$

Note: You can cancel the $\dfrac{11}{14}$ because you are *dividing* both sides by the same nonzero number.

Suppose you had a problem like the following:

If $R \times a = a \times \dfrac{4}{5}$, then $R =$

  (A) $\dfrac{2}{3}$

  (B) $\dfrac{4}{5}$

  (C) 1

  (D) $\dfrac{5}{4}$

  (E) cannot be determined

What do you think the answer is? It's not Choice B! It is Choice E, because you cannot cancel the a, because a may be 0 and you cannot divide by 0. So if $a = 0$, R can be *any* number.

Example 2

If $y + \dfrac{7}{13} + \dfrac{6}{19} = \dfrac{3}{5} + \dfrac{7}{13} + \dfrac{6}{19}$, then $y =$

  (A) $\dfrac{6}{19}$

  (B) $\dfrac{13}{32}$

  (C) $\dfrac{7}{13}$

  (D) $\dfrac{3}{5}$

  (E) $\dfrac{211}{247}$

Choice D is correct. *Do not add the fractions!*

Don't add $\dfrac{3}{5} + \dfrac{7}{13} + \dfrac{6}{19}$! You waste a lot of time! There is a much shorter way to do the problem. Cancel $\dfrac{7}{13} + \dfrac{6}{19}$ from both sides of the equation. Thus,

$$y + \dfrac{\cancel{7}}{\cancel{13}} + \dfrac{\cancel{6}}{\cancel{19}} = \dfrac{3}{5} + \dfrac{\cancel{7}}{\cancel{13}} + \dfrac{\cancel{6}}{\cancel{19}}$$

$$y = \dfrac{3}{5} \ (Answer)$$

Example 3

$$\frac{2}{5} \times \frac{5}{6} \times \frac{6}{7} \times \frac{7}{8} \times \frac{8}{9} \times \frac{9}{10} \times \frac{10}{11} =$$

(A) $\frac{9}{11}$

(B) $\frac{2}{11}$

(C) $\frac{11}{36}$

(D) $\frac{10}{21}$

(E) $\frac{244}{360}$

Choice B is correct.

Cancel numerators/denominators:

$$\frac{2}{\cancel{5}} \times \frac{\cancel{5}}{\cancel{6}} \times \frac{\cancel{6}}{\cancel{7}} \times \frac{\cancel{7}}{\cancel{8}} \times \frac{\cancel{8}}{\cancel{9}} \times \frac{\cancel{9}}{\cancel{10}} \times \frac{\cancel{10}}{11} = \frac{2}{11}$$

Example 4

If $a + b > a - b$, which must follow?

(A) $a < 0$
(B) $b < 0$
(C) $a > b$
(D) $b > a$
(E) $b > 0$

Choice E is correct.

$a + b > a - b$

Cancel common a's:

$$\cancel{a} + b > \cancel{a} - b$$
$$b > -b$$
Add b: $b + b > b - b$
$$2b > 0$$
$$b > 0$$

Example 5

If $7\frac{2}{9} = 6 + \frac{y}{27}$, then $y =$

(A) 8
(B) 30
(C) 35
(D) 37
(E) 33

Choice E is correct.

Subtract 6 from both sides:

$$7\frac{2}{9} - 6 = 6 + \frac{y}{27} - 6$$
$$1\frac{2}{9} = \frac{y}{27}$$
$$\frac{11}{9} = \frac{y}{27}$$
$$\frac{33}{27} = \frac{y}{27}$$
$$y = 33$$

Math Strategy   **2**

Very Important Strategy:

Translate English Words into Mathematical Expressions

Many of the ACT problems are word problems. Being able to translate word problems from English into mathematical expressions or equations will help you to score high on the test. The following table translates some commonly used words into their mathematical equivalents.

By knowing this table, you will find word problems much easier to do.

TRANSLATION TABLE

Words	Math Way to Say It
is, was, has, cost	$=$ (equals)
of	$\times$ (times)
percent	$\overline{\quad}\,100$ (the percent number over 100)
x percent	$\dfrac{x}{100}$
which, what	x (or any other variable)
x and y	$x + y$
the sum of x and y	$x + y$
the difference between x and y	$x - y$
x more than y	$x + y$
x less than y	$y - x$
the product of x and y	xy
the square of x	x^2
x is greater than y	$x > y$ (or $y < x$)
x is less than y	$x < y$ (or $y > x$)
y years ago	$-y$
y years from now	$+y$
c times as old as John	$c \times$ (John's age)
x older than y	$x + y$
x younger than y	$y - x$
the increase from x to y	$y - x$
the decrease from x to y	$x - y$
the percent increase from x to y ($y > x$)	$\left(\dfrac{y - x}{x}\right)100$
the percent decrease from x to y ($y < x$)	$\left(\dfrac{x - y}{x}\right)100$
the percent of increase	$\left(\dfrac{\text{amount of increase}}{\text{original amount}}\right) \times 100$
the percent of decrease	$\left(\dfrac{\text{amount of decrease}}{\text{original amount}}\right) \times 100$
n percent greater than x	$x + \left(\dfrac{n}{100}\right)x$
n percent less than x	$x - \left(\dfrac{n}{100}\right)x$

Optional Quiz on Translation Table

Take this quiz to see if you understand the translation table before attempting the problems in Strategy 2 that follow.

1. **Mila is five years older than Juan** translates to:

    (A) $J = 5 + M$
    (B) $M + J = 5$
    (C) $M > 5 + J$
    (D) $M = 5 + J$
    (E) none of these

    Answer
    (D) Translate: **Mila** to M; **Juan** to J; **is** to $=$; **older than** to $+$
    So **Mila is five years older than Juan** becomes:

    $$M = 5 \quad + \quad J$$

2. **3 percent of 5** translates to:

    (A) $\dfrac{3}{5}$
    (B) $\dfrac{3}{100} \div 5$
    (C) $\left(\dfrac{3}{100}\right) \times 5$
    (D) $3 \times 100 \times 5$
    (E) none of these

    Answer
    (C) percent or $\% = \dfrac{}{100}$; of $= \times$; so

    3% of 5 translates to:

    $$\dfrac{3}{100} \times 5$$

3. **What percent of 3** translates to:

    (A) $x(100) \times 3$
    (B) $\left(\dfrac{x}{100}\right) \times 3$
    (C) $\left(\dfrac{x}{100}\right) \div 3$
    (D) $\left(\dfrac{3}{100}\right)x$
    (E) none of these

    Answer
    (B) Translate: what to x; percent to $\dfrac{}{100}$. Thus
    What percent of 3 becomes:

    $$x \quad \dfrac{}{100} \quad \times 3$$

4. **Six years ago, Sophia was 4 times as old as Jacob was then** translates to:

    (A) $S - 6 = 4J$
    (B) $6 - S = 4J$
    (C) $6 - S = 4(J - 6)$
    (D) $S - 6 = 4(J - 6)$
    (E) none of these

    Answer
    (D) **Six years ago, Sophia was** translates to $S - 6$. **4 times as old as Jacob is** would be $4J$. However, **4 times as old as Jacob *was* then** translates to $4(J - 6)$. Thus **six years ago, Sophia was 4 times as old as Jacob was then** translates to:

    $$S - 6 = 4 \times (J - 6)$$

5. **The percent increase from 5 to 10** translates to:

    (A) $\left[\dfrac{(10 - 5)}{5}\right] \times 100$
    (B) $\left[\dfrac{(5 - 10)}{5}\right] \times 100$
    (C) $\left[\dfrac{(10 - 5)}{10}\right] \times 100$
    (D) $\left[\dfrac{(5 - 10)}{10}\right] \times 100$
    (E) none of these

    Answer
    (A) Percent increase from a to b is $\left[\dfrac{(b - a)}{a}\right] \times 100$.
    So **the percent increase from 5 to 10** would be $\left[\dfrac{(10 - 5)}{5}\right] \times 100$.

6. **Hudson is older than John and John is older than Madison** translates to:

    (A) $H > J > M$
    (B) $H > J < M$
    (C) $H > M > J$
    (D) $M > H > J$
    (E) none of these

    Answer
    (A) **Hudson is older than John** translates to: $H > J$. **John is older than Madison** translates to $J > M$. So we have $H > J$ and $J > M$, which, consolidated, becomes $H > J > M$.

7. **Even after Phil gives Sam 6 DVDs, he still has 16 more DVDs than Sam has** translates to:

   (A) $P - 6 = 16 + S$
   (B) $P - 6 = 16 + S + 6$
   (C) $P + 6 = 16 + S + 6$
   (D) $P + 6 + 16 + S$
   (E) none of these

   Answer

   (B) **Even after Phil gives Sam 6 DVDs** translates to:

   $$P - 6 \qquad \boxed{1}$$

   He still has 16 more DVDs than Sam has translates to:

   $$= 16 + S + 6 \qquad \boxed{2}$$

   since Sam has gotten 6 additional DVDs. Thus, combining $\boxed{1}$ and $\boxed{2}$, we get:
   $P - 6 = 16 + S + 6$.

8. *q* is **10% greater than** *p* translates to:

   (A) $q = \left(\dfrac{10}{100}\right)q + p$

   (B) $q > \left(\dfrac{10}{100}\right)p$

   (C) $q = \left(\dfrac{10}{100}\right)p + p$

   (D) $q = \left(\dfrac{10}{100}\right) + p$

   (E) none of these

   Answer

   (C) *q* **is** translates to $q =$ $\boxed{1}$

   10% greater than *p* translates to $\boxed{2}$

   $\left(\dfrac{10}{100}\right)p + p$ so

   q is 10% greater than p

   translates to:
   $$q = \left(\dfrac{10}{100}\right)p + p$$

9. **200 is what percent of 20** translates to:

   (A) $200 = x \times 100 \times 20$

   (B) $200 = \left(\dfrac{x}{100}\right) \div 20$

   (C) $200 = \left(\dfrac{x}{100}\right) \times 20$

   (D) $200 = x \times 20$

   (E) none of these

Answer

(C) Translate **is** to $=$; **what** to x; **percent** to $\dfrac{}{100}$; **of** to $\times$ so we get:

200 is what percent of 20 translates to:

$$200 = \quad x \quad \dfrac{}{100} \quad \times 20$$

10. **The product of the sums of *x* and *y* and *y* and *z* is 5** translates to:

    (A) $xy + yz = 5$
    (B) $x + y + y + z = 5$
    (C) $(x + y)(yz) = 5$
    (D) $(x + y)(y + z) = 5$
    (E) none of these

Answer

(D) **The sum of *x* and *y* is** $x + y$. **The sum of *y* and *z* is** $y + z$. So the **product of those sums** is $(x + y)(y + z)$.

Thus **The product of the sums of *x* and *y* and *y* and *z* is 5** translates to:
$(x + y)(y + z) = 5$

Math Strategy 2: Examples

Example 1

Sarah is twice as old as John. Six years ago, Sarah was 4 times as old as John was then. How old is John now?

(A) 3
(B) 9
(C) 18
(D) 20
(E) impossible to determine

Choice B is correct. Translate:

Sarah is twice as old as John.

$$S = 2 \times J$$

$$S = 2J \qquad \boxed{1}$$

Six years ago Sarah was 4 times as old as John was then

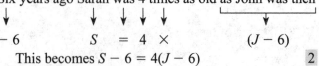

$$-6 \qquad S = 4 \times (J - 6)$$

This becomes $S - 6 = 4(J - 6)$ $\boxed{2}$

Substituting $\boxed{1}$ into $\boxed{2}$:

$$2J - 6 = 4(J - 6)$$
$$2J - 6 = 4J - 24$$
$$18 = 2J$$
$$9 = J \ (Answer)$$

Example 2

200 is what percent of 20?

(A) $\dfrac{1}{10}$

(B) 10

(C) 100

(D) 1,000

(E) 10,000

Choice D is correct. Translate:

200 is what percent of 20

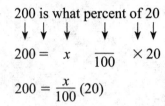

$$200 = x \quad \dfrac{}{100} \quad \times 20$$

$$200 = \dfrac{x}{100}(20)$$

Divide by 20: $10 = \dfrac{x}{100}$

Multiply by 100: $1,000 = x$ (*Answer*)

Example 3

If A is 250 percent of B, what percent of A is B?

(A) 125%

(B) $\dfrac{1}{250}$%

(C) 50%

(D) 40%

(E) 400%

Choice D is correct.

If A is 250 percent of B becomes:

$$A = 250 \quad \dfrac{}{100} \quad \times B$$

What percent of A is B? becomes:

$$x \quad \dfrac{}{100} \quad \times A = B$$

Set up the equations:

$$A = \dfrac{250}{100}B \qquad \boxed{1}$$

$$\dfrac{x}{100}A = B \qquad \boxed{2}$$

Divide Equation $\boxed{1}$ by Equation $\boxed{2}$:

$$\dfrac{A}{\dfrac{x}{100}A} = \dfrac{\dfrac{250}{100}B}{B}$$

We get:

$$\dfrac{1}{\dfrac{x}{100}} = \dfrac{250}{100}$$

Inverting, we get:

$$\dfrac{x}{100} = \dfrac{100}{250}$$

$$x = \dfrac{10,000}{250}$$

To simplify, multiply both numerator and denominator by 4 (the number that will convert the denominator to a power of 10, and therefore give us the simplest way to state the answer as a percentage):

$$x = \dfrac{10,000 \times 4}{250 \times 4} = 40$$

$$x = \dfrac{40,000}{1,000} = 40$$

Alternate way:

Let $B = 100$ (choose any number for B).

We get (after translation):

$$A = \left(\dfrac{250}{100}\right)100 \qquad \boxed{1}$$

$$\left(\dfrac{x}{100}\right)A = 100 \qquad \boxed{2}$$

From $\boxed{1}$,

$$A = 250 \qquad \boxed{3}$$

Substituting $\boxed{3}$ into $\boxed{2}$, we get:

$$\left(\dfrac{x}{100}\right)250 = 100 \qquad \boxed{4}$$

Multiplying both sides of $\boxed{4}$ by 100,

$$(x)(250) = (100)(100)$$

Dividing by 250:

$$x = \dfrac{100 \times 100}{250}$$

Simplify by multiplying numerator and denominator by 4:

$$x = \dfrac{100 \times 100 \times 4}{250 \times 4} = \dfrac{40,000}{1,000}$$

$$= 40$$

Example 4

John is now m years old and Sally is 4 years older than John. Which represents Sally's age 6 years ago?

(A) $m + 10$

(B) $m - 10$

(C) $m - 2$

(D) $m - 4$

(E) $4m - 6$

Choice C is correct.

Translate:

John is now *m* years old

$$J \quad = \quad m$$

Sally is 4 years older than John

$$S \quad = 4 \quad + \quad J$$

Sally's age 6 years ago

$$S \quad - \quad 6$$

So we get: $J = m$
$$S = 4 + J$$

and find: $S - 6 = 4 + J - 6$
$$S - 6 = J - 2$$
$$S - 6 = m - 2 \text{ (substituting } m \text{ for } J)$$

See Math Strategy 7, Example 2 (page 62) for an alternate approach to solving this problem, using a different strategy: *Use Specific Numerical Examples to Prove or Disprove Your Guess.*

Example 5

Phil has three times as many DVDs as Sam has. Even after Phil gives Sam 6 DVDs, he still has 16 more DVDs than Sam has. What was the original number of DVDs that Phil had?

(A) 20
(B) 24
(C) 28
(D) 33
(E) 42

Choice E is correct.

Translate:

Phil has three times as many DVDs as Sam has

$$P \quad = \quad 3 \quad \times \quad S$$

Even after Phil gives Sam 6 DVDs, he still has 16

$$P \quad - \quad 6 \quad\quad = 16$$

more DVDs than Sam has

$$+ \quad\quad S + 6$$

Sam now has $S + 6$ DVDs because Phil gave Sam 6 DVDs. So we end up with the equations:

$$P = 3S$$
$$P - 6 = 16 + S + 6$$

Find *P*; get rid of *S*:

$$P = 3S; \frac{P}{3} = S$$

$$P - 6 = 16 + \frac{P}{3} + 6$$

$$P - 6 = \frac{48 + P + 18}{3}$$

$$3P - 18 = 48 + P + 18$$
$$2P = 84$$
$$P = 42$$

Example 6

If *q* is 10% greater than *p* and *r* is 10% greater than *y*, *qr* is what percent greater than *py*?

(A) 1%
(B) 20%
(C) 21%
(D) 30%
(E) 100%

Choice C is correct.

Translate:

If *q* is 10% greater than *p*

$$q = \quad \frac{10}{100}p + p$$

and *r* is 10% greater than *y*

$$r = \quad \frac{10}{100}y + y$$

qr is what percent greater than *py*?

$$qr = \quad \frac{x}{100}py + py$$

So we have three equations:

$$q = \frac{10}{100}p + p = \left(\frac{10}{100} + 1\right)p \qquad \boxed{1}$$

$$r = \frac{10}{100}y + y = \left(\frac{10}{100} + 1\right)y \qquad \boxed{2}$$

$$qr = \frac{x}{100}py + py = \left(\frac{x}{100} + 1\right)py \qquad \boxed{3}$$

Multiply $\boxed{1}$ and $\boxed{2}$:

$$qr = \left(\frac{10}{100} + 1\right)^2 py \qquad \boxed{4}$$

Now equate $\boxed{4}$ with $\boxed{3}$:

$$qr = \left(\frac{x}{100} + 1\right)py = \left(\frac{10}{100} + 1\right)^2 py$$

You can see that $\left(\frac{10}{100} + 1\right)^2 = \frac{x}{100} + 1$, canceling py.

So, $\left(\frac{10}{100} + 1\right)^2 = \frac{100}{10,000} + 2\left(\frac{10}{100}\right) + 1 = \frac{x}{100} + 1$

$$\frac{100}{10,000} + \frac{20}{100} = \frac{21}{100} = \frac{x}{100}$$

$$21 = x$$

The answer is $x = 21$.

Alternate approach:

Choose numbers for p and for y:

Let $p = 10$ and $y = 20$

Then, since q is 10% greater than p:

$q = 10\%$ greater than 10

$q = \left(\frac{10}{100}\right)10 + 10 = 11$

Next, r is 10% greater than y:

$r = 10\%$ greater than 20

Or, $r = \frac{10}{100}(20) + 20 = 22$

Then:

$$qr = 11 \times 22$$
$$\text{and } py = 20 \times 10$$

So, to find what percent qr is greater than py, you would need to find:

$$\frac{qr - py}{py} \times 100 \text{ or}$$

$$\frac{11 \times 22 - 20 \times 10}{20 \times 10} \times 100$$

This is:

$$\frac{42}{200} \times 100 = 21$$

Example 7

Sales of Item X Jan–Jun 2016	
Month	**Sales ($)**
Jan	800
Feb	1,000
Mar	1,200
Apr	1,300
May	1,600
Jun	1,800

According to the table above, the monthly percent increase in sales was greatest for which of the following periods?

   (A) Jan–Feb
   (B) Feb–Mar
   (C) Mar–Apr
   (D) Apr–May
   (E) May–Jun

Choice A is correct.

The percent increase from Month A to Month B =

$$\frac{\text{sales (month B)} - \text{sales (month A)}}{\text{sales (month A)}} \times 100$$

You can see that $\frac{200}{800} \times 100$ (Jan–Feb) is the greatest.

Month	Sales ($)	Period	% Increase in Sales
Jan	800	Jan–Feb	$\frac{1,000 - 800}{800} \times 100 = \frac{200}{800} \times 100$
Feb	1,000	Feb–Mar	$\frac{1,200 - 1,000}{1,000} \times 100 = \frac{200}{1,000} \times 100$
Mar	1,200	Mar–Apr	$\frac{1,300 - 1,200}{1,200} \times 100 = \frac{100}{1,200} \times 100$
Apr	1,300	Apr–May	$\frac{1,600 - 1,300}{1,300} \times 100 = \frac{300}{1,300} \times 100$
May	1,600	May–Jun	$\frac{1,800 - 1,600}{1,600} \times 100 = \frac{200}{1,600} \times 100$
Jun	1,800		

Math Strategy — 3

Know How to Find Unknown Quantities (Areas, Lengths, Arc and Angle Measurements) from Known Quantities (The Whole Equals the Sum of Its Parts)

When asked to find a particular area or length, instead of trying to calculate it directly, find it by subtracting two other areas or lengths—a method based on the fact that the whole minus a part equals the remaining part.

This strategy is very helpful in many types of geometry problems. A very important equation to remember is

$$\text{The whole} = \text{the sum of its parts} \qquad \boxed{1}$$

Equation $\boxed{1}$ is often disguised in many forms, as seen in the following examples:

Example 1

In the diagram below, $\triangle XYZ$ has been inscribed in a circle. If the circle encloses an area of 64, and the area of $\triangle XYZ$ is 15, then what is the area of the shaded region?

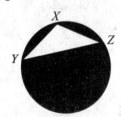

(A) 25
(B) 36
(C) 49
(D) 79
(E) It cannot be determined from the information given.

Choice C is correct. Use Equation $\boxed{1}$. Here, the whole refers to the area within the circle, and the parts refer to the areas of the shaded region and the triangle. Thus,

$$\text{Area within circle} =$$
$$\text{Area of shaded region} +$$
$$\text{Area of } \triangle XYZ$$

$64 = \text{Area of shaded region} + 15$

or Area of shaded region $= 64 - 15 = 49$ (*Answer*)

Example 2

In the diagram below, $\overline{AE}$ is a straight line, and F is a point on $\overline{AE}$. Find an expression for $m\angle DFE$.

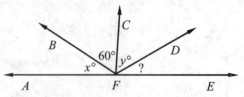

(A) $x + y - 60$
(B) $x + y + 60$
(C) $90 - x - y$
(D) $120 - x - y$
(E) $180 - x - y$

Choice D is correct. Use Equation $\boxed{1}$. Here, the whole refers to the straight angle, $\angle AFE$, and its parts refer to $\angle AFB$, $\angle BFC$, $\angle CFD$, and $\angle DFE$. Thus,

$$m\angle AFE = m\angle AFB + m\angle BFC +$$
$$m\angle CFD + m\angle DFE$$
$$180 = x + 60 + y + m\angle DFE$$
$$\text{or} \quad m\angle DFE = 180 - x - 60 - y$$
$$m\angle DFE = 120 - x - y \,(\textit{Answer})$$

Example 3

In the diagram below, $AB = m$, $BC = n$, and $AD = 10$. Find an expression for CD.

(*Note*: Diagram represents a straight line.)

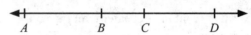

(A) $10 - mn$
(B) $10 - m - n$
(C) $m - n + 10$
(D) $m + n - 10$
(E) $m + n + 10$

Choice B is correct. Use Equation $\boxed{1}$. Here, the whole refers to AD, and its parts refer to AB, BC, and CD. Thus,

$$AD = AB + BC + CD$$
$$10 = m + n + CD$$
$$\text{or} \quad CD = 10 - m - n \,(\textit{Answer})$$

Example 4

The area of triangle $ACE = 64$. The sum of the areas of the shaded triangles ABF and FDE is 39. What is the side of square $BFDC$?

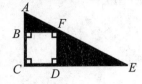

(A) 5
(B) 4
(C) $\sqrt{5}$
(D) $\sqrt{44}$
(E) cannot be determined

Choice A is correct.

Since we are dealing with areas, let's establish the area of the square $BFDC$, which will then enable us to get its side (the positive square root of its area).

Now, the area of square $BFDC$ = area of triangle ACE − (area of triangles ABF + FDE)

Area of square $BFDC = 64 - 39$
$\qquad\qquad\qquad\quad = 25$

Therefore, the side of square $BFDC$ = the square root of 25 = 5.

Example 5

In the figure below, O is the center of the circle. Triangle AOB has side 3 and angle $AOB = 90°$. What is the area of the shaded region?

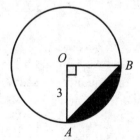

(A) $9\left(\dfrac{\pi}{4} - \dfrac{1}{2}\right)$

(B) $9\left(\dfrac{\pi}{2} - 1\right)$

(C) $9(\pi - 1)$

(D) $9\left(\dfrac{\pi}{4} - \dfrac{1}{4}\right)$

(E) cannot be determined

Choice A is correct.

Subtract knowns from knowns:

Area of shaded region = area of quarter circle AOB − area of triangle AOB

Area of quarter circle $AOB = \dfrac{\pi(3)^2}{4}$ (since $OA = 3$ and area of a quarter of a circle $= \dfrac{1}{4} \times \pi \times$ radius^2)

Area of triangle $AOB = \dfrac{3 \times 3}{2}$ (since $OB = 3$ and area of a triangle $= \dfrac{1}{2}$ base $\times$ height)

Thus, area of shaded region $= \dfrac{9\pi}{4} - \dfrac{9}{2} = 9\left(\dfrac{\pi}{4} - \dfrac{1}{2}\right)$

Example 6

The sides in the square below are each divided into five equal segments. What is the value of

$$\dfrac{\text{area of square}}{\text{area of shaded region}}?$$

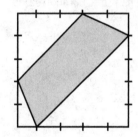

(A) $\dfrac{50}{29}$

(B) $\dfrac{50}{21}$

(C) $\dfrac{25}{4}$

(D) $\dfrac{29}{25}$

(E) none of these

Choice B is correct.

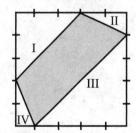

Subtract knowns from knowns:

Area of square = $5 \times 5 = 25$

Area of shaded region = area of square − area of
I − area of II − area of III − area of IV

$$\text{Area of I} = \frac{3 \times 3}{2} = \frac{9}{2}$$

$$\text{Area of II} = \frac{2 \times 1}{2} = 1$$

$$\text{Area of III} = \frac{4 \times 4}{2} = 8$$

$$\text{Area of IV} = \frac{2 \times 1}{2} = 1$$

Area of shaded region = $25 - \frac{9}{2} - 1 - 8 - 1 = \frac{21}{2}$

$$\frac{\text{area of square}}{\text{area of shaded region}} = \frac{25}{\frac{21}{2}} = 25 \times \frac{2}{21} = \frac{50}{21}$$

Example 7

Two concentric circles are shown below with inner
radius of m and outer radius of n. What is the area of
the shaded region?

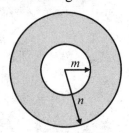

(A) $\pi(n - m)^2$
(B) $\pi(n^2 + m^2)$
(C) $\pi(n^2 - m^2)$
(D) $2\pi(n - m)$
(E) $2\pi(n + m)$

Choice C is correct.

Subtract knowns from knowns:

Area of shaded region = area of circle of radius n
− area of circle of radius m

Area of circle of radius $n = \pi n^2$

Area of circle of radius $m = \pi m^2$

Area of shaded region = $\pi n^2 - \pi m^2$
$$= \pi(n^2 - m^2)$$

Math Strategy 4

Very Important Strategy:

Remember Classic Expressions Such as

$$x^2 - y^2, x^2 + 2xy + y^2, x^2 - 2xy + y^2, \frac{x + y}{xy}$$

Memorize the following factorizations and expressions:

$x^2 - y^2 = (x + y)(x - y)$	Equation 1
$x^2 + 2xy + y^2 = (x + y)(x + y) = (x + y)^2$	Equation 2
$x^2 - 2xy + y^2 = (x - y)(x - y) = (x - y)^2$	Equation 3
$\frac{x + y}{xy} = \frac{1}{x} + \frac{1}{y} \quad x, y \neq 0$	Equation 4
$\frac{x - y}{xy} = \frac{1}{y} - \frac{1}{x} \quad x, y \neq 0$	Equation 4A
$xy + xz = x(y + z)$	Equation 5
$xy - xz = x(y - z)$	Equation 5A

Examples 1, 3, and 9 can also be solved with the aid
of a calculator, and some examples can be solved
with the aid of a calculator allowing for exponential
calculations. However, to illustrate the effectiveness of
Math Strategy 4, we did not use the calculator method
of solution for these examples.

Use algebra to see patterns.

Example 1

$66^2 + 2(34)(66) + 34^2 =$

(A) 4,730
(B) 5,000
(C) 9,860
(D) 9,950
(E) 10,000

Choice E is correct. Notice that there is a 34 and 66
running through the left side of the equality. To see a
pattern, *use algebra*. Substitute a for 66 and b for 34.
You get:

$$66^2 + 2(34)(66) + 34^2 =$$
$$a^2 + 2(b)(a) + b^2$$

But from Equation 2,

$$a^2 + 2ab + b^2 =$$
$$(a + b)(a + b) =$$
$$(a + b)^2$$

1

Now substitute the numbers 34 and 66 *back into* $\boxed{1}$ to get:

$$66^2 + 2(34)(66) + 34^2 =$$
$$(66 + 34)(66 + 34) =$$
$$100 \times 100 =$$
$$10,000 \quad (Answer)$$

Example 2

If $(x + y) = 9$ and $xy = 14$, find $\dfrac{1}{x} + \dfrac{1}{y}$.

(*Note*: $x, y > 0$)

(A) $\dfrac{1}{9}$

(B) $\dfrac{2}{7}$

(C) $\dfrac{9}{14}$

(D) 5

(E) 9

Choice C is correct. We are given:

$$(x + y) = 9 \qquad \boxed{1}$$
$$xy = 14 \qquad \boxed{2}$$
$$x, y > 0 \qquad \boxed{3}$$

I hope that you did not solve $\boxed{2}$ for x (or y), and then substitute it into $\boxed{1}$. If you did, you obtained a quadratic equation.

Here is the FAST method. Use Equation 4:

$$\frac{1}{x} + \frac{1}{y} = \frac{x + y}{xy} \qquad \boxed{4}$$

From $\boxed{1}$ and $\boxed{2}$, we find that $\boxed{4}$ becomes

$$\frac{1}{x} + \frac{1}{y} = \frac{9}{14} \; (Answer)$$

Example 3

The value of $100 \times 100 - 99 \times 99 =$

(A) 1

(B) 2

(C) 99

(D) 199

(E) 299

Choice D is correct.

Write a for 100 and b for 99 to see a pattern:
$$100 \times 100 - 99 \times 99$$

$a \times a - b \times b = a^2 - b^2$. Use Equation 1:
Use the fact that $a^2 - b^2 = (a + b)(a - b)$ $\boxed{1}$

Put back 100 for a and 99 for b in $\boxed{1}$:
$$a^2 - b^2 = 100^2 - 99^2 = (100 + 99)(100 - 99) = 199$$

Example 4

Use factoring to make problems simpler.

$$\frac{8^7 - 8^6}{7} =$$

(A) $\dfrac{8}{7}$

(B) 8^7

(C) 8^6

(D) 8^5

(E) 8^4

Choice C is correct.

Factor: $8^7 - 8^6 = 8^6(8^1 - 1)$ Equation 5A
$$= 8^6(8 - 1)$$
$$= 8^6(7)$$

So $\dfrac{8^7 - 8^6}{7} = \dfrac{8^6(7)}{7} = \dfrac{8^6(\not7)}{\not7} = 8^6$

Represented algebraically, the problem would look like this.

Where $a \neq 1$,

$$\frac{a^7 - a^6}{a - 1} =$$

(A) $\dfrac{a}{a - 1}$

(B) $\dfrac{1}{a - 1}$

(C) $a^6 - a^5$

(D) a^5

(E) a^6

Choice E is correct.

Factor: $a^7 - a^6 = a^6(a - 1)$ Equation 5A

The expression

$$\frac{a^7 - a^6}{a - 1}$$

becomes

$$\frac{a^6(a - 1)}{a - 1}$$

Since $a \neq 1$, this becomes a^6

Example 5

If $y + \dfrac{1}{y} = 9$, then $y^2 + \dfrac{1}{y^2} =$

(A) 76
(B) 77
(C) 78
(D) 79
(E) 81

Choice D is correct.

Square $\left(y + \dfrac{1}{y}\right) = 9$

Substituting y for x and $\dfrac{1}{y}$ for y in Equation 2, we get:

$$\left(y + \dfrac{1}{y}\right)^2 = 81 = y^2 + 2(y)\left(\dfrac{1}{y}\right) + \left(\dfrac{1}{y}\right)^2$$

$$= y^2 + 2 + \left(\dfrac{1}{y}\right)^2$$

$$= y^2 + 2 + \dfrac{1}{y^2}$$

$$79 = y^2 + \dfrac{1}{y^2}$$

Example 6

If $a - b = 4$ and $a + b = 7$, then $a^2 - b^2 =$

(A) $5\dfrac{1}{2}$
(B) 11
(C) 28
(D) 29
(E) 56

Choice C is correct.

Use $(a - b)(a + b) = a^2 - b^2$ Equation 1
$$a - b = 4$$
$$a + b = 7$$
$(a - b)(a + b) = a^2 - b^2 = 28$

Example 7

What is the least possible value of $\dfrac{x + y}{xy}$ if
$2 \leq x < y \leq 11$ and x and y are integers?

(A) $\dfrac{22}{121}$

(B) $\dfrac{5}{6}$

(C) $\dfrac{21}{110}$

(D) $\dfrac{13}{22}$

(E) 1

Choice C is correct.

Use $\dfrac{x + y}{xy} = \dfrac{1}{x} + \dfrac{1}{y}$ Equation 4

$\dfrac{1}{x} + \dfrac{1}{y}$ is *least* when x is *greatest* and y is *greatest*.

Since it was given that x and y are integers and that $2 \leq x < y \leq 11$, the greatest value of x is 10 and the greatest value of y is 11.

So the *least* value of $\dfrac{1}{x} + \dfrac{1}{y} = \dfrac{x + y}{xy} = \dfrac{10 + 11}{10 \times 11} = \dfrac{21}{110}$.

Example 8

If $(a + b)^2 = 20$ and $ab = -3$, then $a^2 + b^2 =$

(A) 14
(B) 20
(C) 26
(D) 32
(E) 38

Choice C is correct.

Use $(a + b)^2 = a^2 + 2ab + b^2 = 20$ Equation 2

$ab = -3$

So, $2ab = -6$

Substitute $2ab = -6$ in:

$a^2 + 2ab + b^2 = 20$

We get:
$$a^2 - 6 + b^2 = 20$$
$$a^2 + b^2 = 26$$

Example 9

If $998 \times 1{,}002 > 10^6 - x$, x could be

(A) 4 but not 3
(B) 4 but not 5
(C) 5 but not 4
(D) 3 but not 4
(E) 3, 4, or 5

Choice C is correct.

Use $(a + b)(a - b) = a^2 - b^2$ Equation 1

$$998 \times 1{,}002 = (1{,}000 - 2)(1{,}000 + 2) > 10^6 - x$$
$$= 1{,}000^2 - 4 > 10^6 - x$$
$$= (10^3)^2 - 4 > 10^6 - x$$
$$= 10^6 - 4 > 10^6 - x$$

Multiply by -1; *reverse inequality sign*:

$$-1(-4 > -x)$$
$$+4 < +x$$

Example 10

If $x^2 + y^2 = 2xy$ and $x > 0$ and $y > 0$, then

(A) $x = 0$ only
(B) $y = 0$ only
(C) $x = 1, y = 1$, only
(D) $x > y > 0$
(E) $x = y$

Choice E is correct. In the given equation $x^2 + y^2 = 2xy$, subtract $2xy$ from both sides to get it to look like what you have in Equation 3.

$$x^2 + y^2 - 2xy = 2xy - 2xy = 0$$
$$\text{so} \quad x^2 - 2xy + y^2 = 0$$

We have:

$$x^2 - 2xy + y^2 = (x - y)^2 = 0 \quad \boxed{\text{Equation 3}}$$
$$x - y = 0, \text{ and thus } x = y$$

Example 11

If $x + y = 7$ and $xy = 4$, then $x^2 + y^2 =$

(A) 16
(B) 28
(C) 41
(D) 49
(E) 65

Choice C is correct. Since we are trying to find $x^2 + y^2$, square $x + y = 7$ to get:

$$(x + y)^2 = 49$$

Use Equation 2 to get:

$$x^2 + 2xy + y^2 = 49$$

Since $xy = 4$, substitute that quantity into the expanded equation.
We get:

$$x^2 + 8 + y^2 = 49$$
$$x^2 + y^2 = 41$$

Math Strategy 5

Know How to Manipulate Averages

Almost all problems involving averages can be solved by remembering that

$$\text{Average} = \frac{\text{sum of the individual quantities or measurements}}{\text{number of quantities or measurements}}$$

Note: Average is also called Arithmetic Mean.

Example 1

The average height of three students is 68 inches. If two of the students have heights of 70 inches and 72 inches respectively, then what is the height (in inches) of the third student?

(A) 60
(B) 62
(C) 64
(D) 65
(E) 66

Choice B is correct. Recall that

$$\text{Average} = \frac{\text{sum of the individual measurements}}{\text{number of measurements}}$$

Let $x = $ height (in inches) of the third student. Thus,

$$68 = \frac{70 + 72 + x}{3}$$

Multiplying by 3,

$$204 = 70 + 72 + x$$
$$204 = 142 + x$$
$$x = 62 \text{ inches}$$

Example 2

The average of 30 numbers is 65. If one of these numbers is 65, the sum of the remaining numbers is

(A) 65×64
(B) 30×64
(C) 29×30
(D) 29×64
(E) 29×65

Choice E is correct.

$$\text{Average} = \frac{\text{sum of numbers}}{30}$$

Call the numbers a, b, c, d, etc.

$$\text{So } 65 = \frac{a + b + c + d + \dots}{30}$$

Now immediately get rid of the fractional part: Multiply by 30 to get: $65 \times 30 = a + b + c + d + \dots$

Since we were told *one of the numbers is 65*, let $a = 65$:

$65 \times 30 = 65 + b + c + d + \dots$

So $65 \times 30 - 65 = b + c + d + \dots$

$b + c + d + \dots = $ sum of remaining numbers

Factor:

$65 \times 30 - 65 = 65(30 - 1) = $ sum of remaining numbers
$65 \times 29 = $ sum of remaining numbers

Example 3

The average length of 6 objects is 25 cm. If 5 objects are each 20 cm in length, what is the length of the sixth object in cm?

(A) 55
(B) 50
(C) 45
(D) 40
(E) 35

Choice B is correct.

Use the formula:

$$\text{Average} = \frac{\text{sum of the individual items}}{\text{number of items}}$$

Now call the length of the sixth item, x. Then:

$$25 = \frac{20 + 20 + 20 + 20 + 20 + x}{6}$$

$$\text{or} \quad 25 = \frac{20 \times 5 + x}{6}$$

Multiply by 6:

$$25 \times 6 = 20 \times 5 + x$$
$$150 = 100 + x$$
$$50 = x$$

Example 4

Scores on five tests range from 0 to 100 inclusive. If Don gets 70 on the first test, 76 on the second, and 75 on the third, what is the minimum score Don may get on the fourth test to average 80 on all five tests?

(A) 76
(B) 79

(C) 82
(D) 89
(E) 99

Choice B is correct.

Use the formula:

$$\text{Average} = \frac{\text{sum of scores on tests}}{\text{number of tests}}$$

Let x be the score on the fourth test and y be the score on the fifth test.

Then:

$$80 = \text{Average} = \frac{70 + 76 + 75 + x + y}{5}$$

The minimum score x Don can get is the *lowest* score he can get. The higher the score y is, the lower the score x can be. The greatest value of y can be 100. So:

$$80 = \frac{70 + 76 + 75 + x + 100}{5}$$

$$80 = \frac{321 + x}{5}$$

Multiply by 5:

$$400 = 321 + x$$
$$79 = x$$

Example 5

Eighteen students attained an average score of 70 on a test, and 12 students on the same test scored an average of 90. What is the average score for all 30 students on the test?

(A) 78
(B) 80
(C) 82
(D) 85
(E) cannot be determined

Choice A is correct.

Use the formula:

$$\text{Average} = \frac{\text{sum of scores}}{\text{number of students}}$$

"Eighteen students attained an average of 70 on a test" translates mathematically to:

$$70 = \frac{\text{sum of scores of 18 students}}{18} \qquad \boxed{1}$$

"Twelve students on the same test scored an average of 90" translates to:

$$90 = \frac{\text{sum of scores of other 12 students}}{12} \qquad \boxed{2}$$

Now what you are looking for is the *average score of all 30 students*. That is, you are looking for:

$$\frac{\text{Average of}}{\text{30 students}} = \frac{\text{sum of scores of all 30 students}}{30} \qquad \boxed{3}$$

So, if you can find the *sum of scores of all 30 students*, you can find the required average.

Now, the sum of all 30 students = sum of scores of 18 students + sum of scores of other 12 students.

And this can be gotten from $\boxed{1}$ and $\boxed{2}$:

From $\boxed{1}$: 70×18 = sum of scores of 18 students

From $\boxed{2}$: 90×12 = sum of scores of other 12 students

So adding:

$70 \times 18 + 90 \times 12$ = sum of scores of 18 students + sum of scores of other 12 students = sum of scores of 30 students

Put all this in $\boxed{3}$:

$$\text{Average of 30 students} = \frac{70 \times 18 + 90 \times 12}{30}$$
$$= \frac{7\!\!\!/0 \times 18 + 9\!\!\!/0 \times 12}{3\!\!\!/0}$$
$$= \frac{7 \times 18 + 9 \times 12}{3}$$
$$= \frac{7 \times \overset{6}{1\!\!\!/8} + \overset{3}{9\!\!\!/} \times 12}{3\!\!\!/}$$
$$= 42 + 36 = 78$$

Example 6

The average length of 10 objects is 25 inches. If the average length of 2 of these objects is 20 inches, what is the average length of the remaining 8 objects?

(A) $22\frac{1}{2}$ inches

(B) 24 inches

(C) $26\frac{1}{4}$ inches

(D) 28 inches

(E) cannot be determined

Choice C is correct.

Denote the lengths of the objects by *a, b, c, d,* etc. Since the average length of 10 objects is given to be 25 inches, establish an equation for the average length:

sum of 10 lengths

$$\text{Average length} = 25 = \frac{a + b + c + d + \ldots + j}{10} \qquad \boxed{1}$$

number of objects

The question also says that the average length of 2 of these objects is 20. Let the lengths of two we choose be *a* and *b*. So,

lengths of 2 objects

$$\text{Average length of } a \text{ and } b = 20 = \frac{a + b}{2} \qquad \boxed{2}$$

number of objects

Now we want to find the average length of the *remaining* objects. There are 8 remaining objects of lengths *c, d, e, . . . j*. Call the average of these lengths *x*, which is what we want to find.

sum of lengths of remaining objects (a + b are not present because only c + d + . . . + j remain)

$$\text{Average length} = x = \frac{c + d + e + \ldots + j}{8}$$

number of remaining objects

Use Equations $\boxed{1}$ and $\boxed{2}$:

$$25 = \frac{a + b + c + \ldots + j}{10} \qquad \boxed{1}$$

$$20 = \frac{a + b}{2} \qquad \boxed{2}$$

Now, remember, we want to find the value of *x*:

$$x = \frac{c + d + e + \ldots + j}{8}$$

Multiply Equation $\boxed{1}$ by 10 to get rid of the denominator. We get:

$$25 \times 10 = 250 = a + b + c + \ldots + j$$

Now multiply Equation $\boxed{2}$ by 2 to get rid of the denominator:

$$20 \times 2 = 40 = a + b$$

Subtract these two new equations:

$$250 = a + b + c + \ldots + j$$
$$- [40 = a + b]$$

You get: $\qquad 210 = c + d + \ldots + j$

Now you just have to divide by 8 to get:

$$\frac{210}{8} = \frac{c + d + \ldots + j}{8} = x$$

$$= 26\frac{1}{4}$$

Math Strategy 6

Know How to Manipulate Inequalities

Most problems involving inequalities can be solved by remembering one of the following statements.

If $x > y$, then $x + z > y + z$	Statement 1
If $x > y$ and $w > z$, then $x + w > y + z$	Statement 2

(Note that Statement 1 and Statement 2 are also true if all the $>$ signs are changed to $<$ signs.)

If $w > 0$ and $x > y$, then $wx > wy$	Statement 3
If $w < 0$ and $x > y$, then $wx < wy$	Statement 4
If $x > y$ and $y > z$, then $x > z$	Statement 5
$x > y$ is the same as $y < x$	Statement 6
$a < x < b$ is the same as both $a < x$ and $x < b$	Statement 7
If $x > y > 0$ and $w > z > 0$, then $xw > yz$	Statement 8
If $x > 0$ and $z = x + y$, then $z > y$	Statement 9
If $x < 0$, then $\begin{cases} x^n < 0 \text{ if } n \text{ is odd} \\ x^n > 0 \text{ if } n \text{ is even} \end{cases}$	Statement 10 Statement 11
If $xy > 0$, then $x > 0$ and $y > 0$ or $x < 0$ and $y < 0$	Statement 12
If $xy < 0$, then $x > 0$ and $y < 0$ or $x < 0$ and $y > 0$	Statement 13

Example 1

If $0 < x < 1$, then which of the following must be true?

I. $2x < 2$
II. $x - 1 < 0$
III. $x^2 < x$

(A) I only
(B) II only
(C) I and II only
(D) II and III only
(E) I, II, and III

Choice E is correct. We are told that $0 < x < 1$. Using Statement 7, we have

$$0 < x \qquad\qquad 1$$
$$x < 1 \qquad\qquad 2$$

For Item I, we multiply 2 by 2.

See Statement 3

$$2x < 2$$

Thus, Item I is true.

For Item II, we add -1 to both sides of 2.

See Statement 1 to get

$$x - 1 < 0$$

Thus, Item II is true.

For Item III, we multiply 2 by x.

See Statement 3 to get

$$x^2 < x$$

Thus, Item III is true.

All items are true, so Choice E is correct.

Example 2

Given that $\dfrac{a}{b}$ is less than 1, $a > 0$, $b > 0$. Which of the following must be greater than 1?

(A) $\dfrac{a}{2b}$

(B) $\dfrac{b}{2a}$

(C) $\dfrac{\sqrt{b}}{a}$

(D) $\dfrac{b}{a}$

(E) $\left(\dfrac{a}{b}\right)^2$

Choice D is correct.

Given: $\quad \dfrac{a}{b} < 1 \qquad\qquad\qquad$ 1
$\qquad\qquad a > 0 \qquad\qquad\qquad$ 2
$\qquad\qquad b > 0 \qquad\qquad\qquad$ 3

See Statement 3: Multiply 1 by b. We get:

$$\cancel{b}\left(\dfrac{a}{\cancel{b}}\right) < b \,(1)$$
$$a < b \qquad\qquad\qquad 4$$

Use Statement 3 where $w = \dfrac{1}{a}$. Divide 4 by a. We get:

$$\dfrac{a}{a} < \dfrac{b}{a}$$
$$1 < \dfrac{b}{a}$$
$$\text{or} \quad \dfrac{b}{a} > 1$$

Example 3

Which combination of the following statements can be used to demonstrate that x is positive?

   I. $x > y$
  II. $1 < y$

(A) I alone but not II
(B) II alone but not I
(C) I and II taken together but neither taken alone
(D) Both I alone and II alone
(E) Neither I nor II nor both

Choice C is correct. We want to know which of the following

$$x > y \qquad \boxed{1}$$
$$1 < y \qquad \boxed{2}$$

is enough information to conclude that

$$x > 0 \qquad \boxed{3}$$

$\boxed{1}$ alone is not enough to determine $\boxed{3}$ because $0 > x > y$ could be true. (*Note*: x is greater than y, but they both could be negative.)

$\boxed{2}$ alone is not enough to determine $\boxed{3}$ because we don't know whether x is greater than, less than, or equal to y.

However, if we use $\boxed{1}$ and $\boxed{2}$ together, we can compare the two:

$$1 < y \text{ is the same as } y > 1.$$

Therefore, $x > y$ with $y > 1$ yields   Statement 5

$$x > 1. \qquad \boxed{4}$$

Since $1 > 0$ is always true, then from $\boxed{4}$

$$x > 0 \text{ is always true.}$$

Example 4

What are all values of x such that $(x - 7)(x + 3)$ is positive?

(A) $x > 7$
(B) $-7 < x < 3$
(C) $-3 < x < 7$
(D) $x > 7$ or $x < -3$
(E) $x > 3$ or $x < -7$

Choice D is correct.

$$(x - 7)(x + 3) > 0 \text{ when}$$
$$x - 7 > 0 \text{ and } x + 3 > 0 \qquad \boxed{1}$$
$$\text{or} \quad x - 7 < 0 \text{ and } x + 3 < 0 \qquad \boxed{2}$$

Statement 12

From $\boxed{1}$ we have $x > 7$ and $x > -3$ $\boxed{3}$
Thus $x > 7$ $\boxed{4}$
From $\boxed{2}$, we have $x < 7$ and $x < -3$ $\boxed{5}$
Thus $x < -3$ $\boxed{6}$

Example 5

If p and q are nonzero real numbers and if $p^2 + q^3 < 0$ and if $p^3 + q^5 > 0$, which of the following number lines shows the relative positions of p, q, and 0?

Choice B is correct.

Method I:

$$\text{Given: } p^2 + q^3 < 0 \qquad \boxed{1}$$
$$p^3 + q^5 > 0 \qquad \boxed{2}$$

Subtracting p^2 from $\boxed{1}$ and q^5 from $\boxed{2}$, we have

$$q^3 < -p^2 \qquad \boxed{3}$$
$$p^3 > -q^5 \qquad \boxed{4}$$

Since the square of any real number is greater than 0, $p^2 > 0$ and $-p^2 < 0$. $\boxed{5}$

Using Statement 5, combining $\boxed{3}$ and $\boxed{5}$ we get:

$$q^3 < -p^2 < 0 \qquad \boxed{6}$$
$$\text{and get: } \quad q^3 < 0. \qquad \boxed{7}$$
$$\text{Therefore, } \quad q < 0. \qquad \boxed{8}$$

From $\boxed{8}$, we can say $q^5 < 0$ or $-q^5 > 0$. $\boxed{9}$

Using Statement 5, combining $\boxed{4}$ and $\boxed{9}$,

$$p^3 > -q^5 > 0 \text{ and } p^3 > 0. \text{ Thus } p > 0. \qquad \boxed{10}$$

Using $\boxed{8}$ and $\boxed{10}$, it is easily seen that Choice B is correct.

Method II:

Use Strategy 6: ***Know How to Manipulate Inequalities***

$$\text{Given: } p^2 + q^3 < 0 \qquad \boxed{1}$$
$$p^3 + q^5 > 0 \qquad \boxed{2}$$

Since p^2 is always > 0, using this with $\boxed{1}$, we know that

$$q^3 < 0 \text{ and, therefore, } q < 0. \qquad \boxed{3}$$

If $q^3 < 0$ then $q^5 < 0$.   **4**

Using **4** and **2**, we know that
$$p^3 > 0, \text{ and therefore } p > 0 \qquad \textbf{5}$$

Using **3** and **5**, we can discern that only Choice B is correct.

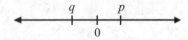

Example 6

Janie is older than Tammy, but she is younger than Lori. Let *j, t,* and *l* be the ages in years of Janie, Tammy, and Lori, respectively. Which of the following is true?

    (A) $j < t < l$
    (B) $t < j < l$
    (C) $t < l < j$
    (D) $l < j < t$
    (E) $l < t < j$

Choice B is correct.

First, use Strategy 2: ***Translate English Words into Mathematical Expressions***

"Janie is older than Tammy, but she is younger than Lori" translates to:

Janie's age > Tammy's age	**1**
Janie's age < Lori's age	**2**
Given: Janie's age $= j$	**3**
Tammy's age $= t$	**4**
Lori's age $= l$	**5**

Substituting **3**, **4**, and **5** into **1** and **2**, we get:

$$j > t \qquad \textbf{6}$$
$$j < l \qquad \textbf{7}$$

Use Statement 5. Reversing **6**, we get:

$$t < j \qquad \textbf{8}$$

Combining **8** and **7**, we get:

$$t < j < l$$

Use Specific Numerical Examples to Prove or Disprove Your Guess

When you do not want to do a lot of algebra, or when you are unable to prove what you think is the answer, you may want to substitute numbers.

Example 1

The sum of the cubes of any two consecutive positive integers is always

    (A) an odd integer
    (B) an even integer
    (C) the cube of an integer
    (D) the square of an integer
    (E) the product of an integer and 3

Choice A is correct. *Try specific numbers.* Call consecutive positive integers 1 and 2.

Sum of cubes:

$$1^3 + 2^3 = 1 + 8 = 9$$

You have now eliminated Choices B and C. You are left with Choices A, D, and E.

Now try two other consecutive integers: 2 and 3.

$$2^3 + 3^3 = 8 + 27 = 35$$

Choice A is acceptable. Choice D is false. Choice E is false.

Thus, Choice A is the only choice remaining.

Example 2

Jason is now *m* years old, and Serena is 4 years older than Jason. Which represents Serena's age 6 years ago?

    (A) $m + 10$
    (B) $m - 10$
    (C) $m - 2$
    (D) $m - 4$
    (E) $4m - 6$

Choice C is correct.

Try a specific number.

Let $m = 10$

Jason is 10 years old. Serena is 4 years older than Jason, so Serena is 14 years old. Serena's age 6 years ago was 8 years.

Now look for the choice that gives you 8 with $m = 10$.

(A) $m + 10 = 10 + 10 = 20$
(B) $m - 10 = 10 - 10 = 0$
(C) $m - 2 = 10 - 2 = 8$—that's the one

See Math Strategy 2, Example 4 (page 49) for an alternate approach to solving this problem, using a different strategy: **Translate English Words into Mathematical Expressions**.

Example 3

If $x \neq 0$, then $\dfrac{(-3x)^3}{-3x^3} =$

(A) -9
(B) -1
(C) 1
(D) 3
(E) 9

Choice E is correct.

Try a specific number.

Let $x = 1$. Then:

$$\frac{(-3x)^3}{-3x^3} = \frac{[-3(1)]^3}{-3(1^3)} = \frac{(-3)^3}{-3} = 9$$

Example 4

If $a = 4b$, then the average of a and b is

(A) $\frac{1}{2}b$

(B) $\frac{3}{2}b$

(C) $\frac{5}{2}b$

(D) $\frac{7}{2}b$

(E) $\frac{9}{2}b$

Choice C is correct.

Try a specific number.

Let $b = 1$. Then $a = 4b = 4$. So the average $=$

$$\frac{1 + 4}{2} = \frac{5}{2}.$$

Look at choices where $b = 1$. The only choice that gives $\frac{5}{2}$ is Choice C.

Example 5

The sum of three consecutive even integers is P. Find the sum of the next three consecutive *odd* integers that follow the greatest of the three even integers.

(A) $P + 9$
(B) $P + 15$
(C) $P + 12$
(D) $P + 20$
(E) none of these

Choice B is correct.

Try specific numbers.

Let the three consecutive even integers be 2, 4, 6.

So, $2 + 4 + 6 = P = 12$.

The next three consecutive odd integers that follow 6 are:

$$7, 9, 11$$

So the sum of

$$7 + 9 + 11 = 27.$$

Now, where $P = 12$, look for a choice that gives you 27:

(A) $P + 9 = 12 + 9 = 21$—NO
(B) $P + 15 = 12 + 15 = 27$—YES

Example 6

If $3 > a$, which of the following is *not* true?

(A) $3 - 3 > a - 3$
(B) $3 + 3 > a + 3$
(C) $3(3) > a(3)$
(D) $3 - 3 > 3 - a$
(E) $\frac{3}{3} > \frac{a}{3}$

Choice D is correct.

Try specific numbers.

Work backward from Choice E if you wish.

Let $a = 1$.

Choice E:

$$\frac{3}{3} > \frac{a}{3} = \frac{1}{3} \qquad \text{TRUE STATEMENT}$$

Choice D:

$3 - 3 > 3 - a = 3 - 1$, or $0 > 2$ FALSE STATEMENT

Example 7

In the figure of intersecting lines below, which of the following is equal to $180 - a$?

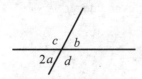

(A) $a + d$
(B) $a + 2d$
(C) $c + b$
(D) $b + 2a$
(E) $c + d$

Choice A is correct.

Try a specific number.

Let $a = 20°$

Then $2a = 40°$

Be careful now—all of the other angles are now determined, so don't choose any more.

Because vertical angles are equal, $2a = b$, so

$$b = 40°.$$

Now $c + b = 180°$, so $c + 40 = 180$ and

$$c = 140°.$$

Thus, $d = 140°$ (vertical angles are equal).

Now look at the question:

$$180 - a = 180 - 20 = 160$$

Which is the correct choice?

   (A) $a + d = 20 + 140 = 160$—that's the one!

See Math Strategy 17, Example 2 (page 85) for an alternate approach to solving this problem, using a different strategy: ***Use the Given Information Effectively (and Ignore Irrelevant Information).***

Math Strategy   8

Very Important Strategy:

When Each Choice Must Be Tested, Start with the Last Choice and Work Backward

If you must check each choice for the correct answer, start with the last choice (whether D or E) and work backward. The reason for this is that the test maker of a question *in which each choice must be tested* often puts the correct answer as Choice D or E (or J or K). In this way, the student must check all or most of the choices, starting with Choice A, before finding the correct one. So if you're trying all the choices, start with the last choice, then the next to last choice, etc. See Example 8 for an example of when this strategy should *not* be used.

Example 1

If p is a positive integer, which *could* be an odd integer?

(A) $2p + 2$
(B) $p^3 - p$
(C) $p^2 + p$
(D) $p^2 - p$
(E) $7p - 3$

Choice E is correct. Start with Choice E first, since you have to *test* the choices.

Method I:

Try a number for p. Let $p = 1$. Then (starting with Choice E),

$7p - 3 = 7(1) - 3 = 4$. 4 is even, so try another number for p to see whether $7p - 3$ is odd. Let $p = 2$.

$7p - 3 = 7(2) - 3 = 11$. 11 is odd. Therefore, Choice E is correct.

Method II:

Look at Choice E. $7p$ could be even or odd, depending on what p is. If p is even, $7p$ is even. If p is odd, $7p$ is odd. Accordingly, $7p - 3$ is either even or odd. Thus, Choice E is correct.

Note: When using either Method I or Method II, you have eliminated the need to test the other choices.

Example 2

If $y = x^2 + 3$, then for which value of x is y divisible by 7?

(A) 10
(B) 8
(C) 7
(D) 6
(E) 5

Choice E is correct. Since you must check all of the choices, start with Choice E:

$$y = 5^2 + 3 = 25 + 3 = 28$$
$$28 \text{ is divisible by } 7$$

If you had started with Choice A, you would have had to test four choices instead of one choice before finding the correct answer.

Example 3

Which fraction is greater than $\frac{1}{2}$?

(A) $\frac{4}{9}$

(B) $\frac{17}{35}$

(C) $\frac{6}{13}$

(D) $\frac{12}{25}$

(E) $\frac{8}{15}$

Choice E is correct.

Look at Choice E first.

$$\text{Is } \frac{8}{15} > \frac{1}{2}?$$

Use the cross-multiplication method.

$$\left(\frac{1}{2} \quad \frac{8}{15}\right)$$
$$15 \qquad 16$$
$$15 \quad < \quad 16$$

So, $\frac{1}{2} < \frac{8}{15}$.

You also could have looked at Choice E and said $\frac{8}{16} = \frac{1}{2}$ and realized that $\frac{8}{15} > \frac{1}{2}$ because $\frac{8}{15}$ has a smaller denominator than $\frac{8}{16}$.

Example 4

If n is an even integer, which of the following is an odd integer?

(A) $n^2 - 2$

(B) $n - 4$

(C) $(n - 4)^2$

(D) n^3

(E) $n^2 - n - 1$

Choice E is correct.

Look at Choice E first.

$$n^2 - n - 1$$
$$\text{If } n \text{ is even}$$
$$n^2 \text{ is even}$$
$$n \text{ is even}$$
$$1 \text{ is odd}$$

So, $n^2 - n - 1 = \text{even} - \text{even} - \text{odd} = \text{odd}$.

Example 5

Which of the following is an odd number?

(A) 7×22

(B) $59 - 15$

(C) $55 + 35$

(D) $75 \div 15$

(E) 4^7

Choice D is correct.

Look at Choice E first.

4^7 is even because all positive integral powers of an even number are even.

So now look at Choice D: $\frac{75}{15} = 5$, which is odd.

Example 6

$$\begin{array}{r} 3 \# 2 \\ \times \quad 8 \\ \hline 28 \star 6 \end{array}$$

If # and ⋆ are different digits in the correctly calculated multiplication problem above, then # could be

(A) 1

(B) 2

(C) 3

(D) 4

(E) 6

Choice E is correct.

Try Choice E first.

$$\begin{array}{r} 3 \# 2 \\ \times \quad 8 \\ \hline 28 \star 6 \end{array} \qquad \begin{array}{r} 3 ⑥ 2 \\ \times \quad 8 \\ \hline 28 ⑨ 6 \end{array}$$

9 and 6 are different numbers, so Choice E is correct.

Example 7

Which choice describes a pair of numbers that are *unequal*?

(A) $\frac{1}{6}, \frac{11}{66}$

(B) $3.4, \frac{34}{10}$

(C) $\frac{15}{75}, \frac{1}{5}$

(D) $\frac{3}{8}, 0.375$

(E) $\frac{86}{24}, \frac{42}{10}$

Choice E is correct.

Look at Choice E first.

$$\frac{86}{24} \quad ? \quad \frac{42}{10}$$

Cross multiply:

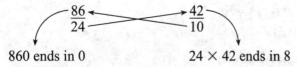

860 ends in 0   24 × 42 ends in 8

Thus, the numbers must be *different* and *unequal*.

When *Not* to Use This Strategy:

If you can spot something in the question that shows you how to solve the problem readily without having to test each choice, there's no need to go through every answer by working backward.

Example 8

If $|6 - 5y| > 20$, which of the following is a possible value of y?

(A) -3
(B) -1
(C) 1
(D) 3
(E) 5

Choice A is correct.

Instead of plugging in values for y, starting with Choice E, you should realize there will only be one answer listed for which $6 - 5y > 20$. So which choice gives you the largest product for $-5y$? Start by checking the *most negative* choice, or $y = -3$.

This gives you $|6 - 5(-3)| = |6 + 15| = |21|$, which is greater than 20.

Math Strategy   9

Know How to Solve Problems Using the Formula
R × T = D

Almost every problem involving motion can be solved using the formula

$$R \times T = D$$

or

$$\text{rate} \times \text{elapsed time} = \text{distance}$$

Example 1

The diagram below shows two paths: Path 1 is 10 miles long, and Path 2 is 12 miles long. If Person X runs along Path 1 at 5 miles per hour and Person Y runs along Path 2 at y miles per hour, and if it takes exactly the same amount of time for both runners to run their whole path, then what is the value of y?

A   Path 1   B

C   Path 2   D

(A) 2
(B) $4\frac{1}{6}$
(C) 6
(D) 20
(E) 24

Choice C is correct. Let T = Time (in hours) for either runner to run the whole path.

Using $R \times T = D$, for Person X, we have

$$\left(\frac{5 \text{ mi}}{\text{hr}}\right)(T \text{ hours}) = 10 \text{ miles}$$

$$\text{or} \quad 5T = 10 \qquad \boxed{1}$$
$$\text{or} \quad T = 2$$

For Person Y, we have

$$\left(\frac{y \text{ mi}}{\text{hr}}\right)(T \text{ hours}) = 12 \text{ miles}$$

$$\text{or} \quad yT = 12$$

Using $\boxed{1}$ $y(2) = 12$ or $y = 6$.

Example 2

A car traveling at 50 miles per hour for 2 hours travels the same distance as a car traveling at 20 miles per hour for x hours. What is x?

(A) $\frac{4}{5}$
(B) $\frac{5}{4}$
(C) 5
(D) 2
(E) $\frac{1}{2}$

Choice C is correct.

Use $R \times T = D$.

Call the distance both cars travel D (since distance is the same for both cars).

So we get:

$$50 \times 2 = D = 100 \qquad \boxed{1}$$
$$20 \times x = D = 100 \qquad \boxed{2}$$

Solving $\boxed{2}$ you can see that $x = 5$.

Example 3

John walks at a rate of 4 miles per hour. Sally walks at a rate of 5 miles per hour. If John and Sally both start at the same starting point, how many miles is one person from the other after t hours of walking? (*Note*: Both are walking on the same road in the same direction.)

(A) $\frac{t}{2}$

(B) t

(C) $2t$

(D) $\frac{4}{5}t$

(E) $\frac{5}{4}t$

Choice B is correct.
Draw a diagram:

John (4 mph)   (*t hours*)

$\vdash\!\!-D_J\!-\!\!\dashrightarrow$

Sally (5 mph)   (*t hours*)

$\vdash\!\!-D_S\!-\!\!\dashrightarrow$

Let D_J be the distance that John walks in t hours.
Let D_S be the distance that Sally walks in t hours.
Then, using $R \times t = D$,

for John: $4 \times t = D_J$
for Sally: $5 \times t = D_S$

The distance between Sally and John after t hours of walking is:

$$D_S - D_J = 5t - 4t = t$$

Example 4

A man rode a bicycle a straight distance at a speed of 10 miles per hour and came back the same distance at a speed of 20 miles per hour. What was the man's total number of miles for the trip back and forth, if his total traveling time was 1 hour?

(A) 15

(B) $7\frac{1}{2}$

(C) $6\frac{1}{3}$

(D) $6\frac{2}{3}$

(E) $13\frac{1}{3}$

Choice E is correct.

Always use $R \times T = D$ (Rate $\times$ Time = Distance) in problems like this. Call the first distance D and the time for the first part T_1. Since he rode at 10 mph:

$$10 \times T_1 = D \qquad \boxed{1}$$

Now for the trip back. He rode at 20 mph. Call the time it took to go back T_2. Since he came back the *same* distance, we can call that distance D also. So for the trip back using $R \times T = D$, we get:

$$20 \times T_2 = D \qquad \boxed{2}$$

Since it was given that the total traveling time was 1 hour, the total traveling time is:

$$T_1 + T_2 = 1$$

Now here's the trick: Let's make use of the fact that $T_1 + T_2 = 1$. Dividing Equation $\boxed{1}$ by 10, we get:

$$T_1 = \frac{D}{10}$$

Dividing $\boxed{2}$ by 20, we get:

$$T_2 = \frac{D}{20}$$

Now add $T_1 + T_2$ and we get:

$$T_1 + T_2 = 1 = \frac{D}{10} + \frac{D}{20}$$

Factor D:

$$1 = D\left(\frac{1}{10} + \frac{1}{20}\right)$$

Add $\frac{1}{10} + \frac{1}{20}$. Remember the fast way of adding fractions?

$$\frac{1}{10} + \frac{1}{20} = \frac{20 + 10}{20 \times 10} = \frac{30}{200}$$

So:

$$1 = (D)\frac{30}{200}$$

Multiply by 200 and divide by 30 and we get:

$$\frac{200}{30} = D; D = 6\frac{2}{3}$$

Don't forget, we're looking for $2D$: $2D = 13\frac{1}{3}$

Example 5

What is the average rate of a bicycle traveling at 10 mph a distance of 5 miles and at 20 mph the same distance?

- (A) 15 mph
- (B) 20 mph
- (C) $12\frac{1}{2}$ mph
- (D) $13\frac{1}{3}$ mph
- (E) 16 mph

Choice D is correct.

Ask yourself, what does *average rate* mean? It *does not* mean the average of the rates! If you thought it did, you would have selected Choice A as the answer (averaging 10 and 20 to get 15)—the "lure" choice.

Average is a word that *modifies* the word *rate* in this case. So you must define the word *rate* first, before you do anything with averaging.

Since rate × time = distance,

$$\text{rate} = \frac{\text{distance}}{\text{time}}$$

Then *average* rate must be:

$$\text{Average rate} = \frac{\text{total distance}}{\text{total time}}$$

The *total distance* is the distance covered on the whole trip, which is 5 + 5 = 10 miles.

The *total time* is the time traveled the first 5 miles at 10 mph added to the time the bicycle traveled the next 5 miles at 20 mph.

Let t_1 be the time the bicycle traveled the first 5 miles.

Let t_2 be the time the bicycle traveled the next 5 miles.

Then the *total time* = $t_1 + t_2$.

Since $R \times T = D$,

for the first 5 miles: $10 \times t_1 = 5$
for the next 5 miles: $20 \times t_2 = 5$

Finding t_1: $t_1 = \frac{5}{10}$

Finding t_2: $t_2 = \frac{5}{20}$

So, $t_1 + t_2 = \frac{5}{10} + \frac{5}{20}$

$$= \frac{1}{2} + \frac{1}{4} \quad \text{(remembering how to quickly add fractions)}$$

$$= \frac{4+2}{8}$$

$$= \frac{6}{8} = \frac{3}{4}$$

$$\text{Average rate} = \frac{\text{total distance}}{\text{total time}}$$

$$= \frac{5+5}{\frac{3}{4}}$$

$$= (5+5) \times \frac{4}{3}$$

$$= 10 \times \frac{4}{3} = \frac{40}{3} = 13\frac{1}{3} \ (\textit{Answer})$$

Here's a formula you can memorize:
If a vehicle travels a certain distance at a mph and travels the same distance at b mph, the *average rate* is

$$\frac{2ab}{a+b}$$

Try doing the problem using this formula:

$$\frac{2ab}{a+b} = \frac{2 \times 10 \times 20}{10 + 20} = \frac{400}{30} = 13\frac{1}{3}$$

Caution: Use this formula only when you are looking for *average* rate, and when the distance is the same for both speeds.

Math Strategy   **10**

Know How to Use Units of Time, Distance, Area, or Volume to Find or Check Your Answer

By knowing what the units in your answer must be, you will often have an easier time finding or checking your answer. A very helpful thing to do is to treat the units of time or space as variables (like x or y). Thus, you should substitute, multiply, or divide these units as if they were ordinary variables. The following examples illustrate this idea.

Example 1

What is the distance in miles covered by a car that traveled at 50 miles per hour for 5 hours?

- (A) 10
- (B) 45
- (C) 55
- (D) 200
- (E) 250

Choice E is correct. Although this is an easy $R \times T = D$ problem, it illustrates this strategy very well.

Recall that

$$\text{rate} \times \text{time} = \text{distance}$$

$$\left(\frac{50 \text{ mi}}{\text{hr}}\right)(5 \text{ hours}) = \text{distance}$$

Notice that when I substituted into $R \times T = D$, *I kept the units of rate and time* (miles/hour and hours). Now I will *treat these units as if they were ordinary variables.* Thus,

$$\text{distance} = \left(\frac{50 \text{ mi}}{\text{hr}}\right)(5 \text{ hours})$$

I have canceled the variable "hour(s)" from the numerator and denominator of the right side of the equation. Hence,

$$\text{distance} = 250 \text{ miles}$$

The distance has units of "miles," as I would expect. In fact, if the units in my answer had been "miles/hour" or "hours," then I would have been in error.

Thus, *the general procedure* for problems using this strategy is:

Step 1. *Keep the units given in the question.*

Step 2. *Treat the units as ordinary variables.*

Step 3. *Make sure the answer has units that you would expect.*

Example 2

How many inches are equivalent to 2 yards, 2 feet, and 7 inches?

(A) 11
(B) 37
(C) 55
(D) 81
(E) 103

Choice E is correct.

Remember that

1 yard = 3 feet	1
1 foot = 12 inches	2

Treat the units of length as variables! Divide 1 by 1 yard, and 2 by 1 foot, to get

$$1 = \frac{3 \text{ feet}}{1 \text{ yard}} \qquad 3$$

$$1 = \frac{12 \text{ inches}}{1 \text{ foot}} \qquad 4$$

We can multiply any expression by 1 and get the same value. Thus, 2 yards + 2 feet + 7 inches =

$$(2 \text{ yards})(1)(1) + (2 \text{ feet})(1) + 7 \text{ inches} \qquad 5$$

Substituting 3 and 4 into 5, 2 yards + 2 feet + 7 inches

$$= 2 \text{ yards}\left(\frac{3 \text{ feet}}{\text{yard}}\right)\left(\frac{12 \text{ inches}}{\text{foot}}\right) + 2 \text{ feet}\left(\frac{12 \text{ inches}}{\text{foot}}\right)$$
$$+ 7 \text{ inches}$$
$$= 72 \text{ inches} + 24 \text{ inches} + 7 \text{ inches}$$
$$= 103 \text{ inches}$$

Notice that the answer is in "inches," as I expected. If the answer had come out in "yards" or "feet," then I would have been in error.

Example 3

A car wash cleans x cars per hour, for y hours, at z dollars per car. How much money in *cents* does the car wash receive?

(A) $\dfrac{xy}{100z}$

(B) $\dfrac{xyz}{100}$

(C) $100xyz$

(D) $\dfrac{100x}{yz}$

(E) $\dfrac{yz}{100x}$

Choice C is correct.

Use units:

$$\left(\frac{x \text{ cars}}{\text{hour}}\right)(y \text{ hours})\left(\frac{z \text{ dollar}}{\text{car}}\right) = xyz \text{ dollars} \qquad 1$$

Since there are 100 cents to a dollar, we multiply 1 by 100. We get $100xyz$ cents.

Example 4

There are 3 feet in a yard and 12 inches in a foot. How many yards are there altogether in 1 yard, 1 foot, and 1 inch?

(A) $1\dfrac{1}{3}$

(B) $1\dfrac{13}{36}$

(C) $1\dfrac{11}{18}$

(D) $2\dfrac{5}{12}$

(E) $4\dfrac{1}{12}$

Choice B is correct.

Know how to work with units.

Given: 3 feet = 1 yard

12 inches = 1 foot

Thus,

1 yard + 1 foot + 1 inch =

$1 \text{ yard} + 1 \text{ foot}\left(\dfrac{1 \text{ yard}}{3 \text{ feet}}\right) + 1 \text{ inch}\left(\dfrac{1 \text{ foot}}{12 \text{ inches}}\right) \times \left(\dfrac{1 \text{ yard}}{3 \text{ feet}}\right)$

$= \left(1 + \dfrac{1}{3} + \dfrac{1}{36}\right) \text{ yards}$

$= \left(1 + \dfrac{12}{36} + \dfrac{1}{36}\right) \text{ yards}$

$= 1\dfrac{13}{36} \text{ yards}$

Math Strategy 11

Use New Definitions and Functions Carefully

Some ACT questions use new symbols, functions, or definitions that were created in the question. At first glance, these questions may seem difficult because you are not familiar with the new symbol, function, or definition. *However, most of these questions can be solved through simple substitution or application of a simple definition.*

Example 1

If the symbol ϕ is defined by the equation

$$a \phi b = a - b - ab$$

for all a and b, then $\left(-\dfrac{1}{3}\right) \phi (-3) =$

(A) $\dfrac{5}{3}$

(B) $\dfrac{11}{3}$

(C) $-\dfrac{13}{3}$

(D) -4

(E) -5

Choice A is correct. All that is required is substitution:

$$a \phi b = a - b - ab$$

$$\left(-\dfrac{1}{3}\right) \phi (-3)$$

Substitute $-\dfrac{1}{3}$ for a and -3 for b in $a - b - ab$:

$$\left(-\dfrac{1}{3}\right) \phi (-3) = -\dfrac{1}{3} - (-3) - \left(-\dfrac{1}{3}\right)(-3)$$

$$= -\dfrac{1}{3} + 3 - 1$$

$$= 2 - \dfrac{1}{3}$$

$$= \dfrac{5}{3} \ (Answer)$$

Example 2

Let $x = \begin{cases} \dfrac{5}{2}(x + 1) & \text{if } x \text{ is an odd integer} \\ \dfrac{5}{2}x & \text{if } x \text{ is an even integer} \end{cases}$

Find $2y$, where y is an integer.

(A) $\dfrac{5}{2}y$

(B) $5y$

(C) $\dfrac{5}{2}y + 1$

(D) $5y + \dfrac{5}{2}$

(E) $5y + 5$

Choice B is correct. All we have to do is substitute $2y$ into the definition of x. In order to know which definition of x to use, we want to know if $2y$ is even. Since y is an integer, then $2y$ is an even integer. Thus,

$$2y = \dfrac{5}{2}(2y)$$

$$\text{or} \quad 2y = 5y \ (Answer)$$

Example 3

As in the previous Example 1, ϕ is defined as

$$a \phi b = a - b - ab.$$

If $a \phi 3 = 6$, $a =$

(A) $\dfrac{9}{2}$

(B) $\dfrac{9}{4}$

(C) $-\dfrac{9}{4}$

(D) $-\dfrac{4}{9}$

(E) $-\dfrac{9}{2}$

Choice E is correct.

$$a \phi b = a - b - ab$$

$$a \phi 3 = 6$$

Substitute 3 for b:

$$a \, \phi \, 3 = a - 3 - a(3) = 6$$
$$= a - 3 - 3a = 6$$
$$= -2a - 3 = 6$$
$$2a = -9$$
$$a = -\frac{9}{2}$$

Example 4

The symbol $\left(\, x \,\right)$ is defined as the greatest integer less than or equal to x.

$$\left(-3.4\right) + \left(21\right) =$$

 (A) 16
 (B) 16.6
 (C) 17
 (D) 17.6
 (E) 18

Choice C is correct.

$\left(-3.4\right)$ is defined as the *greatest integer less than or equal to* -3.4. This is -4, since $-4 < -3.4$.

$\left(21\right)$ is defined as the *greatest integer less than or equal to* 21. That is just 21, since $21 = 21$. Thus, $-4 + 21 = 17$.

Example 5

$\left(\begin{smallmatrix} x & y \\ z & t \end{smallmatrix}\right)$ is defined as $xz - yt$

$$\left(\begin{smallmatrix} 2 & 1 \\ 1 & 1 \end{smallmatrix}\right) =$$

 (A) $\left(\begin{smallmatrix} 1 & 1 \\ 1 & 1 \end{smallmatrix}\right)$

 (B) $\left(\begin{smallmatrix} 3 & 2 \\ 2 & 1 \end{smallmatrix}\right)$

 (C) $\left(\begin{smallmatrix} 4 & 3 \\ 2 & 1 \end{smallmatrix}\right)$

 (D) $\left(\begin{smallmatrix} 5 & 4 \\ 4 & 2 \end{smallmatrix}\right)$

 (E) $\left(\begin{smallmatrix} 3 & 1 \\ 1 & 2 \end{smallmatrix}\right)$

Choice E is correct.

$$\left(\begin{smallmatrix} x & y \\ z & t \end{smallmatrix}\right) = xz - yt; \quad \left(\begin{smallmatrix} 2 & 1 \\ 1 & 1 \end{smallmatrix}\right) = ?$$

Substituting 2 for x, 1 for z, 1 for y, and 1 for t,

$$\left(\begin{smallmatrix} 2 & 1 \\ 1 & 1 \end{smallmatrix}\right) = (2)(1) - (1)(1)$$
$$= 1$$

Now work from Choice E:

(E) $\left(\begin{smallmatrix} 3 & 1 \\ 1 & 2 \end{smallmatrix}\right) = xz - yt = (3)(1) - (1)(2)$
$$= 3 - 2 = 1$$

Example 6

If for all numbers a, b, c, the operation $\bullet$ is defined as

$$a \bullet b = ab - a$$

then

$$a \bullet (b \bullet c) =$$

 (A) $a(bc - b - 1)$
 (B) $a(bc + b + 1)$
 (C) $a(bc - c - b - 1)$
 (D) $a(bc - b + 1)$
 (E) $a(b - a + c)$

Choice A is correct.

$$a \bullet b = ab - a$$
$$a \bullet (b \bullet c) = ?$$

Find $(b \bullet c)$ first. *Use substitution*:

$$a \bullet b = ab - a$$
$$\uparrow \qquad \uparrow$$
$$b \bullet c$$

Substitute b for a and c for b:

$$b \bullet c = b(c) - b$$

Now, $a \bullet (b \bullet c) = a \bullet (bc - b)$

Use definition $a \bullet b = ab - a$

Substitute a for a and $bc - b$ for b:

$$a \bullet b = ab - a$$

$$a \bullet (bc - b) = a(bc - b) - a$$
$$= abc - ab - a$$
$$= a(bc - b - 1)$$

Math Strategy   12

Very Important Strategy:

Try Not to Make Tedious Calculations, Since There Is Usually an Easier Way

In many of the examples given in these strategies, it has been explicitly stated that one should not calculate complicated quantities. In some of the examples, we have demonstrated a fast and a slow way of solving the same problem. On the actual exam, if you find that your solution to a problem involves a tedious and complicated method, then you are probably doing the problem in a long, hard way. Many times, you can DIVIDE, MULTIPLY, ADD, SUBTRACT, or FACTOR to simplify. Almost always, there will be an easier way.

Examples 3, 7, and 8 can also be solved with the aid of a calculator and some with the aid of a calculator allowing for exponential calculations. However, to illustrate the effectiveness of Math Strategy 12, we did not use the calculator method of solving these examples.

Example 1

If $y^8 = 4$ and $y^7 = \dfrac{3}{x}$, what is the value of y in terms of x?

(A) $\dfrac{4x}{3}$

(B) $\dfrac{3x}{4}$

(C) $\dfrac{4}{x}$

(D) $\dfrac{x}{4}$

(E) $\dfrac{12}{x}$

Choice A is correct.

Don't solve for the *value* of y first, by finding $y = 4^{\frac{1}{8}}$.

Just divide the two equations:

Step 1. $y^8 = 4$

Step 2. $y^7 = \dfrac{3}{x}$

Step 3. $\dfrac{y^8}{y^7} = \dfrac{4}{\frac{3}{x}}$

Step 4. $y = 4 \times \dfrac{x}{3}$

Step 5. $y = \dfrac{4x}{3}$

Example 2

What is the value of
$2^1 + 2^2 + 2^3 + 2^4 + 2^5 + 2^6 + 2^7 + 2^8 + 2^9$?

(A) $2^{11} - 2$

(B) 2^{10}

(C) $2^{10} - 2$

(D) $2^{10} - 4$

(E) $2^{10} - 8$

Choice C is correct.

Let $x = 2^1 + 2^2 + 2^3 + 2^4 + 2^5 + 2^6 + 2^7 + 2^8 + 2^9$ **1**

Now multiply **1** by 2:

$2x = 2(2^1 + 2^2 + 2^3 + 2^4 + 2^5 + 2^6 + 2^7 + 2^8 + 2^9)$

Thus,

$2x = 2^2 + 2^3 + 2^4 + 2^5 + 2^6 + 2^7 + 2^8 + 2^9 + 2^{10}$ **2**

Subtracting **1** from **2**, we get:

$2x - x = x = 2^{10} - 2^1 = 2^{10} - 2$

Example 3

Use factoring to make problems simpler.

$\sqrt{(88)^2 + (88)^2(3)} =$

(A) 88

(B) 176

(C) 348

(D) 350

(E) 352

Choice B is correct. Factor:

$(88)^2 + (88)^2(3) = 88^2(1 + 3) = 88^2(4)$

So:

$$\sqrt{(88)^2 + (88)^2(3)} = \sqrt{88^2(4)}$$
$$= \sqrt{88^2} \times \sqrt{4}$$
$$= 88 \times 2$$
$$= 176$$

Example 4

If $16r - 24q = 2$, then $2r - 3q =$

(A) $\dfrac{1}{8}$

(B) $\dfrac{1}{4}$

(C) $\dfrac{1}{2}$

(D) 2

(E) 4

Choice B is correct.

Divide by 8:

$$\frac{16r - 24q}{8} = \frac{2}{8}$$

$$2r - 3q = \frac{1}{4}$$

Example 5

If $(a^2 + a)^3 = x(a + 1)^3$, where $a + 1 \neq 0$, then $x =$

   (A) a

   (B) a^2

   (C) a^3

   (D) $\dfrac{a + 1}{a}$

   (E) $\dfrac{a}{a + 1}$

Choice C is correct.

Isolate x first:

$$x = \frac{(a^2 + a)^3}{(a + 1)^3}$$

Now use the fact that $\left(\dfrac{x^3}{y^3}\right) = \left(\dfrac{x}{y}\right)^3$:

$$\frac{(a^2 + a)^3}{(a + 1)^3} = \left(\frac{a^2 + a}{a + 1}\right)^3$$

Now *factor* $a^2 + a = a(a + 1)$

So:

$$\left(\frac{a^2 + a}{a + 1}\right)^3 = \left[\frac{a(a + 1)}{a + 1}\right]^3$$

$$= \left[\frac{a\cancel{(a + 1)}}{\cancel{a + 1}}\right]^3$$

$$= a^3$$

Example 6

If $\dfrac{p + 1}{r + 1} = 1$ and $p,\ r$ are nonzero, and p is not equal to -1, and r is not equal to -1, then

   (A) $2 > \dfrac{p}{r} > 1$ always

   (B) $\dfrac{p}{r} < 1$ always

   (C) $\dfrac{p}{r} = 1$ always

   (D) $\dfrac{p}{r}$ can be greater than 2

   (E) $\dfrac{p}{r} = 2$ always

Choice C is correct.

Get rid of the fraction. *Multiply* both sides of the equation

$$\frac{p + 1}{r + 1} = 1 \text{ by } r + 1$$

$$\left(\frac{p + 1}{\cancel{r + 1}}\right)\cancel{r + 1} = r + 1$$

$$p + 1 = r + 1$$

Cancel the 1s:

$$p = r$$

So:

$$\frac{p}{r} = 1$$

Example 7

$$\frac{4}{250} =$$

   (A) 0.16

   (B) 0.016

   (C) 0.0016

   (D) 0.00125

   (E) 0.000125

Choice B is correct.

Don't divide 4 into 250! *Multiply:*

$$\frac{4}{250} = \frac{4}{4} = \frac{16}{1{,}000}$$

Now $\dfrac{16}{100} = 0.16$, so $\dfrac{16}{1{,}000} = 0.016$.

Example 8

$(3 \times 4^{14}) - 4^{13} =$

   (A) 4

   (B) 12

   (C) 2×4^{13}

   (D) 3×4^{13}

   (E) 11×4^{13}

Choice E is correct.

Factor 4^{13} from $(3 \times 4^{14}) - 4^{13}$

We get:

$$4^{13}[(3 \times 4^1) - 1]$$

$$\text{or} \quad 4^{13}(12 - 1)$$

$$= 4^{13}(11)$$

You will see more of the technique of dividing, multiplying, adding, and subtracting in the next strategy, Math Strategy 13.

Math Strategy 13

Very Important Strategy:

Know How to Find Unknown Expressions by Adding, Subtracting, Multiplying, or Dividing Equations or Expressions

When you want to calculate composite quantities like $x + 3y$ or $m - n$, often you can do it by adding, subtracting, multiplying, or dividing the right equations or expressions.

Example 1

If $4x + 5y = 10$ and $x + 3y = 8$, then $\dfrac{5x + 8y}{3} =$

(A) 18
(B) 15
(C) 12
(D) 9
(E) 6

Choice E is correct. Don't solve for x, then for y.

Try to get the quantity $\dfrac{5x + 8y}{3}$ by adding or subtracting the equations. In this case, *add* equations.

$$
\begin{array}{r}
4x + 5y = 10 \\
+ \quad x + 3y = 8 \\
\hline
5x + 8y = 18
\end{array}
$$

Now divide by 3:

$$\frac{5x + 8y}{3} = \frac{18}{3} = 6 \ (Answer)$$

Example 2

If $25x + 8y = 149$ and $16x + 3y = 89$, then $\dfrac{9x + 5y}{5} =$

(A) 12
(B) 15
(C) 30
(D) 45
(E) 60

Choice A is correct. We are told

$$25x + 8y = 149 \qquad \boxed{1}$$
$$16x + 3y = 89 \qquad \boxed{2}$$

The long way to do this problem is to solve $\boxed{1}$ and $\boxed{2}$ for x and y, and then substitute these values into $\dfrac{9x + 5y}{5}$.

The fast way to do this problem is to *subtract* $\boxed{2}$ from $\boxed{1}$ and get

$$9x + 5y = 60 \qquad \boxed{3}$$

Now all we have to do is to divide $\boxed{3}$ by 5:

$$\frac{9x + 5y}{5} = 12 \ (Answer)$$

Example 3

If $21x + 39y = 18$, then $7x + 13y =$

(A) 3
(B) 6
(C) 7
(D) 9
(E) It cannot be determined from the information given.

Choice B is correct. We are given

$$21x + 39y = 18 \qquad \boxed{1}$$

Divide $\boxed{1}$ by 3:

$$7x + 13y = 6 \ (Answer)$$

Example 4

If $x + 2y = 4$, then $5x + 10y - 8 =$

(A) 10
(B) 12
(C) −10
(D) −12
(E) 0

Choice B is correct.

Multiply $x + 2y = 4$ by 5 to get:

$$5x + 10y = 20$$

Now subtract 8:

$$5x + 10y - 8 = 20 - 8$$
$$= 12$$

Example 5

If $6x^5 = y^2$ and $x = \dfrac{1}{y}$, then $y =$

(A) x^6
(B) $\dfrac{x^5}{6}$
(C) $6x^6$
(D) $\dfrac{6x^5}{5}$
(E) $\dfrac{x^5}{5}$

Choice C is correct.

Multiply $6x^5 = y^2$ *by* $x = \dfrac{1}{y}$ *to get:*

$$6x^6 = y^2\left(\dfrac{1}{y}\right) = y$$

Example 6

If $x > 0$, $y > 0$ and $x^2 = 27$ and $y^2 = 3$, then $\dfrac{x^3}{y^3} =$

(A) 9
(B) 27
(C) 36
(D) 48
(E) 54

Choice B is correct.

Divide: $\dfrac{x^2}{y^2} = \dfrac{27}{3} = 9$

Take square root: $\dfrac{x}{y} = 3$

So $\left(\dfrac{x}{y}\right)^3 = \dfrac{x^3}{y^3} = 3^3 = 27$

Example 7

If $\dfrac{m}{n} = \dfrac{3}{8}$ and $\dfrac{m}{q} = \dfrac{4}{7}$, then $\dfrac{n}{q} =$

(A) $\dfrac{12}{15}$

(B) $\dfrac{12}{56}$

(C) $\dfrac{56}{12}$

(D) $\dfrac{32}{21}$

(E) $\dfrac{21}{32}$

Choice D is correct.

First get rid of fractions!

Cross-multiply $\dfrac{m}{n} = \dfrac{3}{8}$ to get $8m = 3n$.   1

Now cross-multiply $\dfrac{m}{q} = \dfrac{4}{7}$ to get $7m = 4q$.   2

Now divide Equations 1 and 2 :

$$\dfrac{8m}{7m} = \dfrac{3n}{4q}$$ 3

The m's cancel and we get:

$$\dfrac{8}{7} = \dfrac{3n}{4q}$$ 4

Multiply equation 4 by 4 and divide by 3 to get

$$\dfrac{8 \times 4}{7 \times 3} = \dfrac{n}{q}$$

Thus $\dfrac{n}{q} = \dfrac{32}{21}$.

Example 8

If $\dfrac{a + b + c + d}{4} = 20$

and $\dfrac{b + c + d}{3} = 10$

Then $a =$

(A) 50
(B) 60
(C) 70
(D) 80
(E) 90

Choice A is correct.

We have

$$\dfrac{a + b + c + d}{4} = 20$$ 1

$$\dfrac{b + c + d}{3} = 10$$ 2

Multiply Equation 1 by 4:

We get: $a + b + c + d = 80$ 3

Now *multiply* Equation 2 by 3:

We get: $b + c + d = 30$ 4

Now *subtract* Equation 4 from Equation 3 :

$$a + b + c + d = 80$$ 3
$$- \quad (b + c + d = 30)$$ 4

We get: $a = 50$.

Example 9

If $y + 2q = 15$, $q + 2p = 5$, and $p + 2y = 7$, then $p + q + y =$

(A) 81
(B) 45
(C) 27
(D) 18
(E) 9

Choice E is correct.

There's no need to solve for each variable. Just *add* the equations and divide by 3! To do this, write one equation below the other. Be sure to line up the common variables.

$$
\begin{array}{r}
y + 2q \quad\quad = 15 \\
+ \quad q + 2p = \ 5 \\
+ 2y + \quad\quad p = \ 7 \\
\hline
3y + 3q + 3p = 27
\end{array}
$$

$$y + 2q + q + 2p + p + 2y = 27$$
$$3y + 3q + 3p = 27$$

Factor by 3:

$$3(y + q + p) = 27$$

So

$$p + q + y = 9$$

Example 10

If $x > 0$, $xy = 2$, $yz = 5$, and $xz = 10$, then $xyz =$

(A) 10
(B) 17
(C) 50
(D) 100
(E) 200

Choice A is correct. Since we are dealing with multiplication in all of the equations, *multiply* the expressions xy, yz, and xz.

We get:

$$(xy)(yz)(xz) = 2 \times 5 \times 10 = 100$$

This becomes

$$x^2 y^2 z^2 = 100$$

This is the same as

$$(xyz)^2 = 100$$

Take the square root of both sides to get

$$xyz = 10$$

Math Strategy   14

Very Important Strategy:

Draw or Extend Lines in a Diagram to Make a Problem Easier; Label Unknown Quantities

Remember when you took geometry in your early years in high school and the teacher drew a perpendicular line from the top of the triangle to the base of the triangle to prove that "if two sides of a triangle

are equal, the base angles are equal"? By drawing this line, the teacher was able to prove the theorem.

Unfortunately, the teacher did not say that whenever you draw a line in a diagram, you usually get more information to work with. If the teacher had said this, you would then use the strategy of drawing lines in diagrams to get more information and results. This strategy is a very powerful one and is used in many questions on tests and in figuring out many geometric problems.

When you see a diagram, be curious as to what lines you can draw to get more information to solve a problem. Also, label lines, angles, etc.

Example 1

The circle with center A and radius AB is inscribed in the square below. AB is extended to C. What is the ratio of AB to AC?

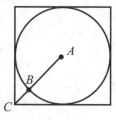

(A) $\sqrt{2}$

(B) $\dfrac{\sqrt{2}}{4}$

(C) $\dfrac{\sqrt{2} - 1}{2}$

(D) $\dfrac{\sqrt{2}}{2}$

(E) none of these

Choice D is correct. Always draw or extend lines to get more information. Also label unknown lengths, angles, or arcs with letters.

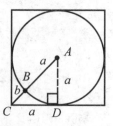

Label $AB = a$ and $BC = b$.
Draw perpendicular AD. Note it is just the radius, a.
CD also $= a$, because each side of the square is length $2a$ (the diameter) and CD is $\dfrac{1}{2}$ the side of the square.

We want to find $\dfrac{AB}{AC} = \dfrac{a}{a+b}$

Now $\triangle ADC$ is an isosceles right triangle, so $AD = CD = a$.

For an isosceles right triangle, we can restate the Pythagorean theorem,
$a^2 + a^2 = (a + b)^2$ where $a + b$ is the hypotenuse.

We get: $2a^2 = (a + b)^2$

Divide by $(a + b)^2$:
$$\frac{2a^2}{(a+b)^2} = 1$$

Divide by 2:
$$\frac{a^2}{(a+b)^2} = \frac{1}{2}$$

Take square roots of both sides:
$$\frac{a}{(a+b)} = \frac{1}{\sqrt{2}}$$
$$= \frac{1}{\sqrt{2}}\left(\frac{\sqrt{2}}{\sqrt{2}}\right)$$
$$= \frac{\sqrt{2}}{2} \ (Answer)$$

Example 2

What is the perimeter of the figure below if B and C are right angles?

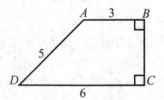

(A) 14
(B) 16
(C) 18
(D) 20
(E) cannot be determined

Choice C is correct.

Draw perpendicular AE. Label side $BC = h$. You can see that $AE = h$.

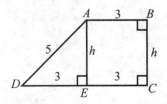

$ABCE$ is a rectangle, so $CE = 3$. This makes $ED = 3$ since the whole $DC = 6$.

Now use the Pythagorean theorem for triangle AED:
$$h^2 + 3^2 = 5^2$$
$$h^2 = 5^2 - 3^2$$
$$h^2 = 25 - 9$$
$$h^2 = 16$$
$$h = 4$$

So the perimeter is
$3 + h + 6 + 5 = 3 + 4 + 6 + 5 = 18.$ (*Answer*)

Example 3

In the figure below, O is the center of a circle with a radius of 6, and $AOCB$ is a square. If point B is on the circumference of the circle, the length of $AC =$

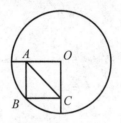

(A) $6\sqrt{2}$
(B) $3\sqrt{2}$
(C) 3
(D) 6
(E) $6\sqrt{3}$

Choice D is correct.

This is tricky if not impossible if you don't draw OB. *So draw OB:*

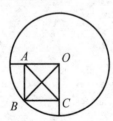

Since $AOCB$ is a square, $OB = AC$; and since $OB =$ radius $= 6$, $AC = 6$.

Example 4

In the figure below, lines ℓ_1 and ℓ_2 are parallel.
$AB = \dfrac{1}{3}AC$.

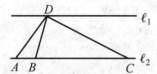

$$\frac{\text{area of triangle } ABD}{\text{area of triangle } DBC} =$$

(A) $\dfrac{1}{4}$

(B) $\dfrac{1}{3}$

(C) $\dfrac{3}{8}$

(D) $\dfrac{1}{2}$

(E) cannot be determined

Choice D is correct.

$$AB = \frac{1}{3}AC$$

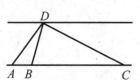

Ask yourself, what is the area of a triangle? It is $\dfrac{1}{2}$ (height $\times$ base). So let's get the heights and the bases of the triangles ABD and DBC. First *draw the altitude* (call it h).

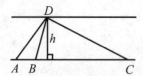

Now label $AB = \dfrac{1}{3}AC$ (given).

This makes $BC = \dfrac{2}{3}AC$, since $AB + BC = AC$

Thus the area of $\triangle ABD = \dfrac{1}{2}h(AB) = \dfrac{1}{2}h\left(\dfrac{1}{3}AC\right)$

Area of $\triangle DBC = \dfrac{1}{2}h(BC) = \dfrac{1}{2}h\left(\dfrac{2}{3}AC\right)$

$$\frac{\text{Area of } ABD}{\text{Area of } DBC} = \frac{\dfrac{1}{2}h\left(\dfrac{1}{3}AC\right)}{\dfrac{1}{2}h\left(\dfrac{2}{3}AC\right)}$$

$$= \frac{\dfrac{1}{3}}{\dfrac{2}{3}} = \frac{1}{3} \times \frac{3}{2} = \frac{1}{2}$$

Example 5

The area of the figure $ABCD$

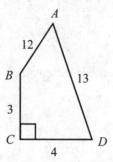

(*Note*: Figure is not drawn to scale.)

(A) is 36
(B) is 108
(C) is 156
(D) is 1,872
(E) cannot be determined

Choice A is correct.

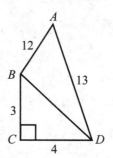

Draw BD. BCD is a 3–4–5 right triangle, so $BD = 5$. Now remember that a 5–12–13 triangle is also a right triangle, so angle ABD is a right angle. The area of triangle BCD is $\dfrac{(3 \times 4)}{2} = 6$ and the area of triangle BAD is $\dfrac{(5 \times 12)}{2} = 30$, so the total area is 36.

Example 6

In the figure, two points, B and C, are placed to the right of point A such that $4AB = 3AC$. The value of $\dfrac{BC}{AB}$

(A) equals $\dfrac{1}{3}$

(B) equals $\dfrac{2}{3}$

(C) equals $\dfrac{3}{2}$

(D) equals 3

(E) cannot be determined

Choice A is correct.

Place B and C to the right of A:

$$\bullet_{A} \quad \bullet_{B} \quad \bullet_{C} \quad \ell$$

Now label $AB = a$ and $BC = b$:

$$\overset{a}{\bullet_{A}} \quad \overset{b}{\bullet_{B}} \quad \bullet_{C} \quad \ell$$

$\dfrac{BC}{AB} = \dfrac{b}{a} \left(\dfrac{b}{a} \text{ is what we want to find}\right)$

We are given $4AB = 3AC$.

So, $4a = 3(a + b)$

Expand: $4a = 3a + 3b$

Subtract $3a$: $a = 3b$

Divide by 3 and a: $\dfrac{1}{3} = \dfrac{b}{a}$

But remember $\dfrac{BC}{AB} = \dfrac{b}{a}$, so $\dfrac{BC}{AB} = \dfrac{1}{3}$

So, $x = \dfrac{1}{2}(b + a + 40)$

Likewise, $y = \dfrac{1}{2}(c + d + 40)$

You want to find $x + y$, so add:

$$x = \dfrac{1}{2}(b + a + 40)$$

$$+ \; y = \dfrac{1}{2}(c + d + 40)$$

$$\overline{x + y = \dfrac{1}{2}(b + a + 40 + c + d + 40)}$$

But what is $a + b + c + d + 40$? It is the total number of degrees around the circumference, which is 360.

So, $x + y = \dfrac{1}{2}(\underbrace{b + a + c + d + 40} + 40)$

$$= \dfrac{1}{2}(360 + 40)$$

$$= \dfrac{1}{2}(400) = 200$$

Example 7

In the figure below, $ABCDE$ is a pentagon inscribed in the circle with center at O. $\angle DOC = 40°$. What is the value of $x + y$?

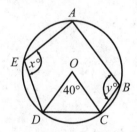

(A) 80
(B) 100
(C) 180
(D) 200
(E) cannot be determined

Choice D is correct.

Label degrees in each arc.

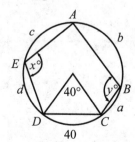

$\angle x$ is measured by $\dfrac{1}{2}$ the arc it cuts.

Example 8

In the figure below, if $\angle ABE = 40°$, $\angle DBC = 60°$, and $\angle ABC = 90°$, what is the measure of $\angle DBE$?

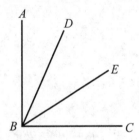

(A) 10°
(B) 20°
(C) 40°
(D) 100°
(E) cannot be determined

Choice A is correct.

Label angles first.

Now $\angle ABE = 40$, so $a + b = 40$
$\angle DBC = 60$, so $b + c = 60$
$\angle ABC = 90$, so $a + b + c = 90$

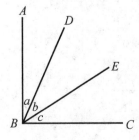

You want to find $\angle DBE$. $\angle DBE = b$, and you want to get the value of b from:

$$a + b = 40 \qquad \boxed{1}$$
$$b + c = 60 \qquad \boxed{2}$$
$$a + b + c = 90 \qquad \boxed{3}$$

Add $\boxed{1}$ and $\boxed{2}$:

$$\begin{aligned} a + b &= 40 \\ + b + c &= 60 \\ \hline a + 2b + c &= 100 \end{aligned}$$

Subtract $\boxed{3}$:

$$\begin{aligned} -(a + b + c &= 90) \\ \hline b &= 10 \end{aligned}$$

Example 9

In the figure below, three lines intersect at the points shown. What is the value of $A + B + C + D + E + F$?

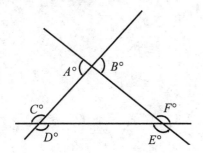

(A) 1,080
(B) 720
(C) 540
(D) 360
(E) cannot be determined

Choice B is correct.

Relabel, using the fact that *vertical angles are equal*.

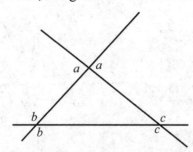

Now use the fact that a straight angle has 180° in it:

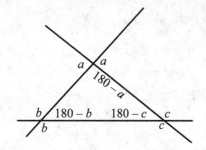

Now use the fact that the sum of the angles of a triangle = 180°:

$$180 - a + 180 - b + 180 - c = 180$$
$$540 - a - b - c = 180$$
$$540 - 180 = a + b + c$$
$$360 = a + b + c$$

Now remember what we are looking to find (the sum):

$$a + a + b + b + c + c = 2a + 2b + 2c$$

But this is just $2(a + b + c) = 2(360) = 720$.

Example 10

In the figure below, lines l and q are shown to be perpendicular on a coordinate plane. If line l contains the points $(0,0)$ and $(2,1)$, and line q contains the points $(2,1)$ and $(0,t)$, what is the value of t?

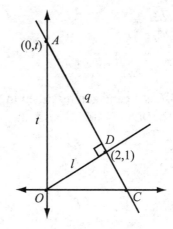

(A) −3
(B) −2
(C) 2
(D) 3
(E) 5

Choice E is correct. You want to find the value of t.

Start by drawing line DE, the altitude of $\triangle DOC$. Then label $EC = x$.

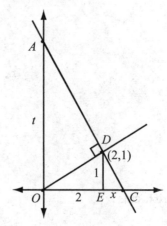

Because the altitude drawn to the hypotenuse of a right triangle forms two similar triangles, $\Delta AOC \sim \Delta DOC \sim \Delta OED$.

This gives $\dfrac{t}{(2 + x)} = \dfrac{2}{1}$ 1

We need to find the value of x in order to find the value of t.

Look at other similar triangles that involve just the variable x:

ΔDEC and ΔOED

This gives: $\dfrac{2}{1} = \dfrac{1}{x}$

So, we get: $x = \dfrac{1}{2}$

Plug $x = \dfrac{1}{2}$ into Equation 1 and we get:

$$\frac{t}{\frac{5}{2}} = \frac{2}{1}$$

$$t = 5$$

Alternate way:

If the lines are perpendicular, the slope of one line is the negative reciprocal of the other line. (See Math Refresher 416.)

Line l contains the points $(0,0)$ and $(2,1)$, so the slope is $\dfrac{(y_2 - y_1)}{(x_2 - x_1)} = \dfrac{(1 - 0)}{(2 - 0)} = \dfrac{1}{2}$.

The slope of line q is $\dfrac{(y_2 - y_1)}{(x_2 - x_1)} = \dfrac{(t - 1)}{(0 - 2)} = \dfrac{(t - 1)}{-2}$.

The slope of line $l = \dfrac{1}{2}$. Since lines l and q are perpendicular, the slope of line q is the negative reciprocal of line l.

$$\frac{t - 1}{-2} = -2$$

$$t - 1 = -2(-2)$$

$$t - 1 = 4$$

$$t = 5$$

Example 11

Here's an example where only a handful of students got the right answer. However, by using one or two powerful strategies, we can solve it.

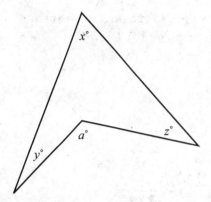

In the figure above, which is true?

(A) $x + y + z = 180 - a$
(B) $2x + y + z = a$
(C) $x - y + x - z = a$
(D) $x + y + z + a = 270$
(E) $x + y + z = a$

There are essentially two ways to effectively solve this problem. The first way is the most direct way:

Label the unmarked angle t (Math Strategy 14).

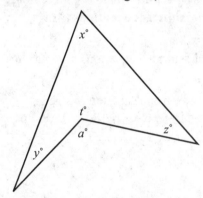

Then
(1) $x + y + t + z = 360$ because in a quadrilateral, the sum of the angles is 360°.

But
(2) $a + t = 360$ since the sum of the angles around a circle is 360.

Subtract equations (Math Strategy 13) and we get:

$x + y + t + z - a - t = 360 - 360 = 0$ and so

$x + y + z - a = 0$ giving us

$x + y + z = a$ *(Answer)*

Although the second method is a little longer and uses a different version of one of the strategies, I like this second method because it reinforces the use of the "drawing lines" strategy.

The first is to **draw lines to extend a diagram and label parts (Math Strategy 14).** Draw line *BC* and label the extra angles, *b* and *c*. We get:

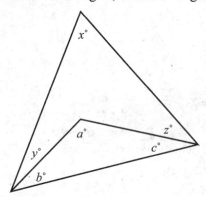

Now use the fact that the sum of the interior angles of any triangle equals 180°. We get:

$x + y + b + z + c = 180$ for the larger triangle   1

and $a + b + c = 180$ for the smaller triangle   2

Now use the second powerful strategy: **Don't just solve for variables, especially when you have many of them. Just add or subtract equations (Math Strategy 13).**

In this case we would subtract equations to reduce the amount of variables.

Subtracting Equation 2 from Equation 1, we get:
$x + y + b + z + c - a - b - c = 180 - 180 = 0$

We end up with: $x + y + z - a = 0$ or
$x + y + z = a$ (*Answer*).

| Math Strategy | 15 |

Know How to Eliminate Certain Choices

Instead of working out a lot of algebra, you may be able to eliminate several of the choices at first glance. In this way you can save yourself a lot of work. The key is to remember to use pieces of the given information to eliminate several of the choices at once.

Example 1

The sum of the digits of a three-digit number is 15. If this number is not divisible by 2 but is divisible by 5, which of the following is the number?

   (A) 384
   (B) 465
   (C) 635

   (D) 681
   (E) 780

Choice B is correct. Use pieces of the given information to eliminate several of the choices.

Which numbers are divisible by 2? Choices A and E are divisible by 2 and, thus, can be eliminated. Of Choices B, C, and D, which are *not* divisible by 5? Choice D can be eliminated because the units digit of the number must be 0 or 5 for the number to be divisible by 5. We are left with Choices B and C.

Only Choice B (465) has the sum of its digits equal to 15. Thus, 465 is the only number that satisfies all the pieces of the given information.

If you learn to use this method well, you can save loads of time.

Example 2

Which of the following numbers is divisible by 5 and 9, but not by 2?

   (A) 625
   (B) 639
   (C) 650
   (D) 655
   (E) 675

Choice E is correct. Clearly, a number is divisible by 5 if, and only if, its last digit is either 0 or 5. A number is also divisible by 2 if, and only if, its last digit is divisible by 2. *Certain choices are easily eliminated.* Thus we can *eliminate* Choices B and C.

Method I:

To eliminate some more choices, remember that a number is divisible by 9 if, and only if, the sum of its digits is divisible by 9. Thus, Choice E is the only correct answer.

Method II:

If you did not know the test for divisibility by 9, divide the numbers in Choices A, D, and E by 9 to find the answer.

Example 3

If the last digit and the first digit are interchanged in each of the numbers below, which will result in the number with the *largest* value?

(A) 5,243
(B) 4,352
(C) 4,235
(D) 2,534
(E) 2,345

Choice E is correct.

Certain choices are easily eliminated.

One of the numbers with the largest last digit (the *units* digit) will be the answer.   `1`

Using `1`, we see that Choices C and E each end in 5. All others end in digits less than 5 and may be eliminated. Starting with Choice E (see Strategy 8),

Choice E, 2,345, becomes 5,342.   `2`

Choice C, 4,235, becomes 5,234.   `3`

`2` is larger than `3`.

Example 4

Which of the following could be the value of 3^x where x is an integer?

(A) 339,066
(B) 376,853
(C) 411,282
(D) 422,928
(E) 531,441

Choice E is correct. Let's look at what 3^x looks like for integral values of x:

$3^1 = 3$
$3^2 = 9$
$3^3 = 27$
$3^4 = 81$
$3^5 = 243$
$3^6 = \ldots 9$
$3^7 = \ldots 7$
$3^8 = \ldots 1$

Note that 3^x always has the *units* digit of 3, 9, 7, or 1. So we can eliminate Choices A, C, and D, since those choices end in numbers other than 3, 9, 7, or 1. We are left with Choices B and E. The number in the correct choice must be exactly divisible by 3, since it is of the form 3^x ($= 3 \times 3 \times 3 \ldots$) where x is an integer. This is a good time to use your calculator. Divide the number in Choice B by 3: You get 125,617.66. That's *not* an integer. So the only remaining choice is Choice E.

Math Strategy   16

Watch Out for Questions That Seem Very Easy but That Can Be Tricky—Beware of Choice A as a "Lure Choice"

When questions appear to be solved very easily, think again! Watch out especially for the "lure," Choice A.

Example 1*

The diagram below shows a 12-hour digital clock whose hours value is the same as the minutes value. Consider each time when the same number appears for both the hour and the minutes as a "double time" situation. What is the shortest elapsed time period between the appearance of one double time and an immediately succeeding double time?

6:06

(A) 61 minutes
(B) 60 minutes
(C) 58 minutes
(D) 50 minutes
(E) 49 minutes

Choice E is correct. Did you think that just by subtracting something like 8:08 from 9:09 you would get the answer (1 hour and 1 minute = 61 minutes)? That's Choice A, which is wrong. So beware, because your answer came too easily for a test like the ACT. You must realize that there is another possibility of "double time" occurrence—12:12 and 1:01, whose difference is 49 minutes. This is Choice E, the correct answer.

Example 2

The letters d and m are integral digits in a certain number system. If $0 \le d \le m$, how many different possible values are there for d?

(A) m
(B) $m - 1$
(C) $m - 2$
(D) $m + 1$
(E) $m + 2$

*This problem also appears in Strategy 1 of the 5 General Strategies on page 40.

Choice D is correct. Did you think that the answer was *m*? Do not be careless! The list 1, 2, 3, . . ., *m* contains *m* elements. If 0 is included in the list, then there are *m* + 1 elements. Hence, if $0 \leq d \leq m$ where *d* is integral, then *d* can have *m* + 1 different values.

Example 3

There are some flags hanging in a horizontal row. Starting at one end of the row, the U.S. flag is 25th. Starting at the other end of the row, the U.S. flag is 13th. How many flags are in the row?

(A) 36
(B) 37
(C) 38
(D) 39
(E) 40

Choice B is correct. **The obvious may be tricky!**

Method I:

Given:
The U.S. flag is 25th from one end.   1
The U.S. flag is 13th from the other end.   2

At first glance it may appear that adding 1 and 2, 25 + 13 = 38, will be the correct answer. This is WRONG!

If you add 25 + 13 you are counting the U.S. flag twice: once as the 25th and again as the 13th from the other end. The correct answer is

$$25 + 13 - 1 = 37$$

Method II:

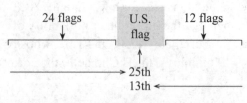

$$24 + \text{U.S. flag} (1) + 12 = 37$$

Example 4

OR = RQ in the figure below. If the coordinates of *Q* are (5,*m*), find the value of *m*.

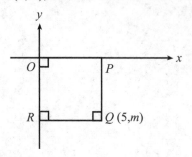

(A) −5
(B) −√5
(C) 0
(D) √5
(E) 5

Choice A is correct.

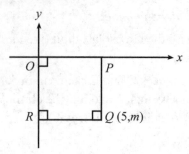

Given: *OR = RQ*   1
Coordinates of *Q* = (5,*m*)   2
From 2, we get: *RQ* = 5   3
Substitute 3 into 1. We get:

$$OR = 5$$

The obvious may be tricky! Since *Q* is below the *x*-axis, its *y*-coordinate is negative. Thus *m* = −5.

Math Strategy   17

Very Important Strategy:

Use the Given Information Effectively (and Ignore Irrelevant Information)

You should always first use the piece of information that tells you the most, gives you a useful idea, or brings you closest to the answer.

Example 1

In the figure below, *BD* is a straight line. What is the value of *a*?

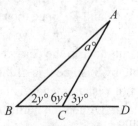

(*Note*: Figure is not drawn to scale.)

(A) 15
(B) 17
(C) 20

(D) 24
(E) 30

Choice C is correct.

Use the piece of information that will give you something definite. You might at first think of using the fact that the sum of the angles of a triangle = 180°. However, that will give you

$$a + 2y + 6y = 180$$

That's not very useful. But if you use the fact that the sum of the angles in a straight angle is 180, we get:

$$6y + 3y = 180$$
and we get: $9y = 180$
$$y = 20$$

Now we have something useful. At this point, we can apply the fact that the sum of the angles in a triangle is 180.

$$a + 2y + 6y = 180$$

Substituting 20 for y, we get:

$$a + 2(20) + 6(20) = 180$$
$$a = 20 \ (Answer)$$

Example 2

Avriel, Braden, and Carlos will be seated at random in three chairs, each denoted by X below. What is the probability that Avriel will be seated next to Carlos?

X   X   X

(A) $\frac{1}{8}$

(B) $\frac{1}{3}$

(C) $\frac{3}{8}$

(D) $\frac{5}{8}$

(E) $\frac{2}{3}$

Represent the students as A, B, and C respectively. However, don't make the mistake of representing the students in an unorganized or random fashion, such as ABC, BAC, CAB, and then try to get all the other possibilities.

Represent the students systematically. Start with A at the extreme left, B at the extreme left, and then C at the extreme left.

Like this:

ABC
ACB   only two possibilities

BAC
BCA   only two possibilities

CAB
CBA   again only two possibilities

Thus, there are 6 total possibilities: ABC, ACB, BAC, BCA, CAB, CBA.

Probability is defined as the favorable number of ways divided by the total number of ways.

The favorable number of ways is the number of ways where Avriel is seated next to Carlos. This is:

ACB, BAC, BCA, and CAB—4 ways.

Thus, the probability is $\frac{4}{6}$, or $\frac{2}{3}$.

Note that by organizing the information like this, we get all the possibilities in a systemized manner.

Example 3

In the figure of intersecting lines below, which of the following is equal to $180 - a$?

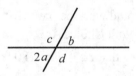

(A) $a + d$
(B) $a + 2d$
(C) $c + b$
(D) $b + 2a$
(E) $c + d$

Choice A is correct. Try to get something you can work with. From the diagram,

$$2a + d = 180.$$

So, to find $180 - a$, just subtract a from both sides of the equation above.

$$2a + d - a = 180 - a.$$

You get:

$$a + d = 180 - a.$$

See Math Strategy 7, Example 7 (page 64) for an alternate approach to solving this problem, using a different strategy: **Use Specific Numerical Examples to Prove or Disprove Your Guess.**

Example 4

Which of the angles in the figure below has a degree measure that can be determined?

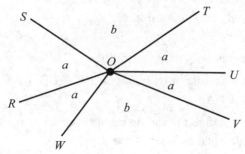

(*Note*: Figure is not drawn to scale.)

(A) $\angle WOS$
(B) $\angle SOU$
(C) $\angle WOT$
(D) $\angle ROV$
(E) $\angle WOV$

Choice C is correct.

Use information that will get you something useful.

$$4a + 2b = 360 \text{ (sum of all angles = 360°)}$$

Divide by 2 to simplify:

$$2a + b = 180$$

Now try all the choices. You could work backward from Choice E, but we'll start with Choice A:

(A) $\angle WOS = 2a$. You know that $2a + b = 180$ but don't know the value of $2a$.
(B) $\angle SOU = b + a$. You know $2a + b = 180$ but don't know the value of $b + a$.
(C) $\angle WOT = b + 2a$. You know that $2a + b = 180$, so you know the value of $b + 2a$.

Example 5

If a ranges in value from 0.003 to 0.3 and b ranges in value from 3.0 to 300.0, then the minimum value of $\frac{a}{b}$ is:

(A) 0.1
(B) 0.01
(C) 0.001
(D) 0.0001
(E) 0.00001

Choice E is correct.

Start by using the definitions of *minimum* and *maximum*.

The minimum value of $\frac{a}{b}$ is when a is *minimum* and b is *maximum*.

The minimum value of $a = .003$
The maximum value of $b = 300$

So the minimum value of $\frac{a}{b} = \frac{.003}{300} = \frac{.001}{100} = .00001$.

Example 6

If $xry = 0$, $yst = 0$, and $rxt = 1$, then which must be 0?

(A) r
(B) s
(C) t
(D) x
(E) y

Choice E is correct.

Use information that will give you something to work with.

$rxt = 1$ tells you that $r \neq 0$, $x \neq 0$, and $t \neq 0$. So if $xry = 0$ then y must be 0.

Example 7

On a street with 25 houses, 10 houses have *fewer than 6 rooms,* 10 houses have *more than 7 rooms,* and 4 houses have *more than 8 rooms.* What is the total number of houses on the street that are either 6-, 7-, or 8-room houses?

(A) 5
(B) 9
(C) 11
(D) 14
(E) 15

Choice C is correct.

There are three possible situations:

(a) Houses that have *fewer than 6 rooms* (call the number a)
(b) Houses that have *6, 7, or 8 rooms* (call the number b)
(c) Houses that have *more than 8 rooms* (call the number c)

$a + b + c$ must total 25 (given).   1

a is 10 (given).   2

c is 4 (given).   3

Substituting 2 and 3 in 1, we get: $10 + b + 4 = 25$. Therefore b must be 11.

Example 8

Mr. Martinez's tenth-grade class took a survey to see what activities each student engages in one hour before bed. When the survey was complete, 5 students selected "Play video games" and "Watch TV," 14 students selected "Watch TV," and 8 students selected "Play video games." How many students are in Mr. Martinez's class? (Assume that every student in the class watches TV only, plays video games only, or does both.)

(A) 11
(B) 17
(C) 22
(D) 25
(E) 27

Choice B is correct.

Method I:

Draw two intersecting circles.

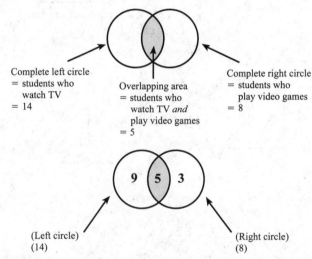

Complete left circle = students who watch TV = 14

Overlapping area = students who watch TV *and* play video games = 5

Complete right circle = students who play video games = 8

(Left circle) (14)

(Right circle) (8)

Above, subtracting: all students who watch TV (14) − students who watch TV *and* also play video games (5), we get 9.

Above, subtracting: all students who play video games (8) − students who watch TV *and* also play video games (5), we get 3.

So the total number of students is 9 + 5 + 3 = 17.

Method II:

Total number of students are:
(a) students who only watch TV
(b) students who only play video games
(c) students who watch TV *and* also play video games

(a) There are 14 students who watch TV and 5 students who watch TV *and* play video games, so subtracting, *there are 9 students who watch TV only.*

(b) There are 8 students who play video games and 5 students who watch TV *and* also play video games, so subtracting, *there are 3 students who play video games only.*

(c) The number of students who watch TV *and* also play video games is 5 (given).

Adding the number of students in (a), (b), and (c) we get: 9 + 3 + 5 = 17.

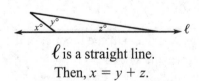

Math Strategy 18

Very Important Strategy:

Know and Use Facts about Triangles

By remembering the following facts about triangles, you can often save yourself a lot of time and trouble.

Statements about Triangles

I.

If $a = b$, then $x = y$.

a b
$x°$ $y°$

The base angles of an isosceles triangle are equal.
If $x = y$, then $a = b$.

a b
$x°$ $y°$

If the base angles of a triangle are equal, the triangle is isosceles.

II.

$x°$ $y°$ $z°$ ℓ

ℓ is a straight line.
Then, $x = y + z$.

The measure of an exterior angle is equal to the sum of the measures of the remote interior angles.

III.

If $a < b$, then $y < x$.

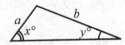

If $y < x$, then $a < b$.

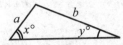

In a triangle, the greater angle lies opposite the greater side.

IV.

Similar Triangles

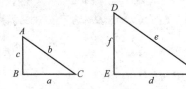

If $\triangle ABC \sim \triangle DEF$, then

$$m\angle A = m\angle D$$
$$m\angle B = m\angle E$$
$$m\angle C = m\angle F$$

and $\dfrac{a}{d} = \dfrac{b}{e} = \dfrac{c}{f}$

V.

$$m\angle A + m\angle B + m\angle C = 180°$$

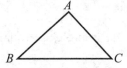

The sum of the interior angles of a triangle is 180°.

VI.

Area of $\triangle ABC = \dfrac{AD \times BC}{2}$

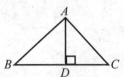

The area of a triangle is one-half the product of the altitude to a side times the side.

Note: If $m\angle A = 90°$, area also $= \dfrac{AD \times BC}{2}$.

VII.

In a right triangle, $c^2 = a^2 + b^2$ and $x° + y° = 90°$.

VIII. Memorize the following standard triangles:

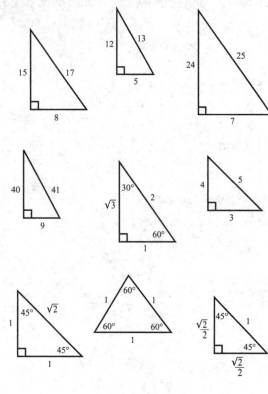

IX.

$a + b > c$
$a + c > b$
$b + c > a$

The sum of the lengths of two sides of a triangle is greater than the length of the third side. (This is like saying that the shortest distance between two points is a straight line.)

Example 1

In the diagram below, what is the value of x?

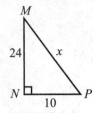

(A) 20
(B) 25
(C) 26
(D) 45
(E) 48

Choice C is correct.

Method I:

Use Statement VII. Then,

$$x^2 = 24^2 + 10^2$$
$$= 576 + 100$$
$$= 676$$

Thus, $x = 26$ (*Answer*)

Method II:

Look at Statement VIII. Notice that $\triangle MNP$ is similar to one of the standard triangles:

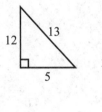 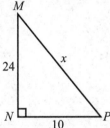

This is true because

$$\frac{12}{24} = \frac{5}{10} \text{ (Look at Statement IV)}$$

Hence, $\frac{12}{24} = \frac{13}{x} = $ or $x = 26$ (*Answer*)

Example 2

If Masonville is 50 kilometers due north of Adamston and Elvira is 120 kilometers due east of Adamston, then the minimum distance between Masonville and Elvira is

(A) 125 kilometers
(B) 130 kilometers
(C) 145 kilometers
(D) 160 kilometers
(E) 170 kilometers

Choice B is correct. *Draw a diagram first.*

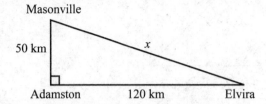

The given information translates into the diagram above. Note Statement VIII. The triangle above is a multiple of the special 5–12–13 right triangle.

$$50 = 10(5)$$
$$120 = 10(12)$$
Thus, $x = 10(13) = 130$ kilometers

(*Note*: The Pythagorean theorem could also have been used: $50^2 + 120^2 = x^2$.)

Example 3

In triangle ABC, if $a > c$, which of the following is true?

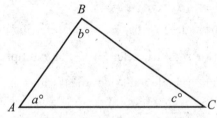

(*Note*: Figure is not drawn to scale.)

(A) $BC = AC$
(B) $AB > BC$
(C) $AC > AB$
(D) $BC > AB$
(E) $BC > AC$

Choice D is correct. *(Remember triangle inequality facts.)* From basic geometry, Statement III, we know that, since $m\angle BAC$ is greater than $m\angle BCA$, the leg opposite $\angle BAC$ is greater than the leg opposite $\angle BCA$, or

$$BC > AB$$

Example 4

In the triangle below, side $BC = 10$, angle $B = 45°$, and angle $A = 90°$.

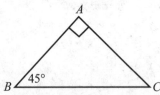

(*Note*: Figure is not drawn to scale.)

The area of the triangle

(A) is 15
(B) is 20
(C) is 25
(D) is 30
(E) cannot be determined

Choice C is correct.

First find angle C using Statement V.

$$90° + 45° + m\angle C = 180°$$

$$\text{so } m\angle C = 45°.$$

Using Statement I, we find $AB = AC$, since

$$m\angle B = m\angle C = 45°.$$

Since our right triangle ABC has $BC = 10$, referring to Statement VIII (the right triangle $\frac{\sqrt{2}}{2}, \frac{\sqrt{2}}{2}, 1$), multiply by 10 to get a right triangle with sides measuring:

$$\frac{10\sqrt{2}}{2}, \frac{10\sqrt{2}}{2}, 10$$

Thus side $AB = \frac{10\sqrt{2}}{2} = 5\sqrt{2}$

$$\text{side } AC = \frac{10\sqrt{2}}{2} = 5\sqrt{2}$$

Now the area of triangle ABC, according to Statement VI, is

$$\frac{5\sqrt{2} \times 5\sqrt{2}}{2} = \frac{25 \times 2}{2} = 25$$

Example 5

In the figure below, what is the value of x?

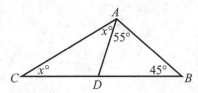

(A) 30
(B) 40

(C) 50
(D) 80
(E) 100

Choice B is correct.

Remember triangle facts. Use Statement II.

$\angle ADB$ is an exterior angle of $\triangle ACD$, so

$$m\angle ADB = x + x = 2x \qquad \boxed{1}$$

In $\triangle ADB$, the sum of its angles $= 180$ (Statement V),

$$\text{so} \quad m\angle ADB + 55 + 45 = 180$$

$$\text{or} \quad m\angle ADB + 100 = 180$$

$$\text{or} \quad m\angle ADB = 80 \qquad \boxed{2}$$

Equating $\boxed{1}$ and $\boxed{2}$ we have

$$2x = 80$$

$$x = 40 \; (\textit{Answer})$$

Example 6

Which of the following represents all of the possibilities for the value of a in the figure below?

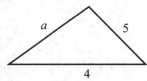

(*Note*: Figure is not drawn to scale.)

(A) $1 < a < 9$
(B) $4 < a < 5$
(C) $0 < a < 9$
(D) $4 < a < 9$
(E) $5 < a < 9$

Choice A is correct. From Statement IX, since the sum of the lengths of two sides of a triangle is greater than the length of the third side, we have:

$$a + 5 > 4 \qquad \boxed{1}$$
$$a + 4 > 5 \qquad \boxed{2}$$
$$5 + 4 > a \qquad \boxed{3}$$

From $\boxed{2}$ we get:

$$a > 1$$

From $\boxed{3}$ we get:

$$9 > a$$

This means that

$$9 > a > 1, \text{ or } 1 < a < 9$$

Math Strategy   19

When Calculating Answers, Never Multiply and/or Do Long Division If You Can Reduce First

On the ACT exam, because calculators are permitted, you may do the following problems with a calculator also. But it would be wise for you to see the other approach too—how the problem can be solved *without* the use of a calculator.

Example 1

If $w = \dfrac{81 \times 150}{45 \times 40}$, then $w =$

   (A) 3

   (B) $6\dfrac{3}{4}$

   (C) $7\dfrac{1}{4}$

   (D) 9

   (E) $20\dfrac{1}{4}$

Choice B is correct.

Do *not* multiply 81×150 and 45×40 to get:

$$\frac{12,150}{1,800}$$

$$\overset{81}{\overbrace{9 \times 9}} \times \overset{150}{\overbrace{15 \times 10}}$$

Factor first: $\dfrac{9 \times 9 \times 15 \times 10}{9 \times 5 \times 4 \times 10}$

$$\underset{45}{\underbrace{9 \times 5}} \times \underset{40}{\underbrace{4 \times 10}}$$

Then cancel like factors in numerator and denominator:

$$\frac{\cancel{9} \times 9 \times 15 \times \cancel{10}}{\cancel{9} \times 5 \times 4 \times \cancel{10}}$$

Reduce further: $\dfrac{9 \times \cancel{5} \times 3}{\cancel{5} \times 4}$

Then simplify: $\dfrac{27}{4} = 6\dfrac{3}{4}$ *(Answer)*

Example 2

$$\frac{4^2 + 4^2 + 4^2}{3^3 + 3^3 + 3^3} =$$

   (A) $\dfrac{16}{27}$

   (B) $\dfrac{8}{9}$

   (C) $\dfrac{4}{3}$

   (D) $\dfrac{64}{27}$

   (E) $\dfrac{512}{81}$

Choice A is correct.

$$\frac{4^2 + 4^2 + 4^2}{3^3 + 3^3 + 3^3} =$$

Factor and reduce: $\dfrac{\cancel{3}(4^2)}{\cancel{3}(3^3)} = \dfrac{16}{27}$

Example 3

If $6 \times 7 \times 8 \times 9 = \dfrac{12 \times 14 \times 18}{x}$, then $x =$

   (A) $\dfrac{1}{2}$

   (B) 1

   (C) 4

   (D) 8

   (E) 12

Choice B is correct.

Given: $6 \times 7 \times 8 \times 9 = \dfrac{12 \times 14 \times 18}{x}$ ⬛1

so that $x = \dfrac{12 \times 14 \times 18}{6 \times 7 \times 8 \times 9}$ ⬛2

Do *not* multiply the numbers out in the numerator and denominator of ⬛2 ! It is too much work! Rewrite ⬛2 .

Factor and reduce:

$$x = \frac{12 \times 14 \times 18}{6 \times 7 \times 8 \times 9}$$

$$= \frac{2 \times \cancel{6} \times 2 \times \cancel{7} \times 2 \times \cancel{9}}{\cancel{6} \times \cancel{7} \times 8 \times \cancel{9}}$$

$$= \frac{2 \times 2 \times 2}{8} = \frac{\cancel{8}}{\cancel{8}} = 1 \ (Answer)$$

Example 4

If $\dfrac{81 \times y}{27} = 21$, then $y =$

(A) $\dfrac{1}{21}$

(B) $\dfrac{1}{7}$

(C) 3

(D) 7

(E) 21

Choice D is correct.

$$\text{Given: } \frac{81 \times y}{27} = 21$$

Multiply both sides by 27 to get $81 \times y = 21 \times 27$.

$$y = \frac{21 \times 27}{81}$$

Factor and reduce:

$$y = \frac{3 \cdot 7 \times 3 \cdot \cancel{9}}{9 \cdot \cancel{9}}$$

$$= \frac{\cancel{3} \cdot 7 \times \cancel{3}}{\cancel{3} \cdot \cancel{3}}$$

$$y = 7 \ (Answer)$$

Example 5

Find the value of $\dfrac{y^2 - 7y + 10}{y - 2}$ rounded to the nearest whole number if $y = 8.000001$.

(A) 2

(B) 3

(C) 5

(D) 6

(E) 16

Choice B is correct.

$$\text{Given: } \frac{y^2 - 7y + 10}{y - 2} \qquad \boxed{1}$$

Factor and reduce:

Factor the numerator of $\boxed{1}$. We get:

$$\frac{(y - 5)\cancel{(y - 2)}}{\cancel{y - 2}} = y - 5 \qquad \boxed{2}$$

Substitute 8.000001 in $\boxed{2}$. We have:

$$8.000001 - 5 =$$

$$3.000001 \approx 3 \ (Answer)$$

READING STRATEGIES AND QUIZZES

Using Critical-Thinking Skills for the ACT Reading Section

Note: There are only 4 choices for the questions in the Reading Section of the actual ACT. For instructional purposes we have chosen to use 5 choices in this strategy section.

Introduction to Passage Reading

Before getting into the detailed strategies, I want to say that the most important way to really understand what you're reading is to *get involved* with the passage—as if a friend of yours were reading the passage to you and you wanted to be interested so you wouldn't hurt your friend's feelings. When you see the passage on paper it is also a good idea to *underline* important parts of the passage, which we'll also go over later in one of the strategies.

So many students ask, How do I answer reading comprehension questions? How do I read the passage effectively? Do I look at the questions before reading the passage? Do I underline things in the passage? Do I have to memorize details and dates? How do I get interested and involved in the passage?

All of these are good questions. They will be answered carefully and in the right sequence.

What Reading Comprehension Questions Ask

First of all, it is important to know that most reading comprehension questions ask about one of four things:

1. The MAIN IDEA of the passage.

2. INFORMATION SPECIFICALLY MENTIONED in the passage.

3. INFORMATION IMPLIED (not directly stated) in the passage.

4. The TONE or MOOD of the passage.

For example, following are some typical question stems. Each lets you immediately know which of the above is being asked about.

1. It can be inferred from the passage that . . . (IMPLIED INFORMATION)

2. According to the author . . . (MAIN IDEA)

3. The passage is primarily concerned with . . . (MAIN IDEA)

4. The author's statement that . . . (SPECIFIC INFORMATION)

5. Which of the following describes the mood of the passage? (TONE or MOOD)

6. The author implies that . . . (IMPLIED INFORMATION)

7. The use of paper is described in lines 14–16 . . . (SPECIFIC INFORMATION)

8. The main purpose of the passage . . . (MAIN IDEA)

9. The author's tone is best described as . . . (TONE or MOOD)

10. One could easily see the author as . . . (IMPLIED INFORMATION)

Getting Involved with the Passage

Now, let's first answer the burning question: Should I read the questions first before reading the passage? The answer is NO! If you have in mind the four main question types given above, you will not likely be in for any big surprises. Many questions, when you get to them, will be reassuringly familiar in the way they're framed and in their intent. You can best answer them by reading the passage first, allowing yourself to become involved with it.

To give you an idea of what I mean, look over the following passage. When you have finished, I'll show you how you might read it so as to get involved with it and with the author's intent.

Introductory Passage 1*

Yesterday, December 7, 1941—a date which will live in infamy—the United States of America was suddenly and deliberately attacked by naval and air forces of the Empire of Japan.

The United States was at peace with that nation, and, at the solicitation of Japan, was still in conversation with its government and its Emperor looking toward the maintenance of peace in the Pacific.

Indeed, one hour after Japanese air squadrons had commenced bombing in the American island of Oahu, the Japanese Ambassador to the United States and his colleague delivered to our Secretary of State a formal reply to a recent American message. And, while this reply stated that it seemed useless to continue the existing diplomatic negotiations, it contained no threat or hint of war or of armed attack.

It will be recorded that the distance of Hawaii from Japan makes it obvious that the attack was deliberately planned many days or even weeks ago. During the intervening time the Japanese Government has deliberately sought to deceive the United States by false statements and expressions of hope for continued peace.

The attack yesterday on the Hawaiian Islands has caused severe damage to American naval and military forces. I regret to tell you that very many American lives have been lost. In addition, American ships have been reported torpedoed on the high seas between San Francisco and Honolulu.

Yesterday the Japanese Government also launched an attack against Malaya.

Last night Japanese forces attacked Hong Kong.

Last night Japanese forces attacked Guam.

Last night Japanese forces attacked the Philippine Islands.

Last night the Japanese attacked Wake Island.

And this morning the Japanese attacked Midway Island.

Japan has therefore undertaken a surprise offensive extending throughout the Pacific area. The facts of yesterday and today speak for themselves. The people of the United States have already formed their opinions and well understand the implications to the very life and safety of our nation.

As Commander-in-Chief of the Army and Navy I have directed that all measures be taken for our defense, that always will our whole nation remember the character of the onslaught against us.

No matter how long it may take us to overcome this premeditated invasion, the American people, in their righteous might, will win through to absolute victory.

I believe that I interpret the will of the Congress and of the people when I assert that we will not only defend ourselves to the uttermost but will make it very certain that this form of treachery shall never again endanger us.

Hostilities exist. There is no blinking at the fact that our people, our territory and our interests are in grave danger.

With confidence in our armed forces, with the unbounding determination of our people, we will gain the inevitable triumph, so help us God.

I ask that the Congress declare that since the unprovoked and dastardly attack by Japan on Sunday, December 7, 1941, a state of war has existed between the United States and the Japanese Empire.

*From President Franklin Delano Roosevelt's address to the U.S. Congress on December 8, 1941.

Breakdown and Underlining of the Passage

Before going over the passage with you, I want to suggest some underlining you might want to make and show what different parts of the passage refer to.

Yesterday, December 7, 1941—a date which will live in infamy—the United States of America was suddenly and deliberately attacked by naval and air forces of the Empire of Japan.

The United States was at peace with that nation, and, at the solicitation of Japan, was still in conversation with its government and its Emperor looking toward the maintenance of peace in the Pacific.

→ Sets the stage.

Indeed, one hour after Japanese air squadrons had commenced bombing in the American island of Oahu, the Japanese Ambassador to the United States and his colleague delivered to our Secretary of State a formal reply to a recent American message. And, while this reply stated that it seemed useless to continue the existing diplomatic negotiations, it contained no threat or hint of war or of armed attack.

It will be recorded that the distance of Hawaii from Japan makes it obvious that the attack was deliberately planned many days or even weeks ago. During the intervening time the Japanese Government has deliberately sought to deceive the United States by false statements and expressions of hope for continued peace.

→ This should interest and surprise you.

The attack yesterday on the Hawaiian Islands has caused severe damage to American naval and military forces. I regret to tell you that very many American lives have been lost. In addition, American ships have been reported torpedoed on the high seas between San Francisco and Honolulu.

Yesterday the Japanese Government also launched an attack against Malaya.

Last night Japanese forces attacked Hong Kong.

Last night Japanese forces attacked Guam.

Last night Japanese forces attacked the Philippine Islands.

Last night the Japanese attacked Wake Island.

And this morning the Japanese attacked Midway Island.

→ Examples of hostility.

Japan has therefore undertaken a surprise offensive extending throughout the Pacific area. The facts of yesterday and today speak for themselves. The people of the United States have already formed their opinions and well understand the implications to the very life and safety of our nation.

As Commander-in-Chief of the Army and Navy I have directed that all measures be taken for our defense, that always will our whole nation remember the character of the onslaught against us.

No matter how long it may take us to overcome this premeditated invasion, the American people, in their righteous might, will win through to absolute victory.

I believe that I interpret the will of the Congress and of the people when I assert that we will not only defend ourselves to the uttermost but will make it very certain that this form of treachery shall never again endanger us.

→ Leading to a conclusion.

Hostilities exist. There is no blinking at the fact that our people, our territory and our interests are in grave danger.

With confidence in our armed forces, with the unbounding determination of our people, we will gain the inevitable triumph, so help us God.

I ask that the Congress declare that since the unprovoked and dastardly attack by Japan on Sunday, December 7, 1941, a state of war has existed between the United States and the Japanese Empire.

Now I'll go over the passage with you, showing you what might go through your mind as you read. This will let you see how to get involved with the passage and how this involvement facilitates answering the questions that follow the passage. In many cases, you'll actually be able to anticipate the questions. Of course, when you are preparing for the SAT, you'll have to develop this skill so that you do it rapidly and almost automatically.

Let's look at the first sentence:

Yesterday, December 7, 1941—a date which will live in infamy—the United States of America was suddenly and deliberately attacked by naval and air forces of the Empire of Japan.

Immediately you should say to yourself, "Something catastrophic has happened—what is the president going to do about it?" Read on:

The United States was at peace with that nation, and, at the solicitation of Japan, was still in conversation with its government and its Emperor looking toward the maintenance of peace in the Pacific.

Now you might say to yourself, "Why did they attack? Was it a mistake or did they trick us deliberately?" Read on:

Indeed, one hour after Japanese air squadrons had commenced bombing in the American island of Oahu, the Japanese Ambassador to the United States and his colleague delivered to our Secretary of State a formal reply to a recent American message. . . . it contained no threat or hint of war or of armed attack.

You are now probably saying to yourself, "Hmmm, this sounds bad if the attack occurred only an hour after that benign, neutral message. What is the president about to suggest?" Read on:

The attack yesterday on the Hawaiian Islands has caused severe damage to American naval and military forces. I regret to tell you that very many American lives have been lost. . . . Yesterday the Japanese Government also launched an attack against. . . .

Now you are probably both sad and angered by the news of the losses. And the list of other nations Japan has attacked at the same time probably has you saying to yourself, "We must do something—what are we going to do?!" Read on:

As Commander-in-Chief of the Army and Navy I have directed that all measures be taken for our defense, that

always will our whole nation remember the character of the onslaught against us.

This has probably boosted your confidence in the president's leadership, but you are also worried: Will I or a member of my family be fighting in a war? What will happen to us? Can we win? Read on:

. . . the American people, in their righteous might, will win through to absolute victory.
. . . we . . . will make it very certain that this form of treachery shall never again endanger us.
. . . There is no blinking at the fact that our people, our territory and our interests are in grave danger.
. . . we will gain the inevitable triumph, so help us God.

Now you are probably saying to yourself, "We are going to war. We must go to war not only to defend ourselves now but to make the world safe for our future." You should easily anticipate the conclusion that the president has prepared you for:

I ask that the Congress declare that since the unprovoked and dastardly attack by Japan on Sunday, December 7, 1941, a state of war has existed between the United States and the Japanese Empire.

How to Answer Reading Comprehension Questions Most Effectively

Before we start to answer the questions, let me tell you the best and most effective way of answering passage questions. You should read the question and proceed to look at the choices in the order of Choice A, Choice B, etc. If a choice (such as Choice A) doesn't give you the definite feeling that it is correct, don't try to analyze it further. Go on to Choice B, and so forth. Read all of the choices and choose the best one.

Suppose you have gone through all five choices, and you don't see any one that stands out as obviously being correct. Then quickly guess or leave the question blank and go on to the next question. You can go back after you have answered the other questions relating to the passage. But remember, when you return to the questions you weren't sure of, don't spend too much time on them. Try to forge ahead on the test.

Let's proceed to answer the questions now. Look at the first question:

1. This passage assumes the desirability of
   (A) maintaining peace at any price
   (B) instigating war before the enemy does
   (C) defending against unprovoked aggression

(D) conducting diplomacy when attacked

(E) declaring war on Japan

Choice A is incorrect, because the president is recommending a declaration of war because of the attack. Choice B is incorrect because the president is declaring war after the attack. Choice D is incorrect because the suggested response to the bombing of U.S. ships and the loss of American lives is war, not a delegation of diplomats. Choice E might be seen as correct, but the passage does not support the desirability of declaring war on Japan, in and of itself. Choice C is correct: The president begins by telling Americans that the attack was a surprise and unprovoked—"The United States was at peace with that nation"—and emphasizes that the purpose of the declaration of war against Japan is self-defense: "all measures be taken for our defense" and "we will . . . defend ourselves to the uttermost."

Let's look at Question 2:

2. According to this passage, the Japanese government probably instigated the surprise attack

(A) by mistake

(B) after being forced to do so

(C) because it wanted to increase its territory

(D) deliberately to provoke a war with the United States

(E) to avenge past offenses

Choice D, according to the passage, is the best answer: ". . . the distance of Hawaii from Japan makes it obvious that the attack was deliberately planned many days or even weeks ago. During the intervening time the Japanese Government has deliberately sought to deceive the United States by . . . expressions of hope for continued peace." Choices A, B, C, and E are not supported by the passage. While the Japanese may in fact have wanted to increase their territory (Choice C), nowhere in his speech does the president suggest that as a motivation for their attack.

Let's look at Question 3:

3. The passage indicates that the U.S. president can declare war

(A) by making an announcement to the American people

(B) when provoked by foreign aggression

(C) only with the approval of Congress

(D) when there is a threat to the mainland

(E) as soon as we are attacked

Choice C is correct: At the end of the passage the president asks Congress to declare that a state of war

exists between Japan and the United States. The other choices may be reasons for war, but only Congress can declare war.

Let's look at Question 4:

4. The purpose of the president's address was to

(A) explain why the United States was going to war

(B) justify U.S. aggression against Japan

(C) announce the loss of American lives

(D) prepare Americans for a justifiable war

(E) encourage Americans to distrust Japanese people

The best answer is Choice D. The structure of the speech makes this clear: First the president announces the atrocity against Americans in detail ("lives lost" etc.), next he lists other nations Japan simultaneously attacked, and finally he asserts that Americans will not stand for the aggression and will defend themselves "to the uttermost" to make certain that "this form of treachery shall never again endanger us." Choice A is incorrect because the speech requests a declaration of war from Congress. Choice B is incorrect because no U.S. aggression against Japan is indicated. Choice C is incorrect; the loss of American lives is announced, but the purpose of the speech is not to stop with that. Choice E is clearly incorrect—although some Americans may have formed anti-Japanese prejudice as a result of the aggression, that is not the purpose of the speech.

Introductory Passage 2*

Some scraps of evidence bear out those who hold a very high opinion of the average level of culture among the Athenians of the great age. The funeral speech of Pericles is the most famous indication from Athenian literature that its level was indeed high. Pericles was, however, a politician, and he may have been flattering his audience. We know that thousands of Athenians sat hour after hour in the theater listening to the plays of the great Greek dramatists. These plays, especially the tragedies, are at a very high intellectual level throughout. There are no letdowns, no concessions to the lowbrows or to the demands of "realism," such as the scene of the gravediggers in *Hamlet*. The music and dancing woven into these plays were almost certainly at an equally high level. Our opera—not Italian opera, not even Wagner, but the restrained, difficult opera of

*Adapted from Arthur Whimbey, "Teaching Sequential Thought: The Cognitive-Skills Approach," *The Phi Delta Kappan* vol. 59, no. 4 (December 1977), pp 255–259.

the 18th century—is probably the best modern parallel. The comparison is no doubt dangerous, but can you imagine almost the entire population of an American city (in suitable installments, of course) sitting through performances of Mozart's *Don Giovanni* or Gluck's *Orpheus*? Perhaps the Athenian masses went to these plays because of a lack of other amusements. They could at least understand something of what went on, since the subjects were part of their folklore. For the American people, the subjects of grand opera are not part of their folklore.

Let's start reading the passage:

Some scraps of evidence bear out those who hold a very high opinion of the average level of culture among the Athenians of the great age.

Now this tells you that the author is going to talk about the culture of the Athenians. Thus the stage is set. Go on reading now:

The funeral speech of Pericles is the most famous indication from Athenian literature that its level was indeed high.

At this point you should say to yourself, "That's interesting, and there was an example of the high level of culture." Read on:

Pericles was, however, a politician, and he may have been flattering his audience.

Now you can say, "So that's why those people were so attentive in listening—they were being flattered." Read on:

We know that thousands of Athenians sat hour after hour in the theater listening to the plays of the great Greek dramatists. These plays, especially the tragedies, are at a very high intellectual level throughout. There are no letdowns, no concessions to the lowbrows or to the demands of "realism"...

At this point you should say to yourself, "That's strange—it could not have been just flattery that kept them listening hour after hour. How is this possible?" You can almost anticipate that the author will now give examples and contrast what he is saying to our plays and our audiences. Read on:

The music and dancing woven into these plays were almost certainly at an equally high level. Our opera—not Italian opera ... is probably the best modern parallel. The comparison is no doubt dangerous, but can you

imagine almost the entire population of an American city ... sitting through performances of ...

Your feeling at this point should be, "No, I cannot imagine that. Why is that so?" So you should certainly be interested to find out. Read on:

Perhaps the Athenian masses went to these plays because of a lack of other amusements. They could at least understand something of what went on, since the subjects were part of their folklore.

Now you can say, "So that's why those people were able to listen hour after hour—the material was all part of their folklore!" Read on:

For the American people, the subjects ... are not part of their folklore.

Now you can conclude, "So that's why the Americans cannot sit through these plays and perhaps cannot understand them—they were not part of their folklore!"

Here are the questions that follow the passage:

1. The author seems to question the sincerity of
   (A) politicians
   (B) playwrights
   (C) operagoers
   (D) lowbrows
   (E) gravediggers

2. The author implies that the average American
   (A) enjoys *Hamlet*
   (B) loves folklore
   (C) does not understand grand opera
   (D) seeks a high cultural level
   (E) lacks entertainment

3. The author's attitude toward Greek plays is one of
   (A) qualified approval
   (B) grudging admiration
   (C) studied indifference
   (D) partial hostility
   (E) great respect

4. The author suggests that Greek plays
   (A) made great demands upon their actors
   (B) flattered their audiences
   (C) were written for a limited audience
   (D) were dominated by music and dancing
   (E) stimulated their audiences

Let's try to answer them.

Question 1:

Remember the statement about Pericles? This statement was almost unrelated to the passage since it was not discussed or referred to again. And here we have a question about it. Usually, if you see something that you think is irrelevant in a passage you may be pretty sure that a question will be based on that irrelevancy. It is apparent that the author seems to question the sincerity of politicians (*not* playwrights), since Pericles was a politician. Therefore Choice A is correct.

Question 2:

We know that it was implied that the average American does not understand grand opera. Therefore Choice C is correct.

Question 3:

From the passage, we see that the author is very positive about the Greek plays. Thus the author must have great respect for the plays. Note that the author may not have respect for Pericles, but Pericles was not a playwright; he was a politician. Therefore Choice E (not Choice A) is correct.

Question 4:

It is certainly true that the author suggests that the Greek plays stimulated their audiences. They didn't necessarily flatter their audiences—there was only one indication of flattery, and that was by Pericles, who was not a playwright, but a politician. Therefore Choice E (not Choice B) is correct.

Example of Underlinings

Some scraps of evidence bear out those who hold a very high opinion of the average level of culture among the Athenians of the great age. The funeral speech of Pericles is the most famous indication from Athenian literature that its level was indeed high. Pericles was, however, a politician, and he may have been flattering his audience. We know that thousands of Athenians sat hour after hour in the theater listening to the plays of the great Greek dramatists. These plays, especially the tragedies, are at a very high intellectual level throughout. There are no letdowns, no concessions to the lowbrows or to the demands of "realism," such as the scene of the gravediggers in *Hamlet*. The music and dancing woven into these plays were almost certainly at an equally high level. Our opera—not Italian opera, not even Wagner, but the restrained, difficult opera of the 18th century—is probably the best modern parallel. The comparison is no doubt dangerous, but can you imagine almost the entire population of an American city (in suitable installments, of course) sitting through performances of Mozart's *Don Giovanni* or Gluck's *Orpheus*? Perhaps the Athenian masses went to these plays because of a lack of other amusements. They could at least understand something of what went on, since the subjects were part of their folklore. For the American people, the subjects of grand opera are not part of their folklore.

- Sets stage.
- Example.
- Qualification.
- Further examples.
- Comparison.
- Explanation of previous statements.

Now the whole purpose of analyzing this passage the way I did was to show you that if you get involved and interested in the passage, you will not only antici-pate many of the questions, but when you answer them you will be able to zero in on the right question choice without having to necessarily analyze or eliminate the wrong choices first. That's a great time-saver on a stan-dardized test such as the ACT.

Now here's a short passage from which four ques-tions were derived. Let's see if you can answer them after you've read the passage.

Introductory Passage 3*

Sometimes the meaning of the glowing water is omi-nous. Off the Pacific Coast of North America, it may mean that the sea is filled with . . . a minute plant that contains a poison of strange and terrible virulence.

5 About four days after this minute plant comes to alter the coastal plankton, some of the fishes and shellfish in the vicinity become toxic. This is because in their nor-mal feeding, they have strained the poisonous plankton out of the water.

1. Fish and shellfish become toxic when they

   (A) swim in poisonous water
   (B) feed on poisonous plants
   (C) change their feeding habits
   (D) give off a strange glow
   (E) take strychnine into their systems

2. One can most reasonably conclude that plankton are

   (A) minute organisms
   (B) mussels
   (C) poisonous fish
   (D) shellfish
   (E) fluids

3. In the context of the passage, the word *virulence* in line 4 means

   (A) strangeness
   (B) color
   (C) calamity
   (D) toxicity
   (E) powerful odor

4. The paragraph preceding this one most probably discussed

   (A) phenomena of the Pacific coastline
   (B) poisons that affect man
   (C) the culture of the early Indians
   (D) characteristics of plankton
   (E) phenomena of the sea

Explanatory Answers

1. Choice B is correct. See the last three sentences. Fish become toxic when they feed on poisonous plants. Don't be fooled into using the first sentence, which seemingly leads to Choice A.

2. Choice A is correct. Since we are talking about *minute* plants (second sentence), it is reasonable to assume that plankton are *minute* organisms.

3. Choice D is correct. We understand that the poison is very strong and noxious. Thus it is "toxic," virulent.

4. Choice E is correct. Since the second and not the first sentence was about the Pacific Coast, the para-graph preceding this one probably didn't discuss the phenomena of the Pacific coastline. It might have, if the first sentence—the sentence that links the ideas in the preceding paragraph—were about the Pacific coastline. Now, since we are talking about glowing water being ominous (first sentence), the paragraph preceding the passage is probably about the sea or the phenomena of the sea.

Summary

So in summary:

1. Make sure that you get involved with the passage. You may even want to select first the passage that interests you most. For example, if you're interested in science, you may want to choose the science pas-sage first. Just make sure that you make some nota-tion so that you don't mismark your answer sheet by putting the answers in the wrong answer boxes.

2. Pay attention to material that seems unrelated in the passage—there will probably be a question or two based on that material.

---

*This example also appears in Part 1, "The World's Shortest Practice Test for the ACT Exam," on page 3. From *The Sea Around Us*, 1950.

3. Pay attention to the mood created in the passage or the tone of the passage. Here again, especially if the mood is striking, there will probably be a question relating to mood.

4. Don't waste valuable time looking at the questions before reading the passage.

5. When attempting to answer the questions (after reading the passage) it is sometimes wise to try to figure out the answer before going through the choices. This will enable you to zero in on the correct answer without wasting time with all of the choices.

6. You may want to underline any information in the passages involving dates, specific names, etc., on your test to have as a ready reference when you come to the questions.

7. Always try to see the overall attempt of the author of the passage or try to get the main gist of why the passage was being written. Try to get involved by asking yourself if you agree or disagree with the author, etc.

The 9 Reading Comprehension Strategies begin on page 102.

9 READING COMPREHENSION STRATEGIES

This section of Reading Comprehension Strategies includes several passages. These passages, though somewhat shorter than the passages that appear on the actual ACT and in the 3 ACT Practice Tests in this book, illustrate the general nature of the "real" ACT reading passages.

Each of the 9 Reading Comprehension Strategies that follow is accompanied by at least two different passages followed by questions and explanatory answers in order to explain how the strategy is used.

Reading Comprehension Strategy   1

Very Important Strategy:

As You Read Each Question, Determine the Type: Main Idea, Detecting Details, Inferential Reasoning, or Tone/Mood

Here are the four major abilities tested in Reading Comprehension questions:

1. **Main Idea**: The main idea of a passage is the central topic of the passage. As you are reading the passage, try to understand the general point of what the author is trying to convey. Try to ascertain the purpose and feel of the piece. The main idea will summarize the complete passage in a short and succinct way.

2. **Detecting Details**: To detect the details of a passage, pay close attention to the specific references of the piece. Curious statements such as "Einstein doesn't believe that nature plays dice with the universe" are clues to the details in the passage. When you see a curious statement, underline that statement so you can reference it again easily. Pay close attention when the author describes a specific example.

3. **Inferential Reasoning**: You must be able to ascertain what the author is trying to convey through the passage. For example, in the quote, "Einstein doesn't believe that nature plays dice with the universe," you will have to infer what the author means by this statement. You'll need to detect the author's viewpoint via the passage.

4. **Tone or Mood**: The tone or mood of a passage can be found by determining how the author or narrator *feels* in the passage. Is the passage angry or light, happy or melancholy, humorous or frightening? What feeling do you get from the passage? Knowing this will also give you insight as you are reading the passage, and offer psychological insight into the passage.

Example 1*

The fight crowd is a beast that lurks in the darkness behind the fringe of white light shed over the first six rows by the incandescents atop the ring, and is not to be trusted with pop bottles or other hardware.

5   People who go to prize fights are sadistic.

When two prominent pugilists are scheduled to pummel one another in public on a summer's evening, men and women file into the stadium in the guise of human beings, and thereafter become a part of a gray thing that
10 squats in the dark until, at the conclusion of the bloodletting, they may be seen leaving the arena in the same guise they wore when they entered.

As a rule, the mob that gathers to see men fight is unjust, vindictive, swept by intense, unreasoning
15 hatreds, and proud of its swift recognition of what it believes to be sportsmanship. It is quick to greet the purely phony move of the boxer who extends his gloves to his rival who has slipped or been pushed to

---

*Adapted from Paul Gallico.

the floor, and to reward this stimulating but still balo-
20 ney gesture with a pattering of hands that indicates the
following: "You are a good sport. We recognize that
you are a good sport, and we know a sporting gesture
when we see one. Therefore we are all good sports too.
Hurrah for us!"

25 The same crowd doesn't see the same boxer stick
his thumb in his opponent's eye or try to cut him with
the laces of his glove, butt him or dig him a low one
when the referee isn't in a position to see. It roots consistently for the smaller man, and never for a moment
30 considers the desperate psychological dilemma of the
larger of the two. It howls with glee at a good finisher
making his kill. The Roman hordes were more civilized. Their gladiators asked them whether the final
blow should be administered or not. The main attraction
35 at the modern prize fight is the spectacle of a man club-
bing a helpless and vanquished opponent into complete
insensibility. The referee who stops a bout to save a
slugged and punch-drunken man from the final igno-
miny is hissed by the assembled sportsmen.

Questions

1. The tone of the passage is chiefly

   (A) disgusted
   (B) jovial
   (C) matter-of-fact
   (D) satiric
   (E) devil-may-care

2. Which group of words from the passage best indicates the author's opinion?

   (A) referee, opponent, finisher
   (B) gladiators, slugged, sporting gesture
   (C) stimulating, hissing, pattering
   (D) beast, lurks, gray thing
   (E) dilemma, hordes, spectacle

3. Apparently, the author believes that boxing crowds
   find the referee both

   (A) gentlemanly and boring
   (B) entertaining and essential
   (C) blind and careless
   (D) humorous and threatening
   (E) necessary and bothersome

Explanatory Answers

1. Choice A is correct. The author is obviously much
   offended (disgusted) by the inhuman attitude of the
   crowd watching the boxing match. For example, see
   these lines:

   Line 1: "The fight crowd is a beast. . . ."
   Line 5: "People who go to prize fights are sadistic."
   Lines 13–15: ". . . the mob that gathers to see men
   fight is unjust, vindictive, swept by
   intense . . . hatreds."
   Lines 32–33: "The Roman hordes were more
   civilized."

   To answer this question, you must be able to determine
   the tone that is dominant in the passage. Accordingly,
   this is a TONE/MOOD type of question.

2. Choice D is correct. The author's opinion is clearly
   one of disgust and discouragement because of the
   behavior of the fight crowd. Accordingly, you would
   expect the author to use words that were condemnatory, like *beast*, and gloom-filled words like *lurks*
   and *gray thing*. To answer this question, you must
   see relationships between words and feelings. So,
   we have here an INFERENTIAL REASONING
   question type.

3. Choice E is correct. Lines 25–28 show that the
   referee is *necessary:* "The same crowd doesn't see
   the same boxer stick his thumb into his opponent's
   eye . . . when the referee isn't in a position to see."
   Lines 37–39 show that the referee is *bothersome*:
   "The referee who stops a bout . . . is hissed by the
   assembled sportsmen." To answer this question, you
   must have the ability to understand the writer's specific statements. Accordingly, this is a DETECTING
   DETAILS type of question.

Example 2*

Mist continues to obscure the horizon, but above us the
sky is suddenly awash with lavender light. At once the
geese respond. Now, as well as their cries, a beating
roar rolls across the water as if five thousand house-
5 wives have taken it into their heads to shake out blankets all at one time. Ten thousand housewives. It keeps
up—the invisible rhythmic beating of all those goose

---

*This passage is attributed to D. G. Schueler.

wings—for what seems a long time. Even Lonnie is
held motionless with suspense.

10   Then the geese begin to rise. One, two, three hundred—then a thousand at a time—in long horizontal
lines that unfurl like pennants across the sky. The horizon actually darkens as they pass. It goes on and on like
that, flock after flock, for three or four minutes, each
15 new contingent announcing its ascent with an acceler-
ating roar of cries and wingbeats. Then gradually the
intervals between flights become longer. I think the
spectacle is over, until yet another flock lifts up, following the others in a gradual turn toward the northeastern
20 quadrant of the refuge.

Finally the sun emerges from the mist; the mist
itself thins a little, uncovering the black line of willows
on the other side of the wildlife preserve. I remember
to close my mouth—which has been open for some
25 time—and inadvertently shut two or three mosqui-
toes inside. Only a few straggling geese oar their way
across the sun's red surface. Lonnie wears an exasperated, proprietary expression, as if he had produced and
directed the show himself and had just received a bad
30 review. "It would have been better with more light,"
he says; "I can't always guarantee just when they'll
start moving." I assure him I thought it was a fantastic
sight. "Well," he rumbles, "I guess it wasn't too bad."

Questions

1. In the descriptive phrase "shake out blankets all at
one time" (lines 5–6), the author is appealing chiefly
to the reader's
   (A) background
   (B) sight
   (C) emotions
   (D) thoughts
   (E) hearing

2. The mood created by the author is one of
   (A) tranquility
   (B) excitement
   (C) sadness
   (D) bewilderment
   (E) unconcern

3. The main idea expressed by the author about the
geese is that they
   (A) are spectacular to watch
   (B) are unpredictable
   (C) disturb the environment

   (D) produce a lot of noise
   (E) fly in large flocks

4. Judging from the passage, the reader can conclude
that
   (A) the speaker dislikes nature's inconveniences
   (B) the geese's timing is predictable
   (C) Lonnie has had the experience before
   (D) both observers are hunters
   (E) the author and Lonnie are the same person

Explanatory Answers

1. Choice E is correct. See lines 3–6: ". . . a beating
roar rolls across the water . . . shake out blankets
all at one time." The author, with these words, is no
doubt appealing to the reader's hearing. To answer
this question, the reader has to identify those words
dealing with sound and noise. Therefore, we have
here a DETECTING DETAILS type of question.
It is also an INFERENTIAL REASONING question type in that the "sound" words such as *beating*
and *roar* lead the reader to infer that the author is
appealing to the auditory (hearing) sense.

2. Choice B is correct. Excitement courses right
through this passage. Here are examples:

   Lines 7–8: ". . . the invisible rhythmic beating of all
       those goose wings. . . ."
   Lines 8–9: "Even Lonnie is held motionless with
       suspense."
   Lines 10–11: "Then the geese begin to rise . . . a
       thousand at a time. . . ."
   Lines 14–16: ". . . flock after flock . . . roar of cries
       and wingbeats."

   To answer this question, you must determine the
   dominant tone in this passage. Therefore, we have
   here a TONE/MOOD question type.

3. Choice A is correct. The word *spectacular* means
"dramatic," "thrilling," or "impressive." There is
considerable action expressed throughout the passage. Sometimes there is a lull—then the action
begins again. See lines 17–19: "I think the spectacle
is over, until yet another flock lifts up, following the
others. . . ." To answer this question, you must have
the ability to judge the general significance of the
passage. Accordingly, we have here a MAIN IDEA
type of question.

4. Choice C is correct. See lines 27–32: "Lonnie wears an exasperated, proprietary expression . . . when they'll start moving.'" To answer this question, you must be able to draw a correct inference. Therefore, we have here an INFERENTIAL REASONING type of question.

Reading Comprehension Strategy 2

Very Important Strategy:
Underline the Key Parts of the Reading Passage*

The underlinings will help you to answer questions. Again, practically every question will ask you to detect the following:

(a) the main idea
or
(b) information that is specifically mentioned in the passage
or
(c) information that is implied (not directly stated) in the passage
or
(d) the tone or mood of the passage.

If you find out quickly what the question is aiming for, you will more easily arrive at the correct answer by referring to your underlinings in the passage.

Example 1**

That one citizen is as good as another is a favorite American axiom, supposed to express the very essence of our Constitution and way of life. But just what do we mean when we utter that platitude? One surgeon
5 is not as good as another. One plumber is not as good as another. We soon become aware of this when we require the attention of either. Yet in political and economic matters we appear to have reached a point where

knowledge and specialized training count for very little.
10 A newspaper reporter is sent out on the street to collect the views of various passers-by on such a question as "Should the United States defend Formosa?" The answer of the bar-fly who doesn't even know where the island is located, or that it is a island, is quoted in
15 the next edition just as solemnly as that of the college teacher of history. With the basic tenets of democracy—that all men are born free and equal and are entitled to life, liberty, and the pursuit of happiness— no decent American can possibly take issue. But that
20 the opinion of one citizen on a technical subject is just as authoritative as that of another is manifestly absurd. And to accept the opinions of all comers as having the same value is surely to encourage a cult of mediocrity.

Questions

1. Which phrase best expresses the main idea of this passage?
   (A) the myth of equality
   (B) a distinction about equality
   (C) the essence of the Constitution
   (D) a technical subject
   (E) knowledge and specialized training

2. The author most probably included the example of the question on Formosa (lines 12–16) in order to
   (A) move the reader to rage
   (B) show that he is opposed to opinion sampling
   (C) show that he has thoroughly researched his project
   (D) explain the kind of opinion sampling he objects to
   (E) provide a humorous but temporary diversion from his main point

3. The author would be most likely to agree that
   (A) some men are born to be masters; others are born to be servants
   (B) the Constitution has little relevance for today's world
   (C) one should never express an opinion on a specialized subject unless he is an expert in that subject
   (D) every opinion should be treated equally
   (E) all opinions should not be given equal weight

---

*Strategy 2 is considered the Master Reading Comprehension Strategy because it can be used effectively in every Reading Comprehension question. However, it is important that you learn the other Reading Comprehension Strategies because you may need to use them in conjunction with this strategy to find the answer efficiently.

**From Claude M. Fuess, "The Retreat from Excellence," *Saturday Review*, March 26, 1960, p 21.

Explanatory Answers

1. Choice B is correct. See lines 1–7: "That one citizen . . . attention of either." These lines indicate that there is quite a distinction about equality when we are dealing with all the American people.

2. Choice D is correct. See lines 10–16: "A newspaper reporter . . . college teacher of history." These lines show that the author probably included the example of the question of Formosa in order to explain the kind of opinion sampling he objects to.

3. Choice E is correct. See lines 19–23: "But that the opinion . . . to encourage a cult of mediocrity." Accordingly, the author would be most likely to agree that all opinions should *not* be given equal weight.

Example 2

She walked along the river until a policeman stopped her. It was one o'clock, he said. Not the best time to be walking alone by the side of a half-frozen river. He smiled at her, then offered to walk her home. It was the

5 first day of the new year, 1946, eight and a half months after the British tanks had rumbled into Bergen-Belsen.

That February, my mother turned twenty-six. It was difficult for strangers to believe that she had ever been a concentration-camp inmate. Her face was smooth and

10 round. She wore lipstick and applied mascara to her large, dark eyes. She dressed fashionably. But when she looked into the mirror in the mornings before leaving for work, my mother saw a shell, a mannequin who moved and spoke but who bore only a superficial

15 resemblance to her real self. The people closest to her had vanished. She had no proof that they were truly dead. No eyewitnesses had survived to vouch for her husband's death. There was no one living who had seen her parents die. The lack of confirmation haunted her. At

20 night before she went to sleep and during the day as she stood pinning dresses, she wondered if, by some chance, her parents had gotten past the Germans or had crawled out of the mass grave into which they had been shot and were living, old and helpless, somewhere in Poland.

25 What if only one of them had died? What if they had survived and had died of cold or hunger after she had been liberated, while she was in Celle* dancing with British officers?

She did not talk to anyone about these things. No one,

30 she thought, wanted to hear them. She woke up in the mornings, went to work, bought groceries, went to the Jewish Community Center and to the housing office like a robot.

Questions

1. The policeman stopped the author's mother from walking along the river because

   (A) the river was dangerous
   (B) it was the wrong time of day
   (C) it was still wartime
   (D) it was so cold
   (E) she looked suspicious

2. The author states that his mother thought about her parents when she

   (A) walked along the river
   (B) thought about death
   (C) danced with officers
   (D) arose in the morning
   (E) was at work

3. When the author mentions his mother's dancing with the British officers, he implies that his mother

   (A) compared her dancing to the suffering of her parents
   (B) had clearly put her troubles behind her
   (C) felt it was her duty to dance with them
   (D) felt guilty about dancing
   (E) regained the self-confidence she once had

Explanatory Answers

1. Choice B is correct. See lines 1–4: "She walked along . . . offered to walk her home." The policeman's telling her that it was not the best time to be walking alone indicates clearly that "it was the wrong time of day."

2. Choice E is correct. Refer to lines 20–21: ". . . and during the day as she stood pinning dresses, she wondered. . . ."

3. Choice D is correct. See lines 25–28: "What if they had survived . . . dancing with British officers?"

---

*Celle is a small town in Germany.

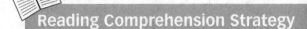

Reading Comprehension Strategy 3

Look Back at the Passage When in Doubt

Sometimes while you are answering a question, you are not quite sure whether you have chosen the correct answer. Often, the underlinings that you have made in the reading passage will help you to determine whether a certain choice is the only correct choice.

Example 1*

A critic of politics finds himself driven to deprecate the power of words, while using them copiously in warning against their influence. It is indeed in politics that their influence is most dangerous, so that one is almost
5 tempted to wish that they did not exist and that society might be managed silently, by instinct, habit, and ocular perception, without this supervening Babel of reports, arguments, and slogans.

Question

1. Which statement is true, according to the passage?

   (A) Critics of politics are often driven to take desperate measures.
   (B) Words, when used by politicians, have the greatest capacity for harm.
   (C) Politicians talk more than other people.
   (D) Society would be better managed if mutes were in charge.
   (E) Reports and slogans are not to be trusted.

Explanatory Answer

1. Choice B is correct. An important part that you might have underlined is in the second sentence: "It is indeed in politics that their influence is most dangerous...." It's also important to note that in the first sentence the word *their* refers to *words*.

Example 2

All museum adepts are familiar with examples of *ostrakoi*, the oystershells used in balloting. As a matter of fact, these "oystershells" are usually shards of pottery, conveniently glazed to enable the voter to express

5 his wishes in writing. In the Agora, a great number of these have come to light, bearing the thrilling name Themistocles. Into rival jars were dropped the ballots for or against his banishment. On account of the huge vote taken on that memorable date, it was to be expected
10 that many ostrakoi would be found, but the interest of this collection is that a number of these ballots are inscribed in an *identical* handwriting. There is nothing mysterious about it! The Boss was on the job, then as now. He prepared these ballots and voters cast them—
15 no doubt for the consideration of an obol or two. *The ballot box was stuffed.*
   How is the glory of the American boss diminished! A vile imitation, he. His methods as old as Time!

Question

1. The title that best expresses the ideas of this passage is

   (A) An Odd Method of Voting
   (B) Themistocles, an Early Dictator
   (C) Democracy in the Past
   (D) Political Trickery—Past and Present
   (E) The Diminishing American Politician

Explanatory Answer

1. Choice D is correct. An important idea that you might have underlined is expressed in lines 13–18: "The Boss was on the job, then as now.... His methods as old as Time!" These lines reveal that stuffing the ballot box is a time-honored tradition.

Example 3

But the weather predictions that an almanac always contains are, we believe, mostly wasted on the farmer. He can take a squint at the moon before turning in. He can "smell" snow or tell if the wind is shifting danger-
5 ously east. He can register forebodingly an extra twinge in a rheumatic shoulder. With any of these to go by, he can be reasonably sure of tomorrow's weather. He can return the almanac to the nail behind the door and put a last stick of wood in the stove. For an almanac, a zero
10 night or a morning's drifted road—none of these has changed much since Poor Richard wrote his stuff and barns were built along the Delaware.

---

*Adapted from George Santayana, "Words, Words, Words," in *Dominations and Powers: Reflections on Liberty, Society, and Government*, 1950.

Question

1. The author implies that, in predicting weather, there is considerable value in

   (A) reading the almanac
   (B) placing the last stick of wood in the stove
   (C) sleeping with one eye on the moon
   (D) keeping an almanac behind the door
   (E) noting rheumatic pains

Explanatory Answer

1. Choice E is correct. Important ideas that you might have underlined are the following:

   Line 3: "He can take a squint at the moon. . . ."
   Lines 3–4: "He can 'smell' snow. . . ."
   Lines 5–6: "He can register forebodingly an extra twinge in a rheumatic shoulder."

   These underlinings will reveal the quote, in lines 5–6, that gives you the correct answer.

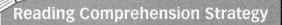

Reading Comprehension Strategy   4

Before You Start Answering the Questions, Read the Passage **Carefully**

A great advantage of careful reading of the passage is that you will, thereby, get a very good idea of what the passage is about. If a particular sentence is not clear to you as you read, then reread that sentence to get a better idea of what the author is trying to say.

Example 1

Underlining important ideas as you are reading this passage is strongly urged:

The American Revolution is the only one in modern history which, rather than devouring the intellectuals who prepared it, carried them to power. Most of the signatories of the Declaration of Independence were
5 intellectuals. This tradition is ingrained in America, whose greatest statesmen have been intellectuals— Jefferson and Lincoln, for example. These statesmen performed their political function, but at the same time they felt a more universal responsibility, and they
10 actively defined this responsibility. Thanks to them

there is in America a living school of political science. In fact, it is at the moment the only one perfectly adapted to the emergencies of the contemporary world, and one that can be victoriously opposed to commu-
15 nism. A European who follows American politics will be struck by the constant reference in the press and from the platform to this political philosophy, to the historical events through which it was best expressed, to the great statesmen who were its best representatives.

Questions

1. The title that best expresses the ideas of this passage is

   (A) Fathers of the American Revolution
   (B) Jefferson and Lincoln—Ideal Statesmen
   (C) The Basis of American Political Philosophy
   (D) Democracy vs. Communism
   (E) The Responsibilities of Statesmen

2. According to the passage, intellectuals who pave the way for revolutions are usually

   (A) honored
   (B) misunderstood
   (C) destroyed
   (D) forgotten
   (E) elected to office

3. Which statement is true according to the passage?

   (A) America is a land of intellectuals.
   (B) The signers of the Declaration of Independence were well educated.
   (C) Jefferson and Lincoln were revolutionaries.
   (D) Adaptability is a characteristic of American political science.
   (E) Europeans are confused by American politics.

Explanatory Answers

1. Choice C is correct. Throughout this passage, the author speaks about the basis of American political philosophy. For example, see lines 5–11: "This tradition is ingrained in America, . . . a living school of political science."

2. Choice C is correct. See lines 1–3: "The American Revolution is the only one . . . carried them to power." These lines may be interpreted to mean that

intellectuals who pave the way for revolutions—other than the American Revolution—are usually destroyed (devoured).

3. Choice D is correct. The word *adaptability* means "the ability to adapt"—to adjust to a specified use or situation. Now see lines 11–15: ". . . there is in America . . . opposed to communism."

Example 2*

Underlining important ideas as you are reading this passage is strongly urged:

The activities of the microscopic vegetables of the sea, of which the diatoms are most important, make the mineral wealth of the water available to the animals. Feeding directly on the diatoms and other groups of minute uni-
5 cellular algae are the marine protozoa, many crustaceans, the young of crabs, barnacles, sea worms, and fishes. Hordes of small carnivores, the first link in the chain of flesh eaters, move among these peaceful grazers. There are fierce little dragons half an inch long, the sharp-
10 jawed arrow-worms. There are gooseberrylike comb jellies, armed with grasping tentacles, and there are the shrimplike euphausiids that strain food from the water with their bristly appendages. Since they drift where the currents carry them, with no power or will to oppose
15 that of the sea, this strange community of creatures and the marine plants that sustain them are called *plankton*, a word derived from the Greek, meaning "wandering."

Questions

1. According to the passage, diatoms are a kind of
   (A) mineral
   (B) alga
   (C) crustacean
   (D) protozoan
   (E) fish

2. Which characteristic of diatoms does the passage emphasize?
   (A) size
   (B) feeding habits
   (C) activeness
   (D) numerousness
   (E) cellular structure

*From Rachel Carson, *The Sea Around Us*, 1950.

Explanatory Answers

1. Choice B is correct. See lines 3–5: "Feeding directly on the diatoms . . . minute unicellular algae are the marine protozoa. . . ." These lines indicate that diatoms are a kind of alga.

2. Choice A is correct. See lines 1–5: "The activities of the microscopic vegetables of the sea . . . minute unicellular algae. . . ." In these lines, the words *microscopic* and *minute* emphasize the small size of the diatoms.

Reading Comprehension Strategy 5

Get the Meanings of "Tough" Words by Using the Context Method

Suppose you don't know the meaning of a certain word in a passage. Then try to determine the meaning of that word from the context—that is, from the words that are close in position to that word whose meaning you don't know. Knowing the meanings of difficult words in the passage will help you to better understand the passage as a whole.

Example 1

Like all insects, it wears its skeleton on the outside—a marvelous chemical compound called *chitin* which sheathes the whole of its body. This flexible armor is tremendously tough, light, shatterproof, and resistant
5 to alkali and acid compounds that would eat the clothing, flesh, and bones of man. To it are attached muscles so arranged around catapult-like hind legs as to enable the hopper to hop, if so diminutive a term can describe so prodigious a leap as ten or twelve feet—about 150
10 times the length of the one-or-so-inch-long insect. The equivalent feat for a man would be a casual jump, from a standing position, over the Washington Monument.

Questions

1. The word *sheathes* (line 3) means
   (A) strips
   (B) provides
   (C) exposes
   (D) encases
   (E) excites

2. The word *prodigious* (line 9) means

   (A) productive
   (B) frightening
   (C) criminal
   (D) enjoyable
   (E) enormous

Explanatory Answers

1. Choice D is correct. The words in line 1, "it wears its skeleton on the outside," give us the idea that *sheathes* probably means "covers" or "encases."

2. Choice E is correct. See the surrounding words in lines 7–10: "enable the hopper to hop . . . so prodigious a leap as ten or twelve feet—about 150 times the length of the one-or-so-inch-long insect." We may easily infer that the word *prodigious* means "great in size" or "enormous."

Example 2*

Since the days when the thirteen colonies, each so jealous of its sovereignty, got together to fight the lobsterbacks, the American people have exhibited a tendency—a genius—to maintain widely divergent viewpoints in
5 normal times, but to unite and agree in times of stress. One reason the federal system has survived is that it has demonstrated this same tendency. Most of the time the three coequal divisions of the general government tend to compete. In crises they tend to cooperate. And
10 not only during war. A singular instance of cooperation took place in the opening days of the first administration of Franklin D. Roosevelt, when the harmonious efforts of the executive and the legislature to arrest the havoc of depression brought the term *rubber-stamp*
15 *Congress* into the headlines. On the other hand, when in 1937 Roosevelt attempted to bend the judiciary to the will of the executive by "packing" the Supreme Court, Congress rebelled. This frequently proved flexibility—this capacity of both people and government to
20 shift from competition to cooperation and back again as circumstances warrant—suggests that the federal system will be found equal to the very real dangers of the present world situation.

*From Milton Lomask, "When Congress Tried to Rule." *American Heritage*, vol. 11, no. 1 (December 1959).

Questions

1. The word *havoc* (line 14) means

   (A) possession
   (B) benefit
   (C) destruction
   (D) symptom
   (E) enjoyment

2. The word *divergent* (line 4) means

   (A) interesting
   (B) discussed
   (C) flexible
   (D) differing
   (E) appreciated

Explanatory Answers

1. Choice C is correct. The prepositional phrase "of depression," which modifies "havoc," should indicate that this word has an unfavorable meaning. The only choice that has an unfavorable meaning is Choice C—"destruction."

2. Choice D is correct. See lines 3–5: ". . . the American people . . . widely divergent viewpoints . . . but to unite and agree in times of stress." The word *but* in this sentence is an *opposition indicator*. We may, therefore, assume that a "divergent viewpoint" is a "differing" one from the idea expressed in the words "to unite and agree in times of stress."

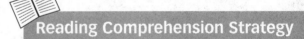

Reading Comprehension Strategy 6

Circle Transitional Words in the Passage

There are certain transitional words—also called "bridge" or "key" words—that will help you to discover logical connections in a reading passage. *Circling* these transitional words will help you to get a better understanding of the passage.

Here are examples of commonly used transitional words and what these words may indicate.

Transitional Word	Indicating
although however in spite of rather than nevertheless on the other hand but	OPPOSITION
moreover besides additionally furthermore in fact	SUPPORT
therefore consequently accordingly because when so	RESULT

Example 1

Somewhere between 1860 and 1890, the dominant emphasis in American literature was radically changed. But it is obvious that this change was not necessarily a matter of conscious concern to all writers. In fact, many
5 writers may seem to have been actually unaware of the shifting emphasis. Moreover, it is not possible to trace the steady march of the realistic emphasis from its first feeble notes to its dominant trumpet-note of unquestioned leadership. The progress of realism is to change
10 the figure to that of a small stream, receiving accessions from its tributaries at unequal points along its course, its progress now and then balked by the sandbars of opposition or the diffusing marshes of error and compromise. Again, it is apparent that any attempt to
15 classify rigidly, as romanticists or realists, the writers of this period is doomed to failure, since it is not by virtue of the writer's conscious espousal of the romantic or realistic creed that he does much of his best work, but by virtue of that writer's sincere surrender to the atmo-
20 sphere of the subject.

Questions

1. The title that best expresses the ideas of this passage is

   (A) Classifying American Writers
   (B) Leaders in American Fiction
   (C) The Sincerity of Writers
   (D) The Values of Realism
   (E) The Rise of Realism

2. Which characteristic of writers does the author praise?

   (A) their ability to compromise
   (B) their allegiance to a "school"
   (C) their opposition to change
   (D) their awareness of literary trends
   (E) their intellectual honesty

Explanatory Answers

1. Choice E is correct. Note some of the transitional words that help you to interpret the passage and see why a title of "The Rise of Realism" would be warranted. In line 6, "Moreover" is a key word that is connected to "realistic emphasis" in line 7. This idea is also connected to the sentence involving the "progress of realism" in line 9. The word *again* in line 14 is also connected with this rise in realism.

2. Choice E is correct. See lines 16–20: ". . . since it is not by virtue of . . . but by virtue of that writer's sincere . . . of the subject." The transitional word *but* helps us to arrive at the correct answer, which is "their intellectual honesty."

Example 2*

A humorous remark or situation is, furthermore, always a pleasure. We can go back to it and laugh at it again and again. One does not tire of the *Pickwick Papers,* or of the humor of Mark Twain, any more than the child
5 tires of a nursery tale that he knows by heart. Humor is a feeling, and feelings can be revived. But wit, being an intellectual and not an emotional impression, suffers by repetition. A witticism is really an item of knowledge. Wit, again, is distinctly a gregarious quality, whereas
10 humor may abide in the breast of a hermit. Those who

---

*Adapted from "Wit and Humor," in *The Atlantic Monthly: A Magazine of Literature, Science, Art, and Politics, Volume C*, Boston, Houghton Mifflin, 1907, p 427.

live by themselves almost always have a dry humor. Wit is a city, humor a country, product. Wit is the accomplishment of persons who are busy with ideas; it is the fruit of intellectual cultivation and abounds

15 in coffeehouses, in salons, and in literary clubs. But humor is the gift of those who are concerned with persons rather than ideas, and it flourishes chiefly in the middle and lower classes.

Question

1. It is probable that the paragraph preceding this one discussed the

    (A) *Pickwick Papers*
    (B) characteristics of literature
    (C) characteristics of human nature
    (D) characteristics of humor
    (E) nature of human feelings

Explanatory Answer

1. Choice D is correct. See lines 1–2: "A humorous remark or situation is, furthermore, always a pleasure." The transitional word *furthermore* means "in addition." We may, therefore, assume that something dealing with humor has been discussed in the previous paragraph.

Reading Comprehension Strategy 7

Don't Answer a Question on the Basis of Your Own Opinion

Answer each question on the basis of the information given or suggested in the passage itself. Your own views or judgments may sometimes conflict with what the author of the passage is expressing. Answer the question according to what the author believes.

Example 1

The drama critic, on the other hand, has no such advantages. He cannot be selective; he must cover everything that is offered for public scrutiny in the principal playhouses of the city where he works.

5 The column space that seemed, yesterday, so pitifully inadequate to contain his comments on *Long Day's Journey into Night* is roughly the same as that

which yawns today for his verdict on some inane comedy that has chanced to find for itself a numskull

10 backer with five hundred thousand dollars to lose. This state of affairs may help to explain why the New York theater reviewers are so often, and so unjustly, stigmatized as baleful and destructive fiends. They spend most of their professional lives attempting to

15 pronounce intelligent judgments on plays that have no aspiration to intelligence. It is hardly surprising that they lash out occasionally; in fact, what amazes me about them is that they do not lash out more violently and more frequently. As Shaw said of his fellow-critics

20 in the 1890s, they are "a culpably indulgent body of men." Imagine the verbal excoriations that would be inflicted if Lionel Trilling, or someone of comparable eminence, were called on to review five books a month of which three were novelettes composed

25 of criminal confessions. The butchers of Broadway would seem lambs by comparison.

Questions

1. In writing this passage, the author's purpose seems to have been to

    (A) comment on the poor quality of our plays
    (B) show why book reviewing is easier than play reviewing
    (C) point out the opinions of Shaw
    (D) show new trends in literary criticism
    (E) defend the work of the play critic

2. The passage suggests that, as a play, *Long Day's Journey into Night* was

    (A) inconsequential
    (B) worthwhile
    (C) poorly written
    (D) much too long
    (E) much too short

Explanatory Answers

1. Choice E is correct. Throughout the passage, the author is defending the work of the play critic. See, for example, lines 11–16: "This state of affairs . . . plays that have no aspiration to intelligence." Be sure that you do not answer a question on the basis of your own views. You yourself may believe that the plays presented on the stage today are of poor

quality (Choice A) generally. The question, however, asks about the *author's opinion*—not yours.

2. Choice B is correct. See lines 5–10: "The column space . . . dollars to lose." *Long Day's Journey into Night* is contrasted here with an inane comedy. This implies that *Long Day's Journey into Night* is a worthwhile play. You yourself may believe that it is a bad or underwhelming play (Choice A or C or D or E). But remember—the author's opinion, not yours, is asked for.

Example 2

History has long made a point of the fact that the magnificent flowering of ancient civilization rested upon the institution of slavery, which released opportunity at the top of the art and literature that became the
5 glory of antiquity. In a way, the mechanization of the present-day world produces the condition of the ancient in that the enormous development of labor-saving devices and of contrivances that amplify the capacities of mankind affords the base for the leisure necessary
10 for widespread cultural pursuits. Mechanization is the present-day slave power, with the difference that in the mechanized society there is no group of the community that does not share in the benefits of its inventions.

Question

1. The author's attitude toward mechanization is one of
   (A) awe
   (B) acceptance
   (C) distrust
   (D) fear
   (E) devotion

Explanatory Answer

1. Choice B is correct. Throughout the passage, the author's attitude toward mechanization is one of acceptance. Such acceptance on the part of the author is indicated particularly in lines 10–13: "Mechanization is . . . the benefits of its inventions." You yourself may have a feeling of distrust (Choice C) or fear (Choice D) toward mechanization. But the author does not have such feelings.

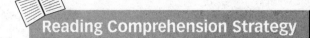

Reading Comprehension Strategy 8

After Reading the Passage, Read Each Question Carefully

Be sure that you read *with care* not only the stem (beginning) of a question but also *each* of the choices. Some students select a choice just because it is a true statement—or because it answers part of a question. This can get you into trouble.

Example 1

The modern biographer's task becomes one of discovering the "dynamics" of the personality he is studying rather than allowing the reader to deduce that personality from documents. If he achieves a reasonable like-
5 ness, he need not fear too much that the unearthing of still more material will alter the picture he has drawn; it should add dimension to it, but not change its lineaments appreciably. After all, he has had more than enough material to permit him to reach conclusions and
10 to paint his portrait. With this abundance of material he can select moments of high drama and find episodes to illustrate character and make for vividness. In any event, biographers, I think, must recognize that the writing of a life may not be as "scientific" or as "defini-
15 tive" as we have pretended. Biography partakes of a large part of the subjective side of man; and we must remember that those who walked abroad in our time may have one appearance for us—but will seem quite different to posterity.

Question

1. According to the author, which is the real task of the modern biographer?
   (A) interpreting the character revealed to him by study of the presently available data
   (B) viewing the life of the subject in the biographer's own image
   (C) leaving to the reader the task of interpreting the character from contradictory evidence
   (D) collecting facts and setting them down in chronological order
   (E) being willing to wait until all the facts on his subject have been uncovered

Explanatory Answer

1. Choice A is correct. See lines 1–8: "The modern biographer's task . . . but not change its lineaments appreciably." The word *dynamics* is used here to refer to the physical and moral forces that exerted influence on the main character of the biography. The lines quoted indicate that the author believes that the real task of the biographer is to study the *presently available data*. Choice D may also appear to be a correct choice since a biographer is likely to consider his job to be collecting facts and setting them down in chronological order. But the passage does not directly state that a biographer has such a procedure.

Example 2

Although patience is the most important quality a trea-sure hunter can have, the trade demands a certain amount of courage too. I have my share of guts, but make no boast about ignoring the hazards of diving. As all good
5 divers know, the business of plunging into an alien world with an artificial air supply as your only link to the world above can be as dangerous as stepping into a den of lions. Most of the danger rests within the diver himself.
    The devil-may-care diver who shows great bravado
10 underwater is the worst risk of all. He may lose his bearings in the glimmering dim light that penetrates the sea and become separated from his diving companions. He may dive too deep, too long and suffer painful, sometimes fatal, bends.

Question

1. According to the author, an underwater treasure hunter needs above all to be

    (A) self-reliant
    (B) adventuresome
    (C) mentally alert
    (D) patient
    (E) physically fit

Explanatory Answer

1. Choice D is correct. See lines 1–3: "Although patience is the most important . . . courage too." Choice E ("physically fit") may also appear to be a correct choice, since an underwater diver certainly has to be physically fit. Nevertheless, the passage nowhere states this directly.

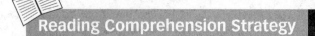

Very Important Strategy:

Increase Your Vocabulary to Boost Your Reading Comprehension Score

You can increase your vocabulary tremendously by learning Latin and Greek roots, prefixes, and suffixes. Knowing the meanings of difficult words will thereby help you to understand a passage better.

Sixty percent of all the words in our English lan-guage are derived from Latin and Greek. By learning certain Latin and Greek roots, prefixes, and suffixes, you will be able to understand the meanings of over 110,000 additional English words. See "Hot Prefixes and Roots" beginning on page 128.

Example 1

Acting, like much writing, is probably a compensation for and release from the strain of some profound malad-justment of the psyche. The actor lives most intensely by proxy. He has to be somebody else to be himself.
5 But it is all done openly and for our delight. The dan-gerous man, the enemy of nonattachment or any other wise way of life, is the born actor who has never found his way into the Theater, who never uses a stage door, who does not take a call and then wipe the paint off his
10 face. It is the intrusion of this temperament into politi-cal life, in which at this day it most emphatically does not belong, that works half the mischief in the world. In every country you may see them rise, the actors who will not use the Theater, and always they bring down
15 disaster from the angry gods who like to see mounte-banks in their proper place.

Questions

1. The meaning of *maladjustment* (lines 2–3) is a

    (A) replacement of one thing with another
    (B) profitable experience in business
    (C) consideration for the feelings of others
    (D) disregard of advice offered by others
    (E) poor relationship with one's environment

2. The meaning of *psyche* (line 3) is

   (A) person
   (B) mind
   (C) personality
   (D) psychology
   (E) physique

3. The meaning of *intrusion* (line 10) is

   (A) entering without being welcome
   (B) acceptance after considering the facts
   (C) interest that has developed after a period of time
   (D) fear as the result of imagination
   (E) refusing to obey a command

4. The meaning of *mountebanks* (lines 15–16) is

   (A) mountain climbers
   (B) cashiers
   (C) high peaks
   (D) fakers
   (E) mortals

Explanatory Answers

1. Choice E is correct. The prefix *mal-* means "bad." Obviously a maladjustment is a bad adjustment— that is, a poor relationship with one's environment.

2. Choice B is correct. The root *psyche* means "the mind" functioning as the center of thought, feeling, and behavior.

3. Choice A is correct. The prefix *in-* means "into" in this case. The root *trud* or *trus* means "pushing into"—or entering without being welcome.

4. Choice D is correct. The root *mont* means "to climb." The root *banc* means a "bench." A mountebank means literally "one who climbs on a bench." The actual meaning of *mountebank* is a "quack" (faker) who sells useless medicines from a platform in a public place.

Example 2

The American Museum of Natural History has long portrayed various aspects of man. Primitive cultures have been shown through habitat groups and displays of man's tools, utensils, and art. In more recent years,
5 there has been a tendency to delineate man's place

in nature, displaying his destructive and constructive activities on the earth he inhabits. Now, for the first time, the Museum has taken man apart, enlarged the delicate mechanisms that make him run, and examined
10 him as a biological phenomenon.

In the new Hall of the Biology of Man, Museum technicians have created a series of displays that are instructive to a degree never before achieved in an exhibit hall. Using new techniques and new materials,
15 they have been able to produce movement as well as form and color. It is a human belief that beauty is only skin deep. But nature has proved to be a master designer, not only in the matter of man's bilateral symmetry but also in the marvelous packaging job
20 that has arranged all man's organs and systems within his skin-covered case. When these are taken out of the case, greatly enlarged, and given color, they reveal form and design that give the lie to that old saw. Visitors will be surprised to discover that man's insides,
25 too, are beautiful.

Questions

1. The meaning of *bilateral* (line 18) is

   (A) biological
   (B) two-sided
   (C) natural
   (D) harmonious
   (E) technical

2. The meaning of *symmetry* (line 19) is

   (A) simplicity
   (B) obstinacy
   (C) sincerity
   (D) appearance
   (E) proportion

Explanatory Answers

1. Choice B is correct. The prefix *bi-* means "two." The root *latus* means "side." Therefore, *bilateral* means "two-sided."

2. Choice E is correct. The prefix *sym-* means "together." The root *metr* means "measure." The word *symmetry*, therefore, means "proportion," "harmonious relation of parts," "balance."

14 READING QUIZZES

Here Are 14 Reading Quizzes.
See How You Do.

Answer Sheet for Reading Quizzes

It is recommended that you use a No. 2 pencil. It is very important that you fill in the entire circle darkly and completely. If you change your response, erase as completely as possible. Incomplete marks or erasures may affect your score.

Complete Mark ●   **Examples of Incomplete Marks** ◐ ⊗ ⊖ ◯ ⊘ ◝ ◒ ◔

	A B C D E		A B C D E		A B C D E		A B C D E		A B C D E
1	○ ○ ○ ○ ○	12	○ ○ ○ ○ ○	23	○ ○ ○ ○ ○	34	○ ○ ○ ○ ○	45	○ ○ ○ ○ ○
2	○ ○ ○ ○ ○	13	○ ○ ○ ○ ○	24	○ ○ ○ ○ ○	35	○ ○ ○ ○ ○	46	○ ○ ○ ○ ○
3	○ ○ ○ ○ ○	14	○ ○ ○ ○ ○	25	○ ○ ○ ○ ○	36	○ ○ ○ ○ ○	47	○ ○ ○ ○ ○
4	○ ○ ○ ○ ○	15	○ ○ ○ ○ ○	26	○ ○ ○ ○ ○	37	○ ○ ○ ○ ○	48	○ ○ ○ ○ ○
5	○ ○ ○ ○ ○	16	○ ○ ○ ○ ○	27	○ ○ ○ ○ ○	38	○ ○ ○ ○ ○	49	○ ○ ○ ○ ○
6	○ ○ ○ ○ ○	17	○ ○ ○ ○ ○	28	○ ○ ○ ○ ○	39	○ ○ ○ ○ ○	50	○ ○ ○ ○ ○
7	○ ○ ○ ○ ○	18	○ ○ ○ ○ ○	29	○ ○ ○ ○ ○	40	○ ○ ○ ○ ○	51	○ ○ ○ ○ ○
8	○ ○ ○ ○ ○	19	○ ○ ○ ○ ○	30	○ ○ ○ ○ ○	41	○ ○ ○ ○ ○	52	○ ○ ○ ○ ○
9	○ ○ ○ ○ ○	20	○ ○ ○ ○ ○	31	○ ○ ○ ○ ○	42	○ ○ ○ ○ ○	53	○ ○ ○ ○ ○
10	○ ○ ○ ○ ○	21	○ ○ ○ ○ ○	32	○ ○ ○ ○ ○	43	○ ○ ○ ○ ○	54	○ ○ ○ ○ ○
11	○ ○ ○ ○ ○	22	○ ○ ○ ○ ○	33	○ ○ ○ ○ ○	44	○ ○ ○ ○ ○	55	○ ○ ○ ○ ○

Turn to your answer sheet (page 116) to answer the questions in this section.

Quiz 1

Questions 1–4 are based on the following passage.

This passage is from James E. Counsilman, "Life's Challenges Can Be Overcome at Every Age," which appeared in The New York Times *on July 1, 1979.*

A little over a year ago I began training to swim the English Channel this September. I will be 58 years old then.

5 My friends thought I had lost my mind; my wife, though not fearful for my sanity, was somewhat apprehensive. The question I was asked over and over was this: Why?

When a student reporter at Indiana recently asked me this question, I said, "First let me ask you a ques-
10 tion. What are your plans for this summer?" He replied that he was going to bag groceries in a supermarket. I didn't have to say more; he understood my point.

A challenge and an element of adventure are welcome whether you are 20 or 58 and preparing to swim
15 the Channel has it all over bagging groceries especially when you have a choice.

But why did I decide to swim the Channel at 58? Perhaps the answer to it may even evade me.

The Channel has always been the supreme challenge
20 to swimmers; a test of ability, endurance, luck and even bravery. It is this challenge that appeals to about 100 swimmers a year who are willing to spend time, effort and money to try it.

One fact that contributes to my interest is that, if I
25 succeed, I will be the oldest person ever to swim the Channel.

I don't think I'm a superman. I do think I have at least three things going for me:

First, I am training hard—presently swimming 7½
30 miles a day. Prior to that time I also kept physically fit by training moderately hard.

Second, I am a very goal-oriented person for whom this swim has long been a goal. I have a feeling I will be psychologically ready and won't do as one Chan-
35 nel swimmer did a few years ago. He trained hard for a couple of years, made the arrangements and even went to England weeks early to train in the Channel before his attempt. The great day came and he started swimming toward France. After swimming only one hour, he got
40 out of the water and climbed aboard the boat, saying that he suddenly had lost the desire to swim the Channel and it no longer meant anything to him.

On the other hand there was the young girl who was attempting to finish her swim when the ocean got
45 rough. She was having a tough time with the rough and cold water, when her trainer shouted to her from the boat that he thought she should give up and get out of the water. She shouted back, "I'm doing the swimming and I'll decide when to get out." She made it.

Quiz 1 Questions

1. Most likely, the author of this passage decided to swim the Channel because he
   (A) enjoys a challenge
   (B) wants to upset his wife
   (C) does not recognize the difficulties involved
   (D) is basically a show-off
   (E) has made a bet that he could do so

2. The author of this passage would most readily agree with which of the following statements?
   (A) People should limit their self-expectations.
   (B) Old people lose their sense of adventure.
   (C) Only an unrealistic person would attempt the Channel.
   (D) Will and drive are more important than age when it comes to overcoming a challenge.
   (E) People should recognize the dangers of physical stress.

3. According to the author,
   (A) the young girl (line 43) who swam the Channel during a storm was foolish
   (B) physical training is more important than being goal-oriented
   (C) the student reporter (line 8) was young at heart
   (D) the Channel swimmer (lines 34–42) who did not finish needed more training
   (E) many swimmers attempt the Channel every year

4. The author of this passage can best be described as
   (A) determined
   (B) cautious
   (C) friendly
   (D) unrealistic
   (E) disappointed

Quiz 2

Questions 5–8 are based on the following passage.

In New York, as much as in most communities in America, basketball is more religious rite than sport. Kids are at the playground as long as ten hours a day, actually playing as many as six. Seventeen- and
5 eighteen-year-olds already have rheumatoid knees from the constant pounding of their feet on the asphalt. They play in the heat of the afternoon with not much more to fuel them than a can of soda and a store-bought pastry, and they play at night in the dim illu-
10 mination of nearby street lights and flashing neon. In a single summer, typical city ballplayers will wear out four or five pairs of sneakers. They play even in the dead of winter, bundled in jackets and sweaters and belching up little puffs of steam as they bang away at
15 the netless rims.

Quiz 2 Questions

5. When the author states that basketball is a religious rite, he is referring to the players'

   (A) joy
   (B) pride
   (C) team spirit
   (D) dedication
   (E) skill

6. This passage as a whole tends to

   (A) create an image
   (B) defend religion
   (C) ridicule basketball players
   (D) uphold the American tradition of fair play
   (E) describe an exception to city life

7. In writing the passage, the author points out the

   (A) many advantages of playing basketball
   (B) values of basketball as an escape from reality
   (C) reasons basketball should be curtailed
   (D) possible dangers to health of playing basketball
   (E) cost of many items of basketball equipment

8. Which statement can best be defended on the basis of the passage?

   (A) The basketball court is open twenty-four hours.
   (B) The playground is not fenced off.

(C) The playground has a hard surface.
(D) Kids would rather play in the afternoon than at night.
(E) The kids are easily fatigued.

Quiz 3

Questions 9–12 are based on the following passage.

This passage is from Richard Katz, "A Solo-Survival Experience as Education for Personal Growth," available at http://files.eric.ed.gov/fulltext/ED038101.pdf.

I was exploring the far side of the island on the third day. I was also observing myself, an animal covering his territory. It was very quiet, even still. Suddenly a thunderous sound in the leaves and there was a pheas-
5 ant, frozen in fear, three feet from my face. I wasn't sure whether I looked as scared; I certainly had been deeply frightened. The stillness had become noise, and since I was alone on the island, my fantasies at that instant were elaborate. But I unfroze and the pheasant
10 did not. The myth of man, the primitive hunter, began to unfold as I reached for a stick. But before any action, another myth took hold and there was no taking of life. The basic need of hunger; the basic force of life. I can't forget that encounter.

Quiz 3 Questions

9. As used in line 9, the word *elaborate* most nearly means

   (A) quiet
   (B) great
   (C) groundless
   (D) expensive
   (E) unnecessary

10. In line 12, the phrase "another myth" refers to

    (A) a need for food
    (B) a respect for primitive customs
    (C) a need for action
    (D) a respect for living things
    (E) the powerlessness of animals

11. From the passage, we can most safely conclude that the

    (A) pheasant was an easy prey
    (B) narrator disliked exploring

(C) narrator was familiar with the island

(D) pheasant flew away

(E) island was a noisy place

12. By the end of this episode, the narrator feels that he has

(A) created a new myth

(B) learned how to survive

(C) grown in perception

(D) become a creature of fantasy

(E) exploded several myths

Quiz 4

Questions 13–15 are based on the following passage.

The ancient Egyptians believed strongly in life after death. They also believed that a person would need his body to exist in this afterlife. Therefore, they carefully preserved the body by treating it with spices and oils
5 and wrapping it in linen cloth. The wrapped body was then placed in a tomb. A body that is treated in this way is called a mummy.

Egyptian kings and nobles wanted to be certain that their mummies would be kept in safe places for-
10 ever. They had great tombs built for themselves and their families. Many kings were buried in secret tombs carved out of solid rock in a place near Thebes called the Valley of the Kings.

About eighty kings built towering pyramid-shaped
15 stone tombs. These pyramids have become famous as one of the Seven Wonders of the Ancient World.

One of the most amazing things about these pyramids is that they were constructed without using wheels or heavy equipment to move or raise the rocks. Egypt did
20 not learn about the wheel until long after the pyramids were built. Workmen used levers to get large blocks of stone on and off sledges and hauled them into place over long ramps built around the pyramids.

Quiz 4 Questions

13. The term *mummy* was used to describe

(A) kings of ancient Egypt

(B) ancient Egyptian nobles

(C) the place where Egyptian kings were buried

(D) the preserved body of a dead person

(E) one of the Seven Wonders of the Ancient World

14. The pyramids were built

(A) before the Egyptians developed a sophisticated technology

(B) after the Egyptians developed a sophisticated technology

(C) to house the tombs of all ancient Egyptian kings and nobles

(D) with the use of spices, oils, and linen cloth

(E) to keep mummies safe forever

15. Which of the following practices is most closely associated with ancient Egyptian belief in an afterlife?

(A) placing the dead in tombs carved out of solid rock

(B) building pyramids to house the bodies of dead kings

(C) preserving dead bodies with oils and spices

(D) creating the Valley of the Kings near Thebes

(E) constructing tombs without the use of wheels or heavy equipment

Quiz 5

Questions 16–18 are based on the following passage.

This passage is Walt Whitman's poem "I Hear America Singing," 1860.

I hear America singing, the varied carols I hear,

Those of mechanics, each one singing his as it should be blithe and strong,

The carpenter singing his as he measures his plank or
5   beam,

The mason singing his as he makes ready for work, or leaves off work,

The boatman singing what belongs to him in his boat, the deckhand singing on the steamboat deck,

10 The shoemaker singing as he sits on his bench, the hatter singing as he stands.

The wood-cutter's song, the ploughboy's on his way in the morning, or at noon intermission or at sundown,

15 The delicious singing of the mother, or of the young wife at work, or of the girl sewing or washing,

Each singing what belongs to him or her and to none else,

The day what belongs to the day—at night the party of
20   young fellows, robust, friendly,
Singing with open mouths their strong melodious
    songs.

Quiz 5 Questions

16. Judging from this poem, it is most probable that
    the poet favors

    (A) teachers
    (B) workingmen
    (C) executives
    (D) singers
    (E) athletes

17. The poet's main purpose in this poem is to

    (A) indicate that women belong in the house
    (B) criticize America's economy
    (C) celebrate the American worker
    (D) speak out in favor of socialism
    (E) show that all work is basically the same

18. The tone of this poem can best be described as

    (A) joyful
    (B) humorous
    (C) impatient
    (D) peaceful
    (E) careless

Quiz 6

Questions 19–24 are based on the following passage.

This passage is adapted from Jacques Barzun's Teacher in America, *1945.*

The whole aim of good teaching is to turn the young
learner, by nature a little copycat, into an independent,
self-propelling creature who can work as his own boss
to the limit of his powers. This is to turn pupils into
5   students, and it can be done on any rung of the ladder of learning. When I was a child, the multiplication
table was taught from a printed sheet which had to be
memorized one square at a time—the ones and the twos
and so on up to nine. It never occurred to the teacher
10   to show us how the answers could be arrived at also by
addition, which we already knew. No one said, "Look:

if four times four is sixteen, you ought to be able to figure out, without aid from memory, what five times four
is, because that amounts to four more ones added to the
15   sixteen." This would at first have been puzzling, *more*
complicated and difficult than memory work, but once
explained and grasped, it would have been an instru-
ment for learning and checking the whole business of
multiplication. We could temporarily have dispensed
20   with the teacher and cut loose from the printed table.

    This is another way of saying that the only thing
worth teaching anybody is a principle. Naturally, principles involve facts and some facts must be learned
"bare" because they do not rest on any principle. The
25   capital of Alaska is Juneau and, so far as I know, that is
all there is to it; but a European child ought not to learn
that Washington is the capital of the United States without fixing firmly in his mind the relation between the
city and the man who led his countrymen to freedom.
30   That would be missing an association, which is the
germ of a principle. And just as a complex athletic feat
is made possible by rapid and accurate coordination, so
all valuable learning hangs together and *works* by asso-
ciations which make sense.

Quiz 6 Questions

19. The title that best expresses the ideas of this
    passage is:

    (A) How to Teach Arithmetic
    (B) A Good Memory Makes a Good Student
    (C) Principles—the Basis of Learning
    (D) Using Addition to Teach Multiplication
    (E) How to Dispense with the Teacher

20. The author implies that the difference between a
    pupil and a student is the difference between

    (A) youth and maturity
    (B) learning and knowing
    (C) beginning and ending
    (D) memorizing and understanding
    (E) learning and teaching

21. The author indicates that children are naturally

    (A) deceitful
    (B) perceptive
    (C) independent
    (D) logical
    (E) imitative

22. The author would be most likely to agree that the most desirable way to teach is by

    (A) relating facts to principles
    (B) stressing the importance of learning
    (C) insisting that pupils work independently
    (D) recognizing that a knowledge of facts is useless
    (E) developing pupils' ability to memorize

23. As it is used in the passage, the word *germ* (line 31) most nearly means

    (A) result
    (B) beginning
    (C) polish
    (D) image
    (E) weakness

24. In this passage, the author develops his paragraphs primarily by the use of

    (A) narration
    (B) comparison
    (C) definitions
    (D) description
    (E) examples

Quiz 7

Questions 25–30 are based on the following passage.

This passage is from W. Douglas Burden, Look to the Wilderness, *1956.*

Next morning I saw for the first time an animal that is rarely encountered face to face. It was a wolverine. Though relatively small, rarely weighing more than 40 pounds, he is, above all animals, the one most hated by
5 the Indians and trappers. He is a fine tree climber and a relentless destroyer. Deer, reindeer, and even moose succumb to his attacks. We sat on a rock and watched him come, a bobbing rascal in blackish-brown. Since the male wolverine occupies a very large hunting area
10 and fights to the death any other male that intrudes on his domain, wolverines are always scarce, and in order to avoid extinction need all the protection that man can give. As a trapper, Henry wanted me to shoot him, but I refused, for this is the most fascinating and little known
15 of all our wonderful predators. His hunchback gait was awkward and ungainly, lopsided yet tireless. He advanced through all types of terrain without change of pace and with a sense of power that seemed indestructible. His course brought him directly to us, and he did

20 not notice our immobile figures until he was ten feet away. Obviously startled, he rose up on his hind legs with paws outstretched and swayed from side to side like a bear undecided whether to charge. Then he tried to make off at top speed and watch us over his shoulder
25 at the same time, running headlong into everything in his path.

Quiz 7 Questions

25. Wolverines are very scarce because

    (A) their food supply is limited
    (B) they are afraid of all humankind
    (C) they are seldom protected by man
    (D) trappers take their toll of them
    (E) they suffer in the survival of the fittest

26. The reason the author did not kill the wolverine seems to be that

    (A) the wolverine's ungainly gait made him miss the target
    (B) conservation laws protected the animal
    (C) the roughness of the terrain made tracking difficult
    (D) he admired the skill of the animal
    (E) he felt sorry for the animal

27. The wolverine ran headlong into everything in his path because of his

    (A) anxiety and curiosity
    (B) helplessness in the face of danger
    (C) snow blindness
    (D) ferocious courage
    (E) pursuit by the trappers

28. The author of this selection is most probably

    (A) an experienced hunter
    (B) a conscientious naturalist
    (C) an inexperienced trapper
    (D) a young Indian
    (E) a farmer

29. The author's chief purpose in writing this passage seems to be to

    (A) defend the wolverine from further attacks by man
    (B) point out the fatal weakness of the wolverine
    (C) show why the wolverine is scarce
    (D) characterize a rarely seen animal
    (E) criticize Henry's action

30. As a whole, this passage suggests that the wolverine

    (A) is every bit as awesome as his reputation
    (B) will eventually destroy the deer herds
    (C) will one day be able to outwit man
    (D) does not really need the protection of man
    (E) is too smart for other animals

33. The author implies that growth and perpetuity in nature and in history are the result of

    (A) quiet changes
    (B) a period of silence
    (C) undiscovered action
    (D) storms and tornadoes
    (E) violence and disruptions

Quiz 8

Questions 31–33 are based on the following passage.

This passage is from John Burroughs, "The Still Small Voice," in The Atlantic Monthly: A Magazine of Literature, Science, Art, and Politics, Volume CXVIII, *1916, p. 329.*

In the ordinary course of nature, the great beneficent changes come slowly and silently. The noisy changes, for the most part, mean violence and disruption. The roar of storms and tornadoes, the explosions of volca-
5 noes, the crash of thunder, are the result of a sudden break in the equipoise of the elements; from a condition of comparative repose and silence they become fearfully swift and audible. The still small voice is the voice of life and growth and perpetuity. . . . In the his-
10 tory of a nation it is the same.

Quiz 8 Questions

31. The title below that best expresses the ideas of this passage is:

    (A) Upsetting Nature's Balance
    (B) Repose and Silence
    (C) The Voice of Life and Growth
    (D) Nature's Intelligence
    (E) The Violent Elements

32. As used in the passage, the word *equipoise* (line 6) most nearly means

    (A) stress
    (B) balance
    (C) course
    (D) slowness
    (E) condition

Quiz 9

Questions 34–37 are based on the following passage.

It is here, perhaps, that poetry may best act nowadays as corrective and complementary to science. When science tells us that the galaxy to which our solar system belongs is so enormous that light, traveling at
5 186,000 miles per second, takes between 60,000 and 100,000 years to cross from one rim to the other of the galaxy, we laymen accept the statement but find it meaningless—beyond the comprehension of heart or mind. When science tells us that the human eye has
10 about 137 million separate "seeing" elements, we are no less paralyzed, intellectually and emotionally. Man is appalled by the immensities and the minuteness which science has disclosed for him. They are indeed unimaginable. But may not poetry be a possible way
15 of mediating them to our imagination? Of scaling them down to imaginative comprehension? Let us remember Perseus, who could not look directly at the nightmare Gorgon without being turned to stone, but could look at her image reflected in the shield the goddess of wisdom
20 lent him.

Quiz 9 Questions

34. The title below that best expresses the ideas of this passage is:

    (A) Poetry and Imagination
    (B) A Modern Gorgon
    (C) Poetry as a Mediator
    (D) The Vastness of the Universe
    (E) Imaginative Man

35. According to the passage, the average man

    (A) should have a better memory
    (B) is impatient with science

(C) cannot trust the scientists

(D) is overwhelmed by the discoveries of science

(E) does not understand either science or poetry

36. Perseus was most probably

(A) a scientist

(B) a legendary hero

(C) an early poet

(D) a horrible creature

(E) a minor god

37. This passage is chiefly developed by means of

(A) examples

(B) cause and effect

(C) narration

(D) definition

(E) anecdotes

Quiz 10

Questions 38–40 are based on the following passage.

Hail is at once the cruelest weapon in Nature's armory, and the most incalculable. It can destroy one farmer's prospects of a harvest in a matter of seconds; it can leave his neighbor's unimpaired. It can slay a flock
5 of sheep (it has killed children before now) in one field, while the sun continues to shine in the next. To the harassed meteorologist its behavior is even more Machiavellian than that of an ice storm. Difficult as it undoubtedly is for him to forecast the onset of an ice
10 storm, he knows pretty well what its course and dura- tion will be once it has started; just about all he can do with a hailstorm is to measure the size of the stones— and they have a habit of melting as soon as he gets his hands on them. He is not even too sure any more about
15 the way in which hail forms—and until he knows this, of course, he isn't likely to stumble upon any very sat- isfactory prognostic rules.

Quiz 10 Questions

38. The title below that best expresses the ideas of this passage is:

(A) Forecasting Ice Storms

(B) The Way That Hail Forms

(C) The Harassed Meteorologist

(D) The Unpredictability of Hailstorms

(E) Hail—the Killer

39. As used in the passage, the word *prognostic* (last line) most nearly means

(A) restraining

(B) breakable

(C) day-by-day

(D) foretelling

(E) regular

40. The author capitalized "Nature's" (line 1) most probably because he wished to

(A) talk with nature directly

(B) contrast nature and science

(C) emphasize the power of nature

(D) show off his knowledge of figures of speech

(E) call the reader's attention to the subject of the passage

Quiz 11

Questions 41–43 are based on the following passage.

This passage is from the Janesville [Wisconsin] Daily Gazette, *October 19, 1954, p. 6.*

Windstorms have recently established a record which meteorologists hope will not be equaled for many years to come. Disastrous tornadoes along with devastating typhoons and hurricanes have cost thousands of lives
5 and left property damage totaling far into the millions. The prominence these storms have held in the news has led many people to ask about the difference between the three. Is a typhoon the same as a hurricane? Is a tornado the same as a typhoon? Basically, there is no
10 difference. All three consist of wind rotating counter- clockwise (in the Northern Hemisphere) at a tremen- dous velocity around a low-pressure center. However, each type does have its own definite characteristics. Of the three the tornado is certainly the most treacherous.
15 The Weather Bureau can, with some degree of accu- racy, forecast the typhoon and the hurricane; however, it is impossible to determine where or when the tornado will strike. And out of the three, if one had a choice, perhaps it would be safer to choose to withstand the
20 hurricane.

Quiz 11 Questions

41. The title below that best expresses the ideas of this passage is:

    (A) Recent Storms
    (B) Record-Breaking Storms
    (C) Predicting Windstorms
    (D) Treacherous Windstorms
    (E) Wind Velocity and Direction

42. Which is *not* common to all of the storms mentioned?

    (A) fairly accurate forecasting
    (B) violently rotating wind
    (C) high property damage
    (D) loss of human lives
    (E) public interest

43. The author indicates that

    (A) typhoons cannot be forecast
    (B) the Southern Hemisphere is free from hurricanes
    (C) typhoons are more destructive than hurricanes
    (D) hurricanes are not really dangerous
    (E) tornadoes occur around a low-pressure center

Quiz 12 Questions

44. The phrase "summer's lease hath all too short a date" (line 4) means that summer

    (A) ends in the first few days of September
    (B) cannot be dated because it lasts forever
    (C) rents time in our memories
    (D) is eternal
    (E) lasts for only a brief time

45. What does the poet mean by "eye of heaven" in line 5

    (A) the moon
    (B) the sun
    (C) the rain
    (D) the stars
    (E) lightning

46. In the final line (line 14), what does Shakespeare mean by "this"?

    (A) eternal summer
    (B) his beloved
    (C) time
    (D) his sonnet
    (E) Death

Quiz 12

Questions 44–46 are based on the following passage.

The following is William Shakespeare's Sonnet 18.

Shall I compare thee to a summer's day?
Thou art more lovely and more temperate:
Rough winds do shake the darling buds of May,
And summer's lease hath all too short a date:
5 Sometime too hot the eye of heaven shines,
And often is his gold complexion dimm'd;
And every fair from fair sometime declines,
By chance or nature's changing course untrimm'd;
But thy eternal summer shall not fade
10 Nor lose possession of that fair thou owest;
Nor shall Death brag thou wander'st in his shade,
When in eternal lines to time thou growest:
So long as men can breathe or eyes can see,
So long lives this and this gives life to thee.

Quiz 13

Questions 47–50 are based on the following passage.

The man who reads well is the man who thinks well, who has a background for opinions and a touchstone for judgment. He may be a Lincoln who derives wisdom from a few books or a Roosevelt who ranges 5 from Icelandic sagas to *Penrod*. But reading makes him a full man, and out of his fullness he draws that example and precept which stand him in good stead when confronted with problems which beset a chaotic universe. Mere reading, of course, is nothing. It is but 10 the veneer of education. But wise reading is a help to action. American versatility is too frequently dilettantism, but reinforced by knowledge it becomes motive power. "Learning," as James L. Mursell says, "cashes the blank check of native versatility." And learning is a 15 process not to be concluded with the formal teaching of schooldays or to be enriched only by the active experience of later years, but to be broadened and deepened

by persistent and judicious reading. "The true University of these days is a Collection of Books," said Carlyle. If that is not the whole of the truth it is enough of
20 it for every young person to hug to this bosom.

Quiz 13 Questions

47. The title that best expresses the ideas of this passage is:

    (A) The Veneer of Education
    (B) The Wise Reader
    (C) The Reading Habits of Great Men
    (D) The Versatility of Americans
    (E) The Motivation of Readers

48. Which advice would the author of this passage most likely give to young people?

    (A) Develop a personal reading program.
    (B) Avoid reading too many books of the same type.
    (C) Spend more time in a library.
    (D) Read only serious books.
    (E) Learn to read more rapidly and accurately.

49. The quotation "Learning cashes the blank check of native versatility" (lines 13–14) means that

    (A) a good education is like money in the bank
    (B) to be versatile is to be learned
    (C) native intelligence has more value than acquired knowledge
    (D) education can make possible an effective use of natural capabilities
    (E) he who learns well will keep an open mind at all times

50. The author apparently believes that

    (A) the answer to the world's problems lies in a nation of learned men
    (B) America can overcome her dilettantism by broader reading programs for her citizens
    (C) people with wide reading backgrounds are likely to find right courses of action
    (D) active experience is the second-best teacher
    (E) the best book is one that is serious in tone

Quiz 14

Questions 51–55 are based on the following passage.

This passage is from Aaron Copland, What to Listen for in Music, *1939.*

Most people want to know how things are made. They frankly admit, however, that they feel completely at sea when it comes to understanding how a piece of music is made. Where a composer begins, how he manages
5 to keep going—in fact, how and where he learns his trade—all are shrouded in impenetrable darkness. The composer, in short, is a man of mystery, and the composer's workshop an unapproachable ivory tower.

One of the first things the layman wants to hear
10 about is the part inspiration plays in composing. He finds it difficult to believe that composers are not much preoccupied with that question, that composing is as natural for the composer as eating or sleeping. Composing is something that the composer happens to have
15 been born to do, and because of that, it loses the character of a special virtue in the composer's eyes.

The composer, therefore, does not say to himself: "Do I feel inspired?" He says to himself: "Do I feel like composing today?" And if he feels like composing, he
20 does. It is more or less like saying to himself: "Do I feel sleepy?" If you feel sleepy, you go to sleep. If you don't feel sleepy, you stay up. If the composer doesn't feel like composing, he doesn't compose. It's as simple as that.

Quiz 14 Questions

51. The author of the passage indicates that creating music is an activity that is

    (A) difficult
    (B) rewarding
    (C) inspirational
    (D) fraught with anxiety
    (E) instinctive

52. When considering the work involved in composing music, the layman often

    (A) exaggerates the difficulties of the composer in commencing work
    (B minimizes the mental turmoil that the composer undergoes

(C) is unaware that a creative process is involved

(D) loses the ability to enjoy the composition

(E) loses his ability to judge the work apart from the composer

53. In this passage, composing music is compared with

(A) having a feast

(B) climbing an ivory tower

(C) visualizing problems

(D) going to sleep

(E) going to sea

54. The author's approach toward his subject is

(A) highly emotional

(B) casually informative

(C) negative

(D) deeply philosophical

(E) consciously prejudiced

55. We may most safely conclude that the author is

(A) a layman

(B) a violinist

(C) a working composer

(D) an amateur musician

(E) a novelist

ANSWERS

To Reading Quizzes

Quiz 1
1. A
2. D
3. E
4. A

Quiz 2
5. D
6. A
7. D
8. C

Quiz 3
9. B
10. D
11. A
12. C

Quiz 4
13. D
14. E
15. C

Quiz 5
16. B
17. C
18. A

Quiz 6
19. C
20. D
21. E
22. A
23. B
24. E

Quiz 7
25. E
26. D
27. A
28. B
29. D
30. A

Quiz 8
31. C
32. B
33. A

Quiz 9
34. C
35. D
36. B
37. A

Quiz 10
38. D
39. D
40. C

Quiz 11
41. D
42. A
43. E

Quiz 12
44. E
45. B
46. D

Quiz 13
47. B
48. A
49. D
50. C

Quiz 14
51. E
52. A
53. D
54. B
55. C

HOT PREFIXES AND ROOTS

Here is a list of the most important prefixes and roots that impart
a certain meaning or feeling. They can be instant clues to the
meanings of more than 110,000 words.

PREFIXES THAT MEAN "TO," "WITH," "BETWEEN," OR "AMONG"

Prefix	Meaning	Examples
ad, ac, af, an, ap, as, at	to, toward	adapt—to fit into adhere—to stick to attract—to draw near
com, con, co, col	with, together	combine—to bring together contact—to touch together collect—to bring together coworker—one who works together with another worker
in, il, ir, im	into	inject—to put into impose—to force into illustrate—to put into example irritate—to put into discomfort
inter	between, among	international—among nations interact—to act among the people
pro	forward, going ahead	proceed—to go forward promote—to move forward

PREFIXES THAT MEAN "BAD"

Prefix	Meaning	Examples
mal	wrong, bad	malady—illness malevolent—evil malfunction—poor function
mis	wrong, badly	mistreat—to treat badly mistake—to get wrong

PREFIXES THAT MEAN "AWAY FROM," "NOT," OR "AGAINST"

Prefix	Meaning	Examples
ab	away from	absent—not present, away abscond—to run away
de, dis	away from, down, the opposite of, apart, not	depart—to go away from decline—to turn down dislike—not to like dishonest—not honest distant—apart
ex, e, ef	out, from	exit—to go out eject—to throw out efface—to rub out, erase
in, il, ir, im	not	inactive—not active impossible—not possible illiterate—not literate irreversible—not reversible
non	not	nonsense—no sense nonstop—having no stops
un	not	unhelpful—not helpful uninterested—not interested
anti	against	antifreeze—a substance used to prevent freezing antisocial—someone who is not social
ob	against, in front of	obstacle—something that stands in the way of obstinate—inflexible

PREFIXES THAT DENOTE DISTANCE

Prefix	Meaning	Examples
circum	around	circumscribe—to write or inscribe in a circle circumspect—very careful
equ, equi	equal, the same	equalize—to make equal equitable—fair, equal
post	after	postpone—to do after postmortem—after death
pre	before	preview—a viewing that goes before another viewing prehistorical—before written history
re	back, again	retell—to tell again recall—to call back, to remember
sub	under, behind, less than	subordinate—under something else subconscious—under the consciousness
super	over, above	superimpose—to put something over something else superstar—a star greater than other stars
trans	across	transcontinental—across the continent transit—act of going across
un, uni	one	unity—oneness unanimous—sharing one view unidirectional—having one direction

ROOTS

Root	Meaning	Examples
cap, capt, cept, ceive	to take, to hold	captive—one who is held capable—to be able to take hold of things concept—an idea or thought held in mind receive—to take
cred	to believe	credible—believable credit—belief, trust
curr, curs, cours	to run	current—now in progress, running cursor—a movable indicator recourse—running for help
dic, dict	to say	indicate—to say by demonstrating diction—verbal saying
duc, duct	to lead	induce—to lead to action aquaduct—a pipe or waterway that leads 　water somewhere
fac, fic, fect, fy	to make, to do	facile—easy to do fiction—something that has been made up satisfy—to make happy or to fulfill affect—to have an influence on effect—to make happen or bring about
jec, ject	to throw	project—to put forward trajectory—a path of an object that has been 　thrown
mit, mis	to send	admit—to send in missile—something that gets sent through 　the air
pon, pos	to place	transpose—to place across compose—to put in place from pieces or parts deposit—to place in something
scrib, script	to write	describe—to write or tell about scripture—a written tablet
spec, spic	to look	specimen—an example to look at inspect—to look over
ten, tain	to hold	maintain—to keep up retain—to hold on to, keep (back)
ven, vent	to come	advent—a coming to, an arrival convene—to come together

PART 4

The ACT Science Test

SCIENCE TEST

Introduction

The Science Test of the ACT consists of a series of graphs, charts, tables, etc., including descriptions of the experiment and an explanation of how the data sets were produced. The experiment could come from biology, chemistry, physics, or any other field of science. Although some questions may require you to know some discipline-specific content for science courses taught at the high school level (such as biology), you don't need to remember obscure chemistry facts or to have even taken a physics class. You can answer the questions just by analyzing the data presented on the test page and working through the scientific method.

Examples

Ants are attracted to the seeds of some plants that contain *elaiosomes* (oil-rich bodies on seeds or fruits that attract ants, which act as dispersal agents). The ants transport the seed nests and eat the elaiosomes. The seeds are then left in a waste pile, and some seeds start to grow (*germinate*). The process was examined in the following studies.

Study 1

For two species of plants (X and Y), the following were recorded: seed mass per seed (mg), elaiosome mass per seed (mg), and percentage of seed mass composed of elaiosome. See Table 1 for the complete record.

TABLE 1

Species	Seed Mass (mg)	Elaiosome Mass per Seed (mg)	Percentage of Seed Mass Composed of Elaiosome
X	6.8	0.42	6.2
Y	14.9	0.92	6.2

Study 2

In order to determine the seed collection rate by a single ant species for the plants from Study 1, three study sites were chosen.

At each site, two dishes of seeds were placed. One dish contained 20 seeds of Species X, and the other contained 20 seeds of Species Y. After the dishes were left for 48 hours, the number of seeds taken from each dish was recorded. The results are represented in Table 2.

TABLE 2

Site	Plant Species Absent	Seeds Taken from Seed Dishes Containing	
		Species X	Species Y
1	X	13	3
2	Y	2	12
3	X and Y	8	9

Study 3

Ants planted 2,550 seeds of a third species, Species Z. Researchers hand-planted an additional 2,550 seeds in similar environments. All seeds were observed for a period of two years. The results are represented in Table 3.

TABLE 3

Maturation of Species Z Seeds	Results From	
	Hand-Planted Seeds	Ant-Planted Seeds
Seeds germinated	26	39
Plants alive after 1 year	9	30
Plants alive after 2 years	4	13
Seeds produced per plant after 2 years	2,187	2,163

Study Questions

1. In Study 2, which variable was controlled at each site?
   - (A) the time at which most of the seeds were taken from the dishes
   - (B) the specific type of seed which was taken by the ants
   - (C) the number of ants
   - (D) the number of seed dishes placed

2. From the results of the studies, Species X and Species Y are most alike in which area?
   - (F) the number of seeds removed from seed dishes
   - (G) the seed mass
   - (H) the rates of germination on ant waste piles
   - (J) the percentage of elaiosome mass per seed

3. As seen in Study 3, compared to the ant-planted seeds, the process of hand-planting seeds produces
   - (A) decreased seed germination
   - (B) increased seed production per plant after 1 year
   - (C) increased plant survival after 1 year
   - (D) increased plant survival after 2 years

4. A researcher can argue which possible flaw in the design of Study 2?
   - (F) There may have been seeds not accounted for at each site.
   - (G) There may have been plants not accounted for at each site.
   - (H) Animals may have eaten the plants.
   - (J) Animals may have taken the seeds from the dishes.

5. According to Study 2, which of the following may affect the ants' seed preference?
   - (A) abundance of a type of plant in a given area
   - (B) elaiosome mass
   - (C) seed mass
   - (D) percentage of seed mass composed of elaiosome

6. For Study 2, Sites 1 and 2 were used to study
   - (F) ants' seed preference in an area where one plant species was absent
   - (G) survival of only one plant species where ants were not present
   - (H) the time by which ants had taken all the seed from the dishes
   - (J) the relation between elaiosome mass and seed mass

Explanatory Answers

1. Choice D is correct. The key to answering this question is to remember what it means for a variable to be "controlled." It means that the condition is the same everywhere and does not change. Although you may be tempted to look at the chart, the control is usually listed in the description of the design of the experiment. Note that in the second sentence of Study 2, it says: "At each site, two dishes of seeds were placed." The control was the two dishes. The other choices do not represent a control element.

2. Choice J is correct. When you are looking for two things that are "most alike," you want to spot some quantity that is the same or nearly the same. Look at Table 1: the "percentage of seed mass composed of elaiosome" for both Species X and Y is 6.2. Choices A and B don't fit this criterion, and we have no data for Choice C.

3. Choice A is correct. According to Table 3, only 26 hand-planted seeds germinated, while 39 ant-planted seeds did, so hand-planting seeds produces *decreased* seed germination. Choice B is incorrect, although tricky. We can see in the table that hand-planting produces more new seeds than ant-planting (2,187 to 2,163) . . . *after two years*. It provides no data about seed generation after one year, so we cannot know what occurs at this point. Choices C and D are incorrect. According to Table 3, more ant-plantings survive after both one year and two years; therefore, hand-planting produces *decreased* plant survival during either length of time.

4. Choice J is correct. Note that the design of Study 2 does not include observations of ants taking the seeds yet assumes this in the results. If animals take some of the seeds, it will obscure the study. The other choices do not affect the study because the measure was seeds *removed from dishes*, not seeds at the site, and the results are not dependent on the cause of the plants' absence.

5. Choice A is correct. Notice that in Table 2, depending on which plant species is absent, we get a different number of seeds taken from the two dishes. This would suggest that the abundance (or absence) of a particular plant species affects the ants' behavior. The other three choices refer to data collected in Study 1, which did not examine the ants' preferences.

6. Choice F is correct. In Site 1 (see Table 2) when Plant Species X is absent (and Y remains) or in Site 2 when Plant Species Y is absent (and X remains), we see the number of seeds taken from seed dishes, showing the ants' seed preference. Choice B is incorrect because the statement is not true. Choice C is incorrect. Although time is mentioned (48 hours), this is not the time by which ants had taken all the seed from the dishes. Choice D is incorrect. It refers to Table 1 and not to Table 2.

Strategies

Experimental Design

There are certain terms you should know when it comes to this science test.

You should know the meaning of an *independent variable*, that is, the variable or quantity that is adjusted and varied or changed. When this variable is changed, it affects the value of the *dependent variable*, which by definition is dependent on the *independent variable*. For instance, if pressure changes with temperature, when you have a certain temperature, you'll get an associated pressure. Pressure is dependent on temperature, so temperature is the *independent variable* while pressure is the *dependent variable*.

Identifying and Converting Units

Know your units. For example, are we discussing speed or acceleration? *Speed* is defined as distance covered divided by time lapsed. *Acceleration* is defined as the change in speed divided by the change in time.

How to Read Science Charts

Information on how to read and interpret charts, tables, and graphs can be found in the Math Refresher Sections 701, 702, 703, 704, 705, and 706, beginning on page 272.

PART 5

Mini Math Refresher

The Most Important Basic Math Rules and Concepts You Need to Know

Make sure that you understand each of the following math rules and concepts. It is a good idea to memorize them all. Refer to the section of the Complete ACT Math Refresher (Part 6 starting on page 147) shown in parentheses, e.g., (409), for a complete explanation of each.

ALGEBRA AND ARITHMETIC

Percentage Problems

(107)

Percentage

$x\% = \dfrac{x}{100}$

Example:

$5\% = \dfrac{5}{100}$

(107)

RULE:

"What" becomes x

"percent" becomes $\dfrac{x}{100}$

"of" becomes $\times$ (times)

"is" becomes $=$ (equals)

Examples:

(1) What percent of 5 is 2?

$\dfrac{x}{100} \quad \times 5 = 2$

or

$\left(\dfrac{x}{100}\right)(5) = 2$

$\dfrac{5x}{100} = 2$

$5x = 200$

$x = 40$

Answer $= 40\%$

(2) 6 is what percent of 24?

$6 = \dfrac{x}{100} \quad \times 24$

$6 = \dfrac{24x}{100}$

$600 = 24x$

$100 = 4x$ (dividing both sides by 6)

$25 = x$

Answer $= 25\%$

Equations

(407)

Example:

$x + y = 1; x - y = 2.$ Solve for x and y.

Procedure:

Add equations:

$$x + y = 1$$
$$\underline{x - y = 2}$$
$$2x + 0 = 3$$

Therefore $2x = 3$ and $x = \dfrac{3}{2}$

Substitute $x = \dfrac{3}{2}$ back into one of the equations:

$x + y = 1$

$\dfrac{3}{2} + y = 1$

$y = -\dfrac{1}{2}$

Factoring

(409)

Example:

$x^2 - 2x + 1 = 0$. Solve for x.

Note that in general:

$(mx + b)(nx + c) = mnx^2 + bnx + mxc + bc$

Procedure:

Factor: $(x - 1)(x - 1) = 0$

$$x - 1 = 0$$
$$x = 1$$

In the example $x^2 - 2x + 1 = 0$, $m = 1$, $n = 1$, $b = -1$, $c = -1$, so

$$(x - 1)(x - 1) = (1)(1)x^2 + (-1)(1)x + (1)x(-1) + (-1)(-1)$$
$$= x^2 + -x + -x + 1$$
$$= x^2 - 2x + 1$$

(409)

$(a + b)(c + d) = ac + ad + bc + bd$

Example:

$$(2 + 3)(4 - 6) = (2)(4) + (2)(-6) + (3)(4) + (3)(-6)$$
$$= 8 - 12 + 12 - 18$$
$$= -10$$

(409)

$a(b + c) = ab + ac$

Example:

$$5(4 + 5) = 5(4) + 5(5)$$
$$= 20 + 25$$
$$= 45$$

(409)

$(a + b)^2 = a^2 + 2ab + b^2$

Example:

$$(9 + 1)^2 = 9^2 + 2(9)(1) + 1^2$$
$$= 81 + 18 + 1$$
$$= 100$$

(409)

$(a - b)^2 = a^2 - 2ab + b^2$

Example:

$$(9 - 1)^2 = 9^2 - 2(9)(1) + 1^2$$
$$= 81 - 18 + 1$$
$$= 64$$

(409)

$(a + b)(a - b) = a^2 - b^2$

Example:

$$(10 + 9)(10 - 9)$$
$$= (10)(10) - (9)(9)$$
$$100 - 81 = 19$$

(409)

$-(a - b) = b - a$

Example:

$$-(5 - 4) = 4 - 5 = -1$$

Exponents and Roots

(429)

$a^2 = (a)(a)$

Examples:

$2^2 = (2)(2) = 4$

$a^3 = (a)(a)(a)$

(429)

$a^x a^y = a^{x+y}$

Examples:

$a^2 \times a^3 = a^5$

$2^2 \times 2^3 = 2^5 = 32$

(429)

$(a^x)^y = a^{xy}$

Examples:

$(a^3)^5 = a^{15}$

$(2^3)^5 = 2^{15}$

(429)

$(ab)^x = a^x b^x$

Examples:

$(2 \times 3)^3 = 2^3 \times 3^3$

$(ab)^2 = a^2 b^2$

(429)

$a^{-y} = \dfrac{1}{a^y}$

Example:

$2^{-3} = \dfrac{1}{2^3} = \dfrac{1}{8}$

(429)

$a^0 = 1$

$10^0 = 1$

$10^1 = 10$

$10^2 = 100$

$10^3 = 1,000$, etc.

Example:

$8.6 \times 10^4 = 8.6\,0\,0\,0.0$

Move decimal 4   1 2 3 4
places to the right

The end result is 86,000.

(429)

$\dfrac{a^x}{a^y} = a^{x-y}$

Examples:

$\dfrac{a^3}{a^2} = a^{3-2} = a$

$\dfrac{2^3}{2^2} = 2^{3-2} = 2$

(430)

If $y^2 = x$, then $y = \pm \sqrt{x}$.

Example:

If $y^2 = 4$, then $y = \pm \sqrt{4} = \pm 2$.

Equalities

(402)

$$
\begin{array}{l}
\;a + b = c \\
+ \qquad d = d \\
\hline
a + b + d = c + d
\end{array}
\qquad
\begin{array}{l}
\;3 + 4 = 7 \\
+ \qquad 2 = 2 \\
\hline
3 + 4 + 2 = 7 + 2
\end{array}
$$

Inequalities

(419–425)

$>$ means "greater than," $<$ means "less than," $\geq$ means "greater than or equal to," $\leq$ means "less than or equal to."

$$
\begin{array}{l}
\;b > c \\
+ \;d > e \\
\hline
b + d > c + e
\end{array}
\qquad
\begin{array}{l}
\;4 > 3 \\
+ \;7 > 6 \\
\hline
11 > 9
\end{array}
\qquad
\begin{array}{l}
\;4 > 3 \\
+ \;{-6} > -7 \\
\hline
-2 > -4
\end{array}
$$

Note: Multiplying both sides of an inequality by -1 reverses the order of the inequality.

$$
\begin{array}{l}
5 > 4 \\
(6)5 > (6)4 \\
\text{Thus} \\
30 > 24
\end{array}
\qquad
\begin{array}{l}
-5 < -4 \\
-(-5) > -(-4) \\
\text{Thus} \\
5 > 4
\end{array}
$$

If $\quad -2 < x < +2 \quad$ then $\quad +2 > -x > -2$

If $\quad a > b > 0 \quad$ then $\quad a^2 > b^2$

GEOMETRY

Angles

(501)

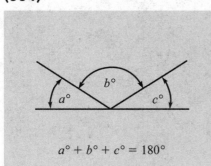

$$a° + b° + c° = 180°$$

(504)

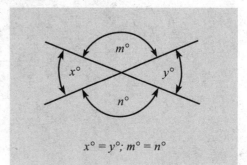

$$x° = y°; \; m° = n°$$

(504)

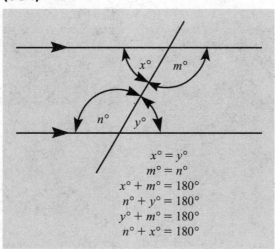

$$x° = y°$$
$$m° = n°$$
$$x° + m° = 180°$$
$$n° + y° = 180°$$
$$y° + m° = 180°$$
$$n° + x° = 180°$$

Triangles

(501)

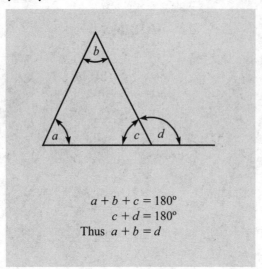

$$a + b + c = 180°$$
$$c + d = 180°$$
Thus $a + b = d$

(506)

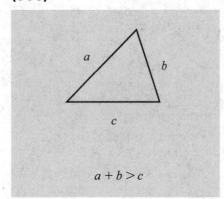

$$a + b > c$$

(506)

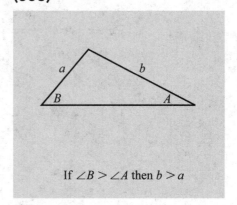

If $\angle B > \angle A$ then $b > a$

(507)

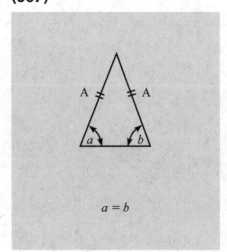

$$a = b$$

(510)

Similar Triangles

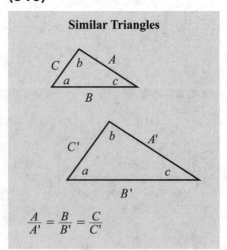

$$\frac{A}{A'} = \frac{B}{B'} = \frac{C}{C'}$$

Triangles—Pythagorean Theorem

Note: Figures are not drawn to scale.

(509)

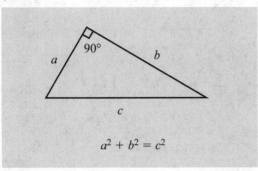

$$a^2 + b^2 = c^2$$

(509)

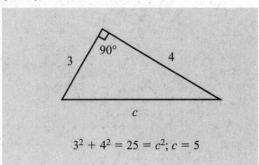

$$3^2 + 4^2 = 25 = c^2; c = 5$$

(509)

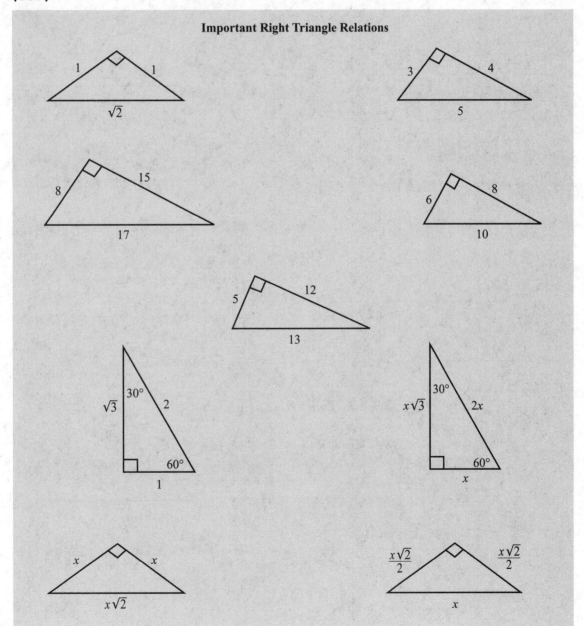

Important Right Triangle Relations

Areas and Perimeters

(304)

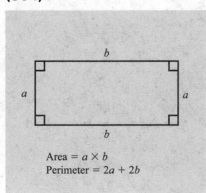

Area = $a \times b$
Perimeter = $2a + 2b$

(305)

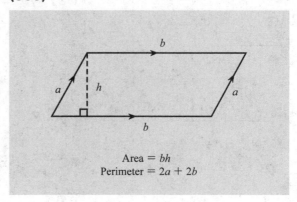

Area = bh
Perimeter = $2a + 2b$

(306)

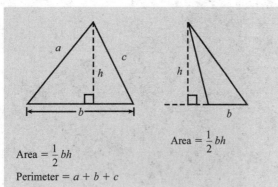

Area = $\frac{1}{2}bh$

Area = $\frac{1}{2}bh$
Perimeter = $a + b + c$

(310)

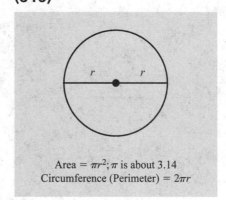

Area = πr^2; π is about 3.14
Circumference (Perimeter) = $2\pi r$

Circles

(526–527)

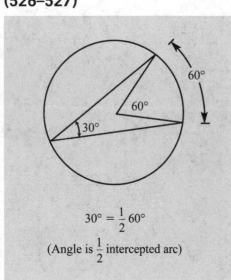

$30° = \frac{1}{2}60°$

(Angle is $\frac{1}{2}$ intercepted arc)

(527)

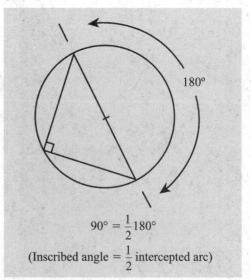

$90° = \frac{1}{2}180°$

(Inscribed angle = $\frac{1}{2}$ intercepted arc)

Coordinate Geometry

(410a)

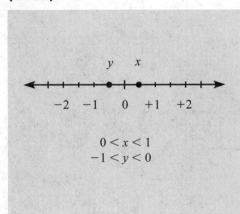

$$0 < x < 1$$
$$-1 < y < 0$$

(410b)

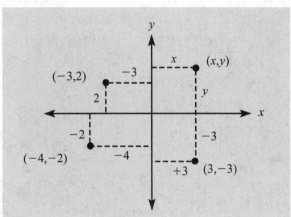

(411)

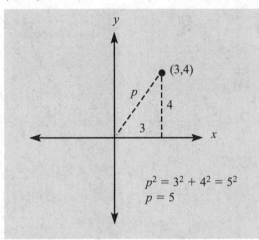

$$p^2 = 3^2 + 4^2 = 5^2$$
$$p = 5$$

(416)

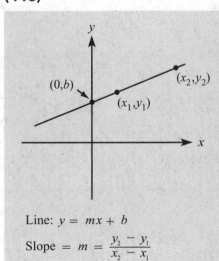

Line: $y = mx + b$

Slope $= m = \dfrac{y_2 - y_1}{x_2 - x_1}$

(416)

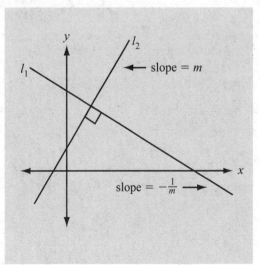

slope $= m$

slope $= -\dfrac{1}{m}$

TRIGONOMETRY

(901)

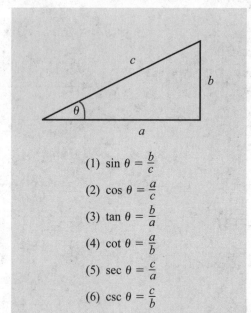

(1) $\sin \theta = \dfrac{b}{c}$

(2) $\cos \theta = \dfrac{a}{c}$

(3) $\tan \theta = \dfrac{b}{a}$

(4) $\cot \theta = \dfrac{a}{b}$

(5) $\sec \theta = \dfrac{c}{a}$

(6) $\csc \theta = \dfrac{c}{b}$

PART 6

Complete ACT Math Refresher

There are many ACT exam takers whose math backgrounds are not quite up to par—probably because their basic math skills are rusty or because they never did do well in their math classes. For these math-troubled students, this Math Refresher section will be "manna from heaven." The pages that follow constitute a complete basic math course that will help students greatly in preparing for the math part of the ACT. *Note*: Many of the examples or methods can be done with a calculator, but it is wise for students to know how to solve problems without a calculator.

This Math Refresher offers the following:

1. a systematic review of every math area covered by the questions in the math part of the ACT

   and

2. short review tests throughout the Refresher to check whether the student has grasped the math principles that he or she has just studied.

The review tests will also provide students with valuable reinforcement so that they will remember how to go about solving math problems they would otherwise have difficulty with on the actual ACT.

Each of the 8 "Sessions" in this Math Refresher has a review test or "Practice Test." Almost every review test has 50 questions followed by 50 detailed solutions. All of the solutions for the 8 review tests include a number (or numbers) in parentheses *after each solution*. The number refers to a specific instructional section where the rules and principles involved in the question are explain simply and clearly.

There is another very important purpose that this Math Refresher serves. You will find, after every solution in the math sections of the 3 ACT Practice Tests in this book, a key to the mathematical principles of this Math Refresher. For example, a solution may direct you to Math Refresher 202, which deals with distance and time problems. If you happen to be weak in this mathematical operation, the Math Refresher 202 explanation will immediately clarify for you how to do Distance and Time problems. In other words, for those who are weak in any area of Basic Math, this invaluable keying system will help you get the right answer to your ACT math question—and thereby increase your ACT score.

Mathematical Symbols

· multiplication dot; as in $x \cdot y$

( ) parentheses; used to group expressions

% percent

÷ division

: ratio

= equals

≠ does not equal

< less than

> greater than

≤ less than or equal to

≥ greater than or equal to

√ square root

π pi, the ratio of the circumference of a circle to its diameter, which is approximately equal to $\frac{22}{7}$ or 3.14.

∠ angle

‖ is parallel to

⊥ is perpendicular to

∧ and

∨ or

~ is similar to, or approximately

→ implies

∈ belongs to

⊂ is a subset of

MATH REFRESHER SESSION 1

Fractions, Decimals, Percentages, Deviations, Ratios and Proportions, Variations, and Comparison of Fractions

Fractions, Decimals, Percentages

These problems involve the ability to perform numerical operations quickly and correctly. It is essential that you learn the arithmetical procedures outlined in this section.

101. Four different ways to write "a divided by b" are

$$a \div b, \frac{a}{b}, a : b, b\overline{)a}.$$

Example: 7 divided by 15 is

$$7 \div 15 = \frac{7}{15} = 7 : 15 = 15\overline{)7}.$$

102. The numerator of a fraction is the upper number and the denominator is the lower number.

Example: In the fraction $\frac{8}{13}$, the numerator is 8 and the denominator is 13.

103. Moving a decimal point one place to the right multiplies the value of a number by 10, whereas moving the decimal point one place to the left divides a number by 10. Likewise, moving a decimal point two places to the right multiplies the value of a number by 100, whereas moving the decimal point two places to the left divides a number by 100.

Example: $24.35 \times 10 = 243.5$
(decimal point moved to *right*)
$24.35 \div 10 = 2.435$
(decimal point moved to *left*)

104. To change a fraction to a decimal, divide the numerator of the fraction by its denominator.

Example: Express $\frac{5}{6}$ as a decimal. We divide 5 by 6, obtaining 0.83.

$$\frac{5}{6} = 5 \div 6 = 0.833 \ldots$$

105. To convert a decimal to a fraction, delete the decimal point and divide by whatever unit of 10 the number of decimal places represents.

Example: Convert 0.83 to a fraction. First, delete the decimal point. Second, two decimal places represent hundredths, so divide 83 by 100: $\frac{83}{100}$.

$$0.83 = \frac{83}{100}$$

106. To change a fraction to a percent, find its decimal form, multiply by 100, and add a percent sign.

Example: Express $\frac{3}{8}$ as a percent. To convert $\frac{3}{8}$ to a decimal, divide 3 by 8, which gives us 0.375. Multiplying 0.375 by 100 gives us 37.5%.

107. To change a percent to a fraction, drop the percent sign and divide the number by 100.

Example: Express 17% as a fraction. Dropping the % sign gives us 17, and dividing by 100 gives us $\frac{17}{100}$.

108. To *reduce* a fraction, divide the numerator and denominator by the largest number that divides them both evenly.

Example: Reduce $\frac{10}{15}$. Dividing both the numerator and denominator by 5 gives us $\frac{2}{3}$.

Example: Reduce $\frac{12}{36}$. The largest number that divides into both 12 and 36 is 12. Reducing the fraction, we have

$$\frac{\overset{1}{\cancel{12}}}{\underset{3}{\cancel{36}}} = \frac{1}{3}.$$

Note: In both examples, the reduced fraction is exactly equal to the original fraction:

$$\frac{2}{3} = \frac{10}{15} \text{ and } \frac{12}{36} = \frac{1}{3}.$$

109. To add fractions with like denominators, add the numerators of the fractions, keeping the same denominator.

Example: $\frac{1}{7} + \frac{2}{7} + \frac{3}{7} = \frac{6}{7}$.

110. To add fractions with different denominators, you must first change all of the fractions to *equivalent fractions* with the same denominator.

Step 1. Find the *lowest (or least) common denominator*, the smallest number divisible by all of the denominators.

Example: If the fractions to be added are $\frac{1}{3}$, $\frac{1}{4}$, and $\frac{5}{6}$, then the lowest common denominator is 12, because 12 is the smallest number that is divisible by 3, 4, and 6.

Step 2. Convert all of the fractions to *equivalent fractions,* each having the lowest common denominator as its denominator. To do this, multiply the numerator of each fraction by the number of times that its denominator goes into the lowest common denominator. The product of this multiplication will be the *new numerator.* The denominator of the equivalent fractions will be the lowest common denominator. (See Step 1 above.)

Example: The lowest common denominator of $\frac{1}{3}$, $\frac{1}{4}$, and $\frac{5}{6}$ is 12. Thus, $\frac{1}{3} = \frac{4}{12}$, because 12 divided by 3 is 4, and 4 times 1 = 4. $\frac{1}{4} = \frac{3}{12}$, because 12 divided by 4 is 3, and 3 times 1 = 3. $\frac{5}{6} = \frac{10}{12}$, because 12 divided by 6 is 2, and 2 times 5 = 10.

Step 3. Now add all of the equivalent fractions by adding the numerators.

Example: $\frac{4}{12} + \frac{3}{12} + \frac{10}{12} = \frac{17}{12}$

Step 4. Reduce the fraction if possible, as shown in Section 108.

Example: Add $\frac{4}{5}$, $\frac{2}{3}$, and $\frac{8}{15}$. The lowest common denominator is 15, because 15 is the smallest number that is divisible by 5, 3, and 15. Then, $\frac{4}{5}$ is equivalent to $\frac{12}{15}$; $\frac{2}{3}$ is equivalent to $\frac{10}{15}$; and $\frac{8}{15}$ remains as $\frac{8}{15}$. Adding these numbers gives us

$\frac{12}{15} + \frac{10}{15} + \frac{8}{15} = \frac{30}{15}$. Both 30 and 15 are divisible by 15, giving us $\frac{2}{1}$, or 2.

111. To *multiply fractions,* follow this procedure:

Step 1. To find the numerator of the product, multiply all the numerators of the fractions being multiplied.

Step 2. To find the denominator of the product, multiply all of the denominators of the fractions being multiplied.

Step 3. Reduce the product.

Example: $\frac{5}{7} \times \frac{2}{15} = \frac{\cancel{5}^{1}}{7} \times \frac{2}{\cancel{15}_{3}} = \frac{2}{21}$.

We reduced by dividing both the numerator and denominator by 5, the common factor.

112. To *divide fractions,* follow this procedure:

Step 1. Invert the divisor. That is, switch the positions of the numerator and denominator in the fraction you are dividing *by.*

Step 2. Replace the division sign with a multiplication sign.

Step 3. Carry out the multiplication indicated.

Step 4. Reduce the product.

Example: Find $\frac{3}{4} \div \frac{7}{8}$. Inverting $\frac{7}{8}$, the divisor, gives us $\frac{8}{7}$. Replacing the division sign with a multiplication sign gives us $\frac{3}{4} \times \frac{8}{7}$. Carrying out the multiplication gives us $\frac{3}{4} \times \frac{8}{7} = \frac{24}{28}$. The fraction $\frac{24}{28}$ may then be reduced to $\frac{6}{7}$ by dividing both the numerator and the denominator by 4.

113. To *multiply decimals,* follow this procedure:

Step 1. Disregard the decimal point. Multiply the factors (the numbers being multiplied) as if they were whole numbers.

Step 2. In each factor, count the number of digits to the *right* of the decimal point. Find the total number of these digits in all the factors. In the product, start at the right and count to the left this (total) number of places. Put the decimal point there.

Example: Multiply 3.8×4.01. First, multiply 38 and 401, getting 15,238. There is a total of 3 digits to the right of the decimal points in the factors. Therefore, the decimal point in the product is placed 3 units to the left of the digit farthest to the right (8).

$$3.8 \times 4.01 = 15.238$$

Example: 0.025×3.6. First, multiply 25×36, getting 900. In the factors, there is a total of 4 digits to the right of the decimal points; therefore, in the product, we place the decimal point 4 units to the left of the digit farthest to the right in 900. However, there are only 3 digits in the product, so we add a 0 to the left of the 9, getting 0900. This makes it possible to place the decimal point correctly, thus: 0.0900, or 0.09. This example illustrates the rule that in the product we add as many zeros as are needed to provide the proper number of digits to the left of the digit farthest to the right.

114. To find a percent of a given quantity:

Step 1. Replace the word "of" with a multiplication sign.

Step 2. Convert the percent to a decimal: drop the percent sign and divide the number by 100. This is done by moving the decimal point two places to the left, adding zeros where necessary.

Examples:
$30\% = 0.30 \quad 2.1\% = 0.021 \quad 78\% = 0.78$

Step 3. Multiply the given quantity by the decimal.

Example: Find 30% of 200.

$$30\% \text{ of } 200 = 30\% \times 200 = 0.30 \times 200 = 60.00$$

Deviations

Estimation problems arise when dealing with approximations, that is, numbers that are not mathematically precise. The error, or *deviation*, in an approximation is a measure of the closeness of that approximation.

115. *Absolute error,* or *absolute deviation,* is the difference between the estimated value and the real value (or between the approximate value and the exact value).

Example: If the actual value of a measurement is 60.2 and we estimate it as 60, then the absolute deviation (absolute error) is $60.2 - 60 = 0.2$.

116. *Fractional error,* or *fractional deviation,* is the ratio of the absolute error to the exact value of the quantity being measured.

Example: If the exact value is 60.2 and the estimated value is 60, then the fractional error is

$$\frac{60.2 - 60}{60.2} = \frac{0.2}{60.2} = \frac{0.2 \times 5}{60.2 \times 5} = \frac{1}{301}$$

117. *Percent error,* or *percent deviation,* is the fractional error expressed as a percent. (See Section 106 on page 149 for the method of converting fractions to percents.)

118. Many business problems, including the calculation of loss, profit, interest, and so forth, are treated as deviation problems. Generally, these problems concern the difference between the original value of a quantity and some new value after taxes, after interest, etc. The following chart shows the relationship between business and estimation problems.

Business Problems	Estimation Problems
original value	= exact value
new value	= approximate value
net profit, net loss, net interest	= absolute error
fractional profit, fractional loss, fractional interest	= fractional error
percent profit, percent loss, percent interest	= percent error

Example: An item that originally cost $50 is resold for $56.

Thus the *net profit* is $56 - 50 = 6$.

The *fractional profit* is $\dfrac{\$56 - \$50}{\$50} = \dfrac{\$6}{\$50} = \dfrac{3}{25}$.

The *percent profit* is equal to the percent equivalent of $\dfrac{3}{25}$, which is 12%. (See Section 106 for converting fractions to percents.)

119. When there are two or more *consecutive changes in value,* remember that the new value of the first change becomes the original value of the second; consequently, successive fractional or percent changes may not be added directly.

    Example: Suppose that a $100 item is reduced by 10% and then by 20%. The first reduction puts the price at $90 (10% of $100 = $10; $100 − $10 = $90). Then, reducing the $90 (the new original value) by 20% gives us $72 (20% of $90 = $18; $90 − $18 = $72). Therefore, it is *not* correct to simply add 10% and 20% and then take 30% of $100.

Ratios and Proportions

120. A *proportion* is an equation stating that two ratios are equal. For example, 3 : 2 = 9 : x and 7 : 4 = a : 15 are proportions. To solve for a variable in a proportion:

    Step 1. First change the ratios to fractions. To do this, remember that $a : b$ is the same as $\frac{a}{b}$, or 1 : 2 is equivalent to $\frac{1}{2}$, or 7 : 4 = a : 15 is the same as $\frac{7}{4} = \frac{a}{15}$.

    Step 2. Now cross-multiply. That is, multiply the numerator of the first fraction by the denominator of the second fraction. Also multiply the denominator of the first fraction by the numerator of the second fraction. Set the first product equal to the second. This rule is sometimes stated as "The product of the means equals the product of the extremes."

    Example: When cross-multiplying in the equation $\frac{3}{2} = \frac{9}{y}$, we get $3 \times y = 2 \times 9$, or $3y = 18$. Dividing by 3, we get y = 6.

    When we cross-multiply in the equation $\frac{a}{2} = \frac{4}{8}$, we get $8a = 8$, and by dividing each side of the equation by 8 to reduce, a = 1.

    Step 3. Solve the resulting equation. This is done algebraically.

    Example: Solve for a in the proportion 7 : a = 6 : 18.

Change the ratios to the fractional relation $\frac{7}{a} = \frac{6}{18}$. Cross-multiply: $7 \times 18 = 6 \times a$, or $126 = 6a$.

Solving for a gives us a = 21.

121. In solving proportions that have units of measurement (feet, seconds, miles, etc.), each ratio must have the same units. For example, if we have the ratio 5 inches : 3 feet, we must convert the 3 feet to 36 inches and then set up the ratio 5 inches : 36 inches, or 5 : 36. We might wish to convert inches to feet. Noting that 1 inch = $\frac{1}{12}$ foot, we get 5 inches : 3 feet = $5\left(\frac{1}{12}\right)$ feet: 3 feet = $\frac{5}{12}$ feet : 3 feet.

    Example: On a blueprint, a rectangle measures 6 inches in width and 9 inches in length. If the actual width of the rectangle is 16 inches, how many feet are there in the length?

    Solution: We set up the proportions, 6 inches : 9 inches = 16 inches : x feet. Since x feet is equal to 12x inches, we substitute this value in the proportion. Thus, 6 inches : 9 inches = 16 inches : 12x inches. Since all of the units are now the same, we may work with the numbers alone. In fractional terms we have $\frac{6}{9} = \frac{16}{12x}$. Cross-multiplication gives us $72x = 144$, and solving for x gives us x = 2. The rectangle is 2 feet long.

Variations

122. In a *variation* problem, you are given a relationship between certain variables. The problem is to determine the change in one variable when one or more of the other variables change.

    Direct Variation (Direct Proportion)
    If x varies directly with y, this means that $\frac{x}{y} = k$ (or x = ky) where k is a constant.

    Example: If the cost of a piece of glass varies directly with the area of the glass, and a piece of glass of 5 square feet costs $20, then how much does a piece of glass of 15 square feet cost?

    Represent the cost of the glass as c and the area of the piece of glass as A. Then we have $\frac{c}{A} = k$.

Now since we are given that a piece of glass of 5 square feet costs \$20, we can write $\frac{20}{5} = k$, and we find $k = 4$.

Let's say a piece of glass of 15 square feet costs \$x. Then we can write $\frac{x}{15} = k$. But we found $k = 4$, so $\frac{x}{15} = 4$ and $x = 60$. \$60 is then the answer.

Inverse Variation (Inverse Proportion)

If x varies inversely with y, this means that $xy = k$ where k is a constant.

Example: If a varies inversely with b, and when $a = 5$, $b = 6$, then what is b when $a = 10$?

We have $ab = k$. Since $a = 5$ and $b = 6$, $5 \times 6 = k = 30$. So if $a = 10$, $10 \times b = k = 30$ and $b = 3$.

Other Variations

Example: In the formula $A = bh$, if b doubles and h triples, what happens to the value of A?

Step 1. Express the new values of the variables in terms of their original values, that is, $b' = 2b$ and $h' = 3h$.

Step 2. Substitute these values in the formula and solve for the desired variable: $A' = b'h' = (2b)(3h) = 6bh$.

Step 3. Express this answer in terms of the original value of the variable, that is, since the new value of A is $6bh$, and the old value of A was bh, we can express this as $A_{new} = 6A_{old}$. The new value of the variable is expressed with a prime mark and the old value of the variable is left as it was. In this problem, the new value of A would be expressed as A' and the old value as A. $A' = 6A$.

Example: If $V = e^3$ and e is doubled, what happens to the value of V?

Solution: Replace e with $2e$. The new value of V is $(2e)^3$. Since this is a new value, V becomes V'. Thus $V' = (2e)^3$, or $8e^3$. Remember, from the original statement of the problem, that $V = e^3$. Using this, we may substitute V for e^3 found in the equation $V' = 8e^3$. The new equation is $V' = 8V$. Therefore, the new value of V is 8 times the old value.

Comparison of Fractions

In *fraction comparison* problems, you are given two or more fractions and are asked to arrange them in increasing or decreasing order, or to select the larger or the smaller. The following rules and suggestions will be very helpful in determining which of two fractions is greater.

123. If fractions A and B have the same denominator, and A has a larger numerator, then fraction A is larger. (We are assuming here, and for the rest of this Refresher Session, that numerators and denominators are positive.)

Example: $\frac{56}{271}$ is greater than $\frac{53}{271}$ because the numerator of the first fraction is greater than the numerator of the second.

124. If fractions A and B have the same numerator, and A has a larger denominator, then fraction A is smaller.

Example: $\frac{37}{256}$ is smaller than $\frac{37}{254}$.

125. If fraction A has a larger numerator and a smaller denominator than fraction B, then fraction A is larger than B.

Example: $\frac{6}{11}$ is larger than $\frac{4}{13}$. (If this does not seem obvious, compare both fractions with $\frac{6}{13}$.)

126. Another method is to convert all of the fractions to equivalent fractions. To do this follow these steps:

Step 1. First find the *lowest common denominator* of the fractions. This is the smallest number that is divisible by all of the denominators of the original fractions. See Section 110 for the method of finding lowest common denominators.

Step 2. The fraction with the greatest numerator is the largest fraction.

127. Still another method is the *conversion to approximating decimals*.

Example: To compare $\frac{5}{9}$ and $\frac{7}{11}$, we might express both as decimals to a few places of accuracy: $\frac{5}{9}$ is approximately equal to 0.555, while $\frac{7}{11}$ is approximately equal to 0.636, so $\frac{7}{11}$ is obviously greater.

To express a fraction as a decimal, divide the numerator by the denominator.

128. If all of the fractions being compared are very close in value to some easy-to-work-with number, such as $\frac{1}{2}$ or 5, you may subtract this number from each of the fractions without changing this order.

    Example: To compare $\frac{151}{75}$ with $\frac{328}{163}$, we notice that both of these fractions are approximately equal to 2. If we subtract 2 (that is, $\frac{150}{75}$ and $\frac{326}{163}$, respectively) from each, we get $\frac{1}{75}$ and $\frac{2}{163}$, respectively. Since $\frac{1}{75}$ (or $\frac{2}{150}$) exceeds $\frac{2}{163}$, we see that $\frac{151}{75}$ must also exceed $\frac{328}{163}$.

    An alternative method of comparing fractions is to change the fractions to their decimal equivalents and then compare the decimals. (See Sections 104 and 127.) You should weigh the relative amount of work and difficulty involved in each method when you face each problem.

129. The following is a quick way of comparing fractions.

    Example: Which is greater, $\frac{3}{8}$ or $\frac{7}{18}$?

    Procedure:

    $$\frac{3}{8} \overset{\text{multiply}}{\underset{\text{multiply}}{\times}} \frac{7}{18}$$

    Multiply the 18 by the 3. We get 54. Put the 54 on the *left* side.

    54

    Now *multiply* the 8 by the 7. We get 56. Put the 56 on the *right* side.

    54   56

    Since 56 > 54 and 56 is on the *right* side, the fraction $\frac{7}{18}$ (which was also originally on the *right* side) is *greater* than the fraction $\frac{3}{8}$ (which was originally on the *left* side).

Example: If $y > x$, which is greater, $\frac{1}{x}$ or $\frac{1}{y}$? (x and y are positive numbers.)

Procedure:

$$\frac{1}{x} \overset{\text{multiply}}{\underset{\text{multiply}}{\times}} \frac{1}{y}$$

Multiply y by 1. We get y. Put y on the left side:

    y

Multiply x by 1. We get x. Put x on the right side:

    y   x

Since $y > x$ (given), $\frac{1}{x}$ (which was originally on the left) is greater than $\frac{1}{y}$ (which was originally on the right).

Example: Which is greater?

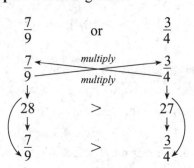

$$\frac{7}{9} \quad \text{or} \quad \frac{3}{4}$$

SESSION 1 PRACTICE TEST

Fractions, Decimals, Percentages, Deviations, Ratios and Proportions, Variations, and Comparison of Fractions

Correct answers and solutions follow this test.

1. Which of the following answers is the sum of the following numbers:

$$2\frac{1}{2}, \frac{21}{4}, 3.350, \frac{1}{8}?$$

(A) 8.225
(B) 9.825
(C) 10.825
(D) 11.225
(E) 12.350

A B C D E
○ ○ ○ ○ ○

2. A chemist was preparing a solution that should have included 35 milligrams of a chemical. If she actually used 36.4 milligrams, what was her percentage error (to the nearest 0.01%)?

(A) 0.04%
(B) 0.05%
(C) 1.40%
(D) 3.85%
(E) 4.00%

A B C D E
○ ○ ○ ○ ○

3. A retailer buys a popular brand of athletic shoe from the wholesaler for $75. He then marks up the price by $\frac{1}{3}$ and sells each pair at a discount of 20%. What profit does the retailer make on each pair of athletic shoes?

(A) $5.00
(B) $6.67
(C) $7.50
(D) $10.00
(E) $13.33

A B C D E
○ ○ ○ ○ ○

4. On a blueprint, $\frac{1}{4}$ inch represents 1 foot. If a window is supposed to be 56 inches wide, how wide would its representation be on the blueprint?

(A) $1\frac{1}{6}$ inches
(B) $4\frac{2}{3}$ inches
(C) $9\frac{1}{3}$ inches
(D) 14 inches
(E) $18\frac{2}{3}$ inches

A B C D E
○ ○ ○ ○ ○

5. If the radius of a circle is increased by 50%, what will be the percent increase in the circumference of the circle? (Circumference $= 2\pi r$)

(A) 25%
(B) 50%
(C) 100%
(D) 150%
(E) 225%

A B C D E
○ ○ ○ ○ ○

6. Which of the following fractions is the greatest?

(A) $\frac{403}{134}$
(B) $\frac{79}{26}$
(C) $\frac{527}{176}$
(D) $\frac{221}{73}$
(E) $\frac{99}{34}$

A B C D E
○ ○ ○ ○ ○

7. A store usually sells a certain item at a 40% profit. One week the store has a sale, during which the item is sold for 10% less than the usual price. During the sale, what is the percent profit the store makes on each of these items?

(A) 4%
(B) 14%
(C) 26%
(D) 30%
(E) 36%

A B C D E
○ ○ ○ ○ ○

8. What is 0.05 percent of 6.5?

(A) 0.00325
(B) 0.013
(C) 0.325
(D) 1.30
(E) 130.0

A B C D E
○ ○ ○ ○ ○

9. What is the value of $\dfrac{\left(3\frac{1}{2} + 3\frac{1}{4} + 3\frac{1}{4} + 3\frac{1}{2}\right)}{4\frac{1}{2}}$?

(A) $1\frac{1}{2}$
(B) $2\frac{1}{4}$
(C) 3
(D) $3\frac{1}{4}$
(E) $3\frac{3}{8}$

A B C D E
○ ○ ○ ○ ○

10. If 8 loggers can chop down 28 trees in one day, how many trees can 20 loggers chop down in one day?

(A) 28 trees
(B) 160 trees
(C) 70 trees
(D) 100 trees
(E) 80 trees

A B C D E
○ ○ ○ ○ ○

11. What is the product of the following fractions: $\dfrac{3}{100}$, $\dfrac{15}{49}$, $\dfrac{7}{9}$?

(A) $\dfrac{215}{44,100}$
(B) $\dfrac{1}{140}$
(C) $\dfrac{1}{196}$
(D) $\dfrac{25}{158}$
(E) $\dfrac{3}{427}$

A B C D E
○ ○ ○ ○ ○

12. In calculating the height of an object, Mrs. Downs mistakenly observed the height to be 72 cm instead of 77 cm. What was her percentage error (to the nearest hundredth of a percent)?

(A) 6.49%
(B) 6.69%
(C) 6.89%
(D) 7.09%
(E) 7.19%

A B C D E
○ ○ ○ ○ ○

13. A retailer buys 1,440 dozen pens at $2.50 a dozen and then sells them at a price of 25¢ apiece. What is the total profit after the retailer sells all the pens?

(A) $60.00
(B) $72.00
(C) $720.00
(D) $874.00
(E) $8,740.00

A B C D E
○ ○ ○ ○ ○

14. On a map, 1 inch represents 1,000 miles. If the area of a country is actually 16 million square miles, what is the area of the country's representation on the map?

(A) 4 square inches
(B) 16 square inches
(C) 4,000 square inches
(D) 16,000 square inches
(E) 4,000,000 square inches

A B C D E
○ ○ ○ ○ ○

15. The formula for the volume of a cone is $V = \frac{1}{3}\pi r^2 h$. If the radius (r) is doubled and the height (h) is divided by 3, what will be the ratio of the new volume to the original volume?

    (A) 2 : 3
    (B) 3 : 2
    (C) 4 : 3
    (D) 3 : 4
    (E) none of these

    A B C D E
    ○ ○ ○ ○ ○

16. Which of the following fractions has the smallest value?

    (A) $\frac{34.7}{163}$

    (B) $\frac{125}{501}$

    (C) $\frac{173}{700}$

    (D) $\frac{10.9}{42.7}$

    (E) $\frac{907}{3,715}$

    A B C D E
    ○ ○ ○ ○ ○

17. Mr. Cutler usually makes a 45% profit on every flat-screen TV he sells. During a sale, he reduces his margin of profit to 40%, while his sales increase by 10%. What is the ratio of his new total profit to the original profit?

    (A) 1 : 1
    (B) 9 : 8
    (C) 9 : 10
    (D) 11 : 10
    (E) 44 : 45

    A B C D E
    ○ ○ ○ ○ ○

18. What is 1.3 percent of 0.26?

    (A) 0.00338
    (B) 0.00500
    (C) 0.200
    (D) 0.338
    (E) 0.500

    A B C D E
    ○ ○ ○ ○ ○

19. What is the average of the following numbers: $3.2, \frac{47}{12}, \frac{10}{3}$?

    (A) 3.55

    (B) $\frac{10}{3}$

    (C) $\frac{103}{30}$

    (D) $\frac{209}{60}$

    (E) $\frac{1,254}{120}$

    A B C D E
    ○ ○ ○ ○ ○

20. If it takes 16 faucets 10 hours to fill 8 tubs, how long will it take 12 faucets to fill 9 tubs?

    (A) 10 hours
    (B) 12 hours
    (C) 13 hours
    (D) 14 hours
    (E) 15 hours

    A B C D E
    ○ ○ ○ ○ ○

21. If the 8% tax on a sale amounts to 96¢, what is the final price (tax included) of the item?

    (A) $1.20
    (B) $2.16
    (C) $6.36
    (D) $12.00
    (E) $12.96

    A B C D E
    ○ ○ ○ ○ ○

22. In a certain class, 40% of the students are girls, and 20% of the girls wear glasses. What percent of the children in the class are girls who wear glasses?

    (A) 6%
    (B) 8%
    (C) 20%
    (D) 60%
    (E) 80%

    A B C D E
    ○ ○ ○ ○ ○

23. What is 1.2% of 0.5?

    (A) 0.0006
    (B) 0.006
    (C) 0.06
    (D) 0.6
    (E) 6.0

    A B C D E
    ○ ○ ○ ○ ○

24. Which of the following quantities is the largest?

    (A) $\frac{275}{369}$

    (B) $\frac{134}{179}$

    (C) $\frac{107}{144}$

    (D) $\frac{355}{476}$

    (E) $\frac{265}{352}$

    A B C D E
    ○ ○ ○ ○ ○

25. If the length of a rectangle is increased by 120%, and its width is decreased by 20%, what happens to the area of the rectangle?

    (A) It decreases by 4%.
    (B) It remains the same.
    (C) It increases by 24%.
    (D) It increases by 76%.
    (E) It increases by 100%.

    A B C D E
    ○ ○ ○ ○ ○

26. A merchant buys an old carpet for $25.00. He spends $15.00 to have it restored to good condition and then sells the rug for $50.00. What is the percent profit on his total investment?

    (A) 20%
    (B) 25%
    (C) 40%
    (D) $66\frac{2}{3}$%
    (E) 100%

    A B C D E
    ○ ○ ○ ○ ○

27. Of the following sets of fractions, which one is arranged in *decreasing* order?

    (A) $\frac{5}{9}, \frac{7}{11}, \frac{3}{5}, \frac{2}{3}, \frac{10}{13}$

    (B) $\frac{2}{3}, \frac{3}{5}, \frac{7}{11}, \frac{5}{9}, \frac{10}{13}$

    (C) $\frac{3}{5}, \frac{5}{9}, \frac{7}{11}, \frac{10}{13}, \frac{2}{3}$

    (D) $\frac{10}{13}, \frac{2}{3}, \frac{7}{11}, \frac{3}{5}, \frac{5}{9}$

    (E) none of these

    A B C D E
    ○ ○ ○ ○ ○

28. If the diameter of a circle doubles, the circumference of the larger circle is how many times the circumference of the original circle? (Circumference $= \pi d$)

    (A) π
    (B) 2π
    (C) 1
    (D) 2
    (E) 4

    A B C D E
    ○ ○ ○ ○ ○

29. The scale on a set of plans is 1 : 8. If a man reads a certain measurement on the plans as 5.6″ instead of 6.0″, what will be the resulting approximate percent error on the full-size model?

    (A) 6.7%
    (B) 7.1%
    (C) 12.5%
    (D) 53.6%
    (E) 56.8%

    A B C D E
    ○ ○ ○ ○ ○

30. G&R Electronics bought 2 dozen megapixel digital cameras for $300 each. The company sold two-thirds of them at a 25% profit but was forced to take a 30% loss on the rest. What was the total profit (or loss) on the digital cameras?

    (A) a loss of $200
    (B) a loss of $15
    (C) no profit or loss
    (D) a profit of $20
    (E) a profit of $480

    A B C D E
    ○ ○ ○ ○ ○

31. The sum of $\frac{1}{2}, \frac{1}{3}, \frac{1}{8}, \frac{1}{15}$ is:

   (A) $\frac{9}{8}$

   (B) $\frac{16}{15}$

   (C) $\frac{41}{40}$

   (D) $\frac{65}{64}$

   (E) $\frac{121}{120}$

32. What is $\frac{2}{3}$% of 90?

   (A) 0.006
   (B) 0.06
   (C) 0.6
   (D) 6.0
   (E) 60

   A B C D E
   ○ ○ ○ ○ ○

33. Lucas borrows $360. If he pays it back in 12 monthly installments of $31.50, what is the interest rate?

   (A) 1.5%
   (B) 4.5%
   (C) 10%
   (D) 5%
   (E) 7.5%

   A B C D E
   ○ ○ ○ ○ ○

34. A merchant marks up a certain lighting fixture 30% above original cost. Then the merchant gives a customer a loyalty discount of 15%. If the final selling price for the lighting fixture was $86.19, what was the original cost?

   (A) $66.30
   (B) $73.26
   (C) $78.00
   (D) $99.12
   (E) $101.40

   A B C D E
   ○ ○ ○ ○ ○

35. In a certain recipe, $2\frac{1}{4}$ cups of flour are called for to make a cake that serves 6. If Mrs. Jenkins wants to use the same recipe to make a cake for 8, how many cups of flour must she use?

   (A) $2\frac{1}{3}$ cups

   (B) $2\frac{3}{4}$ cups

   (C) 3 cups

   (D) $3\frac{3}{8}$ cups

   (E) 4 cups

   A B C D E
   ○ ○ ○ ○ ○

36. If 10 people can survive for 24 days on 15 cans of rations, how many cans will be needed for 8 people to survive for 36 days?

   (A) 15 cans
   (B) 16 cans
   (C) 17 cans
   (D) 18 cans
   (E) 19 cans

   A B C D E
   ○ ○ ○ ○ ○

37. If, on a map, $\frac{1}{2}$ inch represents 1 mile, how long is a border whose representation is $1\frac{1}{15}$ feet long?

   (A) $2\frac{1}{30}$ miles

   (B) $5\frac{1}{15}$ miles

   (C) $12\frac{4}{5}$ miles

   (D) $25\frac{3}{5}$ miles

   (E) $51\frac{1}{5}$ miles

   A B C D E
   ○ ○ ○ ○ ○

38. In the formula $e = hf$, if e is doubled and f is halved, what happens to the value of h?

    (A) h remains the same.
    (B) h is doubled.
    (C) h is divided by 4.
    (D) h is multiplied by 4.
    (E) h is halved.

    A B C D E
    ○ ○ ○ ○ ○

39. Which of the following expresses the ratio of 3 inches to 2 yards?

    (A) $3 : 2$
    (B) $3 : 9$
    (C) $3 : 12$
    (D) $3 : 24$
    (E) $3 : 72$

    A B C D E
    ○ ○ ○ ○ ○

40. If it takes Mark twice as long to earn $6.00 as it takes Carl to earn $4.00, what is the ratio of Mark's pay per hour to Carl's pay per hour?

    (A) $2 : 1$
    (B) $3 : 1$
    (C) $3 : 2$
    (D) $3 : 4$
    (E) $4 : 3$

    A B C D E
    ○ ○ ○ ○ ○

41. What is the lowest common denominator of the following set of fractions:
$$\frac{1}{6}, \frac{13}{27}, \frac{4}{5}, \frac{3}{10}, \frac{2}{15}?$$

    (A) 27
    (B) 54
    (C) 135
    (D) 270
    (E) none of these

    A B C D E
    ○ ○ ○ ○ ○

42. The average grade on a certain examination was 85. Raul scored 90 on the same examination. What was Raul's *percent* deviation from the average score (to the nearest tenth of a percent)?

    (A) 5.0%
    (B) 5.4%
    (C) 5.5%
    (D) 5.8%
    (E) 5.9%

    A B C D E
    ○ ○ ○ ○ ○

43. Successive discounts of 20% and 12% are equivalent to a single discount of:

    (A) 16.0%
    (B) 29.6%
    (C) 31.4%
    (D) 32.0%
    (E) 33.7%

    A B C D E
    ○ ○ ○ ○ ○

44. On a blueprint of a park, 1 foot represents $\frac{1}{2}$ mile. If an error of $\frac{1}{2}$ inch is made in reading the blueprint, what will be the corresponding error on the actual park? (1 mile = 5,280 feet)

    (A) 110 feet
    (B) 220 feet
    (C) 330 feet
    (D) 440 feet
    (E) none of these

    A B C D E
    ○ ○ ○ ○ ○

45. A manufacturer decreases the width of its cereal packaging from 2 inches to 1 inch. If the original packaging measured 10 inches by 2 inches by 12 inches, which statement is true about the volume of the new packaging?

    (A) It decreased by 100%.
    (B) It decreased by 50%.
    (C) It decreased by 16.7%.
    (D) It decreased by 8.3%.
    (E) It remained the same.

    A B C D E
    ○ ○ ○ ○ ○

46. Which of the following fractions has the smallest value?

    (A) $\frac{6,043}{2,071}$

    (B) $\frac{4,290}{1,463}$

    (C) $\frac{5,107}{1,772}$

    (D) $\frac{8,935}{2,963}$

    (E) $\frac{8,016}{2,631}$

    A B C D E
    ◯ ◯ ◯ ◯ ◯

47. A certain company increased its prices by 30% during 2016. Then, in 2017, it was forced to cut back its prices by 20%. What was the net change in price?

    (A) −4%
    (B) −2%
    (C) +2%
    (D) +4%
    (E) 0%

    A B C D E
    ◯ ◯ ◯ ◯ ◯

48. What is 0.04%, expressed as a fraction?

    (A) $\frac{2}{5}$

    (B) $\frac{1}{25}$

    (C) $\frac{4}{25}$

    (D) $\frac{1}{250}$

    (E) $\frac{1}{2,500}$

    A B C D E
    ◯ ◯ ◯ ◯ ◯

49. What is the value of the fraction

    $$\frac{16 + 12 + 88 + 34 + 66 + 21 + 79 + 11 + 89}{25}?$$

    (A) 15.04
    (B) 15.44
    (C) 16.24
    (D) 16.64
    (E) none of these

    A B C D E
    ◯ ◯ ◯ ◯ ◯

50. If coconuts are twice as expensive as bananas, and bananas are one-third as expensive as grapefruits, what is the ratio of the price of one coconut to one grapefruit?

    (A) 2 : 3
    (B) 3 : 2
    (C) 6 : 1
    (D) 1 : 6
    (E) none of these

    A B C D E
    ◯ ◯ ◯ ◯ ◯

Answer Key for Session 1 Practice Test

1. D	14. B	27. D	39. E
2. E	15. C	28. D	40. D
3. A	16. A	29. A	41. D
4. A	17. E	30. E	42. E
5. B	18. A	31. C	43. B
6. B	19. D	32. C	44. A
7. C	20. E	33. D	45. B
8. A	21. E	34. C	46. C
9. C	22. B	35. C	47. D
10. C	23. B	36. D	48. E
11. B	24. E	37. D	49. D
12. A	25. D	38. D	50. A
13. C	26. B		

Answers and Solutions for Session 1 Practice Test

1. Choice D is correct. First, convert the fractions to decimals, as the final answer must be expressed in decimals: $2.500 + 5.250 + 3.350 + 0.125 = 11.225$. (Refreshers 104, 127, 128)

2. Choice E is correct. This is an estimation problem. Note that the correct value was 35, not 36.4. Thus the *real* value is 35 mg and the *estimated* value is 36.4 mg. Thus, percent error is equal to $(36.4 - 35) \div 35$, or 0.04, expressed as a percent, which is 4%. (Refreshers 115, 116, 117)

3. Choice A is correct. This is a business problem. First, the retailer marks up the wholesale price by $\frac{1}{3}$, so the marked-up price equals $75(1 + \frac{1}{3})$, or $100; then it is reduced 20% from the $100 price, leaving a final price of $80. Thus, the net profit on each pair of athletic shoes is $5.00. (Refresher 118)

4. Choice A is correct. Here we have a proportion problem: length on blueprint : actual length $= \frac{1}{4}$ inch : 1 foot. The second ratio is the same as 1 : 48, because 1 foot $=$ 12 inches. In the problem the actual length is 56 inches, so that if the length on the blueprint equals x, we have the proportion $x : 56 = 1 : 48; \frac{x}{56} = \frac{1}{48}$. $48x = 56$; so $x = \frac{56}{48}$, or $1\frac{1}{6}$ inches. (Refresher 120)

5. Choice B is correct. $C = 2\pi r$ (where r is the radius of the circle, and C is its circumference). The new value of r, r', is $(1.5)r$ since r is increased by 50%. Using this value of r', we get the new C, $C' = 2\pi r' = 2\pi(1.5)r = (1.5)2\pi r$. Remembering that $C = 2\pi r$, we get that $C' = (1.5)C$. Since the new circumference is 1.5 times the original, there is an increase of 50%. (Refresher 122)

6. Choice B is correct. In this numerical comparison problem, it is helpful to realize that all of these fractions are approximately equal to 3. If we subtract 3 from each of the fractions, we get $\frac{1}{134}$, $\frac{1}{26}$, $-\frac{1}{176}$, $\frac{2}{73}$, and $-\frac{3}{34}$, respectively. Clearly, the greatest of these is $\frac{1}{26}$, which therefore shows the greatest of the five given fractions. Another method of solving this type of numerical comparison problem is to convert the fractions to decimals by dividing the numerator by the denominator. (Refreshers 127, 128)

7. Choice C is correct. This is another business problem, this time asking for percentage profit. Let the original price be P. A 40% profit means that the store will sell the item for $100\%P + 40\%P$, which is equal to $140\%P$, which in turn is equal to $\left(\frac{140}{100}\right)P = 1.4P$. Then the marked-up price will be $1.4(P)$. Ten percent is taken off this price, to yield a final price of $(0.90)(1.40)(P)$, or $(1.26)(P)$. Thus, the fractional increase was 0.26, so the percent increase was 26%. (Refresher 118)

8. Choice A is correct. Remember that in the phrase "percent of," the "of" may be replaced by a multiplication sign. Thus, $0.05\% \times 6.5 = 0.0005 \times 6.5$, so the answer is 0.00325. (Refresher 114)

9. Choice C is correct. First, add the fractions in the numerator to obtain $13\frac{1}{2}$. Then divide $13\frac{1}{2}$ by $4\frac{1}{2}$. If you cannot see immediately that the answer is 3, you can convert the halves to decimals and divide, or you can express the fractions in terms of their common denominator, thus: $13\frac{1}{2} = \frac{27}{2}$; $4\frac{1}{2} = \frac{9}{2}$; $\frac{27}{2} \div \frac{9}{2} = \frac{27}{2} \times \frac{2}{9} = \frac{54}{18} = 3$. (Refreshers 110, 112)

10. Choice C is correct. This is a proportion problem. If x is the number of loggers needed to chop down 20 trees, then we form the proportion 8 loggers : 28 trees = 20 loggers : x trees, or $\frac{8}{28} = \frac{20}{x}$. Solving for x, we get $x = \frac{(28)(20)}{8}$, or $x = 70$.
(Refresher 120)

11. Choice B is correct. $\frac{3}{100} \times \frac{15}{49} \times \frac{7}{9} = \frac{3 \times 15 \times 7}{100 \times 49 \times 9}$. Canceling 7 out of the numerator and denominator gives us $\frac{3 \times 15}{100 \times 7 \times 9}$. Canceling 5 out of the numerator and denominator gives us $\frac{3 \times 3}{20 \times 7 \times 9}$. Finally, canceling 9 out of both numerator and denominator gives us $\frac{1}{20 \times 7}$, or $\frac{1}{140}$.
(Refresher 111)

12. Choice A is correct. Percent error = (absolute error) ÷ (correct measurement) = 5 ÷ 77 = 0.0649 (approximately) × 100 = 6.49%.
(Refreshers 115, 116, 117)

13. Choice C is correct. Profit on each dozen pens = selling price − cost = 12(25¢) − $2.50 = $3.00 − $2.50 = 50¢ profit per dozen. Total profit = profit per dozen × number of dozens = 50¢ × 1,440 = $720.00.
(Refresher 118)

14. Choice B is correct. If 1 inch represents 1,000 miles, then 1 square inch represents 1,000 miles squared, or 1,000,000 square miles. Thus, the area would be represented by 16 squares of this size, or 16 square inches.
(Refresher 120)

15. Choice C is correct. Let V' equal the new volume. Then if $r' = 2r$ is the new radius, and $h' = \frac{h}{3}$ is the new height, $V' = \frac{1}{3}\pi(r')^2(h') = \frac{1}{3}\pi(2r)^2\left(\frac{h}{3}\right) = \frac{4}{9}\pi r^2 h = \frac{4}{3}V$, so the ratio $V' : V$ is equal to 4 : 3.
(Refresher 122)

16. Choice A is correct. Using a calculator, we get: $\frac{34.7}{163} = 0.2128$ for Choice A; $\frac{125}{501} = 0.2495$ for Choice B; $\frac{173}{700} = 0.2471$ for Choice C; $\frac{10.9}{42.7} = 0.2552$ for Choice D; and $\frac{907}{3,715} = 0.2441$ for Choice E. Choice A is the smallest value.
(Refreshers 104, 127)

17. Choice E is correct. Let N = the original cost of a flat-screen TV. Then, original profit = 45% × N. New profit = 40% × 110%N = 44% × N. Thus, the ratio of new profit to original profit is 44 : 45.
(Refresher 118)

18. Choice A is correct.
1.3% × 0.26 = 0.013 × 0.26 = 0.00338.
(Refresher 114)

19. Choice D is correct. Average = $\frac{1}{3}\left(3.2 + \frac{47}{12} + \frac{10}{3}\right)$. The decimal $3.2 = \frac{320}{100} = \frac{16}{5}$, and the lowest common denominator of the three fractions is 60, so $\frac{16}{5} = \frac{192}{60}, \frac{47}{12} = \frac{235}{60}$, and $\frac{10}{3} = \frac{200}{60}$. Then, $\frac{1}{3}\left(\frac{192}{60} + \frac{235}{60} + \frac{200}{60}\right) = \frac{1}{3}\left(\frac{627}{60}\right) = \frac{209}{60}$.
(Refreshers 101, 105, 109)

20. Choice E is correct. This is an inverse proportion. If it takes 16 faucets 10 hours to fill 8 tubs, then it takes 1 faucet 160 hours to fill 8 tubs (16 faucets : 1 faucet = x hours : 10 hours; $\frac{16}{1} = \frac{x}{10}$; $x = 160$).

If it takes 1 faucet 160 hours to fill 8 tubs, then (dividing by 8) it takes 1 faucet 20 hours to fill 1 tub. If it takes 1 faucet 20 hours to fill 1 tub, then it takes 1 faucet 180 hours (9 × 20 hours) to fill 9 tubs. If it takes 1 faucet 180 hours to fill 9 tubs, then it takes 12 faucets $\frac{180}{12}$, or 15 hours, to fill 9 tubs.
(Refresher 120)

21. Choice E is correct. Let P be the original price. Then $0.08P = 96$¢, so that $8P = \$96$, or $P = \$12$. Adding the tax, which equals 96¢, we obtain our final price of $12.96.
(Refresher 118)

22. Choice B is correct. The number of girls who wear glasses is 20% of 40% of the children in the class. Thus, the indicated operation is multiplication; 20% × 40% = 0.20 × 0.40 = 0.08 = 8%.
(Refresher 114)

23. Choice B is correct.
1.2% × 0.5 = 0.012 × 0.5 = 0.006.
(Refresher 114)

24. Choice E is correct. Using a calculator to find the answer to three decimal places, we get: $\frac{275}{369} = 0.745$ for Choice A; $\frac{134}{179} = 0.749$ for Choice B; $\frac{107}{144} = 0.743$ for Choice C; $\frac{355}{476} = 0.746$ for Choice D;

$\frac{265}{352} = 0.753$ for Choice E. Choice E is the largest value. **(Refreshers 104, 127)**

25. Choice D is correct. Area = length × width. The new area will be equal to the new length × the new width. The new length = (100% + 120%) × old length = 220% × old length = $\frac{220}{100}$ × old length = 2.2 × old length. The new width = (100% − 20%) × old width = 80% × old width = $\frac{80}{100}$ × old width = 0.8 × old width. The new area = new width × new length = 2.2 × 0.8 × old length × old width. So the new area = 1.76 × old area, which is 176% of the old area. This is an increase of 76% from the original area. **(Refresher 122)**

26. Choice B is correct. Total cost to merchant = $25.00 + $15.00 = $40.00.
Profit = selling price − cost = $50 − $40 = $10.
Percent profit = profit ÷ cost = $10 ÷ $40 = 25%. **(Refresher 118)**

27. Choice D is correct. We can convert the fractions to decimals or to fractions with a lowest common denominator. Inspection will show that all sets of fractions contain the same members; therefore, if we convert one set to decimals or find the lowest common denominator for one set, we can use our results for all sets. Converting a fraction to a decimal involves only one operation, a single division, whereas converting to the lowest common denominator involves a multiplication, which must be followed by a division and a multiplication to change each fraction to one with the lowest common denominator. Thus, conversion to decimals is often the simpler method: $\frac{10}{13} = 0.769$; $\frac{2}{3} = 0.666$; $\frac{7}{11} = 0.636$; $\frac{3}{5} = 0.600$; $\frac{5}{9} = 0.555$.
However, in this case there is an even simpler method. Convert two of the fractions to equivalent fractions: $\frac{3}{5} = \frac{6}{10}$ and $\frac{2}{3} = \frac{8}{12}$. We now have $\frac{5}{9}$, $\frac{6}{10}$, $\frac{7}{11}$, $\frac{8}{12}$, and $\frac{10}{13}$. Remember this rule: When the numerator and denominator of a fraction are both positive, adding 1 to both will bring the value of the fraction closer to 1. (For example, $\frac{3}{4} = \frac{2+1}{3+1}$, so $\frac{3}{4}$ is closer to 1 than $\frac{2}{3}$ and is therefore the

greater fraction.) Thus we see that $\frac{5}{9}$ is less than $\frac{6}{10}$, which is less than $\frac{7}{11}$, which is less than $\frac{8}{12}$, which is less than $\frac{9}{13}$. $\frac{9}{13}$ is obviously less than $\frac{10}{13}$, so $\frac{10}{13}$ must be the greatest fraction. Thus, in decreasing order, the fractions are $\frac{10}{13}$, $\frac{2}{3}$, $\frac{7}{11}$, $\frac{3}{5}$, and $\frac{5}{9}$. This method is a great time-saver once you become accustomed to it. **(Refresher 104)**

28. Choice D is correct. The formula governing this situation is $C = \pi d$, where C = circumference and d = diameter. Thus, if the new diameter is $d' = 2d$, then the new circumference is $C' = \pi d' = 2\pi d = 2C$. Thus, the new, larger circle has a circumference twice that of the original circle. **(Refresher 122)**

29. Choice A is correct. The most important feature of this problem is recognizing that the scale does not affect percent (or fractional) error, since it simply results in multiplying the numerator and denominator of a fraction by the same factor. Thus, we need only calculate the original percent error. Although it would not be incorrect to calculate the full-scale percent error, it would be time-consuming and might result in unnecessary errors. Absolute error = 0.4″. Actual measurement = 6.0″. Therefore, percent error = (absolute error ÷ actual measurement) × 100% = $\frac{0.4}{6.0}$ × 100%, which equals 6.7% (approximately). **(Refresher 117)**

30. Choice E is correct. Total cost = number of cameras × cost of each = 24 × $300 = $7,200.
Revenue = (number sold at 25% profit × price at 25% profit) + (number sold at 30% loss × price at 30% loss)
= (16 × $375) + (8 × $210) = $6,000 + $1,680 = $7,680.
Profit = revenue − cost = $7,680 − $7,200 = $480. **(Refresher 118)**

31. Choice C is correct. $\frac{1}{2} + \frac{1}{3} + \frac{1}{8} + \frac{1}{15} = \frac{60}{120} + \frac{40}{120} + \frac{15}{120} + \frac{8}{120} = \frac{123}{120} = \frac{41}{40}$. **(Refresher 110)**

32. Choice C is correct. $\frac{2}{3}\% \times 90 = \frac{2}{300} \times 90 = \frac{180}{300} = \frac{6}{10} = 0.6$. **(Refresher 114)**

33. Choice D is correct. If Lucas makes 12 payments of $31.50, he pays back a total of $378.00. Since the loan is for $360.00, his net interest is $18.00. Therefore, the rate of interest is $\dfrac{\$18.00}{\$360.00}$, which can be reduced to 0.05, or 5%. (Refresher 118)

34. Choice C is correct. Final selling price = 85% × 130% × cost = 1.105 × cost. Thus, $86.19 = 1.105$C$, where C = cost. C = $86.19 ÷ 1.105 = $78.00 (exactly). (Refresher 118)

35. Choice C is correct. If x is the amount of flour needed for 8 people, then we can set up the proportion $2\dfrac{1}{4}$ cups : 6 people = x : 8 people. Solving for x gives us $x = \dfrac{8}{6} \times 2\dfrac{1}{4}$ or $\dfrac{8}{6} \times \dfrac{9}{4} = 3$. (Refresher 120)

36. Choice D is correct. If 10 people can survive for 24 days on 15 cans, then 1 person can survive for 240 days on 15 cans. If 1 person can survive for 240 days on 15 cans, then 1 person can survive for $\dfrac{240}{15}$, or 16 days, on 1 can. If 1 person can survive for 16 days on 1 can, then 8 people can survive for $\dfrac{16}{8}$, or 2 days, on 1 can. If 8 people can survive for 2 days on 1 can, then for 36 days 8 people need $\dfrac{36}{2}$, or 18 cans, to survive. (Refresher 120)

37. Choice D is correct. $1\dfrac{1}{15}$ feet = $1\dfrac{1}{15} \times 12$ inches = $\dfrac{16}{15} \times 12$ inches = 12.8 inches. So we have a proportion, $\dfrac{\frac{1}{2} \text{ inch}}{1 \text{ mile}} = \dfrac{12.8 \text{ inches}}{x \text{ miles}}$. Cross-multiplying, we get $\dfrac{1}{2}x = 12.8$, so $x = 25.6 = 25\dfrac{3}{5}$. (Refresher 120)

38. Choice D is correct. If $e = hf$, then $h = \dfrac{e}{f}$. If e is doubled and f is halved, then the new value of h, $h' = \left(\dfrac{2e}{\frac{1}{2}f}\right)$. Multiplying the numerator and denominator by 2 gives us $h' = \dfrac{4e}{f}$. Since $h = \dfrac{e}{f}$ and $h' = \dfrac{4e}{f}$ we see that $h' = 4h$. This is the same as saying that h is multiplied by 4. (Refresher 122)

39. Choice E is correct. 3 inches : 2 yards = 3 inches : 72 inches = 3 : 72. (Refresher 121)

40. Choice D is correct. If Carl and Mark work for the same length of time, then Carl will earn $8.00 for every $6.00 Mark earns (since in the time Mark can earn one $6.00 wage, Carl can earn *two* $4.00 wages). Thus, their hourly wage rates are in the ratio $6.00 (Mark) : $8.00 (Carl) = 3 : 4. (Refresher 120)

41. Choice D is correct. The lowest common denominator is the smallest number that is divisible by all of the denominators. Thus we are looking for the smallest number that is divisible by 6, 27, 5, 10, and 15. The smallest number that is divisible by 6 and 27 is 54. The smallest number that is divisible by 54 and 5 is 270. Since 270 is divisible by 10 and 15 also, it is the lowest common denominator. (Refreshers 110, 126)

42. Choice E is correct. Percent deviation = $\dfrac{\text{absolute deviation}}{\text{average score}} \times 100\%$. Absolute deviation = Raul's score − average score = 90 − 85 = 5. Percent deviation = $\dfrac{5}{85} \times 100\% = 500\% \div 85 = $ 5.88% (approximately). 5.88% is closer to 5.9% than to 5.8%, so 5.9% is correct. (Refresher 117)

43. Choice B is correct. If we discount 20% and then 12%, we are, in effect, taking 88% of 80% of the original price. Since "of" represents multiplication, when we deal with percent we can multiply 88% × 80% = 70.4%. This is a deduction of 29.6% from the original price. (Refreshers 119, 114)

44. Choice A is correct. This is a simple proportion: $\dfrac{1 \text{ foot}}{\frac{1}{2} \text{ mile}} = \dfrac{\frac{1}{2} \text{ inch}}{x}$. Our first step must be to convert all these measurements to one unit. The most logical unit is the one our answer will take—feet. Thus, $\dfrac{1 \text{ foot}}{2{,}640 \text{ feet}} = \dfrac{\frac{1}{24} \text{ foot}}{x}$. (1 mile equals 5,280 feet.) Solving for x, we find $x = \dfrac{2{,}640}{24}$ feet = 110 feet. (Refreshers 120, 121)

45. Choice B is correct. The original volume is $10 \times 2 \times 12 = 240$ cubic inches. The new width is 1 inch, so the new volume is $10 \times 1 \times 12 = 120$ cubic inches. 120 is $\frac{1}{2}$ of 240, and $\frac{1}{2} = 50\%$. The volume decreased by 50%. (Refreshers 122, 106)

46. Choice C is correct. Using a calculator, we get: $\frac{6,043}{2,071} = 2.9179$ for Choice A; $\frac{4,290}{1,463} = 2.9323$ for Choice B; $\frac{5,107}{1,772} = 2.8820$ for Choice C; $\frac{8,935}{2,963} = 3.0155$ for Choice D; and $\frac{8,016}{2,631} = 3.0467$ for Choice E. Choice C has the smallest value. (Refreshers 104, 127)

47. Choice D is correct. Let's say that the price was $100 during 2016. 30% of $100 = $30, so the new price in 2016 was $130. In 2017, the company cut back its prices 20%, so the new price in 2017 =
$$\$130 - \left(\frac{20}{100}\right)\$130 =$$
$$\$130 - \left(\frac{1}{5}\right)\$130 =$$
$$\$130 - \$26 = \$104.$$
The net change is $104 - $100 = $4.
$$\frac{\$4}{\$100} = 4\% \text{ increase.}$$ (Refresher 118)

48. Choice E is correct. $0.04\% = \frac{0.04}{100} = \frac{4}{10,000} = \frac{1}{2,500}$. (Refresher 107)

49. Choice D is correct. Before adding you should examine the numbers to be added. They form pairs, like this: $16 + (12 + 88) + (34 + 66) + (21 + 79) + (11 + 89)$, which equals $16 + 100 + 100 + 100 + 100 = 416$. Dividing 416 by 25, we obtain $16\frac{16}{25}$, which equals 16.64. (Refresher 112)

50. Choice A is correct. We can set up a proportion as follows:
$$\frac{1 \text{ coconut}}{1 \text{ banana}} = \frac{2}{1}, \frac{1 \text{ banana}}{1 \text{ grapefruit}} = \frac{1}{3},$$ so by multiplying the two equations together
$$\left(\frac{1 \text{ coconut}}{1 \text{ banana}} \times \frac{1 \text{ banana}}{1 \text{ grapefruit}} = \frac{2}{1} \times \frac{1}{3}\right)$$ and canceling the bananas and the 1's in the numerators and denominators, we get: $\frac{1 \text{ coconut}}{1 \text{ grapefruit}} = \frac{2}{3}$, which can be written as 2 : 3. (Refresher 120)

MATH REFRESHER SESSION 2

Rate Problems: Distance and Time, Work, Mixture, and Cost

Word Problem Setup

200. Some problems require translation of words into algebraic expressions or equations. For example: 8 more than 7 times a number is 22. Find the number. Let n = the number. We have

$$7n + 8 = 22 \qquad 7n = 14 \qquad n = 2$$

Another example: There are 3 times as many boys as girls in a class. What is the ratio of boys to the total number of students? Let n = number of girls. Then

$$3n = \text{number of boys}$$
$$4n = \text{total number of students}$$
$$\frac{\text{number of boys}}{\text{total students}} = \frac{3n}{4n} = \frac{3}{4}$$

201. Rate problems concern a special type of relationship that is very common: rate × input = output. This results from the definition of *rate* as *the ratio between output and input*. In these problems, input may represent any type of "investment," but the most frequent quantities used as inputs are time, work, and money. Output is usually distance traveled, work done, or money spent.

Note that the word *per*, as used in rates, signifies a ratio. Thus a rate of 25 miles per hour signifies the ratio between an output of 25 miles and an input of 1 hour.

Frequently, the word *per* will be represented by the fraction sign, thus $\frac{25 \text{ miles}}{1 \text{ hour}}$.

Example: Peter can walk a mile in 10 minutes. He can travel a mile on his bicycle in 2 minutes. How far away is his uncle's house if Peter can walk there and bicycle back in 1 hour exactly?

To solve a rate problem such as the one above, follow these steps:

Step 1. Determine the names of the quantities that represent input, output, and rate in the problem you are doing. In the example, Peter's input is *time*, and his output is *distance*. His rate will be *distance per unit of time*, which is commonly called *speed*.

Step 2. Write down the fundamental relationship in terms of the quantities mentioned, making each the heading of a column. In the example, set up the table like this:

$$\text{speed} \times \text{time} = \text{distance}$$

Step 3. Directly below the name of each quantity, write the unit of measurement in terms of the answer you want. Your choice of unit should be the most convenient one, but remember, once you have chosen a unit, you must convert all quantities to that unit.

We must select a unit of time. Since a *minute* was the unit used in the problem, it is the most logical choice. Similarly, we will choose a *mile* for our unit of distance. *Speed* (which is the ratio of distance to time) will therefore be expressed in *miles per minute*, usually abbreviated as mi/min. Thus, our chart now looks like this:

speed	×	time	=	distance
mi/min		*minutes*		*miles*

Step 4. The problem will mention various situations in which some quantity of input is used to get a certain quantity of output. Represent each of these situations on a different line of the table, leaving blanks for unknown quantities.

In the sample problem, four situations are mentioned: Peter can walk a mile in 10 minutes; he can bicycle a mile in 2 minutes; he walks to his uncle's house; and he bicycles home. On the diagram, with the appropriate boxes filled, the problem will look like this:

	speed	× time	= distance
	mi/min	minutes	miles
1. walking		10	1
2. bicycling		2	1
3. walking			
4. bicycling			

Step 5. From the chart and from the relationship at the top of the chart, quantities for filling some of the empty spaces may become obvious. Fill in these values directly.

In the example, on the first line of the chart, we see that the walking speed × 10 equals 1.

Thus, the walking *speed* is 0.1 mi/min

(mi/min × 10 = 1 mi; mi/min = $\frac{1 \text{ mi}}{10 \text{ min}}$ = 0.1).

Similarly, on the second line we see that the bicycle speed equals 0.5 mi/min. Furthermore, his walking speed shown on line 3 will be 0.1, the same speed as on line 1; and his bicycling speed shown on line 4 will equal the speed (0.5) shown on line 2. Adding this information to our table, we get:

	speed	× time	= distance
	mi/min	minutes	miles
1. walking	0.1	10	1
2. bicycling	0.5	2	1
3. walking	0.1		
4. bicycling	0.5		

Step 6. Next, fill in the blanks with algebraic expressions to represent the quantities indicated, being careful to take advantage of simple relationships stated in the problem or appearing in the chart.

Continuing the example, we represent the time spent traveling shown on line 3 by x. According to the fundamental relationship, the distance traveled

on this trip must be $(0.1)x$. Similarly, if y represents the time shown on line 4, the distance traveled is $(0.5)y$. Thus our chart now looks like this:

	speed	× time	= distance
	mi/min	minutes	miles
1. walking	0.1	10	1
2. bicycling	0.5	2	1
3. walking	0.1	x	$(0.1)x$
4. bicycling	0.5	y	$(0.5)y$

Step 7. Now, from the statement of the problem, you should be able to set up enough equations to solve for all the unknowns. In the example, there are two facts that we have not used yet. First, since Peter is going to his uncle's house and back, it is assumed that the distances covered on the two trips are equal. Thus we get the equation $(0.1)x = (0.5)y$. We are told that the total time to and from his uncle's house is one hour. Since we are using minutes as our unit of time, we convert the one hour to 60 minutes. Thus we get the equation: $x + y = 60$. Solving these two equations $(0.1x = 0.5y$ and $x + y = 60)$ algebraically, we find that $x = 50$ and $y = 10$. (See Section 407 for the solution of simultaneous equations.)

Step 8. Now that you have all the information necessary, you can calculate the answer required. In the sample problem, we are required to determine the distance to the uncle's house, which is $(0.1)x$ or $(0.5)y$. Using $x = 50$ or $y = 10$ gives us the distance as 5 miles.

Now that we have shown the fundamental steps in solving a rate problem, we shall discuss various types of rate problems.

Distance and Time

202. In *distance and time problems* the fundamental relationship that we use is *speed × time = distance*. Speed is the rate, time is the input, and distance is the output. The example in Section 201 is this type of problem.

Example: In a sports-car race, Danica gives Pablo a head start of 10 miles. Danica's car goes 80 miles per hour and Pablo's car goes 60 miles per hour. How long should it take Danica to catch up to Pablo if they both leave their starting marks at the same time?

Step 1. Here the fundamental quantities are *speed*, *time*, and *distance*.

Step 2. The fundamental relationship is speed $\times$ time = distance. Write this at the top of the chart.

Step 3. The unit for *distance* in this problem will be a *mile*. The unit for *speed* will be *miles per hour*. Since the speed is in miles per hour, our *time* will be in *hours*. Now our chart looks like this:

speed	$\times$	time	=	distance
mi/hr		*hours*		*miles*

Step 4. The problem offers us certain information that we can add to the chart. First we must make two horizontal rows, one for Pablo and one for Danica. We know that Pablo's speed is 60 miles per hour and that Danica's speed is 80 miles per hour.

Step 5. In this case, none of the information in the chart can be used to calculate other information in the chart.

Step 6. Now we must use algebraic expressions to represent the unknowns. We know that both Pablo and Danica travel for the same amount of time, but we do not know for how much time, so we will place an x in the space for each driver's time. Now from the relationship of speed $\times$ time = distance, we can calculate Pablo's distance as $60x$ and Danica's distance as $80x$. Now the chart looks like this:

	speed	$\times$	time	=	distance
	mi/hr		*hours*		*miles*
Pablo	60		x		$60x$
Danica	80		x		$80x$

Step 7. From the statement of the problem we know that Danica gave Pablo a 10-mile head start. In other words, Danica's distance is 10 more miles than Pablo's distance. This can be stated algebraically as $60x + 10 = 80x$. That is,

Pablo's distance + 10 miles = Danica's distance. Solving for x gives us $x = \frac{1}{2}$.

Step 8. The question asks how much time is required for Danica to catch up to Pablo. If we look at the chart, we see that this time is x, and x has already been calculated as $\frac{1}{2}$, so the answer is $\frac{1}{2}$ hour.

Work

203. In *work problems* the input is time and the output is the amount of work done. The rate is the work per unit of time.

Example: Jack can chop down 20 trees in 1 hour, whereas it takes Ted $1\frac{1}{2}$ hours to chop down 18 trees. If the two of them work together, how long will it take them to chop down 48 trees?

Solution: By the end of Step 5 your chart should look like this:

	rate	$\times$	time	=	work
	trees/hr		*hours*		*trees*
1. Jack	20		1		20
2. Ted	12		$1\frac{1}{2}$		18
3. Jack	20				
4. Ted	12				

In Step 6, we represent the time that it takes Jack by x in line 3. Since we have the relationship that rate $\times$ time = work, we see that in line 3 the work is $20x$. Since the two boys work together (therefore, for the same amount of time), the time in line 4 must be x, and the work must be $12x$. Now, in Step 7, we see that the total work is 48 trees. From lines 3 and 4, then, $20x + 12x = 48$. Solving for x gives us $x = 1\frac{1}{2}$. We are asked to find the number of hours needed by the boys to chop down the 48 trees together, and we see that this time is x, or $1\frac{1}{2}$ hours.

Mixture

204. In *mixture problems* you are given a percent or a fractional composition of a substance, and you are asked questions about the weights and compositions of the substance. The basic relationship here is that the percentage of a certain substance in a mixture $\times$ the amount of the mixture = the amount of substance.

Note that it is often better to change percentages to decimals because it makes it easier to avoid errors.

Example: A chemist has two quarts of 25% acid solution and one quart of 40% acid solution. If he mixes these, what will be the concentration of the mixture?

Solution: Let x = concentration of the mixture. At the end of Step 6, our table will look like this:

	concentration $\times$	amount of sol	=	amount of acid
	$\dfrac{qt\ (acid)}{qt\ (sol)}$	qts (sol)		qts (acid)
25% solution	0.25	2		0.50
40% solution	0.40	1		0.40
mixture	x	3		$3x$

We now have one additional bit of information: The amount of acid in the mixture must be equal to the total amount of acid in each of the two parts, so $3x = 0.50 + 0.40$. Therefore x is equal to 0.30, which is the same as a 30% concentration of the acid in the mixture.

Cost

205. In *cost problems* the rate is the *price per item*, the input is the *number of items*, and the output is the *value* of the items considered. When you are dealing with dollars and cents, you must be very careful to use the decimal point correctly.

Example: Jim has $3.00 in nickels and dimes in his pocket. If he has twice as many nickels as he has dimes, how many coins does he have altogether?

Solution: After Step 6, our chart should look like this (where c is the number of dimes Jim has):

	rate $\times$	number	=	value
	cents/coin	coins		cents
nickels	5	$2c$		$10c$
dimes	10	c		$10c$

Now we recall the additional bit of information that the total value of the nickels and dimes is $3.00, or 300 cents. Thus, $5(2c) + 10c = 300$; $20c = 300$; so $c = 15$, the number of dimes. Jim has twice as many nickels, so $2c = 30$.

The total number of coins is $c + 2c = 3c = 45$.

The following table will serve as review for this Refresher Session.

Type of Problem	Fundamental Relationship
distance	speed $\times$ time = distance
work	rate $\times$ time = work done
mixture	concentration $\times$ amount of solution = amount of ingredient
cost	rate $\times$ number of items = cost

SESSION 2 PRACTICE TEST

Rate Problems: Distance and Time, Work, Mixture, and Cost

Correct answers and solutions follow this test.

1. A person rowed 3 miles upstream (against the current) in 90 minutes. If the river flowed with a current of 2 miles per hour, how long did the person's return trip take?

   (A) 20 minutes
   (B) 30 minutes
   (C) 45 minutes
   (D) 60 minutes
   (E) 80 minutes

   A B C D E
   ○ ○ ○ ○ ○

2. Aaron can do a job in 1 hour, Camilla can do the same job in 2 hours, and Bob can do the job in 3 hours. How long does it take them to do the job working together?

   (A) $\frac{6}{11}$ hour

   (B) $\frac{1}{2}$ hour

   (C) 6 hours

   (D) $\frac{1}{3}$ hour

   (E) $\frac{1}{6}$ hour

   A B C D E
   ○ ○ ○ ○ ○

3. Mr. Cheung had $2,000 to invest. He invested part of it at 5% per year and the remainder at 4% per year. After one year, his investment grew to $2,095. How much of the original investment was at the 5% rate?

   (A) $500
   (B) $750
   (C) $1,000
   (D) $1,250
   (E) $1,500

   A B C D E
   ○ ○ ○ ○ ○

4. Gabriel walks down the road for half an hour at an average speed of 3 miles per hour. He waits 10 minutes for a bus, which brings him back to his starting point at 3:15. If Gabriel began his walk at 2:25 the same afternoon, what was the average speed of the bus?

   (A) 1.5 miles per hour
   (B) 3 miles per hour
   (C) 4.5 miles per hour
   (D) 6 miles per hour
   (E) 9 miles per hour

   A B C D E
   ○ ○ ○ ○ ○

5. Faucet A lets water flow into a 5-gallon tub at a rate of 1.5 gallons per minute. Faucet B lets water flow into the same tub at a rate of 1.0 gallon per minute. Faucet A runs alone for 100 seconds; then the two of them together finish filling up the tub. How long does the whole operation take?

   (A) 120 seconds
   (B) 150 seconds
   (C) 160 seconds
   (D) 180 seconds
   (E) 190 seconds

   A B C D E
   ○ ○ ○ ○ ○

6. Coffee A normally costs 75¢ per pound. It is mixed with Coffee B, which normally costs 80¢ per pound, to form a mixture that costs 78¢ per pound.

If there are 10 pounds of the mix, how many pounds of Coffee A were used in the mix?

(A) 3
(B) 4
(C) 4.5
(D) 5
(E) 6

A B C D E
○ ○ ○ ○ ○

7. If an athlete can run p miles in x minutes, how long will it take her to run q miles at the same rate?

(A) $\dfrac{pq}{x}$ minutes

(B) $\dfrac{px}{q}$ minutes

(C) $\dfrac{q}{px}$ minutes

(D) $\dfrac{qx}{p}$ minutes

(E) $\dfrac{x}{pq}$ minutes

A B C D E
○ ○ ○ ○ ○

8. A train went 300 miles from City X to City Y at an average rate of 80 mph. At what speed did it travel on the way back if its average speed for the whole trip was 100 mph?

(A) 120 mph
(B) 125 mph
(C) $133\frac{1}{3}$ mph
(D) $137\frac{1}{2}$ mph
(E) 150 mph

A B C D E
○ ○ ○ ○ ○

9. Kaylee spent exactly $2.50 on 3¢, 6¢, and 10¢ stamps. If she bought ten 3¢ stamps and twice as many 6¢ stamps as 10¢ stamps, how many 10¢ stamps did she buy?

(A) 5
(B) 10
(C) 12
(D) 15
(E) 20

A B C D E
○ ○ ○ ○ ○

10. If 6 workers can complete 9 identical jobs in 3 days, how long will it take 4 workers to complete 10 such jobs?

(A) 3 days
(B) 4 days
(C) 5 days
(D) 6 days
(E) more than 6 days

A B C D E
○ ○ ○ ○ ○

11. A barge travels twice as fast when it is empty as when it is full. If it travels 20 miles north with a cargo, spends 20 minutes unloading, and returns to its original port empty, taking 8 hours to complete the entire trip, what is the speed of the barge when it is empty?

(A) less than 3 mph
(B) less than 4 mph but not less than 3 mph
(C) less than 6 mph but not less than 4 mph
(D) less than 8 mph but not less than 6 mph
(E) 8 mph or more

A B C D E
○ ○ ○ ○ ○

12. Liam can hammer 20 nails in 6 minutes. Jordan can do the same job in only 5 minutes. How long will it take them to finish if Liam hammers the first 5 nails, then Jordan hammers for 3 minutes, then Liam finishes the job?

(A) 4.6 minutes
(B) 5.0 minutes
(C) 5.4 minutes
(D) 5.8 minutes
(E) 6.0 minutes

A B C D E
○ ○ ○ ○ ○

13. Jessica has 2 quarts of a 30% acid solution and 3 pints of a 20% solution. If she mixes them, what will be the concentration (to the nearest percent) of the resulting solution? (1 quart = 2 pints.)

(A) 22%
(B) 23%
(C) 24%
(D) 25%
(E) 26%

A B C D E
○ ○ ○ ○ ○

14. Selena has $1.50 in coins. She has one quarter and twice as many dimes as nickels. Which of the following equations can be used to find out how many dimes Selena has?

    (A) $5c + 20c = 175$
    (B) $5c + 10c = 150$
    (C) $5c + 20c = 125$
    (D) $5c + 10c = 125$
    (E) $5c + 20c = 150$

    A B C D E
    ◯ ◯ ◯ ◯ ◯

15. Olivia's allowance is $1.20 per week. Colton's is 25¢ per day. If they save both their allowances together, how long will they have to save before they can get a model car set that costs $23.60?

    (A) 6 weeks
    (B) 8 weeks
    (C) 10 weeks
    (D) 13 weeks
    (E) 16 weeks

    A B C D E
    ◯ ◯ ◯ ◯ ◯

16. Matt can earn money at the following schedule: $2.00 for the first hour, $2.50 an hour for the next two hours, and $3.00 an hour after that. He also has the opportunity to take a different job that pays $2.75 an hour. He wants to work until he has earned $15.00. Which of the following is true?

    (A) The first job will take him longer by 15 minutes or more.
    (B) The first job will take him longer by less than 15 minutes.
    (C) The two jobs will take the same length of time.
    (D) The second job will take him longer by 30 minutes or more.
    (E) The second job will take him longer by less than 10 minutes.

    A B C D E
    ◯ ◯ ◯ ◯ ◯

17. If Kaitlin can seal 40 envelopes in one minute, and Tyler can do the same job in 80 seconds, how many minutes (to the nearest minute) will it take the two of them, working together, to seal 350 envelopes?

    (A) 4 minutes
    (B) 5 minutes
    (C) 6 minutes
    (D) 7 minutes
    (E) 8 minutes

    A B C D E
    ◯ ◯ ◯ ◯ ◯

18. Towns A and B are 400 miles apart. If a train leaves A in the direction of B at 50 miles per hour, how long will it take before that train meets another train, going from B to A, at a speed of 30 miles per hour? (*Note*: The train that leaves B departs at the same time as the train that leaves A.)

    (A) 4 hours
    (B) $4\frac{1}{3}$ hours
    (C) 5 hours
    (D) $5\frac{2}{3}$ hours
    (E) $6\frac{2}{3}$ hours

    A B C D E
    ◯ ◯ ◯ ◯ ◯

19. A rectangular tub has internal measurements of 2 feet × 2 feet × 5 feet. If two faucets, each with an output of 2 cubic feet of water per minute, pour water into the tub simultaneously, how many minutes does it take to fill the tub completely?

    (A) less than 3 minutes
    (B) less than 4 minutes, but not less than 3
    (C) less than 5 minutes, but not less than 4
    (D) less than 6 minutes, but not less than 5
    (E) 6 minutes or more

    A B C D E
    ◯ ◯ ◯ ◯ ◯

20. A 30% solution of barium chloride is mixed with 10 grams of water to form a 20% solution. How many grams were in the original solution?

    (A) 10
    (B) 15
    (C) 20
    (D) 25
    (E) 30

    A B C D E
    ◯ ◯ ◯ ◯ ◯

21. Mr. Chan had a coin collection including only nickels, dimes, and quarters. He had twice as many dimes as he had nickels, and half as many quarters as he had nickels. If the total face value of his collection was $300.00, how many quarters did the collection contain?

    (A) 75
    (B) 100
    (C) 250
    (D) 400
    (E) 800

    A B C D E
    ○ ○ ○ ○ ○ _____

22. Pullig's Office Supply Store stocks a higher-priced pen and a lower-priced pen. If the store sells the higher-priced pens, which yield a profit of $1.20 per pen sold, it can sell 30 in a month. If the store sells the lower-priced pens, making a profit of 15¢ per pen sold, it can sell 250 pens in a month. Which type of pen will yield more profit per month, and by how much?

    (A) The cheaper pen will yield a greater profit, by $1.50.
    (B) The more expensive pen will yield a greater profit, by $1.50.
    (C) The cheaper pen will yield a greater profit, by 15¢.
    (D) The more expensive pen will yield a greater profit, by 15¢.
    (E) Both pens will yield exactly the same profit.

    A B C D E
    ○ ○ ○ ○ ○ _____

23. At a cost of $2.50 per square yard, what would be the price of carpeting a rectangular floor, 18 feet × 24 feet?

    (A) $120
    (B) $360
    (C) $750
    (D) $1,000
    (E) $1,080

    A B C D E
    ○ ○ ○ ○ ○ _____

24. Sarita and Elizabeth agreed to race across a 50-foot pool and back again. They started together, but Sarita finished 10 feet ahead of Elizabeth. If their rates were constant, and Sarita finished the race in 27 seconds, how long did it take Elizabeth to finish?

    (A) 28 seconds
    (B) 30 seconds
    (C) $33\frac{1}{3}$ seconds
    (D) 35 seconds
    (E) 37 seconds

    A B C D E
    ○ ○ ○ ○ ○ _____

25. If four campers need $24.00 worth of food for a three-day camping trip, how much will two campers need for a two-week trip?

    (A) $12.00
    (B) $24.00
    (C) $28.00
    (D) $42.00
    (E) $56.00

    A B C D E
    ○ ○ ○ ○ ○ _____

26. Wilson walks 15 blocks to work every morning at a rate of 2 miles per hour. If there are 20 blocks in a mile, how long does it take him to walk to work?

    (A) $12\frac{1}{2}$ minutes
    (B) 15 minutes
    (C) $22\frac{1}{2}$ minutes
    (D) $37\frac{1}{2}$ minutes
    (E) 45 minutes

    A B C D E
    ○ ○ ○ ○ ○ _____

27. Two buses leave for an away game. Bus A travels at a rate of 45 miles per hour for 15 miles. Bus B travels at 50 miles per hour but takes a route that is 10 miles longer. If the buses leave at the same time, by how many minutes will Bus A arrive before Bus B?

    (A) 5
    (B) 10

(C) 15

(D) 25

(E) 30

A B C D E
○ ○ ○ ○ ○
_____

28. Raj can run 10 miles per hour, whereas Sheldon can run only 8 miles per hour. If they start at the same time from the same point and run in opposite directions, how far apart (to the nearest mile) will they be after 10 minutes?

(A) 1 mile

(B) 2 miles

(C) 3 miles

(D) 4 miles

(E) 5 miles

A B C D E
○ ○ ○ ○ ○
_____

29. Machine A can produce 40 bolts per minute, whereas Machine B can produce only 30 per minute. Machine A begins alone to make bolts, but it breaks down after $1\frac{1}{2}$ minutes, and Machine B must complete the job. If the job requires 300 bolts, how long does the whole operation take?

(A) $7\frac{1}{2}$ minutes

(B) 8 minutes

(C) $8\frac{1}{2}$ minutes

(D) 9 minutes

(E) $9\frac{1}{2}$ minutes

A B C D E
○ ○ ○ ○ ○
_____

30. Ten pints of 15% salt solution are mixed with 15 pints of 10% salt solution. What is the concentration of the resulting solution?

(A) 10%

(B) 12%

(C) 12.5%

(D) 13%

(E) 15%

A B C D E
○ ○ ○ ○ ○
_____

31. Jeff makes $50 every day, from which he must spend $30 a day for various expenses. Pete makes $100 a day but has to spend $70 each day for expenses. If the two of them save together, how long will it take before they can buy a $1,500 used car?

(A) 10 days

(B) 15 days

(C) 30 days

(D) 50 days

(E) 75 days

A B C D E
○ ○ ○ ○ ○
_____

32. Two cities are 800 miles apart. At 3:00 P.M., Plane A leaves one city, traveling toward the other city at a speed of 600 miles per hour. At 4:00 the same afternoon, Plane B leaves the first city, traveling in the same direction at a rate of 800 miles per hour. Which of the following answers represents the actual result?

(A) Plane A arrives first, by an hour or more.

(B) Plane A arrives first, by less than an hour.

(C) The two planes arrive at exactly the same time.

(D) Plane A arrives after Plane B, by less than an hour.

(E) Plane A arrives after Plane B, by an hour or more.

A B C D E
○ ○ ○ ○ ○
_____

33. Emma has $6 in change in a jar. If she has twice as many dimes and three times as many nickels as she does quarters, how many dimes does she have?

(A) 5

(B) 10

(C) 15

(D) 20

(E) 200

A B C D E
○ ○ ○ ○ ○
_____

34. A delivery truck can travel 120 miles in either of two ways. It can travel at a constant rate of 40 miles per hour, or it can travel halfway at 50 miles per hour, then slow down to 30 miles per hour for the second 60 miles. Which way is faster, and by how much?

    (A) The constant rate is faster by 10 minutes or more.
    (B) The constant rate is faster by less than 10 minutes.
    (C) The two ways take exactly the same time.
    (D) The constant rate is slower by less than 10 minutes.
    (E) The constant rate is slower by 10 minutes or more.

    A B C D E
    ○ ○ ○ ○ ○

35. John walks 10 miles at an average rate of 2 miles per hour and returns on a bicycle at an average rate of 10 miles per hour. How long (to the nearest hour) does the entire trip take him?

    (A) 3 hours
    (B) 4 hours
    (C) 5 hours
    (D) 6 hours
    (E) 7 hours

    A B C D E
    ○ ○ ○ ○ ○

36. If a plane can travel P miles in Q hours, how long will it take to travel R miles?

    (A) $\dfrac{PQ}{R}$ hours

    (B) $\dfrac{P}{QR}$ hours

    (C) $\dfrac{QR}{P}$ hours

    (D) $\dfrac{Q}{PR}$ hours

    (E) $\dfrac{PR}{Q}$ hours

    A B C D E
    ○ ○ ○ ○ ○

37. Alison can swim 75 feet in 12 seconds. What is her rate to the nearest mile per hour?

    (A) 1 mph
    (B) 2 mph

(C) 3 mph
(D) 4 mph
(E) 5 mph

A B C D E
○ ○ ○ ○ ○

38. How many pounds of a \$1.20-per-pound nut mixture must be mixed with two pounds of a 90¢-per-pound mixture to produce a mixture that sells for \$1.00 per pound?

    (A) 0.5
    (B) 1.0
    (C) 1.5
    (D) 2.0
    (E) 2.5

    A B C D E
    ○ ○ ○ ○ ○

39. A broken clock is set correctly at 12:00 noon. However, it registers only 20 minutes for each hour. In how many hours will it again register the correct time?

    (A) 12
    (B) 18
    (C) 24
    (D) 30
    (E) 36

    A B C D E
    ○ ○ ○ ○ ○

40. If a man travels p hours at an average rate of q miles per hour, and then r hours at an average rate of s miles per hour, what is his overall average rate of speed?

    (A) $\dfrac{pq + rs}{p + r}$

    (B) $\dfrac{q + s}{2}$

    (C) $\dfrac{q + s}{p + r}$

    (D) $\dfrac{p}{q} + \dfrac{r}{s}$

    (E) $\dfrac{p}{s} + \dfrac{r}{q}$

    A B C D E
    ○ ○ ○ ○ ○

41. If Lily can paint 25 feet of fence in an hour, and Samantha can paint 35 feet in an hour, how many minutes will it take them to paint a 150-foot fence, if they work together?

    (A) 150
    (B) 200
    (C) 240
    (D) 480
    (E) 500

    A B C D E
    ○ ○ ○ ○ ○

42. If an athlete travels for a half hour at a rate of 20 miles per hour, and for another half hour at a rate of 30 miles per hour, what is the athlete's average speed?

    (A) 24 miles per hour
    (B) 25 miles per hour
    (C) 26 miles per hour
    (D) 26.5 miles per hour
    (E) The answer cannot be determined from the given information.

    A B C D E
    ○ ○ ○ ○ ○

43. New York is 3,000 miles from Los Angeles. Sol leaves New York aboard a plane heading toward Los Angeles at the same time that Robert leaves Los Angeles aboard a plane heading toward New York. If Sol is moving at 200 miles per hour and Robert is moving at 400 miles per hour, how soon will one plane pass the other?

    (A) 2 hours
    (B) $22\frac{1}{2}$ hours
    (C) 5 hours
    (D) 4 hours
    (E) 12 hours

    A B C D E
    ○ ○ ○ ○ ○

44. When Amelia deposited her paycheck, she requested $170 back in cash. Her cash was counted out in fives, tens, and twenties. If Amelia received twice as many tens as fives and three times as many twenties as fives, how much did she receive in twenties?

    (A) $20
    (B) $60
    (C) $100
    (D) $120
    (E) $170

    A B C D E
    ○ ○ ○ ○ ○

45. A chemist adds two quarts of pure alcohol to a 30% solution of alcohol in water. If the new concentration is 40%, how many quarts of the original solution were there?

    (A) 12
    (B) 15
    (C) 18
    (D) 20
    (E) 24

    A B C D E
    ○ ○ ○ ○ ○

46. The Energy Value Power Company charges 8¢ per kilowatt-hour for the first 1,000 kilowatt-hours, and 6¢ per kilowatt-hour after that. If a man uses a 900-watt toaster for 5 hours, a 100-watt lamp for 25 hours, and a 5-watt clock for 400 hours, how much is he charged for the power he uses? (1 kilowatt = 1,000 watts.)

    (A) 56¢
    (B) 64¢
    (C) 72¢
    (D) $560.00
    (E) $720.00

    A B C D E
    ○ ○ ○ ○ ○

47. At 30¢ per yard, what is the price of 96 inches of ribbon?

    (A) 72¢
    (B) 75¢
    (C) 80¢
    (D) 84¢
    (E) 90¢

    A B C D E
    ○ ○ ○ ○ ○

48. Maya travels for 6 hours at a rate of 50 miles per hour. Her return trip takes her $7\frac{1}{2}$ hours. What is her average speed for the whole trip?

    (A) 44.4 miles per hour
    (B) 45.0 miles per hour
    (C) 46.8 miles per hour
    (D) 48.2 miles per hour
    (E) 50.0 miles per hour

    A B C D E
    ○ ○ ○ ○ ○

49. Lucas puts $100 in the bank for two years at 5% interest compounded annually. At the end of the two years, what is his balance? (Interest = principal × rate × time)

    (A) $100.00
    (B) $105.00
    (C) $105.25
    (D) $110.00
    (E) $110.25

    A B C D E
    ○ ○ ○ ○ ○

50. A 12-gallon tub has a faucet that lets water in at a rate of 3 gallons per minute, and a drain that lets water out at a rate of 1.5 gallons per minute. If you start with 3 gallons of water in the tub, how long will it take to fill the tub completely? (Note that the faucet is on and the drain is open.)

    (A) 3 minutes
    (B) 4 minutes
    (C) 6 minutes
    (D) 7.5 minutes
    (E) 8 minutes

    A B C D E
    ○ ○ ○ ○ ○

Answer Key for Session 2 Practice Test

1. B	14. C	27. B	39. B
2. A	15. B	28. C	40. A
3. E	16. B	29. E	41. A
4. E	17. B	30. B	42. B
5. C	18. C	31. C	43. C
6. B	19. D	32. B	44. D
7. D	20. C	33. D	45. A
8. C	21. D	34. A	46. C
9. B	22. A	35. D	47. C
10. C	23. A	36. C	48. A
11. D	24. B	37. D	49. E
12. C	25. E	38. B	50. C
13. E	26. C		

Answers and Solutions for Session 2 Practice Test

1. Choice B is correct. The fundamental relationship here is: rate × time = distance. The easiest units to work with are miles per hour for the rate, hours for time, and miles for distance. Note that the word *per* indicates division, because when calculating a rate, we *divide* the number of miles (distance units) by the number of hours (time units).

   We can set up our chart with the information given. We know that the upstream trip took $1\frac{1}{2}$ hours (90 minutes) and that the distance was 3 miles. Thus the upstream rate was 2 miles per hour. The downstream distance was also 3 miles, but we use t for the time, which is unknown. Thus the downstream rate was $\frac{3}{t}$. Our chart looks like this:

	rate ×	time =	distance
	miles/hour	hours	miles
upstream	2	$1\frac{1}{2}$	3
downstream	$\frac{3}{t}$	t	3

   We use the rest of the information to solve for t. We know that the speed of the current is 2 miles per hour. We assume the boat to be in still water and assign it a speed, s; then the upstream (against the current) speed of the boat is $s - 2$ miles per hour. Since $s - 2 = 2$, $s = 4$.

Now the speed of the boat downstream (with the current) is $s + 2$, or 6 miles per hour. This is equal to $\frac{3}{t}$, and we get the equation $\frac{3}{t} = 6$, so $t = \frac{1}{2}$ hour. We must be careful with our units because the answer must be in minutes. We can convert $\frac{1}{2}$ hour to 30 minutes to get the final answer.

   (Refreshers 201, 202)

2. Choice A is correct.

	rate ×	time =	work
	jobs/hour	hours	jobs
Aaron	1	1	1
Camilla	$\frac{1}{2}$	2	1
Bob	$\frac{1}{3}$	3	1
together	r	t	1

   Let r = rate together and t = time together. Now, $r = 1 + \frac{1}{2} + \frac{1}{3} = \frac{11}{6}$ because *whenever two or more people are working together, their joint rate is the sum of their individual rates*. This is not necessarily true of the time or the work done. In this case, we know that $r \times t = 1$ and $r = \frac{11}{6}$, so $t = \frac{6}{11}$.

   (Refreshers 201, 203)

3. Choice E is correct.

	rate ×	principal =	interest
	$/$	$	$
5%	0.05	x	$0.05x$
4%	0.04	y	$0.04y$

   Let x = the part of the $2,000 invested at 5%. Let y = the part of $2,000 invested at 4%. We know that since the whole $2,000 was invested, $x + y$ must equal $2,000. Furthermore, we know that the sum of the interests on both investments equaled $95, so $0.05x + 0.04y = 95$. Since we have to solve only for x, we can express this as $0.01x + 0.04x + 0.04y = 95$. Then we factor out 0.04. Thus $0.01x + 0.04(x + y) = 95$. Since we know that $x + y = 2,000$, we have $0.01x + 0.04(2,000) = 95$; $0.01x + 80 = 95$; and $x = 1,500$. Thus, $1,500 was invested at 5%.

   (Refreshers 201, 205)

4. **Choice E is correct.**

	rate	×	time	=	distance
	miles/min		minutes		miles
walk	$\frac{1}{20}$		30		a
wait	0		10		0
bus	r		t		a

Let a = distance Gabriel walks. Since Gabriel walks at 3 miles per hour, he walks at $\frac{3 \text{ mi}}{60 \text{ min}}$ or $\frac{1 \text{ mi}}{20 \text{ min}}$.

From this we can find $a = \frac{1 \text{ mi}}{20 \text{ min}} \times 30 \text{ min} = 1\frac{1}{2}$ miles. The total time he spent was 50 minutes (the difference between 3:15 and 2:25), and $30 + 10 + t = 50$, so t must be equal to 10 minutes. This reduces our problem to the simple equation $10r = 1\frac{1}{2}$ (where r = rate of the bus), and, on solving, $r = 0.15$ mile per minute. But the required answer is in miles per hour. In one hour, or 60 minutes, the bus can travel 60 times as far as the 0.15 mile it travels in one minute, so the bus travels $60 \times 0.15 = 9$ miles per hour.

(Refreshers 201, 202)

5. **Choice C is correct.**

	rate	×	time	=	water
	gallons/min		minutes		gallons
A only	1.5		$\frac{5}{3}$*		2.5
B only	1.0		0		0
A and B	2.5		t		x

*$\frac{5}{3}$ min = 100 sec.

Let t = time faucets A and B run together.

Let x = amount of water delivered when A and B run together.

We know that the total number of gallons is 5, and A alone delivers 2.5 gallons (1.5 gal/min $\times \frac{5}{3}$ min = 2.5 gal), so x equals 2.5. This leads us to the simple equation $2.5t = 2.5$, so $t = 1$ minute, or 60 seconds. Thus, the whole operation takes $\frac{5}{3} + t$ minutes, or $100 + 60$ seconds, totaling 160 seconds.

(Refreshers 201, 203)

6. **Choice B is correct.**

	rate	×	amount	=	cost
	¢/lb		lb		¢
Coffee A	75		x		$75x$
Coffee B	80		y		$80y$
mix	78		10		780

Let x = weight of Coffee A in the mix.

Let y = weight of Coffee B in the mix.

We know that the weight of the mix is equal to the sum of the weights of its components. Thus, $x + y = 10$. Similarly, the cost of the mix is equal to the sum of the costs of the components. Thus, $75x + 80y = 780$. So we have $x + y = 10$ and $75x + 80y = 780$. Now $y = 10 - x$, so substituting $y = 10 - x$ in the second equation, we get

$$75x + 80(10 - x) = 780$$
$$75x + 800 - 80x = 780$$
$$800 - 5x = 780$$
$$20 = 5x$$
$$4 = x$$

Thus 4 pounds of Coffee A were used.

(Refreshers 201, 204, 407)

7. **Choice D is correct.**

	rate	×	time	=	distance
	miles/min		minutes		miles
first run	r		x		p
second run	r		t		q

Let r = rate of the athlete.

Let t = time it takes her to run q miles.

From the first line, we know that $rx = p$, then $r = \frac{p}{x}$. Substituting this in the second line, we get $\left(\frac{p}{x}\right)t = q$, so $t = q\left(\frac{x}{p}\right)$, or $\frac{qx}{p}$ minutes.

(Refreshers 201, 202)

8. Choice C is correct.

| | rate × | time = | distance |
	miles/hour	hours	miles
X to Y	80	t	300
Y to X	r	s	300
whole trip	100	s + t	600

Let t = time from city X to city Y.

Let s = time from city Y to city X.

Let r = rate of the train from Y to X.

We know that $80t = 300$, so $t = \frac{300}{80}$, or $\frac{15}{4}$. Also, $100(s + t) = 600$, so $s + t = 6$. This and the last equation lead us to the conclusion that $s = 6 - \frac{15}{4}$, or $\frac{9}{4}$. Now, from the middle line, we have $r\left(\frac{9}{4}\right) = 300$, so $r = \frac{400}{3}$, or $133\frac{1}{3}$ miles per hour.

(Note that the reason we chose the equations in this particular order was that it is easiest to concentrate first on those with the most data already given.)

(Refreshers 201, 202)

9. Choice B is correct.

| | rate × | number = | cost |
	¢/stamp	stamps	¢
3¢ stamps	3	10	30
10¢ stamps	10	x	10x
6¢ stamps	6	2x	12x

Let x = the number of 10¢ stamps bought.

We know that the total cost is 250¢, so $30 + 10x + 12x = 250$. This is the same as $22x = 220$, so $x = 10$. Therefore, she bought ten 10¢ stamps.

(Refreshers 201, 205)

10. Choice C is correct.

| | rate × | time = | work |
	jobs/day	days	jobs
6 workers	6r	3	9
4 workers	4r	t	10

Let r = rate of one worker.

Let t = time for 4 workers to do 10 jobs.

From the first line, we have $18r = 9$, so $r = \frac{1}{2}$.

Substituting this in the second line, $4r = 2$, so $2t = 10$. Therefore $t = 5$. The workers will take 5 days.

(Refreshers 201, 203)

11. Choice D is correct.

| | rate × | time = | distance |
	miles/hour	hours	miles
north	r	$\frac{20}{r}$	20
unload	0	$\frac{1}{3}$	0
return	2r	$\frac{10}{r}$	20

Let r = loaded rate; then
$$2r = \text{empty rate}$$
Total time $= \frac{20}{r} + \frac{1}{3} + \frac{10}{r} = 8$ hours.

Multiplying by $3r$ on both sides, we get $90 = 23r$, so $r = 90 \div 23$, or about 3.9 miles per hour. However, the problem asks for the speed *when empty*, which is $2r$, or 7.8. This is less than 8 mph, but not less than 6 mph.

(Refreshers 201, 202)

12. Choice C is correct.

| | rate × | time = | work |
	nails/min	minutes	nails
Liam	r	6	20
Jordan	s	5	20
Liam	r	$\frac{5}{r}$	5
Jordan	s	3	3s
Liam	r	$\frac{x}{r}$	x

Let r = Liam's rate.

Let s = Jordan's rate.

x = number of nails left after Jordan takes her turn.

$6r = 20$, so $r = 3\frac{1}{3}$.

$5s = 20$, so $s = 4$.

Total work $= 5 + 3s + x = 20 = 5 + 12 + x = 20$,

so $x = 3$. Thus $\frac{x}{r} = 0.9$.

Total time $= \frac{5}{r} + 3 + \frac{x}{r}$

$= \dfrac{5}{\left(\dfrac{10}{3}\right)} + 3 + 0.9$

$= \dfrac{15}{10} + 3 + 0.9$

$= 1.5 + 3 + 0.9$

$= 5.4$ (Refreshers 201, 203)

13. Choice E is correct.

| | concentration | × volume | = amount of acid |
	% acid	pts	pts
old solution	30%	4	1.2
	20%	3	0.6
new solution	$x\%$	7	1.8

(2 qts = 4 pts)

Let $x\%$ = concentration of new solution.

4 pts of 30% + 3 pts of 20% = 7 pts of $x\%$

1.2 pts + 0.6 pt = 1.8 pts

$(x\%)(7) = 1.8$, so $x = 180 \div 7 = 25.7$ (approximately), which is closest to 26%.

(Refreshers 201, 204)

14. Choice C is correct.

| | rate | × number | = value |
	¢/coin	coins	¢
nickels	5	c	$5c$
dimes	10	$2c$	$20c$

Let c = the number of nickels and $5c$ = the value of the nickels. There are double the number of dimes, so $2c$ = the number of dimes and $10(2c)$ = the value of the dimes. Write an equation with values in cents ($0.25 = 25 cents and $1.50 = 150 cents):

$$25 + 5c + 2(10c) = 150$$
$$5c + 20c = 125$$

(Refresher 205)

15. Choice B is correct.

| | rate | × time | = money |
	¢/week	weeks	¢
Olivia	120	w	$120w$
Colton	175	w	$175w$
together	295	w	$295w$

(25¢/day = $1.75/week)

Let w = the number of weeks they save.

Total money $= 295w = 2,360$.

Therefore, $w = 2,360 \div 295 = 8$.

So, they must save for 8 weeks.

(Refreshers 201, 205)

16. Choice B is correct.

| | rate | × time | = pay |
	¢/hour	hours	¢
first job	200	1	200
	250	2	500
	300	x	$300x$
second job	275	y	$275y$

Let x = hours at $3.00.

Let y = hours at $2.75.

Total pay, first job $= 200 + 500 + 300x = 1,500$, so $x = 2\frac{2}{3}$.

Total time, first job $= 1 + 2 + 2\frac{2}{3} = 5\frac{2}{3}$.

Total pay, second job $= 275y = 1,500$, so $y = 5\frac{5}{11}$.

Total time, second job $= 5\frac{5}{11}$.

$\frac{2}{3}$ hour = 40 minutes

$\frac{5}{11}$ hour = 27.2727 minutes (less than $\frac{2}{3}$ hour).

Thus, the first job will take him longer by less than 15 minutes. (Refreshers 201, 203)

17. Choice B is correct.

	rate ×	time =	work
	envelopes/min	min	envelopes
Kaitlyn	40	t	$40t$
Tyler	30	t	$30t$
both	70	t	$70t$

Let t = time to seal 350 envelopes.

Tyler's rate is 30 envelopes/minute, as shown by the proportion:

$$\text{rate} = \frac{40 \text{ envelopes}}{80 \text{ seconds}} = \frac{30 \text{ envelopes}}{60 \text{ seconds}}$$

Total work = $70t = 350$, so $t = 5$ minutes.

(Refreshers 201, 203)

18. Choice C is correct.

	rate ×	time =	distance
	miles/hour	hours	miles
A to B	50	t	$50t$
B to A	30	t	$30t$

Let t = time to meet.

Total distance traveled by two trains together equals $50t + 30t = 80t = 400$ miles, so $t = 5$ hrs.

(Refreshers 201, 202)

19. Choice D is correct.

	rate ×	time =	amount of water
	cu ft/min	minutes	cu ft
2 faucets	4	t	20

Let t = time to fill the tub.

Volume of tub = 2 ft × 2 ft × 5 ft = 20 cu ft

Rate = 2 × rate of each faucet

$$= 2 \times \frac{2 \text{ cu ft}}{\min} = \frac{4 \text{ cu ft}}{\min}$$

Therefore, $t = 5$ minutes. (Refreshers 201, 203)

20. Choice C is correct.

	concentration ×	weight =	amount of barium chloride
	%	grams	grams
original	30%	x	$0.30x$
water	0%	10	0
new	20%	$10 + x$	$0.30x$

Let x = number of grams of original solution.

Total weight and amounts of barium chloride may be added by column.

$(20\%) \times (10 + x) = 0.30x$, so $10 + x = 1.50x$, $x = 20$. (Refreshers 201, 204)

21. Choice D is correct.

	coin ×	number =	value
	¢/coin	coins	¢
nickels	5	n	$5n$
dimes	10	$2n$	$20n$
quarters	25	$\frac{n}{2}$	$\frac{25n}{2}$

Let n = number of nickels.

Total value = $5n + 20n + \frac{25n}{2} = \left(37\frac{1}{2}\right)n = 30{,}000$.

Thus, $n = 30{,}000 \div 37\frac{1}{2} = 800$.

The number of quarters is then $\frac{n}{2} = \frac{800}{2} = 400$.

(Refreshers 201, 205)

22. Choice A is correct.

	rate ×	number =	profit
	¢/pen	pens	¢
high-price	120	30	3,600
low-price	15	250	3,750

Subtracting 3,600¢ from 3,750¢, we get 150¢.

Thus, the cheaper pen yields a profit of 150¢, or $1.50, more per month than the more expensive one. (Refreshers 201, 205)

23. Choice A is correct.

price	×	area	=	cost
$/sq yd		sq yd		$
2.50		48		120

Area must be expressed in square yards; 18 ft = 6 yd, and 24 ft = 8 yd, so 18 ft × 24 ft = 6 yd × 8 yd = 48 sq yd. The cost would then be $2.50 × 48 = $120.00.   (Refreshers 201, 205)

24. Choice B is correct.

	rate	×	time	=	distance
	feet/sec		sec		feet
Sarita	r		27		100
Elizabeth	s		27		90
Elizabeth	s		t		100

Let r = Sarita's rate.

Let s = Elizabeth's rate.

Let t = Elizabeth's time to finish the race.

$27s = 90$, so $s = \dfrac{90}{27} = \dfrac{10}{3}$;

$st = 100$, and $s = \dfrac{10}{3}$, so $\dfrac{10t}{3} = 100$; thus $t = 30$.

(Refreshers 201, 202)

25. Choice E is correct. This is a rate problem in which the fundamental relationship is rate × time × number of campers = cost. The rate is in $\dfrac{\text{dollars}}{\text{camper-days}}$.

Thus, our chart looks like this:

	rate	×	time	×	number	=	cost
	$/camper-days		days		campers		$
1st trip	r		3		4		12r
2nd trip	r		14		2		28r

The cost of the first trip is $24, so $12r = 24$ and $r = 2$.

The cost of the second trip is $28r$, or $56.

(Refreshers 201, 205)

26. Choice C is correct.

rate	×	time	=	distance
blocks/min		minutes		blocks
$\frac{2}{3}$		t		15

Let t = time to walk to work.

$$\dfrac{2 \text{ miles}}{\text{hr}} = 2\dfrac{(20 \text{ blocks})}{(60 \text{ min})} = \dfrac{\frac{2}{3} \text{ blocks}}{\text{min}}.$$

$t = 15 \div \dfrac{2}{3} = 22\dfrac{1}{2}$ minutes.

(Refreshers 201, 202)

27. Choice B is correct.

	rate	×	time	=	distance
	miles/hour		hours		miles
A	45		t_1		15
B	50		t_2		10 + 15

Let t_1 and t_2 equal times. To solve, rewrite the equation to solve for time (t_1 and t_2).

$$\text{time} = \dfrac{\text{distance}}{\text{rate}}$$

Bus A: $t_1 = \dfrac{d}{r} = \dfrac{15}{45} = \dfrac{1}{3}$; there are 60 minutes in an hour, so $\dfrac{1}{3} \times 60 = 20$ minutes.

Bus B: $t_2 = \dfrac{d}{r} = \dfrac{25}{50} = \dfrac{1}{2}$, and $\dfrac{1}{2} \times 60 = 30$ minutes.

Bus A arrives 10 minutes before Bus B even though Bus B traveled at a faster rate.

(Refreshers 201, 202)

28. Choice C is correct. We could treat this as a regular distance problem and make up a table that would solve it, but there is an easier way here, if we consider the quantity representing the distance between the boys. This distance starts at zero and increases at the rate of 18 miles per hour. Thus, in 10 minutes, or $\dfrac{1}{6}$ hour, they will be 3 miles apart.

($\dfrac{1}{6}$ hr $\times 18\dfrac{\text{mi}}{\text{hr}} = 3$ mi).   (Refreshers 201, 202)

29. Choice E is correct.

	rate ×	time =	work
	bolts/min	minutes	bolts
A	40	$1\frac{1}{2}$	60
B	30	t	240

Let t = time B works.

Since A produces only 60 out of 300 that must be produced, B must produce 240; then, $30t = 240$, so $t = 8$.

Total time = $t + 1\frac{1}{2} = 8 + 1\frac{1}{2} = 9\frac{1}{2}$.

(Refreshers 201, 203)

30. Choice B is correct.

	concentration ×	volume =	amount of salt
	%	pints	pints of salt
15%	15	10	1.5
10%	10	15	1.5
total	x	25	3.0

Let x = concentration of resulting solution.

$(x\%)(25) = 3.0$, so $x = 300 \div 25 = 12$.

(Refreshers 201, 204)

31. Choice C is correct.

	rate ×	time =	pay (net)
	$/day	days	$
Jeff	20	d	$20d$
Pete	30	d	$30d$
total	50	d	$50d$

(Net pay = pay − expenses.)

Let d = the number of days it takes to save.

Total net pay = $1,500, so $1,500 = 50d$, thus $d = 30$.

Do not make the mistake of using 50 and 100 as the rates!

(Refreshers 201, 205)

32. Choice B is correct.

	rate ×	time =	distance
	miles/hour	hours	miles
plane A	600	h	800
plane B	0	1	0
plane B	800	t	800

Let h = time for trip at 600 mph.

Let t = time for trip at 800 mph.

Plane A: $600h = 800$, so $h = \frac{800}{600} = 1\frac{1}{3}$ hours = 1 hour, 20 minutes.

Plane B: $800t = 800$, so $t = 1$.

Total time for plane A = 1 hour, 20 minutes.

Total time for plane B = 1 hour + 1 hour = 2 hours.

Thus, plane A arrives before plane B by 40 minutes (less than an hour).

(Refreshers 201, 202)

33. Choice D is correct.

	rate ×	number =	value
	¢/coin	coins	¢
nickels	5	$3c$	$15c$
dimes	10	$2c$	$20c$
quarters	25	c	$25c$

Since the other coins are described in terms of quarters, let c = the number of quarters. If c = the number of quarters, $25c$ = the value of the quarters. There are double the number of dimes, so $2c$ = the number of dimes and $10(2c)$ = the value of the dimes. There are three times the number of nickels, so $3c$ = the number of nickels and $5(3c)$ = the value of the nickels. Write an equation with values in cents ($6 = 600 cents):

$$15c + 20c + 25c = 600$$
$$60c = 600$$
$$c = 10$$

There are 10 quarters. The problem asks for the number of dimes. Since there are twice as many dimes as quarters, there are 20 dimes.

$$2c = 2(10) = 20$$

(Refresher 205)

34. Choice A is correct.

	rate ×	time =	distance
	miles/hour	hours	miles
constant rate	40	h	120
two rates	50	m	60
	30	n	60

Let h = time to travel 120 miles at the constant rate.

Let m = time to travel 60 miles at 50 mi/hr.

Let n = time to travel 60 miles at 30 mi/hr.

Forming the equations for h, m, and n, and solving, we get:

$$40h = 120; h = \frac{120}{40}; h = 3$$

$$50m = 60; m = \frac{60}{50}; m = 1.2$$

$$30n = 60; n = \frac{60}{30}; n = 2$$

Total time with constant rate = h = 3 hours.

Total time with changing rate = $m + n$ = 3.2 hours.

Thus, the constant rate is faster by 0.2 hour, or 12 minutes. (Refreshers 201, 202)

35. Choice D is correct.

	rate ×	time =	distance
	miles/hour	hours	miles
walking	2	h	10
bicycling	10	t	10

Let h = time to walk.

Let t = time to bicycle.

Forming equations: $2h = 10$, so $h = 5$; and $10t = 10$, so $t = 1$.

Total time = $h + t = 5 + 1 = 6$. (Refreshers 201, 202)

36. Choice C is correct.

	rate ×	time =	distance
	miles/hour	hours	miles
	x	Q	P
	x	y	R

Let x = rate at which the airplane travels.

Let y = time to travel R miles.

$Qx = P$, so $x = \frac{P}{Q}$.

$xy = \left(\frac{P}{Q}\right) y = R$, so $y = \frac{QR}{P}$ hours = time to travel R miles. (Refreshers 201, 202)

37. Choice D is correct.

rate ×	time =	distance
miles/hour	hours	miles
r	$\frac{1}{300}$	$\frac{75}{5,280}$

Let r = rate of swimming.

75 feet = $75\left(\frac{1}{5,280} \text{ mile}\right) = \frac{75}{5,280}$ mile

12 seconds = $12\left(\frac{1}{3,600} \text{ hour}\right) = \frac{1}{300}$ hour

$r = \frac{75}{5,280} \div \frac{1}{300} = \frac{22,500}{5,280}$

= 4.3 (approximately)

= 4 mi/hr (approximately). (Refreshers 201, 202)

38. Choice B is correct.

	price ×	amount =	value
	¢/lb	lbs	¢
$1.20 nuts	120	x	120x
$0.90 nuts	90	2	180
mixture	100	x + 2	180 × 120x

Let x = pounds of $1.20 mixture.

Total value of mixture = $100(x + 2) = 180 + 120x$.

$100x + 200 = 180 + 120x$, so $x = 1$ pound. (Refreshers 201, 204)

39. Choice B is correct.

rate ×	time =	loss
hours/hour	hours	hours
$\frac{2}{3}$	t	12

(Loss is the amount by which the clock time differs from real time.)

Let t = hours to register the correct time.

If the clock registers only 20 minutes each hour, it loses 40 minutes, or $\frac{2}{3}$ hour each hour. The clock will register the correct time only if it has lost some multiple of 12 hours. The first time this can occur is after it has lost 12 hours. $\left(\frac{2}{3}\right)t = 12$, so $t = 18$ hours. (Refresher 201)

40. Choice A is correct.

	rate	×	time	=	distance
	miles/hour		*hours*		*miles*
	q		p		pq
	s		r		rs
total	x		$p + r$		$pq + rs$

Let x = average speed.

We may add times of travel at the two rates, and also add the distances. Then, $x(p + r) = pq + rs$; thus,

$$x = \frac{pq + rs}{p + r}.$$ (Refreshers 201, 202)

41. Choice A is correct.

	rate	×	time	=	work
	feet/hour		*hours*		*feet*
Samantha	35		x		$35x$
Lily	25		x		$25x$
both	60		x		$60x$

Let x = the time the job takes.

Since they are working together, we add their rates and the amount of work they do. Thus, $60x = 150$, so $x = 2.5$ (hours) = 150 minutes.

(Refreshers 201, 203)

42. Choice B is correct.

	rate	×	time	=	distance
	miles/hour		*hours*		*miles*
first $\frac{1}{2}$ hour	20		$\frac{1}{2}$		10
second $\frac{1}{2}$ hour	30		$\frac{1}{2}$		15
total		x		1	25

Let x = average speed.

We add the times and distances; then, using the rate formula, $(x)(1) = 25$, so $x = 25$ mi/hr.

(Refreshers 201, 202)

43. Choice C is correct.

	rate	×	time	=	distance
	miles/hour		*hours*		*miles*
Sol	200		t		$200t$
Robert	400		t		$400t$

Let t = time from simultaneous departure to meeting.

Sol's time is equal to Robert's time because they leave at the same time and then they meet. Their combined distance is 3,000 miles, so $200t + 400t = 3,000$, or $t = 5$ hours. (Refreshers 201, 202)

44. Choice D is correct.

	rate	×	number	=	value
	$/bill		*bills*		*$*
fives	5		n		$5n$
tens	10		$2n$		$20n$
twenties	20		$2n$		$60n$

Since the other bills are described in terms of five-dollar bills, let n = the number of fives. There are twice as many tens, so write the number of tens as $2n$. Since there are three times as many twenties as fives, write the number of twenties as $3n$. Use each bill's value with the number of bills to show the value in dollars. Let $5n$ = the value of the fives, $20n$ = the value of the tens, and $60n$ = the value of the twenties. Write an equation with values in dollars:

$$5n + 20n + 60n = 170$$
$$85n = 170$$
$$n = 2$$

Substitute 2 for n in $60n$ to find how much Amelia received in twenty-dollar bills. $60(2) = 120$ dollars

(Refresher 205)

45. Choice A is correct.

concentration $\times$	amount of solution	$=$	amount of alcohol
	%	quarts	quarts
pure alcohol	100%	2	2
solution	30%	x	$0.30x$
mixture	40%	$2 + x$	$2 + 0.30\,x$

Let x = quarts of original solution.

Amounts of solution and of alcohol may be added.

$(40\%)(2 + x) = 2 + 0.30x$; so $0.8 + 0.4x = 2.0 + 0.30x$; thus, $x = 12$.   (Refreshers 201, 204)

46. Choice C is correct.

	rate $\times$	time $=$	cost
	¢/kWh	kWh	¢
first 1,000 kWh	8	t	$8t$

(time expressed in kilowatt-hours, or kWh)

Let t = number of kWh.

This problem must be broken up into two different parts: (1) finding the total power or the total number of kilowatt-hours (kWh) used, and (2) calculating the charge for that amount. (1) Total power used, $t =(900w)(5 \text{ hr})+(100w)(25 \text{ hr})+(5w)(400 \text{ hr})$ $= (4,500 + 2,500 + 2,000)$ watt-hours $= 9,000$ watt-hours. (2) 1,000 watt-hours $= 1$ kilowatt-hour. Thus, $t = 9$ kilowatt-hours, so that the charge is $(8¢)(9) = 72¢$.   (Refreshers 201, 205)

47. Choice C is correct.

	rate $\times$	amount $=$	cost
	¢/inch	inches	¢
1 yard	r	36	30
96 inches	r	96	$96r$

Let r = cost per inch of ribbon.

From the table, $r \times 36 \text{ in} = 30¢$; $r = \dfrac{30¢}{36 \text{ in.}} = \dfrac{5¢}{6 \text{ in.}}$.

Thus, $96r = 96\left(\dfrac{5}{6}\right) = 80¢$.   (Refreshers 201, 205)

48. Choice A is correct.

	rate $\times$	time $=$	distance
	miles/hour	hours	miles
trip	50	6	300
return	r	$7\frac{1}{2}$	300
total	s	$13\frac{1}{2}$	600

Let r = rate for return.

Let s = average overall rate.

$(13\frac{1}{2})(s) = 600$; thus, $s = 600 \div 13\frac{1}{2} = 44.4$ (approximately).   (Refreshers 201, 202)

49. Choice E is correct.

	rate $\times$	principal $=$	interest
	%/year	$	$/year
first year	5	100	5
second year	5	105	5.25

Interest first year equals rate $\times$ principal = 5% $\times$ $100 = $5.

New principal = $105.00.

Interest second year = rate $\times$ new principal = 5% $\times$ $105 = $5.25.

Final principal = $105.00 + $5.25 = $110.25.   (Refreshers 201, 205)

50. Choice C is correct.

	rate $\times$	time $=$	amount
	gallons/min	minutes	gallons
in	3	x	$3x$
out	$1\frac{1}{2}$	x	$1\frac{1}{2}x$
net	$1\frac{1}{2}$	x	$1\frac{1}{2}x$

(Net = in − out.)

Let x = time to fill the tub completely.

Since only 9 gallons are needed (there are already 3 in the tub), we have $1\frac{1}{2}x = 9$, so $x = 6$.   (Refresher 201)

MATH REFRESHER SESSION 3

Area, Perimeter, and Volume Problems

301. *Formula Problems.* Here, you are given certain data about one or more geometric figures, and you are asked to supply some missing information. To solve this type of problem, follow this procedure:

Step 1. If you are not given a diagram, draw your own; this may make the answer readily apparent or may suggest the best way to solve the problem. You should try to make your diagram as accurate as possible, but *do not waste time perfecting your diagram.*

Step 2. Determine the formula that relates to the quantities involved in your problem. In many cases it will be helpful to set up tables containing the various data. (See Sections 303–317.)

Step 3. Substitute the given information for the unknown quantities in your formulas to get the desired answer.

When doing volume, area, and perimeter problems, keep this hint in mind: Often the solutions to such problems can be expressed as the sum of the areas *or* volumes *or* perimeters of simpler figures. In such cases, do not hesitate to break down your original figure into simpler parts.

In doing problems involving the following figures, these approximations and facts will be useful:

$\sqrt{2}$ is approximately 1.4.

$\sqrt{3}$ is approximately 1.7.

$\sqrt{10}$ is approximately 3.16.

π is approximately $\frac{22}{7}$ or 3.14.

$\sin 30° = \frac{1}{2}$

$\sin 45° = \frac{\sqrt{2}}{2}$, which is approximately 0.71.

$\sin 60° = \frac{\sqrt{3}}{2}$, which is approximately 0.87.

Example: The following figure contains a square, a right triangle, and a semicircle. If $ED = CD$ and the length of CD is 1 unit, find the area of the entire figure.

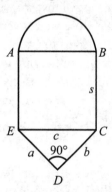

Solution: To calculate the area of the entire figure, we calculate the areas of the triangle, square, and semicircle and then add these together. In a right triangle, the area is $\frac{1}{2}ab$ where a and b are the sides of the triangle. In this case we will call side ED, a, and side CD, b. $ED = CD = 1$, so the area of the triangle is $\frac{1}{2}(1)(1)$, or $\frac{1}{2}$.

The area of a square is s^2, where s is a side. We see that the side EC of the square is the hypotenuse of the right triangle. We can calculate this length by using the formula $c^2 = a^2 + b^2$. Where $a = b = 1$, then $c = \sqrt{2}$. Thus, in this case, $s = \sqrt{2}$ so the area of the square is $(\sqrt{2})^2 = 2$.

AB is the diameter of the semicircle, so $\frac{1}{2}AB$ is the radius. Since all sides of a square are equal, $AB = \sqrt{2}$, and the radius is $\frac{1}{2}\sqrt{2}$. Further, the area of a semicircle is $\frac{1}{2}\pi r^2$, where r is the radius, so the area of this semicircle is $\frac{1}{2}\pi \left(\frac{1}{2}\sqrt{2}\right)^2 = \frac{1}{4}\pi$.

The total area of the whole figure is equal to the area of the triangle plus the area of the square plus the area of the semicircle $= \frac{1}{2} + 2 + \frac{1}{4}\pi = 2\frac{1}{2} + \frac{1}{4}\pi$.

Example: If water flows into a rectangular tank with dimensions of 12 inches, 18 inches, and 30 inches at the rate of 0.25 cubic foot per minute, how long will it take to fill the tank?

Solution: This problem is really a combination of a rate problem and a volume problem. First we must calculate the volume, and then we must substitute in a rate equation to get our final answer. The formula for the volume of a rectangular solid is $V = lwh$, where l, w, and h are the length, width, and height, respectively. We must multiply the three dimensions of the tank to get the volume. However, if we look ahead to the second part of the problem, we see that we want the volume in cubic *feet;* therefore we convert 12 inches, 18 inches, and 30 inches to 1 foot, 1.5 feet, and 2.5 feet, respectively. Multiplying gives us a volume of 3.75 cubic feet. Now substituting in the equation *rate* × *time* = *volume*, we get $0.25 \times time = 3.75$; $time = \dfrac{3.75}{0.25}$; thus, the time is 15 minutes.

302. *Comparison problems.* Here you are asked to identify the largest, or smallest, of a group of figures, or to place them in ascending or descending order of size. The following procedure is the most efficient one:

Step 1. Always diagram each figure before you come to any conclusions. Whenever possible, try to include two or more of the figures in the same diagram, so that their relative sizes are most readily apparent.

Step 2. If you have not already determined the correct answer, then (and only then) determine the size of the figures (as you would have done in Section 301) and compare the results. (Note that even if Step 2 is necessary, Step 1 should eliminate most of the possible choices, leaving only a few formula calculations to be done.)

Example: Which of the following is the greatest in length?

(A) The perimeter of a square with a side of 4 inches.

(B) The perimeter of an isosceles right triangle whose equal sides are 8 inches each.

(C) The circumference of a circle with a diameter of $4\sqrt{2}$ inches.

(D) The perimeter of a pentagon whose sides are all equal to 3 inches.

(E) The perimeter of a semicircle with a radius of 5 inches.

Solution: Diagramming the five figures mentioned, we obtain the following illustration:

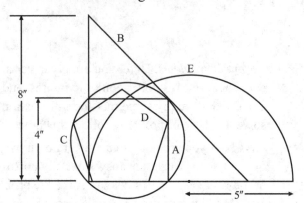

From the diagram, it is apparent that the square and the pentagon are both smaller than the circle. Further observation should show that the circle is smaller than the triangle. Thus we need only to see which is larger—the semicircle or the triangle. The perimeter of the semicircle is found by the formula $P = 2r + \pi r$ (the sum of the diameter and the semicircular arc, where r is the radius). Since r in this case is 5 inches, the perimeter is approximately $10 + (3.14)5$, or 25.7 inches. The formula for the perimeter of a triangle is the sum of the sides. In this case, two of the sides are 8 inches and the third side can be found by using the relationship $c^2 = a^2 + b^2$, where a and b are the sides of a right triangle and c is the hypotenuse. Since in our problem $a = b = 8$ inches, $c = \sqrt{8^2 + 8^2} = \sqrt{128} = \sqrt{2(64)} = 8\sqrt{2}$, which is the third side of the triangle. The perimeter is $8 + 8 + 8\sqrt{2}$, which is $16 + 8\sqrt{2}$. This is approximately equal to $16 + 8(1.4)$, or 27.2, so the triangle is the largest of the figures.

Formulas Used in Area, Perimeter, and Volume Problems

It is important that you know as many of these formulas as possible. Problems using these formulas appear frequently on tests of all kinds. You should not need to refer to the tables that follow when you do problems. Learn these formulas before you go any further.

303. *Square.* The area of a square is the square of one of its sides. Thus, if A represents the area and s represents the length of a side, $A = s^2$. The area of a square is also one-half of the square of its diagonal and may be written as $A = \frac{1}{2}d^2$, where d represents the length of a diagonal. The perimeter of a square is 4 times the length of one of its sides, or $4s$.

Square	
quantity	*formula*
area	$A = s^2$
	$A = \frac{1}{2}d^2$
perimeter	$P = 4s$

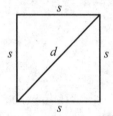

304. *Rectangle.* Let a and b represent the lengths of two adjacent sides of a rectangle, and let A represent the area. Then the area of a rectangle is the product of the two adjacent sides: $A = ab$. The perimeter, P, is the sum of twice one side and twice the adjacent side: $P = 2a + 2b$.

Rectangle	
quantity	*formula*
area	$A = ab$
perimeter	$P = 2a + 2b$

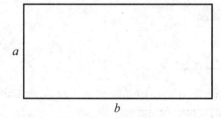

305. *Parallelogram.* The area of a parallelogram is the product of a side and the altitude, h, to that side. $A = bh$ (in this case the altitude to side b). Let a and b represent the length of 2 adjacent sides of a parallelogram. Then, C is the included angle. The area can also be expressed as the product of two adjacent sides and the sine of the included angle: $A = ab \sin C$, where C is the angle included between side a and side b. The perimeter is the sum of twice one side and twice the adjacent side. $P = 2a + 2b$. A represents its area, P its perimeter, and h the altitude to one of its sides.

Parallelogram	
quantity	*formula*
area	$A = bh$
	$A = ab \sin C$
perimeter	$P = 2a + 2b$

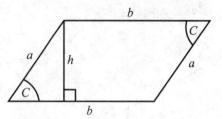

306. *Triangle.* The area of any triangle is one-half of the product of any side and the altitude to that side. $A = \frac{1}{2}bh$, where b is a side and h the altitude to that side. The area may be written also as one-half of the product of any two adjacent sides and the sine of the included angle. $A = \frac{1}{2}ab \sin C$, where A is the area, a and b are two adjacent sides, and C is the included angle. The perimeter of a triangle is the sum of the sides of the triangle. $P = a + b + c$, where P is the perimeter and c is the third side.

Triangle	
quantity	*formula*
area	$A = \frac{1}{2}bh$
	$A = \frac{1}{2}ab \sin C$
perimeter	$P = a + b + c$

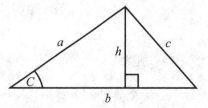

307. *Right triangle.* The area of a right triangle is one-half of the product of the two sides adjacent to the right angle. $A = \frac{1}{2}ab$, where A is the area and a and b are the adjacent sides. The perimeter is the sum of the sides. $P = a + b + c$, where c is the third side, or hypotenuse.

Right Triangle	
quantity	*formula*
area	$A = \frac{1}{2}ab$
perimeter	$P = a + b + c$
hypotenuse	$c^2 = a^2 + b^2$

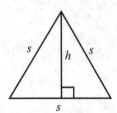

308. *Equilateral triangle.* The area of an equilateral triangle is one-fourth the product of a side squared and $\sqrt{3}$. $A = \frac{1}{4}s^2\sqrt{3}$, where A is the area and s is one of the equal sides. The perimeter of an equilateral triangle is 3 times one side, $P = 3s$, where P is the perimeter.

Equilateral Triangle	
quantity	*formula*
area	$A = \frac{1}{4}s^2\sqrt{3}$
perimeter	$P = 3s$
altitude	$h = \frac{1}{2}s\sqrt{3}$

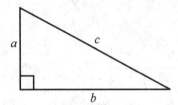

Note: The equilateral triangle and the right triangle are special cases of the triangle, and any law that applies to the triangle applies to both the right triangle and the equilateral triangle.

309. *Trapezoid.* The area of a trapezoid is one-half of the product of the altitude and the sum of the bases. $A = \frac{1}{2}h(B + b)$, where A is the area, B and b are the bases, and h is their altitude. The perimeter is the sum of the 4 sides. $P = B + b + c + d$, where P is the perimeter, and c and d are the other 2 sides.

Trapezoid	
quantity	*formula*
area	$A = \frac{1}{2}h(B + b)$
perimeter	$P = B + b + c + d$

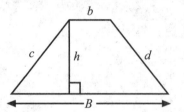

310. *Circle.* The area of a circle is π (pi) times the square of the radius, $A = \pi r^2$, where A is the area and r is the radius. The circumference is pi times the diameter, or pi times twice the radius. $C = \pi d = 2\pi r$, where C is the circumference, d is the diameter, and r is the radius.

Circle	
quantity	*formula*
area	$A = \pi r^2$
circumference	$C = \pi d = 2\pi r$

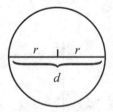

311. *Semicircle.* The area of a semicircle is one-half pi times the square of the radius.

$A = \frac{1}{2}\pi r^2$, where A is the area and r is the radius.

The length of the curved portion of the semicircle is one-half pi times the diameter, or pi times the radius. $C = \frac{1}{2}\pi d = \pi r$, where C is the circumference, d is the diameter, and r is the radius. The perimeter of a semicircle is equal to the circumference plus the length of the diameter. $P = C + d = \frac{1}{2}\pi d + d$, where P is the perimeter.

Semicircle

quantity	formula
area	$A = \frac{1}{2}\pi r^2$
circumference	$C = \frac{1}{2}\pi d = \pi r$
perimeter	$P = d\left(\frac{1}{2}\pi + 1\right)$

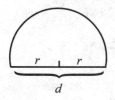

312. *Rectangular solid.* The volume of a rectangular solid is the product of the length, width, and height. $V = lwh$, where V is the volume, l is the length, w is the width, and h is the height. The volume is also the product of the area of one side and the altitude to that side. $V = Bh$, where B is the area of its base and h the altitude to that side. The surface area is the sum of the area of the six faces. $S = 2wh + 2hl + 2wl$, where S is the surface area.

Rectangular Solid

quantity	formula
volume	$V = lwh$
	$V = Bh$
surface area	$S = 2wh + 2hl + 2wl$

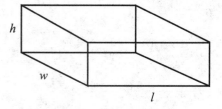

313. *Cube.* The volume of a cube is its edge cubed. $V = e^3$, where V is the volume and e is an edge. The surface area is the sum of the areas of the six faces. $S = 6e^2$, where S is the surface area.

Cube

quantity	formula
volume	$V = e^3$
surface area	$S = 6e^2$

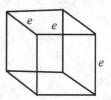

314. *Cylinder.* The volume of a cylinder is the area of the base times the height. $V = Bh$, where V is the volume, B is the area of the base, and h is the height. Note that the area of the base is the area of the circle $= \pi r^2$, where r is the radius of a base. The surface area not including the bases is the circumference of the base times the height. $S_1 = Ch = 2\pi rh$, where S_1 is the surface area without the bases, C is the circumference, and h is the height. The area of the bases $= 2\pi r^2$. Thus, the area of the cylinder, including the bases, is $S_2 = 2\pi rh + 2\pi r^2 = 2\pi r(h + r)$.

Cylinder

quantity	formula
volume	$V = Bh$
	$V = \pi r^2 h$
surface area	$S_1 = 2\pi rh$ (without bases)
	$S_2 = 2\pi r(h + r)$ (with bases)

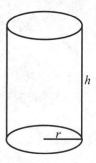

315. *Sphere*. The volume of a sphere is four-thirds π times the cube of the radius. $V = \frac{4}{3}\pi r^3$, where V is the volume and r is the radius. The surface area is 4π times the square of the radius. $S = 4\pi r^2$, where S is the surface area.

Sphere	
quantity	*formula*
volume	$V = \dfrac{4}{3}\pi r^3$
surface area	$S = 4\pi r^2$

316. *Hemisphere*. The volume of a hemisphere is two-thirds π times the cube of the radius. $V = \frac{2}{3}\pi r^3$, where V is the volume and r is the radius. The surface area not including the area of the base is 2π times the square of the radius. $S_1 = 2\pi r^2$, where S_1 is the surface area without the base. The total surface area, including the base, is equal to the surface area without the base plus the area of the base. $S_2 = 2\pi r^2 + \pi r^2 = 3\pi r^2$, where S_2 is the surface area including the base.

Hemisphere	
quantity	*formula*
volume	$V = \dfrac{2}{3}\pi r^3$
surface area	$S_1 = 2\pi r^2$ (without base)
	$S_2 = 3\pi r^2$ (with base)

317. *Pythagorean theorem*. The Pythagorean theorem states a very important geometrical relationship. It states that in a right triangle, if c is the hypotenuse (the side opposite the right angle), and a and b are the sides adjacent to the right angle, then $c^2 = a^2 + b^2$.

Pythagorean Theorem	
quantity	*formula*
square of hypotenuse	$c^2 = a^2 + b^2$
length of hypotenuse	$c = \sqrt{a^2 + b^2}$

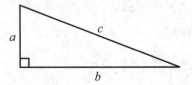

Examples of right triangles are triangles with sides of 3, 4, and 5, or 5, 12, and 13. Any multiples of these numbers also form right triangles—for example, 6, 8, and 10, or 30, 40, and 50.

Using the Pythagorean theorem to find the diagonal of a square, we get $d^2 = s^2 + s^2$ or $d^2 = 2s^2$, where d is the diagonal and s is a side. Therefore, $d = s\sqrt{2}$, or the diagonal of a square is $\sqrt{2}$ times the side.

Square	
quantity	*formula*
diagonal	$d = s\sqrt{2}$

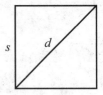

318. Another important fact to remember in doing area problems is that areas of two similar figures (figures having the same shape) are in the same ratio as the squares of corresponding parts of the figures.

Example: Triangles P and Q are similar. Side p of triangle P is 2 inches, the area of triangle P is 3 square inches, and corresponding side q of triangle Q is 4 inches. What is the area of triangle Q?

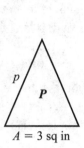

$A = 3$ sq in

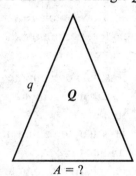

$A = ?$

Solution: The square of side p is to the square of side q as the area of P is to the area of Q. If we call x the area of triangle Q, then we get the following relationship: The square of side p is to the square of side q as the area of P is to the area of Q, or

$$\frac{2^2}{4^2} = \frac{3}{x} \text{ or } \frac{4}{16} = \frac{3}{x}$$

Therefore, $x = 12$ square inches.

SESSION 3 PRACTICE TEST

Area, Perimeter, and Volume Problems

Correct answers and solutions follow this test.

1. Which of the following figures has the largest area?

   (A) a square with a perimeter of 12 inches
   (B) a circle with a radius of 3 inches
   (C) a right triangle with sides of 3, 4, and 5 inches
   (D) a rectangle with a diagonal of 5 inches and sides of 3 and 4 inches
   (E) a regular hexagon with a perimeter of 18 inches

   A B C D E
   ○ ○ ○ ○ ○ _____

2. If the area of the base of a rectangular solid is tripled, what is the percent increase in its volume?

   (A) 200%
   (B) 300%
   (C) 600%
   (D) 800%
   (E) 900%

   A B C D E
   ○ ○ ○ ○ ○ _____

3. How many yards of carpeting that is 26 inches wide will be needed to cover a floor that is 12 feet by 13 feet?

   (A) 22 yards
   (B) 24 yards
   (C) 27 yards
   (D) 36 yards
   (E) 46 yards

   A B C D E
   ○ ○ ○ ○ ○ _____

4. If water flows into a rectangular tank at the rate of 6 cubic feet per minute, how long will it take to fill the tank, which measures $18'' \times 32'' \times 27''$?

   (A) less than one minute
   (B) less than two minutes, but not less than one minute
   (C) less than three minutes, but not less than two minutes
   (D) less than four minutes, but not less than three minutes
   (E) four minutes or more

   A B C D E
   ○ ○ ○ ○ ○ _____

5. The ratio of the area of a circle to the radius of the circle is

   (A) π
   (B) 2π
   (C) π^2
   (D) $4\pi^2$
   (E) not determinable

   A B C D E
   ○ ○ ○ ○ ○ _____

6. Which of the following figures has the smallest perimeter or circumference?

   (A) a circle with a diameter of 2 feet
   (B) a square with a diagonal of 2 feet
   (C) a rectangle with sides of 6 inches and 4 feet
   (D) a pentagon with each side equal to 16 inches
   (E) a hexagon with each side equal to 14 inches

   A B C D E
   ○ ○ ○ ○ ○ _____

7. In the figure shown, triangle ABC is similar to triangle ADE. The area of triangle ADE is 12 centimeters squared. If DE is 6 centimeters and BC is 9 centimeters, what is the area of triangle ABC in centimeters squared?

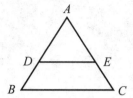

(A) 18
(B) 27
(C) 36
(D) 81
(E) 108

A B C D E
○ ○ ○ ○ ○

8. At a speed of 22 revolutions per minute, how long will it take a wheel of radius 10 inches, rolling on its edge, to travel 10 feet? (Assume π equals $\frac{22}{7}$, and express answer to nearest 0.1 second.)

(A) 0.2 second
(B) 0.4 second
(C) 5.2 seconds
(D) 6.3 seconds
(E) 7.4 seconds

A B C D E
○ ○ ○ ○ ○

9. If the diagonal of a square is 16 inches long, what is the area of the square?

(A) 64 square inches
(B) $64\sqrt{2}$ square inches
(C) 128 square inches
(D) $128\sqrt{2}$ square inches
(E) 256 square inches

A B C D E
○ ○ ○ ○ ○

10. In the diagram shown, $ACDF$ is a rectangle, and $GBHE$ is a circle. If $CD = 4$ inches and $AC = 6$ inches, what is the number of square inches in the shaded area?

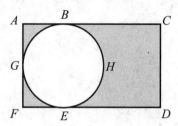

(A) $16 - 4\pi$ square inches
(B) $24 - 4\pi$ square inches
(C) $24 - 16\pi$ square inches
(D) $16 - 2\pi$ square inches
(E) $24 - 2\pi$ square inches

A B C D E
○ ○ ○ ○ ○

11. What is the area of an equilateral triangle with a side of 1 inch?

(A) 1 square inch
(B) $\frac{\sqrt{3}}{2}$ square inch
(C) $\frac{1}{2}$ square inch
(D) $\frac{\sqrt{3}}{4}$ square inch
(E) $\frac{1}{3}$ square inch

A B C D E
○ ○ ○ ○ ○

12. A right triangle with legs measuring 12 feet and 16 feet is inscribed in a circle. If the hypotenuse of the triangle is also the diameter of the circle, how many square feet is the area of the circle?

(A) 10π
(B) 20π
(C) 96π
(D) 100π
(E) 400π

A B C D E
○ ○ ○ ○ ○

13. A couple wishes to cover their floor with tiles, each one measuring $\frac{3}{4}$ inch by 2 inches. If the room is a rectangle, measuring 12 feet by 18 feet, how many such tiles will they need?

(A) 144
(B) 1,152
(C) 1,728
(D) 9,216
(E) 20,736

A B C D E
〇 〇 〇 〇 〇
_____

14. The volume of a sphere is equal to the volume of a cylinder. If the radius of the sphere is 4 meters and the radius of the cylinder is 8 meters, what is the height of the cylinder?

(A) 8 meters
(B) $\frac{4}{3}$ meters
(C) 4 meters
(D) $\frac{16}{3}$ meters
(E) 1 meter

A B C D E
〇 〇 〇 〇 〇
_____

15. A wheel travels 33 yards in 15 revolutions. What is its diameter? (Assume $\pi = \frac{22}{7}$.)

(A) 0.35 foot
(B) 0.70 foot
(C) 1.05 feet
(D) 1.40 feet
(E) 2.10 feet

A B C D E
〇 〇 〇 〇 〇
_____

16. If a rectangle with a perimeter of 48 inches is equal in area to a right triangle with legs of 12 inches and 24 inches, what is the rectangle's diagonal?

(A) 12 inches
(B) $12\sqrt{2}$ inches
(C) $12\sqrt{3}$ inches
(D) 24 inches
(E) The answer cannot be determined from the given information.

A B C D E
〇 〇 〇 〇 〇
_____

17. What is the approximate area that remains after a circle $3\frac{1}{2}''$ in diameter is cut from a square piece of cloth with a side of 8"? (Use $\pi = \frac{22}{7}$.)

(A) 25.5 square inches
(B) 54.4 square inches
(C) 56.8 square inches
(D) 142.1 square inches
(E) 284.2 square inches

A B C D E
〇 〇 〇 〇 〇
_____

18. A container is shaped like a rectangular solid with sides of 3 inches, 3 inches, and 11 inches. What is its approximate capacity, if 1 gallon equals 231 cubic inches? (1 gallon = 128 fluid ounces.)

(A) 14 ounces
(B) 27 ounces
(C) 55 ounces
(D) 110 ounces
(E) 219 ounces

A B C D E
〇 〇 〇 〇 〇
_____

19. The 20-inch-diameter wheels of one car travel at a rate of 24 revolutions per minute, while the 30-inch-diameter wheels of a second car travel at a rate of 18 revolutions per minute. What is the ratio of the speed of the second car to that of the first?

(A) 1 : 1
(B) 3 : 2
(C) 4 : 3
(D) 6 : 5
(E) 9 : 8

A B C D E
〇 〇 〇 〇 〇
_____

20. A circular garden 20 feet in diameter is surrounded by a path 3 feet wide. What is the area of the path?

(A) 9π square feet
(B) 51π square feet
(C) 60π square feet
(D) 69π square feet
(E) 90π square feet

A B C D E
〇 〇 〇 〇 〇
_____

21. What is the area of a semicircle with a diameter of 16 inches?

(A) 32π square inches
(B) 64π square inches
(C) 128π square inches
(D) 256π square inches
(E) 512π square inches

A B C D E
◯ ◯ ◯ ◯ ◯

22. If the edges of a cube add up to 4 feet in length, what is the volume of the cube?

(A) 64 cubic inches
(B) 125 cubic inches
(C) 216 cubic inches
(D) 512 cubic inches
(E) none of these

A B C D E
◯ ◯ ◯ ◯ ◯

23. The inside of a trough is shaped like a rectangular solid, 25 feet long, 6 inches wide, and filled with water to a depth of 35 inches. If we wish to raise the depth of the water to 38 inches, how much water must be let into the tank?

(A) $\dfrac{25}{96}$ cubic foot

(B) $\dfrac{25}{8}$ cubic feet

(C) $\dfrac{75}{2}$ cubic feet

(D) 225 cubic feet
(E) 450 cubic feet

A B C D E
◯ ◯ ◯ ◯ ◯

24. If 1 gallon of water equals 231 cubic inches, approximately how much water will fill a cylindrical vase 7 inches in diameter and 10 inches high? (Assume $\pi = \dfrac{22}{7}$.)

(A) 1.7 gallons
(B) 2.1 gallons
(C) 3.3 gallons
(D) 5.3 gallons
(E) 6.7 gallons

A B C D E
◯ ◯ ◯ ◯ ◯

25. Tiles of linoleum, measuring 8 inches × 8 inches, cost 9¢ apiece. At this rate, what will it cost a man to cover a floor with these tiles, if his floor measures 10 feet by 16 feet?

(A) $22.50
(B) $25.00
(C) $28.00
(D) $32.40
(E) $36.00

A B C D E
◯ ◯ ◯ ◯ ◯

26. Which of the following figures has the largest area?

(A) a 3–4–5 triangle with a hypotenuse of 25 inches
(B) a circle with a diameter of 20 inches
(C) a square with a 20-inch diagonal
(D) a regular hexagon with a side equal to 10 inches
(E) a rectangle with sides of 10 inches and 30 inches

A B C D E
◯ ◯ ◯ ◯ ◯

27. If the radius of the base of a cylinder is tripled and its height is divided by three, what is the ratio of the volume of the new cylinder to the volume of the original cylinder?

(A) 1 : 9
(B) 1 : 3
(C) 1 : 1
(D) 3 : 1
(E) 9 : 1

A B C D E
◯ ◯ ◯ ◯ ◯

28. If 1 cubic foot of water equals 7.5 gallons, how long will it take for a faucet that flows at a rate of 10 gal/min to fill a cube 2 feet on each side (to the nearest minute)?

(A) 4 minutes
(B) 5 minutes
(C) 6 minutes
(D) 7 minutes
(E) 8 minutes

A B C D E
◯ ◯ ◯ ◯ ◯

29. The ratio of the area of a square to the *square of its diagonal* is which of the following?

    (A) 2 : 1
    (B) √2 : 1
    (C) 1 : 1
    (D) 1 : √2
    (E) 1 : 2

    A B C D E
    ○ ○ ○ ○ ○

30. If *ABCD* is a square, with side *AB* = 4 inches, and *AEB* and *CED* are semicircles, what is the area of the shaded portion of the diagram below?

    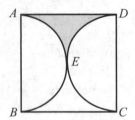

    (A) 8 − π square inches
    (B) 8 − 2π square inches
    (C) 16 − 2π square inches
    (D) 16 − 4π square inches
    (E) 16 − 8π square inches

    A B C D E
    ○ ○ ○ ○ ○

31. If the area of a circle is equal to the area of a rectangle, one of whose sides is equal to π, express the other side of the rectangle, *x*, in terms of the radius of the circle, *r*.

    (A) $x = r$
    (B) $x = \pi r$
    (C) $x = r^2$
    (D) $x = \sqrt{r}$
    (E) $x = \dfrac{1}{r}$

    A B C D E
    ○ ○ ○ ○ ○

32. If the volume of a cube is 27 cubic meters, find the surface area of the cube.

    (A) 9 square meters
    (B) 18 square meters
    (C) 54 square meters
    (D) 3 square meters
    (E) 1 square meter

    A B C D E
    ○ ○ ○ ○ ○

33. What is the area of a circle with a diameter of 5 inches?

    (A) 5π square inches
    (B) $\dfrac{5}{2}$π square inches
    (C) $\dfrac{25}{4}$π square inches
    (D) 10π square inches
    (E) 25π square inches

    A B C D E
    ○ ○ ○ ○ ○

34. What is the area of the triangle pictured below?

    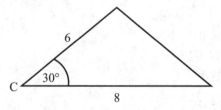

    (A) 18 square units
    (B) 32 square units
    (C) 24 square units
    (D) 12 square units
    (E) 124 square units

    A B C D E
    ○ ○ ○ ○ ○

35. If a wheel travels 1 mile in 1 minute, at a rate of 600 revolutions per minute, what is the diameter of the wheel, in feet? (Use $\pi = \dfrac{22}{7}$, 1 mile = 5,280 feet.)

    (A) 2.2 feet
    (B) 2.4 feet
    (C) 2.6 feet
    (D) 2.8 feet
    (E) 3.0 feet

    A B C D E
    ○ ○ ○ ○ ○

36. Which of the following figures has the largest perimeter?

    (A) a square with a diagonal of 5 feet
    (B) a rectangle with sides of 3 feet and 4 feet
    (C) an equilateral triangle with a side of 48 inches
    (D) a regular hexagon whose longest diagonal is 6 feet
    (E) a parallelogram with sides of 6 inches and 7 feet

    A B C D E
    ○ ○ ○ ○ ○

37. A man has two containers: The first is a rectangular solid, measuring 3 inches × 4 inches × 10 inches; the second is a cylinder having a base with a radius of 2 inches and a height of 10 inches. If the first container is filled with water, and then this water is poured into the second container, which of the following occurs?

    (A) There is room for more water in the second container.
    (B) The second container is completely filled, without overflowing.
    (C) The second container overflows by less than 1 cubic inch.
    (D) The second container overflows by less than 2 (but not less than 1) cubic inches.
    (E) The second container overflows by 2 or more cubic inches.

    A B C D E
    ○ ○ ○ ○ ○
    _____

38. If, in this diagram, A represents a square with a side of 4 inches and B, C, D, and E are semicircles, what is the area of the entire figure?

    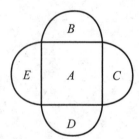

    (A) $16 + 4\pi$ square inches
    (B) $16 + 8\pi$ square inches
    (C) $16 + 16\pi$ square inches
    (D) $16 + 32\pi$ square inches
    (E) $16 + 64\pi$ square inches

    A B C D E
    ○ ○ ○ ○ ○
    _____

39. The area of a square is $81p^2$. What is the length of the square's diagonal?

    (A) $9p$
    (B) $9p\sqrt{2}$
    (C) $18p$
    (D) $9p^2$
    (E) $18p^2$

    A B C D E
    ○ ○ ○ ○ ○
    _____

40. The following diagram represents the floor of a room that is to be covered with carpeting at a price of $2.50 per square yard. What will be the cost of the carpeting?

    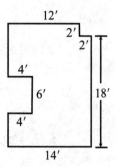

    (A) $70
    (B) $125
    (C) $480
    (D) $630
    (E) none of these

    A B C D E
    ○ ○ ○ ○ ○
    _____

41. Which of the following has the largest perimeter?

    (A) a square with a diagonal of 10 inches
    (B) a 3–4–5 right triangle with a hypotenuse of 15 inches
    (C) a pentagon, each of whose sides is 5 inches
    (D) a right isosceles triangle with an area of 72 square inches
    (E) a regular hexagon with a radius of 5 inches

    A B C D E
    ○ ○ ○ ○ ○
    _____

42. If you double the area of the base of a rectangular solid and also triple the solid's height, what is the ratio of the new volume to the old volume?

    (A) 2 : 3
    (B) 3 : 2
    (C) 1 : 6
    (D) 6 : 1
    (E) none of these

    A B C D E
    ○ ○ ○ ○ ○
    _____

43. A certain type of linoleum costs $1.50 per square yard. If a room measures 27 feet by 14 feet, what will be the cost of covering it with linoleum?

    (A) $44.10
    (B) $51.60
    (C) $63.00
    (D) $132.30
    (E) $189.00

    A B C D E
    ○ ○ ○ ○ ○

44. How many circles, each with a 4-inch radius, can be cut from a rectangular sheet of paper measuring 16 inches × 24 inches?

    (A) 6
    (B) 7
    (C) 8
    (D) 12
    (E) 24

    A B C D E
    ○ ○ ○ ○ ○

45. The ratio of the area of an equilateral triangle, in square inches, to its perimeter, in inches, is

    (A) 3 : 4
    (B) 4 : 3
    (C) $\sqrt{3}$: 4
    (D) 4 : $\sqrt{3}$
    (E) The answer cannot be determined from the given information.

    A B C D E
    ○ ○ ○ ○ ○

46. What is the volume of a cylinder whose radius is 4 inches and whose height is 10 inches? (Assume that $\pi = 3.14$.)

    (A) 125.6 cubic inches
    (B) 134.4 cubic inches
    (C) 144.0 cubic inches
    (D) 201.2 cubic inches
    (E) 502.4 cubic inches

    A B C D E
    ○ ○ ○ ○ ○

47. The area of a square is $144s^2$. What is the square's diagonal?

    (A) $12s$
    (B) $12s\sqrt{2}$
    (C) $24s$
    (D) $144s$
    (E) $144s^2$

    A B C D E
    ○ ○ ○ ○ ○

48. A circular pool is 10 feet in diameter and 5 feet deep. What is its volume, in cubic feet?

    (A) 50 cubic feet
    (B) 50π cubic feet
    (C) 125π cubic feet
    (D) 250π cubic feet
    (E) 500π cubic feet

    A B C D E
    ○ ○ ○ ○ ○

49. A certain type of carpeting is 30 inches wide. How many yards of this carpet will be needed to cover a floor that measures 20 feet by 24 feet?

    (A) 48
    (B) 64
    (C) 144
    (D) 192
    (E) none of these

    A B C D E
    ○ ○ ○ ○ ○

50. With each rotation of the blade, a push mower cuts a circular area of about 380 square inches. Approximately what is the circumference of the rotation of the blade in inches?

    (A) 11
    (B) 22
    (C) 35
    (D) 69
    (E) 121

    A B C D E
    ○ ○ ○ ○ ○

Answer Key for Session 3 Practice Test

1. B	14. B	27. D	39. B
2. A	15. E	28. C	40. A
3. B	16. B	29. E	41. D
4. B	17. B	30. B	42. D
5. E	18. C	31. C	43. C
6. B	19. E	32. C	44. A
7. B	20. D	33. C	45. E
8. C	21. A	34. D	46. E
9. C	22. A	35. D	47. B
10. B	23. B	36. D	48. C
11. D	24. A	37. A	49. B
12. D	25. D	38. B	50. D
13. E	26. B		

Answers and Solutions for Session 3 Practice Test

1. Choice B is correct. This is a fairly difficult comparison problem, but the use of diagrams simplifies it considerably.

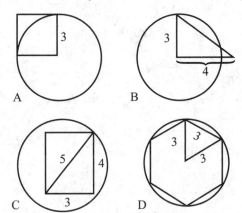

From diagram A it is apparent that the circle is larger than the square. Diagram B shows that the circle is larger than the right triangle. And, since a rectangle with a diagonal of 5 inches is made up of two right triangles, as shown in diagram C, the circle is larger than the rectangle. Finally, as shown in diagram D, the circle is larger than the hexagon. Thus, the circle is the largest of the five figures described. (Refresher 302)

2. Choice A is correct. This is a formula problem: Letting V_o represent the original volume, B_o represent the original area of the base, and h_o represent

the original height of the figure, we have the formula $V_o = h_o B_o$. The new volume, V, is equal to $3h_o B_o$. Thus, the new volume is three times the original volume—an *increase* of 200%. (Refresher 301)

3. Choice B is correct. Here, we must find the length of carpeting needed to cover an area of 12 feet × 13 feet, or 156 square feet. The formula needed is: $A = lw$, where $l =$ length and $w =$ width, both expressed in *feet*. Now, since we know that $A = 156$ square feet, and $w = 26$ inches, or $\frac{26}{12}$ feet, we can calculate l as $156 \div \left(\frac{26}{12}\right)$, or 72 feet. But since the answer must be expressed in yards, we express 72 feet as 24 yards. (Refresher 304)

4. Choice B is correct. First we must calculate the volume of the tank in cubic feet. Converting the dimensions of the box to feet, we get $1\frac{1}{2}$ feet × $2\frac{2}{3}$ feet × $2\frac{1}{4}$ feet, so the total volume is $\frac{3}{2} \times \frac{8}{3} \times \frac{9}{4}$, or 9, cubic feet. Thus, at a rate of 6 cubic feet per minute, it would take $\frac{9}{6}$, or $1\frac{1}{2}$, minutes to fill the tank. (Refreshers 312, 201)

5. Choice E is correct. Here, we use the formula $A = \pi r^2$, where $A =$ area, and $r =$ radius. Thus, the ratio of A to r is just $\frac{A}{r} = \pi r$. Since r is not a constant, the ratio cannot be determined. (Refresher 310)

6. Choice B is correct.

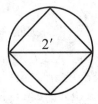

First, we diagram the circle and the square and see that the square has a smaller perimeter. Next, we notice that the circle, which has a larger circumference than the square, has circumference 2π, or about 6.3 feet. But the perimeters of the rectangle (9 feet), of the pentagon (5 × 16 inches = 80 inches = 6 feet, 8 inches), and of the hexagon (6 × 14 inches = 84 inches = 7 feet) are all greater than the circumference of the circle, and therefore also greater than the perimeter of the square. Thus, the square has the smallest perimeter. (Refresher 302)

7. Choice B is correct. Because the triangles are similar, the sides are proportional. However, we want to find the area of triangle ABC, so set up a proportion comparing the square of DE to the square of BC and the area of ADE to the area of ABC.

$$\frac{6^2}{9^2} = \frac{12}{x} \quad \text{or} \quad \frac{36}{81} = \frac{12}{x}$$

Therefore, the area of ABC equals 27 centimeters squared. (Refresher 318)

8. Choice C is correct. Since the radius of the circle is 10 inches, its circumference is $2\pi(10 \text{ inches})$, or $2\left(\frac{22}{7}\right)(10 \text{ inches})$, which equals $\frac{440}{7}$ inches. This is the distance the wheel will travel in one revolution. To travel 10 feet, or 120 inches, it must travel $120 \div \frac{440}{7}$, or $\frac{21}{11}$ revolutions. At a speed of 22 revolutions per minute, or $\frac{11}{30}$ revolutions per second, it will take $\frac{21}{11} \div \frac{11}{30}$, or $\frac{630}{121}$ seconds. Carrying the division to the nearest tenth of a second, we get 5.2 seconds. (Refresher 310)

9. Choice C is correct. If we let d represent the diagonal of a square, s represent the length of one side, and A represent the area, then we have two formulas: $d = s\sqrt{2}$ and $A = s^2$, relating the three quantities. However, from the first equation, we can see that $s^2 = \frac{d^2}{2}$, so we can derive a third formula, $A = \frac{d^2}{2}$, relating A and d. We are given that d equals 16 inches, so we can calculate the value of A as $\frac{(16 \text{ inches})^2}{2}$, or 128 square inches. (Refresher 303)

10. Choice B is correct. The area of the shaded figure is equal to the difference between the areas of the rectangle and the circle. The area of the rectangle is defined by the formula $A = bh$, where b and h are the two adjacent sides of the rectangle. In this case, A is equal to 4 inches $\times$ 6 inches, or 24 square inches. The area of the circle is defined by the formula $A = \pi r^2$, where r is the radius. Since BE equals the diameter of the circle and is equal to 4 inches, then the radius must be 2 inches. Thus, the area of the circle is $\pi(2 \text{ inches})^2$, or 4π square inches. Subtracting, we obtain the area of the shaded portion: $24 - 4\pi$ square inches. (Refreshers 304, 310)

11. Choice D is correct. We use the formula for the area of an equilateral triangle, $\frac{\sqrt{3}s^2}{4}$, where s is a side. If $s = 1$, then the area of the triangle is $\frac{\sqrt{3}}{4}$. (Refresher 308)

12. Choice D is correct.

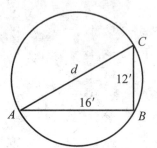

Use the Pythagorean theorem to find the length of the hypotenuse, which is also the diameter of the circle: $\sqrt{12^2 + 16^2} = \sqrt{400} = 20$ feet. Therefore, if we call d the diameter, the area of the circle is $A = \pi\left(\frac{d}{2}\right)^2 = \pi\left(\frac{20}{2}\right)^2 = 100\pi$ square feet. (Refreshers 310, 317)

13. Choice E is correct. The area of the room $= 12$ feet $\times$ 18 feet $= 216$ square feet. The area of one tile $= \frac{3}{4}$ inch $\times$ 2 inches $= \frac{3}{2}$ square inches. The number of tiles $=$ area of the room $\div$ area of one tile

$$= \frac{216 \text{ square feet}}{\frac{3}{2} \text{ square inches}} = \frac{216 \times 144 \text{ square inches}}{\frac{3}{2} \text{ square inches}}$$

$$= 216 \times \overset{48}{\cancel{144}} \times \frac{2}{\cancel{3}} = 20{,}736 \text{ tiles.} \quad \text{(Refresher 304)}$$

14. Choice B is correct. The volume of a sphere is found by using the formula $\frac{4}{3}\pi r^3$, where r is the radius. In this case, the radius is 4 meters, so the volume is $\frac{256}{3}\pi$ cubic meters. This is equal to the volume of a cylinder of radius 8 meters, so $\frac{256}{3}\pi = \pi 8^2 h$, since the volume of a cylinder is $\pi r^2 h$, where h is the height and r is the radius of the base. Solving $\frac{256\pi}{3} = \pi 8^2 h$:

$$h = \frac{\frac{256\cancel{\pi}}{3}}{\cancel{\pi}64} = \frac{\overset{4}{\cancel{256}}}{3} \times \frac{1}{\cancel{64}} = \frac{4}{3} \text{ meters}$$

(Refreshers 314, 315)

15. Choice E is correct. 33 yards = 99 feet = 15 revolutions. Thus, 1 revolution = $\frac{99}{15}$ feet = $\frac{33}{5}$ feet = 6.6 feet. Since 1 revolution = the circumference of the wheel, the wheel's diameter = circumference ÷ π. 6.6 feet ÷ $\frac{22}{7}$ = 2.10 feet.   (Refresher 310)

16. Choice B is correct. The area of the right triangle is equal to $\frac{1}{2}ab$, where a and b are the legs of the triangle. In this case, the area is $\frac{1}{2} \times 12 \times 24$, or 144 square inches. If we call the sides of the rectangle x and y we get $2x + 2y = 48$, or $y = 24 - x$. The area of the rectangle is xy, or $x(24 - x)$. This must be equal to 144, so we get the equation $24x - x^2 = 144$. Adding $x^2 - 24x$ to both sides of this last equation gives us $x^2 - 24x + 144 = 0$, or $(x - 12)^2 = 0$. Thus, $x = 12$. Since $y = 24 - x$, $y = 24 - 12$, or $y = 12$. By the Pythagorean theorem, the diagonal of the rectangle = $\sqrt{12^2 + 12^2}$ = $\sqrt{144 + 144}$ = $\sqrt{2(144)}$ = $(\sqrt{2})(\sqrt{144})$ = $12\sqrt{2}$.
    (Refreshers 304, 306, 317)

17. Choice B is correct. The area of the square is 64 square inches, since $A = s^2$ where s is the length of a side and A is the area. The area of the circle is $\pi\left(\frac{7}{4}\right)^2 = \frac{22}{7} \times \frac{49}{16} = \frac{77}{8} = 9.625$. Subtracting, $64 - 9.625 = 54.375 = 54.4$ (approximately).
    (Refreshers 304, 310)

18. Choice C is correct. The volume of the container ($V = lwh$, where l, w, h are the adjacent sides of the solid) = (3 inches)(3 inches)(11 inches) = 99 cubic inches. Since 1 gallon equals 231 cubic inches, 99 cubic inches equal $\frac{99}{231}$ gallon (the fraction reduces to $\frac{3}{7}$). One gallon equals 128 ounces (1 gallon = 4 quarts; 1 quart = 2 pints; 1 pint = 16 ounces), so the container holds $\frac{384}{7}$ ounces = 55 ounces (approximately).   (Refresher 312)

19. Choice E is correct. The speed of the first wheel is equal to its rate of revolution multiplied by its circumference, which equals 24×20 inches $\times \pi = 480\pi$ inches per minute. The speed of the second is 18×30 inches $\times \pi = 540\pi$ inches per minute. Thus, their ratio is $540\pi : 480\pi = 9 : 8$.
    (Refresher 310)

20. Choice D is correct.

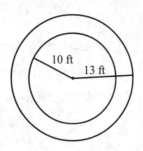

The area of the path is equal to the area of the ring between two concentric circles of radii 10 feet and 13 feet. This area is obtained by subtracting the area of the smaller circle from the area of the larger circle. The area of the larger circle is equal to $\pi \times$ its radius squared = $\pi(13)^2$ square feet = 169π square feet. By the same process, the area of the smaller circle = 100π square feet. The area of the path = $169\pi - 100\pi = 69\pi$ square feet.   (Refresher 310)

21. Choice A is correct. The diameter = 16 inches, so the radius = 8 inches. Thus, the area of the whole circle = $\pi(8 \text{ inches})^2 = 64\pi$ square inches. The area of the semicircle is one-half of the area of the whole circle, or 32π square inches.   (Refresher 311)

22. Choice A is correct.

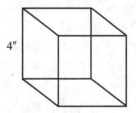

A cube has 12 equal edges, so the length of one side of the cube is $\frac{1}{12}$ of 4 feet, or 4 inches. Thus, its volume is 4 inches $\times$ 4 inches $\times$ 4 inches = 64 cubic inches.   (Refresher 313)

23. Choice B is correct.

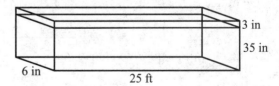

The additional water will take the shape of a rectangular solid measuring 25 feet $\times$ 6 inches $\times$ 3 inches (3″ = the added depth) = $25 \times \frac{1}{2} \times \frac{1}{4}$ cubic feet = $\frac{25}{8}$ cubic feet.   (Refresher 312)

24. Choice A is correct. The volume of the cylinder $= \pi r^2 h = \left(\frac{22}{7}\right)\left(\frac{7}{2}\right)^2(10)$ cubic inches $= 385$ cubic inches. 231 cubic inches $= 1$ gallon, so 385 cubic inches $= \frac{385}{231}$ gallons $= \frac{5}{3}$ gallons $= 1.7$ gallons (approximately).   (Refresher 314)

25. Choice D is correct. The area of floor $= 10$ feet $\times$ 16 feet $= 160$ square feet. Area of one tile $=$ 8 inches $\times$ 8 inches $= 64$ square inches $= \frac{64}{144}$ square feet $= \frac{4}{9}$ square foot. (Remember, 1 square foot equals 144 square inches.) Thus, the number of tiles $=$ area of floor $\div$ area of tile $= 160 \div \frac{4}{9} =$ 360. At 9¢ apiece, the tiles will cost $32.40.
                    (Refresher 304)

26. Choice B is correct. Looking at the following three diagrams, we can observe that the triangle, square, and hexagon are all smaller than the circle.

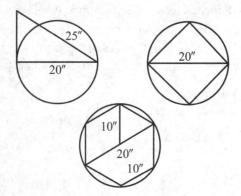

Comparing the areas of the circle and the rectangle, we notice that the area of the circle is $\pi(10 \text{ inches})^2 = 100\pi$ square inches, which is greater than $(10 \text{ inches})(30 \text{ inches}) = 300$ square inches, the area of the rectangle. (π is approximately 3.14.)   (Refresher 302)

27. Choice D is correct. In a cylinder, $V = \pi r^2 h$, where r is the radius of the base and h is the height. The new volume $V' = \pi(3r)^2 \left(\frac{h}{3}\right) = 3\pi r^2 h = 3V$.

Thus, the ratio of the new volume to the old volume is $3 : 1$.   (Refresher 314)

28. Choice C is correct. A cube 2 feet on each side has a volume of $2 \times 2 \times 2 = 8$ cubic feet. Since 1 cubic foot equals 7.5 gallons, 8 cubic feet equals 60 gallons. If the faucet flows at the rate of 10 gallons/minute, it will take 6 minutes to fill the cube.
                    (Refresher 313)

29. Choice E is correct. Let $s =$ the side of the square. Then, the area of the square is equal to s^2. The diagonal of the square is $s\sqrt{2}$, so the square of the diagonal is $2s^2$. Thus, the ratio of the area of the square to the square of the diagonal is $s^2 : 2s^2$, or $1 : 2$.   (Refresher 303)

30. Choice B is correct. The area of the square $ABCD$ is equal to 4 inches $\times$ 4 inches $= 16$ square inches. The two semicircles can be placed together diameter-to-diameter to form a circle with a radius of 2 inches, and thus, an area of 4π. Subtracting the area of the circle from the area of the square, we obtain the combined areas of AED and BEC. But, since the figure is symmetrical, AED and BEC must be equal. The area of the remainder is $16 - 4\pi$; AED is one-half of this remainder, or $8 - 2\pi$ square inches.
                    (Refreshers 303, 310)

31. Choice C is correct. The area of the circle is equal to πr^2, and the area of the rectangle is equal to πx. Since these areas are equal, $\pi r^2 = \pi x$, and $x = r^2$.   (Refreshers 304, 310)

32. Choice C is correct. The volume of a cube is e^3, where e is the length of an edge. If the volume is 27 cubic meters, then $e^3 = 27$ and $e = 3$ meters. The surface area of a cube is $6e^2$, and if $e = 3$ meters, then the surface area is 54 square meters.
                    (Refresher 313)

33. Choice C is correct. The formula for the area of a circle is $A = \pi r^2$, where r is the radius. Since the diameter of this circle is 5 inches, it will have a radius of $\frac{5}{2}$ inches. Therefore, that area is $A = \pi\left(\frac{5}{2}\right)^2 = \frac{25}{4}\pi$ square inches.   (Refresher 310)

34. Choice D is correct. Draw a perpendicular line from the top of the triangle to the side, which is 8. You have created a 30–60–90 right triangle. The line drawn is $\frac{1}{2}$ of $6 = 3$. The area of the whole triangle is the altitude multiplied by the base divided by 2. The altitude is 3 and the base is 8, so the area is $3 \times \frac{8}{2} = 12$.   (Refresher 307)

35. Choice D is correct. Since the wheel takes 1 minute to make 600 revolutions and travels 1 mile in that time, we have the relation 1 mile = 5,280 feet = 600 revolutions. Thus 1 revolution = $\frac{5,280}{600}$ feet = 8.8 feet = circumference = π(diameter) = $\left(\frac{22}{7}\right)$ (diameter). Therefore, the diameter = 8.8 feet ÷ $\left(\frac{22}{7}\right)$ = 2.8 feet. (Refresher 310)

36. Choice D is correct. In this case, it is easiest to calculate the perimeters of the 5 figures. According to the Pythagorean theorem, a square with a diagonal of 5 feet has a side of $\frac{5}{\sqrt{2}}$, which is equal to $\frac{5\sqrt{2}}{2}$. (This is found by multiplying the numerator and denominator of $\frac{5}{\sqrt{2}}$ by $\sqrt{2}$.) If each side of the square is $\frac{5\sqrt{2}}{2}$, then the perimeter is $\overset{2}{\cancel{4}} \times \frac{5\sqrt{2}}{\cancel{2}} = 10\sqrt{2}$ feet. A rectangle with sides of 3 feet and 4 feet has a perimeter of 2(3) + 2(4), or 14 feet. An equilateral triangle with a side of 48 inches, or 4 feet, has a perimeter of 12 feet. A regular hexagon whose longest diagonal is 6 feet has a side of 3 feet and, therefore, a perimeter of 18 feet. (See the diagram for Solution 41.) Finally, a parallelogram with sides of 6 inches, or $\frac{1}{2}$ foot, and 7 feet has a perimeter of 15 feet. Therefore, the hexagon has the largest perimeter. (Refreshers 302, 317)

37. Choice A is correct. The volume of the first container is equal to 3 inches × 4 inches × 10 inches, or 120 cubic inches. The volume of the second container, the cylinder, is equal to $\pi r^2 h$ = π(2 inches)²(10 inches), or 40π cubic inches, which is greater than 120 cubic inches (π is greater than 3). So the second container can hold more than the first. If the first container is filled and the contents poured into the second, there will be room for more water in the second. (Refreshers 312, 314)

38. Choice B is correct. The area of the square is 16 square inches. The four semicircles can be added to form two circles, each of radius 2 inches, so the area of each circle is 4π square inches, and the two circles add up to 8π square inches. Thus, the total area is 16 + 8π square inches. (Refreshers 303, 311)

39. Choice B is correct. Since the area of the square is $81p^2$, one side of the square will equal $9p$. According to the Pythagorean theorem, the diagonal will equal $\sqrt{81p^2 + 81p^2} = 9p\sqrt{2}$. (Refreshers 303, 317)

40. Choice A is correct. We can regard the area as a rectangle, 20 ft × 14 ft, with two rectangles, measuring 4 ft × 6 ft and 2 ft × 2 ft, cut out. Thus, the area is equal to 280 sq ft − 24 sq ft − 4 sq ft = 252 sq ft = $\frac{252}{9}$ sq yd = 28 sq yds. (Remember, 1 square yard equals 9 square feet.) At $2.50 per square yard, 28 square yards will cost $70. (Refresher 304)

41. Choice D is correct.

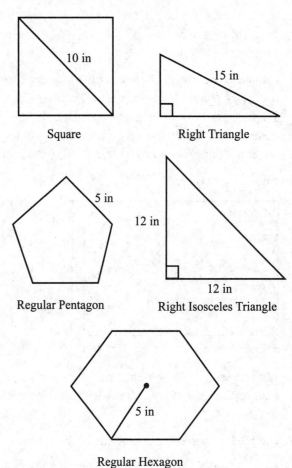

Square   Right Triangle

10 in

15 in

5 in   12 in

12 in

Regular Pentagon   Right Isosceles Triangle

5 in

Regular Hexagon

The perimeter of the square is equal to four times its side; since a side is $\frac{1}{\sqrt{2}}$, or $\frac{\sqrt{2}}{2}$ times the diagonal, the perimeter of the square in question is 4 × 5$\sqrt{2}$ = 20$\sqrt{2}$, which is approximately equal to 28.28 inches. The perimeter of a right triangle with sides that are in a 3–4–5 ratio, i.e., 9 inches, 12 inches, and 15 inches, is 9 + 12 + 15 = 36 inches. The perimeter of the pentagon is 5 × 5 inches, or 25 inches. The perimeter of the right isosceles triangle (with sides of 12 inches, 12 inches, and 12√2 inches) is 24 + 12√2 inches, which is approximately equal to 40.968 inches. The perimeter of the hexagon is 6 × 5 inches, or 30 inches. Thus, the isosceles right triangle has the largest perimeter of those figures mentioned. You should become familiar with the approximate value of √2, which is 1.414. (Refresher 302)

42. Choice D is correct. For rectangular solids, the following formula holds:

$$V = Ah, \text{ where } A \text{ is the area of the base,}$$
$$\text{and } h \text{ is the height.}$$

If we replace A with $2A$, and h with $3h$, we get $V' = (2A)(3h) = 6V$. Thus, $V' : V = 6 : 1$.
(Refresher 312)

43. Choice C is correct. The area of the room is 27 feet × 14 feet = 378 square feet. 9 square feet = 1 square yard, so the area of the room is 42 square yards. At $1.50 per square yard, the linoleum to cover the floor will cost $63.00. (Refresher 304)

44. Choice A is correct.

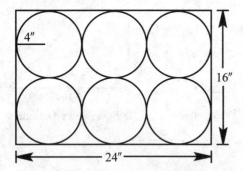

A circle with a 4-inch radius has an 8-inch diameter, so there can be only 2 rows of 3 circles each, or 6 circles. (Refresher 310)

45. Choice E is correct. Let one side of the triangle be s. Then the area of the triangle is $\frac{s^2\sqrt{3}}{4}$. (Either memorize this formula or remember that it is derived by drawing an altitude to divide the triangle into two congruent 30°–60°–90° right

triangles.) The perimeter of the equilateral triangle is $3s$, so the ratio of the area to the perimeter is $\frac{s^2\sqrt{3}}{4} : 3s$, or $s : 4\sqrt{3}$, which cannot be determined unless we know the value of s. (Refresher 308)

46. Choice E is correct. The formula for volume of a cylinder is $V = \pi r^2 h$, where r is the radius of the base and h is the height. Here, $r = 4$ inches and $h = 10$ inches, while $\pi \approx 3.14$. (The symbol $\approx$ means "approximately equal to.") Thus $V \approx (4)^2(10)(3.14) = 160(3.14) = 502.4$ cubic inches.
(Refresher 314)

47. Choice B is correct. If the area of a square is $144s^2$, then one side will equal $12s$, so the diagonal will equal $12s\sqrt{2}$. (The Pythagorean theorem may be used here to get $d = \sqrt{144s^2 + 144s^2}$, where d is the diagonal.) (Refreshers 303, 317)

48. Choice C is correct. The inside of the pool forms a cylinder of radius 5 feet and height 5 feet. The volume is $\pi r^2 h$, or $\pi \times 5 \times 5 \times 5 = 125\pi$ cubic feet. (Refresher 314)

49. Choice B is correct. The area of the floor is 20 feet × 24 feet = 480 square feet. 30 inches is equal to $2\frac{1}{2}$ feet, and we must find the length that, when multiplied by $2\frac{1}{2}$ feet, will yield 480 square feet. This length is 192 feet, which equals 64 yards (3 feet = 1 yard). (Refresher 304)

50. Choice D is correct. The area of each rotation is about 380 inches ($A = \pi r^2$). Divide 380 by 3.14: $r^2 \approx 121$, so $r \approx 11$. Since $r \approx 11$, we now know that $d \approx 2(11)$ and the circumference is approximately 69 inches [$C = d\pi \approx 22(3.14)$].
(Refresher 310)

MATH REFRESHER SESSION 4

Algebra Problems

Algebraic Properties

Algebra is the branch of mathematics that applies the laws of arithmetic to symbols that represent unknown quantities. The most commonly used symbols are the letters of the alphabet, such as A, B, C, x, y, z, etc. These symbols can be added, subtracted, multiplied, and divided like numbers. For example, $3a + 2a = 5a$, $2x - x = x$, $3(5b) = 15b$, $\frac{6x}{3x} = 2$. These symbols can be raised to powers like a^3 or y^2. Remember that raising a number to a power means multiplying the number by itself a number of times. For example, $a^3 = a \cdot a \cdot a$. The power is 3, and a is multiplied by itself 3 times.

Generally, in algebra, a *variable* (an unknown represented by a symbol) appears in an expression that defines the relationship (whether an equation or an inequality) between certain quantities. The numerical value of a variable that satisfies this relationship can usually be found if the expressions contain numerical values (e.g., 26, -5, $\frac{1}{2}$). and values of the variable that *satisfy* the equation must be found. For example, the equation $6a = 12$ is satisfied when the variable a is equal to 2. This section is a discussion on how to solve complicated algebraic equations and other related topics.

Fundamental Laws of Our Number System

The following list of laws applies to all numbers, and it is necessary to adhere to these laws when doing arithmetic and algebra problems. Remember these laws and use them in solving problems.

401. If $x = y$ and $y = z$, then $x = z$. This is called *transitivity*. For example, if $a = 3$ and $b = 3$, then $a = b$.

402. If $x = y$, then $x + z = y + z$, and $x - z = y - z$. This means that the same quantity can be added to or subtracted from both sides of an equation. For example, if $a = b$, then add any number to both sides, say 3, and $a + 3 = b + 3$. Or if $a = b$, then $a - 3 = b - 3$.

403. If $x = y$, then $x \cdot z = y \cdot z$ and $x \div z = y \div z$, unless $z = 0$ (see Section 404). This means that both sides of an equation can be multiplied by the same number. For example, if $a = n$, then $5a = 5n$. It also means that both sides of an equation can be divided by the same nonzero number. If $a = b$, then $\frac{a}{3} = \frac{b}{3}$.

404. *Never divide by zero.* This is a very important rule that must be remembered. The quotient of *any* quantity (except zero) divided by zero is infinity.

405. $x + y = y + x$, and $x \cdot y = y \cdot x$. Therefore, $2 + 3 = 3 + 2$, and $2 \cdot 3 = 3 \cdot 2$. Remember that this does not work for division and subtraction. $3 \div 2$ does not equal $2 \div 3$, and $3 - 2$ does not equal $2 - 3$. The property described above is called *commutativity*.

Algebraic Expressions

405a. Since the letters in an algebraic expression stand for numbers, and since we add, subtract, multiply, or divide them to get the algebraic expression, the algebraic expression itself stands for a number. When we are told what value each of the letters in the expression has, we can evaluate the expression. Note that $(+a) \times (+b) = +ab;$ $(+a) \times (-b) = -ab; (-a) \times (+b) = -ab;$ and $-a \times -b = +ab$.

In evaluating algebraic expressions, place the value you are substituting for a letter in parentheses. (This is important when a letter has a negative value.)

Example: What is the value of the expression $a^2 - b^3$ when $a = -2$, and $b = -1$?
$a^2 - b^3 = (-2)^2 - (-1)^3 = 4 - (-1) = 4 + 1 = 5$.

If you can, simplify the algebraic expression before you evaluate it.

Example: Evaluate $\dfrac{32a^6b^2}{8a^4b^3}$ if $a = 4$, and $b = -2$.

First we divide:

$\dfrac{32a^6b^2}{8a^4b^3} = \dfrac{4a^2}{b}$. Then $\dfrac{4a^2}{b} = \dfrac{4(+4)^2}{-2} = -32$.

Note: $\dfrac{a^6}{a^4} = a^2$ and $\dfrac{b^2}{b^3} = \dfrac{1}{b}$. Remember, in division, you subtract the exponents if they belong to the same variable.

Equations

406. *Linear equations in one unknown.* An equation of this type has only one variable, and that variable is always in the first power, i.e., x or y or a, but never a higher or fractional power, i.e., x^2, y^3, or $a^{\frac{1}{2}}$. Examples of linear equations in one unknown are $x + 5 = 7$, $3a - 2 = 7a + 1$, $2x - 7x = 8 + x$, $8 = -4y$, etc. To solve these equations, follow these steps:

Step 1. Combine the terms on the left and right sides of the equality. That is, (1) add all of the numerical terms on each side, and (2) add all of the terms with variables on each side. For example, if you have $7 + 2x + 9 = 4x - 3 - 2x + 7 + 6x$, combining terms on the left gives you $16 + 2x$, because $7 + 9 = 16$, and $2x$ is the only variable term on that side. On the right we get $8x + 4$, since $4x - 2x + 6x = 8x$ and $-3 + 7 = 4$. Therefore the new equation is $16 + 2x = 8x + 4$.

Step 2. Put all of the numerical terms on the right side of the equation and all of the variable terms on the left side. This is done by subtracting the numerical term on the left from both sides of the equation and by subtracting the variable term on the right side from both sides of the equation. In the example $16 + 2x = 8x + 4$, subtract 16 from both sides and obtain $2x = 8x - 12$; then subtracting $8x$ from both sides gives $-6x = -12$.

Step 3. Divide both sides by the coefficient of the variable. In this case, where $-6x = -12$, dividing

by -6 gives $x = 2$. This is the final solution to the problem.

Example: Solve for a in the equation $7a + 4 - 2a = 18 + 17a + 10$.

Solution: From Step 1, we combine terms on both sides to get $5a + 4 = 28 + 17a$. As in Step 2, we then subtract 4 and $17a$ from both sides to give $-12a = 24$. In Step 3, we then divide both sides of the equation by the coefficient of a, which is -12, to get $a = -2$.

Example: Solve for x in $2x + 6 = 0$.

Solution: Here Step 1 is eliminated because there are no terms to combine on either side. Step 2 requires that 6 be subtracted from both sides to get $2x = -6$. Then Step 3, dividing by 2, gives $x = -3$.

407. *Simultaneous equations in two unknowns.* These are problems in which two equations, each with two unknowns, are given. These equations must be solved together (simultaneously) in order to arrive at the solution.

Step 1. Rearrange each equation so that both have the x term on the left side and the y term and the constant on the right side. The first equation should be in the form $Ax = By + C$, and the second equation should be in the form $Dx = Ey + F$, where A, B, C, D, E, and F are numerical constants. For example, if one of the equations is $9x - 10y + 30 = 11y + 3x - 6$, then subtract $-10y$ and 30 from both sides to get $9x = 21y + 3x - 36$. Subtracting $3x$ from both sides gives $6x = 21y - 36$, which is in the form of $Ax = By + C$.

Step 2. Multiply the first equation by the coefficient of x in the second equation (D). Multiply the second equation by the coefficient of x in the first equation (A). Now the equations are in the form $ADx = BDy + CD$ and $ADx = AEy + AF$. For example, in the two equations $2x = 7y - 12$ and $3x = y + 1$, multiply the first by 3 and the second by 2 to get $6x = 21y - 36$ and $6x = 2y + 2$.

Step 3. Equate the right sides of both equations. This can be done because both sides are equal to ADx. (See Section 401 on transitivity.) Thus, $BDy + CD = AEy + AF$. So $21y - 36$ and $2y + 2$ are both equal to $6x$ and are equal to each other: $21y - 36 = 2y + 2$.

Step 4. Solve for y. This is done in the manner outlined in Section 406. In the equation $21y - 36 = 2y + 2$, $y = 2$. By this method $y = \dfrac{AF - CD}{BD - AE}$.

Step 5. Substitute the value of y into either of the original equations and solve for x. In the general equations we would then have either

$$x = \frac{B}{A}\left[\frac{AF - CD}{BD - AE}\right] + \frac{C}{A} \text{ or } x = \frac{E}{D}\left[\frac{AF - CD}{BD - AE}\right] + \frac{F}{D}.$$

In the example, if $y = 2$ is substituted into either $2x = 7y - 12$ or $3x = y + 1$, then $2x = 14 - 12$ or $3x = 3$ can be solved to get $x = 1$.

Example: Solve for a and b in the equations $3a + 4b = 24$ and $2a + b = 11$.

Solution: First note that it makes no difference in these two equations whether the variables are a and b instead of x and y. Subtract $4b$ from the first equation and b from the second equation to get the equations $3a = 24 - 4b$ and $2a = 11 - b$. Multiply the first by 2 and the second by 3. Thus, $6a = 48 - 8b$ and $6a = 33 - 3b$. Equate $48 - 8b$ and $33 - 3b$ to get $48 - 8b = 33 - 3b$. Solving for b in the usual manner gives us $b = 3$. Substituting the value of $b = 3$ into the equation $3a + 4b = 24$ obtains $3a + 12 = 24$. Solving for a gives $a = 4$. Thus the complete solution is $a = 4$ and $b = 3$.

408. *Quadratic equations.* Quadratic equations are expressed in the form $ax^2 + bx + c = 0$, where a, b, and c are constant numbers (for example, $\frac{1}{2}$, 4, -2, etc.) and x is a variable. An equation of this form may be satisfied by two values of x, one value of x, or no values of x. (Actually, when there are no values of x that satisfy the equation, there are only *imaginary* solutions. On the ACT, you will not have questions where you will have to use these formulas.) To determine the number of solutions, find the value of the expression $b^2 - 4ac$, where a, b, and c are the constant coefficients of the equation $ax^2 + bx + c = 0$.

If $b^2 - 4ac$ is *greater* than 0, there are two solutions.

If $b^2 - 4ac$ is *less* than 0, there are no solutions.

If $b^2 - 4ac$ is *equal* to 0, there is one solution.

If solutions exist, they can be found by using the formulas:

$$x = \frac{-b + \sqrt{b^2 - 4ac}}{2a} \text{ and } x = \frac{-b - \sqrt{b^2 - 4ac}}{2a}$$

Note that if $b^2 - 4ac = 0$, the two solutions above will be the same and there will be one solution.

Example: Determine the solutions, if they exist, to the equation $x^2 + 6x + 5 = 0$.

Solution: First, noting $a = 1$, $b = 6$, and $c = 5$, calculate $b^2 - 4ac$, or $6^2 - 4(1)(5)$. Thus, $b^2 - 4ac = 16$. Since this is greater than 0, there are two solutions. They are, from the formulas:

$$x = \frac{-6 + \sqrt{6^2 - 4 \cdot 1 \cdot 5}}{2 \cdot 1}$$

$$\text{and } x = \frac{-6 - \sqrt{6^2 - 4 \cdot 1 \cdot 5}}{2 \cdot 1}$$

Simplify these to:

$$x = \frac{-6 + \sqrt{16}}{2} \text{ and } x = \frac{-6 - \sqrt{16}}{2}$$

As $\sqrt{16} = 4$, $x = \dfrac{-6 + 4}{2} = \dfrac{-2}{2}$ and $x = \dfrac{-6 - 4}{2} = \dfrac{-10}{2}$. Thus, the two solutions are $x = -1$ and $x = -5$.

Another method of solving quadratic equations is to *factor* the $ax^2 + bx + c$ into two expressions. This will be explained in the next section.

409. *Factoring.* Factoring is breaking down an expression into two or more expressions, the product of which is the original expression. For example, 6 can be factored into 2 and 3 because $2 \cdot 3 = 6$. $x^2 - x$ can be factored into x and $(x - 1)$ because $x^2 - x = x(x - 1)$. Then, if $x^2 + bx + c$ is factorable, it will be factored into two expressions in the form $(x + d)$ and $(x + e)$, such that $d + e = b$ and $de = c$. If the expression $(x + d)$ is multiplied by the expression $(x + e)$, their product is $x^2 + (d + e)x + de$. For example, $(x + 3) \cdot (x + 2)$ equals $x^2 + 5x + 6$. To factor an expression such as $x^2 + 6x + 8$, find d and e such that $d + e = 6$ and $de = 8$. Of the various factors of 8, we find that $d = 4$ and $e = 2$. Thus $x^2 + 6x + 8$ can be factored into the expressions $(x + 4)$ and $(x + 2)$. Below are factored expressions.

$$x^2 + 2x + 1 = (x + 1)(x + 1)$$
$$x^2 + 4x + 4 = (x + 2)(x + 2)$$
$$x^2 - 4x + 3 = (x - 3)(x - 1)$$
$$x^2 + 10x + 16 = (x + 8)(x + 2)$$

$$x^2 - 5x + 6 = (x - 2)(x - 3)$$
$$x^2 + 3x + 2 = (x + 2)(x + 1)$$
$$x^2 + 5x + 6 = (x + 3)(x + 2)$$
$$x^2 - 4x - 5 = (x - 5)(x + 1)$$
$$x^2 + 4x - 5 = (x + 5)(x - 1)$$
$$x^2 - x - 6 = (x - 3)(x + 2)$$

An important rule to remember in factoring is that $a^2 - b^2 = (a + b)(a - b)$. For example, $x^2 - 9 = (x + 3)(x - 3)$. You don't get a middle term in x because the $3x$ cancels with the $-3x$ in the product $(x + 3)(x - 3)$. To apply factoring in solving quadratic equations, factor the quadratic expression into two terms and set each term equal to zero. Then, solve the two resulting equations.

Example: Solve $x^2 - x - 6 = 0$.

Solution: First factor the expression $x^2 - x - 6$ into $x - 3$ and $x + 2$. Setting each of these equal to 0 gives $x - 3 = 0$ and $x + 2 = 0$. Solving these equations gives us $x = 3$ and $x = -2$.

Algebra of Graphs

410a. *Number lines*. Numbers, positive and negative, can be represented as points on a straight line. Conversely, points on a line can also be represented by numbers. This is done by use of the number line.

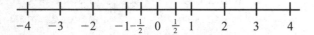

The diagram above is an example of a number line. On a number line, a point is chosen to represent the number zero. Then a point that is 1 unit to the right of 0 represents $+1$; a point that is $\frac{1}{2}$ unit to the right of 0 is $+\frac{1}{2}$; a point that is 2 units to the right of 0 is $+2$; and so on. A point that is 1 unit to the left of 0 is -1; a point that is $\frac{1}{2}$ unit to the left of 0 is $-\frac{1}{2}$; a point that is 2 units to the left of 0 is -2; and so on. As you can see, all points to the right of the 0 point represent positive numbers, and all those to the left of the 0 point represent negative numbers.

To find the distance between two points on the line:

1. Find the numbers that represent the points.
2. The distance is the smaller number subtracted from the larger.

Example: Find the distance between point A and point B on the number line.

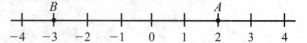

Solution: Point A is $+2$ on the number line and point B is -3. $+2$ is larger than -3, so the distance is $+2 - (-3)$ or $+2 + 3 = 5$. By counting the number of units between A and B, we can also find the distance to be 5.

410b. *Coordinate geometry*. These problems deal with the algebra of graphs. A graph consists of a set of points whose position is determined with respect to a set of axes, usually labeled the x-axis and the y-axis and divided into appropriate units. Locate a point on the graph with an "x-coordinate" of a units and a "y-coordinate" of b units. First move a units along the x-axis (either to the left or the right depending on whether a is negative or positive). Then move b units along the y-axis (either up or down depending on the sign of b). A point with an x-coordinate of a and a y-coordinate of b is represented by (a,b). The points $(2,3)$, $(-1,4)$, $(-2,-3)$, and $(4,-2)$ are shown on the following graph.

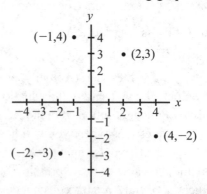

411. *Distance between two points*. If the coordinates of point A are (x_1, y_1) and the coordinates of point B are (x_2, y_2), then the distance on the graph between the two points is $d = \sqrt{(x_2 - x_1)^2 + (y_2 - y_1)^2}$.

Example: Find the distance between the point $(2,-3)$ and the point $(5,1)$.

Solution: In this case $x_1 = 2$, $x_2 = 5$, $y_1 = -3$, and $y_2 = 1$. Substituting into the above formula gives us

$$d = \sqrt{(5-2)^2 + [1-(-3)]^2} = \sqrt{3^2 + 4^2} = \sqrt{25} = 5$$

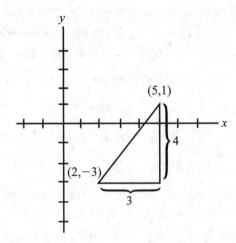

Note: This formula is a consequence of the Pythagorean theorem. Pythagoras, an ancient Greek mathematician, discovered that the square of the length of the hypotenuse (longest side) of a right triangle is equal to the sum of the squares of the lengths of the other two sides. See Sections 317 and 509.

412. *Midpoint of the line segment joining two points.*
If the coordinates of the first point are (x_1, y_1) and the coordinates of the second point are (x_2, y_2), then the coordinates of the midpoint will be $\left(\dfrac{x_1 + x_2}{2}, \dfrac{y_1 + y_2}{2}\right)$. In other words, each coordinate of the midpoint is equal to the *average* of the corresponding coordinates of the endpoints.

Example: Find the midpoint of the segment connecting the points (2,4) and (6,2).

Solution: The average of 2 and 6 is 4, so the first coordinate is 4. The average of 4 and 2 is 3; thus the second coordinate is 3. The midpoint is (4,3).

$$\left[\frac{2+6}{2} = 4, \frac{4+2}{2} = 3\right]$$

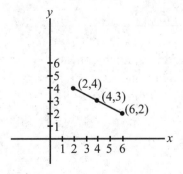

413. *Plotting the graph of a line.* An equation that can be put in the form of $y = mx + b$, where m and b are numerical constants, can be represented as a line on a graph. This means that all of the points on the graph that the line passes through will satisfy the equation. Remember that each point has an x and a y value that can be substituted into the equation. To plot a line, follow the steps below:

Step 1. Select two values of x and two values of y that will satisfy the equation. For example, in the equation $y = 2x + 4$, the point ($x = 1$, $y = 6$) will satisfy the equation, as will the point ($x = -2$, $y = 0$). There is an infinite number of such points on a line.

Step 2. Plot these two points on the graph. In this case, the two points are (1,6) and (-2,0). These points are represented below.

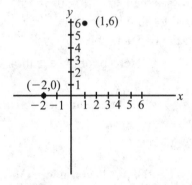

Step 3. Draw a line connecting the two points. This is the line representing the equation.

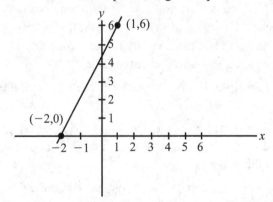

(*Note*: A straight line is completely specified by two points.)

Example: Graph the equation $2y + 3x = 12$.

Solution: Two points that satisfy this equation are (2,3) and (0,6). Plotting these points and drawing a line between them gives:

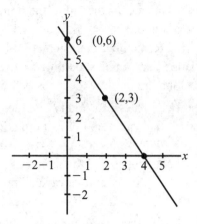

414. *y-intercept.* The *y*-intercept of a line is the point where the line crosses the *y*-axis. At any point where a line crosses the *y*-axis, $x = 0$. To find the *y*-intercept of a line, simply substitute $x = 0$ into the equation of the line, and solve for *y*.

Example: Find the *y*-intercept of the equation $2x + 3y = 6$.

Solution: If $x = 0$ is substituted into the equation, it simplifies to $3y = 6$. Solving for *y* gives $y = 2$. Thus, 2 is the *y*-intercept.

> **If an equation can be put into the form of $y = mx + b$, then b is the *y*-intercept.**

415. *x-intercept.* The point where a line intersects the *x*-axis is called the *x*-intercept. At this point $y = 0$. To find the *x*-intercept of a line, substitute $y = 0$ into the equation and solve for *x*.

Example: Given the equation $2x + 3y = 6$, find the *x*-intercept.

Solution: Substitute $y = 0$ into the equation, getting $2x = 6$. Solving for *x*, find $x = 3$. Thus the *x*-intercept is 3.

In the diagram below, the *y*- and *x*-intercepts of the equation $2x + 3y = 6$ are illustrated.

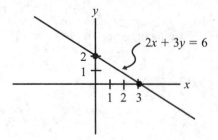

416. *Slope.* The slope of a line is the change in *y* caused by a 1-unit increase in *x*. If an equation is in the form of $y = mx + b$, then as *x* increases 1 unit, *y* will increase *m* units. Therefore the slope is *m*.

Example: Find the slope of the line $2x + 3y = 6$.

Solution: First put the equation into the form of $y = mx + b$. Subtract 2*x* from both sides and divide by 3. The equation becomes $y = -\frac{2}{3}x + 2$. Therefore the slope is $-\frac{2}{3}$.

The slope of the line joining two points, (x_1, y_1) and (x_2, y_2), is given by the expression $m = \frac{y_2 - y_1}{x_2 - x_1}$.

Example: Find the slope of the line joining the points (3,2) and (4,−1).

Solution: Substituting into the formula above gives us $m = \frac{-3}{1} = -3$, where $x_1 = 3$, $x_2 = 4$, $y_1 = 2$, $y_2 = -1$.

If two lines are perpendicular, the slope of one is the negative reciprocal of the other.

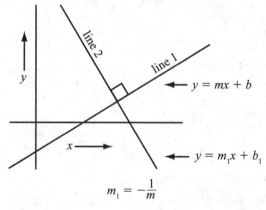

Example: What is the slope of a line perpendicular to the line $y = -3x + 4$?

Solution: Since the slope of the line $y = -3x + 4$ is −3, the slope of the line perpendicular to that line is the negative reciprocal, or $\frac{-1}{-3} = \frac{+1}{+3}$.

417. *Graphing simultaneous linear equations.* Recall that simultaneous equations are a pair of equations in two unknowns. Each of these equations is graphed separately, and each is represented by

a straight line. The solution of the simultaneous equations (i.e., the pair of values that satisfies *both* at the same time) is represented by the intersection of two lines. Now, for any pair of lines, there are three possible relationships:

1. The lines intersect at one and only one point; in this case, this point represents the unique solution to the pair of equations. This is most often the case. Such lines are called *consistent*.

2. The lines coincide exactly; this represents the case where the two equations are equivalent (just different forms of the same mathematical relation). Any point that satisfies *either* of the two equations automatically satisfies *both*.

3. The lines are parallel and never intersect. In this case the equations are called *inconsistent*, and they have *no* solution at all. Two lines that are parallel will have the same slope.

Example: Solve graphically the equations $4x - y = 5$ and $2x + 4y = 16$.

Solution: Plot the two lines represented by the two equations. (See Section 413.) The graph is shown below.

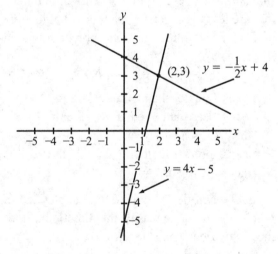

The two lines intersect in the point (2,3), which represents the solution $x = 2$ and $y = 3$. This can be checked by solving the equations as is done in Section 407.

Example: Solve $x + 2y = 6$ and $2x + 4y = 8$.

Solution: Find a point that satisfies each equation. You cannot.

The two graphs will look like this:

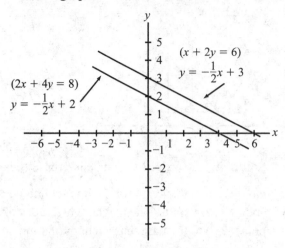

These lines will never intersect, and these equations are termed inconsistent. There is no solution.

Remember that two parallel lines have the same slope. This is an easy way to see whether two lines are consistent or inconsistent.

Example: Find the solution to $2x - 3y = 8$ and $4x = 6y + 16$.

Solution: On the graph these two lines are identical. This means that there is an infinite set of points that satisfy both equations.

Equations of identical lines are multiples of each other and can be reduced to a single equation.

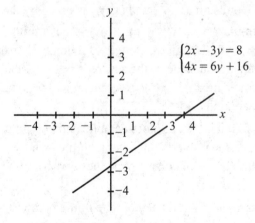

418. *Areas of polygons.* Often, an elementary geometric figure is placed on a graph to calculate its area. This is usually simple for figures such as triangles, rectangles, squares, parallelograms, etc.

Example: Calculate the area of the triangle in the figure below.

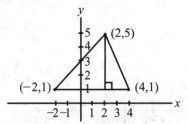

Solution: The area of a triangle is $\frac{1}{2}$(base)(height). On the graph the length of the line joining $(-2,1)$ and $(4,1)$ is 6 units. The height, which goes from point $(2,5)$ to the base, has a length of 4 units. Therefore the area is $\frac{1}{2}(6)(4) = 12$.

Example: Calculate the area of the square pictured below.

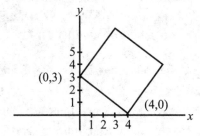

Solution: The area of a square is given by the square of the side. To find this area, first find the length of one side. The length of a segment whose endpoints are (x_1,y_1) and (x_2,y_2) is given by the formula $\sqrt{(x_2 - x_1)^2 + (y_2 - y_1)^2}$. Substituting in $(0,3)$ and $(4,0)$ gives a length of 5 units. Thus the length of one side of the square is 5. Using the formula area $=$ (side)^2 gives an area of 5^2, or 25 square units.

To find the area of more complicated polygons, divide the polygon into simple figures whose areas can be calculated. Add these areas to find the total area.

Example: Find the area of the figure below:

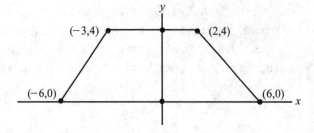

Solution: Divide the figure into two triangles and a rectangle by drawing vertical lines at $(-3,4)$ and $(2,4)$. Thus the polygon is now two triangles and a rectangle.

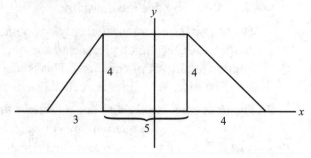

The height of the left triangle is 4 units, and the base is 3. Using $A = \frac{1}{2}bh$ gives the area as 6. The height of the right triangle is 4, and the base is 4. The area is 8. The length of one side of the rectangle is 4, and the other side is 5. Using the formula area $=$ base $\cdot$ height gives the area as 20. Thus the total area is $6 + 8 + 20 = 34$.

Inequalities

419. *Inequalities.* These problems deal with numbers that are less than, greater than, or equal to other numbers. The following laws apply to all inequalities:

$<$ means "less than," thus $3 < 4$

$>$ means "greater than," thus $5 > 2$

$\leq$ means "less than or equal to," thus $x \leq y$ means $x < y$ or $x = y$

$\geq$ means "greater than or equal to," thus $x \geq y$ means $x > y$ or $x = y$

420. If equal quantities are added to or subtracted from both sides of an inequality, the direction of the inequality does *not* change.

If $x < y$, then $x + z < y + z$ and $x - z < y - z$.
If $x > y$, then $x + z > y + z$ and $x - z > y - z$.

For example, given the inequality $4 > 2$, with 1 added to or subtracted from both sides, the results, $5 > 3$ and $3 > 1$, have the same inequality sign as the original. If the problem is algebraic, e.g., $x + 3 < 6$, it is possible to subtract 3 from both sides to get the simple inequality $x < 3$.

421. Subtracting parts of an inequality from an equation *reverses* the order of the inequality.

Given $z = z$ and $x < y$, then $z - x > z - y$.
Given $z = z$ and $x > y$, then $z - x < z - y$.

For example, given that $3 < 5$, subtracting 3 from the left-hand side and 5 from the right-hand side of the equation $10 = 10$ results in $7 > 5$. Thus the direction of the inequality is reversed.

Note: Subtracting parts of an equation from an inequality does not reverse the inequality. For example, if $3 < 5$, then $3 - 10 < 5 - 10$.

422. Multiplying or dividing an inequality by a number greater than zero does not change the order of the inequality.

If $x > y$ and $a > 0$, then $xa > ya$ and $\frac{x}{a} > \frac{y}{a}$.

If $x < y$ and $a > 0$, then $xa < ya$ and $\frac{x}{a} < \frac{y}{a}$.

For example, if $4 > 2$, multiplying both sides by any arbitrary number (for instance, 5) gives $20 > 10$, which is still true. Or, if algebraically $6h < 3$, dividing both sides by 6 gives $h < \frac{1}{2}$, which is true.

423. Multiplying or dividing an inequality by a number less than 0 reverses the order of the inequality.

If $x > y$ and $a < 0$, then $xa < ya$ and $\frac{x}{a} < \frac{y}{a}$.

If $x < y$ and $a < 0$, then $xa > ya$ and $\frac{x}{a} > \frac{y}{a}$.

If $-3 < 2$ is multiplied through by -2 it becomes $6 > -4$, and the order of the inequality is reversed.

> **Note that negative numbers are always less than positive numbers. Note also that the greater the absolute value of a negative number, the smaller it actually is. Thus, $-10 < -9$, $-8 < -7$, etc.**

424. The product of two numbers with like signs is positive.

If $x > 0$ and $y > 0$, then $xy > 0$.
If $x < 0$ and $y < 0$, then $xy > 0$.

For example, -3 times -2 is 6.

425. The product of two numbers with unlike signs is negative.

If $x < 0$ and $y > 0$, then $xy < 0$.
If $x > 0$ and $y < 0$, then $xy < 0$.

For example, -2 times 3 is -6; 8 times -1 is -8; etc.

426. *Linear inequalities in one unknown.* In these problems a first-power variable is given in an inequality, and this variable must be solved for in terms of the inequality. Examples of linear inequalities in one unknown are $2x + 7 > 4 + x$, $8y - 3 \le 2y$, etc.

Step 1. By ordinary algebraic addition and subtraction (as if it were an equality), get all of the constant terms on one side of the inequality and all of the variable terms on the other side. In the inequality $2x + 4 < 8x + 16$ subtract 4 and $8x$ from both sides and get $-6x < 12$.

Step 2. Divide both sides by the coefficient of the variable. Important: If the coefficient of the variable is negative, you must reverse the inequality sign. For example, in $-6x < 12$, dividing by -6 gives $x > -2$. (The inequality is reversed.) In $3x < 12$, dividing by 3 gives $x < 4$.

Example: Solve for y in the inequality $4y + 7 \ge 9 - 2y$.

Solution: Subtracting $-2y$ and 7 from both sides gives $6y \ge 2$. Dividing both sides by 6 gives $y \ge \frac{1}{3}$.

Example: Solve for a in the inequality $10 - 2a < 0$.

Solution: Subtracting 10 from both sides gives $-2a < -10$. Dividing both sides by -2 gives $a > \frac{-10}{-2}$ or $a > 5$. Note that the inequality sign has been reversed because of the division by a negative number.

427. *Simultaneous linear inequalities in two unknowns.* These are two inequalities, each one in two unknowns. The same two unknowns are to be solved for in each equation. This means the equations must be solved simultaneously.

Step 1. Plot both inequalities on the same graph. Replace the inequality sign with an equals sign and plot the resulting line. The side of the line that makes the inequality true is then shaded in. For example, graph the inequality $2x - y > 4$. First replace the inequality sign, getting $2x - y = 4$; then, plot the line. The x-intercept is where $y = 0$. The y-intercept is where $x = 0$. So in the equation $2x - y = 4$, the x-intercept is where $2x = 4$, or where $x = 2$. Similarly, in the equation $2x - y = 4$, the y-intercept is where $-y = 4$, or where $y = -4$. (See Sections 414 and 415 for determining x- and y-intercepts.)

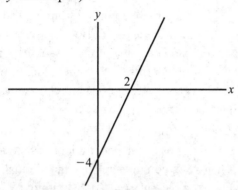

To decide which side of the line satisfies the inequality, choose a convenient point on each side and determine which point satisfies the inequality. Shade in that side of the line. In this case, choose the point $(0,0)$. With this point the equation becomes $2(0) - 0 > 4$, or $0 > 4$. This is not true. Therefore, shade in the other side of the line.

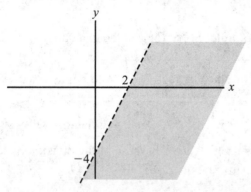

Step 2. After both inequalities have been solved, the area that is common to both shaded portions is the solution to the problem.

Example: Solve $x + y > 2$ and $3x < 6$.

Solution: First graph $x + y > 2$ by plotting $x + y = 2$ and using the point $(4,0)$ to determine the region where the inequality is satisfied:

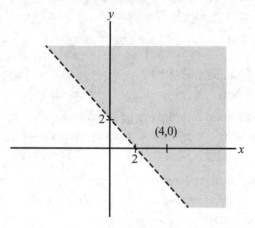

Graph the inequality $3x < 6$ on the same axes:

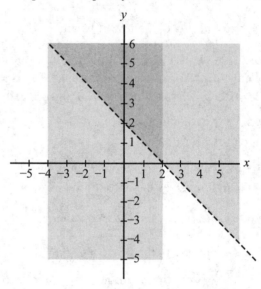

The solution is $x < 2$, $y > 0$, double-shaded area.

428. *Higher-order inequalities in one unknown.* These are inequalities that deal with variables multiplied by themselves. For example, $x^2 + 3 \geq 0$, $(x - 1)(x + 2) < 4$, and $x^3 - 7x > 0$ are such inequalities. The basic rules to remember in doing such problems are:

> **1. The product of any number of positive numbers is positive.**

For example, $2 \times 3 \times 4 \times 5 = 120$, which is positive, or $\frac{1}{2} \times \frac{1}{2} = \frac{1}{4}$, which is positive.

2. The product of an even number of negative numbers is positive.

For example, $(-3)(-2) = 6$ or $(-3)(-1)(-9)(-2) = 54$, which is positive.

3. The product of an odd number of negative numbers is negative.

For example, $(-1)(-2)(-3) = -6$ or $(-\frac{1}{2})(-2)(-3)(-6)(-1) = -18$.

4. Any real number squared or raised to an even power is always positive or zero.

For example, $x^2 \geq 0$ or $a^4 \geq 0$ for all x and for all a. Often these basic rules will make the solution to an inequality problem obvious.

Example: Which of the following values can x^2 not have?

(A) 5   (B) -2 (C) 0   (D) 144   (E) 9

Solution: We know that $x^2 \geq 0$ for all x, so x^2 cannot be negative. -2 is negative, so x^2 cannot equal -2.

The steps in solving a higher-order inequality are:

Step 1. Bring all of the terms to one side of the inequality, making the other side zero. For example, in the inequality $x^2 > 3x - 2$, subtract $3x - 2$ from both sides to get $x^2 - 3x + 2 > 0$.

Step 2. Factor the resulting expression. To factor a quadratic expression means to write the original expression as the product of two terms in the first power, i.e., $x^2 = x \cdot x$. x is a factor of x^2. (See Section 409 for a detailed explanation of factoring.) The quadratic expression $x^2 - 3x + 2$ when factored is $(x - 2)(x - 1)$. Note that $x \cdot x = x^2$, $-2x - x = -3x$, and $(-1)(-2) = 2$. Most quadratic expressions can easily be factored by taking factors of the last term (in this case 2 and 1) and adding or subtracting them to or from x. Through trial and error, the right combination is found. An important fact to remember when factoring is: $(a + b)(c + d) = ac + ad + bc + bd$. Example: $(x + 4)(x + 2) = x^2 + 4x + 2x + 8 = x^2 + 6x + 8$. Another is that $a^2 - b^2 = (a + b)(a - b)$. Example: $x^2 - 16 = (x + 4)(x - 4)$.

Step 3. Investigate which terms are positive and which terms are negative. For example, in $(x - 3)(x + 2) > 0$, either $(x - 3)$ and $(x + 2)$ are both positive or $(x - 3)$ and $(x + 2)$ are both negative. If one were positive and the other were negative, the product would be negative and would not satisfy the inequality. If the factors are positive, then $x - 3 > 0$ and $x + 2 > 0$, which yields $x > 3$ and $x > -2$. For x to be greater than 3 and to be greater than -2, it must be greater than 3. If it is greater than 3, it is automatically greater than -2. Thus, with positive factors $x > 3$ is the answer. If the factors are negative, $x - 3 < 0$ and $x + 2 < 0$, or $x < -2$. For x to be less than 3 and less than -2, it must be less than -2. Thus, with negative factors $x < -2$ is the answer. As both answers are possible from the original equation, the solution to the original problem is $x > 3$ or $x < -2$.

Example: For which values of x is $x^2 + 5 < 6x$?

Solution: First subtract $6x$ from both sides to get $x^2 - 6x + 5 < 0$. The left side factors into $(x - 5)(x - 1) < 0$. Now for this to be true, one factor must be positive and one must be negative, that is, their product is less than zero. Thus, $x - 5 > 0$ and $x - 1 < 0$, or $x - 5 < 0$ and $x - 1 > 0$. If $x - 5 < 0$ and $x - 1 > 0$, then $x < 5$ and $x > 1$, or $1 < x < 5$. If $x - 5 > 0$ and $x - 1 < 0$, then $x > 5$ and $x < 1$, which is impossible because x cannot be less than 1 *and* greater than 5. Therefore, the solution is $1 < x < 5$.

Example: For what values of x is $x^2 < 4$?

Solution: Subtract 4 from both sides to get $x^2 - 4 < 0$. Remember that $a^2 - b^2 = (a + b)(a - b)$; thus $x^2 - 4 = (x + 2)(x - 2)$. Hence, $(x + 2)(x - 2) < 0$. For this to be true, $x + 2 > 0$ and $x - 2 < 0$, or $x + 2 < 0$ and $x - 2 > 0$. In the first case $x > -2$ and $x < 2$, or $-2 < x < 2$. The second case is $x < -2$ and $x > 2$, which is impossible because x cannot be less than -2 *and* greater than 2. Thus, the solution is $-2 < x < 2$.

Example: When is $(x^2 + 1)(x - 2)^2(x - 3)$ greater than or equal to zero?

Solution: This inequality can be written as $(x^2 + 1)(x - 2)^2(x - 3) \geq 0$. This is already in factors. The individual terms must be investigated.

$x^2 + 1$ is always positive because $x^2 \geq 0$, so $x^2 + 1$ must be greater than 0. $(x - 2)^2$ is a number squared, so this is always greater than or equal to zero. Therefore, the product of the first two terms is positive or equal to zero for all values of x. The third term, $x - 3$, is positive when $x > 3$ and negative when $x < 3$. For the entire expression to be positive, $x - 3$ must be positive, that is, $x > 3$. For the expression to be equal to zero, $x - 3 = 0$, that is, $x = 3$, or $(x - 2)^2 = 0$, that is, $x = 2$. Thus, the entire expression is positive when $x > 3$ and zero when $x = 2$ or $x = 3$.

Exponents and Roots

429. *Exponents.* An exponent is an easy way to express repeated multiplication. For example, $5 \times 5 \times 5 \times 5 = 5^4$. The 4 is the exponent. In the expression $7^3 = 7 \times 7 \times 7$, 3 is the exponent. 7^3 means 7 is multiplied by itself three times. If the exponent is 0, the expression always has a value of 1. Thus, $6^0 = 15^0 = 1$, etc. If the exponent is 1, the value of the expression is the number base. Thus, $4^1 = 4$ and $9^1 = 9$.

In the problem $5^3 \times 5^4$, we can simplify by counting the factors of 5. Thus, $5^3 \times 5^4 = 5^{3+4} = 5^7$. When we multiply and the base number is the same, we keep the base number and add the exponents. For example, $7^4 \times 7^8 = 7^{12}$.

For division, we keep the same base number and subtract exponents. Thus, $8^8 \div 8^2 = 8^{8-2} = 8^6$.

A negative exponent indicates the reciprocal of the expression with a positive exponent, thus $3^{-2} = \dfrac{1}{3^2}$.

430. *Roots.* The square root of a number is a number whose square is the original number. For example, $\sqrt{16} = 4$, since $4 \times 4 = 16$. (The $\sqrt{}$ symbol always means a positive number.) Note that $(-4)(-4) = 16$, so if we have an equation such as $x^2 = 16$, then $x = \pm\sqrt{16} = \pm 4$.

To simplify a square root, we factor the number.

$$\sqrt{32} = \sqrt{16 \cdot 2} = \sqrt{16} \cdot \sqrt{2} = 4\sqrt{2}$$
$$\sqrt{72} = \sqrt{36 \cdot 2} = \sqrt{36} \cdot \sqrt{2} = 6\sqrt{2}$$
$$\sqrt{300} = \sqrt{25 \cdot 12} = \sqrt{25} \cdot \sqrt{12}$$
$$= 5 \cdot \sqrt{12}$$
$$= 5 \cdot \sqrt{4 \cdot 3}$$
$$= 5 \cdot \sqrt{4} \cdot \sqrt{3}$$
$$= 5 \cdot 2\sqrt{3}$$
$$= 10\sqrt{3}$$

We can add expressions with the square roots only if the numbers inside the square root sign are the same. For example,

$$3\sqrt{7} + 2\sqrt{7} = 5\sqrt{7}$$
$$\sqrt{18} + \sqrt{2} = \sqrt{9 \cdot 2} + \sqrt{2}$$
$$= \sqrt{9} \cdot \sqrt{2} + \sqrt{2}$$
$$= 3\sqrt{2} + \sqrt{2}$$
$$= 4\sqrt{2}$$

431. *Evaluation of expressions.* To evaluate an expression means to substitute a value in place of a letter. For example:

Evaluate $3a^2 - c^3$ if $a = -2$, $c = -3$.

$$3a^2 - c^3 = 3(-2)^2 - (-3)^3$$
$$= 3(4) - (-27)$$
$$= 12 + 27$$
$$= 39$$

Example: Given: $f(a,b) = ab + b^2$.

Find: $f(-2,3)$.

Using the definition, by inserting -2 for a and 3 for b in $ab + b^2$, we get

$$f(-2,3) = (-2)(3) + (3)^2$$
$$= -6 + 9$$
$$f(-2,3) = 3$$

SESSION 4 PRACTICE TEST

Algebra Problems

Correct answers and solutions follow this test.

1. For what values of x is the following equation satisfied: $3x + 9 = 21 + 7x$?

   (A) -3 only
   (B) 3 only
   (C) 3 or -3 only
   (D) no values
   (E) an infinite number of values

   A B C D E
   ○ ○ ○ ○ ○
   _____

2. What values may z have if $2z + 4$ is greater than $z - 6$?

   (A) any values greater than -10
   (B) any values greater than -2
   (C) any values less than 2
   (D) any values less than 10
   (E) none of these

   A B C D E
   ○ ○ ○ ○ ○
   _____

3. If $ax^2 + 2x - 3 = 0$ when $x = -3$, what value(s) can a have?

   (A) -3 only
   (B) -1 only
   (C) 1 only
   (D) -1 and 1 only
   (E) $-3, -1,$ and 1 only

   A B C D E
   ○ ○ ○ ○ ○
   _____

4. If the coordinates of point P are (0,8), and the coordinates of point Q are (4,2), which of the following points represents the midpoint of PQ?

   (A) (0,2)
   (B) (2,4)
   (C) (2,5)
   (D) (4,8)
   (E) (4,10)

   A B C D E
   ○ ○ ○ ○ ○
   _____

5. In the formula $V = \pi r^2 h$, what is the value of r, in terms of V and h?

   (A) $\dfrac{\sqrt{V}}{\pi h}$

   (B) $\pi\sqrt{\dfrac{V}{h}}$

   (C) $\sqrt{\pi V h}$

   (D) $\dfrac{\pi h}{\sqrt{V}}$

   (E) $\sqrt{\dfrac{V}{\pi h}}$

   A B C D E
   ○ ○ ○ ○ ○
   _____

6. Solve the inequality $x^2 - 3x < 0$.

   (A) $x < -3$
   (B) $-3 < x < 0$
   (C) $x < 3$
   (D) $0 < x < 3$
   (E) $3 < x$

   A B C D E
   ○ ○ ○ ○ ○
   _____

7. Which of the following lines is parallel to the line represented by $2y = 8x + 32$?

   (A) $y = 8x + 32$
   (B) $y = 8x + 16$
   (C) $y = 16x + 32$
   (D) $y = 4x + 32$
   (E) $y = 2x + 16$

   A B C D E
   ○ ○ ○ ○ ○
   _____

8. In the equation $4.04x + 1.01 = 9.09$, what value of x is necessary to make the equation true?

(A) -1.5
(B) 0
(C) 1
(D) 2
(E) 2.5

A B C D E
○ ○ ○ ○ ○

9. What values of x satisfy the equation $(x + 1)(x - 2) = 0$?

(A) 1 only
(B) -2 only
(C) 1 and -2 only
(D) -1 and 2 only
(E) any values between -1 and 2

A B C D E
○ ○ ○ ○ ○

10. Solve the inequality $(x - 5)(2x + 4) \geq 0$.

(A) $x = -2, x = 5$
(B) $x \geq -2$
(C) $x \geq 5$
(D) $x \leq -2, x \geq 5$
(E) $-2 \leq x \leq 5$

A B C D E
○ ○ ○ ○ ○

11. For what value(s) of k is the following equation satisfied:

$$2k - 9 - k = 4k + 6 - 3k?$$

(A) -5 only
(B) 0
(C) $\frac{5}{2}$ only
(D) no values
(E) more than one value

A B C D E
○ ○ ○ ○ ○

12. In the equation $p = aq^2 + bq + c$, if $a = 1$, $b = -2$, and $c = 1$, which of the following expresses p in terms of q?

(A) $p = (q - 2)^2$
(B) $p = (q - 1)^2$
(C) $p = q^2$
(D) $p = (q + 1)^2$
(E) $p = (q + 2)^2$

A B C D E
○ ○ ○ ○ ○

13. If $A + B + C = 10$, $A + B = 7$, and $A - B = 5$, what is the value of C?

(A) 1
(B) 3
(C) 6
(D) 7
(E) The answer cannot be determined from the given information.

A B C D E
○ ○ ○ ○ ○

14. If $5x + 15$ is greater than 20, which of the following best describes the possible values of x?

(A) x must be greater than 5.
(B) x must be greater than 3.
(C) x must be greater than 1.
(D) x must be less than 5.
(E) x must be less than 1.

A B C D E
○ ○ ○ ○ ○

15. If $\frac{t^2 - 1}{t - 1} = 2$, then what value(s) may t have?

(A) 1 only
(B) -1 only
(C) 1 or -1
(D) no values
(E) an infinite number of values

A B C D E
○ ○ ○ ○ ○

16. If $4m = 9n$, what is the value of $7m$, in terms of n?

(A) $\frac{63n}{4}$
(B) $\frac{9n}{28}$
(C) $\frac{7n}{9}$
(D) $\frac{28n}{9}$
(E) $\frac{7n}{4}$

A B C D E
○ ○ ○ ○ ○

17. The coordinates of a triangle's vertices are (0,2), (0,6), and (3,4). What is the area of the triangle in square units?

    (A) 6
    (B) 8
    (C) 9
    (D) 12
    (E) 18

    A B C D E
    ○ ○ ○ ○ ○
    _____

18. In the formula $s = \frac{1}{2}gt^2$, what is the value of t, in terms of s and g?

    (A) $\dfrac{2s}{g}$

    (B) $2\sqrt{\dfrac{s}{g}}$

    (C) $\dfrac{s}{2g}$

    (D) $\sqrt{\dfrac{s}{2g}}$

    (E) $\sqrt{\dfrac{2s}{g}}$

    A B C D E
    ○ ○ ○ ○ ○
    _____

19. In the triangle ABC, angle A is a 30° angle, and angle B is obtuse. If x represents the number of degrees in angle C, which of the following best represents a possible value of x?

    (A) 0°
    (B) 50°
    (C) 90°
    (D) 120°
    (E) 180°

    A B C D E
    ○ ○ ○ ○ ○
    _____

20. Which of the following sets of coordinates does *not* represent the vertices of an isosceles triangle?

    (A) (0,2), (0,−2), (2,0)
    (B) (1,3), (1,5), (3,4)
    (C) (1,3), (1,7), (4,5)
    (D) (2,2), (2,0), (1,1)
    (E) (2,3), (2,5), (3,3)

    A B C D E
    ○ ○ ○ ○ ○
    _____

21. If $2 < a < 5$, and $3 < b < 6$, what are the possible values of $a + b$?

    (A) $a + b$ must equal 8.
    (B) $a + b$ must be between 2 and 6.
    (C) $a + b$ must be between 3 and 5.
    (D) $a + b$ must be between 5 and 8.
    (E) $a + b$ must be between 5 and 11.

    A B C D E
    ○ ○ ○ ○ ○
    _____

22. The area of a square will be doubled if:

    (A) the length of the diagonal is divided by 2
    (B) the length of the diagonal is divided by $\sqrt{2}$
    (C) the length of the diagonal is multiplied by 2
    (D) the length of the diagonal is multiplied by $\sqrt{2}$
    (E) none of the above

    A B C D E
    ○ ○ ○ ○ ○
    _____

23. Find the value of y that satisfies the equation $8.8y - 4 = 7.7y + 7$.

    (A) 1.1
    (B) 7.7
    (C) 8.0
    (D) 10.0
    (E) 11.0

    A B C D E
    ○ ○ ○ ○ ○
    _____

24. Which of the following is a factor of the expression $2x^2 + 1$?

    (A) $x + 2$
    (B) $x - 2$
    (C) $x + \sqrt{2}$
    (D) $x - \sqrt{2}$
    (E) none of these

    A B C D E
    ○ ○ ○ ○ ○
    _____

25. A manager has ten employees. The manager's salary is equal to six times the *average* of the employees' salaries. If the eleven of them received a total of $640,000 in one year, what was the manager's salary that year?

    (A) $40,000
    (B) $60,000
    (C) $240,000
    (D) $400,000
    (E) $440,000

    A B C D E
    ○ ○ ○ ○ ○

26. If $6x + 3 = 15$, what is the value of $12x - 3$?

    (A) 21
    (B) 24
    (C) 28
    (D) 33
    (E) 36

    A B C D E
    ○ ○ ○ ○ ○

27. If $2p + 7$ is greater than $3p - 5$, which of the following best describes the possible values of p?

    (A) p must be greater than 2.
    (B) p must be greater than 12.
    (C) p must be less than 2.
    (D) p must be less than 12.
    (E) p must be greater than 2 but less than 12.

    A B C D E
    ○ ○ ○ ○ ○

28. What is the value of q if $x^2 + qx + 1 = 0$, if $x = 1$?

    (A) -2
    (B) -1
    (C) 0
    (D) 1
    (E) 2

    A B C D E
    ○ ○ ○ ○ ○

29. What is the area (to the nearest unit) of the shaded figure in the diagram below, assuming that each of the squares has an area of 1?

    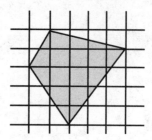

    (A) 12
    (B) 13
    (C) 14
    (D) 15
    (E) 16

    A B C D E
    ○ ○ ○ ○ ○

30. Which of the following statements is *false*?

    (A) Any two numbers, a and b, have a sum equal to $a + b$.
    (B) Any two numbers, a and b, have a product equal to $a \cdot b$.
    (C) Any two numbers, a and b, have a difference equal to $a - b$.
    (D) Any two numbers, a and b, have a quotient equal to $\frac{a}{b}$.
    (E) Any two numbers, a and b, have an average equal to $\frac{(a + b)}{2}$.

    A B C D E
    ○ ○ ○ ○ ○

31. If $(x - 1)(x - 2)(x^2 - 4) = 0$, what are the possible values of x?

    (A) -2 only
    (B) $+2$ only
    (C) $-1, -2,$ or -4 only
    (D) $+1, +2,$ or $+4$ only
    (E) $+1, -2,$ or $+2$ only

    A B C D E
    ○ ○ ○ ○ ○

32. If $P + Q = R$ and $P + R = 2Q$, what is the ratio of P to R?

    (A) $1:1$
    (B) $1:2$
    (C) $2:1$
    (D) $1:3$
    (E) $3:1$

    A B C D E
    ○ ○ ○ ○ ○

33. For what value(s) of r is $\dfrac{r^2 + 5r + 6}{r + 2}$ equal to 0?

    (A) -2 only
    (B) -3 only
    (C) $+3$ only
    (D) -2 or -3
    (E) $+2$ or $+3$

    A B C D E
    ○ ○ ○ ○ ○

34. What is the value of $a^2b + 4ab^2 + 4b^3$, if $a = 15$ and $b = 5$?

    (A) 1,625
    (B) 2,125
    (C) 2,425
    (D) 2,725
    (E) 3,125

    A B C D E
    ○ ○ ○ ○ ○

35. If $m + 4n = 2n + 8m$, what is the ratio of n to m?

    (A) $1:4$
    (B) $1:-4$
    (C) $-4:1$
    (D) $2:7$
    (E) $7:2$

    A B C D E
    ○ ○ ○ ○ ○

36. If the value of a lies between -5 and $+2$, and the value of b lies between -7 and $+1$, what are the possible values for the product $a \cdot b$?

    (A) between -14 and $+2$
    (B) between -35 and $+2$
    (C) between $+2$ and $+35$
    (D) between -12 and $+3$
    (E) between -14 and $+35$

    A B C D E
    ○ ○ ○ ○ ○

37. What is the area, in square units, of a triangle whose vertices lie on points $(-5,1)$, $(-5,4)$, and $(2,4)$?

    (A) 10.5 square units
    (B) 12.5 square units
    (C) 15.0 square units
    (D) 20.0 square units
    (E) 21.0 square units

    A B C D E
    ○ ○ ○ ○ ○

38. If $A + B = 12$ and $B + C = 16$, what is the value of $A + C$?

    (A) -4
    (B) -28
    (C) $+4$
    (D) $+28$
    (E) The answer cannot be determined from the given information.

    A B C D E
    ○ ○ ○ ○ ○

39. What is the solution to the equation $x^2 + 2x + 1 = 0$?

    (A) $x = 1$
    (B) $x = 0$
    (C) $x = 1$ and $x = -1$
    (D) $x = -1$
    (E) no real solutions

    A B C D E
    ○ ○ ○ ○ ○

40. Which of the following equations will have a vertical line as its graph?

    (A) $x + y = 1$
    (B) $x - y = 1$
    (C) $x = 1$
    (D) $y = 1$
    (E) $xy = 1$

    A B C D E
    ○ ○ ○ ○ ○

41. For what value(s) of x does $x^2 + 3x + 2$ equal zero?

    (A) -1 only
    (B) $+2$ only
    (C) -1 or -2 only
    (D) 1 or 2 only
    (E) none of these

    A B C D E
    ○ ○ ○ ○ ○

42. If $a + b$ equals 12, and $a - b$ equals 6, what is the value of b?

(A) 0
(B) 3
(C) 6
(D) 9
(E) The answer cannot be determined from the given information.

A B C D E
○ ○ ○ ○ ○

43. For what value(s) of m is $m^2 + 4$ equal to $4m$?

(A) −2 only
(B) 0 only
(C) +2 only
(D) +4 only
(E) more than one value

A B C D E
○ ○ ○ ○ ○

44. If $x = 0$, $y = 2$, and $x^2yz + 3xz^2 + y^2z + 3y + 4x = 0$, what is the value of z?

(A) $-\dfrac{4}{3}$

(B) $-\dfrac{3}{2}$

(C) $+\dfrac{3}{4}$

(D) $+\dfrac{4}{3}$

(E) The answer cannot be determined from the given information.

A B C D E
○ ○ ○ ○ ○

45. If $c + 4d = 3c - 2d$, what is the ratio of c to d?

(A) 1 : 3
(B) 1 : −3
(C) 3 : 1
(D) 2 : 3
(E) 2 : −3

A B C D E
○ ○ ○ ○ ○

46. If $3 < x < 7$ and $2 < x < 6$, which of the following best describes x?

(A) $2 < x < 6$
(B) $2 < x < 7$
(C) $3 < x < 6$

(D) $3 < x < 7$
(E) No value of x can satisfy both of these conditions.

A B C D E
○ ○ ○ ○ ○

47. What are the coordinates of the midpoint of the line segment whose endpoints are (4,9) and (5,15)?

(A) (4,5)
(B) (5,9)
(C) (4,15)
(D) (4.5,12)
(E) (9,24)

A B C D E
○ ○ ○ ○ ○

48. If $\dfrac{t^2 + 2t}{2t + 4} = \dfrac{t}{2}$, what does t equal?

(A) −2 only
(B) +2 only
(C) any value except +2
(D) any value except −2
(E) any value

A B C D E
○ ○ ○ ○ ○

49. If $x + y = 4$, and $x + z = 9$, what is the value of $(y - z)$?

(A) −5
(B) +5
(C) −13
(D) +13
(E) The answer cannot be determined from the given information.

A B C D E
○ ○ ○ ○ ○

50. Of the following statements, which are equivalent?

   I. $-3 < x < 3$
   II. $x^2 < 9$
   III. $\dfrac{1}{x} < \dfrac{1}{3}$

(A) I and II only
(B) I and III only
(C) II and III only
(D) I, II, and III
(E) none of the above

A B C D E
○ ○ ○ ○ ○

Answer Key for Session 4 Practice Test

1. A	14. C	27. D	39. D
2. A	15. D	28. A	40. C
3. C	16. A	29. B	41. C
4. C	17. A	30. D	42. B
5. E	18. E	31. E	43. C
6. D	19. B	32. D	44. B
7. D	20. E	33. B	45. C
8. D	21. E	34. E	46. C
9. D	22. D	35. E	47. D
10. D	23. D	36. E	48. D
11. D	24. E	37. A	49. A
12. B	25. C	38. E	50. A
13. B	26. A		

Answers and Solutions for Session 4 Practice Test

1. Choice A is correct. The original equation is $3x + 9 = 21 + 7x$. First subtract 9 and $7x$ from both sides to get $-4x = 12$. Now divide both sides by the coefficient of x, -4, obtaining the solution, $x = -3$.
(Refresher 406)

2. Choice A is correct. Given $2z + 4 > z - 6$. Subtracting equal quantities from both sides of an inequality does not change the order of the inequality. Therefore, subtracting z and 4 from both sides gives a solution of $z > -10$.
(Refreshers 419, 420)

3. Choice C is correct. Substitute -3 for x in the original equation to get the following:
$$a(-3)^2 + 2(-3) - 3 = 0$$
$$9a - 6 - 3 = 0$$
$$9a - 9 = 0$$
$$a = 1$$
(Refresher 406)

4. Choice C is correct. To find the midpoint of the line segment connecting two points, find the point whose x-coordinate is the average of the two given x-coordinates, and whose y-coordinate is the average of the two given y-coordinates. The midpoint here will be $\left(\dfrac{0 + 4}{2}, \dfrac{8 + 2}{2}\right)$, or $(2,5)$.
(Refresher 412)

5. Choice E is correct. Divide both sides of the equation by πh:
$$\frac{V}{\pi h} = r^2$$
Take the square root of both sides:
$$r = \sqrt{\frac{V}{\pi h}}$$
(Refresher 403)

6. Choice D is correct. Factor the original expression into $x(x - 3) < 0$. In order for the product of two expressions to be less than 0 (negative), one must be positive and the other must be negative. Thus, $x < 0$ and $x - 3 > 0$; or $x > 0$ and $x - 3 < 0$. In the first case, $x < 0$ and $x > 3$. This is impossible because x cannot be less than 0 *and* greater than 3 at the same time. In the second case $x > 0$ and $x < 3$, which can be rewritten as $0 < x < 3$.
(Refresher 428)

7. Choice D is correct. Divide both sides of the equation $2y = 8x + 32$ by 2 to get $y = 4x + 16$. Now it is in the form of $y = mx + b$, where m is the slope of the line and b is the y-intercept. Thus the slope of the line is 4. Any line parallel to this line must have the same slope. The answer must have a slope of 4. This is the line $y = 4x + 32$. Note that all of the choices are already in the form of $y = mx + b$.
(Refresher 416)

8. Choice D is correct. Subtract 1.01 from both sides to give: $4.04x = 8.08$. Dividing both sides by 4.04 gives a solution of $x = 2$.
(Refresher 406)

9. Choice D is correct. If a product is equal to zero, then one of the factors must equal zero. If $(x + 1)(x - 2) = 0$, either $x + 1 = 0$, or $x - 2 = 0$. Solving these two equations, we see that either $x = -1$ or $x = 2$.
(Refreshers 408, 409)

10. Choice D is correct. For $(x - 5)(2x + 4) \geq 0$ to be a true statement, both factors must be negative, both must be positive, or one factor must be 0.

    Set $x - 5 \geq 0$ and $2x + 4 \geq 0$.

    From this we get:
    $$x \geq 5 \quad \text{and} \quad 2x \geq -4$$
    This becomes:
    $$x \geq 5 \quad \text{and} \quad x \geq -2$$
    Thus, $x \geq 5$ or $x = -2$.

Now set $x - 5 \leq 0$ and $2x + 4 \leq 0$.

From this we get:
$$x \leq 5 \quad \text{and} \quad 2x \leq -4$$

This becomes:
$$x \leq 5 \quad \text{and} \quad x \leq -2$$

Thus, $x \leq -2$.

So we end up with:
$$x \leq -2, x \geq 5$$

(Refresher 428)

11. Choice D is correct. Combine like terms on both sides of the given equations and obtain the equivalent form: $k - 9 = k + 6$. This is true for no values of k. If k is subtracted from both sides, -9 will equal 6, which is impossible. (Refresher 406)

12. Choice B is correct. Substitute for the given values of a, b, and c, and obtain $p = q^2 - 2q + 1$; or, rearranging terms, $p = (q - 1)^2$. (Refresher 409)

13. Choice B is correct. $A + B + C = 10$. Also, $A + B = 7$. Substitute the value 7 for the quantity $(A + B)$ in the first equation and obtain the new equation: $7 + C = 10$ or $C = 3$. $A - B = 5$ could be used with the other two equations to find the values of A and B. (Refresher 406)

14. Choice C is correct. If $5x + 15 > 20$, then subtract 15 from both sides to get $5x > 5$. Now divide both sides by 5. This does not change the order of the inequality because 5 is a positive number. The solution is $x > 1$. (Refreshers 419, 426)

15. Choice D is correct. Factor $(t^2 - 1)$ to obtain the product $(t + 1)(t - 1)$. For any value of t, except 1, the equation is equivalent to $(t + 1) = 2$, or $t = 1$. One is the only possible value of t. However, this value is not possible as $t - 1$ would equal 0, and the quotient $\frac{t^2 - 1}{t - 1}$ would not be defined. (Refreshers 404, 409)

16. Choice A is correct. If $4m = 9n$, then $m = \frac{9n}{4}$. Multiplying both sides of the equation by 7, we obtain: $7m = \frac{63n}{4}$. (Refresher 403)

17. Choice A is correct. The easiest way to find the area of the triangle is to first draw a sketch. As the diagram shows, the base falls on the y-axis.

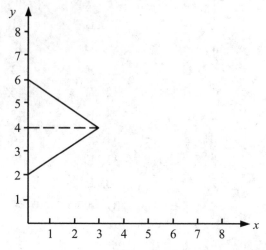

We can either subtract the y-coordinates of the vertices of the base or count the number of units to find the base (4 units). Since the base is on the y-axis, the height is the x-coordinate of the third vertex (3 units). $A = \frac{1}{2}bh = \frac{1}{2}(4)(3) = 6$ square units. (Refresher 418)

18. Choice E is correct. Since $s = \frac{1}{2}gt^2$, divide both sides of the equation by $\frac{1}{2}g$ to obtain the form, $\frac{2s}{g} = t^2$. Then, after taking the square roots, $t = \sqrt{\frac{2s}{g}}$. (Refresher 403)

19. Choice B is correct. The sum of the angles in a triangle must add up to 180°. If A is a 30° angle, and angle B is obtuse (or greater than 90°), this implies that angle C must be less than 60°. $180° - 90° - 30° = 60°$. To have a proper triangle, C must be a positive angle. Therefore the only possible value is 50°. (Refresher 419)

20. Choice E is correct. An isosceles triangle has two equal sides. To find the length of the sides, we use the distance formula, $\sqrt{(x_2 - x_1)^2 + (y_2 - y_1)^2}$. In the first case the lengths of the sides are 4, $2\sqrt{2}$, and $2\sqrt{2}$. Thus two sides have the same length, and it is an isosceles triangle. The only set of points that is not an isosceles triangle is the last one. (Refresher 411)

21. Choice E is correct. The smallest possible value of a is greater than 2, and the smallest possible value of b is greater than 3, so the smallest possible value of $a + b$ must be greater than $2 + 3 = 5$. Similarly,

the largest values of a and b are less than 5 and 6, respectively, so the largest possible value of $a + b$ is less than 11. Therefore, the sum must be between 5 and 11. (Refresher 419)

22. Choice D is correct. If the sides of the original square are each equal to s, then the area of the square is s^2, and the diagonal is $s\sqrt{2}$. Now, a new square, with an area of $2s^2$, must have a side of $s\sqrt{2}$. Thus, the diagonal is $2s$, which is $\sqrt{2}$ times the original length of the diagonal.
(Refreshers 303, 406)

23. Choice D is correct. First place all of the variable terms on one side and all of the numerical terms on the other side. Subtracting $7.7y$ and adding 4 to both sides of the equation gives $1.1y = 11$. Now divide both sides by 1.1 to solve for $y = 10$.
(Refresher 406)

24. Choice E is correct. To determine whether an expression is a factor of another expression, give the variable a specific value in both expressions. An expression divided by its factor will be a whole number. If we give x the value 0, then the expression $2x^2 + 1$ has the value of 1 and $x + 2$ has the value of 2. 1 is not divisible by 2, so the first choice is not a factor. The next choice has the value of -2, also not a factor of 1. Similarly $x + \sqrt{2}$ and $x - \sqrt{2}$ take on the values of $\sqrt{2}$ and $-\sqrt{2}$, respectively, when $x = 0$, and are not factors of $2x^2 + 1$. Therefore, the correct choice is (E). (Refresher 409)

25. Choice C is correct. Let x equal the average salary of the employees. Then the employees receive a total of $10x$ dollars, and the manager receives six times the average, or $6x$. Together, the eleven of them receive a total of $10x + 6x = 16x$, which equals $\$640,000$. Thus, x equals $\$40,000$, and the manager's salary is $6x$, or $\$240,000$.
(Refresher 406)

26. Choice A is correct. We are given $6x + 3 = 15$. Subtract 3 from both sides of the equation. We get $6x = 12$. Now divide this equation by 6. We get $x = 2$. Substituting $x = 2$ into the expression $12x - 3$ gives $24 - 3$, which equals 21.
(Refresher 406)

27. Choice D is correct. $2p + 7 > 3p - 5$. To both sides of the inequality add 5. We get $2p + 12 > 3p$. Now subtract $2p$. We get $12 > p$. Thus, p is less than 12.
(Refreshers 419, 426)

28. Choice A is correct. Substituting 1 for x in the given equation obtains $1 + q + 1 = 0$, or $q + 2 = 0$. This is solved only for $q = -2$. (Refresher 406)

29. Choice B is correct.

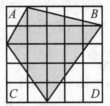

The area of the shaded figure can most easily be found by taking the area of the square surrounding it (25) and subtracting the areas of the four triangles marked A (1), B (2), C (3), and D (6), leaving an area of $25 - (1 + 2 + 3 + 6) = 13$ square units.
(Refresher 418)

30. Choice D is correct. If the number b is equal to zero, the quotient $\frac{a}{b}$ is not defined. For all other pairs, all five statements are true.
(Refreshers 401–405)

31. Choice E is correct. If a product equals zero, one of the factors must be equal to zero also. Thus, either $x - 1 = 0$, or $x - 2 = 0$, or $x^2 - 4 = 0$. The possible solutions, therefore, are $x = 1$, $x = 2$, and $x = -2$. (Refresher 408)

32. Choice D is correct. Solve the equation $P + Q = R$, for Q (the variable we wish to eliminate), to get $Q = R - P$. Substituting this for Q in the second equation yields $P + R = 2(R - P) = 2R - 2P$, or $3P = R$. Therefore, the ratio of P to R is $\frac{P}{R}$, or $\frac{1}{3}$.
(Refresher 406)

33. Choice B is correct. The fraction in question will equal zero if the numerator equals zero and the denominator is nonzero. The expression $r^2 + 5r + 6$ can be factored into $(r + 2)(r + 3)$. As long as r is not equal to -2, the equation is defined, and $r + 2$ can be canceled in the original equation to yield $r + 3 = 0$, or $r = -3$. For r equals -2, the denominator is equal to zero, and the fraction in the original equation is not defined.
(Refreshers 404, 409)

34. Choice E is correct. This problem can be shortened considerably by factoring the expression $a^2b + 4ab^2 + 4b^3$ into the product $(b)(a + 2b)^2$.

Now, since $b = 5$ and $(a + 2b) = 25$, our product equals $5 \times 25 \times 25$, or $3,125$.   (Refresher 409)

35. Choice E is correct. Subtract $m + 2n$ from both sides of the given equation and obtain the equivalent form, $2n = 7m$. Dividing this equation by $2m$ gives $\dfrac{n}{m} = \dfrac{7}{2}$, the ratio of n to m.   (Refresher 406)

36. Choice E is correct. To find the range of the values of the product ab, find the smallest value of the product and the largest value of the product. If a lies between -5 and $+2$ and b lies between -7 and $+1$, then the largest value of ab is $-5 \times -7 = +35$. The smallest value of ab is $+2 \times -7 = -14$. So the possible values of ab are between -14 and 35.

(Refresher 419)

37. Choice A is correct.

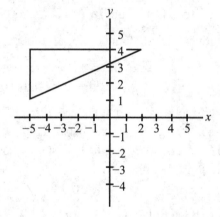

As can be seen from a diagram, this triangle must be a right triangle, since the line from $(-5,1)$ to $(-5,4)$ is vertical, and the line from $(-5,4)$ to $(2,4)$ is horizontal. The lengths of these two perpendicular sides are 3 and 7, respectively. Since the area of a right triangle is half the product of the perpendicular sides, the area is equal to $\dfrac{1}{2} \times 3 \times 7$, or 10.5.

(Refreshers 410, 418)

38. Choice E is correct. Solving the first equation for A gives $A = 12 - B$. Solving the second equation for C gives $C = 16 - B$. Thus, the sum $A + C$ is equal to $28 - 2B$. There is nothing to determine the value of B, so the sum of A and C is not determined from the information given.

(Refresher 406)

39. Choice D is correct. Factor $x^2 + 2x + 1$ to get $(x + 1)(x + 1) = 0$. Thus $x + 1 = 0$, so $x = -1$.

(Refresher 409)

40. Choice C is correct. If we graph the five choices we will get:

A
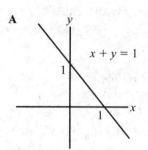

B
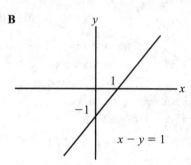

C
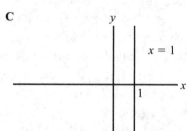

D
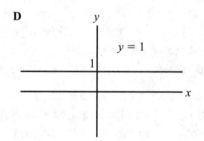

E
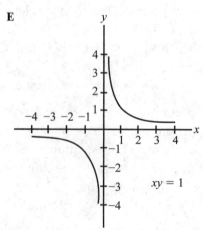

The only choice that is a vertical line is Choice C, $x = 1$.   (Refresher 413)

41. Choice C is correct. The factors of $x^2 + 3x + 2$ are $(x + 1)$ and $(x + 2)$. Either $x + 1 = 0$ or $x + 2 = 0$. x may equal either -1 or -2.   (Refresher 408)

42. Choice B is correct. $a + b = 12$ and $a - b = 6$. Rewrite these equations as $a = 12 - b$ and $a = 6 + b$. $12 - b$ and $6 + b$ are both equal to a. Or, $12 - b = 6 + b$. Thus, $6 = 2b$ and $b = 3$.
    (Refresher 407)

43. Choice C is correct. Let $m^2 + 4 = 4m$. Subtracting $4m$ from both sides yields $m^2 - 4m + 4 = 0$. Factor to get the following equation: $(m - 2)^2 = 0$. Thus, $m = 2$ is the only solution.   (Refresher 408)

44. Choice B is correct. Substitute for the given values of x and y, obtaining: $(0)^2(2)(z) + (3)(0)(z)^2 + (2)^2(z) + (3)(2) + (4)(0) = 0$. Perform the indicated multiplications, and combine terms. $0(z) + 0(z^2) + 4z + 6 + 0 = 4z + 6 = 0$. This equation has $z = -\dfrac{3}{2}$ as its only solution.   (Refresher 406)

45. Choice C is correct. $c + 4d = 3c - 2d$. Add $2d - c$ to each side and get $6d = 2c$. (Be especially careful about your signs here.) Dividing by $2d$: $\dfrac{c}{d} = \dfrac{6}{2} = \dfrac{3}{1}$. Thus, $c : d = 3 : 1$.   (Refresher 406)

46. Choice C is correct. x must be greater than 3, less than 7, greater than 2, and less than 6. These conditions can be reduced as follows: If x is less than 6, it is also less than 7. Similarly, x must be greater than 3, which automatically makes it greater than 2. Thus, x must be greater than 3 *and* less than 6.
    (Refresher 419)

47. Choice D is correct. To obtain the coordinates of the midpoint of a line segment, average the corresponding coordinates of the endpoints. Thus, the midpoint will be $\left(\dfrac{4 + 5}{2}, \dfrac{9 + 15}{2}\right)$, or $(4.5, 12)$.
    (Refresher 412)

48. Choice D is correct. If both sides of the equation are multiplied by $2t + 4$, we obtain: $t^2 + 2t = t^2 + 2t$, which is true for every value of t. However, when $t = -2$, the denominator of the fraction on the left side of the original equation is equal to zero. Since division by zero is not a permissible operation, this fraction will not be defined for $t = -2$. The equation cannot be satisfied for $t = -2$.
    (Refreshers 404, 406, 409)

49. Choice A is correct. If we subtract the second of our equations from the first, we will be left with the following: $(x + y) - (x + z) = 4 - 9$, or $y - z = -5$.   (Refresher 402)

50. Choice A is correct. If x^2 is less than 9, then x may take on any value greater than -3 and less than $+3$; other values will produce squares greater than or equal to 9. If $\dfrac{1}{x}$ is less than $\dfrac{1}{3}$, x is restricted to positive values greater than 3 and all negative values. For example, if $x = 1$, then conditions I and II are satisfied, but $\dfrac{1}{x}$ equals 1, which is greater than $\dfrac{1}{3}$.   (Refresher 419)

MATH REFRESHER SESSION 5

Geometry Problems

Basic Definitions

500. *Plane geometry* deals with points and lines. A point has no dimensions and is generally represented by a dot (·). A line has no thickness, but it does have length. Lines can be straight or curved, but here it will be assumed that a line is straight unless otherwise indicated. All lines have infinite length. A part of a line that has a finite length is called a line segment.

> Remember that the *distance* between two lines or from a point to a line always means the perpendicular distance. Thus, the distance between the two parallel lines pictured below (top diagram) is the length of line segment A, as this is the only perpendicular line segment. Also, as shown in bottom diagram, the distance from a line to a point is the length of perpendicular line segment AB from the point to the line. Thus, AB is the distance from point A to the line segment CBD.

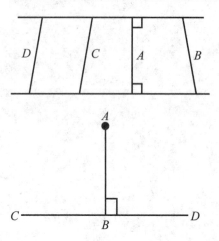

501. *Angles.* An angle is formed when two lines intersect at a point. Angle B, angle ABC, $\angle B$, and $\angle ABC$ are all possible names for the angle shown.

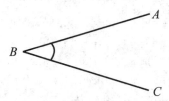

The measure of the angle is given in degrees. If the sides of the angle form a straight line, then the angle is said to be a straight angle and has 180°. A circle has 360°, and a straight angle is a turning through a half circle. All other angles are either greater or less than 180°.

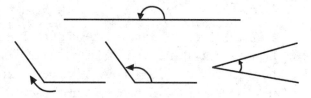

Angles are classified in different ways:

An *acute* angle has less than 90°.

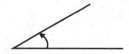

A *right* angle has exactly 90°. In the diagram, the small square in the corner of the angle indicates a right angle (90°).

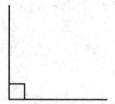

An *obtuse* angle has between 90° and 180°.

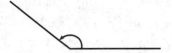

A *straight* angle has exactly 180°.

A *reflex* angle has between 180° and 360°.

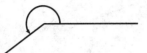

502. Two angles are *complementary* if their sum is 90°. For example, an angle of 30° and an angle of 60° are complementary. Two angles are *supplementary* if their sum is 180°. If one angle is 82°, then its supplement is 98°.

503. *Vertical angles.* These are pairs of opposite angles formed by the intersection of two straight lines. Vertical angles are always equal to each other.

   Example: In the diagram shown, angles *AEC* and *BED* are equal because they are vertical angles. For the same reason, angles *AED* and *BEC* are equal.

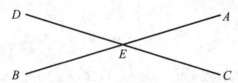

504. When two parallel lines are crossed by a third straight line (called a *transversal*), then all the acute angles formed are equal, and all of the obtuse angles are equal.

   Example: In the diagram below, angles 1, 4, 5, and 8 are all equal. Angles 2, 3, 6, and 7 are also equal.

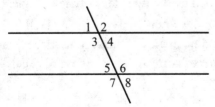

Triangles

505. *Triangles.* A triangle is a closed figure with three sides, each side being a line segment. The sum of the angles of a triangle is *always* 180°.

506. *Scalene triangles* are triangles with no two sides equal. Scalene triangles also have no two angles equal.

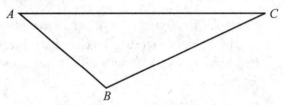

507. *Isosceles triangles* have two equal sides and two equal angles formed by the equal sides and the unequal side. See the figure below.

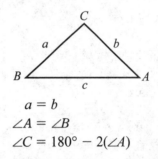

   $a = b$
   $\angle A = \angle B$
   $\angle C = 180° - 2(\angle A)$

508. *Equilateral triangles* have all three sides and all three angles equal. Since the sum of the three angles of a triangle is 180°, each angle of an equilateral triangle is 60°.

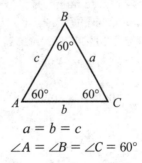

   $a = b = c$
   $\angle A = \angle B = \angle C = 60°$

509. A *right triangle* has one angle equal to a right angle (90°). The sum of the other two angles of a right triangle is, therefore, 90°. The most important relationship in a right triangle is expressed by the Pythagorean theorem. It states that $c^2 = a^2 + b^2$, where c, the hypotenuse, is the length of the

side opposite the right angle, and a and b are the lengths of the other two sides. Recall that this was discussed in Section 317.

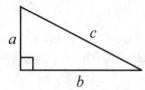

Example: If the two sides of a right triangle adjacent to the right angle are 3 inches and 4 inches respectively, find the length of the side opposite the right angle.

Solution:

Use the Pythagorean theorem, $c^2 = a^2 + b^2$, where $a = 3$ and $b = 4$. Then, $c = 3^2 + 4^2$ or $c^2 = 9 + 16 = 25$. Thus $c = 5$.

> Certain sets of integers will always fit the formula $c^2 = a^2 + b^2$. These integers can always represent the lengths of the sides of a right triangle. For example, a triangle whose sides are 3, 4, and 5 will always be a right triangle. Further examples are 5, 12, and 13, and 8, 15, and 17. Any multiples of these numbers also satisfy this formula. For example, 6, 8, and 10; 9, 12, and 15; 10, 24, and 26; 24, 45, and 51; etc.

509a. In a triangle, the greater angle lies opposite the greater side.

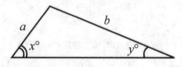

If $a < b$, then $y < x$
If $y < x$, then $a < b$

Properties of Triangles

510. Two triangles are said to be *similar* (having the same shape) if their corresponding angles are equal. The sides of similar triangles are in the same proportion. The two triangles below are similar because they have the same corresponding angles.

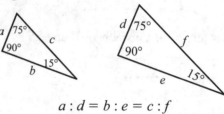

$$a : d = b : e = c : f$$

Example: Two triangles both have angles of 30°, 70°, and 80°. If the sides of the triangles are as indicated below, find the length of side x.

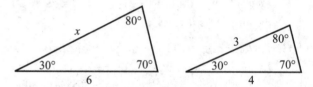

Solution: The two triangles are similar because they have the same corresponding angles. The corresponding sides of similar triangles are in proportion, so $x : 3 = 6 : 4$. This can be rewritten as $\frac{x}{3} = \frac{6}{4}$. Multiplying both sides by 3 gives $x = \frac{18}{4}$, or $x = 4\frac{1}{2}$.

511. Two triangles are *congruent* (*identical* in shape and size) if any one of the following conditions is met:

1. Each side of the first triangle equals the corresponding side of the second triangle.

2. Two sides of the first triangle equal the corresponding sides of the second triangle, and their included angles are equal. The included angle is formed by the two sides of the triangle.

3. Two angles of the first triangle equal the corresponding angles of the second triangle, and any pair of corresponding sides are equal.

Example: Triangles *ABC* and *DEF* in the diagrams below are congruent if any one of the following conditions can be met:

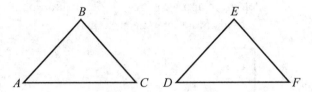

1. The three sides are equal (*sss*) = (*sss*).

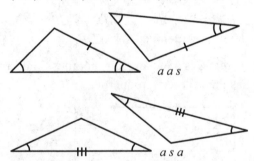

2. Two sides and the included angle are equal (*sas*) = (*sas*).

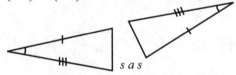

3. Two angles and any one side are equal (*aas*) = (*aas*) or (*asa*) = (*asa*).

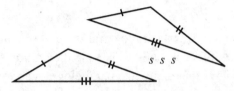

Example: In the equilateral triangle below, line *AD* is perpendicular (forms a right angle) to side *BC*. If the length of *BD* is 5 feet, what is the length of *DC*?

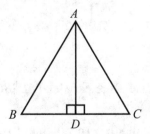

Solution: Since the large triangle is an equilateral triangle, each angle is 60°. Therefore ∠*B* is 60° and ∠*C* is 60°. Thus, ∠*B* = ∠*C*. *ADB* and *ADC*

are both right angles and are equal. Two angles of each triangle are equal to the corresponding two angles of the other triangle. Side *AD* is shared by both triangles and side *AB* = side *AC*. Thus, according to condition 3 in Section 511, the two triangles are congruent. Then *BD* = *DC* and, since *BD* is 5 feet, *DC* is 5 feet.

512. The *medians* of a triangle are the lines drawn from each vertex to the midpoint of its opposite side. The medians of a triangle cross at a point that divides each median into two parts: one part is one-third the length of the median and the other part is two-thirds the length.

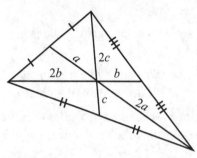

513. The *angle bisectors* of a triangle are the lines that divide each angle of the triangle into two equal parts. These lines meet in a point that is the center of a circle inscribed in the triangle.

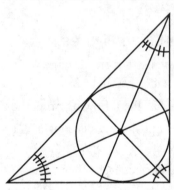

514. The *altitudes* of the triangle are lines drawn from the vertices perpendicular to the opposite sides. The lengths of these lines are useful in calculating the area of the triangle, since the area of the triangle is $\frac{1}{2}$(base)(height), and the height is identical to the altitude.

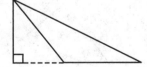
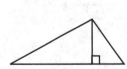

515. The *perpendicular bisectors* of the triangle are the lines that bisect and are perpendicular to each of the three sides. The point where these lines meet is the center of the circumscribed circle.

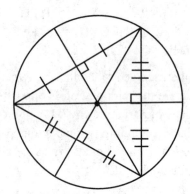

516. The sum of any two sides of a triangle is greater than the third side.

Example: If the three sides of a triangle are 4, 2, and x, then what is known about the value of x?

Solution: Since the sum of two sides of a triangle is always greater than the third side, then $4 + 2 > x$, $4 + x > 2$, and $2 + x > 4$. These three inequalities can be rewritten as $6 > x$, $x > -2$, and $x > 2$. For x to be greater than -2 and 2, it must be greater than 2. Thus, the values of x are $2 < x < 6$.

Four-Sided Figures

517. A *parallelogram* is a four-sided figure with each pair of opposite sides parallel.

A parallelogram has the following properties:

1. Each pair of opposite sides is equal. ($AD = BC$, $AB = DC$)

2. The diagonals bisect each other. ($AE = EC$, $DE = EB$)

3. The opposite angles are equal. ($\angle A = \angle C$, $\angle D = \angle B$)

4. One diagonal divides the parallelogram into two congruent triangles. Two diagonals divide the parallelogram into two pairs of congruent triangles.

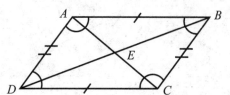

518. A *rectangle* is a parallelogram in which all the angles are right angles. Since a rectangle is a parallelogram, all of the laws that apply to a parallelogram apply to a rectangle. In addition, the diagonals of a rectangle are equal.

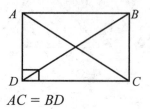

$AC = BD$

519. A *rhombus* is a parallelogram with four equal sides. Since a rhombus is a parallelogram, all of the laws that apply to a parallelogram apply to a rhombus. In addition, the diagonals of a rhombus are perpendicular to each other and bisect the vertex angles.

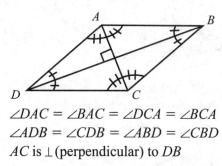

$\angle DAC = \angle BAC = \angle DCA = \angle BCA$
$\angle ADB = \angle CDB = \angle ABD = \angle CBD$
AC is $\perp$ (perpendicular) to DB

520. A *square* is a rectangular rhombus. Thus a square has the following properties:

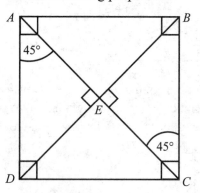

1. All four sides are equal. ($AB = BC = CD = DA$)

2. Opposite pairs of sides are parallel. ($AD\|BC$, $AB\|DC$)

3. Diagonals are equal, are perpendicular to each other, and bisect each other. ($AC = BD$, $AC \perp BD$, $AE = EC = DE = EB$)

4. All the angles are right angles (90°). ($\angle A = \angle B$ $= \angle C = \angle D = 90°$)

5. Diagonals intersect the vertices at 45°. ($\angle DAC$ $= \angle BCA = 45°$, and similarly for the other 3 vertices.)

Many-Sided Figures

521. A *polygon* is a closed plane figure whose sides are straight lines. The sum of the angles in any polygon is equal to $180(n - 2)°$, where n is the number of sides. Thus, in a polygon of 3 sides (a triangle), the sum of the angles is $180(3 - 2)°$, or 180°.

522. A *regular polygon* is a polygon all of whose sides are equal and all of whose angles are equal. These polygons have special properties:

1. A regular polygon can be inscribed in a circle and can be circumscribed about another circle. For example, a hexagon is inscribed in a circle in the diagram below.

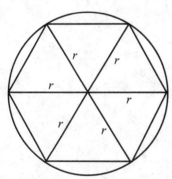

2. Each angle of a regular polygon is equal to the sum of the angles divided by the number (n) of sides, $\dfrac{180(n - 2)°}{n}$. Thus, a square, which is a regular polygon of 4 sides, has each angle equal to $\dfrac{180(4 - 2)°}{4}$ or 90°.

523. An important regular polygon is the *hexagon*. The diagonals of a regular hexagon divide it into 6 equilateral triangles, the sides of which are equal to the sides of the hexagon. If a hexagon is inscribed in a circle, the length of each side is equal to the length of the radius of the circle. (See diagram of hexagon above.)

Circles

524. A *circle* (also see Section 310) is a set of points equidistant from a given point, the *center*. The distance from the center to the circle is the *radius*. Any line that connects two points on the circle is a *chord*. A chord through the center of the circle is a *diameter*. On the circle below, O is the center, line segment OF is a radius, DE is a diameter, and AC is a chord.

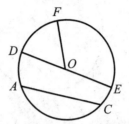

The length of the diameter of a circle is twice the length of the radius. The circumference (distance around the circle) is 2π times the length of the radius. π is a constant approximately equal to $\dfrac{22}{7}$ or 3.14. The formula for the circumference of a circle is $C = 2\pi r$, where C = circumference and r = radius.

525. A *tangent* to a circle is a line that is perpendicular to a radius and that passes through only one point of the circle. In the diagram below, AB is a tangent.

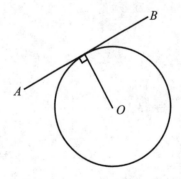

526. A *central angle* is an angle whose sides are two radii of the circle. The vertex of this angle is the center of the circle. The number of degrees in a central angle is equal to the amount of arc length that the radii intercept. As the complete circumference has 360°, any other arc lengths are less than 360°.

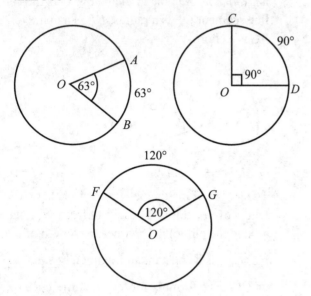

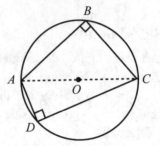

Angles *AOB*, *COD*, and *FOG* are all central angles.

527. An *inscribed angle* of a circle is an angle whose sides are two chords. The vertex of the angle lies on the circumference of the circle. The number of degrees in the inscribed angle is equal to one-half the intercepted arc.

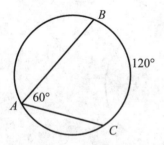

∠*BAC* is an inscribed angle.

528. An angle inscribed in a semicircle is always a right angle. ∠*ABC* and ∠*ADC* are inscribed in semicircles *AOCB* and *AOCD*, respectively, and are thus right angles.

Note: A semicircle is one-half of a circle.

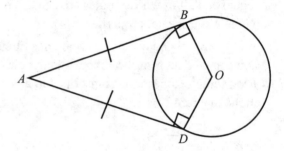

529. Two tangents to a circle from the same point outside of the circle are always equal.

Tangents *AB* and *AD* are equal.

Formulas

(Also see 301–317.)

530. Triangle: Area = $\frac{1}{2}bh$ (b = base, h = height)

Perimeter = $a + b + c$ (a, b, and c are the 3 sides)

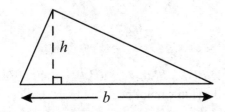

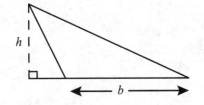

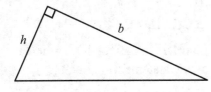

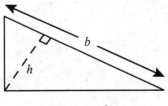

Area = $\frac{1}{2}bh$

The area of any triangle is $\frac{1}{2}bh$, where b is the length of *any* side and h is the length of the altitude (height) to that side. Note that the altitude is defined as the perpendicular distance from the vertex of the triangle to the opposite side.

Rectangle: Area = lw (l = length, w = width)

Perimeter = sum of sides = $2(l + w)$

Square: Area = s^2 (s = side of square)

Perimeter = sum of sides = $4s$

Parallelogram: Area = bh (b = base, h = height)

Perimeter = sum of 4 sides

Trapezoid: Area = $\frac{1}{2}(a + b)h$ (a and b are the two bases, h = height)

Median = $\frac{1}{2}(a + b)$

Circle: $d = 2r$ (d = diameter, r = radius)

Circumference = $2\pi r = \pi d$

(π is about 3.14)

Area = πr^2

Rectangular Box: Volume = lwh (l = length, w = width, h = height)

Cube: Volume = s^3 (s = side of cube)

Note: The perimeter of a polygon is the sum of the sides of the polygon.

SESSION 5 PRACTICE TEST

Geometry Problems

Correct answers and solutions follow this test.

1. In the following diagram, angle 1 is equal to 40°, and angle 2 is equal to 150°. What is the number of degrees in angle 3?

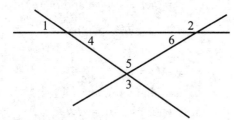

(A) 70°
(B) 90°
(C) 110°
(D) 190°
(E) The answer cannot be determined from the given information.

A B C D E
○ ○ ○ ○ ○

2. In this diagram, AB and CD are both perpendicular to BE. If $EC = 5$ and $CD = 4$, what is the ratio of AB to BE?

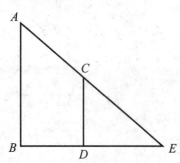

(A) 1 : 1
(B) 4 : 3
(C) 5 : 4
(D) 5 : 3
(E) none of these

A B C D E
○ ○ ○ ○ ○

3. In triangle PQR, $PR = 7.0$, and $PQ = 4.5$. Which of the following cannot possibly represent the length of QR?

(A) 2.0
(B) 3.0
(C) 3.5
(D) 4.5
(E) 5.0

A B C D E
○ ○ ○ ○ ○

4. In this diagram, $AB = AC$, and $BD = CD$. Which of the following statements is true?

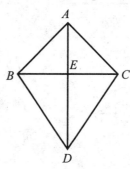

(A) $BE = EC$.
(B) AD is perpendicular to BC.
(C) Triangles BDE and CDE are congruent.
(D) Angle ABD equals angle ACD.
(E) All of these.

A B C D E
○ ○ ○ ○ ○

5. In the following diagram, if $BC = CD = BD = 1$, and angle ADC is a right angle, what is the perimeter of triangle ABD?

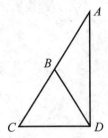

(A) 3
(B) $2 + \sqrt{2}$
(C) $2 + \sqrt{3}$
(D) $3 + \sqrt{3}$
(E) 4

A B C D E
○ ○ ○ ○ ○

6. In this diagram, if $PQRS$ is a parallelogram, which of the following can be deduced?

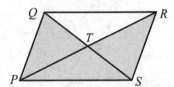

  I. $QT + PT = RT + ST$.
 II. QS is perpendicular to PR.
III.   The area of the shaded portion is exactly three times the area of triangle QRT.

(A) I only
(B) I and II only
(C) II only
(D) I and III only
(E) I, II, and III

A B C D E
○ ○ ○ ○ ○

7. James lives on the corner of a rectangular field that measures 120 yards by 160 yards. If he wants to walk to the opposite corner, he can either travel along the perimeter of the field or cut directly across in a straight line. How many yards does he save by taking the direct route? (Express to the nearest 10 yards.)

(A) 40 yards
(B) 60 yards

(C) 80 yards
(D) 100 yards
(E) 110 yards

A B C D E
○ ○ ○ ○ ○

8. In a square, the perimeter is how many times the length of the diagonal?

(A) $\dfrac{\sqrt{2}}{2}$
(B) $\sqrt{2}$
(C) 2
(D) $2\sqrt{2}$
(E) 4

A B C D E
○ ○ ○ ○ ○

9. How many degrees are there in the angle formed by two adjacent sides of a regular nonagon (nine-sided polygon)?

(A) 40°
(B) 70°
(C) 105°
(D) 120°
(E) 140°

A B C D E
○ ○ ○ ○ ○

10. In the diagram below, $AB = CD$. From this we can deduce that:

(*Note*: Figure is not drawn to scale.)

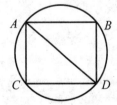

(A) AB is parallel to CD.
(B) AB is perpendicular to BD.
(C) $AC = BD$.
(D) Angle ABD equals angle BDC.
(E) Triangle ABD is congruent to triangle ACD.

A B C D E
○ ○ ○ ○ ○

11. If two lines, *AB* and *CD*, intersect at a point *E*, which of the following statements is *not* true?

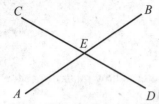

(A) Angle *AEB* equals angle *CED*.
(B) Angles *AEC* and *BEC* are complementary.
(C) Angle *CED* is a straight angle.
(D) Angle *AEC* equals angle *BED*.
(E) Angle *BED* plus angle *AED* equals 180°.

A B C D E
○ ○ ○ ○ ○

12. In the following diagram, *AC* = *CE* and *BD* = *DE*. Which of these statements is (are) true?

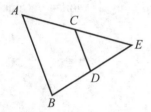

   I. *AB* is twice as long as *CD*.
  II. *AB* is parallel to *CD*.
 III. Triangle *AEB* is similar to triangle *CED*.

(A) I only
(B) II and III only
(C) I and III only
(D) I, II, and III
(E) none of these

A B C D E
○ ○ ○ ○ ○

13. In triangle *ABC,* angle *A* is obtuse, and angle *B* equals 30°. Which of the following statements *best* describes angle *C?*

(A) Angle *C* must be less than 60°.
(B) Angle *C* must be less than or equal to 60°.
(C) Angle *C* must be equal to 60°.
(D) Angle *C* must be greater than or equal to 60°.
(E) Angle *C* must be greater than 60°.

A B C D E
○ ○ ○ ○ ○

14. In this diagram, *ABCD* is a parallelogram, and *BFDE* is a square. If *AB* = 20 and *CF* = 16, what is the perimeter of the parallelogram *ABCD*?

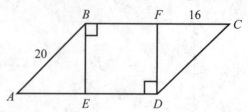

(A) 72
(B) 78
(C) 86
(D) 92
(E) 96

A B C D E
○ ○ ○ ○ ○

15. The hypotenuse of a right triangle is exactly twice as long as the shorter leg. What is the number of degrees in the smallest angle of the triangle?

(A) 30°
(B) 45°
(C) 60°
(D) 90°
(E) The answer cannot be determined from the given information.

A B C D E
○ ○ ○ ○ ○

16. The legs of an isosceles triangle are equal to 17 inches each. If the altitude to the base is 8 inches long, how long is the base of the triangle?

(A) 15 inches
(B) 20 inches
(C) 24 inches
(D) 25 inches
(E) 30 inches

A B C D E
○ ○ ○ ○ ○

17. The perimeter of a right triangle is 18 inches. If the midpoints of the three sides are joined by line segments, they form another triangle. What is the perimeter of this new triangle?

(A) 3 inches
(B) 6 inches
(C) 9 inches

(D) 12 inches

(E) The answer cannot be determined from the given information.

A B C D E
○ ○ ○ ○ ○

18. If the diagonals of a square divide it into four triangles, the triangles *cannot* be

(A) right triangles
(B) isosceles triangles
(C) similar triangles
(D) equilateral triangles
(E) equal in area

A B C D E
○ ○ ○ ○ ○

19. In the diagram below, *ABCDEF* is a regular hexagon. How many degrees are there in angle *ADC*?

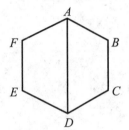

(A) 45°
(B) 60°
(C) 75°
(D) 90°
(E) none of these

A B C D E
○ ○ ○ ○ ○

20. This diagram depicts a rectangle inscribed in a circle. If the measurements of the rectangle are 10″ × 14″, what is the area of the circle in inches?

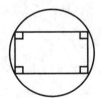

(A) 74π
(B) 92π
(C) 144π
(D) 196π
(E) 296π

A B C D E
○ ○ ○ ○ ○

21. How many degrees are included between the hands of a clock at 5:00?

(A) 50°
(B) 60°
(C) 75°
(D) 120°
(E) 150°

A B C D E
○ ○ ○ ○ ○

22. *ABCD* is a square. If the midpoints of the four sides are joined to form a new square, the perimeter of the old square is how many times the perimeter of the new square?

(A) 1
(B) √2
(C) 2
(D) 2√2
(E) 4

A B C D E
○ ○ ○ ○ ○

23. Angles *A* and *B* of triangle *ABC* are both acute angles. Which of the following *best* describes angle *C*?

(A) Angle *C* is between 0° and 180°.
(B) Angle *C* is between 0° and 90°.
(C) Angle *C* is between 60° and 180°.
(D) Angle *C* is between 60° and 120°.
(E) Angle *C* is between 60° and 90°.

A B C D E
○ ○ ○ ○ ○

24. The angles of a quadrilateral are in the ratio 1 : 2 : 3 : 4. What is the number of degrees in the largest angle?

(A) 72
(B) 96
(C) 120
(D) 144
(E) 150

A B C D E
○ ○ ○ ○ ○

25. *ABCD* is a rectangle; the diagonals *AC* and *BD* intersect at *E*. Which of the following statements is *not necessarily true*?

    (A) *AE* = *BE*.
    (B) Angle *AEB* equals angle *CED*.
    (C) *AE* is perpendicular to *BD*.
    (D) Triangles *AED* and *AEB* are equal in area.
    (E) Angle *BAC* equals angle *BDC*.

    A B C D E
    ○ ○ ○ ○ ○
    _____

26. City A is 200 miles from City B, and City B is 400 miles from City C. Which of the following best describes the distance between City A and City C? (*Note*: The cities A, B, and C do *not* all lie on a straight line.)

    (A) It must be greater than zero.
    (B) It must be greater than 200 miles.
    (C) It must be less than 600 miles and greater than zero.
    (D) It must be less than 600 miles and greater than 200 miles.
    (E) It must be exactly 400 miles.

    A B C D E
    ○ ○ ○ ○ ○
    _____

27. At 7:30, how many degrees are included between the hands of a clock?

    (A) 15°
    (B) 30°
    (C) 45°
    (D) 60°
    (E) 75°

    A B C D E
    ○ ○ ○ ○ ○
    _____

28. If a ship is sailing in a northerly direction and then turns to the right until it is sailing in a southwesterly direction, it has gone through a rotation of:

    (A) 45°
    (B) 90°
    (C) 135°
    (D) 180°
    (E) 225°

    A B C D E
    ○ ○ ○ ○ ○
    _____

29. x, y, and z are the angles of a triangle. If $x = 2y$ and $y = z + 30°$, how many degrees are there in angle x?

    (A) 22.5°
    (B) 37.5°
    (C) 52.5°
    (D) 90.0°
    (E) 105.0°

    A B C D E
    ○ ○ ○ ○ ○
    _____

30. In the diagram below, *AB* is parallel to *CD*. Which of the following statements is *not necessarily true*?

    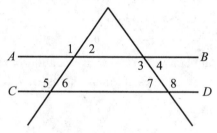

    (A) $\angle 1 + \angle 2 = 180°$
    (B) $\angle 4 = \angle 7$
    (C) $\angle 5 + \angle 8 + \angle 2 + \angle 4 = 360°$
    (D) $\angle 2 + \angle 3 = 180°$
    (E) $\angle 2 = \angle 6$

    A B C D E
    ○ ○ ○ ○ ○
    _____

31. What is the ratio of the diagonal of a square to the hypotenuse of the isosceles right triangle having the same area?

    (A) $1 : 2$
    (B) $1 : \sqrt{2}$
    (C) $1 : 1$
    (D) $\sqrt{2} : 1$
    (E) $2 : 1$

    A B C D E
    ○ ○ ○ ○ ○
    _____

32. How many degrees are there between two adjacent sides of a regular ten-sided figure?

    (A) 36°
    (B) 72°
    (C) 120°
    (D) 144°
    (E) 154°

    A B C D E
    ○ ○ ○ ○ ○
    _____

33. Which of the following sets of numbers *cannot* represent the lengths of the sides of a right triangle?

    (A) 5, 12, 13
    (B) 4.2, 5.6, 7
    (C) 9, 28, 35
    (D) 16, 30, 34
    (E) 7.5, 18, 19.5

    A B C D E
    ○ ○ ○ ○ ○

34. How many degrees are there in the angle that is its own supplement?

    (A) 30°
    (B) 45°
    (C) 60°
    (D) 90°
    (E) 180°

    A B C D E
    ○ ○ ○ ○ ○

35. If a central angle of 45° intersects an arc 6 inches long on the circumference of a circle, what is the radius of the circle?

    (A) $\frac{24}{\pi}$ inches

    (B) $\frac{48}{\pi}$ inches

    (C) 6π inches
    (D) 24 inches
    (E) 48 inches

    A B C D E
    ○ ○ ○ ○ ○

36. What is the length of the line segment connecting the two most distant vertices of a 1-inch cube?

    (A) 1 inch
    (B) $\sqrt{2}$ inches
    (C) $\sqrt{3}$ inches
    (D) $\sqrt{5}$ inches
    (E) $\sqrt{6}$ inches

    A B C D E
    ○ ○ ○ ○ ○

37. Through how many degrees does the hour hand of a clock move in 70 minutes?

    (A) 35°
    (B) 60°
    (C) 80°
    (D) 90°
    (E) 120°

    A B C D E
    ○ ○ ○ ○ ○

38. In the diagram pictured below, *AB* is tangent to circle *O* at point *A*. *CD* is perpendicular to *OA* at *C*. Which of the following statements is (are) true?

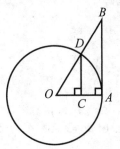

    I.   Triangles *ODC* and *OBA* are similar.
    II. *OA* : *CD* = *OB* : *AB*.
    III. *AB* is twice as long as *CD*.

    (A) I only
    (B) III only
    (C) I and II only
    (D) II and III only
    (E) none of the above combinations

    A B C D E
    ○ ○ ○ ○ ○

39. The three angles of triangle *ABC* are in the ratio 1 : 2 : 6. How many degrees are in the largest angle?

    (A) 45°
    (B) 90°
    (C) 120°
    (D) 135°
    (E) 160°

    A B C D E
    ○ ○ ○ ○ ○

40. In this diagram, $AB = AC$, angle $A = 40°$, and BD is perpendicular to AC at D. How many degrees are there in angle DBC?

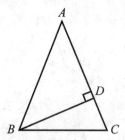

(A) 20°
(B) 40°
(C) 50°
(D) 70°
(E) none of these

A B C D E
○ ○ ○ ○ ○

41. If the line AB intersects the line CD at point E, which of the following pairs of angles need *not* be equal?

(A) $\angle AEB$ and $\angle CED$
(B) $\angle AEC$ and $\angle BED$
(C) $\angle AED$ and $\angle CEA$
(D) $\angle BEC$ and $\angle DEA$
(E) $\angle DEC$ and $\angle BEA$

A B C D E
○ ○ ○ ○ ○

42. All right isosceles triangles must be

(A) similar
(B) congruent
(C) equilateral
(D) equal in area
(E) none of these

A B C D E
○ ○ ○ ○ ○

43. What is the area of a triangle whose sides are 10 inches, 13 inches, and 13 inches?

(A) 39 square inches
(B) 52 square inches
(C) 60 square inches
(D) 65 square inches
(E) The answer cannot be determined from the given information.

A B C D E
○ ○ ○ ○ ○

44. If each side of an equilateral triangle is 2 inches long, what is the triangle's altitude?

(A) 1 inch
(B) $\sqrt{2}$ inches
(C) $\sqrt{3}$ inches
(D) 2 inches
(E) $\sqrt{5}$ inches

A B C D E
○ ○ ○ ○ ○

45. In the parallelogram $ABCD$, diagonals AC and BD intersect at E. Which of the following must be true?

(A) $\angle AED = \angle BEC$
(B) $AE = EC$
(C) $\angle BDC = \angle DBA$
(D) Two of the above must be true.
(E) All three of the statements must be true.

A B C D E
○ ○ ○ ○ ○

46. If $ABCD$ is a square and diagonals AC and BD intersect at point E, how many isosceles right triangles are there in the figure?

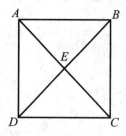

(A) 4
(B) 5
(C) 6
(D) 7
(E) 8

A B C D E
○ ○ ○ ○ ○

47. How many degrees are there in each angle of a regular hexagon?

(A) 60°
(B) 90°
(C) 108°
(D) 120°
(E) 144°

A B C D E
○ ○ ○ ○ ○

48. The radius of a circle is 1 inch. If an equilateral triangle is inscribed in the circle, what will be the length of one of the triangle's sides?

    (A) 1 inch

    (B) $\frac{\sqrt{2}}{2}$ inches

    (C) $\sqrt{2}$ inches

    (D) $\frac{\sqrt{3}}{2}$ inches

    (E) $\sqrt{3}$ inches

    A B C D E
    ○ ○ ○ ○ ○
    _____

49. If the angles of a triangle are in the ratio 2 : 3 : 4, how many degrees are there in the largest angle?

    (A) 20°

    (B) 40°

    (C) 60°

    (D) 80°

    (E) 120°

    A B C D E
    ○ ○ ○ ○ ○
    _____

50. Which of the following combinations may represent the lengths of the sides of a right triangle?

    (A) 4, 6, 8

    (B) 12, 16, 20

    (C) 7, 17, 23

    (D) 9, 20, 27

    (E) none of these

    A B C D E
    ○ ○ ○ ○ ○
    _____

Answer Key for Session 5 Practice Test

1. C	14. E	27. C	39. C
2. B	15. A	28. E	40. A
3. A	16. E	29. E	41. C
4. E	17. C	30. D	42. A
5. C	18. D	31. B	43. C
6. D	19. B	32. D	44. C
7. C	20. A	33. C	45. E
8. D	21. E	34. D	46. E
9. E	22. B	35. A	47. D
10. D	23. A	36. C	48. E
11. B	24. D	37. A	49. D
12. D	25. C and D	38. C	50. B
13. A	26. D		

Answers and Solutions for Session 5 Practice Test

1. Choice C is correct.

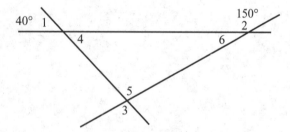

In the problem it is given that ∠1 = 40° and ∠2 = 150°. The diagram makes it apparent that: (1) ∠1 = ∠4 and ∠3 = ∠5 (vertical angles); (2) ∠6 + ∠2 = 180° (straight angle); (3) ∠4 + ∠5 + ∠6 = 180° (sum of angles in a triangle). To solve the problem, ∠3 must be related through the above information to the known quantities in ∠1 and ∠2. Proceed as follows: ∠3 = ∠5, but ∠5 = 180° − ∠4 − ∠6. ∠4 = ∠1 = 40° and ∠6 = 180° − ∠2 = 180° − 150° = 30°. Therefore, ∠3 = 180° − 40° − 30° = 110°.
(Refreshers 501, 503, 505)

2. Choice B is correct. Since CD is perpendicular to DE, CDE is a right triangle, and using the Pythagorean theorem yields DE = 3. Thus, the ratio of CD to DE is 4 : 3. But triangle ABE is similar to triangle CDE. Therefore, AB : BE = CD : DE = 4 : 3.
(Refreshers 509, 510)

3. Choice A is correct. In a triangle, it is impossible for one side to be longer than the sum of the other two (a straight line is the shortest distance between two points). Thus 2.0, 4.5, and 7.0 cannot be three sides of a triangle.
(Refresher 516)

4. Choice E is correct. AB = AC, BD = CD, and AD equal to itself is sufficient information (three sides) to prove triangles ABD and ACD congruent. Also, since AB = AC, AE = AE, and ∠BAE = ∠CAE (by the previous congruence), triangles ABE and ACE are congruent. Since BD = CD, ED = ED, and angle BDE equals angle CDE (by initial congruence), triangles BDE and CDE are congruent. Through congruence of triangle ABE and triangle ACE, angles BEA and CEA are equal, and their sum is a straight angle (180°). They must both be right angles. Thus, from the given information, we can deduce all the properties given as choices.
(Refresher 511)

5. Choice C is correct. The perimeter of triangle ABD is AB + BD + AD. The length of BD is 1. Since BC = CD = BD, triangle BCD is an equilateral triangle. Therefore, angle C = 60° and angle BDC = 60°. Angle A + angle C = 90° (the sum of two acute angles in a right triangle is 90°), and angle BDC + angle BDA = 90° (these two angles form a right angle). Since angle C and angle BDC both equal 60°, angle A = angle BDA = 30°. Now two angles of triangle ADB are equal. Therefore, triangle ADB is an isosceles triangle with side BD = side AB. Since BD = 1, then AB = 1. AD is a leg of the right triangle, with side CD = 1 and hypotenuse AC = 2. (AC = AB + BC = 1 + 1.) Using the relationship $c^2 = a^2 + b^2$ gives us the length of AD as $\sqrt{3}$. Thus the perimeter is $1 + 1 + \sqrt{3}$, or $2 + \sqrt{3}$.
(Refreshers 505, 507, 509)

6. Choice D is correct. Statement I must be true, since the diagonals of a parallelogram bisect each other, so QT = ST, and PT = RT. Thus, since the sums of equals are equal, QT + PT = RT + ST. II is not necessarily true and, in fact, can be true only if the parallelogram is also a rhombus (all four sides equal). III is true, since the four small triangles each have the same area. The shaded portion

contains three such triangles. This can be seen by noting that the altitudes from point P to the bases of triangles PQT and PTS are identical. We have already seen from part (I) that these bases (QT and TS) are also equal. Therefore, only I and III can be deduced from the given information.

(Refreshers 514, 517)

7. Choice C is correct.

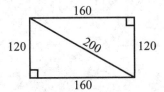

The diagonal path divides the rectangular field into two right triangles. The Pythagorean theorem gives the length of the diagonal as 200 yards. If James takes the route around the perimeter, he will travel 120 + 160, or 280 yards. Thus, the shorter route saves him 80 yards.

(Refreshers 509, 518)

8. Choice D is correct. Let one side of a square be s. Then the perimeter must be $4s$. The diagonal of a square with side s is equal to $s\sqrt{2}$. Dividing the perimeter by the diagonal produces $2\sqrt{2}$. The perimeter is $2\sqrt{2}$ times the diagonal.

(Refreshers 509, 520)

9. Choice E is correct. The sum of the angles of any polygon is equal to $180°(n - 2)$, where n is the number of sides. Thus the total number of degrees in a nonagon = $180°(9 - 2) = 180° \times 7 = 1,260°$. The number of degrees in each angle is $\frac{1,260°}{n} = \frac{1,260°}{9} = 140°$. (Refreshers 521, 522)

10. Choice D is correct.

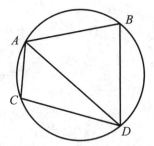

Since chord AB equals chord CD, it must be true that arc AB equals arc CD. By adding arc AC to arc CD and to arc AB, it is apparent that arc ACD

is equal to arc CAB. These arcs are intersected by inscribed angles ABD and BDC. Therefore, the two inscribed angles must be equal. If we redraw the figure as shown above, the falseness of Choices A, B, C, and E becomes readily apparent.

(Refresher 527)

11. Choice B is correct. $\angle AEC + \angle BEC = \angle AEB$, a straight angle (180°). Thus, angles AEC and BEC are *supplementary*. (*Complementary* means that the two angles add up to a *right* angle, or 90°.)

(Refreshers 501, 502)

12. Choice D is correct. Since $AC = CE$ and $BD = DE$, triangles AEB and CED are similar, and AB is twice as long as CD, since by proportionality, $AB : CD = AE : CE = 2 : 1$. From the similarity it is found that angle ABE equals angle CDE, and, therefore, that AB is parallel to CD. Thus, all three statements are true. (Refreshers 504, 510)

13. Choice A is correct. Angle A must be greater than 90°; angle B equals 30°. Thus, the sum of angles A and B must be greater than 120°. Since the sum of the three angles A, B, and C must be 180°, angle C must be *less than* 60°. (It cannot equal 60°, because then angle A would be a right angle instead of an obtuse angle.) (Refreshers 501, 505)

14. Choice E is correct. CDF is a right triangle with one side of 16 and a hypotenuse of 20. Thus, the third side, DF, equals 12. Since $BFDE$ is a square, BF and ED are also equal to 12. Thus, $BC = 12 + 16 = 28$, and $CD = 20$. $ABCD$ is a parallelogram, so $AB = CD$, $AD = BC$. The perimeter is $28 + 20 + 28 + 20 = 96$. (Refreshers 509, 517, 520)

15. Choice A is correct.

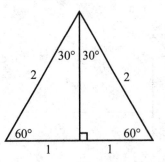

Recognize that the sides of a 30°-60°-90° triangle are in the proportion $1 : \sqrt{3} : 2$, and the problem is solved. 30° is the smallest angle. (Refresher 509)

16. Choice E is correct.

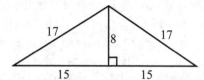

The altitude to the base of an isosceles triangle divides it into two congruent right triangles, each with one leg of 8 inches, and a hypotenuse of 17 inches. By the Pythagorean theorem, the third side of each right triangle must be 15 inches long. The base of the isosceles triangle is the sum of two such sides, totaling 30 inches.

(Refreshers 507, 509, 514)

17. Choice C is correct.

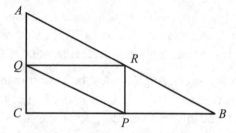

Call the triangle ABC, and the triangle of midpoints PQR, where P is the midpoint of BC, Q is the midpoint of AC, and R is the midpoint of AB. Then, PQ is equal to half the length of AB, $QR = \frac{1}{2}BC$, and $PR = \frac{1}{2}AC$. This has nothing to do with the fact that ABC is a right triangle. Thus, the perimeter of the small triangle is equal to $PQ + QR + PR = \frac{1}{2}(AB + BC + AC)$. The new perimeter is half the old perimeter, or 9 inches.

(Refreshers 509, 510, 512)

18. Choice D is correct.

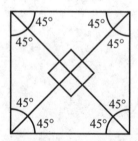

The diagonals of the square form four right triangles, each of which is isosceles because each has two 45° angles. The triangles are all identical in shape and size, so they all are similar and have the same area. The only choice left is equilateral, which cannot be true, since the sum of the angles at the intersection of the diagonals must be 360°. The sum of four 60° angles would be only 240°.

(Refresher 520)

19. Choice B is correct.

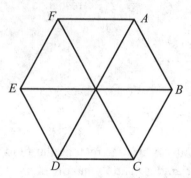

First, draw in the lines CF and BE. These intersect AD at its midpoint (also the midpoint of CF and BE) and divide the hexagon into six equilateral triangles. Since ADC is an angle of one of these equilateral triangles, it must be equal to 60°. (Another way to do this problem is to calculate the number of degrees in one angle of a regular hexagon and divide this by 2.) (Refreshers 508, 523)

20. Choice A is correct. The diagonal of an inscribed rectangle is equal to the diameter of the circle. To find this length, use the Pythagorean theorem on one of the two triangles formed by two of the sides of the rectangle and the diagonal. Thus, the square of the diagonal is equal to $10^2 + 14^2 = 100 + 196 = 296$. The area of the circle is equal to π times the square of the radius. The square of the radius of the circle is one-fourth of the diameter squared (since $d = 2r$, $d^2 = 4r^2$), or 74. Thus, the area is 74π. (Refreshers 509, 518, 524)

21. Choice E is correct.

Each number (or hour marking) on a clock represents an angle of 30°, as 360° divided by 12 is 30° (a convenient fact to remember for other clock problems). Since the hands of the clock are on the 12 and the 5, there are five hour units between the hands; $5 \times 30° = 150°$. (Refreshers 501, 526)

22. **Choice B is correct.**

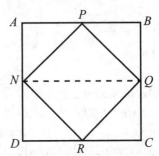

Let S represent the side of the large square. Then the perimeter is $4S$. Let s represent the side of the smaller square. Then the smaller square's perimeter is $4s$. Line NQ is the diagonal of the smaller square, so the length of NQ is $\sqrt{2}s$. (The diagonal of a square is $\sqrt{2}$ times the side.) Now, NQ is equal to DC, or S, which is the side of the larger square. So now $S = \sqrt{2}s$. The perimeter of the large square equals $4S = 4\sqrt{2}s = \sqrt{2}(4s) = \sqrt{2} \times$ perimeter of the small square. (Refresher 520)

23. **Choice A is correct.** Angles A and B are both greater than $0°$ and less than $90°$, so their sum is between $0°$ and $180°$. Then angle C must be between $0°$ and $180°$. (Refreshers 501, 505)

24. **Choice D is correct.** Let the four angles be x, $2x$, $3x$, and $4x$. The sum of the angles in a quadrilateral is $360°$. Thus, the sum, $10x$, must equal $360°$ and therefore $x = 36°$. The largest angle is then $4x$, which is equal to $144°$. (Refresher 505)

25. **Choices C and D are correct.**

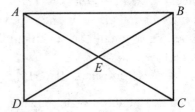

For Choice C, the diagonals of a rectangle are perpendicular only when the rectangle is a square. AE is part of the diagonal AC, so AE will not necessarily be perpendicular to BD. For Choice D, triangles AED and AEB are equal in area when the rectangle is a square. Triangles AED and AEB are also equal in area, in general, when $h_2 \times AD$

$= h_1 \times AB$, where h_2 and h_1 are, respectively, the altitudes to side AD and side AB. When $h_2 \times AD \neq h_1 \times AB$, triangles AED and AEB are not equal in area. (Refresher 518)

26. **Choice D is correct.**

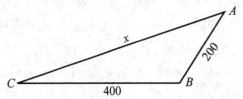

Draw the three cities as the vertices of a triangle. The length of side CB is 400 miles, the length of side AB is 200 miles, and x, the length of side AC, is unknown. The sum of any two sides of a triangle is greater than the third side, or in algebraic terms: $400 + 200 > x$, $400 + x > 200$, and $200 + x > 400$. These simplify to $600 > x$, $x > -200$, and $x > 200$. For x to be greater than 200 and -200, it must be greater than 200. Thus, the values of x are $200 < x < 600$. (Refreshers 506, 516)

27. **Choice C is correct.** At 7:30, the hour hand is *halfway between the 7 and the 8*, and the minute hand is on the 6. Thus, there are one and one-half "hour units," each equal to $30°$, so the whole angle is $45°$. (Refreshers 501, 526)

28. **Choice E is correct.** If a ship is facing north, a right turn of $90°$ will face it eastward. Another $90°$ turn will face it south, and an additional $45°$ turn will bring it to southwest. Thus, the total rotation is $90° + 90° + 45° = 225°$. (Refresher 501)

29. **Choice E is correct.** Since $y = z + 30°$ and $x = 2y$, then $x = 2(z + 30°) = 2z + 60°$. Thus, $x + y + z$ equals $(2z + 60°) + (z + 30°) + z = 4z + 90°$. This must equal $180°$ (the sum of the angles of a triangle). So $4z + 90° = 180°$, and the solution is $z = 22\frac{1}{2}°$; $x = 2z + 60° = 45° + 60° = 105°$. (Refresher 505)

30. **Choice D is correct.** Since AB is parallel to CD, angle 2 = angle 6, and angle 3 + angle 7 = $180°$. If angle 2 + angle 3 equals $180°$, then angle 2 = angle 7 = angle 6. However, since there is no evidence that angles 6 and 7 are equal, angle 2 + angle 3 does not necessarily equal $180°$. Therefore, the answer is (D). (Refresher 504)

31. Choice B is correct. Call the side of the square s. Then, the diagonal of the square is $s\sqrt{2}$ and the area is s^2. The area of an isosceles right triangle with leg r is $\frac{1}{2}r^2$. Now, the area of the triangle is equal to the area of the square, so $s^2 = \frac{1}{2}r^2$. Solving for r gives $r = s\sqrt{2}$. The hypotenuse of the triangle is $\sqrt{r^2 + r^2}$. Substituting $r = s\sqrt{2}$, the hypotenuse is $\sqrt{2s^2 + 2s^2}$ $= \sqrt{4s^2} = 2s$. Therefore, the ratio of the diagonal to the hypotenuse is $s\sqrt{2} : 2s$. Since $s\sqrt{2} : 2s$ is $\frac{s\sqrt{2}}{2s}$ or $\frac{\sqrt{2}}{2}$, multiply by $\frac{\sqrt{2}}{\sqrt{2}}$, which has a value of 1. $\frac{\sqrt{2}}{2} \cdot \frac{\sqrt{2}}{\sqrt{2}}$ $= \frac{2}{2\sqrt{2}} = \frac{1}{\sqrt{2}}$ or $1 : \sqrt{2}$, which is the final result.
(Refreshers 507, 509, 520)

32. Choice D is correct. The formula for the number of degrees in the angles of a polygon is $180(n - 2)$, where n is the number of sides. For a ten-sided figure this is $180°(10 - 2) = 180°(8) = 1,440°$. Since the ten angles are equal, they must each equal 144°. (Refreshers 521, 522)

33. Choice C is correct. If three numbers represent the lengths of the sides of a right triangle, they must satisfy the Pythagorean theorem: The squares of the smaller two combined must equal the square of the largest one. This condition is met in all the sets given except the set 9, 28, 35. There, $9^2 + 28^2 = 81 + 784 = 865$, but $35^2 = 1,225$.
(Refresher 509)

34. Choice D is correct. Let the angle be x. Since x is its own supplement, then $x + x = 180°$, or, since $2x = 180°$, $x = 90°$. (Refresher 502)

35. Choice A is correct. The length of the arc intersected by a central angle of a circle is proportional to the number of degrees in the angle. Thus, if a 45° angle cuts off a 6-inch arc, a 360° angle intersects an arc eight times as long, or 48 inches. The length of the arc of a 360° angle is equal to the circle's circumference, or 2π times the radius. Thus, to obtain the radius, divide 48 inches by 2π. 48 inches $\div 2\pi = \frac{24}{\pi}$ inches.
(Refreshers 524, 526)

36. Choice C is correct.

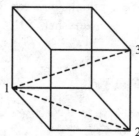

Refer to the diagram above. Calculate the distance from vertex 1 to vertex 2. This is simply the diagonal of a 1-inch square and equal to $\sqrt{2}$ inches. Now, vertices 1, 2, and 3 form a right triangle, with legs of 1 and $\sqrt{2}$. By the Pythagorean theorem, the hypotenuse is $\sqrt{3}$. This is the distance from vertex 1 to vertex 3, the two most distant vertices.
(Refreshers 509, 520)

37. Choice A is correct. In one hour, the hour hand of a clock moves through an angle of 30° (one "hour unit"). 70 minutes equals $\frac{7}{6}$ hours, so during that time the hour hand will move through $\frac{7}{6} \times 30°$, or 35°.
(Refreshers 501, 526)

38. Choice C is correct. In order to be similar, two triangles must have equal corresponding angles. This is true of triangles ODC and OBA, since angle O equals itself, and angles OCD and OAB are both right angles. (The third angles of these triangles must be equal, as the sum of the angles of a triangle is always 180°.) Since the triangles are similar, $OD : CD = OB : AB$. But, OD and OA are radii of the same circle and are equal. Therefore, substitute OA for OD in the proportion above. Hence, $OA : CD = OB : AB$. There is, however, no information given on the relative sizes of any of the line segments, so statement III may or may not be true.
(Refreshers 509, 510, 524)

39. Choice C is correct. Let the three angles equal x, $2x$, and $6x$. The sum of the angles in a triangle is 180°. Thus, $x + 2x + 6x = 180°$, or $9x = 180°$. Therefore, $x = 20°$ and the largest angle is $6x = 120°$.
(Refresher 505)

40. Choice A is correct. Since $AB = AC,$ angle ABC must equal angle ACB. (Base angles of an isosceles triangle are equal.) As the sum of angles BAC, ABC, and ACB is 180°, and angle BAC equals 40°, angle ABC and angle ACB must each equal 70°. Now, DBC is a right triangle, with angle $BDC =$ 90° and angle $DCB = 70°$. (The three angles must add up to 180°.) Angle DBC must equal 20°.

(Refreshers 507, 514)

41. Choice C is correct.

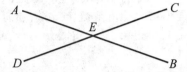

$\angle AEB$ and $\angle CED$ are both straight angles, and are equal; similarly, $\angle DEC$ and $\angle BEA$ are both straight angles. $\angle AEC$ and $\angle BED$ are vertical angles, as are $\angle BEC$ and $\angle DEA$, and are equal. $\angle AED$ and $\angle CEA$ are supplementary and need not be equal.

(Refreshers 501, 502, 503)

42. Choice A is correct. All right isosceles triangles have angles of 45°, 45°, and 90°. Since all triangles with the same angles are similar, all right isosceles triangles are similar. (Refreshers 507, 509, 510)

43. Choice C is correct.

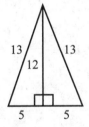

As the diagram shows, the altitude to the base of the isosceles triangle divides it into two congruent right triangles, each with 5–12–13 sides. Thus, the base is 10, the height is 12, and the area is $\frac{1}{2}(10)(12)$ = 60.

(Refreshers 505, 507, 509)

44. Choice C is correct.

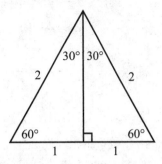

The altitude to any side divides the triangle into two congruent 30°-60°-90° right triangles, each with a hypotenuse of 2 inches and a leg of 1 inch. The other leg equals the altitude. By the Pythagorean theorem, the altitude is equal to $\sqrt{3}$ inches. (The sides of a 30°-60°-90° right triangle are always in the proportion $1 : \sqrt{3} : 2$.)

(Refreshers 509, 514)

45. Choice E is correct.

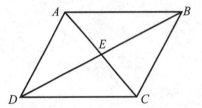

As the diagram illustrates, angles AED and BEC are vertical and, therefore, equal. $AE = EC$, because the diagonals of a parallelogram bisect each other. Angles BDC and DBA are equal because they are alternate interior angles of parallel lines ($AB\|CD$).

(Refreshers 503, 517)

46. Choice E is correct. There are eight isosceles right triangles: ABE, BCE, CDE, ADE, ABC, BCD, CDA, and ABD. (Refresher 520)

47. Choice D is correct.

Recall that a regular hexagon may be broken up into six equilateral triangles. Since the angles of each triangle are 60°, and two of these angles make up each angle of the hexagon, an angle of the hexagon must be 120°. (Refresher 523)

48. Choice E is correct.

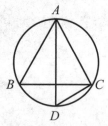

Since the radius equals 1", AD, the diameter, must be 2". Now, since AD is a diameter, ACD must be a right triangle, because an angle inscribed in a semi-circle is a right angle. Thus, because $\angle DAC = 30°$, it must be a 30°-60°-90° right triangle. The sides will be in the proportion $1 : \sqrt{3} : 2$. As $AD : AC = 2 : \sqrt{3}$, so AC, one of the sides of the equilateral triangle, must be $\sqrt{3}$ inches long.

(Refreshers 508, 524)

49. Choice D is correct. Let the angles be $2x$, $3x$, $4x$. Their sum, $9x$, equals 180° and $x = 20°$. Therefore, the largest angle, $4x$, is 80°.   (Refresher 505)

50. Choice B is correct. The sides of a right triangle must obey the Pythagorean theorem. The only group of choices that does so is the second: 12, 16, and 20 are in the 3 : 4 : 5 ratio, and the relationship $12^2 + 16^2 = 20^2$ is satisfied.   (Refresher 509)

MATH REFRESHER SESSION 6

Miscellaneous Problems: Averages, Series, Properties of Integers, Approximations, Combinations, Permutations, Probability, the Absolute Value Sign, Functions, Logarithms, and Imaginary Numbers

Averages, Medians, and Modes

601. *Averages.* The average of n numbers is merely their sum, divided by n.

Example: Find the average of 20, 0, 80, and 12.

Solution: The average is the sum divided by the number of entries, or:

$$\frac{20 + 0 + 80 + 12}{4} = \frac{112}{4} = 28$$

Another way of obtaining an average of a set of numbers that are close together is the following:

Step 1. Choose any number that will approximately equal the average.

Step 2. Subtract this approximate average from each of the numbers (this sum will give some positive and negative results). Add the results.

Step 3. Divide this sum by the number of entries.

Step 4. Add the result of Step 3 to the approximate average chosen in Step 1. This will be the true average.

Example: Find the average of 92, 93, 93, 96, and 97.

Solution: Choose 95 as an approximate average. Subtracting 95 from 92, 93, 93, 96, and 97 gives $-3, -2, -2, 1,$ and 2. The sum is -4. Divide -4 by 5 (the number of entries) to obtain -0.8. Add -0.8 to the original approximation of 95 to get the true average, $95 - 0.8$, or 94.2.

601a. *Medians.* The median of a set of numbers is that number which is in the *middle* of all the numbers.

Example: Find the median of 20, 0, 80, 12, and 30.

Solution: Arrange the numbers in increasing order:

$$0$$
$$12$$
$$20$$
$$30$$
$$80$$

The *middle* number is 20, so 20 is the *median*.

Note: If there is an *even* number of items, such as 0, 12, 20, 24, 30, and 80, there is no *middle* number.

So in this case we take the average of the two middle numbers, 20 and 24, to get 22, which is the *median*.

In the above set of 6 numbers, if 24 was replaced by 22, the median would be 21 (just the average of 20 and 22).

601b. *Modes.* The mode of a set of numbers is the number that occurs most frequently.

If we have numbers 0, 12, 20, 30, and 80, there is *no* mode, since no one number appears with the greatest frequency. But consider this:

Example: Find the mode of 0, 12, 12, 20, 30, and 80.

Solution: 12 appears most frequently, so it is the mode.

Example: Find the mode of 0, 12, 12, 20, 30, 30, and 80.

Solution: Here *both* 12 and 30 are modes.

Series

602. *Number series* or *sequences* are progressions of numbers arranged according to some design. By recognizing the type of series from the first four terms, it is possible to know all the terms in the series. Following are a few different types of number series that appear frequently.

1. *Arithmetic progressions* are very common. In an arithmetic progression, each term exceeds the previous one by some fixed number.

   Example: In the series 3, 5, 7, 9 . . . find the next term.

   Solution: Each term in the series is 2 more than the preceding one, so the next term is 9 + 2, or 11.

   If the difference in successive terms is negative, then the series decreases.

   Example: Find the next term: 100, 93, 86, 79 . . .

   Solution: Each term is 7 less than the previous one, so the next term is 72.

2. In a *geometric progression* each term equals the previous term multiplied by a fixed number.

   Example: What is the next term of the series 2, 6, 18, 54 . . . ?

   Solution: Each term is 3 times the previous term, so the fifth term is 3 times 54 or 162.

   If the multiplying factor is negative, the series will alternate between positive and negative terms.

   Example: Find the next term of $-2, 4, -8, 16 \ldots$

   Solution: Each term is -2 times the previous term, so the next term is -32.

   Example: Find the next term in the series 64, $-32, 16, -8 \ldots$

   Solution: Each term is $-\frac{1}{2}$ times the previous term, so the next term is 4.

3. In a *mixed step progression* the successive terms can be found by repeating a pattern of add 2, add 3, add 2, add 3; or a pattern of add 1, multiply by 5, add 1, multiply 5, etc.

The series is the result of a combination of operations.

   Example: Find the next term in the series 1, 3, 9, 11, 33, 35 . . .

   Solution: The pattern of successive terms is add 2, multiply by 3, add 2, multiply by 3, etc. The next step is to multiply 35 by 3 to get 105.

   Example: Find the next term in the series 4, 16, 8, 32, 16 . . .

   Solution: Here, the pattern is to multiply by 4, divide by 2, multiply by 4, divide by 2, etc. Thus, the next term is 16 times 4 or 64.

4. If no obvious solution presents itself, it may be helpful to calculate the difference between each term and the preceding one. Then if it is possible to determine the next *increment* (the difference between successive terms), add it to the last term to obtain the term in question. Often the series of *increments* is a simpler series than the series of original terms.

   Example: Find the next term in the series 3, 9, 19, 33, 51 . . .

   Solution: Write out the series of increments: 6, 10, 14, 18 . . . (each term is the difference between two terms of the original series). This series is an arithmetic progression whose next term is 22. Adding 22 to the term 51 from the original series produces the next term, 73.

5. If none of the above methods is effective, the series may be a combination of two or three different series. In this case, make a series out of every other term or out of every third term and see whether these terms form a series that can be recognized.

   Example: Find the next term in the series 1, 4, 4, 8, 16, 12, 64, 16 . . .

   Solution: Divide this series into two series by taking out every other term, yielding: 1, 4, 16, 64 . . . and 4, 8, 12, 16 . . . . These series are easy to recognize as a geometric and arithmetic series, respectively, but the first series has the term we must use to find the next term. The next term in this series is 4 times 64, or 256.

Properties of Integers

An integer is a whole number; for example, −5, −2, 0, 1, 3, etc.

603. *Even–Odd.* These are problems that deal with even and odd numbers. An even number is divisible by 2, and an odd number is not divisible by 2. All even numbers end in the digits 0, 2, 4, 6, or 8; odd numbers end in the digits 1, 3, 5, 7, or 9. For example, the numbers 358, 90, 18, 9,874, and 46 are even numbers. The numbers 67, 871, 475, and 89 are odd numbers. It is important to remember the following facts:

604. The sum of *two even* numbers is *even*, and the sum of *two odd* numbers is *even*, but the sum of an *odd* number *and* an *even* number is *odd*. For example, $4 + 8 = 12$, $5 + 3 = 8$, and $7 + 2 = 9$.

Example: If m is any integer, is the number $6m + 3$ an even or odd number?

Solution: $6m$ is even, since 6 is a multiple of 2. 3 is odd. Therefore $6m + 3$ is odd, since even + odd = odd.

605. The product of *two odd* numbers is *odd*, but the product of an *even* number and *any other* number is an *even* number. For example, $3 \times 5 = 15$ (odd); $4 \times 5 = 20$ (even); $4 \times 6 = 24$ (even).

Example: If m is any integer, is the product $(2m + 3)(4m + 1)$ even or odd?

Solution: Since $2m$ is even and 3 is odd, $2m + 3$ is odd. Likewise, since $4m$ is even and 1 is odd, $4m + 1$ is odd. Thus $(2m + 3)(4m + 1)$ is (odd × odd), which is odd.

606. Even numbers are expressed in the form $2k$, where k may be any integer. Odd numbers are expressed in the form of $2k + 1$ or $2k − 1$, where k may be any integer. For example, if $k = 17$, then $2k = 34$ and $2k + 1 = 35$. If $k = 6$, then we have $2k = 12$ and $2k + 1 = 13$.

Example: Prove that the product of two odd numbers is odd.

Solution: Let one of the odd numbers be represented as $2x + 1$. Let the other number be represented as $2y + 1$. Now multiply $(2x + 1)(2y + 1)$. We get $4xy + 2x + 2y + 1$. Since $4xy + 2x + 2y$ is even because it is a multiple of 2, that quantity is even. Since 1 is odd, we have $4xy + 2x + 2y + 1$ is odd, since even + odd = odd.

607. *Divisibility.* If an integer P is divided by an integer Q, and an integer is obtained as the quotient, then P is said to be divisible by Q. In other words, if P can be expressed as an integral multiple of Q, then P is said to be divisible by Q. For example, dividing 51 by 17 gives 3, an integer. 51 is divisible by 17, or 51 equals 17 times 3. On the other hand, dividing 8 by 3 gives $2\frac{2}{3}$, which is not an integer. 8 is not divisible by 3, and there is no way to express 8 as an integral multiple of 3. There are various tests to see whether an integer is divisible by certain numbers. These tests are listed below:

1. Any integer is divisible *by 2* if the last digit of the number is a 0, 2, 4, 6, or 8.

   Example: The numbers 98, 6,534, 70, and 32 are divisible by 2 because they end in 8, 4, 0, and 2, respectively.

2. Any integer is divisible *by 3* if the sum of its digits is divisible by 3.

   Example: Is the number 34,237,023 divisible by 3?

   Solution: Add the digits of the number. $3 + 4 + 2 + 3 + 7 + 0 + 2 + 3 = 24$. Now, 24 is divisible by 3 ($24 \div 3 = 8$), so the number 34,237,023 is also divisible by 3.

3. Any integer is divisible *by 4* if the last two digits of the number make a number that is divisible by 4.

   Example: Which of the following numbers is divisible by 4?

   3,456; 6,787,612; 67,408; 7,877; 345; 98.

   Solution: Look at the last two digits of the numbers: 56, 12, 08, 77, 45, 98. Only 56, 12, and 08 are divisible by 4, so only the numbers 3,456; 6,787,612; and 67,408 are divisible by 4.

4. An integer is divisible *by 5* if the last digit is either a 0 or a 5.

   Example: The numbers 780, 675, 9,000, and 15 are divisible by 5, while the numbers 786, 5,509, and 87 are not divisible by 5.

5. Any integer is divisible *by 6* if it is divisible by both 2 and 3.

   Example: Is the number 12,414 divisible by 6?

   Solution: Test whether 12,414 is divisible by 2 and 3. The last digit is a 4, so it is divisible by 2. Adding the digits yields $1 + 2 + 4 + 1 + 4 = 12$. 12 is divisible by 3, so the number 12,414 is divisible by 3. Since it is divisible by both 2 and 3, it is divisible by 6.

6. Any integer is divisible *by 8* if the last three digits are divisible by 8. (Since 1,000 is divisible by 8, you can ignore all multiples of 1,000 in applying this rule.)

    Example: Is the number 342,169,424 divisible by 8?

    Solution: $424 \div 8 = 53$, so 342,169,424 is divisible by 8.

7. Any integer is divisible *by 9* if the sum of its digits is divisible by 9.

    Example: Is the number 243,091,863 divisible by 9?

    Solution: Adding the digits yields $2 + 4 + 3 + 0 + 9 + 1 + 8 + 6 + 3 = 36$. 36 is divisible by 9, so the number 243,091,863 is divisible by 9.

8. Any integer is divisible *by 10* if the last digit is a 0.

    Example: The numbers 60, 8,900, 5,640, and 34,000 are all divisible by 10 because the last digit in each is a 0.

> Note that if a number P is divisible by a number Q, then P is also divisible by all the factors of Q. For example, 60 is divisible by 12, so 60 is also divisible by 2, 3, 4, and 6, which are all factors of 12.

608. *Prime numbers.* A prime number is one that is divisible only by 1 and itself. The first few prime numbers are 2, 3, 5, 7, 11, 13, 17, 19, 23, 29, 31, 37. . . . Note that the number 1 is not considered a prime number. To determine if a number is prime, follow these steps:

Step 1. Determine a very rough approximate square root of the number. Remember that the square root of a number is that number which, when multiplied by itself, gives the original number. For example, the square root of 25 is 5 because $5 \times 5 = 25$.

Step 2. Divide the number by all of the primes that are less than the approximate square root. If the number is not divisible by any of these

primes, then it is prime. If it is divisible by one of the primes, then it is not prime.

Example: Is the number 97 prime?

Solution: An approximate square root of 97 is 10. All of the primes less than 10 are 2, 3, 5, and 7. Divide 97 by 2, 3, 5, and 7. No integer results, so 97 is prime.

Example: Is the number 161 prime?

Solution: An approximate square root of 161 is 13. The primes less than 13 are 2, 3, 5, 7, and 11. Divide 161 by 2, 3, 5, 7, and 11. 161 is divisible by 7 ($161 \div 7 = 23$), so 161 is not prime.

Approximations

609. *Rounding off numbers with decimal points.* A number expressed to a certain number of places is rounded off when it is approximated as a number with fewer places of accuracy. For example, the number 8.987 is expressed more accurately than the number rounded off to 8.99. To round off to *n* places, look at the digit that is to the right of the *n*th digit. (The *n*th digit is found by counting *n* places to the right of the decimal point.) If this digit is less than 5, eliminate all of the digits to the right of the *n*th digit. If the digit to the right of the *n*th digit is 5 or more, then add 1 to the *n*th digit and eliminate all of the digits to the right of the *n*th digit.

Example: Round off 8.73 to the nearest tenth.

Solution: The digit to the right of the 7 (.7 is seven-tenths) is 3. Since this is less than 5, eliminate it, and the rounded-off answer is 8.7.

Example: Round off 986 to the nearest tens place.

Solution: The number to the right of the tens place is 6. Since this is 5 or more, add 1 to the 8 and replace the 6 with a 0 to get 990.

610. *Approximating sums with decimal points.* When adding a small set of numbers (10 or fewer) and the answer must have a given number of places of accuracy, follow the steps below.

Step 1. Round off each addend (number being added) to one less place than the number of places the answer is to have.

Step 2. Add the rounded addends.

Step 3. Round off the sum to the desired number of places of accuracy.

Example: What is the sum of 12.0775, 1.20163, and 121.303, correct to the nearest hundredth?

Solution: Round off the three numbers to the nearest thousandth (one less place than the accuracy of the sum): 12.078, 1.202, and 121.303. The sum of these is 134.583. Rounded off to the nearest hundredth, this is 134.58.

611. *Approximating products.* To multiply certain numbers and have an answer to the desired number of places of accuracy (significant digits), follow the steps below.

    Step 1. Round off the numbers being multiplied to the number of places of accuracy (significant digits) desired in the answer.

    Step 2. Multiply the rounded-off factors (numbers being multiplied).

    Step 3. Round off the product to the desired number of places (significant digits).

    Example: Find the product of 3,316 and 1,432 to the nearest thousand.

    Solution: First, round off 3,316 to 3 places, to obtain 3,320. Round off 1,432 to 3 places to give 1,430. The product of these two numbers is 4,747,600. Rounded off to 3 places, this is 4,748,000.

612. *Approximating square roots.* The square root of a number is that number which, when multiplied by itself, gives the original number. For example, 6 is the square root of 36. Often on tests, a number with different choices for the square root is given. Follow this procedure to determine which is the best choice.

    Step 1. Square all of the choices given.

    Step 2. Select the closest choice that is too large and the closest choice that is too small (assuming that no choice is the exact square root). Find the average of these two *choices* (not of their squares).

    Step 3. Square this average; if the square is greater than the original number, choose the lower of the two choices; if its square is lower than the original number, choose the higher.

    Example: Which of the following is closest to the square root of 86: 9.0, 9.2, 9.4, 9.6, or 9.8?

Solution: The squares of the five numbers are 81, 84.64, 88.36, 92.16, and 96.04, respectively. (Actually, it is not necessary to calculate the last two, since they are greater than the third square, which is already greater than 86.) The two closest choices are 9.2 and 9.4; their average is 9.3. The square of 9.3 is 86.49. Therefore, 9.3 is greater than the square root of 86. So, the square root must be closer to 9.2 than to 9.4.

Combinations

613. Suppose that a job has 2 different parts. There are m different ways of doing the first part, and there are n different ways of doing the second part. The problem is to find the number of ways of doing the entire job. For each way of doing the first part of the job, there are n ways of doing the second part. Since there are m ways of doing the first part, the total number of ways of doing the entire job is $m \times n$. The formula that can be used is

$$\text{Number of ways} = m \times n$$

For any problem that involves 2 actions or 2 objects, each with a number of choices, and asks for the number of combinations, this formula can be used. For example: A man wants a sandwich and a drink for lunch. If a restaurant has 4 choices of sandwich and 3 choices of drink, how many different ways can he order his lunch?

Since there are 4 choices of sandwich and 3 choices of drink, use the formula

$$\text{Number of ways} = 4(3)$$
$$= 12$$

Therefore, the man can order his lunch 12 different ways.

If we have objects a, b, c, and d and want to arrange them two at a time—that is, like ab, bc, cd, etc.—we have four combinations taken two at a time. This is denoted as $_4C_2$. The rule is that $_4C_2 = \dfrac{(4)(3)}{(2)(1)}$. In general, n combinations taken r at a time is represented by the formula:

$$_nC_r = \frac{(n)(n-1)(n-2)\ldots(n-r+1)}{(r)(r-1)(r-2)\ldots(1)}$$

Examples: $_3C_2 = \dfrac{3 \times 2}{2 \times 1}$; $_8C_3 = \dfrac{8 \times 7 \times 6}{3 \times 2 \times 1}$

Suppose there are 24 people at a party and each person shakes another person's hand (only once). How many handshakes are there?

Solution: Represent the people at the party as a, b, c, d, etc.

The combinations of handshakes would be ab, ac, bc, bd, etc., or 24 combinations taken 2 at a time: $_{24}C_2$. This is $\dfrac{24 \times 23}{2 \times 1} = 276$.

Permutations

613a. *Permutations* are like combinations, except in permutations the order is important. As an example, if we want to find how many permutations there are of 3 objects taken 2 at a time, we would have for a, b, c, ab, ba, ac, ca, bc, cb. Thus, as an example, ba would be one permutation and ab would be another. The permutations of 3 objects taken 2 at a time would be $_3P_2 = 3 \times 2$ and not $\dfrac{(3 \times 3)}{(2 \times 1)}$ as in combinations. The number of permutations of n objects taken r at a time would be

$$_nP_r = (n)(n-1)\ldots(n-r+1).$$

Example: How many permutations of the digits 142 are there, where the digits are taken two at a time?

Solution: You have 14, 41, 12, 21, 42, 24. That is, $_3P_2 = 3 \times 2 = 6$.

Probability

614. The *probability* that an event will occur equals the number of favorable ways divided by the total number of ways. If P is the probability, m is the number of favorable ways, and n is the total number of ways, then

$$P = \frac{m}{n}$$

Example: What is the probability that a head will turn up on a single throw of a penny?

The favorable number of ways is 1 (a head).

The total number of ways is 2 (a head and a tail).

Thus, the probability is $\dfrac{1}{2}$.

If a and b are two mutually exclusive events, then the probability that a or b will occur is the sum of the individual probabilities.

Suppose P_a is the probability that an event a occurs. Suppose that P_b is the probability that a second independent event b occurs. Then the probability that the first event a occurs *and* the second event b occurs subsequently is $P_a \times P_b$.

The Absolute Value Sign

615. The symbol $|\ |$ denotes *absolute value*. The absolute value of a number is the numerical value of the number without the plus or minus sign in front of it. Thus all absolute values are positive. For example, $|+3|$ is 3, and $|-2|$ is 2. Here's another example:

If x is positive and y is negative $|x| + |y| = x - y$. Because y is negative, we must have $x - y$ to make the term positive.

Functions

616. Suppose we have a *function* of x. This is denoted as $f(x)$ or $g(y)$ or $h(z)$, etc. As an example, if $f(x) = x$, then $f(3) = 3$.

In this example we substitute the value 3 wherever x appears in the function. Similarly, $f(-2) = -2$.

Consider another example: If $f(y) = y^2 - y$, then $f(2) = 2^2 - 2 = 2$. $f(-2) = (-2)^2 - (-2) = 6$. $f(z) = z^2 - z$. $f(2z) = (2z)^2 - (2z) = 4z^2 - 2z$.

Let us consider still another example: Let $f(x) = x + 2$ and $g(y) = 2^y$. What is $f[g(-2)]$? Now $g(-2) = 2^{-2} = \dfrac{1}{4}$. Thus $f[g(-2)] = f\left(\dfrac{1}{4}\right)$. Since $f(x) = x + 2$, $f\left(\dfrac{1}{4}\right) = \dfrac{1}{4} + 2 = 2\dfrac{1}{4}$.

Logarithms

617. A logarithm is an exponent. For a description of exponents, see Section 429. If $\log_a b = x$, this means $a^x = b$. Examples are

$$\log_{10}10 = 1, \text{ since } 10^1 = 10$$
$$\log_2 16 = 4, \text{ since } 2^4 = 16$$

It can be seen that the following equalities are true:
$$\log_a(xy) = \log_a x + \log_a y$$
$$\log_a\left(\frac{x}{y}\right) = \log_a x - \log_a y$$
$$\log_a x^n = n(\log_a x)$$

Imaginary Numbers

618. An imaginary number, $i = \sqrt{-1}$, is a number that when multiplied by itself will give you the value -1. Obviously there is no number in the real world that can be multiplied by itself to give a negative number: If the number is positive, positive $\times$ positive = positive, and if the number is negative, negative $\times$ negative = positive, and if it is 0, $0 \times 0 = 0$. Thus the number is called "imaginary." So if $i = \sqrt{-1}$, $i^2 = -1$.

Example: Find another expression for $(2 + 3i)(3 + 5i)$.

Solution: Multiply the factors: We get $2 \times 3 + 3i \times 3 + 2 \times 5i + 3i \times 5i$. This becomes $6 + 9i + 10i + 15i^2 = 6 + 19i + 15(-1) = 6 + 19i - 15 = 19i - 9$.

SESSION 6 PRACTICE TEST

Miscellaneous Problems: Averages, Series, Properties of Integers, Approximations, Combinations, Permutations, Probability, the Absolute Value Sign, Functions, Logarithms, and Imaginary Numbers

Correct answers and solutions follow this test.

1. If n is the first of five consecutive odd numbers, what is their average?

   (A) n
   (B) $n + 1$
   (C) $n + 2$
   (D) $n + 3$
   (E) $n + 4$

   A B C D E
   ○ ○ ○ ○ ○
   ——————

2. What is the average of the following numbers: 35.5, 32.5, 34.0, 35.0, 34.5?

   (A) 33.0
   (B) 33.8
   (C) 34.0
   (D) 34.3
   (E) 34.5

   A B C D E
   ○ ○ ○ ○ ○
   ——————

*3. What is the next number in the following series: 1, 5, 9, 13, . . . ?

   (A) 11
   (B) 15
   (C) 17
   (D) 19
   (E) 21

   A B C D E
   ○ ○ ○ ○ ○
   ——————

*4. Which of the following is the next number in the series: 3, 6, 4, 9, 5, 12, 6, . . . ?

   (A) 7
   (B) 9
   (C) 12

(D) 15
(E) 24

   A B C D E
   ○ ○ ○ ○ ○
   ——————

5. If P is an even number, and Q and R are both odd, which of the following *must* be true?

   (A) $P \cdot Q$ is an odd number.
   (B) $Q - R$ is an even number.
   (C) $PQ - PR$ is an odd number.
   (D) $Q + R$ cannot equal P.
   (E) $P + Q$ cannot equal R.

   A B C D E
   ○ ○ ○ ○ ○
   ——————

6. If a number is divisible by 102, then it is also divisible by:

   (A) 23
   (B) 11
   (C) 103
   (D) 5
   (E) 2

   A B C D E
   ○ ○ ○ ○ ○
   ——————

7. Which of the following numbers is divisible by 36?

   (A) 35,924
   (B) 64,530
   (C) 74,098
   (D) 152,640
   (E) 192,042

   A B C D E
   ○ ○ ○ ○ ○
   ——————

8. How many prime numbers are there between 45 and 72?

   (A) 4
   (B) 5
   (C) 6

———————
*Not tested on current ACT.

(D) 7
(E) 8

A B C D E
○ ○ ○ ○ ○

9. Which of the following represents the smallest possible value of $(M - \frac{1}{2})^2$, if M is an integer?

(A) 0.00
(B) 0.25
(C) 0.50
(D) 0.75
(E) 1.00

A B C D E
○ ○ ○ ○ ○

10. Which of the following best approximates $\frac{7.40096 \times 10.0342}{0.2001355}$?

(A) 0.3700
(B) 3.700
(C) 37.00
(D) 370.0
(E) 3,700

A B C D E
○ ○ ○ ○ ○

11. In a class with 6 boys and 4 girls, the students all took the same test. The boys' scores were 74, 82, 84, 84, 88, and 95, while the girls' scores were 80, 82, 86, and 86. Which of the following statements is true?

(A) The boys' average was 0.1 higher than the average for the whole class.
(B) The girls' average was 0.1 lower than the boys' average.
(C) The class average was 1.0 higher than the boys' average.
(D) The boys' average was 1.0 higher than the class average.
(E) The girls' average was 1.0 lower than the boys' average.

A B C D E
○ ○ ○ ○ ○

*12. If the following series continues to follow the same pattern, what will be the next number: 2, 6, 3, 9, 6, . . . ?

(A) 3
(B) 6
(C) 12
(D) 14
(E) 18

A B C D E
○ ○ ○ ○ ○

13. Which of the following numbers *must* be odd?

(A) The sum of an odd number and an odd number.
(B) The product of an odd number and an even number.
(C) The sum of an odd number and an even number.
(D) The product of two even numbers.
(E) The sum of two even numbers.

A B C D E
○ ○ ○ ○ ○

14. Which of the following numbers is the best approximation of the length of one side of a square with an area of 12 square inches?

(A) 3.2 inches
(B) 3.3 inches
(C) 3.4 inches
(D) 3.5 inches
(E) 3.6 inches

A B C D E
○ ○ ○ ○ ○

15. If n is an odd number, then which of the following *best* describes the number represented by $n^2 + 2n + 1$?

(A) It can be odd or even.
(B) It must be odd.
(C) It must be divisible by four.
(D) It must be divisible by six.
(E) The answer cannot be determined from the given information.

A B C D E
○ ○ ○ ○ ○

*Not tested on current ACT.

*16. What is the next number in the series:
2, 5, 7, 8, . . . ?

(A) 8
(B) 9
(C) 10
(D) 11
(E) 12

A B C D E
○ ○ ○ ○ ○

17. What is the average of the following numbers: $3\frac{1}{2}$, $4\frac{1}{4}$, $2\frac{1}{4}$, $3\frac{1}{4}$, 4?

(A) 3.25
(B) 3.35
(C) 3.45
(D) 3.50
(E) 3.60

A B C D E
○ ○ ○ ○ ○

18. Which of the following numbers is divisible by 24?

(A) 76,300
(B) 78,132
(C) 80,424
(D) 81,234
(E) 83,636

A B C D E
○ ○ ○ ○ ○

19. In order to graduate, a boy needs an average of 65 percent for his five major subjects. His first four grades were 55, 60, 65, and 65. What grade does he need in the fifth subject in order to graduate?

(A) 65
(B) 70
(C) 75
(D) 80
(E) 85

A B C D E
○ ○ ○ ○ ○

20. If t is any integer, which of the following represents an odd number?

(A) $2t$
(B) $2t + 3$
(C) $3t$

(D) $2t + 2$
(E) $t + 1$

A B C D E
○ ○ ○ ○ ○

21. If the average of five whole numbers is an even number, which of the following statements is *not* true?

(A) The sum of the five numbers must be divisible by 2.
(B) The sum of the five numbers must be divisible by 5.
(C) The sum of the five numbers must be divisible by 10.
(D) At least one of the five numbers must be even.
(E) All of the five numbers must be odd.

A B C D E
○ ○ ○ ○ ○

22. What is the product of 23 and 79 to one significant digit?

(A) 1,600
(B) 1,817
(C) 1,000
(D) 1,800
(E) 2,000

A B C D E
○ ○ ○ ○ ○

*23. What is the next term in the series 1, 1, 2, 3, 5, 8, 13, . . . ?

(A) 18
(B) 21
(C) 13
(D) 9
(E) 20

A B C D E
○ ○ ○ ○ ○

*24. What is the next number in the series 1, 4, 2, 8, 6, . . . ?

(A) 4
(B) 6
(C) 8
(D) 15
(E) 24

A B C D E
○ ○ ○ ○ ○

*Not tested on current ACT.

25. Which of the following is closest to the square root of $\frac{1}{2}$?

    (A) 0.25
    (B) 0.5
    (C) 0.6
    (D) 0.7
    (E) 0.8

    A B C D E
    ○ ○ ○ ○ ○

26. How many prime numbers are there between 56 and 100?

    (A) 8
    (B) 9
    (C) 10
    (D) 11
    (E) none of the above

    A B C D E
    ○ ○ ○ ○ ○

27. If you multiply 1,200,176 by 520,204, and then divide the product by 1,000,000,000, your result will be closest to:

    (A) 0.6
    (B) 6
    (C) 600
    (D) 6,000
    (E) 6,000,000

    A B C D E
    ○ ○ ○ ○ ○

28. The number 89.999 rounded off to the nearest tenth is equal to which of the following?

    (A) 90.0
    (B) 89.0
    (C) 89.9
    (D) 89.99
    (E) 89.90

    A B C D E
    ○ ○ ○ ○ ○

29. a, b, c, d, and e are integers; M is their average and S is their sum. What is the ratio of S to M?

    (A) 1 : 5
    (B) 5 : 1
    (C) 1 : 1

    (D) 2 : 1
    (E) depends on the values of a, b, c, d, and e

    A B C D E
    ○ ○ ○ ○ ○

*30. What is the next number in the series 1, 1, 2, 4, 5, 25, . . . ?

    (A) 8
    (B) 12
    (C) 15
    (D) 24
    (E) 26

    A B C D E
    ○ ○ ○ ○ ○

31. The sum of five odd numbers is always:

    (A) even
    (B) divisible by 3
    (C) divisible by 5
    (D) a prime number
    (E) none of the above

    A B C D E
    ○ ○ ○ ○ ○

32. If E is an even number and F is divisible by 3, then what is the *largest* number by which E^2F^3 *must* be divisible?

    (A) 6
    (B) 12
    (C) 54
    (D) 108
    (E) 144

    A B C D E
    ○ ○ ○ ○ ○

33. If the average of five consecutive even numbers is 8, which of the following is the smallest of the five numbers?

    (A) 4
    (B) 5
    (C) 6
    (D) 8
    (E) none of the above

    A B C D E
    ○ ○ ○ ○ ○

*Not tested on current ACT.

*34. What is the next number in the sequence 1, 4, 7, 10, . . . ?

(A) 13
(B) 14
(C) 15
(D) 16
(E) 18

A B C D E
○ ○ ○ ○ ○

35. If a number is divisible by 23, then it is also divisible by which of the following?

(A) 7
(B) 24
(C) 9
(D) 3
(E) none of the above

A B C D E
○ ○ ○ ○ ○

*36. What is the next term in the series 3, 6, 2, 7, 1, . . . ?

(A) 0
(B) 1
(C) 3
(D) 6
(E) 8

A B C D E
○ ○ ○ ○ ○

37. What is the average (to the nearest tenth) of the following numbers: 91.4, 91.5, 91.6, 91.7, 91.7, 92.0, 92.1, 92.3, 92.3, 92.4?

(A) 91.9
(B) 92.0
(C) 92.1
(D) 92.2
(E) 92.3

A B C D E
○ ○ ○ ○ ○

*38. What is the next term in the following series: 8, 3, 10, 9, 12, 27, . . . ?

(A) 8
(B) 14

(C) 18
(D) 36
(E) 81

A B C D E
○ ○ ○ ○ ○

39. Which of the following numbers is divisible by 11?

(A) 30,217
(B) 44,221
(C) 59,403
(D) 60,411
(E) none of the above

A B C D E
○ ○ ○ ○ ○

*40. What is the next number in the series 1, 4, 9, 16, . . . ?

(A) 22
(B) 23
(C) 24
(D) 34
(E) 25

A B C D E
○ ○ ○ ○ ○

41. Which of the following is the best approximation of the product (1.005)(20.0025)(0.0102)?

(A) 0.02
(B) 0.2
(C) 2.0
(D) 20
(E) 200

A B C D E
○ ○ ○ ○ ○

*42. What is the next number in the series 5, 2, 4, 2, 3, 2, . . . ?

(A) 1
(B) 2
(C) 3
(D) 4
(E) 5

A B C D E
○ ○ ○ ○ ○

*Not tested on current ACT.

43. If *a*, *b*, and *c* are all divisible by 8, then their average must be

    (A) divisible by 8
    (B) divisible by 3
    (C) divisible by 5
    (D) divisible by 7
    (E) none of the above

    A B C D E
    ○ ○ ○ ○ ○

44. Which of the following numbers is divisible by 24?

    (A) 13,944
    (B) 15,746
    (C) 15,966
    (D) 16,012
    (E) none of the above

    A B C D E
    ○ ○ ○ ○ ○

45. Which of the following numbers is a prime?

    (A) 147
    (B) 149
    (C) 153
    (D) 155
    (E) 161

    A B C D E
    ○ ○ ○ ○ ○

*46. What is the next number in the following series: 4, 8, 2, 4, 1, . . . ?

    (A) 1
    (B) 2
    (C) 4
    (D) 8
    (E) 16

    A B C D E
    ○ ○ ○ ○ ○

47. The sum of four consecutive odd integers must be:

    (A) even, but not necessarily divisible by 4
    (B) divisible by 4, but not necessarily by 8
    (C) divisible by 8, but not necessarily by 16
    (D) divisible by 16
    (E) none of the above

    A B C D E
    ○ ○ ○ ○ ○

48. Which of the following is closest to the square root of $\frac{3}{5}$?

    (A) $\frac{1}{2}$

    (B) $\frac{2}{3}$

    (C) $\frac{3}{4}$

    (D) $\frac{4}{5}$

    (E) 1

    A B C D E
    ○ ○ ○ ○ ○

*49. What is the next term in the series: 9, 8, 6, 3, . . . ?

    (A) 0
    (B) 22
    (C) 1
    (D) 23
    (E) 21

    A B C D E
    ○ ○ ○ ○ ○

50. The sum of an odd and an even number is

    (A) a perfect square
    (B) negative
    (C) even
    (D) odd
    (E) none of the above

    A B C D E
    ○ ○ ○ ○ ○

*Not tested on current ACT.

Answer Key for Session 6 Practice Test

1. E	14. D	27. C	39. A
2. D	15. C	28. A	40. E
3. C	16. A	29. B	41. B
4. D	17. C	30. E	42. B
5. B	18. C	31. E	43. E
6. E	19. D	32. D	44. A
7. D	20. B	33. A	45. B
8. C	21. E	34. A	46. B
9. B	22. E	35. E	47. C
10. D	23. B	36. E	48. C
11. E	24. E	37. A	49. E
12. E	25. D	38. B	50. D
13. C	26. B		

Answers and Solutions for Session 6 Practice Test

1. Choice E is correct. The five consecutive odd numbers must be $n, n + 2, n + 4, n + 6$, and $n + 8$. Their average is equal to their sum, $5n + 20$, divided by the number of addends, 5, which yields $n + 4$ as the average. (Refresher 601)

2. Choice D is correct. Choosing 34 as an approximate average results in the following addends: $+1.5, -1.5, 0, +1.0$, and $+0.5$. Their sum is $+1.5$. Now, divide by 5 to get $+0.3$ and add this to 34 to get 34.3. (To check this, add the five original numbers and divide by 5.) (Refresher 601)

3. Choice C is correct. This is an arithmetic sequence: Each term is 4 more than the preceding one. The next term is $13 + 4$, or 17. (Refresher 602)

4. Choice D is correct. This series can be divided into two parts: the even-numbered terms: 6, 9, 12, ... and the odd-numbered terms: 3, 4, 5, 6, ... ("Even- and odd-numbered terms" refers to the terms' *place* in the series and not if the term itself is even or odd.) The next term in the series is even-numbered, so it will be formed by adding 3 to the 12 (the last of the even-numbered terms) to get 15. (Refresher 602)

5. Choice B is correct. Since Q is an odd number, it may be represented by $2m + 1$, where m is an integer. Similarly, call $R\ 2n + 1$, where n is an integer. Thus, $Q - R$ is equal to $(2m + 1) - (2n + 1), 2m - 2n$, or $2(m - n)$. Now, since m and n are integers, $m - n$ will be some integer p. Thus, $Q - R = 2p$. Any number in the form of $2p$, where p is any integer, is an even number. Therefore, $Q - R$ *must* be even. (A) and (C) are wrong, because an even number multiplied by an odd is always even. (D) and (E) are only true for specific values of P, Q, and R. (Refresher 604)

6. Choice E is correct. If a number is divisible by 102 then it must be divisible by all of the factors of 102. The only choice that is a factor of 102 is 2. (Refresher 607)

7. Choice D is correct. To be divisible by 36, a number must be divisible by both 4 and 9. Only (A) and (D) are divisible by 4. (Recall that only the last two digits must be examined.) Of these, only (D) is divisible by 9. The sum of the digits of (A) is 23, which is not divisible by 9; the sum of the digits of (D) is 18. (Refresher 607)

8. Choice C is correct. The prime numbers between 45 and 72 are 47, 53, 59, 61, 67, and 71. All of the others have factors other than 1 and themselves. (Refresher 608)

9. Choice B is correct. Since M must be an *integer*, the closest value it can have to $\frac{1}{2}$ is either 1 or 0. In either case, $(M - \frac{1}{2})^2$ is equal to $\frac{1}{4}$, or 0.25. (Refresher 603)

10. Choice D is correct. Approximate each of the numbers to only one significant digit (this is permissible because the choices are so far apart; if they had been closer together, two or three significant digits should be used). After this approximation, the expression is: $\frac{7 \times 10}{0.2}$, which is equal to 350. This is closest to 370. (Refresher 609)

11. Choice E is correct. The average for the boys alone was $\frac{74 + 82 + 84 + 84 + 88 + 95}{6}$, or $507 \div 6 = 84.5$. The girls' average was $\frac{80 + 82 + 86 + 86}{4}$, or $334 \div 4 = 83.5$, which is 1.0 below the boys' average. (Refresher 601)

12. Choice E is correct. To generate this series, start with 2; multiply by 3 to get 6; subtract 3 to get 3; multiply by 3; subtract 3; etc. Thus, the next term will be found by multiplying the previous term, 6, by 3 to get 18. (Refresher 602)

13. Choice C is correct. The sum of an odd number and an even number can be expressed as $(2n + 1) + (2m)$, where n and m are integers. ($2n + 1$ must be odd, and $2m$ must be even.) Their sum is equal to $2n + 2m + 1$, or $2(m + n) + 1$. Since $(m + n)$ is an integer, the quantity $2(m + n) + 1$ *must* represent an odd integer. (Refreshers 604, 605)

14. Choice D is correct. The actual length of one of the sides would be the square root of 12. Square each of the five choices to find the square of 3.4 is 11.56, and the square of 3.5 is 12.25. The square root of 12 must lie between 3.4 and 3.5. Squaring 3.45 (halfway between the two choices) yields 11.9025, which is less than 12. Thus the square root of 12 must be greater than 3.45 and therefore closer to 3.5 than to 3.4. (Refresher 612)

15. Choice C is correct. Factor $n^2 + 2n + 1$ to $(n + 1)(n + 1)$ or $(n + 1)^2$. Now, since n is an odd number, $n + 1$ must be even (the number after every odd number is even). Thus, representing $n + 1$ as $2k$ where k is an integer ($2k$ is the standard representation for an even number), yields the expression: $(n + 1)^2 = (2k)^2$ or $4k^2$. Thus, $(n + 1)^2$ is a multiple of 4, and it must be divisible by 4. A number divisible by 4 must also be even, so (C) is the best choice. (Refreshers 604–607)

16. Choice A is correct. The differences between terms are as follows: 3, 2, and 1. Thus, the next term should be found by adding 0, leaving a result of 8. (Refresher 602)

17. Choice C is correct. Convert to decimals. Then calculate the value of $\frac{3.50 + 4.25 + 2.25 + 3.25 + 4.00}{5}$. This equals $17.25 \div 5$, or 3.45. (Refresher 601)

18. Choice C is correct. If a number is divisible by 24, it must be divisible by 3 and 8. Of the five choices given, only Choice C is divisible by 8. Add the digits in 80,424 to get 18. As this is divisible by 3, the number is divisible by 3. The number, therefore, is divisible by 24. (Refresher 607)

19. Choice D is correct. If the boy is to average 65 for five subjects, the total of his five grades must be five times 65, or 325. The sum of the first four grades is $55 + 60 + 65 + 65$, or 245. Therefore, the fifth mark must be $325 - 245$, or 80. (Refresher 601)

20. Choice B is correct. If t is any integer, then $2t$ is an even number. Adding 3 to an even number always produces an odd number. Thus, $2t + 3$ is always odd. (Refresher 606)

21. Choice E is correct. Call the five numbers a, b, c, d, and e. Then the average is $\frac{(a + b + c + d + e)}{5}$. Since this must be even, $\frac{(a + b + c + d + e)}{5} = 2k$, where k is an integer. Thus $a + b + c + d + e = 10k$. Therefore, the sum of the 5 numbers is divisible by 10, 2, and 5. Thus the first three choices are eliminated. If the five numbers were 1, 1, 1, 1, and 6, then the average would be 2. Thus, the average is even, but not all of the numbers are even. Thus, Choice D can be true. If all the numbers were odd, the sum would have to be odd. This contradicts the statement that the average is even. Thus, Choice E is the answer. (Refreshers 601, 607)

22. Choice E is correct. First, round off 23 and 79 to one significant digit. The numbers become 20 and 80. The product of these two numbers is 1,600, which rounded off to one significant digit is 2,000. (Refresher 611)

23. Choice B is correct. Each term in this series is the sum of the two previous terms. Thus, the next term is $8 + 13$, or 21. (Refresher 602)

24. Choice E is correct. This series can be generated by the following steps: multiply by 4; subtract 2; multiply by 4; subtract 2; etc. Since the term 6 was obtained by subtracting 2, multiply by 4 to obtain $4 \times 6 = 24$, the next term. (Refresher 602)

25. Choice D is correct. 0.7 squared is 0.49. Squaring 0.8 yields 0.64. Thus, the square root of $\frac{1}{2}$ must lie between 0.7 and 0.8. Take the number halfway between these two, 0.75, and square it. This number, 0.5625, is more than $\frac{1}{2}$, so the square root

must be closer to 0.7 than to 0.8. An easier way to do problems concerning the square roots of 2 and 3 and their multiples is to memorize the values of these two square roots. The square root of 2 is about 1.414 (remember fourteen-fourteen), and the square root of 3 is about 1.732 (remember that 1732 was the year of George Washington's birth). Apply these as follows: $\frac{1}{2} = \frac{1}{4} \times 2$. Thus, $\sqrt{\frac{1}{2}} = \sqrt{\frac{1}{4}} \times \sqrt{2} = \frac{1}{2} \times 1.414 = 0.707$, which is very close to 0.7.   (Refresher 612)

26. Choice B is correct. The prime numbers can be found by taking all the odd numbers between 56 and 100 (the even ones cannot be primes) and eliminating all the ones divisible by 3, by 5, or by 7. If a number under 100 is divisible by none of these, it must be prime. Thus, the only primes between 56 and 100 are 59, 61, 67, 71, 73, 79, 83, 89, and 97.   (Refresher 608)

27. Choice C is correct. Since all the answer requires is an order-of-ten approximation, do not calculate the exact answer. Approximate the answer in the following manner: $\frac{1,000,000 \times 500,000}{1,000,000,000} = 500$. The only choice on the same order of magnitude is 600.   (Refresher 609)

28. Choice A is correct. To round off 89.999, look at the number in the hundredths place. 9 is more than 5, so add 1 to the number in the tenths place and eliminate all of the digits to the right. Thus, we get 90.0.   (Refresher 609)

29. Choice B is correct. The average of five numbers is found by dividing their sum by five. Therefore, the sum is five times the average, so $S : M = 5 : 1$ (Refresher 601)

30. Choice E is correct. The series can be generated by the following steps: To get the second term, square the first term; to get the third, add 1 to the second; to get the fourth, square the third; to get the fifth, add 1 to the fourth; etc. The pattern can be written as: square; add 1; repeat the cycle. Following this pattern, the seventh term is found by adding one to the sixth term. Thus, the seventh term is $1 + 25$, or 26.   (Refresher 602)

31. Choice E is correct. None of the first four choices is necessarily true. The sum, $5 + 7 + 9 + 13 + 15 = 49$, is not even, not divisible by 3, not divisible by 5, and not prime.   (Refreshers 604, 607, 608)

32. Choice D is correct. Any even number can be written as $2m$, and any number divisible by 3 can be written as $3n$, where m and n are integers. Thus, E^2F^3 equals $(2m)^2(3n)^3 = (4m^2)(27n^3) = 108(m^2n^3)$, and 108 is the largest number by which E^2F^3 must be divisible.   (Refresher 607)

33. Choice A is correct. The five consecutive even numbers can be represented as $n, n + 2, n + 4, n + 6$, and $n + 8$. Taking the sum and dividing by five yields an average of $n + 4$. Thus, $n + 4 = 8$, the given average, and $n = 4$, the smallest number.   (Refresher 601)

34. Choice A is correct. To find the next number in this sequence, add 3 to the previous number. This is an arithmetic progression. The next term is $10 + 3$, or 13.   (Refresher 602)

35. Choice E is correct. If a number is divisible by 23, then it is divisible by all of the factors of 23. But 23 is a prime with no factors except 1 and itself. Therefore, the correct choice is E.   (Refresher 607)

36. Choice E is correct. The steps generating the successive terms in this series are (to the previous term): add 3; subtract 4; add 5; subtract 6; add 7; etc. The next term is $1 + 7 = 8$.   (Refresher 602)

37. Choice A is correct. To find the average, it is convenient to choose 92.0 as an approximate average and then find the average of the differences between the actual numbers and 92.0. Thus, add up: $(-0.6) + (-0.5) + (-0.4) + (-0.3) + (-0.3) + (0.0) + 0.1 + 0.3 + 0.3 + 0.4 = -1.0$; divide this by 10 (the number of quantities to be averaged) to obtain -0.1. Finally, add this to the approximate average, 92.0, to obtain a final average of 91.9.   (Refresher 601)

38. Choice B is correct. This series is a combination of two sub-series: The odd-numbered terms, 3, 9, 27, etc., form a geometric series; the even-numbered terms, 8, 10, 12, etc., form an arithmetic sequence. The next number in the sequence

is from the arithmetic sequence and is 14. (Note: in the absence of any other indication, assume a series to be as simple as possible, i.e., arithmetic or geometric.) (Refresher 602)

39. Choice A is correct. To determine if a number is divisible by 11, take each of the digits separately and, beginning with either end, subtract the second from the first, add the following digit, subtract the next one, add the one after that, etc. If this result is divisible by 11, the entire number is. Thus, because $3 - 0 + 2 - 1 + 7 = 11$, we know that 30,217 is divisible by 11. Using the same method, we find that the other four choices are not divisible by 11. (Refresher 607)

40. Choice E is correct. This is the series of integers squared: $1^2, 2^2, 3^2, 4^2 \ldots$ the next term is 5^2, or 25. (Refresher 602)

41. Choice B is correct. This is simply an order-of-ten approximation, so round off the numbers and work the following problem. $(1.0)(20.0)(0.01) = 0.20$. The actual answer is closest to 0.2. (Refresher 611)

42. Choice B is correct. The even-numbered terms of this series form the sub-series: 2, 2, 2, ... The odd-numbered terms form the arithmetic series: 5, 4, 3, ... The next term in the series is a 2. (Refresher 602)

43. Choice E is correct. Represent the three numbers as $8p$, $8q$, and $8r$, respectively. Thus, their sum is $8p + 8q + 8r$, and their average is $\dfrac{(8p + 8q + 8r)}{3}$. This need not even be a whole number. For example, the average of 8, 16, and 32 is $\dfrac{56}{3}$, or $18\dfrac{2}{3}$. (Refreshers 601, 607)

44. Choice A is correct. To be divisible by 24, a number must be divisible by both 3 and 8. Only 13,944 and 15,966 are divisible by 3; of these, only 13,944 is divisible by 8 ($13,944 = 24 \times 581$). (Refresher 607)

45. Choice B is correct. The approximate square root of each of these numbers is 13. Merely divide each of these numbers by the primes up to 13, which are 2, 3, 5, 7, and 11. The only number not divisible by any of these primes is 149. (Refreshers 608, 612)

46. Choice B is correct. The sequence is formed by the following operations: Multiply by 2, divide by 4, multiply by 2, divide by 4, etc. Accordingly, the next number is 1×2, or 2. (Refresher 602)

47. Choice C is correct. Call the first odd integer $2k + 1$. (This is the standard algebraic expression for an odd integer.) Thus, the next 3 odd integers are $2k + 3$, $2k + 5$, and $2k + 7$. (Each one is 2 more than the previous one.) The sum of these integers is $(2k + 1) + (2k + 3) + (2k + 5) + (2k + 7) = 8k + 16$. This can be written as $8(k + 2)$, which is divisible by 8, but not necessarily by 16. (Refreshers 606, 607)

48. Choice C is correct. By squaring the five choices, it is evident that the two closest choices are $\left(\dfrac{3}{4}\right)^2 = 0.5625$ and $\left(\dfrac{4}{5}\right)^2 = 0.64$. Squaring the number half-way between $\dfrac{3}{4}$ and $\dfrac{4}{5}$ gives $(0.775)^2 = 0.600625$. This is greater than $\dfrac{3}{5}$, so the square root of $\dfrac{3}{5}$ must be closer to $\dfrac{3}{4}$ than to $\dfrac{4}{5}$. (Refresher 612)

49. Choice E is correct. The terms decrease by 1, then 2, then 3, so the next term is 4 less than 3, or -1. (Refresher 602)

50. Choice D is correct. Let the even number be $2k$, where k is an integer, and let the odd number be $2m + 1$, where m is an integer. Thus, the sum is $2k + (2m + 1)$, $2k + 2m + 1$, or $2(k + m) + 1$. Now $k + m$ is an integer since k and m are integers. Call $k + m$ by another name, p. Thus, $2(k + m) + 1$ is $2p + 1$, which is the representation of an odd number. (Refreshers 604, 606)

MATH REFRESHER SESSION 7

Tables, Charts, and Graphs

Introduction

701. *Graphs* and *charts* show the relationship of numbers and quantities in visual form. By looking at a graph, you can see at a glance the relationship between two or more sets of information. If such information were presented in written form, it would be hard to read and understand.

Here are some things to remember when doing problems based on graphs or charts:

1. Understand what you are being asked to do before you begin figuring.

2. Check the dates and types of information required. Be sure that you are looking in the proper columns, and on the proper lines, for the information you need.

3. Check the units required. Be sure that your answer is in thousands, millions, or whatever the question calls for.

4. In computing averages, be sure that you add the figures you need and no others, and that you divide by the correct number of years or other units.

5. Be careful in computing problems asking for percentages.

   (a) Remember that to convert a decimal into a percent you must multiply it by 100. For example, 0.04 is 4%.

   (b) Be sure that you can distinguish between such quantities as 1% (1 percent) and .01% (one one-hundredth of 1 percent), whether in numerals or in words.

   (c) Remember that if quantity X is greater than quantity Y, and the question asks what percent quantity X is of quantity Y, the answer must be greater than 100 percent.

Tables and Charts

702. A table or chart shows data arranged in rows and columns. Each column usually is headed by a brief description of the type of data in the column, and the far-left column lists items for which these different data points are displayed in the rows.

Example:

Test Score	Number of Students
90	2
85	1
80	1
60	3

Example: How many students took the test?

Solution: To find out the number of students who took the test, just add up the numbers in the column marked "Number of Students." That is, add $2 + 1 + 1 + 3 = 7$.

Example: What was the difference in scores between the highest and the lowest score?

Solution: First look at the highest score: 90. Then look at the lowest score: 60. Now calculate the difference: $90 - 60 = 30$.

Example: What was the *median* score?

Solution: The median score means the score that is in the *middle* of all the scores. That is, there are just as many scores above the median as below it. So in this example, the scores are 90, 90 (there are two 90s), 85, 80, and 60, 60, 60 (there are three 60s). So we have:

$$90$$
$$90$$
$$85$$
$$80$$
$$60$$
$$60$$
$$60$$

80 is right in the middle. That is, there are three scores above it and three scores below it. So 80 is the median.

Example: What was the *mean* score?

Solution: The mean score is defined as the *average* score. That is, it is the

$$\frac{\text{sum of the scores}}{\text{total number of scores}}$$

The sum of the scores is 90 + 90 + 85 + 80 + 60 + 60 + 60 = 525. The total number of scores is 2 + 1 + 1 + 3 = 7, so divide 7 into 525 to get the average: 75.

Graphs

703. To read a graph, you must know what *scale* the graph has been drawn to. Somewhere on the face of the graph will be an explanation of what each division of the graph means. Sometimes the divisions will be labeled. At other times, this information will be given in a small box called a *scale* or *legend*. For instance, a map, which is a specialized kind of graph, will always carry a scale or legend on its face telling you such information as $1'' = 100$ miles or $\frac{1''}{4} = 2$ miles.

Bar Graphs

704. A *bar graph* shows how information is compared by using broad lines, called *bars*, of varying lengths. Sometimes single lines are used as well. Bar graphs are good for showing a quick comparison of the information involved; however, the bars are difficult to read accurately unless the end of the bar falls exactly on one of the divisions of the scale. If the end of the bar falls between divisions of the scale, it is not easy to arrive at the precise figure represented by the bar. In bar graphs, the bars can run either vertically or horizontally. The sample bar graph following is a horizontal graph.

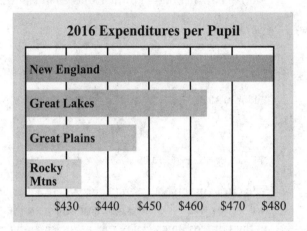

The individual bars in this kind of graph may carry a label within the bar, as in this example. The label may also appear alongside each bar. The scale used on the bars may appear along one axis, as in the example, or it may be noted somewhere on the face of the graph. Each numbered space on the *x*-axis, or horizontal axis, represents an expenditure of $10 per pupil. A wide variety of questions may be answered by a bar graph, such as:

1. Which area of the country spends least per pupil? Rocky Mountains.

2. How much does the New England area spend per pupil? $480.

3. How much less does the Great Plains spend per pupil than the Great Lakes?

$$\$464 - 447 = \frac{\$17}{\text{pupil}}.$$

4. How much more does New England spend on a pupil than the Rocky Mountains area?

$$\$480 - 433 = \frac{\$47}{\text{pupil}}$$

Circle Graphs

705. A *circle graph* or *pie chart* shows how an entire quantity has been divided or apportioned. The circle represents 100 percent of the quantity; the different parts into which the whole has been divided are shown by sections, or wedges, of the circle. Circle graphs are good for showing how money is distributed or collected, and for this reason they are widely used in financial graphing. The information is usually presented on the face of each section, telling you exactly what the section stands for and the value of that section in comparison to the other parts of the graph.

Sources of Income—Public Colleges of the U.S.*

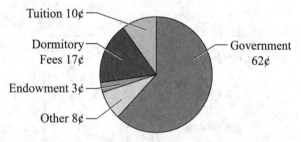

*Amounts represent cents per dollar of income.

The circle graph above indicates where the money originates that is used to maintain public colleges in the United States. The sizes of the sections tell you at a glance which source is most important (government) and which is least important (endowments). The sections total 100¢, or $1.00. This graph may be used to answer the following questions:

1. What is the most important source of income to the public colleges? Government.

2. What part of the revenue dollar comes from tuition? 10¢.

3. Dormitory fees bring in how many times the money that endowments bring in? $5\frac{2}{3}$ times $\left(\frac{17}{3} = 5\frac{2}{3}\right)$.

4. What is the least important source of revenue to public colleges? Endowments.

Line Graphs

706. *Line graphs* display the relationship of two types of information, one arranged vertically on a *y*-axis and the other horizontally on an *x*-axis. When we are asked to compare two values, we subtract the smaller from the larger.

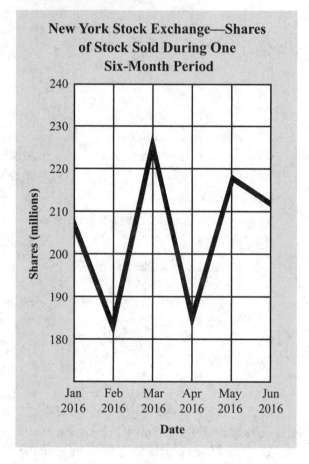

Our sample line graph represents the total shares of stock sold on the New York Stock Exchange between January and June of 2016. The months are placed along the *x*-axis, while the sales, in units of 1,000,000 shares, are placed along the *y*-axis.

1. How many shares were sold in March? 225,000,000.

2. What is the trend of stock sales between April and May? The volume of sales rose.

3. Compare the share sales in January and February. 25,000,000 fewer shares were sold in February.

4. During which months of the period was the increase in sales largest? February to March.

SESSION 7 PRACTICE TEST

Tables, Charts, and Graphs

Correct answers and solutions follow this test.

Table Test

Questions 1–5 are based on this table.

The following table is a record of the performance of a baseball team for the first seven weeks of the season.

	Games Won	Games Lost	Total No. of Games Played
First week	5	3	8
Second week	4	4	16
Third week	5	2	23
Fourth week	6	3	32
Fifth week	4	2	38
Sixth week	3	3	44
Seventh week	2	4	50

1. How many games did the team win during the first seven weeks?

   (A) 32
   (B) 29
   (C) 25
   (D) 21
   (E) 50

   A B C D E
   ○ ○ ○ ○ ○ _____

2. What percent of the games did the team win?

   (A) 75%
   (B) 60%
   (C) 58%
   (D) 29%
   (E) 80%

   A B C D E
   ○ ○ ○ ○ ○ _____

3. According to the table, which week was the worst for the team?

   (A) second week
   (B) fourth week
   (C) fifth week
   (D) sixth week
   (E) seventh week

   A B C D E
   ○ ○ ○ ○ ○ _____

4. Which week was the best week for the team?

   (A) first week
   (B) third week
   (C) fourth week
   (D) fifth week
   (E) sixth week

   A B C D E
   ○ ○ ○ ○ ○ _____

5. If there are fifty more games to play in the season, how many more games must the team win to end up winning 70% of the games?

   (A) 39
   (B) 35
   (C) 41
   (D) 34
   (E) 32

   A B C D E
   ○ ○ ○ ○ ○ _____

Pie Chart Test

Questions 6–10 are based on this pie chart.

Population by Region
Total = 191.3 million = 100%

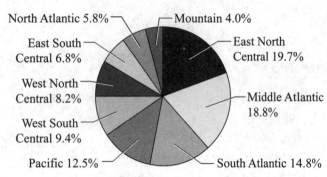

North Atlantic 5.8%

Mountain 4.0%

East South Central 6.8%

East North Central 19.7%

West North Central 8.2%

Middle Atlantic 18.8%

West South Central 9.4%

Pacific 12.5%

South Atlantic 14.8%

6. Which region is the most populated region?

(A) East North Central
(B) Middle Atlantic
(C) South Atlantic
(D) Pacific
(E) North Atlantic

A B C D E
○ ○ ○ ○ ○

7. What part of the entire population lives in the Mountain region?

(A) $\frac{1}{10}$

(B) $\frac{1}{30}$

(C) $\frac{1}{50}$

(D) $\frac{1}{25}$

(E) $\frac{1}{8}$

A B C D E
○ ○ ○ ○ ○

8. What is the approximate population in the Pacific region?

(A) 20 million
(B) 24 million
(C) 30 million
(D) 28 million
(E) 15 million

A B C D E
○ ○ ○ ○ ○

9. Approximately how many more people live in the Middle Atlantic region than in the South Atlantic?

(A) 4.0 million
(B) 7.7 million
(C) 5.2 million
(D) 9.3 million
(E) 8.5 million

A B C D E
○ ○ ○ ○ ○

10. What is the total population in all the regions combined?

(A) 73.3 million
(B) 100.0 million
(C) 191.3 million
(D) 126.8 million
(E) 98.5 million

A B C D E
○ ○ ○ ○ ○

Line Graph Test

Questions 11–15 are based on this line graph.

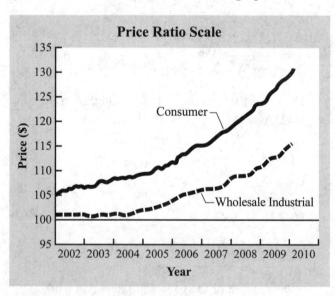

Price Ratio Scale

Price ($)

Consumer

Wholesale Industrial

2002 2003 2004 2005 2006 2007 2008 2009 2010

Year

11. On the ratio scale, what was the consumer price at the end of 2005?

(A) 95
(B) 100
(C) 105
(D) 110
(E) 115

A B C D E
○ ○ ○ ○ ○

12. During what year did consumer prices rise fastest?

(A) 2003
(B) 2005
(C) 2007
(D) 2008
(E) 2009

A B C D E
○ ○ ○ ○ ○

13. When wholesale and industrial prices were recorded as 110, consumer prices were recorded as

(A) between 125 and 120
(B) between 120 and 115
(C) between 115 and 110
(D) between 110 and 105
(E) between 105 and 100

A B C D E
○ ○ ○ ○ ○

14. For the 8 years from 2002 to 2009 inclusive, the average increase in consumer prices was

(A) 1 point
(B) 2 points
(C) 3 points
(D) 4 points
(E) 5 points

A B C D E
○ ○ ○ ○ ○

15. The percentage increase in wholesale and industrial prices between the beginning of 2002 and the end of 2009 was

(A) 1 percent
(B) 5 percent
(C) 10 percent
(D) 15 percent
(E) less than 1 percent

A B C D E
○ ○ ○ ○ ○

Bar Graph Test

Questions 16–18 are based on this bar graph.

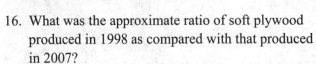

Soft Plywood Shows Growth

Billion Square Feet

16. What was the approximate ratio of soft plywood produced in 1998 as compared with that produced in 2007?

(A) 1 : 1
(B) 2 : 3
(C) 4 : 7
(D) 3 : 4
(E) 1 : 3

A B C D E
○ ○ ○ ○ ○

17. For the years 1998 through 2003, excluding 2002, how many billion square feet of plywood were produced altogether?

(A) 23.2
(B) 29.7
(C) 34.1
(D) 49.8
(E) 52.6

A B C D E
○ ○ ○ ○ ○

18. Between which consecutive odd years and between which consecutive even years did plywood production have the greatest increase?

    (A) 2005 and 2007; 1998 and 2000
    (B) 2003 and 2005; 2004 and 2006
    (C) 1999 and 2001; 2000 and 2002
    (D) 2001 and 2003; 2000 and 2002
    (E) 2003 and 2005; 2002 and 2004

    A B C D E
    ○ ○ ○ ○ ○

Cumulative Graph Test

Questions 19–23 are based on this cumulative graph.

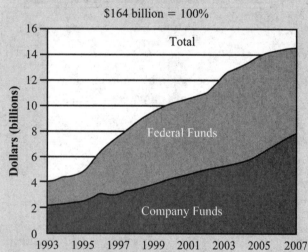

Spending for Research & Development (R&D) by Type of Research, 2007

$164 billion = 100%

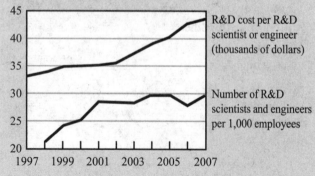

Scientists and engineers engaged full time in R&D and full-time equivalent of those working part time in R&D.

19. About how much in government funds was spent for research and development in 2007?

    (A) $4 billion
    (B) $6 billion

    (C) $12 billion
    (D) $16 billion
    (E) $24 billion

    A B C D E
    ○ ○ ○ ○ ○

20. In 2007, about what percent of the total spending in research and development was company funds?

    (A) 27%
    (B) 37%
    (C) 47%
    (D) 57%
    (E) 67%

    A B C D E
    ○ ○ ○ ○ ○

21. What was the change in the relative number of research and development scientists and engineers with respect to all employees from 2004 to 2005?

    (A) 10%
    (B) 5%
    (C) 2%
    (D) 3%
    (E) 0%

    A B C D E
    ○ ○ ○ ○ ○

22. What was the increase in company funds in research and development from 1993 to 2007?

    (A) $12 billion
    (B) $6 billion
    (C) $8 billion
    (D) $4 billion
    (E) $14 billion

    A B C D E
    ○ ○ ○ ○ ○

23. What was the percent of increase in the company funds spent on research and development from 1993 to 2007?

    (A) 100%
    (B) 50%
    (C) 300%
    (D) 400%
    (E) 1,000%

    A B C D E
    ○ ○ ○ ○ ○

Answer Key for Session 7 Practice Test

1. B	7. D	13. A	19. B
2. C	8. B	14. C	20. D
3. E	9. B	15. D	21. E
4. B	10. C	16. C	22. B
5. C	11. D	17. D	23. C
6. A	12. E	18. E	

Answers and Solutions for Session 7 Practice Test

1. Choice B is correct. To find the total number of games won, add the number of games won for all the weeks, $5 + 4 + 5 + 6 + 4 + 3 + 2 = 29$.
(Refresher 702)

2. Choice C is correct. The team won 29 out of 50 games, or 58%.
(Refresher 702)

3. Choice E is correct. The seventh week was the only week in which the team lost more games than it won.
(Refresher 702)

4. Choice B is correct. During the third week the team won 5 games and lost 2, or it won about 70% of the games that week. Compared with the winning percentages for other weeks, the third week's was the highest.
(Refresher 702)

5. Choice C is correct. To win 70% of all the games, the team must win 70 out of 100. Since it won 29 games out of the first 50 games, it must win $70 - 29$, or 41 games out of the next 50 games.
(Refresher 702)

6. Choice A is correct. East North Central, with 19.7% of the total population, has the largest population.
(Refresher 705)

7. Choice D is correct. The Mountain region has 4.0% of the population. 4.0% is $\frac{1}{25}$.
(Refresher 705)

8. Choice B is correct. Pacific has 12.5% of the population. 12.5% of 191.3 million is $.125 \times 191.3$, or about 24 million.
(Refresher 705)

9. Choice B is correct. Middle Atlantic has 18.8% and South Atlantic has 14.8% of the population. So, Middle Atlantic has 4.0% more. 4.0% of 191.3 million is $.04 \times 191.3$, or about 7.7 million.
(Refresher 705)

10. Choice C is correct. All the regions combined have 100% of the population, or 191.3 million.
(Refresher 705)

11. Choice D is correct. Drawing a vertical line at the end of 2005, we reach the consumer price graph at about the 110 level.
(Refresher 706)

12. Choice E is correct. The slope of the consumer graph is clearly steepest in 2009.
(Refresher 706)

13. Choice A is correct. Wholesale and industrial prices were about 110 at the beginning of 2009, when consumer prices were between 120 and 125.
(Refresher 706)

14. Choice C is correct. At the beginning of 2002 consumer prices were about 105; at the end of 2009 they were about 130. The average increase is $\frac{130 - 105}{8} = \frac{25}{8}$, or about 3 points.
(Refresher 706)

15. Choice D is correct. At the beginning of 2002 wholesale prices were about 100; at the end of 2009 they were about 115. The percent increase is about $\frac{115 - 100}{100} \times 100\%$, or 15%.
(Refresher 706)

16. Choice C is correct. To answer this question, you will have to measure the bars. In 1998, about 8 billion square feet of plywood were produced. In 2007, about 14 billion square feet were produced. The ratio of 8 : 14 is the same as 4 : 7.
(Refresher 704)

17. Choice D is correct. All you have to do is to measure the bar for each year—of course, don't include the 2002 bar—and estimate the length of each bar. Then you add the five lengths. 1998 = 8; 1999 = 10; 2000 = 10; 2001 = 10; 2003 = 12. The total is close to 50.
(Refresher 704)

18. Choice E is correct. The jumps from 2001 to 2003, from 2003 to 2005, and from 2007 to 2009 were all about 2 billion square feet, so you can eliminate answers A and C. The jump from 2002 to 2004 was from 11 to 13.5 = 2.5 billion square feet. None of the other choices shows such broad jumps.
(Refresher 704)

19. Choice B is correct. Total spending was about $14 billion, and company spending was about $8 billion. So, government spending was about $6 billion.
(Refresher 706)

20. Choice D is correct. Company funds totaled about $8 billion, and the total funds were about $14 billion. So, company funds were $\frac{4}{7}$ of total funds, or 57%. (Refresher 706)

21. Choice E is correct. The graph showing the relative employment of research and development scientists and engineers was horizontal between 2004 and 2005. This means no change, or 0%. (Refresher 706)

22. Choice B is correct. Company funds totaled $8 billion in 2007 and $2 billion in 1993. The increase was $6 billion. (Refresher 706)

23. Choice C is correct. Company funds totaled $2 billion in 1993, and the increase from 1993 to 2007 was $6 billion, or 300% of $2 billion. (Refresher 706)

MATH REFRESHER SESSION 8

Modern Math: Sets, Relations, Solution Sets, Axioms, Closed Sets, and Mathematical Symbols

Sets

801. A *set* is a collection of anything: numbers, letters, objects, etc. The members, or elements, of the set are written between braces like this: {1, 2, 3, 4, 5}. The elements of this set are simply the numbers 1, 2, 3, 4, and 5. Another example of a set is {apples, peaches, pears}. Two sets are equal if they have the same elements. The order in which the elements of the set are listed does not matter. Thus {1, 2, 3, 4, 5} = {5, 4, 3, 2, 1}. We can use one letter to stand for a whole set; for example, A = {1, 2, 3, 4, 5}.

802. To find the *union* of two sets:

Write down every member in both of the two sets. The union of two sets is a new set. The union of sets A and B is written $A \cup B$.

For example: If A = {1, 2, 3, 4} and B = {2, 4, 6}, find $A \cup B$. All the elements in both A and B are 1, 2, 3, 4, and 6. Therefore $A \cup B$ = {1, 2, 3, 4, 6}.

803. To find the *intersection* of two sets:

Write down every member that the two sets have in common. The intersection of the sets A and B is a set written $A \cap B$.

Example: If A = {1, 2, 3, 4} and B = {2, 4, 6}, find $A \cap B$. The elements in both A and B are 2 and 4. Therefore $A \cap B$ = {2, 4}.

If two sets have no elements in common, then their intersection is the null or empty set, written as $\varnothing$ or { }.

Example: The intersection of {1, 3, 5, 7} with {2, 4, 6, 8} is $\varnothing$ since they have no members in common.

804. To perform several union and intersection operations, first operate on sets within parentheses.

Example: If A = {1, 2, 3} and B = {2, 3, 4, 5, 6} and C = {1, 4, 6} find $A \cup (B \cap C)$.

First we find $B \cap C$ by listing all the elements in both B and C. $B \cap C$ = {4, 6}.

Then $A \cup (B \cap C)$ is just the set of all members in at least one of the sets A and {4, 6}.

Therefore, $A \cup (B \cap C)$ = {1, 2, 3, 4, 6}.

805. A *subset* of a set is a set, all of whose members are in the original set. Thus, {1, 2, 3} is a subset of the set {1, 2, 3, 4, 5}. Note that the null set (a set with no members) is a subset of every set, and also that every set is a subset of itself. In general, a set with n elements has 2^n subsets. For example: How many subsets does {x, y, z} have? This set has 3 elements and therefore 2^3, or 8 subsets.

Relations

806. When the elements of a set are ordered pairs, then the set is called a *relation*. An ordered pair is written (x, y). The order of the two components of the ordered pair matters. Therefore the ordered pairs (x, y) and (y, x) are not equal.

The *domain* of a relation is the set of the first components of the ordered pairs. The *range* of a relation is the set of the second components of the ordered pairs. A relation is a *function* if each element of the domain occurs only once as a first component.

Example: R = {(a, b), (a, c), (b, c), (c, d)}. Find the domain and range of R. Is the relation R a function?

The domain is the set of first components. These are a, a, b, and c, so that the domain is $\{a, b, c\}$. The range is the set of second components. These are b, c, c, and d. Thus the range is $\{b, c, d\}$. R is not a function since the letter a occurred twice as a first component.

807. The *inverse* of a relation is the relation with all the ordered pairs reversed. Thus, the inverse of $R = \{(1, 2), (3, 4), (5, 6)\}$ is $\{(2, 1), (4, 3), (6, 5)\}$.

Example: Find the domain of the inverse of $\{(m, n), (p, q), (r, s)\}$.

The domain of the inverse is simply the range of the original relation. So, the domain of the inverse is $\{n, q, s\}$. Similarly, the range of the inverse is the domain of the original relation.

Solution Sets

808. Sets can be used to indicate solutions to equations or inequalities. These sets are called *solution sets*. A solution set is just the set of the solutions to an equation. We may also demand that the elements of the solution set meet another condition. Thus, the solution set for the equation $10x - 5 = 0$ is simply $\left\{\frac{1}{2}\right\}$, since only $x = \frac{1}{2}$ solves the equation.

If we demanded that the solution set consist only of whole numbers, then the solution set would be $\varnothing$ since no whole number solves this equation.

The solution set in the positive integers (whole numbers) for the inequality $x < 4$ is $\{1, 2, 3\}$ since these are the only positive integers less than 4.

> When finding a solution set, first solve the equation or inequality and then use only the solutions that satisfy the condition required.

Example: Find the solution set in the positive integers for the inequality $4x < x + 13$.

First, $4x < x + 13$ means $3x < 13$, or $x < 4\frac{1}{3}$. Since x must be a positive integer, the solution set is the set of positive integers less than $4\frac{1}{3}$, or $\{1, 2, 3, 4\}$. Sometimes we use the following notation:

$$R = \{x : x \geq 10\}$$

This would be read as "the set of all x such that x is greater than or equal to 10."

Axioms

809. On your test, there may be a list of *axioms*, or rules, about arithmetical operations with numbers. The list will contain examples of the use of the axioms. Problems will then ask you to identify which axiom is used to make a specific statement. An example of these axioms is the distributive law. A problem may ask you: Which axiom is used to justify $3(4 + 1) = 3 \cdot 4 + 3 \cdot 1$? The *distributive* axiom is used to justify this statement.

Another axiom is the *commutative* axiom of addition and multiplication. The equations $5 + 3 = 3 + 5$ and $5 \cdot 3 = 3 \cdot 5$ illustrate these rules.

The last two rules are the *associative* axioms of addition and multiplication. Examples of these operations are the equations $(3 + 5) + 6 = 3 + (5 + 6)$ and $(3 \cdot 5)6 = 3(5 \cdot 6)$.

Closed Sets

810. A set is called *closed* under an operation if any two members of the set constitute an element of the set. Consider, for example, the set $\{0, 1\}$. This set is closed under the operation of multiplication because $0 \times 0 = 0$, $1 \times 1 = 1$, and $0 \times 1 = 0$. Note that in order for the set to be closed, the elements multiplied by themselves must also be elements of the set $\{0 \times 0 = 0$ and $1 \times 1 = 1\}$.

SESSION 8 PRACTICE TEST

Modern Math: Sets, Relations, Solution Sets, Axioms, Closed Sets, and Mathematical Symbols

Correct answers and solutions follow this test.

Sets Test

1. Which set equals {1, 2, 3, 4}?

   (A) {a, b, c, d}
   (B) {4, 5, 6, 7}
   (C) {1, 3, 5, 7, 9}
   (D) {4, 3, 2, 1}
   (E) none of the above

   A B C D E
   ○ ○ ○ ○ ○

2. $A = \{1, 2, 3, 4, 5\}$. $B = \{2, 4, 6, 8\}$. $A \cap B$ equals

   (A) {1, 2, 3, 4, 5, 6, 7, 8}
   (B) {2, 4}
   (C) {1, 2, 3, 4, 5, 6, 8, 10}
   (D) {9}
   (E) {1, 2, 6, 8}

   A B C D E
   ○ ○ ○ ○ ○

3. $C = \{a, b, c, d\}$. $D = \{3, 4, b\}$. $C \cup D$ equals

   (A) {a, b, c, d, 3, 4}
   (B) {b}
   (C) {3, 4}
   (D) {b, d, 4}
   (E) {a, c, 3, 4}

   A B C D E
   ○ ○ ○ ○ ○

4. $A = \{1, 2, 3\}$. $B = \{2, 3, 4\}$. $C = \{3, 4, 5\}$. $(A \cap B) \cap C$ equals

   (A) {1, 2, 3, 4, 5}
   (B) {1, 3, 5}
   (C) {2, 3, 4}
   (D) {1}
   (E) {3}

   A B C D E
   ○ ○ ○ ○ ○

5. How many elements are there in the set of even integers from 2 through 10 inclusive?

   (A) 3
   (B) 5
   (C) 7
   (D) 9
   (E) 10

   A B C D E
   ○ ○ ○ ○ ○

6. How many subsets does {a, b, c} have?

   (A) 6
   (B) 7
   (C) 8
   (D) 9
   (E) 10

   A B C D E
   ○ ○ ○ ○ ○

Use the following information to answer Questions 7–10.
$A = \{1, 3, 2, 5\}$. $B = \{2, 4, 6\}$. $C = \{1, 3, 5\}$.

7. $(A \cup B) \cap C$ equals

   (A) {1, 2, 3}
   (B) {2, 4, 5}
   (C) {1, 2, 5}
   (D) {1, 3, 5}
   (E) {3, 4, 5}

   A B C D E
   ○ ○ ○ ○ ○

8. $(A \cap B) \cup C$ equals

   (A) {1, 2, 3, 5}
   (B) {4}
   (C) {2, 4}
   (D) {1, 3, 5}
   (E) {1, 2, 3, 4, 5}

   A B C D E
   ○ ○ ○ ○ ○

9. How many subsets does $A \cup (B \cup C)$ have?

   (A) 2
   (B) 4
   (C) 16
   (D) 32
   (E) 64

   A B C D E
   ○ ○ ○ ○ ○

10. Which set is not a subset of $A \cup C$?

   (A) ∅
   (B) A
   (C) C
   (D) {4}
   (E) {1, 2, 5}

   A B C D E
   ○ ○ ○ ○ ○

Relations Test

11. Which of the following sets are relations?

   I.   {(1, 2), (a, c)}
   II. {(3, 8), (8, 3)}
   III. {(1, a), (2, c)}

   (A) I only
   (B) II only
   (C) III only
   (D) I and III only
   (E) I, II, and III

   A B C D E
   ○ ○ ○ ○ ○

12. Which of the following relations equals the relation {(a, b), (1, 2), (x, y)}?

   (A) {(a, b), (1, x), (2, y)}
   (B) {(x, y), (a, b), (1, 2)}
   (C) {(12, xy), (a, b)}
   (D) {(b, a), (2, 1), (x, y)}
   (E) none of the above

   A B C D E
   ○ ○ ○ ○ ○

13. What is the range of {(1, 2), (3, 4), (5, 6)}?

   (A) {1, 2, 3, 4, 5, 6}
   (B) {(1, 2)}
   (C) {(1, 2), (3, 4), (5, 6)}

   (D) {1, 3, 5}
   (E) none of the above

   A B C D E
   ○ ○ ○ ○ ○

14. What is the domain of {(1, 2), (2, 1), (1, 5)}?

   (A) {1, 2}
   (B) {(1, 2)}
   (C) {1, 2, 5}
   (D) {8}
   (E) {3}

   A B C D E
   ○ ○ ○ ○ ○

15. Which relation is a function?

   (A) {(1, 1), (2, 2), (3, 3)}
   (B) {(1, 1), (1, 2), (1, 3)}
   (C) {(a, b), (b, a), (b, b)}
   (D) {(1, 3), (1, 5), (1, 7)}
   (E) {(1, a), (2, b), (2, 1)}

   A B C D E
   ○ ○ ○ ○ ○

16. What is the inverse of {(1, 2), (3, 6), (4, 2)}?

   (A) {1, 2, 3, 4, 5, 6}
   (B) {(1, 3), (1, 4), (1, 6)}
   (C) {(2, 1), (6, 3), (2, 4)}
   (D) {(3, 2), (6, 4), (4, 1)}
   (E) none of the above

   A B C D E
   ○ ○ ○ ○ ○

17. Which relation equals its inverse?

   (A) {(1, 2)}
   (B) {(1, 2), (3, 3)}
   (C) {(1, 2), (3, 3), (2, 1)}
   (D) {(4, 4), (2, 3), (3, 4)}
   (E) {(1, 2), (2, 3), (3, 1)}

   A B C D E
   ○ ○ ○ ○ ○

18. What is the domain of the inverse of {(a, 1), (b, 3), (c, 5)}?

   (A) {a, b, c}
   (B) {1, 3, 5}
   (C) {1, a, 2, b, 3, c}

(D) $\{a, 5\}$

(E) $\{(a, 5)\}$

A B C D E
○ ○ ○ ○ ○
_____

19. The inverse of which of the following is a function?

(A) $\{(1, 1), (1, 2), (1, 3)\}$

(B) $\{(a, 0), (b, 0), (c, 0)\}$

(C) $\{(a, j), (r, j), (a, r)\}$

(D) $\{(1, 2), (2, 3), (3, 2)\}$

(E) $\{(u, v), (w, v), (y, x)\}$

A B C D E
○ ○ ○ ○ ○
_____

20. What is the range of the inverse of $\{(P, Q), (R, S), (T, V)\}$?

(A) $\{1, 2, 3\}$

(B) $\{P, Q, R\}$

(C) $\{Q, S, V\}$

(D) $\{P, R, T\}$

(E) $\{P, Q, R, S, T, V\}$

A B C D E
○ ○ ○ ○ ○
_____

Solution Sets Test

Find the solution sets in Questions 21–23.

21. $2x - 4 = 0$

(A) $\{2\}$

(B) $\{4\}$

(C) $\{-4\}$

(D) $\{0\}$

(E) $\{2, -4\}$

A B C D E
○ ○ ○ ○ ○
_____

22. $x + 9 = 3 - x$

(A) $\{-3\}$

(B) $\{9\}$

(C) $\{3\}$

(D) $\{-3, 9\}$

(E) $\varnothing$

A B C D E
○ ○ ○ ○ ○
_____

23. $(x + 2)(x - 1) = 0$

(A) $\{-1\}$

(B) $\{-2, -1\}$

(C) $\{1\}$

(D) $\{-2, 1\}$

(E) $\{2, 1\}$

A B C D E
○ ○ ○ ○ ○
_____

Find the solution sets in the positive integers for Questions 24–27.

24. $x + 7 = 9$

(A) $\{7\}$

(B) $\{9\}$

(C) $\{16\}$

(D) $\{2\}$

(E) $\{9, 7\}$

A B C D E
○ ○ ○ ○ ○
_____

25. $x - 3 = -4$

(A) $\{-3\}$

(B) $\{-4\}$

(C) $\{1\}$

(D) $\{-1\}$

(E) $\varnothing$

A B C D E
○ ○ ○ ○ ○
_____

26. $x > 2x - 4$

(A) $\{1\}$

(B) $\{2, 3\}$

(C) $\{1, 2, 3\}$

(D) $\{1, 2, 3, 4\}$

(E) $\varnothing$

A B C D E
○ ○ ○ ○ ○
_____

27. $(x + 1)(x - 4) = 0$

(A) $\{4\}$

(B) $\{1, 4\}$

(C) $\{-1, 1, 4\}$

(D) $\{0\}$

(E) $\{-4\}$

A B C D E
○ ○ ○ ○ ○
_____

Find the solution set in the negative integers for Questions 28–30.

28. $(x + 3)(x + 6) = 0$

    (A) $\{3, 6\}$

    (B) $\{-3, -6\}$

    (C) $\{-3\}$

    (D) $\{-6\}$

    (E) $\varnothing$

    A B C D E
    ○○○○○

29. $(2x + 7)(x - 3) = 0$

    (A) $\{2, 7, -3\}$

    (B) $\{-3\}$

    (C) $\left\{-3\frac{1}{2}\right\}$

    (D) $\{2\}$

    (E) $\varnothing$

    A B C D E
    ○○○○○

30. $10 + 2x > 0$

    (A) $\{-1, -2\}$

    (B) $\{-10, -8, -6\}$

    (C) $\{-1, -2, -3, -4, -5\}$

    (D) $\{-1, -2, -3, -4\}$

    (E) $\{1, 2, 3, 4\}$

    A B C D E
    ○○○○○

Axioms Test

Use the following axioms to answer Questions 31–35.

  I. Commutative axiom for addition:
    $a + b = b + a$

  II. Associative axiom for addition:
    $a + (b + c) = (a + b) + c$

  III. Commutative axiom for multiplication:
    $ab = ba$

  IV. Associative axiom for multiplication:
    $(ab)c = a(bc)$

  V. Distributive axiom:
    $a(b + c) = ab + ac$

In Questions 31–34, which axiom can be used to justify the given statements?

31. $3 \cdot 5 = 5 \cdot 3$

    (A) I

    (B) II

    (C) III

    (D) IV

    (E) V

    A B C D E
    ○○○○○

32. $(3 + 7) + 4 = 3 + (7 + 4)$

    (A) I

    (B) II

    (C) III

    (D) IV

    (E) V

    A B C D E
    ○○○○○

33. $(2 \cdot 5) \cdot 3 = (5 \cdot 2) \cdot 3$

    (A) I

    (B) II

    (C) III

    (D) IV

    (E) V

    A B C D E
    ○○○○○

34. $3(6 + 2) = 18 + 6$

    (A) I

    (B) II

    (C) III

    (D) IV

    (E) V

    A B C D E
    ○○○○○

35. Which two axioms can be used to justify the following:

    $5(3 + 4) = 20 + 15$?

    (A) I and II

    (B) I and III

    (C) III and V

    (D) IV and V

    (E) V and I

    A B C D E
    ○○○○○

Answer Key for Session 8 Practice Test

1. D	10. D	19. A	28. B
2. B	11. E	20. D	29. E
3. A	12. B	21. A	30. D
4. E	13. E	22. A	31. C
5. B	14. A	23. D	32. B
6. C	15. A	24. D	33. C
7. D	16. C	25. E	34. E
8. A	17. C	26. C	35. E
9. E	18. B	27. A	

Answers and Solutions for Session 8 Practice Test

1. Choice D is correct. {4, 3, 2, 1} contains the same elements as {1, 2, 3, 4}. Since the order does not matter, the sets are equal. (Refresher 801)

2. Choice B is correct. $A \cap B$ means the set of elements in both A and B, or {2, 4}. (Refresher 803)

3. Choice A is correct. $C \cup D$ means the set of elements in at least one of C and D, or {a, b, c, d, 3, 4}. (Refresher 802)

4. Choice E is correct. $(A \cap B) \cap C$ is the set of elements in all three sets. Only 3 is a member of all three sets, so $(A \cap B) \cap C$ = {3}. (Refresher 803)

5. Choice B is correct. The set of even integers from 2 through 10 inclusive is {2, 4, 6, 8, 10}, which has 5 elements. (Refresher 801)

6. Choice C is correct. {a, b, c} has 3 elements and therefore 2^3, or 8 subsets. (Refresher 805)

7. Choice D is correct. First $(A \cup B)$ = {1, 2, 3, 4, 5, 6}.
Then {1, 2, 3, 4, 5, 6} ∩ {1, 3, 5} = {1, 3, 5}. (Refresher 804)

8. Choice A is correct. First $(A \cap B)$ = {2}.
Then {2} ∪ {1, 3, 5} = {1, 2, 3, 5}. (Refresher 804)

9. Choice E is correct. $A \cup (B \cup C)$ is the set of elements in at least one of the three sets, or {1, 2, 3, 4, 5, 6}, which has 2^6, or 64 subsets. (Refresher 805)

10. Choice D is correct. $A \cup C$ = {1, 2, 3, 5}. Since 4 is not an element of this set, {4} is not a subset of $A \cup C$. (Refreshers 802, 805)

11. Choice E is correct. A set is a relation if all its elements are ordered pairs; I, II, and III meet this condition. (Refresher 806)

12. Choice B is correct. Two relations are equal if their elements are equal. Though it doesn't matter in what order the ordered pairs are listed, if the elements of the ordered pairs are switched, the relation is changed. (Refresher 806)

13. Choice E is correct. The range of a relation is the set of second elements of the ordered pairs. The range of {(1, 2), (3, 4), (5, 6)} is {2, 4, 6}. (Refresher 806)

14. Choice A is correct. The domain is the set of first elements of the ordered pairs. The domain of {(1, 2), (2, 1), (1, 5)} is {1, 2}. (Refresher 806)

15. Choice A is correct. To be a function, a relation must not repeat any of the first elements of its ordered pairs. The first elements of {(1, 1), (2, 2), (3, 3)} are all distinct. (Refresher 806)

16. Choice C is correct. To find the inverse, simply reverse all the ordered pairs. (Refresher 807)

17. Choice C is correct. Reversing (1, 2) we get (2, 1); reversing (3, 3) we get (3, 3); reversing (2, 1) we get (1, 2). Though they are in a different order, the ordered pairs of the inverse of (C) are the same as the ordered pairs of (C). (Refresher 807)

18. Choice B is correct. The domain of the inverse is the range of the relation, or {1, 3, 5}. (Refreshers 806, 807)

19. Choice A is correct. If the inverse of the relation is to be a function, the second elements must all be distinct. The second elements of the ordered pairs of (A) are 1, 2, and 3, all distinct. (Refreshers 806, 807)

20. Choice D is correct. The range of the inverse is the domain of the function, or {P, R, T}. (Refreshers 806, 807)

21. Choice A is correct. $2x - 4 = 0$. $x = 2$, so the solution set is {2}. (Refresher 808)

22. Choice A is correct. $x + 9 = 3 - x$. $2x = -6$, or $x = -3$. The solution set is $\{-3\}$.
    (Refresher 808)

23. Choice D is correct. $(x + 2)(x - 1) = 0$, so $x = -2$ or 1. The solution set is $\{-2, 1\}$.
    (Refresher 808)

24. Choice D is correct. $x + 7 = 9$, or $x = 2$, which is a positive integer. The solution set is $\{2\}$.
    (Refresher 808)

25. Choice E is correct. $x - 3 = -4$, or $x = -1$, which is not a positive integer. The solution set is $\varnothing$.
    (Refresher 808)

26. Choice C is correct. $x > 2x - 4$, or $x < 4$. The positive integers less than 4 are 1, 2, and 3. The solution set is $\{1, 2, 3\}$.
    (Refresher 808)

27. Choice A is correct. $(x + 1)(x - 4) = 0$. $x = -1$, or 4. 4 is a positive integer, but -1 is not, so the solution set is $\{4\}$.
    (Refresher 808)

28. Choice B is correct. $(x + 3)(x + 6) = 0$. $x = -3$, or -6, both of which are negative integers, so the solution set is $\{-3, -6\}$.
    (Refresher 808)

29. Choice E is correct. $(2x + 7)(x - 3) = 0$. $x = -3\frac{1}{2}$, or 3, neither of which is a negative integer. The solution set is $\varnothing$.
    (Refresher 808)

30. Choice D is correct. $10 + 2x > 0$. $2x > -10$ or $x > -5$. The negative integers greater than -5 are $-1, -2, -3$, and -4. The solution set is $\{-1, -2, -3, -4\}$.
    (Refresher 808)

31. Choice C is correct. To go from $3 \cdot 5$ to $5 \cdot 3$, we switch the order of multiplication. The axiom that deals with order of multiplication is the commutative axiom for multiplication, III.
    (Refresher 809)

32. Choice B is correct. Switching parentheses in addition involves the associative axiom for addition, II.
    (Refresher 809)

33. Choice C is correct. To go from $(2 \cdot 5) \cdot 3$ to $(5 \cdot 2) \cdot 3$, we switch the order of multiplying inside the parentheses. This is justified by the commutative axiom for multiplication, III.
    (Refresher 809)

34. Choice E is correct. To go from $3(6 + 2)$ to $3 \cdot 6 + 3 \cdot 2$, or $18 + 6$, we use the distributive axiom, V.
    (Refresher 809)

35. Choice E is correct. To go from $5(3 + 4)$ to $5 \cdot 3 + 5 \cdot 4$, or $15 + 20$, we use the distributive axiom, V. To go from $15 + 20$ to $20 + 15$, we use the commutative axiom of addition, I.
    (Refresher 809)

MATH REFRESHER SESSION 9

Trigonometry

Diagnostic Test on Trigonometry

Questions 1–5 refer to the following diagram:

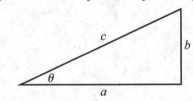

1. $\sin \theta =$

   (A) $\dfrac{a}{b}$

   (B) $\dfrac{b}{c}$

   (C) $\dfrac{a}{c}$

   (D) $\dfrac{c}{b}$

   (E) $\dfrac{b}{a}$

   A B C D E
   ○ ○ ○ ○ ○

2. $\cos \theta =$

   (A) $\dfrac{a}{b}$

   (B) $\dfrac{b}{c}$

   (C) $\dfrac{a}{c}$

   (D) $\dfrac{c}{b}$

   (E) $\dfrac{b}{a}$

   A B C D E
   ○ ○ ○ ○ ○

3. $\tan \theta =$

   (A) $\dfrac{a}{b}$

   (B) $\dfrac{b}{c}$

   (C) $\dfrac{a}{c}$

   (D) $\dfrac{c}{b}$

   (E) $\dfrac{b}{a}$

   A B C D E
   ○ ○ ○ ○ ○

4. $\sin^2 \theta + \cos^2 \theta =$

   (A) 1
   (B) 2
   (C) $\tan \theta$
   (D) $\tan^2 \theta$
   (E) $\dfrac{1}{\tan^2\theta}$

   A B C D E
   ○ ○ ○ ○ ○

5. $1 + \tan^2 \theta =$

   (A) $\dfrac{1}{\cos^2\theta}$
   (B) $\cos^2 \theta$
   (C) $\dfrac{1}{\sin^2\theta}$
   (D) $\sin^2 \theta$
   (E) $\cos^2 \theta$

   A B C D E
   ○ ○ ○ ○ ○

Answers for Diagnostic Test

Refer to the 19 Trig Identities to Know below.

1. Choice B is correct.
   See 19 Trig Identities to Know #1.

2. Choice C is correct.
   See 19 Trig Identities to Know #2.

3. Choice E is correct.
   See 19 Trig Identities to Know #3.

4. Choice A is correct.
   See 19 Trig Identities to Know #7.

5. Choice A is correct.
   See 19 Trig Identities to Know #8.

---

19 Trig Identities to Know

901.

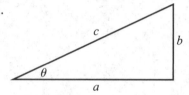

Remember the letter sequence:

S O H C A H T O A

1. **S**in θ = **O**pposite side (from angle θ) divided by **H**ypotenuse (longest side c)

   So we get $\sin \theta = \dfrac{b}{c}$

2. **C**os θ = **A**djacent side (to angle θ) divided by **H**ypotenuse

   So we get $\cos \theta = \dfrac{a}{c}$

3. **T**an θ = **O**pposite side (from angle θ) divided by **A**djacent side

   So we get $\tan \theta = \dfrac{b}{a}$

Other definitions for cotangent θ, secant θ, and cosecant θ are:

4. $\cot \theta = \dfrac{a}{b}$

5. $\sec \theta = \dfrac{c}{a}$

6. $\csc \theta = \dfrac{c}{b}$

$$\sin^2 \theta + \cos^2 \theta = \frac{b^2}{c^2} + \frac{a^2}{c^2} + \frac{(a^2 + b^2)}{c^2} = \frac{c^2}{c^2}$$
$$= 1$$

So

7. $\sin^2 \theta + \cos^2 \theta = 1$

   $$1 + \tan^2 \theta = 1 + \frac{b^2}{a^2} = \frac{(a^2 + b^2)}{a^2} = \frac{c^2}{a^2} = \frac{1}{\cos^2\theta}$$
   $$= \sec^2 \theta$$

So

8. $1 + \tan^2 \theta = \dfrac{1}{\cos^2\theta} = \sec^2 \theta$

   $$\frac{\sin\theta}{\cos\theta} = \frac{\dfrac{b}{c}}{\dfrac{a}{c}} = \frac{b}{a} = \tan \theta$$

So

9. $\dfrac{\sin\theta}{\cos\theta} = \tan \theta$

Other things to know:

10. $\sin(x + y) = \sin(x)\cos(y) + \cos(x)\sin(y)$

11. $\sin(x - y) = \sin(x)\cos(y) - \cos(x)\sin(y)$

12. $\cos(x + y) = \cos(x)\cos(y) - \sin(x)\sin(y)$

13. $\cos(x - y) = \cos(x)\cos(y) + \sin(x)\sin(y)$

You can prove using (10), where $y = x$, and using (12), where $y = x$, that

14. $\sin 2x = 2\sin x \cos x$

15. $\cos 2x = \cos^2 x - \sin^2 x = 1 - 2\sin^2 x$

Also note:

16. $\cos \dfrac{x}{2} = \pm\sqrt{\dfrac{1 + \cos x}{2}}$

and

17. $\sin \dfrac{x}{2} = \pm\sqrt{\dfrac{1 - \cos x}{2}}$

18. $\cos(-x) = +\cos x$

19. $\sin(-x) = -\sin x$

SESSION 9 PRACTICE TEST

Trigonometry

Refer to the following diagrams for questions 1–5:

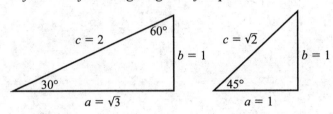

1. sin 30° =

   (A) $\frac{1}{2}$

   (B) $\frac{1}{\sqrt{3}}$

   (C) $\frac{\sqrt{3}}{2}$

   (D) $\sqrt{3}$

   (E) 2

   A B C D E
   ○ ○ ○ ○ ○

2. sin 60° =

   (A) $\frac{1}{2}$

   (B) $\frac{1}{\sqrt{3}}$

   (C) $\frac{\sqrt{3}}{2}$

   (D) $\sqrt{3}$

   (E) 2

   A B C D E
   ○ ○ ○ ○ ○

3. tan 30° =

   (A) $\frac{1}{2}$

   (B) $\frac{1}{\sqrt{3}}$

   (C) $\frac{\sqrt{3}}{2}$

   (D) $\sqrt{3}$

   (E) 2

   A B C D E
   ○ ○ ○ ○ ○

4. tan 45° =

   (A) 1

   (B) $\sqrt{2}$

   (C) 2

   (D) $\frac{1}{2}$

   (E) $\frac{1}{4}$

   A B C D E
   ○ ○ ○ ○ ○

5. sin 45° =

   (A) 1

   (B) $\frac{1}{\sqrt{2}}$

   (C) 2

   (D) $\frac{1}{2}$

   (E) $\frac{1}{4}$

   A B C D E
   ○ ○ ○ ○ ○

Answers and Solutions for Session 9
Practice Test

1. Choice A is correct. $\sin 30° = \dfrac{1}{2}$

2. Choice C is correct. $\sin 60° = \dfrac{\sqrt{3}}{2}$

3. Choice B is correct. $\tan 30° = \dfrac{1}{\sqrt{3}}$

4. Choice A is correct. $\tan 45° = 1$

5. Choice B is correct. $\sin 45° = \dfrac{1}{\sqrt{2}}$

PART 7

A Brief Review of English Grammar

FREQUENT GRAMMATICAL PROBLEMS

Split Infinitive

By the 17th century English had developed a two-word infinitive—*to go*, *to run*, *to talk*, etc. The word *to* was coupled with the verb and stood next to it. Since the Latin infinitive was always treated as one word, scholars decided that the infinitive in English must also be treated as one word. It was considered an error to split these two words by inserting an adverb between them.

But English isn't Latin, so people went on splitting the infinitive whenever it suited their purpose. And we've been doing it ever since.

It isn't necessary to split the infinitive deliberately, of course, but if it sounds better or seems more natural or will add emphasis, then do so. The following sentence is an example of a permissible split infinitive: "After they had won the baseball trophy, they went to the party *to proudly display* their prize." (*Proudly to display* or *to display proudly* makes the sentence stiff. And *they went proudly to the party to display their prize* changes the original meaning.)

Ending a Sentence with a Preposition

The old "rule" that you should never end a sentence with a preposition was another attempt to force Latin on English, and it also is fading out. Often, to avoid this "error," we have to write a much longer and more awkward sentence.

Which sounds better?

This is a rule up with which I won't put.

This is a rule I won't put up with.

Clearly the second example is easier to understand. The choice should be made on the basis of clarity and ease of understanding; sometimes it is better to move the preposition closer to the word or phrase that goes with it:

Acceptable: That is the group I traveled with.

Preferable: That is the group with which I traveled.

Distinction Between "Shall" and "Will"

Formal usage required *shall* in the first person and *will* in the second and third person when forming the simple future. For the emphatic future, these were reversed. Today most of us use *will* in all persons for both simple and emphatic future.

"It Is I"

This question of which pronoun to use probably causes more uncertainty than any other problem in grammar. We do not change the form of a noun, whether we use it as a subject or as an object. But we do have different forms for our pronouns.

For example, *I, you, he, they, we,* etc., are the nominative forms and are used as subjects. *Me, you, him, them, us,* etc., are the objective forms. Normally we use the objective form after a verb, but after the *be* verbs (*am, is, are, was, will be,* etc.) we have traditionally used the nominative form; thus, *it is I* rather than *it is me.*

Usage, however, is divided on this. In informal conversation we often say, "It's me," just as the French do—"*C'est moi.*" The argument for this usage is pretty sound. The predicate is thought of as object territory, and it feels strange to us to use the nominative form here. Still, the traditional use of this form has come to be regarded as a sign of the well-educated individual. So, until "It is me" has become more widely accepted, we should continue to use "It is I."

Examples of the nominative forms for other pronouns may prove helpful:

It was he (not *it was him*)

This is she (not *this is her*)

Had it been they (not *had it been them*)

There should be no question about using the objective case of the pronoun after other verbs. "The chairman appointed *him* and *me*" is considered correct, not "The chairman appointed *he* and *I*." But often in trying to avoid this decision we make an even worse error. Instead of the objective form we use the reflexive—*myself*, *himself*, etc. "He appointed John and myself" is definitely wrong. "He appointed John and me" is correct.

"Who" versus "Whom"

The pronoun *who* is used for the subject and *whom* is used for the object.

Give the letter to *whoever* answers the door (not to *whomever* . . .). The pronoun *whoever* is the subject of its clause.

Tell me *whom* you borrowed the money from (not *who . . . from*). The pronoun *whomever* is the object of the preposition *from*.

The pronoun *who* used as the subject of a verb is not affected by a parenthetical expression such as *I think*, *he believes*, or *they say* intervening between the subject and the verb.

He is the person *who* I think is best qualified.

Mr. Jameson is the attorney *who* we suppose will prepare the brief.

Adverbs and Adjectives

We seem to have more trouble with adverbs than with adjectives. A simple guide is this: An *adverb* may modify a verb, another adverb, or an adjective; an *adjective* may modify only a noun or a pronoun.

Our biggest problem comes in confusing adjectives and adverbs. For example, we may use the adjective *good* when we should use the adverb *well*:

Poor: The engines are running *good*.

Proper: The engines are running *well*.

Note: Both *good* and *well* may be used after a linking verb as predicate adjectives. For example: "I feel good" indicates a state of well-being, but "I feel well" indicates either that you are not sick or that your ability to use your sense of touch is above average.

It is also important to remember that some irregular adverbs take the same form as their adjectival counterparts:

Adverb: He ran *fast*.

Adjective: He was a *fast* runner.

COMMON ERRORS IN GRAMMAR

Most of us do not have too much trouble writing grammatically acceptable sentences. We just habitually follow the basic word order. But sometimes we get careless or we fall into bad habits. When we do, we can interfere with the meaning and with the movement of our sentences.

Here are some common grammatical errors that may confuse a reader. The errors may be so simple that the reader quickly sees the error, revises the sentence in his mind, and gets the proper message. But this is the writer's job, not the reader's. Too often the reader won't catch the error and will get the wrong idea about what the writer is trying to say.

Misplaced Modifiers

1. Avoid dangling modifiers. When a word or phrase seems to modify another word that it cannot logically modify, we say it has been left dangling. Usually it will be a phrase beginning the sentence. From its position we expect it to modify the subject. But the connection is illogical.

Confusing: Approaching the flight line from the east side, the operations building can be easily seen. (The operations building obviously does not approach the flight line.)

Improved: A person approaching the flight line from the east side can easily see the operations building.

Confusing: To make a climbing turn, the throttle is opened wider. (The throttle does not make the turn.)

Improved: To make a climbing turn, open the throttle wider. (The sentence is in the imperative mode, so the subject *you* is understood.)

2. Keep your modifiers close to the words they modify. Sometimes we widely separate a modifier from its modified word and end up confusing the reader.

Confusing: It was impossible to find the book I had been reading in the dark.

Improved: In the dark it was impossible to find the book I had been reading.

Confusing: He had marked on the map the places where we were to watch for turns in red ink.

Improved: He marked on the map in red ink the places where we were to watch for turns.

3. Avoid using "squinting" modifiers that may refer to either of two parts of a sentence. A squinting modifier is so placed in a sentence that it could logically modify either the words that came before it or the words that follow it; it "squints" both ways. This may confuse the reader, who may not realize the ambiguity and may misinterpret the intended meaning.

Confusing: Personnel who drive their cars to work only occasionally can count on finding a parking space.

Improved: Only occasionally can personnel who drive their cars to work count on finding a parking space.

Confusing: The electrician said Wednesday he would repair the light. (Did he make the statement on Wednesday, or did he say that he would repair the light on Wednesday?)

Improved: Wednesday the electrician said he would repair the light.
or
The electrician said that he would repair the light on Wednesday.

By misplacing modifiers we make it easy for the reader to misunderstand the meaning of our sentences, sometimes with dire results. We can eliminate such errors by reading and revising our writing before we release it. Don't confuse your reader or make him do your work. Keep your modifiers close to the words they modify.

Confusing Pronouns and Other Reference Words

1. Make sure that a pronoun agrees in number with the noun it refers to.

   Confusing: Though there may be different teacher unions, the policy of *its* delegates should be similar.

   Improved: Though there may be different teacher unions, the policies of *their* delegates should be similar.

2. Make sure a pronoun or other reference word has a definite and clearly understood antecedent. We often use words or pronouns such as *which, the latter, the former, this, it,* etc., to refer to something we have previously mentioned. This reference must be clear to the reader.

   Confusing: A piece of thread dangled over his belt that was at least eight inches long.

   Improved: A piece of thread that was at least eight inches long dangled over his belt.

   Confusing: The president told the executive he would handle all personnel assignments.

   Improved: The president told the executive to handle all personnel assignments.
   or
   The president told the executive that he, the president, would handle all personnel assignments.

Nonparallel Structure

Express parallel ideas in words with the same grammatical construction. Nothing sounds quite so disorganized in writing as structure that is not parallel.

   Not Parallel: Briefly, the functions of a staff are to advise the general manager, transmit her instructions, and the supervision of the execution of her decisions.

   Parallel: Briefly, the functions of a staff are to advise the general manager, transmit her instructions, and supervise the execution of her decisions.

   Not Parallel: I have learned three things: that one should not argue about legalisms, never expect miracles, and the impropriety of using a singular verb with a compound subject.

   Parallel: I have learned three things: never argue about legalisms, never expect miracles, and never use a singular verb with a compound subject.

   Not Parallel: She was both excited about the project and its potential to help the children.

   Parallel: She was excited about both the project and its potential to help the children.

   Not Parallel: He claimed either that he was sick or injured.

   Parallel: He claimed either that he was sick or that he was injured.

   Parallel: He claimed that he was either sick or injured.

SOME BASIC GRAMMATICAL TERMS

Parts of Speech

Nouns

Names of people, things, qualities, acts, ideas, relationships: *General Smith, Texas, aircraft, confusion, running, predestination, grandfather.*

Pronouns

Words that refer indirectly to nouns: *he, she, that, which, it, someone.*

Adjectives

Words that point out or indicate a quality of nouns or pronouns: *big, lowest, cold, hard.*

Prepositions

Words that link nouns and pronouns to other words by showing the relationship between them: *to, by, between, above, behind, about, of, in, on, from.*

Conjunctions

Words used to join other words, phrases, and clauses: *and, but, however, because, although.*

Verbs

Words that express action or indicate a state, feeling, or simply existence: *go, hate, fly, feel, is.*

Adverbs

Words that indicate a degree of quality or that tell how, where, when, or to what degree acts were performed: *slowly, well, today, much, very.* Adverbs modify verbs, adjectives, and adverbs.

Don runs *slowly.* (modifies verb)

Emily is an *extremely* gifted pianist. (modifies adjective)

Eric skates *incredibly* well. (modifies adverb)

Note: Many of our words can serve as more than one part of speech. Some words may be used as nouns, adjectives, and verbs without any change in spelling: *Drinking* coffee is a popular pastime; He broke the *drinking* glass; The boy *is drinking* a glass of milk. Often words may be both adjectives and adverbs: *better, well, fast.* Ordinarily we add -*ly* to words to form adverbs, while adjectives may be formed by adding -*able*, -*ly*, -*ing*, -*al*, -*ese*, -*ful*, -*ish*, -*ous*, -*y*, etc. But these endings are not always necessary: *college* (noun); *college boy* (noun used as an adjective to modify the noun *boy*).

OTHER GRAMMATICAL TERMS

Subject

A noun or pronoun (or word or phrase used as a noun) that names the actor in a sentence. The term may be used in a broader sense to include all of the words that are related to the actor.

Predicate

The verb with its modifiers and its object or complement.

Predicate complement

A noun or adjective completing the meaning of a linking verb and modifying the subject.

Jones is *chief* (noun). He was *pale* (adjective).

Linking verb

A verb with little or no meaning of its own that usually indicates a state of being or condition. It functions chiefly to connect the subject with an adjective or noun in the predicate. The most common linking verb is the verb *to be* (*am, are, is, was, were, had been*), but there are others.

He *feels* nervous.

He *acts* old.

He *seems* tired.

Clause

A grammatical unit that is part of a complex or compound sentence and has a subject, a verb, and often an object. "Nero killed Agrippina" is a clause but is not ordinarily called one because it is a complete sentence. In the compound sentence *"Nero killed Agrippina*, but *he paid the penalty,"* each italicized group of words is an independent clause. In the complex sentence

"Because he killed Agrippina, Nero paid the penalty," the italicized clause is made dependent or subordinate by the word *because;* it depends upon the rest of the sentence for the complete meaning.

Phrase

Two or more words without a subject and predicate that function as a grammatical unit in a clause or sentence. A phrase may modify another word or may be used as a noun or verb. For example: *beside the radiator, approaching the pier, to fly a kite.*

Verbals

Words made from verbs but used as other parts of speech:

Gerund: a verb used as a noun:
  Swimming was his favorite sport.

Participle: a verb used as an adjective:
  The aircraft *piloted* by Colonel Jones has crashed.

Infinitive: a verb used as a noun, adjective, or adverb:
  To travel is my greatest pleasure. (infinitive used as a noun)

  We have four days *to spend* at home. (infinitive used as an adjective)

  Bruce was glad *to have joined.* (infinitive used as an adverb)

Superlative degree

Indicates the quality described by the adverb, which exists in the greatest or least degree for one person or thing.

Ben works *most carefully* when someone is watching.

COMMON GRAMMATICAL ERRORS CLASSIFIED BY PART OF SPEECH

Nouns

Incorrect form to express plural number:
> *He shot two deers.*

Correction:
> He shot two *deer.*

Incorrect form of the possessive case:
> *Two boy's heads and two sheeps' heads.*

Correction:
> Two *boys'* heads and two *sheep's* heads.

Use of the objective case for the possessive:
> *I was sorry to hear of John doing wrong.*

Correction:
> I was sorry to hear of *John's* doing wrong.

Pronouns

Pronoun *I* placed incorrectly:
> *I and my sister will attend the concert.*

Correction:
> My sister and *I* will attend the concert.

Use of compound personal pronoun for simple personal pronoun:
> *Sam and myself will do it.*

Correction:
> Sam and *I* will do it.

Incorrect choice of relative pronoun:
> *I have a dog who barks at night.*
> *This is the person which did the wrong.*
> *This is the house what Jack built.*
> *Columbus, that discovered America, was an Italian.*

Correction:
> I have a dog *that* barks at night.
> This is the person *who* did the wrong.
> This is the house *that* Jack built.
> Columbus, *who* discovered America, was an Italian.

Lack of agreement between pronoun and antecedent:
> *Every one of the pupils lost their books.*

Correction:
> Every one of the pupils lost *his or her* book.

Incorrect case form:
> *The book is your's or his'. I recognize it's cover.*

Correction:
> The book is *yours* or *his.* I recognize *its* cover.

Use of nominative case for objective:
> *Give it to Kate and I.*
> *I knew it to be she.*

Correction:
> Give it to Kate and *me.*
> I knew it to be *her.*

Use of objective case for nominative:
> *Him and me are brothers.*
> *Whom do you suppose she is?*
> *It was her.*

Correction:
> *He* and *I* are brothers.
> *Who* do you suppose she is?
> It was *she.*

Use of objective case for possessive:
> *There is no chance of me being chosen.*

Correction:
> There is no chance of *my* being chosen.

Redundant use:
> *John, he tried, and then Mary, she tried.*

Correction:
> John *tried,* and then Mary *tried.*

Ambiguous use:
> *The man told his son to take his coat to the tailor.*

Correction:
> The man told his son to take *his (the man's)* coat to the tailor.

Verbs and Verbals

Use of the indicative mood for the subjunctive:

I wish I was you.

Correction:

I wish I *were* you.

Use of the subjunctive mood for the indicative:

If the cavern were of artificial construction, considerable pains had been taken to make it look natural.

Correction:

If the cavern *was* of artificial construction, considerable pains had been taken to make it look natural.

Use of incorrect form to express tense:

I done it.
He seen it.
She come late yesterday.
I see him last week.
The boy has went home.
My hands were froze.
He teached me all I know.
I ain't seen it.

Correction:

I *did* it.
He *saw* it.
She *came* late yesterday.
I *saw* him last week.
The boy *has gone* home.
My hands were *frozen*.
He *taught* me all I know.
I *haven't seen* it.

Error in sequence of tenses:

I meant, when first I came, to have bought all the parts.
He did not know that mercury was a metal.

Correction:

I meant, when first I came, *to buy* all the parts.
He did not know that mercury *is* a metal.

Lack of agreement between verb and subject:

Was you glad to see us?
Neither he nor she have ever been there.
It don't cost much.

Correction:

Were you glad to see us?
Neither he nor she *has* ever been there.
It *doesn't* cost much.

Use of incorrect forms of principal parts of certain verbs (e.g., *sit* and *lie*):

The hen sets on the eggs.
The book lays on the table.
It laid there yesterday.
It has laid there all week.

Correction:

The hen *sits* on the eggs.
The book *lies* on the table.
It *lay* there yesterday.
It *has lain* there all week.

Use of adjective participle without modified word:

Coming into the room, a great noise was heard.

Correction:

Coming into the room, *I* heard a great noise.

Adjectives

Omission of article:

The noun and pronoun are inflected.

Correction:

The noun and *the* pronoun are inflected.

Use of superfluous article:

I do not like this kind of a story.

Correction:

I do not like this *kind of* story.

Use of *a* for *an* and *an* for *a*:

This is an universal custom.
I should like a apple.

Correction:

This is *a* universal custom.
I should like *an* apple.

Use of adverb for predicate adjective:

She looks nicely.

Correction:

She looks *nice*.

Lack of agreement between certain adjectives and the words they modify:

I do not like these kind of grapes.

Correction:

I do not like *this kind* of grapes.

Incorrect forms of comparison:

His ways have become eviler.

Correction:

His ways have become *more evil*.

Use of comparative form not accompanied by certain necessary words:

He is shorter than any boy in his class.

Correction:

He is shorter than any *other* boy in his class.

Use of superlative form accompanied by certain superfluous words:

This is of all others the most important.

Correction:

This is the most important.

Use of double comparative or superlative form:

She is more kinder than you.

Correction:

She is *kinder* than you.

Incorrect placement of adjective phrases and clauses:

The mariner shot the bird with an unfeeling heart.

Correction:

With an unfeeling heart, the mariner shot the bird.

Adverbs

Use of adjective for adverb:

She sings real well.

Correction:

She sings *really* well.

Incorrect use of double negatives:

I cannot go no faster.

Correction:

I cannot go *any* faster.

Incorrect placement of adverbs and of adverbial phrases and clauses:

I only came yesterday, and I go today.

Correction:

I came *only* yesterday, and I go today.

Prepositions

Incorrect choice of prepositions:

I walked from the hall in the room.
Divide this between the three boys.
I was to New York today.

Correction:

I walked from the hall *into* the room.
Divide this *among* the three boys.
I was *in* New York today.

Omission of preposition:

She is an example of what a person in good health is capable.

Correction:

She is an example of what a person in good health is capable *of.*

Use of a superfluous preposition:

The book in which the story appears in is mine.

Correction:

The book in which the story appears *is mine.*

Conjunctions

Incorrect choice of words as conjunctions, especially *like* for *as* and *as* for *whether:*

I cannot write like you do.
I don't know as I can go.

Correction:

I cannot write *as* you do.
I don't know *whether* I can go.

Incorrect choice of correlatives:

Neither this or that will do.

Correction:

Neither this *nor* that will do.

Use of a superfluous conjunction:

I have no doubt but that he will come.
This is a fine picture and which all will admire.

Correction:

I have no doubt *that* he will come.
This is a fine picture, *which* all will admire.

Incorrect placement of correlatives:

He is neither disposed to sanction bloodshed nor deceit.

Correction:

He is disposed to sanction *neither* bloodshed nor deceit.

PART 8

Complete ACT Grammar and Usage Refresher

The following pages will prove very helpful since you will find in these pages a brief but to-the-point review for almost every type of English grammar and usage question that appears on the actual ACT. These are the areas covered in this study section:

Sentence Sense	(SS)
Parts of Speech	(PS)
Phrases	(PH)
Clauses	(CL)
Sentence Logic	(SL)
Sentence Coherence	(SC)
Word Effectiveness	(WE)

SENTENCE SENSE

What Is Sentence Sense?

SS-1

Knowing what a sentence is and how its parts relate to one another is called *sentence sense.* All language skills, and most thinking skills, begin with sentence sense.

How the Sentence Expresses Thought

SS-2

The sentence expresses thought by naming some *person, place,* or *thing* and relating that person, place, or thing to an *action* or *state of being.* Sometimes the action expressed needs a completing word or phrase called a *complement.*

Consider the following sentences:

1. Professor Sanchez will return.
2. The campfire is lit.
3. Each student will carry a laptop.
4. Middletown is where the company is headquartered.
5. The sunset is beautiful.

The words underlined once name some person, place, or thing. These words are called *subjects.*

The words underlined twice relate that person, place, or thing to an action or state of being. These words are called *verbs.*

The words underlined three times provide the completion needed in sentences 3, 4, and 5. These words are called *complements.*

The sentence expresses thought by naming a *subject,* relating that subject to a *verb,* and—when necessary—completing the thought with a *complement.*

The Subject

SS-3

Naming "Professor Sanchez," "campfire," "student," "Middletown," or "sunset" calls a person, place, or thing to the reader's attention. In "Professor Sanchez

will return," the words "Professor Sanchez" cause the reader to think of a certain professor. In "The campfire is lit," the word "campfire" causes the reader to think of a campfire. The reader knows by the positions of "Professor Sanchez" and "campfire" in these sentences that these sentences will say something about "Professor Sanchez" and the "campfire," respectively.

The reader focuses on "Professor Sanchez," "campfire," "student," "Middletown," or "sunset" and prepares to hear a statement (a) because these words name persons, places, or things and (b) because these words hold certain positions in their sentences.

The Verb

SS-4

Placing "will return," "is lit," "will carry," or "is" in the sentence calls a certain action or state of being to the reader's attention. In "Professor Sanchez will return," the words "will return" cause the reader to think of the action "returning." In "Middletown is where the company is headquartered," the word "is" causes the reader to think of a state of being. The reader knows by the positions of "will return" and "is" that these words express the *action* that involves "Professor Sanchez" and the *being* that involves "Middletown."

The Complement

SS-5

Placing the words "laptop," "home," and "beautiful" in sentences 3, 4, and 5 completes the thoughts initiated by subjects and verbs. The subject and verb "Each student will carry . . . " initiate a thought but do not complete that thought. The subject and verb "Middletown is . . . " initiate a thought but do not complete that thought. The subject and verb "The sunset is . . . " initiate a thought but do not complete that thought. Each of these sentences needs a "completer," or *complement.*

When the reader sees the word "laptop" after "will carry," the word calls a certain thing to his attention, a laptop. The reader relates "laptop" to "will carry" and rounds out the thought "Each student will carry a laptop."

When the reader sees the word "headquartered" after "is," the word calls a certain place to his attention, the company's headquarters. The reader relates "company's headquarters" to "is" and rounds out the thought "Middletown is where the company is headquartered."

When the reader sees the word "beautiful" after the verb "is," the word calls a certain quality to his attention, beautiful. The reader relates "beautiful" to "is" and rounds out the thought "The sunset is beautiful."

Note how the word "is" requires either a naming word or a word that describes a naming word to complete its meaning in the *complement* blank.

Word Order, Word Meaning, and Sentence Thought

SS-6

The sentence expresses thought through the word order and through the meanings that words bring into the sentence.

First: Master the Verb

SS-7

The first element to master in the subject-verb-complement pattern is the verb. The verb is the easiest element to identify in the sentence. The verb is the most important element in the sentence. As an *action* or *being* word, the verb gives the sentence movement and life.

Verbs Look Different from Other Kinds of Words

Examine the following sentences and note how the verbs differ from other words:

PJ <u>studies</u> his notes.

I <u>study</u> history.

The test <u>was passed</u> by all students.

He <u>eats</u> in the cafeteria.

Madison <u>will eat</u> in the new restaurant.

Taylor <u>ate</u> in the fraternity house.

I <u>am</u> early.

I <u>was</u> late.

We <u>are</u> hungry.

Lindsay <u>will be</u> tired after the drive.

In each of these sentences, the *action* or *being* is plainly centered in the verb. Whether the verb expresses *action* or *being,* that verb has a liveliness not found in the other words. In addition, the verb changes its shape (*inflects*) more often than other words. Note how "studies" in one sentence becomes "study" in the next. Note the changes "eats," "will eat," and "ate." Note "am," "was," "are," and "will be."

Action Verbs

SS-8

You can identify the action verbs "studies," "study," "was passed," "eats," "will eat," and "ate" very easily, because these words express action. Consider "PJ studies his lecture notes." Is "PJ" an action word? No. Is "studies" an action word? *Yes,* the action "studies" is happening. Is "his" an action word? No. Is "notes" an action word? No—not in this case. The word that expresses the action in "PJ studies his notes" is "studies." "Studies" is the verb in "PJ studies his notes."

In the sentence "The test was passed by the students," the action is centered in "was passed." What action occurs in the sentence? *Answer:* The action of passing expressed in "was passed." "Was passed" is the verb.

Being Verbs

SS-9

You can identify verbs that express *states of being*— "am," "was," "are," and "will be"—even more quickly. These words all belong to the same family, the verb *to be.*

Middletown *is* where the company is headquartered.

Middletown *was* where the company had its headquarters.

Middletown *has been* where the company was headquartered for years.

Middletown *will be* where the company is headquartered for many years to come.

You can recognize these verbs by the way they *link* the subject with the complement.

Consider, for example, "Middletown is where the company is headquartered." The verb "is" serves as a kind of equals sign (=). "Middletown *is* where the company is headquartered" is similar to "3 × 3 = 9" in arithmetic. "Middletown is the company's headquarters" means "Middletown = the company's headquarters" or "Middletown is the same thing as the company's headquarters."

When we say, "The sunset is a beauty," we are actually linking "sunset" and "beauty" and saying "The *sunset* equals a *beauty*" or "The *sunset* is the same thing as a *beauty*."

In the sentence "The sunset is beautiful," the verb "is" links "sunset" with the describing word "beautiful." Again, "is" links the subject with a describing word in the way an equals sign links numbers in arithmetic—"2 + 2 = 4"; "the sunset = beautiful." When we say, "Middletown is prosperous," we link "Middletown" with "prosperous"—"*Middletown* = *prosperous*," placing in full-sentence emphasis the idea "prosperous Middletown."

Verb Inflection

SS-10

You can identify verbs by the way they change their shapes. When a word changes its shape to say something special, that change of shape is called an *inflection*.

Verbs inflect more often than any other word in the language. You can identify verbs by their frequency of inflection. You can identify verbs by their patterns of inflection.

Note some of these more common patterns of inflection that appear when verbs change shape to indicate *tense, person, number,* and *voice*.

SS-11

Tense. Verbs inflect to indicate the time of action or being. The form a verb takes to indicate the time of the action or state of being is called *tense*.

Consider "PJ *studies* his notes." The verb "studies" is shaped, or inflected, to tell us that this studying is occurring now. If John did this studying in the past, the verb would be shaped "studied." If PJ intended to do this studying in the future, the verb would be shaped "will study."

Compare "He *eats* in the cafeteria," "Madison *will eat* in the new restaurant," and "Taylor *ate* in the fraternity house." Compare "I *am* early," "I *was* late," and "Lindsay *will be* tired after the drive."

Verbs tell time by their shapes. When you can tell the time by the shape of a word, you can feel fairly certain that the word is a verb.

SS-12

Person and Number. Verbs inflect to tell us whether the subject is the *person speaking* (the first person), the *person spoken to* (the second person), or the *person or thing discussed* (the third person). These inflections indicate the *person* of the subject.

Compare "I *study* history" with "PJ *studies* history." Compare "I *have studied* history for an hour" with "PJ *has studied* history for an hour."

Verbs inflect to tell whether certain subjects are *singular* (one person or thing) or *plural* (more than one person or thing). Compare "I am" with "We are." Compare "PJ studies" with "They study." This change of shape is called inflection to indicate *number*.

SS-13

Voice. Verbs inflect to tell us whether the subject is the *doer* or *receiver* of verb action. Compare "The students passed the test" with "The test was passed by the students." In "The students passed the test," the subject "students" is the doer of the verb action. In "The test was passed by the students," the subject "test" is the receiver of the verb action. In the first of these two sentences, the shape of the verb "passed" tells us that the subject is the *doer* of the action. This inflection of the verb is called the *active voice*. In the second of these two sentences, the shape of the verb "was passed" tells us that the subject is the *receiver* of the verb action. This inflection of the verb is called the *passive voice*.

The Verb Is the Most Important Word in the Sentence

SS-14

You must learn how to identify verbs because it is the verb that turns the sentence into a thought. *Action verbs* supply the movement in many thoughts. *Being verbs* link other sentence parts in a relationship. The verb relates all the other words of the sentence into a full thought.

A *subject* is a *subject* because it ties to a verb. Consider "PJ" in "PJ studies his notes." "PJ" is the subject because it tells *who* or *what* was involved in the verb action "studies."

A *complement* is a *complement* because (a) it receives verb action or (b) it is linked by the verb to the subject. Consider "Each student will carry a notebook." "A notebook" is a complement because it receives the action of "will carry." Consider "Middletown is where the company is headquartered." "Company's headquarters" is a complement because it is linked to "Middletown" by the verb "is." Consider "The sunset is beautiful." "Beautiful" is a complement because it is linked to "the sunset" by the verb "is."

Second: Master the Subject

SS-15

The second element to master in the subject-verb-complement tie is the *subject*. The subject is important because the reader must know the *who* or *what* of verb action or being. If the reader does not know this *who* or *what,* the thought is incomplete. If we write the verb "arrives" without a subject, the reader will ask, "*Who* arrives? *What* arrives?" The answer to this question is always the name of some person, place, or thing.

The Subject Always Tells *Who* or *What* Is Involved in Verb Action or Being

SS-16

Once you have located the verb, you can easily find the subject by asking yourself, "Who is the person involved in this verb action or state of being?" "What place or thing is involved in this verb action or state of being?" The answer to one of these questions will indicate the subject.

The Subject Is Always a *Noun* or *Noun Equivalent*—Name of a Person, Place, or Thing

SS-17

The subject of a verb always names some person, place, or thing, directly or indirectly. A word or word group that names a person, place, or thing is called a *noun*. For example, the word "student" is a noun. The word group "Professor Sanchez" is a noun.

Some words present persons, places, or things indirectly. Consider "Professor Sanchez called and *he* asked for Reese." The word "he" takes the place of the noun "Professor Sanchez." Words like *I, you, he, she, it, we, they, who,* and *which* can all take the place of nouns. A word that takes the place of a noun is called a *pronoun*. A pronoun is a noun equivalent.

Third: Master the Complement

SS-18

The third element to master in the subject-verb-complement tie is the *complement*. If you are to write effectively, you must know whether a subject and predicate relationship needs a complement.

For example, "The salesperson arrives" does *not* need a complement, but "The salesperson meets," "The client is," and "The salesperson is" *do* need complements.

If you are to write effectively, you must know *what kind* of complement is needed. For example, "client" in "The salesperson meets the *client*" is a *direct object* of the verb "meets." "Cook" in "The client is a *cook*" is a *predicate noun.* "Angry" in "The salesperson is *angry*" is a *predicate adjective.*

Objects

SS-19

As we noted, many verbs like *carry, hit,* or *open* require a receiver of action. For example, the subject and verb "Each student will carry . . ." does not form a thought until a receiver is supplied for the verb action of "will carry." The subject and verb "The traveler requested . . ." do not form a thought until a receiver is supplied for the verb action of "requested." The name of a person, place, or thing (noun, pronoun, or other noun equivalent) that tells *what* each student will carry or *what* the traveler requested is a *direct object.*

Some sentences have *indirect objects* as well as direct objects. Consider the sentence "The doctor gives the patient a prescription." The direct object of the verb "gives" is "a prescription." However, the doctor gives this prescription to a patient. We could say, "The doctor gives a prescription to the patient," but our language permits us take a shortcut: "The doctor gives [to the a patient a prescription." The words "the patient" form an indirect object in the sentence "The doctor gives *the patient* a prescription."

The best way to identify indirect objects is to watch for the pattern in "The doctor gives the patient a prescription." This indirect object pattern is used often, but it usually involves the verb "give" or verbs that suggest something that is done for someone. "The doctor sold *her neighbor* a car," "The doctor built *her family* a home," and "The doctor brought *her patients* great care." The indirect object has a "to" or "for" understood—"The doctor sold [to] her neighbor a car," "The doctor built [for] her family a home."

Predicate Nouns and Predicate Pronouns

SS-20

As we noted, the verb *to be* (*is, are, was, has been, will be*) expresses a state of being rather than action. This verb, as we also noted, links the subject with the complement. For example, the verb "is" in the sentence "The sunset is a beauty" links the word "beauty" to the subject "sunset." When we say, "The sunset is a beauty," we mean "the sunset = a beauty."

The name of a person, place, or thing linked to the subject by the verb *to be* is called a *predicate noun.* The word *predicate* refers to the verb area of the sentence.

The verb *to be* can also link a pronoun to the subject—"The cheerleaders are we." The predicate pronoun is discussed later in this study guide.

When you locate the subject and a verb *to be,* you can find the predicate noun complement by asking *what.* For example, "Middletown is…what?" "Middletown is *where the company is headquartered.*" Sometimes the answer to this question yields a describing word like *prosperous.* We shall discuss the possibility of this describing word immediately below.

Predicate Adjective

SS-21

In the sentences "The salesperson is angry," "Dinner is delicious," and "The beach is sunny," the verb *to be* ("is") links the subjects to words that describe nouns and pronouns. A word that describes a noun or pronoun is called an *adjective.* An adjective linked to the subject by the verb *to be* is called a *predicate adjective.*

You can identify a predicate adjective by asking *what* after a verb *to be,* forming the question: "The salesperson is *what?*" "Dinner is *what?*" or "The beach is *what?*" If the answer is an adjective—"angry," "delicious," or "sunny"—then the complement is a predicate adjective. Sometimes the answer to this question yields a predicate noun. The complement of the linking verb is always a noun (or noun equivalent) or an adjective.

The three main types of complements are illustrated below:

Subject	Verb	Object
Each student	will carry	a laptop.

Subject	Verb	Predicate Noun
Middletown	is	the company's headquarters.

Subject	Verb	Predicate Adjective
The sunset	is	beautiful.

Compound Subjects, Verbs, and Complements

SS-22

In the sentence, "The salesperson arrives," the subject consists of one element, "The salesperson." In the sentence "The salesperson and the client arrive," the subject consists of two elements, "The salesperson and the client." In the sentence "The dean, the professor, and the coach address the freshman team," the subject consists of three elements: "The dean, the professor, and the coach." A subject that consists of two or more elements is called a *compound subject.* A compound subject is two or more nouns, not just two or more elements. "The large dog" has three elements of meaning, but only one noun, so it is not a compound subject.

Complete Subjects and Predicates

SS-23

In the sentence "The salesperson arrives," the word "salesperson" is the subject. If we added the word "the" to "salesperson," we would have the *complete subject.* Sentences are seldom as simple as "The salesperson arrives." Generally, we have words that support the subject like "large," "happy," or "in a brown suit." We might say, "A large, happy salesperson in a brown suit arrives." The *complete subject* is now "A large, happy salesperson in a brown suit."

Statements, Commands, Questions, and Exclamations

The sentences you write serve four different purposes—they state facts or opinions; they give commands; they ask questions; or they express excitement. These purposes affect (a) the structure of the sentence and (b) the punctuation of a sentence.

Sentences That State Facts or Opinions Are Called *Declarative Sentences*

SS-24

Most of the sentences you write are declarative sentences. These sentences are usually built upon one of the ten basic sentence patterns. A declarative sentence always begins with a noun, pronoun, or word (such as a gerund) that functions as a noun. The following sentences are declarative sentences; the first states a fact, the second an opinion.

George Washington was our first president.

George Washington was our greatest president.

Sentences That Give Commands Are Called *Imperative Sentences*

SS-25

As we noted earlier, the command usually omits the subject, since the subject is generally understood to be "you." An imperative sentence always begins with a verb and ends with a period or exclamation point.

Write all answers with a pen.

Write all answers with a pen!

Sentences That Ask Questions Are Called *Interrogative Sentences*

SS-26

As we noted earlier, the question usually requires an inversion of word order and often the insertion of special words. An interrogative sentence always ends with a question mark.

Why is the campfire lit early tonight?

Sentences That Express Excitement Are Called *Exclamatory Sentences*

SS-27

When we get excited, we exclaim our thoughts and feelings. The exclamation may be a word or phrase— "Look!" "This way!"—or a full sentence—"The game is over!" "A tornado is coming!" An exclamatory sentence always begins with a capital letter and ends with an exclamation point.

Subject-Verb Agreement

SS-28

As we have emphasized many times, the subject-verb tie is the key to the sentence and to each clause within the sentence. The subject identifies the person, place, or thing we have in mind. The verb ties that person, place, or thing to an action or state of being.

The subject-verb tie initiates the thought of the sentence or a main clause within the sentence.

The subject-verb tie makes the clause a clause rather than a phrase.

As key elements in the sentence and in clauses within the sentence, subjects and verbs must be in *agreement.*

What Is Subject-Verb Agreement?

SS-29

Every subject and verb must agree in person and in number. If a subject is in the first-person singular, the verb must also be in the first-person singular. If a subject is in the third-person singular, the verb must also be in the third-person singular. If a subject is in the third-person plural, the verb must also be in the third-person plural.

Inverted Order

SS-30

Observe how difficulty arises when the subject and verb do not appear in natural order. Instead of preceding the verb as it does in natural order, the subject follows the verb in inverted order.

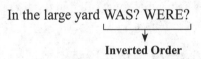

In the large yard WAS? WERE?

Inverted Order
The verb "was" or "were" precedes the subject.

a garage, a lawn, and a shed.

Agreement Problem
We must examine the subject to decide the number of the verb.

When we apply the test "Who was? What was?" "Who were? What were?" we find "a garage, a lawn, **and a** shed" (three things) *were.*

Subject Separated from Verb

SS-31

Observe how difficulty arises when the subject and verb are separated by intervening words.

Subject

The schedule,

Intervening words containing plurals

together with key schedules from three courses,

IS DELAYED?/ARE DELAYED? every day.

Verb

If we ask "What is delayed? What are delayed?" the answer "schedule" presents itself. The subject "schedule" is singular. The verb must therefore be singular—"is delayed." The word group "together with key schedules from three courses" is a modifier, *not* part of the subject. The plurals within the modifier, "schedules" and "courses," deceive our ear. Consider how we might compose the faulty sentence below if we are not careful:

Faulty: The schedule, together with key schedules from three courses, <u>are delayed</u>.

Correct: The schedule, together with key schedules from three courses, <u>is delayed</u>.

Inverted word order and separation of subject and verb are but two of the structures that can complicate subject-verb agreement. Later we will review all of these complicating structures in detail.

Critical Points of Subject-Verb Agreement
SS-32
For action verbs like *walk* or *delay*, subject-verb agreement gives us trouble most often in the *present* and *present perfect* tenses.

Present Tense of Action Verbs
SS-33
All action verbs add an *s* to indicate third-person singular: "He walk*s*" or "He delay*s*." Note how *walk* serves in every person and number but the third-person singular, in the following display:

	Singular	Plural
First person	I walk	We walk
Second person	You walk	You walk
Third person	<u>He (she, it) walks</u>	They walk

Forms of the present tense like the progressive "I am walking" or the passive voice "I am delayed" have additional inflections. These additional inflections are created by the verb *to be* serving as a helping verb. Note how the helping verb *are* serves in the second-person singular, and in all plurals in the passive voice, present

tense, of the verb *to delay*. Contrast these four inflections with the *am* helping verb in the first-person singular and the *is* inflection in the third-person singular:

	Singular	Plural
First person	I <u>am</u> delayed	We are delayed
Second person	You are delayed	You are delayed
Third person	He (she, it) <u>is</u> delayed	They are delayed

Present Perfect Tense of Action Verbs
SS-34
The present perfect tense, as you will recall, is formed by the helping verb *have* and the past participle. Note in the following display how *have* inflects to *has* in the third-person singular:

	Singular	Plural
First person	I have delayed	We have delayed
Second person	You have delayed	You have delayed
Third person	He (she, it) <u>has</u> delayed	They have delayed

Present Tense of the Verb To Be
SS-35
The verb *to be* is the most highly inflected verb in the language. These inflections give the verb *to be* many changes of form when it serves as the main verb or when it serves as a helping verb. Note, for example, how the verb *to be* has the inflection *am* in the first-person singular, present tense; *is* for the third-person singular, present tense; and *are* for all other persons and numbers.

	Singular	Plural
First person	I <u>am</u>	We are
Second person	You are	You are
Third person	He (she, it) <u>is</u>	They are

Past Tense of the Verb To Be

SS-36

Note how the verb *to be* has the inflection *was* for the first- and third-person singular, past tense.

	Singular	**Plural**
First person	I <u>was</u>	We were
Second person	You were	You were
Third person	He (she, it) <u>was</u>	They were

Once you have identified the subject-verb tie, you have little difficulty controlling subject-verb agreement. With the verb located, we can easily identify the subject by asking *who* or *what*.

Controlling Subject-Verb Agreement

SS-37

The secret of controlling subject-verb agreement is to locate the true subject of the verb and determine correctly the person and number of that subject. Difficulties occur when we mistake the wrong noun or pronoun for the subject and when we fail to determine correctly the person and number of the subject after we have located it.

The following rules will provide the guidance you need in controlling subject-verb agreement.

SS-38

> **Rule**
>
> *Do not mistake a noun or pronoun in an intervening word group for the subject of a verb.*

Subject	Intervening word group	Verb
↓	↓	↓
The can	of <u>figs</u>	has arrived.

The noun "figs" is the object of the preposition "of" and helps form a prepositional phrase. Very often subjects of verbs are followed by adjectival prepositional phrases in this kind of structure. These objects of prepositions must never be mistaken for the subjects of the verbs.

Faulty: The can of figs *have arrived.*

Correct: The can of figs *has arrived.*

In the sentence "The schedule, together with key schedules from three courses, is delayed," the plurals "schedules" and "courses" could be mistaken for the subject "schedule." We must watch intervening word groups introduced by *together with, as well as, in addition to, like, accompanied by, along with,* etc.

Faulty: Noah, like his older cousin Logan, <u>speak</u> whatever comes to mind.

Correct: Noah, like his older cousin Logan, <u>speaks</u> whatever comes to mind.

Faulty: Charlotte, along with two friends, <u>walk</u> this way daily.

Correct: Charlotte, along with two friends, <u>walks</u> this way daily.

SS-39

> **Rule**
>
> *Consider compound subjects joined by* and *plural, unless the compound subject stands for a single person or thing.*

In the sentence "The bookcase and typewriter are in the empty room," the subject nouns "bookcase" and "typewriter" are combined by "and" to form a plural.

The "and" adds "bookcase" and "typewriter" to form a plural subject.   *Since the subject is plural, the verb must be plural.*

↘   ↙

The bookcase <u>and</u> typewriter <u>are</u> in the empty room.

Generally, *and* combines the elements of a compound subject in this way to form a plural subject.

Sometimes the elements of a compound subject stand for the same person or thing. For example, many corporations have an office called "treasurer and controller." In these corporations, the treasurer is also the controller.

In the sentence "The treasurer and controller of the firm is Mr. Hengest," the compound joined by "and" identifies a single person—Mr. Hengest. Since the compound "treasurer and controller" applies to a single unit, it is singular. The verb *is* rather than *are* must be used to agree with this singular subject.

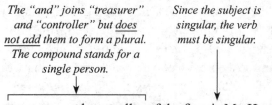

The "and" joins "treasurer" and "controller" but <u>does not add</u> them to form a plural. The compound stands for a single person.

Since the subject is singular, the verb must be singular.

The treasurer and controller of the firm <u>is</u> Mr. Hengest.

SS-40

> **Rule**
>
> *Consider compound subjects joined by* or *or* nor *singular if each noun of the compound is singular.*

The coordinating conjunctions *or* and *nor* do not add elements the way *and* does. Note in the following sentence that the conjunction "or" gives us the choice of "sheriff" or "deputy," but not both together.

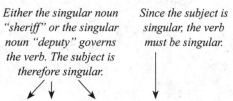

Either the singular noun "sheriff" or the singular noun "deputy" governs the verb. The subject is therefore singular.

Since the subject is singular, the verb must be singular.

The sheriff *or* his deputy *investigates* these reports.

SS-41

> **Rule**
>
> *Consider compound subjects joined by* or *or* nor *plural if each noun of the compound is plural.*

In the sentence "The fishermen or their wives *sell* the day's catch," the choice offered by "or" is plural. The verb must therefore be plural.

SS-42

> **Rule**
>
> *Let the number of the noun nearest the verb govern when singular and plural elements are combined by* or *or* nor *in a compound subject.*

Very often *or* and *nor* combine singular and plural elements in a compound subject. For example, the sentence "The sheriff or his deputies investigate these reports" has a choice of the singular "sheriff" or the

plural "deputies" joined by "or." Since the plural "deputies" is closer to the verb, the verb "investigate" must be plural.

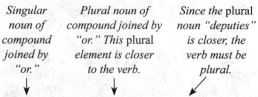

Singular noun of compound joined by "or."

Plural noun of compound joined by "or." This plural element is closer to the verb.

Since the plural noun "deputies" is closer, the verb must be plural.

The sheriff or his *deputies investigate* these reports.

If the sentence reads "The deputies or the sheriff investigates these reports," the singular noun "sheriff" appears closer to the verb. Therefore, the verb must be singular.

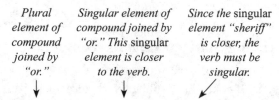

Plural element of compound joined by "or."

Singular element of compound joined by "or." This singular element is closer to the verb.

Since the singular element "sheriff" is closer, the verb must be singular.

The deputies or the *sheriff investigates* these reports.

SS-43

> **Rule**
>
> *Consider a collective noun subject singular when the group identified serves as a unit.*

As we have seen, some nouns like "army," "class," "company," or "jury" combine a group into a unit. Sometimes the group identified acts as a unit—"The crowd rises and cheers." In this sentence, we see the crowd as singular since it acts as a unit. When a collective noun subject is singular, the verb must also be singular.

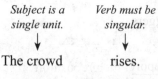

Subject is a single unit.

Verb must be singular.

The crowd   rises.

SS-44

> **Rule**
>
> *Consider a collective noun subject plural when the group identified serve as individual members.*

Sometimes the group identified in a compound noun act as individual members—"The crowd hurry to their automobiles." In this sentence, we see the crowd as plural since each member acts as an individual. When a collective noun subject is plural, the verb must also be plural.

Subject is a group of persons acting as individuals.   *Verb must be plural.*

↓   ↓

The crowd   hurry to their automobiles.

SS-45

> **Rule**
>
> *Consider indefinite pronouns such as* anybody, anyone, each, either (neither)*, everybody, everyone, nobody, and* no one *singular when they serve as subjects of verbs.*

When we use an indefinite pronoun like *anybody*, we mean "any *single* body." When we use the indefinite pronouns *anyone*, *everyone*, and *no one*, we indicate the singular with the "one" in these pronouns. Similarly, *each* means "each *one*," and *either* means "either *one*" in sentences like the following:

Each returns.	**means**	Each *one* returns.
Either returns.	**means**	Either *one* returns.

These indefinite pronouns always form singular subjects. The verbs that these indefinite pronoun subjects govern must also be singular. Note how our ear can mislead us in the faulty examples below.

Faulty: Each of the joggers <u>are circling</u> Brookdale Park.

Correct: Each of the joggers <u>is circling</u> Brookdale Park.

Faulty: Neither <u>have reported</u>.

Correct: Neither <u>has reported</u>.

SS-46

> **Rule**
>
> *Consider indefinite pronouns such as* all, none, *or* some *singular subjects when the context is singular.*

When we say, "All is well," we mean that <u>every single thing</u> is well. When we say, "None has completed his test," we mean that <u>no one has completed his test</u>. When we say, "Some of the oatmeal is burned," we mean <u>a part of the oatmeal is burned</u>.

SS-47

> **Rule**
>
> *Consider indefinite pronouns such as* all, none, *or* some *plural subjects when the context is plural.*

When we say, "All are ready," we mean that <u>all items or all persons are ready</u>. When we say, "None hesitate," we mean that <u>members of some group do not hesitate</u>. When we say, "Some are hesitating," we mean that <u>some members of a group are hesitating</u>.

The real problem in using "all," "none," and "some" is being consistent with the other words in the sentence:

Correct: None <u>has completed</u> his test.

Correct: None <u>have completed</u> their tests.

Correct: Some of the oatmeal <u>is burned</u>.

Correct: Some of the eggs <u>are boiled</u>.

SS-48

> **Rule**
>
> *Consider as singular all plural noun subjects that identify singular ideas.*

Many nouns and noun phrases in our language are plural in form but singular in meaning. For example, the plural noun phrase "twenty-four dollars" is plural in form but singular in meaning in the sentence "Twenty-four dollars was the purchase price for Manhattan Island." The plural compound "two and two" is plural in form but singular in meaning in the sentence "Two and two is four." These nouns are always considered singular and require singular verbs.

It is the singular unit of twenty-four dollars that was the price. The twenty-four dollars are a sum or total.

Since the subject is singular, the verb must be singular.

↓   ↓

Twenty-four dollars was the purchase price for Manhattan.

It is the idea of two and two—a numeric concept— that is four. This plural identifies a singular idea.

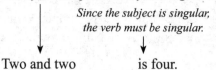

Since the subject is singular, the verb must be singular.

Two and two   is four.

SS-49

Note how the subjects of the following sentences are plural in form but singular in meaning; hence, each of these subjects takes a singular verb.

Subject   Verb

The Clouds is a comedy by Aristophanes.

Subject   Verb

Thousand Islands is a beautiful resort in the St. Lawrence.

Nouns such as "ballistics," "civics," "economics," "mathematics," "news," "physics," and "semantics" are usually considered singular in meaning. When these nouns serve as subjects, they take singular verbs.

SS-50

Nouns such as "athletics," "acoustics," "statistics," and "tactics" may be singular or plural. When we consider these nouns as fields of interest or as disciplines, these nouns are singular. As singular nouns, they form singular subjects and take singular verbs.

Subject   Verb

Athletics has replaced hygiene in the new curriculum.

Subject   Verb

Statistics is required for computer science majors.

When we consider these nouns as activities, events, or properties, these nouns are plural. As plural nouns, they form plural subjects and take plural verbs.

Subject   Verb

Athletics keep the laboratory staff healthy.

Subject   Verb

Statistics have been gathered on wasp stings.

SS-51

> **Rule**
>
> *Watch inverted structures carefully to ensure identification of the true subject.*

When the subject precedes the verb, we call the word order *natural*. When the subject follows the verb, we call the word order *inverted*. For example, the subject "a garage, a lawn, and a shed" follows the verb "were" in the sentence, "In the large yard were a garage, a lawn, and a shed." The word order in this sentence is inverted.

Very often we invert the word order of our sentences by using *there is*, *there are*, and *here are* structures. For example, the structure is inverted in the sentence, "There are a pencil and a printed form on each desk."

As we noted earlier, these inversions can mislead the ear. Note, for example, how we might use the singular verb "is" instead of the plural "are" in the faulty example below.

Faulty: There <u>is</u> a pencil and a printed form on each desk.

Correct: There <u>are</u> a pencil and a printed form on each desk.

SS-52

> **Rule**
>
> *Examine the antecedent to determine the number of a relative pronoun subject.*

A relative pronoun such as "who" does not inflect to indicate the plural. Note in the following display how "who" has the same form in the singular and in the plural.

The pronoun "who" is singular because its antecedent is singular.

The man who <u>wakes</u> the bugler is the corporal of the guard.

The pronoun "who" is plural because its antecedent is plural.

The operators who <u>wake</u> the guests work very hard after six o'clock.

In the first sentence above, we know that "who" is singular because its antecedent, "man," is singular. Since "who" is singular and the subject of the subordinate clause "who wakes the bugler," the verb "wakes" must be singular.

In the second sentence above, we know that "who" is plural because its antecedent, "operators," is plural. Since "who" is plural and the subject of the subordinate clause "who wake the guests," the verb "wake" must be plural.

The number of a relative pronoun sometimes gives us difficulty in "one of those who" structures. Note, for example, in the following display how your ear might mislead you into using a singular verb if you do not examine the antecedent of *who* carefully.

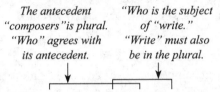

The antecedent "composers" is plural. "Who" agrees with its antecedent.

"Who is the subject of "write." "Write" must also be in the plural.

John is one of those *composers who write* lyrics.

Note how your ear might mislead you into use of the faulty singular verb "writes" in the example below.

Faulty: John is one of those composers who <u>writes</u> lyrics.

Correct: John is one of those composers who <u>write</u> lyrics.

SS-53

> #### Rule
> *Do not let the number of a predicate noun govern the number of the verb.*

A predicate noun, as we learned, is a noun linked to the subject by the verb *to be*. For example, the word "commander" is a predicate noun in the sentence "Scott was the commander."

Sometimes a subject is singular and the predicate noun is plural, and sometimes a subject is plural and the predicate noun is singular.

Singular subject with plural predicate noun.
↓
His dinner is fish and coffee.

Plural subject with singular predicate noun.
↓
Fish and coffee are his dinner.

Notice how your ear can mislead you into using the verb "are" instead of "is" in the sentence "His dinner is fish and coffee." The plural predicate noun "fish and coffee" makes "His dinner are fish and coffee" sound right. The subject, however, and not the predicate noun, must govern the number of the verb.

Notice how your ear can mislead you into using the verb "is" instead of "are" in the sentence "Fish and coffee are his dinner." The singular predicate noun "dinner" makes "Fish and coffee is his dinner" sound right. The subject, however, and not the predicate noun, must govern the number of the verb.

Faulty: His dinner <u>are</u> fish and coffee.

Correct: His dinner <u>is</u> fish and coffee.

Faulty: Fish and coffee <u>is</u> his dinner.

Correct: Fish and coffee <u>are</u> his dinner.

When a subject and a predicate noun clash in number, it is sometimes advisable to revise the sentence and eliminate this awkwardness. For example, "He has fish and coffee for dinner" would eliminate the awkward clash in either of these sentences.

Main Types of Sentences

SS-54

Sentences are generally classified in two ways—by the kind of work they do, that is, by *function*, and by their *structure*.

We have not considered the main *structural classification* of sentences until now, because structural classification is based on the clause. Sentences can be classified by structure as *simple sentences*, *complex sentences*, *compound sentences*, and *compound-complex sentences*.

Simple Sentences

SS-55

A simple sentence consists of one *main* (independent) clause and no other clause, main or *subordinate* (dependent).

The following word groups, which we use to illustrate the main clause, are simple sentences when punctuated as separate sentences. A simple sentence is a main clause punctuated as a sentence.

Mr. Smith telephoned early. (*simple sentence*)

He sounded happy. (*simple sentence*)

The two sentences above, of course, are extremely short. Most simple sentences are shorter than other types of sentences, but a sentence does not have to be short to be a simple sentence. Notice how the following sentence is fairly long and somewhat complicated, yet it too is a simple sentence.

Hoping to see you some time later today, Mr. Smith of Smith & Company telephoned early this morning and sounded very happy about something of interest to you.

The sentence above is a simple sentence because it consists of one main clause and no other clauses, main or subordinate. The complications in this simple sentence are caused by several phrases and a compound verb.

Complex Sentences

SS-56

A complex sentence consists of one main (independent) clause and one or more subordinate (dependent) clauses.

When Mr. Smith telephoned, he sounded very happy. (*complex sentence*)

If you have time, please call Mr. Smith, who sounded happy when he called you this morning. (*complex sentence*)

The first sentence consists of one main clause, "he sounded very happy," and one subordinate clause, "when Mr. Smith telephoned."

The second sentence consists of one main clause, "(You) please call Mr. Smith," and the three subordinate clauses "if you have time," "who sounded happy," and "when he called you this morning." The last-named of these subordinate clauses is actually a modifier within the subordinate clause "who sounded happy when he called you this morning."

Compound Sentences

SS-57

A compound sentence consists of two or more main clauses and no subordinate clause.

Mr. Smith telephoned; he sounded very happy. (*compound sentence*)

Mr. Smith telephoned, and he made two requests: he wants the title of a book by Margaret Mead, and he wants a copy of Ruth Benedict's *Patterns of Culture*. (*compound sentence*)

The first compound sentence above contains two main clauses; the second compound sentence contains four main clauses.

Compound-Complex Sentences

SS-58

A compound-complex sentence consists of two or more independent clauses and one or more subordinate clauses.

Before Dean Smollett spoke, he placed his notes carefully on the table beside the large yearbook, and then he brought forth those remarkable spectacles to the cheers of all. (*compound-complex sentence*)

When we arrived at the city of Ravenna, we looked for evidence of its past greatness, which makes it a city of major historical importance; but we spent most of our time studying mosaics that we had not expected to see. (*compound-complex sentence*)

The first sentence above opens with a subordinate clause, followed by two main clauses. The second sentence opens with a subordinate clause followed by two main clauses; each of these main clauses is followed by a subordinate clause.

THE EIGHT PARTS OF SPEECH

PS-1

You know much more about the parts of speech than you suspect. When you entered the first grade of elementary school, you had already gained a good working command of the parts of speech. You may not have understood the terms *parts of speech* or *classes of words*, but you did know how to manage these word classes when you talked to family and friends.

Nouns

Nouns *Name*

PS-2

Every person, place, or thing in this world has a name. When a child is born, that child is given a name. When a new idea is born, that idea is given a name. Albert Einstein called his theory "relativity." We called men "astronauts" when they visited space for the first time in world history. When atomic energy was first released, we called the process "nuclear fission." If our language is to refer to persons, places, or things, those persons, places, or things must have names. A word that names is called a *noun*.

When a noun names a particular person, place, or thing, we call that noun a *proper noun. New York, Los Angeles, Canada, Texas, Olivia Sanchez, Tyler Jennings*, and *Lake Michigan* are all proper nouns. A proper noun always begins with a capital letter.

When a noun names a whole class of persons, places, or things, we call that noun a *common noun*. The nouns *city, nation, state, man, woman, lake, tree*, and *baseball* are all common nouns. A common noun does *not* begin with a capital letter, except when that noun opens a sentence.

Pronouns

Pronouns Substitute for Nouns

PS-3

If Tyler Jennings speaks to Olivia Sanchez, he does not say, "Tyler Jennings saw Olivia Sanchez from the bus window this morning." He says "*I* saw *you* from the bus window this morning." The pronoun "I" takes the place of "Tyler Jennings." The pronoun "you" takes the place of "Olivia Sanchez."

The pronoun simplifies expressions when the person, place, or thing discussed is clear to the listener or reader. In the sentence "I studied for the *test* very carefully and I am certain that I can pass *it*," the pronoun "it" makes it unnecessary for us to repeat the word "test." In this structure, the noun "test" serves as the *antecedent* of the pronoun "it." Later we shall see how carefully we must watch the pronoun and its antecedent if our writing is to be clear.

Pronouns are identified in five main classes:

personal pronouns

relative pronouns

interrogative pronouns

demonstrative pronouns

indefinite pronouns

These formal class names make the pronoun sound more difficult than it really is. Actually, you already have a good working command of these classes.

The Personal Pronoun

PS-4

Study the following table of personal pronouns for a few minutes and you will have little difficulty recognizing personal pronouns when you meet them in your reading and when you write them in compositions.

Personal Pronouns (Singular)	
First person	I, me, my, mine. (I am)
Second person	You, your, yours. (You are)
Third person	He, his, him. (He is)
	She, her, hers. (She is)
	It, its. (It is)

Personal Pronouns (Plural)	
First person	We, us, our, ours. (We are)
Second person	You, your, yours. (You are)
Third person	They, their, them. (They are)

The Relative Pronoun

PS-5

Study the underlined words in the following sentences and you will see what kind of word we call a *relative pronoun* and how that word operates in the sentence.

The player <u>who</u> is holding the ball is Rick Richards.

The player <u>whom</u> he called is Rick Richards.

The game <u>that</u> they play is rugby, not football.

The game <u>that</u> they play is rugby, <u>which</u> few of us understand.

Note that the relative pronouns are "who," "which," and "that" when these words take the places of nouns and introduce word groups, as in "who is holding the ball" or "that they play."

Note how the relative pronoun, like the personal pronoun, has an antecedent. The relative pronoun "who" in the first sentence stands for the noun "player." The relative pronoun "which" in the last sentence stands for "rugby."

Note how the relative pronoun *who* is inflected "whom" in the second sentence. Later we shall discuss the problem of *who* and *whom* more fully. When *who* is possessive, we use the inflected form "whose." Later we shall stress the importance of distinguishing the possessive *whose* from the contraction *who's*. (Compare "The man whose team won is Rick Richards" and "The man who's going is Rick Richards." In the first sentence "whose team" means "Rick's team." In the second sentence "who's going" means "who is going.")

Note how *who* refers to a person and *which* refers to a thing. The relative pronoun *that* can refer to a thing or an animal.

We shall see in the discussions that follow how *who* (*whom, whose*) and *which* can also serve as interrogative pronouns, and how *that* can serve in several other ways.

The Interrogative Pronoun

PS-6

When the pronouns *who* (*whose, whom*), *which*, and *what* ask a question, we call these pronouns *interrogative pronouns*. Study the underlined words in the following sentences and you will see interrogative pronouns in action.

<u>Who</u> is going?

<u>Whom</u> do you mean?

<u>Which</u> do you prefer?

<u>What</u> is the best way to review French?

Note that the interrogative pronouns are *who*, *which*, and *what*, when these pronouns ask questions. The interrogative pronoun gives us very little trouble, except for the problem of *who* and *whom*, which we shall discuss in full later in this text.

The Demonstrative Pronoun

PS-7

When the pronouns *this, that, these*, or *those* appear in sentences like the following, we call *this, that, these*, and *those* "demonstrative pronouns."

<u>This</u> is a good course for a sophomore to take.

<u>These</u> will make good pies.

<u>That</u> is a good road to travel.

Please do <u>that</u>.

You will prefer <u>these</u>.

The word *demonstrative* means *pointing at*. The word "this" in the first sentence above is a *demonstrative pronoun* because it *points at* a good course.

The Indefinite Pronoun

PS-8

When a pronoun refers *generally* to anyone, everyone, someone, or anything, we call that pronoun an *indefinite pronoun*. Note how the underlined pronouns in the following sentences are general, or *indefinite*, in the persons or things they identify.

Anyone may attend this lecture.

He will repair anything you give him.

I do not have any.

Is everybody happy?

He will listen to anyone's problems.

Someone is needed in the kitchen.

Someone's coat is on the floor.

One seldom has trouble with a crew cut.

Some found economics very interesting.

Nouns and Pronouns: Number

PS-9

Most nouns and many pronouns inflect to indicate number. *Number* is the grammatical property of being singular or plural. The noun *boy* is singular; the noun *boys* is plural. The pronoun *he* is singular; the pronoun *they* is plural. We generally take the number of a noun or pronoun in stride in our speaking and writing, but a few nouns and pronouns do give us trouble.

Singular and Plural Nouns

PS-10

Most nouns are made plural by the addition of *-s*. The plural of *boy* is *boys*; the plural of *street* is *streets*. Some nouns, however, have a singular that ends in *s* or a sound that resembles *s*, and these nouns are pluralized by the addition of *-es*. The word *ash*, for example, ends in a sound that resembles *s*. Since the addition of *-s* would not give *ash* a distinctive plural, the noun *ash* is pluralized by the addition of *-es*—*ashes*. The noun *boss* is pluralized *bosses*. The noun *mix* is pluralized *mixes*.

A few very familiar nouns are pluralized by inflections other than the addition of *-s* or *-es*. For example, the noun *child* is pluralized *children*; the noun *man* is pluralized *men*. These plurals are considered irregular, but words like *child*, *man*, and *woman* are used so often that we employ their plurals as though they were very simple and natural.

We still retain a few Latin and Greek plurals for words we have taken directly from Latin or Greek. We pluralize *alumnus* by its Latin plural *alumni*. We pluralize *hypothesis* by its Greek plural *hypotheses*.

We generally pluralize compound words like *father-in-law* by adding *s* to the noun element *father* to get *fathers-in-law*. The plural of *son-in-law* is *sons-in-law*. The plural of *notary public* is *notaries public*.

Related to the problem of number is the *collective noun*. Nouns like *army*, *committee*, *company*, *group*, *jury*, and *squad* represent a number of individuals within single units. We think of a collective noun like *army* or *committee* as singular when the group represents a unit acting as an individual—"The army holds maneuvers" or "The committee presents its research findings." Occasionally, we think of a collective noun as a number of individuals acting as individuals—"The committee are always dividing themselves into factions based on age." In this plural sense, we think of the committee as a group of individual members.

Singular and Plural Pronouns

PS-11

All the personal pronouns but *you* inflect to form the plural. The pronoun *I* becomes *we*. The pronouns *he*, *she*, and *it* become *they*.

The demonstrative pronoun *this* changes to *these* in the plural, and the demonstrative pronoun *that* changes to *those* in the plural.

Relative pronouns such as *who*, *which*, *what*, and *that* have the same form in the singular and the plural.

Nouns and Pronouns: Case

PS-12

Both nouns and pronouns inflect to indicate *case*. Nouns have two case inflections; many pronouns have three.

Case is a property of a noun or pronoun that relates to function. As we have seen, nouns and noun equivalents perform some half-dozen functions in the sentence, and each of these functions places that noun or pronoun in one of three cases—*subjective* (nominative), *objective*, or *possessive*.

The noun has the *same* form for the *subjective case* and the *objective case* but takes a *special* form to indicate the *possessive case*. The form *boy* (*boys*) serves both the subjective and the objective, but the form *boy's* (*boys'*) must be used in the possessive case.

CASE—NOUNS

Subjective		Objective		Possessive	
Singular	*Plural*	*Singular*	*Plural*	*Singular*	*Plural*
boy	boys	boy	boys	boy's	boys'
man	men	man	men	man's	men's

CASE—PERSONAL, RELATIVE, AND INTERROGATIVE PRONOUNS

Subjective		Objective		Possessive	
Singular	*Plural*	*Singular*	*Plural*	*Singular*	*Plural*
I	we	me	us	my, mine	our, ours
you	you	you	you	your, yours	your, yours
he	they	him	them	his	their, theirs
she	they	her	them	her, hers	their, theirs
it	they	it	them	its	their, theirs
who	who	whom	whom	whose	whose
which	which	which	which	whose	whose

Many pronouns have a *different* form for the *subjective case,* the *objective case,* and the *possessive case.* The form *I* is used in the subjective case; the form *me* in the objective case; the form *my* or *mine* in the possessive case. Indefinite pronouns such as *anyone* and demonstrative pronouns such as *this* do not inflect to indicate case.

A glance at the table above will show you how nouns have two forms for case, but many pronouns have three. The only noun inflection that can offer difficulty is the inflection for the possessive case. Three pronoun inflections, however, can cause difficulty—inflections for the nominative case, the objective case, and the possessive case.

The Subjective (Nominative) Case

PS-13

A noun or pronoun takes the subjective or nominative case when it serves as the subject of a verb, as a predicate noun or pronoun, or as an appositive to some other noun or pronoun in the subjective case.

Subject of a Verb

PS-14

The subject of a verb is always in the subjective case. The nouns and pronouns that could serve as subjects of the verb "will verify" in the following frame are in the subjective case.

Possible Noun Subjects	Possible Pronoun Subjects
(The) boy	I
(The) boys	You
(The) man	We
(The) men	Someone
	Who*
_____ will verify this card.	
(Subject Slot)	

These subjects of this verb would still be in the subjective case in a subordinate clause.

If the <u>boy</u> will verify the card, I will return the book.

If <u>he</u> will verify the card, I will return the book.

---

*If the interrogative pronoun "who" is used, this sentence will become a question: "Who will verify this card?"

Note how the relative pronoun "who" can introduce a subordinate clause and serve as subject of the verb "will verify." We use "who," the subjective case, rather than "whom," the objective case, because "who" is the subject of a verb and the subject of a verb is always in the subjective case.

Relative pronoun introduces the subordinate clause.

↓

We are sending a man <u>who</u> will verify the card.

↑

Relative pronoun serves as a subject of verb.

Predicate Noun and Pronoun
PS-15

A predicate noun or a predicate pronoun is always in the subjective case. A predicate noun or predicate pronoun, as you will recall, is a noun or pronoun linked to the subject by the verb *to be*. The noun "John" is a predicate noun in the sentence "The winner is *John*." The pronoun "she" is a predicate pronoun in the sentence "The winner is *she*."

Predicate nouns and predicate pronouns are actually nouns or pronouns that identify the person, place, or thing named in the subject. These nouns or pronouns are placed in the subjective case because they are essentially the same as the subject.

The nouns and pronouns that could serve as predicate nouns or predicate pronouns in the following frame are in the subjective case.

Possible Predicate Nouns	Possible Predicate Pronouns
John	I
(the) boy	he
(the) girl	she
(the) Jets	someone
Texans	who*
(our) team	we

The winner is _____
(Predicate Noun or Pronoun Slot)

---

*The interrogative pronoun "who" would make this sentence a question: "The winner is who?"

**The term *idiomatic* refers to a grammatical practice that is peculiar but accepted, an *idiom*.

Some authorities would accept "The winner is *me*," as well as "The winner is *I*." These authorities feel that "me" in this structure is *idiomatic*.** The expression "It is me" is now widely accepted. The subjective case, however, is preferred in predicate pronoun structures— "It is *she*," "The winner is *he* who finishes first," "It is *I* who should reply," etc.

Apposition
PS-16

A noun or pronoun in apposition always takes the same case as the noun or pronoun it identifies; hence, a noun or pronoun in apposition to a noun or pronoun in the subjective case is also in the subjective case.

The nouns and pronouns that could serve as appositives in the following frame are in apposition to the subject. Since a subject is in the subjective case, these nouns and pronouns are in the subjective case.

Possible Noun Appositives	Possible Pronoun Appositives
Bob	he
(the) center	I
(his) brother	we
(an) alumnus	another

The basketball players, Cliff and _____, were honored.
(Appositive Slot)

The Objective Case
PS-17

A noun or pronoun takes the objective case when it serves as the direct or indirect object of a verb, as the object of a preposition, as the object of a verbal, as the subject of an infinitive, or as an appositive to another noun or pronoun in the objective case.

Object of a Verb
PS-18

The object of a verb is always in the objective case. The nouns or pronouns that could serve as objects of the verb "will verify" in the following frame are in the objective case.

Possible Noun Objects of Verb	Possible Pronoun Objects of Verb
(the) boy	me
(the) boys	you
(the) man	us
(the) men	someone
	whom*

Ms. Hunter will verify _____

(Object Slot)

Observe how the noun "boy" is the same form in the subjective case and in the objective case:

The boy will verify this card.

Ms. Hunter will verify the boy.

But note how the personal pronoun changes from "I" in the subjective case to "me" in the objective case.

I will verify this card.

Ms. Hunter will verify me.

Consider now the way the relative pronoun operates when it introduces a subordinate clause but serves also as the object of a verb.

Relative pronoun "whom" appears at the beginning of subordinate clause as an introducer of that clause.

↓

We are sending a man whom Ms. Hunter will verify.

↑

Relative pronoun "whom" is inflected because it is in the objective case.

Object of a Preposition
PS-19

The object of a preposition is always in the objective case. The underlined words in the following sentences are objects of prepositions. Compare the noun objects of prepositions with the personal pronoun objects and note how the noun has the same form it would have in the subjective case, but the personal pronouns have a special inflection for the objective case.

The child hurried to Alma.

The child hurried to her.

The fact that the noun does not inflect can mislead us in structures that combine nouns and personal pronouns as objects of the same preposition.

Objects of Verbals
PS-20

The objects of verbals are always in the objective case. Very often the verbal has a receiver of its action in a verbal phrase. Note in the display below how the underlined objects of participles, gerunds, and infinitives can be nouns or pronouns. Note the special inflection for the objective case of the three personal pronoun objects.

Objects of Participles:
The girl addressing the students is Anita.
The girl addressing them is Anita.

Objects of Gerunds:
Meeting Matt was pleasant.
Meeting him was pleasant.

Objects of Infinitives:
I wanted to meet Julie.
I wanted to meet her.

Subjects of Infinitives
PS-21

The subjects of infinitives are always in the objective case. In the sentence, "John asked him to identify the Alcazar on the horizon," the pronoun "him" is the subject of the infinitive "to identify." The subject of an infinitive is always in the objective case, whether that subject is a noun or a pronoun.

John asked Miriam to identify the Alcazar.

John asked her to identify the Alcazar.

Objective-Case Appositives
PS-22

Appositives to nouns or pronouns in the objective case are always in the objective case. The underlined nouns and pronouns in the following sentences are in apposition to nouns or pronouns in the objective case.

Pronoun in apposition to object of verb "suitor"
Marilyn had one persistent suitor, me.

Pronoun in apposition to object of preposition "group"
The girls did extend an invitation to one group, us.

---

*If the interrogative pronoun "whom" is used, this sentence will become a question, "Ms. Hunter will verify whom?" A more likely form of this question would be "Whom will Ms. Hunter verify?"

Noun and pronoun in apposition to object of participle "sweethearts"

The fraternity men sang a touching song honoring two sweethearts, <u>Mary</u> and <u>me</u>.

The Possessive Case
PS-23
A noun or pronoun takes the possessive case to indicate ownership. If a boy owns a wagon, we say, "the boy's wagon." The noun "boy's" is in the possessive case. If the boy's ownership must be indicated by a pronoun, we say, "his wagon."

The possessive case of nouns is always formed with an *apostrophe* (') working with a letter *s*. For example, the possessive of "boy" in "boy's wagon" above is formed by the addition of an apostrophe and an *s* to "boy."

The possessive case of indefinite pronouns such as *anyone* is also formed by an apostrophe and the letter *s*. For example, the possessive of *anyone* is *anyone's*.

The possessive case of personal, relative, and interrogative pronouns is formed by internal inflections. For example, *I* inflects to *my* or *mine*; *who* inflects to *whose*. Earlier in this chapter, we list the possessives of these pronouns along with other pronoun case inflections.

Generally, the possessive is restricted to nouns that identify animate objects. We can ascribe possession to a boy and say, "the boy's wagon," because a boy is animate. We should not ascribe possession to a wagon in structures like "the wagon's handle," because a wagon is an inanimate object. Preferably, we should say, "the handle of the wagon."

Idiom, however, does permit us such inanimate possessives as "a dollar's worth," "a minute's notice," or "the year's end." Idiom is usage established as correct by long practice, even though it contradicts certain rules of language.

PS-24

Rule
Place the apostrophe correctly when you form the possessive sace of nouns.

The possessive case of nouns always requires an apostrophe and the presence of the letter *s*. It is the presence of this *s* that causes many of us difficulty with the noun possessive. Sometimes we must add the *s* to inflect for the possessive, but sometimes an *s* in nouns like *Jones* or *boss*, or in plurals, confuses us.

The Singular Possessive of Nouns
PS-25
The singular possessive is generally formed by the addition of an apostrophe and *s*.

Singular Noun	*Add apostrophe and "s"*	Singular Possessive
boy	's	<u>boy's</u> diary
butcher	's	<u>butcher's</u> coat
man	's	<u>man's</u> car
girl	's	<u>girl's</u> comb
woman	's	<u>woman's</u> purse
boss	's	<u>boss's</u> holiday
Hannah	's	<u>Hannah's</u> piano
Liam	's	<u>Liam's</u> sword
Washington	's	<u>Washington's</u> tactics
Charles	's	<u>Charles's</u> castle

The primary exception to this rule for the singular possessive occurs with certain nouns that end with the sound *-eez*. Consider a name such as Aristophanes (pronounced air-rihs-STAH-fan-eez). It would be most awkward to say, "Aristophanes's plays." Therefore, in such cases the singular possessive is formed simply by adding an apostrophe at the end of the "eez" name, as in "Aristophanes' plays." Names that fall into this category are often proper Greek names, such as Euripides, Eumenides, and Heracles.

Remember that one-syllable common nouns like *boss* must follow the rule for the singular possessive—add apostrophe and *s*. You would never say, "the boss' responsibility." You would always say, "the boss's responsibility," adding the extra *s* sound.

Be careful with names like *James* or *Jones* that you don't place the apostrophe before the *s* at the end of the name and write "Jame's father" or "Jone's report." Always get the full noun on paper before you add the apostrophe.

The Plural Possessive of Nouns

PS-26

The plural possessive of nouns causes much more difficulty than the singular possessive.

When a noun forms its plural by adding *-s* or *-es*, the plural possessive is indicated by the addition of an apostrophe after the *s* of the plural. No additional *s* is needed. For example, the word *boy* forms its plural by adding *s*—*boys*. This plural *boys* is made possessive by the addition of an apostrophe after the *s* of the plural—*boys'*.

PS-27

Plural Formed by Adding *s* or *es* to the Singular	Add Apostrophe but Do NOT Add an "s"	Plural Possessive
boys	'	two boys' diaries
butchers	'	butchers' strike
Joneses	'	Joneses' maple tree
bosses	'	bosses' game
hostesses	'	hostesses' aprons

When a noun forms its plural by an internal change without the addition of s, the plural possessive is indicated by the addition of an apostrophe and an s. For example, the noun *man* forms its plural by an internal change that does not require *s*. The plural of *man* is *men*. This plural *men* is made possessive by the addition of an apostrophe and an *s*—*men's*.

PS-28

Plural Formed by Internal Change without *s*	Add Apostrophe and "s"	Plural Possessive
men	's	men's department
children	's	children's play
women	's	women's club

PS-29

> **Rule**
>
> *Give special attention to compound nouns and nouns in joint possession.*

A compound noun is a word group like "father-in-law" or "attorney general" that serves as a unit. The possessive case is indicated in the compound noun by adding an apostrophe and s to the last word in the unit, whether the compound noun is singular or plural.

Singular possessive of compound nouns
    his father-in-law's home
    an attorney general's case

Plural possessive of compound nouns
    his sons-in-law's homes
    an attorneys general's meeting

Joint ownership occurs when two animate objects own the same thing. For example, Cliff and Al could own the same car. To indicate joint ownership, we inflect the last word only—"Cliff and Al's car."

When ownership is separate, we inflect each noun that identifies an owner—"Cliff's and Al's cars."

PS-30

> **Rule**
>
> *Do not place inanimate nouns in the possessive unless the structure is idiomatic.*

The possessive case is restricted to animate objects, with the exception of a few idioms. We can say, "the woman's dress," and "season's greetings" because "woman" is animate and the possessive "season's greetings" is an idiom, that is, usage established by long practice.

We must not say, "the closet's darkness," or "the floor's slipperiness" because "closet" and "floor" are inanimate.

We must avoid as especially awkward the possessive in long nouns that end in *-ability*, *-ity*, *-ion*, etc., nouns that identify ideas rather than physical things. These abstract nouns make absurd possessives— "amiability's reward," "creativity's achievement," "insurance's coverage."

When we must indicate a relationship like that of a closet and darkness or a floor and slipperiness, we place the inanimate object in an *of-phrase*—"the darkness of the closet," "the slipperiness of the floor," "the reward of amiability," "coverage of the insurance." Sometimes, a *for-phrase* or an *in-phrase* may be needed to express this relationship—"a program for reform," rather than "reform's program," or "an achievement in creativity," rather than "creativity's achievement."

Remember, however, that idiom—long, established usage—does permit abstract possessives like "goodness' sake," "freedom's call," "a month's pay," "five years' experience," etc.

PS-31

> ### Rule
> *Inflect pronouns properly in forming the possessive case.*

Remember that personal, relative, and interrogative pronouns do not use the apostrophe in forming the possessive case. Only the indefinite pronoun uses the apostrophe in forming the possessive case.

Note in the following display the possessive forms of personal, relative, and interrogative pronouns:

Personal, Relative, and Interrogative Pronouns Inflected for Possessive

Singular	Plural
my, mine	our, ours
your, yours	your, yours
his	their, theirs
her, hers	their, theirs
its	their, theirs
whose	whose

Some Examples of Personal, Relative, and Interrogative Pronouns as Possessives

That is my book. The book is ours.

Your brother called. It is yours.

His book is lost. Theirs is lost.

Her book is lost. Their book is lost.

The cat drinks its milk.

The boy whose brother called is Al.

Whose book is this?

Never place an apostrophe in possessives such as *ours*, *yours*, *theirs*, *its*, or *whose*.

Faulty:	The book is our's.
Correct:	The book is ours.
Faulty:	It is your's.
Correct:	It is yours.
Faulty:	Their's is lost.
Correct:	Theirs is lost.
Faulty:	The kitten licks it's paws.
Correct:	The kitten licks its paws.
Faulty:	The boy who's brother called is Al.
Correct:	The boy whose brother called is Al.

Do not confuse the possessive case of personal, relative, or interrogative pronouns with contractions. The possessive of *it* is *its*. When we place an apostrophe between the *t* and the *s*, we create the contraction *it's*, which means "it is." The possessive of *who* is *whose*. When we add an apostrophe and an *s* to *who*, we create the contraction *who's*, which means "who is."

Compare these sentences containing possessives with the sentences containing contractions.

Possessive
> The fox lost its tail.
> The fox whose tail was lost returned to the forest.

Contraction
> It's raining. (It is raining.)
> The man who's going is Glen. (The man who is going is Glen.)

The indefinite pronoun, however, always requires an apostrophe in forming the possessive. To form the possessive of *anyone*, for example, we must add an apostrophe and an *s*—*anyone's*.

PS-32

Place a Noun or Pronoun That Limits a Gerund in the Possessive Case

A *gerund* is an *-ing* verb form that serves as a noun. For example, "jogging" is a gerund in the following sentence because it serves as the subject of the verb "is"—"Jogging is good exercise."

Note in the following display how nouns and pronouns can limit (restrict or modify) the gerund "jogging."

<u>John's</u> jogging helped him lose excess weight.

<u>His</u> jogging frightened the chickens.

He wouldn't give up <u>his</u> jogging.

In the first two sentences, "jogging" serves as a subject. In the third sentence, "jogging" receives the action of the verb and therefore serves as an object.

As we observed in our earlier discussion of verbals, we must watch structures in which a gerund can be mistaken for a present participle. When we say, "The farmer denounced the man's jogging," we indicate that "jogging" is a gerund—a noun—by the possessive "man's." When we say, "The farmer denounced the man jogging," we indicate that "jogging" is a participle—an adjective—by not placing "man" in the possessive.

The farmer denounced the jogging.

The farmer denounced the man.

The farmer denounced the man's jogging.

The farmer denounced the man jogging.

Pronoun Reference

PS-33

By definition, a pronoun is a word that takes the place of a noun. The pronoun "he" in the sentence "<u>He</u> spoke to Tommy about the flag" takes the place of some noun that appeared in a previous sentence. The meaning of "he" depends upon our relating "he" to that preceding noun. Without that preceding noun, the word "he" has very little meaning.

We know the meaning of a pronoun through reference to its antecedent, some noun mentioned earlier. The process of relating a pronoun to its antecedent is called *pronoun reference*.

Faulty pronoun reference can occur very easily, if we are not careful. This fault always blocks clearness and distorts meaning.

Whenever you use a pronoun, be certain that the pronoun refers directly to a specific antecedent and that the pronoun agrees with that antecedent in number and gender.

Clear Pronoun Reference

PS-34

When a reader meets a pronoun, he should be able to grasp instantly the person, place, or thing identified by that pronoun. If the reader has to pause for even a fraction of a second to puzzle out the pronoun, that pronoun is faulty.

The antecedent of a pronoun should be placed close enough to that pronoun for clear, unmistakable reference. An indefinite pronoun like *anyone*, of course, does not need a specific antecedent because it refers broadly to humanity. A few pronouns such as *I*, *we*, or *you* can have an antecedent that is *understood* rather than *expressed*. But, generally, the antecedent must appear earlier in the sentence, in a preceding sentence, or within the paragraph.

PS-35

> ### Rule
>
> *Be certain that the pronoun refers to an antecedent that has been expressed or to an antecedent that is unmistakably an antecedent understood.*

We must always be certain that the pronoun refers to an antecedent that exists as implied. For example, in the following sentence the pronoun "it" refers to an antecedent that doesn't exist:

He studied to become an accountant, and he found <u>it</u> a very rewarding profession.

He could not possibly find "accountant" an interesting profession. The pronoun implies the antecedent "accountancy." The sentence could read:

He studied to enter <u>accountancy</u>, and he found it a very rewarding profession.

Consider "them" in the following sentence:

We saw Bruce Willis rescuing heroes and heroines in the movies, and he made <u>them</u> often in every movie.

The logical antecedent of "them" is "rescues," but that antecedent has not been expressed. The sentence could read:

We saw Bruce Willis rescuing heroes and heroines in the movies, and he made rescues often in every movie.

We must watch the logic of antecedents in the possessive case. Notice how "Sousa's" provides an awkward antecedent for "him" in the following sentence: "After delighting in the concert by Sousa's band, the mayor gave him a fine dinner." Try: "After delighting in the concert by Sousa's band, the mayor gave the famous bandmaster a fine dinner."

PS-36

> ### Rule
>
> *Be certain that the antecedent is close enough to the pronoun for convenient reference.*

We must never overestimate our reader's memory span. When an antecedent is *remote*, we must supply a noun rather than a pronoun to identify the person, place, or thing we mean.

Consider the following paragraph:

> Sam climbed the hill and saw the hostel. Waterfalls were audible and flowers were profuse everywhere. He approached it as a good place for spending the night.

The word "hostel" is too remote for the pronoun "it." The sentence would be clearer if the noun "hostel" were used instead of "it."

> Sam climbed the hill and saw the hostel. Waterfalls were audible and flowers were profuse everywhere. He approached the hostel as a good place for spending the night.

PS-37

> ### Rule
>
> *Be certain that the pronoun refers to the antecedent you mean.*

We must always check for *ambiguous* or *intercepted* reference.

Consider again the following sequence:

> The captain and the first mate stalked into view. He spoke to Tommy about the flag.

The antecedent of "he" is ambiguous; this pronoun could refer to either "captain" or "first mate."

PS-38

> ### Rule
>
> *Be certain that the antecedent is a specific noun and not a general or vague idea.*

We must always watch the pronouns *that*, *this*, and *which* for focus on antecedents. Clarity demands that the antecedent of a pronoun be a specific noun. If we are not careful with *that*, *this*, and *which*, however, we may give these pronouns antecedents that are general ideas rather than specific nouns. When we do, we invite confusion.

Consider the confusion caused by the referent of "that" in the following sequence:

> With his mother away, he had to prepare his own supper. That upset him and he didn't do his homework.

The pronoun "that" has as its antecedent the general idea of preparing his own supper. The noun "supper," however, can be mistaken for the antecedent of "that." What upset him, the supper or preparing the supper?

To correct this ambiguity, we must identify more clearly what upset him:

> With his mother away, he had to prepare his own supper. Having to prepare his own supper upset him and he didn't do his homework.

PS-39

> ### Rule
>
> *Be certain that* you, they, *and* it *have specific antecedents and do not substitute for indefinite pronouns.*

Our everyday conversation is filled with expressions like the following:

> When you apply tar to a roof, you wear the oldest shoes you have.

> They say Chicago is very windy.

> It says in the *Divine Comedy* that pride is very bad.

In these sentences, the pronouns "you," "they," and "it" operate as indefinite pronouns. In the first sentence, the pronoun "you" means "anyone" or "one." In the second sentence, "they" refers to an indefinite group of persons. In the third sentence "it" refers vaguely to the spirit beneath words on a page.

This indefinite use of "you," "they," and "it" is permissible in conversation but is considered substandard in formal speaking and writing.

Avoid Indefinite "You"

If *you* does not refer to the person addressed, substitute a noun or an indefinite pronoun such as *anyone* or *one*.

> When a householder applies tar to a roof, he wears the oldest shoes he has.

> In applying tar to a roof, one wears the oldest shoes one owns.

Avoid Vague "They Say"

Substitute a noun or an indefinite pronoun for vague "they say" structures.

> Chicago has a reputation for being windy.

Avoid "It Says"

Let the document speak for itself in "it says" structures.

> The *Divine Comedy* considers pride a very serious sin.

> Dante ranks pride as a very serious sin in the *Divine Comedy*.

The pronoun "it" is quite acceptable in such idioms as "It is raining," "It is too late," "It is easy to be polite."

Pronoun Agreement

PS-40

A pronoun substitutes for a noun. As a substitute, the pronoun must resemble its antecedent in *person*, *number*, and *gender*.

PS-41

Rule
Check indefinite nouns and pronouns that serve as antecedents carefully.

Nouns such as *kind*, *sort*, *man*, and *woman* can mislead when used with pronouns, if we are not careful.

PS-42

Rule
Check collective noun antecedents carefully.

When we use a collective noun antecedent, we must guard against inconsistency. In the sentence "The group has changed its meeting place," both the verb "has changed" and the pronoun "its" refer to a singular collective noun, "group." Note how inconsistent the structure would be if the verb were singular and the pronoun were plural.

Inconsistent:

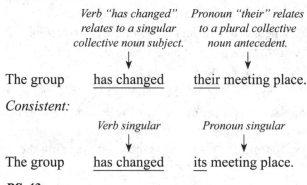

Verb "has changed" relates to a singular collective noun subject.   Pronoun "their" relates to a plural collective noun antecedent.

The group   has changed   their meeting place.

Consistent:

Verb singular   Pronoun singular

The group   has changed   its meeting place.

PS-43

Rule
Check compound element antecedents carefully.

When two or more nouns are joined by a coordinating conjunction such as *and* or *or*, a *compound* element is formed. For example, the coordinating conjunction "and" combines "carpenter" and "electrician" in the following sentence: "The carpenter and the electrician store their tools in the shed." The coordinating conjunction "or" combines "carpenter" and "electrician" in the following sentence: "The carpenter or the electrician stores his tools in the shed."

When compound antecedents are joined by *and*, the pronoun referring to these antecedents is plural.

When compound antecedents are joined by *or*, the pronoun referring to these antecedents can be singular or plural. If each noun in the compound is singular, the pronoun referring to these antecedents is singular.

Adjectives

PS-44

Adjectives describe and limit nouns and pronouns. Sometimes the adjective is defined as the part of speech that *modifies* nouns and pronouns. The term *modify* means "to describe and limit."

The Position of the Adjective

PS-45

We have met one important adjective, the *predicate adjective*. The word "beautiful" in "The sunset is *beautiful*" is a predicate adjective. The verb "is" links "beautiful" to the noun "sunset." When we say, "The sunset is *beautiful*," we describe the sunset as being beautiful.

The predicate adjective structure occurs very often in our language. There is, however, an even more familiar adjective structure in English—the adjective that precedes a noun.

Describing Adjectives and Limiting Adjectives

PS-46

The adjectives *beautiful, delicious, frightened,* and *tired* are *describing adjectives*. When we say, "*beautiful* sunset," we tell what the sunset is like. The adjective "beautiful" describes the sunset. When we say, "The cake is *delicious*" we tell what the cake is like. The adjective "delicious" describes the cake.

Some adjectives *limit* rather than describe. Consider the adjectives "the," "each," "five," and "several" in the following expressions: "*the* men," "*each* student," "*five* freshmen," and "*several* athletes." These adjectives do not tell what the nouns are like the way "beautiful" tells what the sunset is like. Instead, these adjectives pin down or narrow the meaning of the noun. They *restrict* or *qualify* rather than describe. Adjectives such as *the, each, five,* and *several* are *limiting adjectives*.

The limiting adjectives *a, an,* and *the* are most commonly called *articles* or *article adjectives*. When we use "a" or "an," as in "*a* boy" or "*an* arrow," we refer to *any* example of the noun. The words "a boy" indicate *any* boy. The words "an arrow" indicate *any* arrow. When we say, "*a* boy" or "*an* arrow," we are indefinite about which boy or arrow we mean. The articles "a" and "an" are *indefinite articles*.

When we use "the," as in "*the* boy" or "*the* arrow," we refer to a definite example of the noun. The words "*the* boy" and "*the* arrow" indicate a specific boy and a specific arrow. We call the specific article "the" the *definite article*.

An adjective formed from a proper noun is called a *proper adjective*. For example, a person who lives in Canada is identified by the proper noun *Canadian*. This proper noun becomes a proper adjective when it is used in structures like the following: "*Canadian* generosity has relieved much suffering in the world today." The proper adjective "Canadian" modifies the noun "generosity." The people of England are identified by the proper noun "English." This proper noun becomes a proper adjective in structures like the following: "The people of North America follow many *English* customs." The proper adjective "English" modifies the noun "customs."

Note how the underlined adjectives in the following word groups have been formed from proper nouns: "French cooking," "United States interests," "Mexican hospitality," and "Los Angeles residents."

A proper adjective, like a proper noun, is always capitalized.

Comparison of Adjectives

PS-47

Many adjectives *compare*. Consider the following sentences:

Joe is *quick* and makes a good shortstop and quarterback.

Joe is *quicker* than Juan, the former shortstop.

In basketball, Joe is the *quickest* man on the court.

Angela is *intelligent*.

Angela is *more intelligent* than last year's valedictorian.

Angela was the *most intelligent* girl in her class.

When we change "quick" to "quicker" or "quickest," we *compare* the adjective "quick." When we change "intelligent" to "more intelligent" or "most intelligent," we *compare* the adjective "intelligent."

Adjectives are compared to indicate *degree*. We can say that one man is "quick." If we compare that man with another, we can say he is "quicker" than the other. We indicate that he has a greater *degree* of quickness. If we compare that man with two or more other men, we can say that he is the "quickest" man in the group. We indicate that he has the greatest *degree* of quickness.

Similarly, we can say that one girl is "intelligent." If we compare her with another girl, we can say that she is "more intelligent" than the other girl. If we compare that girl with two or more other girls, we can say that she is the "most intelligent" girl in the group.

The three degrees of the adjective have names— *positive*, *comparative*, and *superlative*. When we say that one man is "quick" or one girl is "intelligent," we use the *positive degree*. When we say that one man is "quicker" or one girl "more intelligent" than another, we use the *comparative degree*. When we say that one man is the "quickest" of three or more or one girl is the "most intelligent" of three or more, we use the *superlative degree*.

Adverbs
PS-48
Adverbs modify verbs, adjectives, other adverbs, and whole sentences. The underlined words below are adverbs. Study each of these underlined words to gain a working knowledge of the adverb in operation.

Adverb modifies a verb.
    John adds quickly.

Adverb modifies a verb.
    Angela sings beautifully.

Adverb modifies an adjective.
    Angela is very intelligent.

Adverb modifies another adverb.
    Angela sings quite beautifully.

Adverb modifies whole sentence.
    John, consequently, is the winner.

Adverbs That Modify Verbs
PS-49
When we say, "John adds *quickly*," the adverb "quickly" tells *how* John adds. We might get as an answer to the question "How does John add?" the statement "John adds *quickly*." When we say, "Angela sings *beautifully*," the adverb "beautifully" tells how Angela sings. We might get as an answer to the question "How does Angela sing?" the statement "Angela sings *beautifully*." These two adverbs "quickly" and "beautifully" describe the way a verb action occurs.

Some adverbs tell when the action occurs. When we say, "John works *nightly* on the report," the adverb "nightly" tells *when* John works. When we say, "John is working *now*," the adverb "now" tells *when* John works. These two adverbs, "nightly" and "now," tell *when* an action occurs.

Some adverbs tell *where* the action occurs. When we say, "John works *here*," the adverb "here" tells where John works. When we say, "Angela studies *at the library*," the adverb phrase "at the library" tells *where* Angela studies.

Some adverbs tell *how much* or *how often* the action occurs. When we say, "John called *once* but Angela called *twice*," we tell *how often* John and Angela called. When we say that "John makes *much* of each opportunity," we indicate the *quantity* that John makes. When we say, "Angela practices *little*," we indicate the *quantity* that Angela practices.

The main job of the adverb is to modify the verb. Adverbs that modify verbs usually tell *how* something occurs (adverbs of *manner*); *when* something occurs (adverbs of *time*); *where* something occurs (adverbs of *place*); or *how much* something occurs (adverbs of *degree*).

Adverbs That Modify Adjectives
PS-50
When we say, "Angela is *very* intelligent," the adverb "very" modifies the adjective "intelligent." When we say, "We need an *unusually* able chemist," the adverb "unusually" modifies the adjective "able." When we say, "John is *well* known," the adverb "well" modifies the adjective "known."

Adverbs That Modify Other Adverbs

PS-51

When we say, "Angela sings *quite* beautifully," the adverb "quite" modifies another adverb, "beautifully." When we say, "John works *most* diligently," the adverb "most" modifies another adverb, "diligently." When we say, "He drives *too* fast" or "He drives *very* fast," the adverbs "too" and "very" modify the adverb "fast."

Adverbs That Modify Sentences

PS-52

When we say, "John, consequently, is the winner," the adverb "consequently" modifies the whole sentence. When we say, "Finally, the solution occurred to all of us and the meeting ended," the adverb "finally" modifies the whole sentence.

Very often, adverbs like *however, therefore, moreover, nevertheless,* and *otherwise* provide transition as they modify. The word *transition* means getting from one place to another. The adverb "however" relates what was said before to what follows in the sentence "Five men reported for work; two of them, *however*, came late." The adverb "therefore" relates what was said before to what follows in the sentence "Most members wanted to have parties as well as athletic events; *therefore*, we called the group a social and sports club." These adverbs have a special name to identify this transitional function. We call adverbs such as *consequently, hence, therefore, thus, moreover, nevertheless,* and *otherwise conjunctive adverbs.* Later we shall see why it is important you learn how to recognize *conjunctive adverbs* (also called *sentence adverbs*).

The Position of the Adverb

PS-53

Adverbs can appear in many different positions in the sentence. Usually, adverbs that modify verbs appear after the verb. Consider "He worked quickly" or "She sings beautifully."

Usually adverbs that modify adjectives or other adverbs appear before the words they modify. Consider the adverb "very" as it modifies the adjective "good" in "He is *very* good." Consider the adverb "very" as it modifies the other adverb "quickly" in "He works *very* quickly."

Adverbs that modify whole sentences may appear at the beginning of the sentence, somewhere inside the sentence, or at the end of the sentence. Consider the adverb "however" in the following sentences:

However, he accepted any papers that students submitted by noon.

He accepted, however, any papers that students submitted by noon.

and

He accepted any papers that students submitted by noon, however.

Adverbs may occupy other positions. Often the adverb precedes the verb. Consider "He *quickly* wrote the letter," "She *often* arrives early," or "He *certainly* likes dessert." Later we shall see why we must place adverbs carefully if we are to avoid confusion.

Comparison of Adverbs

PS-54

Many adverbs compare. These adverbs compare in a way that is similar to the comparison of adjectives. Consider the following:

Tom solves mathematical problems *efficiently*. He solves these problems *more efficiently* than his roommate. Of all the men in class, Tom solves these problems *most efficiently*.

Dr. Jones will arrive *soon*. Dr. Jones will arrive *sooner* than Dean Smith. Dr. Jones will arrive *soonest* among the faculty members who will attend the meeting.

Angela sings *beautifully*. Angela sings *more beautifully* than her sister. Of all her family, Angela sings *most beautifully*.

Adverbs have the same three degrees of comparison as adjectives—*positive, comparative,* and *superlative*. When we say that one man solves problems "quickly," we use the *positive* degree. When we say that this man solves problems "more efficiently" than another, we use the *comparative* degree. When we say that this man solves problems "most efficiently" among three or more, we use the *superlative* degree.

Verbs

PS-55

The verb is the *key word*, *heart*, or *motor* of the sentence. The verb activates the *subject-verb* or *subject-verb-complement* tie, which makes the sentence an expression of thought. All grammatical analysis must begin with the verb.

Verbs are grouped in several classes:

Action Verbs

PS-56

Verbs such as *break*, *run*, *talk*, or *vote* express action. When we say, "The girls often *break* dishes in the kitchen," the verb "break" expresses action. When we say, "I *run* to class," the verb "run" expresses action.

Sometimes the verb action needs a receiver, as in "Every student *will carry* a notebook." Sometimes the verb action is complete in itself, as in "Professor Sanchez will return."

Transitive Verbs

When a verb needs a receiver for its action, that verb is a *transitive verb*. The word *transitive* means "going across to." The action of a transitive verb goes across to a receiver—an object. We could define a transitive verb as one that takes an object.

Subject	Transitive Verb	Object
Each student	will carry	a laptop.
The mechanic	opens	the door.
The fielder	catches	the ball.

Intransitive Verbs

When an action verb does *not* need a receiver for its action, that verb is an *intransitive verb*. The prefix *in-* means *not* and the word *intransitive* means "not going across to." The action of an intransitive verb does *not* go across to a receiver. We could define an intransitive verb as one that does *not* take an object.

Subject	Intransitive Verb	Comment
I	travel.	*The verb needs no object.*
I	sit.	*I don't "sit" something the way I might "set" something. The verb needs no object. Compare "I sit" with "I set the table."*
I	rise.	*Compare "I rise" with "I raise my hand."*

Some verbs can be transitive in one sentence and intransitive in another. Compare "Professor Sanchez will return the book" with "Professor Sanchez will return."

In the sentence "Professor Sanchez will return the book," the action of "will return" has a receiver, or object—"book." An action verb that takes an object is a transitive verb.

In the sentence "Professor Sanchez will return," we mean that Professor Sanchez is coming back. Since "will return" needs no object to receive its action, "will return" is an intransitive verb. An action verb that *does not* take an object is an intransitive verb.

Linking Verbs

PS-57

Generally, a linking verb is some form of the verb *to be*, but there are other linking verbs that you must learn to recognize.

The Verb "To Be"

The verb *to be* is the main linking verb in our language. This verb can join a subject to a predicate noun or pronoun. This verb can join a subject to a predicate adjective.

Subject	Verb *To Be* (Linking Verb)	Predicate Noun (Complement)
Hunter Stevenson	is	the treasurer.
The woman	is	the mayor.

Subject	Verb *To Be* (Linking Verb)	Predicate Adjective (Complement)
Hunter Stevenson	is	accurate.
The woman	is	diplomatic.

Other Linking Verbs

Verbs such as *becomes* and *seems* are usually linking verbs. When we say, "It *becomes* late," "It *became* foggy," "He *seemed* happy," or "The coach *seems* quiet," we really mean "It = late," or "It is late"; "It = foggy," or "It is foggy"; "He = happy," or "He was happy"; and "The coach = quiet," or "The coach was quiet." Verbs such as *appears*, *feels*, *grows*, *smells*, and *tastes* can serve as either linking verbs or action verbs.

Linking Verb	Action Verb
She appears silly. (She is silly.)	She appears often at lunch.
His hands feel rough. (His hands are rough.)	His hands feel the wall.
He grows ambitious. (He is ambitious.)	He grows potatoes.
She looks good. (She is good.)	She looks carefully.
The poodle smells clean. (The poodle is clean.)	The poodle smells the plate.
The fish tastes good. (The fish is good.)	The fish tastes the bread crust.

The Inflections of the Verb

PS-58

The verb has more inflections (changes of form) than any other part of speech. Mastering the verb is primarily a challenge in mastering the inflection system of the verb.

Helping Verbs

PS-59

Some verbs assist the main verb in the verb phrase. We call these verbs *helping (auxiliary) verbs*. When we build a verb for our sentence, we must know whether a helping verb is needed, and if so which helping verb to use.

The common helping verbs are *am* (and all other forms of the verb *to be*), *can* (*could*), *do* (*did*, *done*), *have* (*has*, *had*), *may* (*might*), *must*, *shall* (*should*), *will* (*would*), and *ought to*.

Some of these verbs, such as the verb *to be* and *have*, often serve as main verbs. Study the difference between these verbs as helping verbs in the column to the left below and these verbs as main verbs in the column to the right below.

Am and Have as Helping Verbs	Am and Have as Main Verbs
I <u>am</u> eating.	I <u>am</u> ready.
I <u>have</u> eaten.	I <u>have</u> six pence.

Some of these verbs, such as *may*, *must*, and *shall*, are always helping verbs.

Principal Parts of the Verb

PS-60

The true source of power in the sentence, however, is the *verb* or the *main verb* in the verb phrase. For example, the source of power in the sentence "I walk to school every other day" is the verb "walk." The source of power in the sentence "I have walked to school many times" is the main verb "walked" in the verb phrase "have walked."

A verb like *walk* has many inflections—"I walk," "I walked," "I have walked," "I shall have walked," "I shall have been walking," to name a few. Some of these inflections involve a helping verb or helping verbs, but some involve changes from "walk" or "walked" or "walking."

A verb like *eat* has more inflections—"I eat," "I ate," "I have eaten," "I shall have eaten," "I shall have been eating," to name a few. The word *eat* appears also as "ate," "eaten," and "eating."

The key to these many inflections of verbs like *walk* or *eat*, as we have noted several times, is a set of four basic forms called the *principal parts of the verb*.

If you know the following forms of *walk* or *eat*—and, of course, the appropriate helping verbs—you can form any inflection of either of these verbs.

Present	Past	Past Participle	Present Participle
walk (walks)	walked	walked	walking
eat (eats)	ate	eaten	eating

Regular Verbs*

PS-61

We call a verb such as *walk* a *regular verb*. Any verb that forms its past and past participle by adding -*d*, -*ed*, or -*t* to the present is a regular verb.

Note how the following verbs are regular:

Present	Past	Past Participle	Present Participle
walk	walked	walked	walking
agree	agreed	agreed	agreeing
deal	dealt	dealt	dealing

Irregular Verbs**

PS-62

We call a verb such as *eat* an irregular verb. Any verb that changes internally to form the past and past participle is an irregular verb.

Note how the following verbs are irregular:

Present	Past	Past Participle	Present Participle
begin	began	begun	beginning
blow	blew	blown	blowing
break	broke	broken	breaking
burst	burst	burst	bursting
catch	caught	caught	catching
choose	chose	chosen	choosing
come	came	come	coming
do	did	done	doing
drink	drank	drunk	drinking
drive	drove	driven	driving
eat	ate	eaten	eating
fall	fell	fallen	falling
find	found	found	finding
fly	flew	flown	flying
freeze	froze	frozen	freezing
give	gave	given	giving
go	went	gone	going
grow	grew	grown	growing

(table continues)

Present	Past	Past Participle	Present Participle
know	knew	known	knowing
lie	lay	lain	lying
ring	rang	rung	ringing
rise	rose	risen	rising
run	ran	run	running
speak	spoke	spoken	speaking
steal	stole	stolen	stealing
swim	swam	swum	swimming
take	took	taken	taking
throw	threw	thrown	throwing
wear	wore	worn	wearing
write	wrote	written	writing

The Six Verb Tenses

PS-63

Whenever we use a verb, we always tell the time. It is impossible to use a verb without telling time. For example, if we use the verb "went" in the sentence "I *went* to the store," we tell the reader that the action of the verb occurred in the past. If we use the verb "will go" in the sentence "I *will go* to the store," we tell the reader that the action of the verb will occur some time in the future.

The time of verb action or state of being is called *tense*.

PS-64

Our language has six tenses. Three of these six tenses are called *simple* tenses—*present* ("I eat"), *past* ("I ate"), and *future* ("I will eat"). Three of these six tenses are called *perfect* tenses—*present perfect* ("I have eaten), *past perfect* ("I had eaten"), and *future perfect* ("I will have eaten").

Each of these six tenses has a *progressive form*—*present progressive* ("I am eating"), *past progressive* ("I was eating"), *future progressive* ("I will be eating"), *present perfect progressive* ("I have been eating"), *past perfect progressive* ("I had been eating"), and *future perfect progressive* ("I will have been eating").

Certain of these tenses have *emphatic forms* that employ the helping verb *do*—"I do eat," "He does eat," "I did eat."

---

*Some authorities call regular verbs *weak verbs*.

**Some authorities call irregular verbs *strong verbs*.

Study the chart below and you will see the tense inflections of the verb *to eat* charted in time.

PS-65

FORWARD MOVEMENT OF TIME →

Past Tense

Indicates action that occurred before the present moment.

I ate.

Progressive Form	*Emphatic Form*
I was eating.	I did eat.

Present Tense

Indicates action that occurs now.

I eat.

Progressive Form	*Emphatic Form*
I am eating.	I do eat.

Future Tense

Indicates action that will occur after the present moment.

I will eat.

Progressive Form
I will be eating.

Past Perfect Tense

Indicates action *completed* in past before another past action.

I had eaten.

Progressive Form
I had been eating.

Present Perfect Tense

Indicates action that began in the past but continues into present.

I have eaten.
He has eaten.

Progressive Form
I have been eating.
He has been eating.

Future Perfect Tense

Indicates action that *will* be *completed* after the present moment but before another action occurs.

I will have eaten.

Progressive Form
I will have been eating.

Present Tense

PS-66

The present tense is formed from the *present* of the principal parts of the verb, but note how "eat" changes to "eats" in the third person singular— "I eat" but "he eats." The progressive form of the present is formed from the present participle as a main verb and the verb *to be* as a helping verb—"I am eating," "you are eating," "he is eating."

We use the present tense to indicate an action or state of being that occurs now, occurs habitually, or occurs as a general truth.

Sometimes we place past action in the present to gain a dramatic effect. We call this present the *historical present*—"Hannibal looks at the masses of Romans. He *smiles*."

Past Tense

PS-67

The past tense is formed from the *past* of the principal parts of the verb. The past indicates any action or being prior to now—"I just saw Tom," "Socrates lived several thousand years ago," "Angela was the chairman."

The past progressive is formed from the present participle as a main verb and the past-tense verb *to be* as a helping verb. The past progressive indicates an action in progress at some period in the past— "Socrates was earning his living as a stone cutter."

Future Tense

PS-68

The future tense is formed from the present of the principal parts of the verb as a main verb with *will* as a helping verb. The future indicates an action that will occur after the present moment—"I will see Tom in a few minutes," "A million years from now the earth will melt," "Angela will be chairperson next semester."

The future progressive is formed from the present participle as a main verb with *will* and *be* as helping verbs. The future progressive indicates action in progress sometime after the present moment—"I <u>will be holding</u> three offices in the new semester."

Present Perfect Tense

PS-69

The present perfect tense is formed from the past participle as a main verb and *have* or *has* as a helping verb. The present perfect tense indicates an action or state of being that began in the past and continues into the present. When we say, "He <u>has eaten</u> at Maxim's many times," we mean that he started eating at Maxim's in the past and has continued eating there up to the present. He may or may not continue. This tense always includes a touch of the past and a touch of the present.

The progressive form of the present perfect is built from the present participle as a main verb and *have* (*has*) and *been* as helping verbs. The progressive of the present perfect indicates an action in progress from some time in the past to the present moment—"He <u>has been eating</u> at Maxim's all month."

Past Perfect Tense

PS-70

The past perfect tense is formed from the past participle as a main verb and *had* as a helping verb. The past perfect tense indicates an action or state of being that was completed before some other past action or state of being. Often we neglect this tense and overwork the simple past. The verb "had signed" must be placed in the past perfect tense in the following sentence: "The delegates <u>had signed</u> the Treaty of Ghent before Jackson fought the Battle of New Orleans." The past perfect "had signed" indicates an action prior to that indicated by the past tense "fought."

The progressive form of the past perfect tense is built from the present participle as a main verb and *had* and *been* as helping verbs. The progressive of the past perfect indicates an action in progress at some time in the past that preceded another past action— "Demosthenes <u>had been warning</u> the Athenians of the threat of Macedonia for some time before Philip attacked."

Future Perfect Tense

PS-71

The future perfect tense is formed from the past participle as a main verb and *will* and *have* as helping verbs. The future perfect tense indicates an action or state of

being that will be completed before some other action or state of being occurs or before some specified time in the future. This tense is seldom used in the English language because it is cumbersome and sounds stilted. The verb "will have driven" is in the future perfect tense in the following sentence: "He <u>will have driven</u> five hundred miles before he reaches Columbus."

The progressive form of the future perfect tense is built from the present participle as a main verb and *have* and *been* as helping verbs. The progressive form of the future perfect tense indicates an action in progress in the future, but an action that will be completed before something else occurs or before a specified future time—"I <u>will have been clipping</u> these hedges for five hours by lunch time," "Professor Jones <u>will have been teaching</u> here for thirty years when he retires."

Using Tenses Logically and Consistently

PS-72

We must be logical and consistent in the tenses we choose for our verbs. Verbs must indicate logically the time periods we mean to present. Verbs must relate consistently to one another within the sentence and within the whole composition.

PS-73

> **Rule**
>
> *Indicate the time you intend by selecting the appropriate verb tense.*

As we noted in reviewing the six tenses, each of these tenses covers a specified time period. All who use English associate the tense of the verb with its designated time period. If we say, "He has used that bridge many times," we convey accurately the idea that he started using that bridge in the past and that he still uses it. If we say, "He used that bridge many times," we convey the idea that the period of usage is in the past.

Watch sentences that contain a general, universal, or permanent truth. The fact that the earth is round represents a permanent truth in the following sentence: "Magellan demonstrated that the earth *is* round." It would be illogical to say, "Magellan demonstrated that the earth *was* round."

PS-74

Rule
Keep your verb tense consistent with time indicated by other words in the sentence and the whole composition.

Verbs always tell time, but other words are often needed to reinforce that indication of time. Note how the sentence to the left below needs the reinforcing time indicator "when it started in 1920."

Meaning Not Clear without Time Indicator
We learned in the lecture that the radio industry did not have commercials but now earns handsome revenues from advertising.

Meaning Clarified with Insertion of Time Indicator
We learned in the lecture that the radio industry did not have commercials *when it started in 1920* but now earns handsome revenues from advertising.

PS-75

Rule
Maintain consistency of tense among all the verbs in the sentence and in the whole composition.

Verbs must relate logically to life outside the sentence, and they must also relate consistently to other verbs in the sentence and in the whole composition.

Avoid Careless Shifts in Verb Tense
PS-76
Earlier we noted that the present tense can be used to indicate a habitual action or to dramatize some historical event.

Habitual action:
My friend and I rise early each morning when we are at camp. We take our breakfast with us and go fishing or climb mountains.

Historical present:
Labienus hurries to Caesar's assistance. Caesar is grateful to have this able lieutenant.

Whenever we adopt this present-tense viewpoint, we must guard against shifting to the past. For example, the verb *are* could shift inconsistently to the past *were*, if we are not careful—"My friend and I rise early each morning when we were at camp." Or the verbs "take," "go," and "climb" in the second sentence could shift inconsistently to the past, after a first sentence in the present—"My friend and I rise early each morning when we are at camp. We took our breakfast with us and went fishing or climbed mountains."

Keep Sequence of Tenses Logical
PS-77
We must not shift our time viewpoint carelessly and inconsistently, but we must also maintain logic in our *sequence of tenses*.

We mean by *sequence of tenses* the way the tense of one verb follows and relates to the tense of another verb in the same sentence or in a series of sentences. Note in the following sentence how a sequence of three verbs represents three different periods of time:

Before I took trumpet lessons, I had learned triple tonguing on the bugle, and I will always remember the thrill of triple tonguing during my first trumpet lesson.

PS-78

Rule
Keep the tenses of verbs and verbals consistent within the sentence.

As we noted earlier, the main business of the verb is to activate thought in the *subject-verb* and *subject-verb-complement* tie. For example, the verb "walk" activates thought in the subject-verb tie: "I walk." The verb "hit" activates thought in the subject-verb-complement tie: "I hit the ball."

Sometimes verb forms like the participle "eating" or the infinitive "to eat" appear in sentences like "Eating into the cherry pie, I struck several pits" or "I meant to eat the whole pie." In these cases, we call verb forms like "eating" and "to eat" *verbals*—verb forms that serve in a function other than that of verb.

Participles and infinitives—as verbals—do not serve as verbs, but these verbals do inflect for tense. These participial and infinitive tense inflections must relate consistently with the tenses of their *governing verbs*.

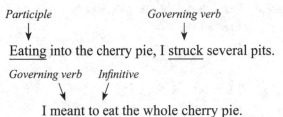

Tense Consistency of Participle and Governing Verb

PS-79

Two tenses of the participle concern us in the problem of tense consistency—the *present* and the *perfect*.

Present participle: eating, being

Perfect participle: having eaten, having been

We use the present participle to represent time that is identical with the time of the governing verb.

We use the perfect participle to represent time that precedes the time of the governing verb.

Tense Consistency of Infinitive and Governing Verb

PS-80

Two tenses of the infinitive concern us in the problem of tense consistency—the *present* and the *perfect*.

Present infinitive: to eat, to be

Perfect infinitive: to have eaten, to have been

The relation of the infinitive to its governing verb is very similar to the relation of the participle to its governing verb.

We use the present infinitive to represent time that is identical with the time of the governing verb, or time that follows that of the governing verb.

We use the perfect infinitive to represent time that precedes the time of the governing verb in the present.

Mood (Mode)

PS-81

Whenever we use a verb, we always think of the verb action or state of being in one of three ways. We think of the verb as helping to indicate a fact. We think of the verb as helping to give a command. We think of the verb as helping to express an idea that is not a fact of life. The form a verb takes to represent our viewpoint is called the *mood* of the verb.

Verbs are inflected to show three moods in English—the *indicative* mood, the *imperative* mood, and the *subjunctive* mood. We take the *indicative* and *imperative* moods easily in stride, but the *subjunctive* mood requires a little care.

Indicative Mood

PS-82

When we think of the verb as *indicating something we believe true*, we use the *indicative mood*. In most of our statements and questions, we deal with the facts of life.

For example, we say, "I <u>am</u> the class representative," "I <u>was</u> the class representative," "I <u>return</u> the book," "He <u>returns</u> the book," "I <u>choose</u> a chairman," and "He <u>chooses</u> a chairman." We never have trouble with the indicative mood, as a mood.

Imperative Mood

PS-83

When we think of the verb as *giving a command*, *issuing a warning*, or *making a request*, we use the *imperative mood*. Generally, commands, warnings, and requests are given directly to another, making it possible to omit the subject—"you" is understood. For example, we say, "Please <u>elect</u> me as class representative," "<u>Return</u> that book at once," or "<u>Choose</u> a chairman now if you want an orderly meeting." Sometimes the command sentence consists of one word—"<u>Hurry</u>!" "<u>Enter</u>!" "<u>Go</u>!" We seldom have trouble with the imperative mood, as a mood.

Subjunctive Mood

PS-84

When we think of the verb as expressing an idea that is *not* a fact of life, but a *condition contrary to fact*, a *wish*, a *desire*, or a *resolution*, we use the *subjunctive mood*. Most inflections for the subjunctive are identical with inflections for the indicative. On a few occasions the subjunctive differs from the indicative, and the difference must appear in our formal expression:

Subjunctive in condition contrary to fact:
If I <u>were</u> President . . . (not <u>was</u>)

Subjunctive in wish:
I wish I <u>were</u> President. (not <u>was</u>)

Subjunctive in "that" structures that express desire or resolution:
I desire that he <u>appoint</u> me chairman. (not appoints)
I move that the representative <u>appoint</u> Tom. (not appoints)
Resolved, that each class representative <u>appoint</u> a chairman of the class history committee. (not appoints)

Subjunctive in certain traditional (idiomatic) expressions:

As it <u>were</u>.
<u>Be</u> that as it may.
Come what <u>may</u>.
<u>Suffice</u> it to say.

Voice

PS-85

Transitive verbs inflect to indicate *voice*. Voice is a property or characteristic of the verb that tells whether the subject performs or receives verb action.

As we noted earlier, a transitive verb is a verb that can take an object. The verb "meets" is a transitive verb in the sentence "The boy <u>meets</u> the girl," since this verb has a receiver for its action, the object "girl." We distinguish the transitive verb from the intransitive "arrives" in the sentence "The boy <u>arrives</u>." The intransitive verb cannot take an object.

Active Voice

PS-86

When we structure a transitive verb in a form such as "meets" in the sentence "The boy <u>meets</u> the girl," we place that verb in the *active voice*. The active voice is that form of the verb that makes the subject the doer of verb action. In the sentence "The boy <u>meets</u> the girl," the subject "boy" performs the action "meets," and this action is received by the object "girl."

Passive Voice

PS-87

Sometimes we structure a transitive verb to make the subject receive the verb action. For example, the inflection "is met" makes the subject the receiver of verb action in the following sentence: "The girl <u>is met</u> by the boy." When we structure the verb "meet" in the form "is met," we place that verb in the *passive voice*. In the sentence, "The girl <u>is met</u> by the boy," the subject "girl" receives the action of "is met," and the doer of this action appears as the object of an adverbial preposition, "boy." Note that when the passive voice is used, the receiver of the action is actually the subject of the sentence.

Compare the active voice structures with the passive-voice structures in the sentences below.

Active Voice: The boy meets the girl.

Passive Voice: The girl is met by the boy.

Active Voice: Hugo wrote *Les Misérables*.

Passive Voice: *Les Misérables* was written by Hugo.

Active Voice: Termites destroyed my cottage.

Passive Voice: My cottage was destroyed by termites.

When to Use the Active Voice

PS-88

As you can see in the display above, the active voice is stronger and simpler than the passive voice. Whenever you cast a sentence or clause containing a transitive verb, prefer the active voice. On some occasions, you will have no choice; logic or paragraph structure will demand the passive. However, make the active, not the passive, your first choice.

When to Use the Passive Voice

PS-89

Consider the active voice first, but use the passive voice when it expresses your idea more effectively.

Conjunctions

PS-90

Conjunctions join parts of sentences. Consider the word "and" in the following sentence: "Tom *and* John went to Chicago *and* spent the day sightseeing." The first "and" joins two subjects, and the second "and" joins two verbs. Consider the word "because" in the following sentence: "He left for the concert early *because* he wanted a seat in the first row." The word "because" joins the word group that follows it to the first part of the sentence.

The words *and* and *because* are both conjunctions, since they join parts of sentences. The conjunctions *and* and *because*, however, differ as conjunctions. The conjunction "and" joins equal elements, like two subjects or two verbs. It is called a *coordinating conjunction*. The conjunction "because" joins a less important group of words to a main group of words. It is called a *subordinating conjunction*. There are several different kinds of conjunctions; only the three most important ones are illustrated here.

Coordinating and Correlative Conjunctions

PS-91

Coordinating conjunctions join equal sentence parts. Correlative conjunctions occur in pairs and balance two related parts of the sentence to demonstrate their relationship to each other. Study the following exhibit and note how these conjunctions operate. Each conjunction is shown in capital letters to the left, and then shown again in action to the right.

Conjunction	Conjunction in the Sentence
AND	Mr. Green and Mr. Carpenter called.
	The professor smiled and continued the lecture.
	We hurried to the store and then to the theater.
	If you do come and if you like the program, tell Helen.
	We studied our linear algebra, and then we had a soda.
BUT	We went to the beach but didn't like the weather.
	The boys played touch football, but they didn't have their hearts in it.
FOR	The dog show was uninteresting after three, for most exhibitors left as soon as their dogs had shown.
EITHER—OR	Either the professor or the proctor will start the quiz.
OR	Tomorrow the professor is going to give a quiz or hold a conference.
NEITHER—NOR	Neither rain nor snow discourages our mail carrier.
NOR	I did not get a letter, nor do I expect one.
YET	We have studied *Hamlet* many times, yet we still cannot explain why he delayed his action.

Subordinating Conjunctions

PS-92

The subordinating conjunction links a dependent word group to the main sentence. Consider the following:

Many customers ordered soup *because* the weather was raw and damp outside.

We did not climb to the peak of the mountain, *since* it was late in the afternoon.

The men stopped the machinery *when* the noon whistle blew.

The hikers accepted the ride, *although* a few of them wanted to walk all the way home.

The students did not know *where* the man had gone.

Prepositions

PS-93

Prepositions connect nouns and pronouns to the sentence. Consider the word "with" in the following sentence: "The plane *with* a high tail is a 727." The word "with" connects the noun "tail" and its modifiers to the sentence. Consider the word "to" in the following sentence: "All orders were sent *to* him." The word "to" connects the pronoun "him" to the sentence.

A good way to learn the prepositions is to recognize what you do to the waves at the beach:

Prepositions

At the beach I swim [among / under / in / into / over / through / around / beneath / above / across / between / after / before / behind / on / to / with / within / *etc.*] the waves.

Interjections

PS-94

Interjections express feeling. Consider the word "oh" in the following sentence: "Oh, what a difficult time I had with my descriptive geometry." Consider the word "ah" in the following sentence: "Ah, that coffee is delicious." The words "oh" and "ah" express feeling in these two sentences. These words are *interjections*.

Interjections are very easily recognized and seldom give us trouble in our writing and speaking. The following table lists some common interjections:

Common Interjections				
ah	bah	heavens	O	well
alas	gosh	hurrah	oh	whew
aha	ha	my	ouch	wow

Interjections such as *ah* or *alas* are always interjections when they appear in sentences. Interjections such as *heavens*, *my*, and *well* are interjections only when structured in sentences like the following:

Heavens, hasn't the mail come yet?

My, you solve these problems so rapidly.

Well, we have a new term beginning today.

PHRASES

What Are Phrases?

PH-1

Both phrases and clauses appear within the sentence as groups of related words. The main difference between a phrase and a clause is the subject-verb tie. A phrase *never* contains a subject and a verb. A clause *always* contains a subject and a verb.

Phrases

A *phrase* is a group of related words *without* a subject and a verb. For example, the prepositional phrase "with red hair" in the sentence "A boy *with red hair* is needed for the part" lacks a subject and a verb.

Phrases appear in various forms in our language— *noun phrases*, *verb phrases*, *prepositional phrases*, *participial phrases*, *gerund phrases*, and *infinitive phrases*.

Clauses

A *clause* is a group of related words *with* a subject and a verb. For example, the dependent clause "who has red hair" in the sentence "A boy *who has red hair* is needed for the part" has both a subject, "who," and a verb, "has."

Clauses appear in two different forms in our language—*main clauses* (independent clauses, principal clauses) and *subordinate clauses* (dependent clauses).

All phrases function as parts of speech within the sentence. For example, the prepositional phrase "with red hair" functions as an adjective in the sentence "A boy *with red hair* is needed in this part." The prepositional phrase "with red hair" describes the boy.

The *subordinate clause* (dependent clause) functions as a part of speech in the sentence. For example, the subordinate clause (dependent clause) "who has red hair" functions as an adjective in the sentence "A boy *who has red hair* is needed for the part." The subordinate clause (dependent clause) describes the boy.

Participial Phrases

PH-2

Participial phrases are common in our language; we use them constantly in our everyday expression. If we are to identify these phrases and control them in precise expression, however, we must understand the participle.

Present	Past	Past Participle	Present Participle
eat	ate	eaten	eating
find	found	found	finding
grow	grew	grown	growing
talk	talked	talked	talking
use	used	used	using

Participial Phrase with an Object
PH-3

Participle	Object
reading	Shakespeare

Participial Phrase with a Single-Word Adverb
PH-4

Participle	Single-Word Adverb
presented	first

Participial Phrase with an Adverbial Prepositional Phrase
PH-5

Participle	Adverbial Prepositional Phrase
reading	in the library

Participial Phrase with an Object and Adverbial Prepositional Phrase
PH-6

Participle	Object	Adverbial Prepositional Phrase
reading	Shakespeare	in the library

Participial Phrase with a Complicated Structure of Object and Modifiers
PH-7

Participle	Complicated Structure of Object and Modifiers
<u>reading</u>	<u>an early American edition of Shakespeare in the rare-books section of the Sussex Campus Library in Wallington</u>

PH-8

> ### Rule
> *Learn how to recognize participles and participial phrases; learn how to distinguish these elements from other elements based on verb forms.*

The participle is one of the three *verbals* of our language. The other two verbals are *gerunds* and *infinitives*, which we shall discuss later in this chapter. As we noted, the participle is a verb form that serves as an adjective, either singly or as part of a participial phrase. *A verbal is a verb form that serves in a capacity other than that of verb.* A *gerund*, we shall see, looks like a participle but serves as a noun rather than as an adjective. An *infinitive*, we shall see, can serve as a noun, an adjective, or an adverb.

We must not confuse a participle or participial phrase with a main verb. Very often we write *fragments* of sentences rather than true sentences because we mistake a participle for a verb. *A fragment is a sentence portion punctuated as though it were a full sentence.* Consider the following word group:

> The man reading an early American edition of Shakespeare in the rare-books section of the Sussex Campus Library in Wallington.

This word group looks like a sentence. It begins with a capital letter and ends with a period. If you read this word group carefully, however, you will note that it is not a complete sentence. This word group does not make sense because it lacks a verb. The word "reading" resembles a verb, but it is actually a participle introducing a long participial phrase. This word group is a *fragment*, a sentence element punctuated as though it were a true sentence.

PH-9

> ### Rule
> *Structure sentences containing participles and participial phrases carefully to avoid distortions of meaning.*

As adjectives, the participle and the participial phrase always modify nouns or pronouns. If we are not careful, we may place these modifiers near the wrong nouns, or we may even forget to include the nouns modified. Consider the following distorted sentences:

> <u>Skating rapidly around the block</u>, the firehouse dissolved in a blur.

> <u>Whispering "Dobbin, Dobbin," softly</u>, the horse was coaxed into the yard by the old farmer.

In the first of these sentences, the noun or pronoun modified by "skating rapidly around the block" is not included in the sentence. In this structure, the participial phrase seems to modify "firehouse." Did the firehouse really skate rapidly around the block?

In the second of these two sentences, the noun that should be modified is "farmer." The participial phrase "whispering 'Dobbin,' 'Dobbin,' softly," however, is closer to the noun "horse." Did the horse whisper, "Dobbin, Dobbin," softly?

We must guard constantly against this kind of distortion when we open a sentence with a participial phrase. We must structure our sentence carefully to see that the noun or pronoun to be modified does appear in the sentence and that it does precede all other nouns and pronouns in the sentence.

Noun modified

<u>Skating rapidly around the block</u>, the boy saw the firehouse dissolve in a blur.

Noun modified

<u>Whispering "Dobbin, Dobbin," softly</u>, the old farmer coaxed the horse into the yard.

A participle or participial phrase that applies to the wrong noun or pronoun is called a *dangling participle*.

Gerund Phrases

PH-10

Like the participial phrase, the gerund phrase is based on a verbal.* Although we use gerund phrases constantly and readily in our everyday speech, we must tighten our written command of the gerund phrase for two reasons:

1. We can confuse gerund phrases with verb phrases and with other verbal phrases like the participial phrase.

2. We can misplace gerund phrases and cause distortions of meaning.

The key to the gerund phrase is a verbal called the *gerund*. In appearance a gerund is identical with a present participle, but the gerund functions as a *noun* rather than an adjective.

The word *reading*, for example, could serve as a gerund or as a participle. In the sentence "*Reading* is educational," the subject of the sentence is the gerund "reading." The subject of a sentence is always a noun; hence, "reading" is a gerund because it serves as a *noun*. Compare "reading" in "*Reading* is educational" with "reading" in "The man *reading* is Tom." In "The man *reading* is Tom," the word "reading" serves as an adjective; hence, "reading" is a participle because it serves as an adjective.

Appearance of the gerund: In appearance, the gerund is identical with a present participle. The gerund is an *-ing* verb form like *reading, talking, using, working*.

Function of the gerund: In function, the gerund serves as a noun. A gerund can operate as a *subject*, an *object of a verb*, a *predicate noun*, or an *object of a preposition*.

Note in the following display how the gerund differs from the present participle, even though the two verbals are identical in appearance. In the left-hand column below, you will see the gerund in action as a verbal noun. In the right-hand column below, you will see the present participle as a verbal adjective.

---

*Remember the definition of *verbal*. A *verbal* is a verb form that serves a function in the sentence other than that of verb. We have three verbals in English—the *participle*, the *gerund*, and the *infinitive*.

PH-11

The Gerund Operates as a Noun	The Participle Operates as an Adjective
<u>Reading</u> is educational.	The man <u>reading</u> is Tom.
He likes <u>boating</u>.	He shouted at the girls <u>boating</u>.
The beautiful terrace is used for <u>jogging</u>.	He looked at the beautiful terrace and saw a man <u>jogging</u>.
He commented on the man's <u>reading</u>.	He commented on the man <u>reading</u>.

PH-12

Rule
Learn how to recognize gerunds and gerund phrases and how to distinguish these elements from other elements based on verb forms.

If we don't distinguish gerunds from verbs, we might punctuate the following fragment as though it were a sentence.

Reading an early American edition of Shakespeare in the rare-books section of the Sussex Campus Library in Wallington.

This fragment could deceive us, because it might serve as a subject and because the verbal "reading" sounds like a verb. We can make a sentence out of this gerund phrase by placing it in any of the positions occupied by a noun.

Gerund Phrase as Subject
PH-13

<u>Reading an early American edition of Shakespeare in the rare-books section of the Sussex Campus Library in Wallington</u> was inspiring.

Gerund Phrase as Object of Verb
PH-14

The professor praised my <u>reading an early American edition of Shakespeare in the rare-books section of the Sussex Campus Library in Wallington</u>.

Gerund Phrase as Predicate Noun
PH-15

His delight was <u>reading</u> an early American edition of Shakespeare in the rare-books section of the Sussex Campus Library in Wallington.

Gerund Phrase as Object of Preposition
PH-16

She referred to my <u>reading</u> an early American edition of Shakespeare in the rare-books section of the Sussex Campus Library in Wallington.

PH-17

Rule
Structure sentences carefully whenever you use gerunds and gerund phrases as objects of prepositions.

As we have noted, gerunds and gerund phrases can serve as objects of prepositions. For example, the gerund "operating" is the object of the preposition "by" in the prepositional phrase "by operating." The gerund phrase "<u>vacuuming the living room rug</u>" is the object of the preposition in the phrase "before <u>vacuuming the living room rug</u>."

Infinitive Phrases

PH-18

Like the participial phrase and the gerund phrase, the infinitive is based on a verbal.* Like these other two verbal phrases, the infinitive phrase is a familiar item of everyday speech. Clearness and precision, however, require that we tighten our command of the infinitive phrase, as we tightened our command of the participial phrase and the gerund phrase.

The key to the infinitive phrase is a verbal called the *infinitive*. The infinitive is much more distinctive in appearance than the participle and the gerund. The infinitive is generally marked by the word "to."** Whenever you meet a verb form preceded by the word "to," you may be certain that you are meeting an infinitive. For example, the verb form "to see" is an infinitive in the sentence "The person *to see* is the librarian."

An infinitive can serve as a *noun*, an *adjective*, or an *adverb* in the sentence.

Infinitive as Noun
PH-19

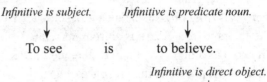

Professor Sanchez intended to return.

Infinitive as Adjective
PH-20

Infinitive modifies noun "person."

The person to see is the librarian.

Infinitive as Adverb
PH-21

Infinitive modifies verb "come."

Mary came to shop.

The infinitive, as we have noted, is the key to the infinitive phrase. An infinitive phrase is a group of related words that contains an infinitive. An infinitive phrase serves as a noun, an adjective, or an adverb in the sentence.

---

*Remember the definition of the verbal. A verbal is a verb form that serves a function in the sentence other than that of verb. We have three verbals in English—the *participle*, the *gerund*, and the *infinitive*.

**When the word "to" precedes a verb form in this structure, we call "to" the *sign of the infinitive*, rather than a *preposition*. The word "to" is the only *sign of the infinitive*. Occasionally, infinitives appear without "to," but these seldom cause trouble. For example, the "to" is omitted before "recite" in the sentence "The professor asked John to rise at once and recite the poem."

CLAUSES

What Are Clauses?

CL-1

A clause is a group of related words with a subject and a verb. Like the phrase, a clause is a sentence element. Like the phrase, a clause is a group of related words that serve as a unit. The main difference between a clause and a phrase is the presence of a subject and verb in the clause.

Some clauses express full thoughts. We call these clauses *main clauses* because they provide the main ideas in our sentences. Some authorities call these clauses *independent clauses* because they operate independently of other sentence elements. If we choose, we can punctuate *main* (or independent) *clauses* as separate sentences.

Some clauses do *not* express full thoughts. We call these clauses *subordinate clauses* because they serve *main clauses*. Some authorities call these clauses *dependent clauses* because they depend on main clauses for full expression of thought. We cannot punctuate subordinate clauses as sentences; if we try, the result is a *fragment*. A subordinate clause *cannot stand alone* as a sentence. Every subordinate clause is introduced by either a *subordinating conjunction* or a *relative pronoun*.

Main Clauses (Independent Clauses)

CL-2

A *main clause* expresses a full thought. This type of clause may stand alone as a sentence, or it may be combined with one or more other clauses within a single sentence. Every sentence must have at least one main clause if it is to make sense. Some authorities call main clauses *independent clauses*. Some authorities call main clauses *principal clauses*.

CL-3

> **Rule**
>
> *Check each unit that you punctuate as a sentence to ensure the presence of at least one main clause.*

If you don't know how to recognize main clauses, you won't be able to distinguish sentences from *fragments*. Remember from our discussion of phrases that a group of related words can *look like a sentence* without really expressing a thought. You must never punctuate a word group as a sentence *if it does not contain at least one main clause*.

CL-4

> **Rule**
>
> *Learn how to separate main clauses into different sentences and how to join main clauses within the same sentence, according to the meaning you intend.*

Some sentences consist of one main clause and no other clauses, main or subordinate. Each of the following sentences consists of one main clause.

Sentence formed from one main clause.	*Sentence formed from one main clause.*
↓	↓
Ms. Riley telephoned early.	She sounded very happy.

Some sentences combine two or more main clauses within a single sentence unit. The following sentence combines two main clauses:

Ms. Riley telephoned early; she sounded very happy.

When we combine two or more main clauses in a single sentence, we sometimes have to provide *coordinating conjunctions* to tell the reader how ideas blend. Note how *and* suggests one blend of meaning and *but* suggests a different blend of meaning when two main clauses are combined in a single sentence.

Main Clauses Joined by a Common and "And"
CL-5

The "and" tells the reader to think of the two main clauses as adding up to a single impact.

Ms. Riley telephoned early, *and* she sounded very happy.

Main Clauses Joined by a Common and "But"
CL-6

The "but" tells the reader that the mood he expected—sad or neutral—wasn't present.

Ms. Riley telephoned early, *but* she sounded very happy.

Sometimes we indicate the blend of ideas with a *conjunctive adverb*.

Main Clauses Joined by a Semicolon and "However"
CL-7

However *conveys an idea somewhat similar to "but." Note the* need for a semicolon *in this structure. The coordinating conjunction* but *is a true conjunction: it has the power to join sentence elements. The conjunctive adverb* however *does not have the power of a conjunction. When you join main clauses with a conjunctive adverb such as* consequently, however, therefore, *or* moreover, *you need a semicolon.*

Ms. Riley telephoned; *however*, she sounded happy.

The Fused Sentence
CL-8

A fused sentence results when one main clause follows another with no punctuation between. Note in the following example how one main clause fuses with another. These two main clauses could be punctuated as separate sentences, or these two main clauses could be joined with a semicolon or with a comma and coordinating conjunction.

Fused Sentence

Reader needs a marker to indicate the end of one thought and the beginning of the next.

Ms. Riley telephoned she sounded happy.

Correction by placing each main clause in a separate sentence.

Ms. Riley telephoned. She sounded happy.

Correction by joining main clauses with semicolon.

Ms. Riley telephoned; she sounded happy.

Correction by joining main clauses with comma and coordinating conjunction.

Ms. Riley telephoned, and she sounded happy.

The Comma Splice
CL-9

A comma splice results when one main clause is linked to another with a comma. A comma is too weak to join two main clauses. Note in the following example how one main clause is spliced to another with a comma. If two main clauses are to be joined, they must be joined with a semicolon or with a comma and a coordinating conjunction.

Comma Splice

Reader needs a stronger link to join two thoughts.

Ms. Riley telephoned, she sounded happy.

Correction by replacing comma with semicolon.

Ms. Riley telephoned; she sounded happy.

Correction by inserting a coordinating conjunction between comma and second main clause.

Ms. Riley telephoned, and she sounded happy.

Correction by joining main clauses with comma and coordinating conjunction.

Ms. Riley telephoned, and she sounded happy.

Subordinate Clauses (Dependent Clauses)
CL-10

A *subordinate clause* cannot stand alone as a sentence. It contains a subject and a verb, but it never expresses a full thought. Instead, it serves as a noun, an adjective, or an adverb within the sentence. We call this type of clause a *subordinate clause* because it is less important than a *main clause*. Some authorities call this clause a *dependent clause* because it depends upon the main clause, the *independent clause* of the sentence.

You can recognize a subordinate clause in two ways:

CL-11

1. **A subordinate clause does not express a full thought.** Consider the subordinate clause "if you are going to the library," in the following sentence:

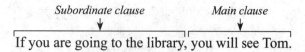

Subordinate clause   *Main clause*

If you are going to the library, you will see Tom.

Without the main clause "you will see Tom," this subordinate clause does not make sense. Consider the subordinate clause "which Tom said is interesting" in the following sentence.

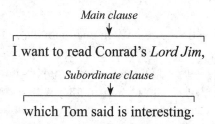

Main clause

I want to read Conrad's *Lord Jim,*

Subordinate clause

which Tom said is interesting.

Without the main clause "I want to read Conrad's *Lord Jim,*" this subordinate clause does not make sense. A subordinate clause without a main clause is a fragment of a thought.

CL-12

2. **A subordinate clause is always introduced by either a subordinating conjunction or a relative pronoun.** *Subordinating conjunctions* are words such as *although, because, if, since, when,* and *where* that introduce dependent word groups containing subjects and verbs. *Relative pronouns,* we noted, are *who, which, what,* and *that. That* is a subordinating conjunction when it introduces a noun clause, e.g., Jane said *that* she was going to class.

Subordinate Clauses Introduced by Subordinating Conjunctions

CL-13

In the display below, main clauses are distinguished from subordinate clauses in five sentences. Each subordinate clause is introduced by an underlined subordinating conjunction. Study each sentence and note how the subordinating conjunction serves as a *marker* for each subordinate clause.

Main Clause	Subordinate Clause
Many patrons ordered soup	<u>because</u> the weather was chilly.
We did not climb Mount Alb	<u>since</u> it was very misty weather.
The men stopped the truck	<u>when</u> the watchman appeared.
John accepted the ride	<u>although</u> he enjoys walking.
The adviser did not know	<u>where</u> Professor Sanchez resides.

Subordinate Clauses Introduced by Relative Pronouns

CL-14

In the display below, subordinate clauses are underlined to distinguish them from main clauses. Each of these subordinate clauses is introduced by a *relative pronoun*, which is underlined twice. The remainder of the subordinate clause is underlined once. Study each sentence and note how the relative pronoun serves as a marker for each subordinate clause.

The player <u>who</u> is holding the ball is Bill Richards.

The player <u>that</u> we meant is Bill Richards.

The game is rugby, <u>which</u> is very popular.

He calls to Bill Richards, <u>who</u> is holding the ball.

A Subordinate Clause Serves as a Noun, Adjective, or Adverb

The Noun Clause

CL-15

Whenever a subordinate clause serves as a noun, we call that subordinate clause a *noun clause*. Subjects, objects, predicate nouns, and objects of prepositions are all positions occupied by nouns.

The Adjective Clause

CL-16

A subordinate clause that modifies a noun or pronoun is called an *adjective clause*. We use an adjective clause when a single-word adjective fails to provide the detail and definition we need in our intended meaning.

The Adverb Clause

CL-17

When a subordinate clause modifies a verb, an adjective, an adverb, or a whole sentence, we call that clause an *adverb clause*. As you can see in the following display, adverb clauses can occupy many different positions in the sentence.

Introductory adverb clause modifying whole sentence.

If you meet Jim at the library,

Adverb clause following a main clause.

you can be friendly as you greet him,
but you must not,
if you want to cooperate, delay him as he works.

Adverb clause interrupting a main clause

Adverb clause at end of sentence.

SENTENCE LOGIC

Parallelism (Parallel Structure)

SL-1

> **Rule**
>
> *Maintain parallel sentence structure.*

Very often we employ a series of two or more words, phrases, or clauses in a sentence. For example, we write, "He asked for *pencils*, *papers*, and *books*" or "He searched *on the bureau*, *under the bed*, and *in the desk*."

Any such series of elements must be placed in the same grammatical structure, that is, must be made *parallel*. Parallelism is phrasing similar, coordinate elements in the same grammatical form. Note how awkward it is to combine a one-word adjective, a subordinate clause, and a prepositional phrase in the same series: "Ms. Hunter likes to find a store *convenient, that has low prices*, and *with a friendly atmosphere*." These elements can be made parallel in several different ways, for example: "Ms. Hunter likes to find a *convenient, inexpensive*, and *friendly* store when she shops" or "Ms. Hunter likes to find a store *that is convenient, that has low prices*, and *that has a friendly atmosphere* when she shops."

Faulty:	To mow, painting, and a swim are his only forms of exercise.
Parallel:	Mowing, painting, and swimming are his only forms of exercise.
Faulty:	My excuses are reluctance and that I am lazy.
Parallel:	My excuses are reluctance and laziness.
Faulty:	We want a government consisting of people, run by people, and for the people.
Parallel:	We want a government of the people, for the people, and by the people.

Items in a Series

SL-2

My philosophy professor stresses the value of <u>love</u>, <u>having reason</u>, <u>justice</u>, and <u>happiness</u>.

↑

Note how the gerund phrase "having reason" weakens coherence. The items in a series should be placed in the same grammatical form.

Items Joined by a Coordinating Conjunction Such as *And* or *But*

SL-3

Sir Charles Grandison proved himself a <u>hero</u> and <u>prompt</u>.

Note how the noun "hero" combines awkwardly with the adjective "prompt." The elements combined by a coordinating conjunction must be parallel.

"And Who" and "And Which" Structures

SL-4

Whenever "and who" or "and which" appears in a sentence, the structure preceding the "and" should be a parallel "who" or "which" clause.

John L. Sullivan was a fighter of great strength <u>and who</u> was feared by most of his opponents.

↑

The elements on each side of this "and" should be parallel. If a "who" dependent clause is used here, another "who" clause must precede the "and."

The elements on each side of this "and" should be parallel. If a "which" dependent clause is used here, another "which" clause must precede the "and."

↓

"Estrellita" is a beautiful serenade <u>and which</u> very few singers have sufficient range to present.

Correlative Conjunctions

SL-5

Correlative conjunctions occur in pairs and balance two related parts of the sentence to demonstrate their relationship to each other. Here are some examples:

> Both . . . and
> Either . . . or
> Neither . . . nor
> Not only . . . but also
> Whether . . . or

The grammatical elements that follow each unit in these pairs must be parallel. Whenever you use a correlative conjunction, be certain that you bracket or underline the grammatical units that follow each word of the correlative pair. Doing this in the following examples shows that they are **faulty**:

> He knew that the orchestra
> either needed a <u>trombone</u> or a <u>bass viol</u>.

> *The word "either" should be placed in front of "a trombone" since the elements to be compared are "trombone" and "bass viol," not "needed" and "bass viol."*

> *The "not only . . . but also" relates the verb "strengthens" with the pronoun "it." The parallelism of this structure is faulty.*

> Walking not only <u>strengthens</u> the body, but also <u>it</u> calms the nerves.

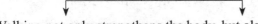

Note how the incoherent structures below are made coherent when similar, coordinate ideas are placed in the same grammatical structure.

Faulty Parallelism:
> My philosophy professor stresses the value of love, having reason, justice, and happiness.

Improved Parallelism:
> My philosophy professor stresses the value of love, reason, justice, and happiness.

Faulty Parallelism:
> Steve Jobs proved himself an innovator and resilient in difficult times.

Improved Parallelism:
> Steve Jobs proved himself innovative and resilient in difficult times.

Faulty Parallelism:
> LeBron James is a basketball player of great talent and who is feared by most of his opponents.

Improved Parallelism:
> LeBron James is a basketball player of great talent who is feared by most of his opponents.

Faulty Parallelism:
> "Estrellita" is a beautiful serenade and which very few singers have sufficient range to present.

Improved Parallelism:
> "Estrellita" is a beautiful serenade, which very few singers have sufficient range to present.

Faulty Parallelism:
> He knew that the orchestra either needed a trombone or a bass viol.

Improved Parallelism:
> He knew that the orchestra needed either a trombone or a bass viol.

Faulty Parallelism:
> Walking not only strengthens the body, but it also calms the nerves.

Improved Parallelism:
> Walking not only strengthens the body but also calms the nerves.

Modifier Placement

SL-6

> **Rule**
>
> *Place modifiers close to the words you want modified.*

A misplaced modifier can destroy the logic of a sentence. Verbal phrases are very easily misplaced and must be watched with special care. Note in the examples below how any modifier can distort meaning if it is carelessly placed:

Dangling Participle:
> Shouting insults, the shields were heaped on the traitorous girl.

> *The participial phrase "shouting insults" seems to modify "shields." How could the shields shout?*

Dangling Gerund:

Before vacuuming the living room rug, the baby was placed in the yard.

The vacuuming seems to apply to the baby. Did the baby vacuum the living room rug?

Dangling Infinitive:

To surprise the little girl, the lovely necklace hung from a branch of the Christmas tree.

Did the necklace want to surprise the little girl?

Dangling Prepositional Phrase:

My brother attracts girls with steadfast, manly glances.

Do the girls have "steadfast, manly glances"?

Dangling Adjective Clause:

The composer carried the piano from camp to camp in a large wagon which he played beautifully before soldiers, nobles, and kings.

Did he play the wagon before soldiers, nobles, and kings?

Note how the revisions below correct these dangling modifiers.

Dangling Modifier:

Shouting insults, the shields were heaped on the traitorous girl.

Revision:

Shouting insults, the invading soldiers heaped their shields on the traitorous girl.

Dangling Modifier:

Before vacuuming the living room rug, the baby was placed in the yard.

Revision:

Before vacuuming the living room rug, the mother placed the baby in the yard.

Dangling Modifier:

To surprise the little girl, the lovely necklace hung from a branch of the Christmas tree.

Revision:

To surprise the little girl, Uncle Charles hung the lovely necklace from a branch of the Christmas tree.

Dangling Modifier:

My brother attracts girls with steadfast, manly glances.

Revision:

With steadfast, manly glances, my brother attracts girls.

Dangling Modifier:

The composer carried the piano from camp to camp in a large wagon which he played beautifully before soldiers, nobles, and kings.

Revision:

Carrying the piano from camp to camp in a large wagon, the composer played that piano beautifully before soldiers, nobles, and kings.

Don't Use Squinting Modifiers

SL-7

> **Rule**
>
> *Guard against the "squinting" modifier, a modifier that could apply to words that precede it or words that follow it.*

Note in the structure below how the phrase "on New Year's Day" could apply to "said," which precedes it, or to "would meet," which follows it. The phrase "on New Year's Day" is a *squinting modifier.*

Squinting modifier

Sir Gawain said on New Year's Day he would meet the Green Knight.

Did Sir Gawain say *this on New Year's Day?*
Would Sir Gawain meet *the Green Knight on New Year's Day?*

Be alert for squinting modifiers. They usually occur in the middle of a sentence. Once detected, a squinting modifier is very easily corrected.

Squinting Modifier:

Sir Gawain said on New Year's Day he would meet the Green Knight.

Revision:

Sir Gawain said he would meet the Green Knight on New Year's Day.

Place Modifiers Next to What They Modify
SL-8

> **Rule**
>
> *Give special attention to modifiers such as* almost, even, hardly, just, merely, nearly, only, *and* scarcely.

Modifiers such as *only* can take many different positions in the sentence. For example, we can say, "*Only* Dave will deposit these payments in the First National Bank" and mean that Dave is the only one permitted to make deposits. If we place the word "only" after the word "payments" in the structure "Dave will deposit these payments *only* in the First National Bank," we mean that certain payments will be deposited only in a particular bank. If we place the word "only" after the word "Bank" in the structure "Dave will deposit these payments in the First National Bank *only*," we also mean that Dave will place these deposits in the First National Bank and in no other place.

The word *almost* can take different positions and change sentence meaning with each change of position.

> He <u>almost</u> qualified for the license by answering all of the technical questions, but he failed in all of the demonstration problems.

> He qualified for the license by answering <u>almost</u> all of the technical questions, but he failed in all of the demonstration problems.

> He qualified for the license by answering all of the technical questions, but he failed in <u>almost</u> all of the demonstration problems.

If misplaced, modifiers such as *almost, even, hardly*, etc., can change the meaning of a sentence or simply create an awkward, illogical structure. Generally, these modifiers go best in front of the words they modify.

Note in the following display how placing the modifiers "hardly," "merely," and "only" in front of the word modified improves sentence logic.

Illogical: He <u>hardly</u> cleared enough snow to get his car into the driveway.

Improved: He cleared <u>hardly</u> enough snow to get his car into the driveway.

Illogical: He <u>merely</u> wrote poetry for his own pleasure.

Improved: He wrote poetry <u>merely</u> for his own pleasure.

Illogical: We <u>only</u> skated for an hour.

Improved: We skated for <u>only</u> an hour.

Use Proper Emphasis
SL-9

> **Rule**
>
> *Emphasize the important ideas in a sentence; subordinate the less important ideas.*

We guide our readers by the emphasis we give to ideas. Our readers consider important the ideas we place in main clauses, and less important the ideas we place in subordinate clauses, phrases, and single words.

When we give a main idea and a subordinate idea the same stress, we confuse the reader. The sentence "My father loves mountain climbing, and he was a sailor when he was a young man" confuses the reader; the sentence has two main points. The sentence "Although my father was a sailor in his youth, he prefers mountain climbing to aquatic sports" does not confuse the reader because the less important idea is subordinated.

Even more confusing is a structure that places the less important idea in a main clause and the important idea in a subordinate clause or phrase. This illogical phrasing is sometimes called upside-down subordination.

In the display below, main ideas are underlined. Note how the illogical subordination confuses or misleads. Note how logical subordination improves clarity.

Illogical Subordination:
<u>Causing Romeo and Juliet to take their own lives</u>, a message went astray.

Logical Subordination:
Because a message went astray, <u>Romeo and Juliet took their own lives</u>.

Illogical Subordination:
<u>Although the great fortress that dominated the city for five hundred years has powdered to dust</u>, the site is still level.

Logical Subordination:
Although the site is still level, <u>the great fortress that dominated the city for five hundred years has powdered to dust</u>.

Structure Sentences Smoothly and Logically

SL-10

> **Rule**
>
> *Combine sentence parts carefully, smoothly, and logically.*

In the give and take of daily conversation, we are permitted great freedom when we combine sentence parts. In our formal speaking and writing, we are expected to combine the parts of our sentences carefully, smoothly, and logically.

Ungrammatical Combinations of Sentence Parts

SL-11

Sometimes through haste or carelessness, we try to combine sentence parts that do not go together. For example, we try to make an adverbial clause serve as the subject of a sentence.

The modifier "when I solve problems without bothering him" tells when something pleases. It does not tell what pleases.

↓

When I solve problems without bothering him pleases my supervisor.

↑

The verb "pleases" needs a noun or noun equivalent as its subject. An adverb cannot serve as a subject.

Even more often we try to make an adverb serve as a predicate noun.

Grammatically, we are permitted a predicate noun, predicate pronoun, or predicate adjective after this linking verb.

↓

The reason is because these plates are expensive.

↑

In formal expression, this adverbial clause must be changed to a noun clause—"The reason is that these plates are expensive."

An adverb substituting for a predicate noun occurs in many definitions.

In defining "documentation," we must tell what it is, not when it is. We need a predicate noun, not an adverbial clause.

↓

Documentation is when you cite the authorities for your statements in footnotes or a bibliography.

In defining "famine," we must tell what kind of thing it is, not where it is. We need a predicate noun, not an adverbial clause.

↓

A famine is where food is scarce and many people starve.

Note in the display below how sentences are improved when sentence parts are combined in a grammatical way.

Ungrammatical Combination:
When I solve problems without bothering him pleases my supervisor.

Grammatical Combination:
Solving problems on my own initiative pleases my supervisor.

Ungrammatical Combination:
The reason is because these plates are expensive.

Grammatical Combination:
The reason is that these plates are expensive.

Ungrammatical Combination:
Documentation is when you cite the authorities for your statements in footnotes or a bibliography.

Grammatical Combination:
Documentation is the citing of authority for your statements in footnotes and bibliographies.

Ungrammatical Combination:
A famine is where food is scarce and many people starve.

Grammatical Combination:
A famine is a scarcity of food that causes many people to starve.

Contradictory Statements

SL-12

Sometimes carelessness leads to contradictory statements or to statements that say the very opposite to what we intend:

Saul was the greatest warrior in the army, but he became envious of David, who was the greatest warrior in the army.

Contradictory statement caused by careless verb tense. Who was the greatest warrior, Saul or David?

Accounting is simply keeping records of business transactions, but it is much more than simply keeping records.

Contradictory statement by using same words—"simply keeping records"—to identify different concepts.

Although I haven't ever bought none of their records, I do like the Magnolia Quartet.

Double negative causes statement to say the very opposite of meaning intended. To say, "haven't bought…none" means "have bought some."

Note in the display that follows how a little care in phrasing corrects these awkward contradictions.

Illogical: Saul was the greatest warrior in the army but he became envious of David, who was the greatest warrior in the army.

Improved: Although Saul had been the greatest warrior in the army, he became envious when David surpassed him.

Illogical: Accounting is simply keeping records of business transactions, but it is much more than simply keeping records.

Improved: Although accounting is basically the recording of business transactions, it involves judgments beyond record keeping.

Illogical: Although I haven't ever bought none of their records, I do like the Magnolia Quartet.

Improved: Although I have never bought any of their records, I do like the Magnolia Quartet.

SENTENCE COHERENCE

Consistency in Point of View

SC-1

Rule
Maintain a consistent point of view throughout the sentence.

Our sentences always imply points of view when they convey our thoughts. Our choice of subject focuses the thought from a viewpoint that is limited or omniscient; singular or plural; first, second, or third person. Our choice of verb focuses the thought in tense, mood, voice, or number. Our choice of tone focuses a level of formality and an emotional attitude about the reader or the subject matter.

Consider the points of view established in the following sentence:

My <u>kid brother</u> <u>loves</u> tennis, and <u>he</u> <u>whacks</u> a tennis ball all day long every Saturday.

Tone: The expressions "kid brother" and "whacks" establish and maintain an informal tone.

Gender, Number, and Person: The subjects "kid brother" and "he" establish and maintain a singular, third-person point of view.

Tense: The verbs "loves" and "whacks" place this idea in the present.

Mood: The indicative mood views the thought as a statement of fact.

Voice: The active voice shows the subjects as the doers of verb action.

Once a point of view has been established in a sentence, that point of view should be maintained, if at all possible. Unnecessary shifts must always be avoided.

Observe the disruptive effect a shift in viewpoint causes.

My <u>kid brother</u> <u>loves</u> tennis, and a <u>tennis ball</u> <u>is parried</u> by this young athlete throughout the course of each Saturday.

Tone: The shift from the informal "kid brother" to the more formal "parried," "young athlete," and "throughout the course of each Saturday" is needless and disturbing.

Identity of Subject: In the first clause the subject is a person, "brother." In the second clause the subject is a thing, "tennis ball."

Voice: The major shift in this sentence is from the active voice, in which the subject is the doer of the verb action, to the passive voice, in which a completely different subject is the receiver of the verb action.

In maintaining a consistent authorial voice, watch the following critical areas:

Unnecessary Shift in Person:

When <u>I</u> get home from basketball practice, <u>you</u> know that my mother has been worrying about me.

Why the shift from "I" to "you"?

Unnecessary Shift in Number:

Every <u>soldier</u> must take good care of <u>their</u> rifle.

Why the shift from singular to plural?

Unnecessary Shift in Tense:

The neighbor's dog <u>has crawled</u> into our yard every day this week and <u>eats</u> from our garbage can on each visit.

Why the shift from the present perfect to the present when both actions occur at the same time?

Unnecessary Shift in Voice:

> We <u>won</u> the log-chopping contest, and an award <u>was received</u> by us.

Why the shift from the active voice to the passive voice?

Unnecessary Shift in Tone:

> We were <u>delighted</u> to sip the fine <u>vintage</u> wine that was served with the <u>chow</u>.

Why drop abruptly from the formal level of "delighted" and "vintage" to the informal "chow"?

Note in the examples below how sentences are improved when abrupt shifts in authorial voice are repaired:

Shift in Point of View:

> When <u>I</u> get home from basketball practice, <u>you</u> know that my mother has been worrying about me.

Consistent Point of View:

> When <u>I</u> get home from basketball practice, <u>I</u> know that my mother has been worrying about me.

Shift in Point of View:

> Every <u>soldier</u> must take good care of <u>their</u> rifle.

Consistent Point of View:

> Every <u>soldier</u> must take good care of <u>his or her</u> rifle.

Shift in Point of View:

> The neighbor's dog <u>has crawled</u> into our yard every day this week and <u>eats</u> from our garbage can on each visit.

Consistent Point of View:

> The neighbor's dog <u>has crawled</u> into our yard every day this week and <u>has eaten</u> from our garbage can on each visit.

Shift in Point of View:

> We <u>won</u> the log-chopping contest, and an award <u>was received</u> by us.

Consistent Point of View:

> We <u>won</u> the log-chopping contest and <u>received</u> an award.

Shift in Point of View:

> We were <u>delighted</u> to sip the fine vintage wine that was served with the <u>chow</u>.

Consistent Point of View:

> We were <u>delighted</u> to sip the fine <u>vintage</u> wine that was served with the <u>dinner</u>.

Inseparables

SC-2

> **Rule**
>
> *Keep related sentence parts as close together as possible.*

Certain sentence parts are called *inseparables* because their relationship is vital to sentence meaning. Subjects and verbs, verbs and complements, the parts of a verb phrase, and adjectives and the nouns modified are all inseparables that must never be separated unnecessarily by intervening words.

Note the awkwardness that results when inseparables are not kept close together.

Awkward Separation of Subject and Verb:

> Baseball, which every American schoolboy knows was popularized if not invented by Abner Doubleday, became popular after the Civil War.

The subject "baseball" does not tie smoothly to the verb "became."

Awkward Separation of Verb and Object:

> The young lawyer had organized before he left on the long mission in the Missouri area not to return for two years a school for Indians.

The verb "had organized" does not tie smoothly to its object, "school."

Awkward Separation of the Parts of a Verb:

> You will, whether you need it or not in whole or in part, receive this monthly ration of detergents.

The helping verb "will" does not tie smoothly to the main verb, "receive."

Awkward Separation of an Adjective from the Noun Modified:

> He was a quiet, and please understand that I use this term in a relative sense because he was noisy enough at times, child of seven.

The adjective "quiet" does not tie smoothly to the noun it modifies, "child."

Awkward Separation of the Parts of an Infinitive:
> To abruptly and without any explanation at all change course frightened the crew.

The sign of the infinitive, "to," is badly split from the element "change."

Observe how the awkwardness in the sentences below is removed when inseparables are brought closer together.

Awkward: Baseball, which every American schoolboy knows was popularized if not invented by Abner Doubleday, became popular after the Civil War.

Improved: Baseball became popular after the Civil War. As every schoolboy knows, this sport was popularized, if not invented, by Abner Doubleday.

Awkward: The young lawyer had organized before he left on the long mission in the Missouri area not to return for two years a school for Indians.

Improved: Before he embarked on a two-year mission in the Missouri area, the young lawyer organized a school for Indians.

Awkward: You will, whether you need it or not in whole or in part, receive this monthly ration of detergents.

Improved: Whether you need it or not, in whole or part, you will receive monthly this ration of detergents.

Awkward: He was a quiet, and please understand that I use this term in a relative sense because he was noisy enough at times, child of seven.

Improved: He was a quiet child of seven. Please understand that I use the term "quiet" in a relative sense, because he was noisy enough at times.

Awkward: To abruptly and without any explanation at all change course frightened the crew.

Improved: To change course abruptly and without any explanation frightened the crew.

Maintain Clarity by Avoiding Omissions
SC-3

Rule
Supply all words needed for clarity and completeness.

Everyday conversation permits many omissions of words and phrases. If we want to know whether a friend is ready, we don't have to use the full sentence "Are you ready?" We simply utter one word with a special inflection of voice: "Ready?" Even when we use full sentences, we often omit verb parts, prepositions, and conjunctions.

In formal expression, particularly in our writing, we must include all needed words when we write our sentences. Moreover, we must check copy carefully to make certain that all words needed for clarity and completeness have been included.

We must watch particularly the following structures:

Omitted Verb Parts:

The helping verbs "has been" are needed.

The guests have returned and the front door locked.

Omitted Prepositions:

The preposition "in" is needed.

A week's time the adviser scheduled an appointment.

The preposition "in" is needed. This "in" goes with "believes" as "for" goes with "hopes."

He neither believes nor hopes for mercy.

Omitted Conjunctions:

The subordinating conjunction "that" is needed.

He heard the cackling of geese saved Rome.

Note in the display below how supplying needed words improves coherence.

Needed Words Omitted:
> The guests have returned and the front door locked.

Needed Words Supplied:
> The guests have returned, and the front door has been locked.

Needed Words Omitted:

A week's time the adviser will meet with me.

Needed Words Supplied:

In a week's time the adviser will meet with me.

Needed Words Omitted:

He neither believes nor hopes for mercy.

Needed Words Supplied:

He neither believes in nor hopes for mercy.

Needed Words Omitted:

He heard the cackling of geese saved Rome.

Needed Words Supplied:

He heard that the cackling of geese saved Rome.

Avoiding Confusing Verb Pairs

SC-4

Rule
Learn the differences between commonly confused verbs.

Four verb pairs trouble many writers of our language— *affect* and *effect*, *lay* and *lie*, *raise* and *rise*, and *set* and *sit*.

Affect and Effect

The verbs *affect* and *effect* are both *transitive verbs*. A transitive verb, you will recall, is a verb that can take an object such as "hit" in the sentence "He hit the ball." The problem of *affect* and *effect* is complicated by the existence of a noun *effect*.

The easiest way to master *affect* and *effect* as verbs is to associate the word *influence* with *affect* and the word *change* with *effect*. You can help remember this distinction by noting that *effect* begins with the letter *e*, and *change* ends with the letter *e*.

Ⓔ F F E C T   C H A N G Ⓔ

For example, we say correctly, "This bad weather will *affect* attendance at the State Fair," meaning "This bad weather will *influence* attendance at the State Fair."

We can also say correctly, "The dean will *effect* a new curriculum," meaning the dean will institute a *change*. It is easy to associate *effect* with *change*

because the expression "He will effect some changes" is something of a cliché in our language.

The noun is always *effect*, except for an uncommon noun, *affect*, used by psychologists and other behavioral scientists. We can say, "The bad weather has an undesirable *effect* on fair attendance," since the noun is invariably "effect."

The easiest way to master the pairs *lay* and *lie*, *raise* and *rise*, and *set* and *sit* is to remember that *lay*, *raise*, and *set* are transitive verbs, and that *lie*, *rise*, and *sit* are intransitive verbs. These pairs are similar in appearance and meaning, but they are best mastered if seen as distinctly different verbs.

Lay and Lie

SC-5

The verb *lay* is a transitive verb; it needs a receiver for its action. The verb *lie* is an intransitive verb; it does not need a receiver for its action.

Associate *lay* with *place*. You *lay* the pencil on the desk when you *place* the pencil on the desk. Relate the *la* in *lay* with the *la* in *place*—LAy and pLAce.

Associate *lie* with *recline*. You *lie* in bed when you *recline* in bed. Relate the *li* in *lie* with the *li* in *recline*—LIe and recLIne.

Compare the principal parts of "lay" with the principal parts of "lie."

Present	Past	Past Participle	Present Participle
lay	laid	laid	laying
lie	lay	lain	lying

Note that the past of *lie* is *lay*, and guard against confusing the present of one member of this troublesome pair with the past of the other. Note that *lie* has a form with n and associate that *n* with the *n* in *recline*. The word *recline* will serve you in two ways when you associate that word with *lie*.

Lay: (To pLAce something)

He will lay the new rug this morning.

Yesterday, we laid a new rug in the hall.

They have laid a new tile roof.

You are not laying that rug straight.

Lie: (To recLIne)

Let a sleeping dog <u>lie</u>.

The basking fish <u>lay</u> on the surface of the lake yesterday afternoon.

He <u>has lain</u> in the hammock since lunch.

A strange dog <u>is lying</u> on the front porch.

Raise and Rise

SC-6

The verb *raise* is a transitive verb; it needs a receiver for its action. The verb *rise* is an intransitive verb; it does not need a receiver for its action. Fortunately, this pair gives us little trouble once we have viewed differences in the principal parts.

Present	Past	Past Participle	Present Participle
raise	raised	raised	raising
rise	rose	risen	rising

Raise:

I <u>raise</u> corn on my farm.

Last year I <u>raised</u> tomatoes.

I <u>have raised</u> a crop of vegetables every year since I moved to Idaho.

He is <u>raising</u> a question we will have difficulty answering.

Rise:

He watched the mist <u>rise</u> from Lake Leman.

The winner <u>rose</u> happily and shouted.

Who is the man who <u>has risen</u> from his chair?

The full moon <u>is rising</u> over the bay.

Set and Sit

SC-7

The verb *set* is a transitive verb; it needs a receiver for its action. The verb *sit* is an intransitive verb; it does not need a receiver for its action.

These two verbs are confused by many persons and often require special drill to eliminate substandard expressions like "I set there all morning" or "I sat the jar on the shelf." Compare the principal parts of this pair to see how their inflections differ.

Present	Past	Past Participle	Present Participle
set	set	set	setting
sit	sat	sat	sitting

Set:

The waiter will <u>set</u> the table.

Yesterday I <u>set</u> my watch by Central Standard Time.

They <u>have set</u> the stage carefully for the musical.

She <u>is setting</u> a plate on each shelf.

Sit:

Let us <u>sit</u> on the front porch.

The old bucket <u>sat</u> on the roof for years.

We could <u>have sat</u> in the waiting room.

This house <u>has been sitting</u> on the ridge for fifty years.

WORD EFFECTIVENESS

Avoid Pretension

WE-1

> ### Rule
>
> *Avoid pretentious expressions at all times, but especially on informal occasions.*

Whenever we discuss serious subjects such as history, literature, or philosophy, we necessarily use the words that identify the concepts of those subjects. For example, a discussion of logic requires the expression "syllogistic reasoning." Learned expressions in scholarly discussions are both desirable and appropriate.

Learned expressions and unusual words should never be used pretentiously, that is, to show off our knowledge. Some people imagine that it is impressive to call the eye the "optic" or to call laziness "voluntary inertia." They fill their speech with expressions like "compatible monitored mobility" or "synergistic applicability."

Always prefer the simple, direct expression to the pretentious and elaborately indirect expression. Use the special vocabulary of scholarly subjects when you need special terms to identify special concepts, but even then do not say, "ocular power" for *eyesight*. When you write a business letter do not say, "We wish to acknowledge receipt of your check in the amount of fifty dollars" when you mean "Thank you for your check for fifty dollars."

Don't Mix Formal and Informal

WE-2

> ### Rule
>
> *Avoid clashing mixtures of informal and formal expressions.*

To be taken seriously we must avoid clashing mixtures of informal expressions like "snappy" with formal expressions like "decor" in such sentences as "The Emperor approved of the *snappy decor* he found in the dining room."

If we establish the tone of informality in our writing, we must not introduce any highly formal expression. For example, the word "inaugurated" is too formal for the following sentence: "The peddler *inaugurated* the practice of selling apples in little paper bags."

If we establish the tone of formality in our writing, we must be careful not to introduce some highly informal expression. For example, the word "bug" is inappropriate in the following sentence: "Wordsworth's poetry on nature was exalted and noble, but when he ventured a poem on human nature there was always a bug in the imagery."

Be Idiomatic

WE-3

> ### Rule
>
> *Avoid unidiomatic expressions.*

An unidiomatic expression is one that breaks with the pattern followed by careful speakers and writers. If English is your mother tongue, you take most of the idiom of our language as *natural*. We say, "I found *logic* in his reasoning," but we do not say, "I found *flaw* in his reasoning." To be idiomatic, we must say, "I found a *flaw* in his reasoning."

One area of idiom that everyone must watch is prepositional idiom. Note: "different *from*" is preferable to "different *than*" because "different from" is idiomatic. The dictionary guides us on prepositional idiom, but it is valuable to master some of the more common prepositional idioms.

Here are only a few examples—there are many more.

accede

We accede *to* something. "The Dean acceded to our request."

agree

We agree *to* a plan or other idea. "The Dean agreed to our program."

We agree *with* a person. "The Dean agreed with the professor on the merits of the new course."

compare

One situation compares *to* another situation when it illustrates similarities. "This protest compares to the protest of New England in 1812."

We compare one thing *with* another to find similarities and differences. "Compare this poem by Tennyson with any poem of Keats and you will note very interesting similarities and differences."

differ

We differ *with* another when we disagree with him. "The Dean differed with the professor on the merits of the new course."

One person, place, or thing differs *from* another when the two are not the same. "The new program differs from the one we used last year."

A Glossary of Usage

WE-4

Rule
Learn the meanings of words and proper usage.

Some words cause us constant trouble if we do not master them. For example, *affect* and *effect* are frequently confused. We can consult our dictionaries each time we use *affect* or *effect*. But we can save ourselves trouble if we master the difference between these two words.

The following word guide, or *glossary*, reviews some of the words that cause constant trouble. Study this glossary and apply the insights it provides for better speaking and writing.

a, an

The indefinite article *a* is used before a consonant sound; the indefinite article *an* is used before a vowel sound: *a plan, an idea.*

accept, except

Accept means *to receive*; *except* when used as a verb means *to exclude*. "We accepted the new program." "Tom's name was excepted from the committee roster."

The word *except* is used most often as a preposition. "Everyone went except me."

affect, effect

The verb *affect* means *to influence*. The verb *effect* means to *bring about*. The noun *effect* means *result*. "The Dean's decision did not affect the program." "The new program will effect many changes." "The new program will have a good effect on student morale."

aggravate

The verb *aggravate* means to *intensify* or *increase* when used formally. "The rain aggravated their suffering."

Many use the word *aggravate* also to mean to *irritate* or to *annoy*. This latter usage should be avoided in formal expression.

ain't

An illiteracy to be avoided by careful speakers and writers.

all the farther, all the faster

Do not use these dialectal expressions in place of *as far as* or *as fast as*.

already, all ready

Already means *before* or *by a certain time*; *all ready* means *fully, completely*, or *entirely ready*. "Mike said that he had already received his voucher." "When the whistle blew, the girls were all ready for the game."

all right, alright

Always spell this expression *all right*.

altogether, all together

Altogether means *completely, entirely, wholly*; *all together* means *as a group*. "We find Peggy altogether too conceited for our choice of friend." "After the explosion, the foreman was relieved to find his group all together in front of the building."

among, between

Among applies to *three or more*; *between* applies to *two*. "She divided the commission evenly among the three college students." "She divided the commission evenly between the two college students."

Occasionally, the word *between* is used with three or more if a give-and-take situation results or a point in a relationship is established. "The cotton triangle required cooperation between the South, the Northeast, and England." "Columbus proved to be the most convenient point between Cleveland, Cincinnati, and Toledo."

amount, number

Amount applies to *bulk*, *mass*, or *quantity*; *number* applies to *a quantity that can be counted*. "There is a larger amount of snow on the lawn today than there was yesterday." "A large number of these books is available in the bookstore."

an, a

See a, an

and etc.

The abbreviation *etc.* stands for the Latin *et cetera*. The *et* means *and*; the *cetera* means *other things*. It is wrong to say *and etc.* because the idea of *and* is already included in the *etc.* Do not use this expression as a substitute for thinking of additional items.

anyways, anywheres, everywheres, somewheres

These expressions are all colloquial. Omit the final *s* after each.

as, as a means of, as a method of, as to

The conjunction *as* provides a useful connective, but it sometimes leads to loose, flabby structures. Do not use *as* when you mean *that* or *whether*. "I am not certain that (*not* as) he will bring the road map." "I am not certain whether (*not* as) he wrote."

Avoid the indirect expressions *as a means of* and *as a method of* when you mean *for*. "You will find walking useful for (*not* as a means of *or* as a method of) reducing nervous tension."

Do not use *as to* for *about*. "He requested information about (*not* as to) your article on wasps."

awful

Never use *awful* when you mean *very* or *extremely* in formal expression. "Rover was very (*not* awfully) excited when we returned."

Never use *awful* to mean *bad*, *undesirable*, or *unsatisfactory*. "His criticism made me feel depressed (*not* awful)."

being as, being that

Do not use these illiteracies for *since* or *that*.

beside, besides

Beside means *alongside of*; *besides* means *in addition to*. "They sat beside the brook all afternoon." "There is nobody besides Tom who understands this code."

between, among

See among, between

but that, but what

Do not use in place of *that* in structures like "I do not question that (*not* but that) you are faster."

can't hardly

Avoid this double negative. Prefer *can hardly*.

complected, complexioned

Avoid the illiteracy *complected*. Prefer *complexioned*.

continual, continuous

Continual applies to a *succession that is steady but broken from time to time*; *continuous* applies to an *unbroken succession*. "The space flight was guided by continual corrections from Houston." "The mud was washed away by the continuous rain from Monday through Wednesday."

could of

Do not use for *could have*.

data

Although *data* is the plural of *datum*, idiom permits the use of this word as a singular. Some authorities still insist on *Data are gathered* rather than *Data is gathered*, or *these data* rather than *this data*. Most persons in computer programming now say *Data is gathered* or *this data*.

deal

Do not use this colloquial term for *arrangement* or *transaction* in formal expression. "He enjoys an excellent arrangement (*not* deal) with the business manager of the *State College Journal*."

different from, different than

Prefer idiomatic *different from*. See discussion of idiom in preceding section of this chapter.

doesn't, don't

Doesn't means *does not*; *don't* means *do not*. Do not say "He don't (do not)" when you mean "He doesn't (does not)."

effect, affect

See affect, effect

enthuse

Do not use this colloquial verb in formal expression. "The art director was enthusiastic (*not* enthused) about the painting."

equally as good

Prefer *equally good.*

etc.

See and etc.

everywheres

See anyways, anywheres, everywheres, somewheres

except, accept

See accept, except

expect

Do not use this word when you mean *believe, suppose,* or *think.* "I do not think (*not* expect) that the postman was here yet."

farther, further

Farther applies to *distance in space*; *further* applies to *additional or advanced degrees or quantities.* "We walked farther east than we did south." "The mayor waited for further information."

fewer, less

Fewer applies to *quantities that can be counted*; *less* applies to *quantities that must be measured rather than counted.* Observe these distinctions in all formal expression. "Our team made fewer errors and displayed less confusion than any other team in the tournament."

former, latter

Former applies to the *first named in a series of two*; *latter* refers to the *last named in a series of two.* Do not use *former* to indicate the first of a series of three or more and *latter* to indicate the last of a series of three or more.

get

Get means to *obtain* or *receive* and may be used in these senses without restriction. This word, however, should not be used formally in the sense of *to excite, to interest,* or *to understand.* "His guitar playing intrigues (*not* gets) me." "When my grandmother talks about music, I just don't understand (*not* get) her."

good, well

Do not use the adjective *good* in place of the adverb *well* in structures like the following: "John works well (*not* good) as committee chairman."

had of

Avoid this illiteracy for *had.* "My father always said that he wished he had (*not* had of) gone to college."

hanged, hung

When a person is *executed,* he is *hanged.* When anything is *suspended in space,* it is *hung.*

hardly

See can't hardly

healthful, healthy

Healthful applies to *conditions that promote health*; *healthy* applies to *a state of health.* "Stevenson found the climate of Saranac Lake very healthful." "Mary is a very healthy girl."

if, whether

Prefer *whether* to *if* in structures that follow verbs such as *ask, doubt, know, learn, say.* "Henry V did not know whether (*not* if) he had won the battle."

imply, infer

Imply means to *hint an idea without expressing it directly*; *infer* means to *draw an understanding or conclusion from someone's expression or a situation.* "The professor implied that the student was not listening carefully." "He inferred from Jane's remark that she was bored."

in, into

In applies to *something located within something else*; *into* applies to *a movement from the outside to the inside.* "John sat in the office." "John walked into the office."

in back of

Prefer *at the back of* or *behind.*

infer, imply

See imply, infer

irregardless

Avoid this impropriety. Say *regardless.*

its, it's

Its is the possessive of *it*; *it's* is the contraction for *it is.*

kind of, sort of

Do not use *kind of* and *sort of* as adverbs in formal expression. "Falstaff was rather (*not* kind of *or* sort of) witty in *Henry IV, Part 1*."

kind of a, sort of a

Omit the *a* in formal structures. "What kind of (*not* kind of a *or* sort of a) wine is Chablis?"

lay, lie

See discussion under transitive and intransitive verbs in "The Eight Parts of Speech" on page 332.

learn, teach

Learn means to *gain knowledge*; *teach* means to *impart knowledge*. "He taught (*not* learned) his brother how to swim."

leave, let

Avoid the nonstandard *leave* him go for *let* him go. The word *leave* means *depart*. "I leave today." The word *let* means to *allow*. "Let me take your place."

less, fewer

See fewer, less

lie, lay

See discussion under transitive and intransitive verbs in "The Eight Parts of Speech" on page 332.

like

Do not use *like* as a subordinating conjunction in formal expression. *Like* is a preposition when used as a connective: A writer like Stephen Crane is rare. Use a subordinating conjunction, not the preposition *like*, in structures like the following: He tries hard, as (*not* like) most players do.

likely, liable

The word *likely* applies to *anything probable*; the word *liable* applies to an *unpleasant possibility*, a *subjection to punishment*, or a *responsibility*. "You are likely (*not* liable) to get the part of François Villon in the play." "You are liable to fall off the stage if you get too excited."

locate

Do not use to mean *settle* or *move to*. "We will move to (*not* locate in) Clear Water next year."

may of

Avoid this illiteracy for *may have*.

might of

Avoid this illiteracy for *might have*.

must of

Avoid this illiteracy for *must have*.

myself, himself, yourself

These pronouns are to be used as intensives, as in "The Dean herself (himself) will open the conclave," or as reflexives, as in "He (she) hit himself when he beat the carpet." Do not use these forms when *me*, *her*, *him*, or *you* will serve. "We shall be honored if John and you (*not* yourself) join us for tea at the Plaza."

nice

Do not use in formal expression for *becoming*, *pleasant*, *pretty*, *winsome*. "John met an attractive (*not* nice) girl at the dance." The word *nice* means *subtle* or *fine*. "He made some nice distinctions between Freudian and interpersonal theory."

number, amount

See amount, number

of, have

Do not use *of* for *have* in structures such as *could have*.

off of

Omit the *of*. "The book fell off (*not* off of) the shelf."

per

Avoid the pretentious Latin preposition in statements such as *per your letter*.

practical, practicable

Practical applies to *actual use as distinguished from theory*; *practicable* means *feasible* or *possible*. "My father is a practical man." "The chairman did not consider the program practicable for May."

principal, principle

Principal applies to *a chief* or *the chief part of something*; *principle* applies to *a basic law*. "Mr. Jones is the principal of the school." "Professor White was the principal speaker." "He paid both the interest and the principal." "Fair play is a good principle to follow."

raise, rise

See discussion under transitive and intransitive verbs in "The Eight Parts of Speech" on page 332.

reason is because, reason is that

Prefer *the reason is that* in formal speaking and writing.

respectfully, respectively

Respectfully means *with respect* as in the complimentary close of a letter *respectfully yours*; *respectively* means that *each item will be considered in the order given.* "This paper is respectfully submitted." "The hero, the heroine, and the villain will be played by Hunter, Selena, and Jake, respectively."

rise, raise

See discussion under transitive and intransitive verbs in "The Eight Parts of Speech" on page 332.

said

Avoid the legalistic use of *said* as in *said letter, said plan*, and *said program* except in legal writing.

should of

Do not use for *should have.*

sit, set

See discussion under transitive and intransitive verbs in "The Eight Parts of Speech" on page 332.

some

Do not use *some* when you mean *somewhat.*

sort of, kind of

See kind of, sort of

sort of a, kind of a

See kind of a, sort of a

such

Do not use *such* as an intensive in formal expression. "My sister has such a wonderful way with children" is permissible in friendly conversation. "My sister has a wonderful way with children" is preferred in formal speaking and writing.

suspicion

Do not use *suspicion* as a verb when you mean *suspect.*

teach, learn

See learn, teach

terrible, terribly

Do not use these words in place of *very* in formal speaking and writing.

try and

Use *try to* in formal expression.

wait for, wait on

Wait for means to *await*; *wait on* means to *serve.* "I am waiting for (*not* waiting on) Tom to call."

way, ways

Do not use *ways* for *way.* "It is a long way (*not* ways) to California."

where

Do not use *where* in place of *that* in expressions like the following: "I see in the newspaper that (*not* where) a jet airport will be built near Hampton."

would of

Do not use for *would have.*

PART 9

The ACT Writing Test

THE ACT WRITING SECTION

The ACT Writing Section will measure a student's mastery of the effective development and expression of ideas. Students will have 40 minutes to write a draft of an original essay. This will be a direct measure of their abilities, under timed conditions, to do the kind of writing required in most college courses—writing that emphasizes precise use of language, logical presentation of ideas, development of a point of view, and clarity of expression.

Unlike the 36-point scale for the other sections of the ACT, scores for the essay range from 2 to 12. Essays not written on the assigned prompt will be given a score of zero.

THE ESSAY ON THE ACT WRITING TEST

On the ACT Writing Test you will be presented with a prompt in which you will have to take a position based on three perspectives. You will have 40 minutes to write about your position. Here are the directions and a sample prompt.

Directions

You may use the unlined pages in this test booklet to plan your essay. These pages will not be scored. **You must write your essay in pencil on the lined pages in the answer folder.** Your writing on those lined pages will be scored. You may not need all the lined pages, but to ensure you have enough room to finish, do NOT skip lines. You may write corrections or additions neatly between the lines of your essay, but do NOT write in the margins of the lined pages. **Illegible essays cannot be scored, so you must write (or print) clearly.**

If you finish before time is called, you may review your work. Lay your pencil down immediately when time is called.

Writing Test Prompt

Many high school libraries use some of their limited funding to subscribe to popular magazines with articles that are interesting to students. Despite limited funding, some educators support this practice because they think having these magazines available encourages students to read. Other educators think school libraries should not use limited funds to subscribe to these magazines because they may not be related to academic subjects. Should high school libraries subscribe to popular magazines?

Carefully read the following perspectives, which describe the consequences of schools providing or not providing popular magazines for their students.

Perspective One

By having students read popular magazines, teachers prevent students from learning about subjects related to their course work and keep them from recognizing the relevance of their courses to the real world. They will not be able to draw examples related to the courses they are taking and their work will not be substantiated with real-world situations.

Perspective Two

By not providing students with popular magazines, schools will be able to use that money for other students' needs, such as computer peripherals. Students will focus more on their course work and its relevance to everyday life, and this focus can be enhanced by material used in place of the popular magazines

Perspective Three

Popular magazines provide insight into all aspects of human endeavors. They connect material taken from standard school curriculum to real-life situations. When courses taught in school can be related to material found in the popular magazines, students are better able to appreciate the relevance of their courses to what is happening in the real world with real people.

Essay Directions

Write a meaningful and logical essay in which you describe and evaluate multiple perspectives on advantages and disadvantages of schools providing popular magazines and articles for their students. In your essay, make sure that you

- clearly state and analyze your own perspective in relation to at least one other perspective
- support your statements with clear reasoning and specific examples

- organize your material logically
- communicate effectively using atandard written English

Note that your perspective may be completely in agreement with any of the others, may be partially in agreement, or may be in complete disagreement. In any case, you must support your essay with logic, making detailed references to the passages and using specific examples to support your points.

Note on Planning the Essay

Develop ideas and plan your essay using the space below. Your notes will not be scored. Consider the following points as you critically think about what you are going to write.

Strengths and weaknesses related to the three perspectives presented:

- What insights can be found in these perspectives and what insights do they fail to show?
- Why is each perspective persuasive or not persuasive?

Your personal experience, knowledge and values:

- What is your own perspective on this issue and what are your perspective's strengths and weaknesses?
- How will you support your perspective in your essay?

6-POINT HOLISTIC SCORING RUBRIC FOR THE ACT WRITING TEST

A Few Words about Scoring the Essay

Even with some errors in spelling, punctuation, and grammar, a student can get a top score on the essay. The highly trained high school and college composition teachers who score the essays will follow a rubric that focuses upon content, organization, and language usage and sentence structure. Each essay will be independently scored on a 1–6 scale by two such readers in *four* domains: Ideas and Analysis, Development and Support, Organization, and Language Use. If the readers' scores differ by more than two points, the test will be evaluated by a third reader. Fewer than 2 percent of all scored essays require a third reader.

Some general points about the scoring rubrics are summarized here. For full descriptions of the criteria for *each* of the four domains, refer to "Preparing for the ACT Test" at https://www.act.org/content/dam/act/unsecured/documents/Preparing-for-the-ACT.pdf. Essays at each level will exhibit all or most of the characteristics described below.

Score = 6

Essays with this score demonstrate effective skill in responding to the task.

The essay shows a clear understanding of the task. The essay takes a position on the issue and may offer a critical context for discussion. The essay addresses complexity by examining different perspectives presented on the issue, and by evaluating the implications and/or complications of the issue, and/or by fully responding to counterarguments to the writer's position. Development of ideas is ample, specific, and logical. Most ideas are fully elaborated. A clear focus on the specific issue in the prompt is maintained. The organization of the essay is clear: the organization may be somewhat predictable or it may grow from the writer's purpose. Ideas are logically sequenced. Most transitions reflect the writer's logic and are usually integrated into the essay.

The introduction and conclusion are effective, clear, and well developed. The essay shows a good command of language. Sentences are varied and word choice is varied and precise. There are few, if any, errors to distract the reader.

Score = 5

Essays with this score demonstrate competent skill in responding to the task.

The essay shows a clear understanding of the task. The essay takes a position on the issue and may offer a broad context for discussion. The essay shows recognition of complexity by partially evaluating the implications and/or complications of the given perspectives, and by responding to counterarguments to the writer's position. Development of ideas is specific and logical. Most ideas are elaborated, with clear movement between general statements and specific reasons, examples, and details. Focus on the specific issue in the prompt is maintained. The organization of the essay is clear, although it may be predictable. Ideas are logically sequenced, although simple and obvious transitions may be used. The introduction and conclusion are clear and generally well developed. Language is competent. Sentences are somewhat varied and word choice is somewhat varied and precise. There may be a few errors, but they are rarely distracting.

Score = 4

Essays with this score demonstrate adequate skill in responding to the task.

The essay shows an understanding of the task. The essay takes a position on the issue and may offer some context for discussion based on the given perspectives. The essay may show some recognition of complexity by providing some response to counterarguments to the writer's position. Development of ideas is adequate, with some movement between general statements and specific reasons, examples, and details. Focus on the specific issue in the prompt is maintained throughout most of the essay. The organization of the essay is apparent but predictable. Some evidence of logical sequencing of ideas is apparent, although most transitions are simple and obvious. The introduction and conclusion are clear and somewhat developed. Language is adequate, with some sentence variety and appropriate word choice. There may be some distracting errors, but they do not impede understanding.

Score = 3

Essays with this score demonstrate some developing skill in responding to the task.

The essay shows some understanding of the task. The essay takes a position on the issue but does not offer a context for discussion. The essay may acknowledge a counterargument to the writer's position, but its development is brief or unclear. Development of ideas is limited and may be repetitious, with little, if any, movement between general statements and specific reasons, examples, and details. Focus on the general topic is maintained, but focus on the specific issue in the prompt may not be maintained. The organization of the essay is simple. Ideas are logically grouped within parts of the essay, but there is little or no evidence of logical sequencing of ideas. Transitions, if used, are simple and obvious. An introduction and conclusion are clearly discernible but underdeveloped. Language shows a basic control. Sentences show a little variety and word choice is appropriate. Errors may be distracting and may occasionally impede understanding.

Score = 2

Essays with this score demonstrate inconsistent or weak skill in responding to the task.

The essay shows a weak understanding of the task. The essay may not take a position on the issue, or the essay may take a position but fail to convey reasons to support that position, or the essay may take a position but fail to maintain a stance. There is little to no recognition of a counterargument to the author's position. The essay is thinly developed. If examples are given, they are general and may not be clearly relevant. The essay may include extensive repetition of the writer's ideas or of ideas in the prompt. Focus on the general topic

is maintained, but focus on the specific issue in the prompt may not be maintained. There is some indication of an organizational structure, and some logical grouping of ideas within parts of the essay is apparent. Transitions, if used, are simple and obvious, and they may be inappropriate or misleading. An introduction and conclusion are discernible but minimal. Sentence structure and word choice are usually simple. Errors may be frequently distracting and may sometimes impede understanding.

Score = 1

Essays with this score show little or no skill in responding to the task.

The essay shows little or no understanding of the task. If the essay takes a position, it fails to convey reasons to support that position. The essay is minimally developed. The essay may include excessive repetition of the writer's ideas or of ideas in the prompt. Focus on the general topic is usually maintained, but focus on the specific issue in the prompt may not be maintained. There is little or no evidence of an organizational structure or of the logical grouping of ideas. Transitions are rarely used. If present, an introduction and conclusion are minimal. Sentence structure and word choice are simple. Errors may be frequently distracting and may significantly impede understanding.

How to Score the Writing Test

Two trained readers will score each essay on the actual Writing Test. These readers are trained by reading examples of papers at each score point and by scoring many practice papers. They are given detailed feedback on the correctness of their scores during practice. During actual scoring, score differences of more than one point will be evaluated by a third trained reader to resolve discrepancies. This method is designed to be as objective and impartial as possible. So—how can you rate your *own* practice Writing Test?

It is difficult to be objective about one's own work, and you have not had the extensive training provided to actual readers of the ACT Writing Test. However, it is to your advantage to read your own writing critically. Becoming your own editor helps you grow as a writer and as a reader. So it makes sense for you to evaluate your own practice essay. It may also be helpful for you to give your practice essay to one or two other readers to get another perspective: perhaps that of a classmate, a parent, or an English teacher, for example. Thinking and talking with others about writing is good preparation for the ACT Writing Test. To rate your essay, you and your reader(s) should read the scoring guidelines and examples, and then assign your practice essay a score of 1 through 6.

In an actual test, each essay will be scored on a scale from 1 (low) through 6 (high). The scores are based on the overall impression that is created by all the elements of the writing: Ideas and Analysis, Development and Support, Organization, and Language Use. The scores given by the two readers are subjected to a computation that yields a Writing Subject Score ranging between 2 and 12.

The guidelines used to score your essay are also called a "rubric." Many papers do not fit the exact description at each score point. You should note that the rubric says: "Papers at each level exhibit *all* or *most* of the characteristics in the descriptors." To score your paper, read it and try to determine which score point and paragraph in the rubric best describes most of the characteristics of your essay. Then (because your Writing Test subscore is the sum of two readers' ratings of your essay), you should multiply your 1–6 score by 2. Or, if both you and someone else read and score your practice essay, add those scores together.

To see the full computation for the actual ACT exam, refer to page 62 of "Preparing for the ACT Test" at https://www.act.org/content/dam/act/unsecured/documents/Preparing-for-the-ACT.pdf.

College and Career Readiness Standards

The College and Career Readiness Standards for Writing can be found at www.act.org/standard.

Example Essays and Scoring Explanations

Readers for the ACT Writing Test practice by scoring many essays before they score "live" essays. Although we cannot provide you with the same extensive training these readers receive, reading the example essays that follow will help you better understand some of the characteristics of essays at each score point. You will also be able to read a brief explanation of how each essay was scored. The example essays are in response to the practice prompt on page 369.

Score = 1

The funding should be used to buy magazines. Some magazines are only for entertainment but some talk about politics and the world. Even the more popular magazine for kids will be chosen, its still the best thing to do. Students like to read about what tells them what movie stars lives are like.

Score Point 1 Scoring Explanation

This essay shows little engagement with the prompt task. The writer does take a clear position (*The funding should be used to buy magazines*) but little is developed in support of that position. Two ideas are offered (*Some magazines are only for entertainment but some talk about politics and the world* and *Students like to read about what tells them what movie stars lives are like*). But ideas are left unexplored and unexplained. No organization is evident. Transitions (*even*, *still*) are used but are unclear. No introduction or conclusion is present, unless the statement of position is considered an introduction. The essay's language is clear at the beginning but later becomes hard to understand. Language errors and a lack of logical sequencing of ideas are also problems.

Score = 2

Popular magazines would be a good thing, it would pull students into the library and encourage them to read. Some articles and magazines have nothing to do with school, but it still encourages students to read more. Reading is education, no matter if its talking about academics or not.

Many of the subjects in the magazine are school related. If an article is about a girl from another country talking about how she lives, that's school related because it has to do with geography. If it's an article about some part of the body, then that has to do with science.

Score Point 2 Scoring Explanation

Essays that earn a score of 2 demonstrate either weak or inconsistent skill in responding to the task. In this essay, the writer takes a clear position (*Popular magazines would be a good thing*) and offers specific supporting reasons (*it would pull students into the library and encourage them to read*, and *Many of the subjects in the magazine are school related*) but development of these ideas is thin. The writer does not attempt to explain the second claim with examples (*If an article is about a girl from another country . . . that's . . . geography. If it's . . . the body, then . . . science*), but much more explanation is needed. The second paragraph might be understood to be responding to a counterargument from the prompt that the magazines aren't related to academic subjects. If so, it is a faint reference that should be clearer. The essay indicates organizational structure by separating the two ideas into two separate paragraphs. However, there is no discernible introduction or conclusion. Language use in the essay contains a variety of errors that distract the reader, including a run-on sentence, disagreements of subject and verb, and several misspellings.

Score = 3

I feel that schools should not subscribe to popular magazines. Sometimes the magazine articles are misleading and don't tell the truth. And some students may not know between right and wrong. I get Seventeen magazine every month. There are some subjects in the articles that I feel should not be allowed, or maybe edited. They put in college searches which are helpful, but other articles have girls talking about things that are not right. Not everybody should be reading them. Why should schools subscribe to magazines that have articles that are not right? These articles could make teenagers spend too much time thinking about things that are misleading or not right or a waist of time. Teenagers are sometimes too young to read some of the articles that the popular magazines have.

Also, popular magazines will not help students to be encouraged to read. Popular magazines have short articles that are based on opinion and gossip and they are filled with quizzes and advertisements and how to loose weight. The advertisements show skinny girls and the articles about loosing weight are not good. They are bad for teenagers to see and to read. And the other articles are a waist of time because they are full of gossip and mostly pictures. If school libraries really want to help students, they need to subscribe to magazines that are academic, like Time and National Geographic.

There is no reason to subscribe to any other kind of popular magazines. If school libraries did, they would find that popular magazines give students something to do instead of the research they should use the library for. It would be a perfect excuse for hanging out to just look at magazines with their friends. School libraries should not subscribe to popular magazines, especially when funding is limited.

Score Point 3 Scoring Explanation

Essays that earn a score of 3 show some developing skill in responding to the task. This essay takes a clear position but does not provide any context for discussion. A counterargument taken from the prompt is vaguely referenced and refuted (*popular magazines will not help students to be encouraged to read*), but further clarification is needed to explain why short, gossipy articles are of no use in encouraging students to read. The essay contains limited movement between general statements and specific examples (*They put in college searches which are helpful, but other articles have girls talking about things that are not right.*). Focus on the specific issue in the prompt wavers because of the somewhat vague discussion the writer gives on the general, negative aspects of popular magazines (*These articles could make teenagers spend too much time thinking about things that are misleading or not right or a waist of time*). All the ideas would benefit from more development. This writer's ideas are grouped logically throughout the essay. There is only a single use of a transition (*Also*). The opening and closing sentences clearly signal an introduction and conclusion, but they lack development. The language usage in this essay demonstrates basic control. Sentences are somewhat varied in length and structure, and words are used correctly. Language errors are at times distracting.

Score = 4

High school libraries have only a very limited fund. The big question is how do they spend the fund. Some people think only the magazines that are about academics should be bought, but others point out that if students are interested in what is being read, they will read more, learn more and like school more. The second group is exactly right.

First, anytime someone reads, their learning. Studies show that students who read thirty minutes a day in their free time perform better than those who don't. Students are not going to want to pick up Shakespeare in their study hall, theyre going to pick up "Seventeen."

If you want them to get in that thirty minutes, you have to give them something they will actually open and look at. Remember its not what we're reading, its just the reading that counts.

Also, popular magazines can help students learn about current events. Its important to keep up with information that hasn't had time to get in the textbooks yet. Many popular magazines contain articles about new health discoveries, wars and events in other countries, and can even provide resources for research papers. This is important for our education.

Most importantly, popular magazines offer a break from the stress of schoolwork. After hours of listening to lectures and taking tests, people need to relax by reading something fun. If there is nothing fun to read, a bad attitude could develop from libraries and school. This could hurt students much more than it would "hurt" us to read about movie stars and new music during study hall.

In conclusion, for student's mental health, knowledge, and love of reading, popular magazines should stay in our library. While some people may want to debate the issue, the right decision is clear. Interesting magazines are important for students in lots of ways.

Score Point 4 Scoring Explanation

Essays that earn a score of 4 demonstrate adequate skill in responding to the task. This essay takes a position on the issue presented in the prompt but first offers a context for the discussion and recognizes two different perspectives. The essay offers three ideas to support the writer's position (*anytime someone reads, their learning*; *popular magazines can help students learn about current events*; and p*opular magazines offer a break*) with adequate development of each idea. The writer moves ably between general statements and some specific details (*Shakespeare*/Seventeen, *health discoveries, wars, hours listening to lectures and taking tests*) and maintains focus throughout the discussion. The essay is clearly organized around a simple five-paragraph framework. The sequencing of ideas is logical, though predictable, and indicated by transitions (*First, Also, Most importantly, In conclusion*). While the transitions are simple and obvious, they are at least effective in moving the reader through the essay systematically. The introduction and conclusion are clear and somewhat developed, with the introduction offering much necessary information to set up the discussion. The conclusion makes very clear the writer's

position and reasoning. Language is adequate, with a variety of sentence constructions and correct word usage. Language errors—mostly spelling—are somewhat distracting.

Score = 5

High school libraries have a dilemma on their hands. Should they buy popular magazines as well as academic books and publications? In a perfect world, our school libraries would be able to offer everything that's possible and appropriate. But with budget limits throughout the school system, the administration must be sure they're making the best choices of books and magazines, so magazines like "Teen People" and "YM" should not be paid for instead of educational books and publications.

The purpose of school, and school libraries, is learning. Supporters of popular magazines argue that there is something to be learned from any reading material, but I believe some kinds of learning are more important to students futures than other kinds. If the school library has to choose between teaching teenage girls about the achievements of Harriet Tubman and letting them read about their favorite movie star, I know which one I would vote for.

Furthermore, one of the school library's most important functions is offering students the learning resources they might not be able to find or afford on their own. Everybody would agree the school library should have Internet access for people who don't have a computer at home. Shouldn't the library also offer full sets of encyclopedia, hard cover books and high quality magazines like "National Geographic" to students who can't buy all these materials, especially when they may only need them for one paper all year? On the other hand, anybody can spend $3.99 at the drugstore to find out about Justin Timberlake's love life if they want to. The school library shouldn't have to finance that. If you're in study hall and you just have an urgent celebrity trivia question that just can't wait, you can always use the Internet, at no extra cost to the school.

Reading for pleasure is a great thing, and one of my personal favorite leisure activities, but magazines just for entertainment shouldn't be a priority for school libraries. Learning is the reason for school, and should be first in mind as this decision is made. When funding is so limited, the school library must always put learning material first.

Score Point 5 Scoring Explanation

Essays that earn a score of 5 show a clear understanding of the task. The writer takes the position of Perspective Two (Teen People *and* YM *should not be paid for instead of educational books and publications*) after establishing a broad context for discussion (*In a perfect world, our school libraries would be able to offer everything that's possible and appropriate. But with budget limits throughout the school system, the administration must be sure they're making the best choices*). The essay shows recognition of complexity by responding succinctly to counterarguments to the writer's position (*Supporters of popular magazines argue that there is something to be learned from any reading material, but I believe some kinds of learning are more important to students futures than other kinds*). Development of the discussion is specific, with clear movement between claims and the details that explain and support them. Development is also logical, assisted by strong, integrated transitions (*Furthermore, On the other hand*) and carefully sequenced ideas. The introduction and conclusion are both clear and generally well developed, offering necessary context and adding emphasis to clarify the argument. Language is highly competent and engaging, with a lot of sentence variety and some precise word choice (*urgent celebrity trivia question*). Language errors are minimally distracting.

Score = 6

High schools nowadays are struggling to draw the line between what is "educational" and what is not. School programs are cut based on how much educational content they're perceived to have. Now the administration is trying to purge the libraries of popular magazines because they contain non academic subjects. It's important that the library buy dictionaries and encyclopedias, but educational purists need to be reminded that if you separate "academic" from "nonacademic" too strictly, you separate school from the real world it's supposed to prepare us for.

Educators are the ones who tell us we should spend more time reading. The only way to build the reading comprehension and vocabulary skills so important for getting into and through college is to practice, and that means reading things other than school assignments. No one ever gained reading proficiency from daily struggles through their Chemistry and History textbooks. We read these because we have to, but we would continue reading—even during precious homework free moments—if we had something interesting to turn to. The magazines that teenagers enjoy reading are the ones that cover our interests and address our concerns, like "Seventeen" and "Teen People". These are the magazines that some would banish from the library.

It's true that not every page in youth magazines is an intellectual challenge. Many pages show young models selling zit cream, or contain "dream date" quizzes. But the critics of popular magazines should take a closer look at them. These same magazines have articles on suicide prevention, the spread of AIDS among teens, and college comparisons—subjects that the adult oriented news media doesn't cover.

Even the frivolous features have something to teach the reader who wants to learn. All those "Great Looks Cheap" may be a first step toward becoming a smarter consumer. The silly quiz may open up questions about the nature of "scientific proof" or lead to more self-knowledge.

Learning is where you find it, and students may find it in places administrators and librarians might not think to look. Learning can be found in popular magazines as well as approved academic texts. There should be room in the school library for both.

Score Point 6 Scoring Explanation

Essays that earn a score of 6 demonstrate effective skill in responding to the task and may deal with one or more perspectives such as Perspective One, Perspective Two, and Perspective Three. The writer takes a clear position, develops it throughout the essay, and states it directly in the conclusion (*Learning can be found in popular magazines as well as approved academic texts*). This position is placed in a wider context without disrupting the essay's focus (*High schools nowadays are struggling to draw the line between what is "educational" and what is not. School programs are cut based on how much educational content they're perceived to have*).

The essay addresses complexity by anticipating counterarguments to the writer's position (*It's true that not every page in the youth magazines is an intellectual challenge*) and fully responding to those counterarguments by showing specifically where they are weak

(*These same magazines have articles on suicide prevention, the spread of AIDS among teens, and college comparisons—subjects that the adult oriented news media doesn't cover*).

The writer's ideas may not be developed evenly throughout all the paragraphs, but their development is succinct and logical. The essay elaborates on general statements (*Even the frivolous features have something to teach the reader who wants to learn*) by moving to specific details and examples (*All those "Great Looks Cheap" may be a first step toward becoming a smarter consumer*).

The organization of the essay is clear and the logical sequence of ideas grows out of the writer's intent to persuade. Transitions help the essay flow smoothly from one paragraph to the next (*It's true that not every page*

in youth magazines is an intellectual challenge. . . . Even the frivolous features have something to teach the reader who wants to learn). The introduction is clear and especially well developed, connecting the writer's position to a strong critical claim (*if you separate "academic" from "nonacademic" too strictly, you separate school from the real world it's supposed to prepare us for*).

This essay shows a good command of language. Word choice is precise and persuasive (*purge the libraries, frivolous features*). Facility with words and sentence structure enables the writer to maintain a light, amused tone (*The silly quiz may open up questions about the nature of "scientific proof" or lead to more self-knowledge*). There are a few language errors in this essay, but they rarely distract the reader.

WHAT MAKES A GREAT ESSAY

The key aim is to engross the reader. Make the reader want to read what you've written and to be involved with your ideas.

Make sure you provide examples and references to support your ideas or theories. For example, if you are arguing against the idea that ignorance is bliss, you could cite how information technology is good for people and contrast that with what happens when one does not use that technology. If you are taking the stance that movies based on books are never as good as the actual books, you should reference a particular book that will support your point. You may want to give an interesting example with which the reader can identify (e.g., in a movie, you get what you see, whereas in a book, you have room to interpret the characters and you may be able to identify with them more, which allows you to enjoy the book more than the movie).

You should also try to get the reader to sympathize or identify with what you have to say by noting a personal experience that is relevant to the essay topic. One of my students, while writing an essay about a father-son relationship, noted that one of the most significant moments in his life was when he went fishing with his father. He mentioned that while he learned the sport of fishing, he bonded with his father through the common activity.

Sometimes it is wise to challenge the reader by describing an example that would make the reader think. For example, if you are writing about music and how it affects and calms people, you might mention and try to explain something controversial, such as Hitler's loving Wagner's operatic music. The reader will become more involved with what you are writing and perhaps look forward to the rest of your essay.

To get the reader interested in what you are writing, show examples so that the reader will say, "That's a good example" or "I never thought about that." Better yet, if you can say something that the reader may not know, the reader will in fact appreciate having learned something new. That is the ultimate goal of creativity in writing.

IMPORTANT TIPS ON HOW TO WRITE THE BEST ESSAY

Making Your Sentences Effective

What Is Style?

Many good ideas are lost because they are expressed in a dull, wordy, involved way. We often have difficulty following—we may even ignore—instructions that are hard to read. Yet we find other instructions written in such a clear and simple way that a child could easily follow them. This way of writing—the words we choose and the way we use them—is called *style*.

No two people write exactly alike. Even when writing about the same thing, they probably will express ideas differently. Some will say what they think more effectively than others; what they say will be more easily read and understood. But there is seldom any one best way to say something. Rather, there are usually several equally good ways. This flexibility is what makes English such a rich language.

Style can't be taught; each person's style is like personality—it is unique to him or her. But we can each improve our styles. Let us consider how we can improve our writing styles by improving our sentences.

How to Write Effective Sentences

We speak in sentences; we write in sentences. A single word or phrase sometimes carries a complete thought, but sentences are more often the real units of thought communication.

Writing good sentences takes concentration, patience, and practice. It involves much more than just stringing words together, one after another, as they tumble from our minds. If writers aren't careful, their sentences may not mean to the reader what they want them to mean. A poorly written sentence might even be misinterpreted to mean what the writer did *not* want it to mean—or it might mean nothing at all.

This section discusses five things writers can do to write better sentences and essays—or to improve work already written:

1. Create interest.
2. Make your meaning clear.
3. Keep your sentences brief.
4. Make every word count.
5. Vary your sentence patterns.

Let's consider interest first.

1. Create Interest

We can make our writing more interesting by writing in an informal, conversational style. This style also makes our writing easier to understand and our readers more receptive to our thoughts.

Listen to two men meeting in the coffee shop. One tells the other, "Let me know when you need more paper clips." But how would he have written it? Probably as follows:

> Request this office be notified when your activity's supply of paper clips, wire, steel gem pattern, large type 1, stock No. 7510-634-6516, falls below 30-day level prescribed in AFR 67-1, Vol. II, Section IV, subject: Office Supplies. Requisition will be submitted as expeditiously as possible to preclude noncompliance with appropriate directives.

Judging from the formal, academic style of much of our writing, we want to *impress* rather than *express*. There seems to be something about writing that brings out our biggest words, our most complex sentences, and our most formal style. Obviously this is not effective writing. We wouldn't dare say it aloud this formally for fear someone would laugh at us, but we will write it.

Write to Express

One of the best ways to make our writing more interesting to the reader and, hence, more effective is to write as we talk. Of course we can't write *exactly* as we talk, and we shouldn't want to. We usually straighten out the sentence structure, make our sentences complete rather than fragmentary or run-on, substitute for obvious slang words, and so on. But we can come close to our conversational style without being folksy, ungrammatical, or wordy. This informal style is far more appropriate for the kind of writing we do and for the kind of readers we have than the old formal style. And it certainly makes better reading.

Be Definite, Specific, and Concrete

Another way—and one of the surest—to arouse and hold the interest and attention of readers is to be definite, specific, and concrete.

2. Make Your Meaning Clear

You do not need to be a grammarian to recognize a good sentence. After all, the first requirement of grammar is that you focus your reader's attention on the meaning you wish to convey. If you take care to make your meaning clear, your grammar will usually take care of itself. You can, however, do three things to make your meaning clearer to your reader: (1) emphasize your main ideas, (2) avoid wandering sentences, and (3) avoid ambiguity.

Emphasize the Main Ideas

When we talk, we use gestures, voice changes, pauses, smiles, frowns, and so on to emphasize our main ideas. In writing, we have to use different methods for emphasis. Some are purely mechanical; others are structural.

Mechanical devices include capital letters, underlining or italics, punctuation, and headings. Printers used to capitalize the first letter of a word they wanted to emphasize. We still occasionally capitalize or use a heavier type to emphasize words, phrases, or whole sentences. Sometimes we underline or italicize words that we want to stand out. Often we label or head main sections or subdivisions, as we have done in this book. This effectively separates main ideas and makes them stand out so that the reader doesn't have to search for them.

But mechanical devices for emphasizing an idea—capitalization, particularly—are often overused. The best way to emphasize an idea is to place it effectively in the sentence. The most emphatic position is at the end of the sentence. The next most emphatic position is at the beginning of the sentence. The place of least importance is anywhere in the middle. Remember, therefore, to put the important clause, phrase, name, or idea at the beginning or at the end of a sentence, and never hide the main idea in a subordinate clause or have it so buried in the middle of the sentence that the reader has to dig it out or miss it altogether.

> *Unemphatic:* People drive on the left side of the road instead of the right side in England.
>
> *Better:* Instead of driving on the right side of the road, people in England drive on the left.

Avoid Wandering Sentences

All parts of a sentence should contribute to one clear idea or impression. Long, straggling sentences usually contain a hodgepodge of unrelated ideas. You should either break long sentences into shorter sentences or put the subordinate thoughts into subordinate form. Look at this sentence:

> The sergeant, an irritable fellow who had been a truck driver, born and brought up in the corn belt of Iowa, strong as an ox and six feet tall, fixed an angry eye on the recruit.

You can see that the main idea is "The sergeant fixed an angry eye on the recruit." That he was an irritable fellow, strong as an ox and six feet tall, adds to the main idea. But the facts that he had been a truck driver and had been born in Iowa add nothing to the main thought, and the sentence is better without them.

> The sergeant, an irritable fellow who was strong as an ox and six feet tall, fixed an angry eye on the recruit.

Avoid Ambiguity

If a sentence can be misunderstood, it will be misunderstood. A sentence that says, "The truck followed the Jeep until its tire blew out," may be perfectly clear to the writer, but the reader will not know which vehicle's tire blew out until the pronoun *its* is identified.

Make Sure That Your Modifiers Say What You Mean

"While eating oats, the farmer took the horse out of the stable." This sentence suggests that the farmer is simultaneously eating his breakfast until you add to the first part of the sentence a logical subject ("the horse"): "While the horse was eating oats, the farmer took him out of the stable." Sometimes simple misplacement of modifiers in sentences leads to misunderstanding: "The young lady went to the dance with her boyfriend wearing a low-cut gown." You can clarify this sentence by simply rearranging it: "Wearing a low-cut gown, the young lady went to the dance with her boyfriend."

3. Keep Your Sentences Brief

Sentences written like ten-word advertisements are hard to read. You cannot get the kind of brevity you want by leaving out the articles (*a*, *an*, and *the*). You can get brevity by dividing complex ideas into bite-sized sentences and by avoiding unnecessary words and phrases and needless repetition and elaboration. Here are some suggestions that will help you to write short, straightforward sentences.

Use Verbs That Work

The verb—the action word—is the most important word in a sentence. It is the power plant that supplies the energy, vitality, and motion in the sentence. So use strong verbs, verbs that really *work* in your sentences.

Use the Active Voice

Sentences written in the basic subject-verb-object pattern are said to be written in the *active voice*. In such sentences, someone or something *does* something to the object—there is a forward movement of the idea. In sentences written in the *passive voice*, the subject merely receives the action—it has something done to it by an unnamed someone or something, and there is no feeling of forward movement of the idea.

The active voice, in general, is preferable to the passive voice because it helps to give writing a sense of energy, vitality, and motion. When we use the passive voice predominantly, our writing doesn't seem to have much life, the actor in the sentences is not identified, and verbs become weak. So don't rob your writing of its power by using the passive voice when you can use the active voice. Nine out of ten sentences will be both shorter (up to 25 percent shorter) and stronger in the active voice.

Let's compare the two voices:

Active: The pilot   flew   the aircraft.
       (Actor)   (action)   (acted upon)

Passive: The aircraft   was flown by the pilot.
       (Acted upon)   (action)   (actor)

Now let's see some typical passive examples:

The committee will be appointed by the principal.

Reports have been received . . .

Provisions will be made by the manager in case of a subway strike.

Aren't these familiar? In most of these, we should be emphasizing the actor rather than leaving out or subordinating him or her.

See how much more effective those sentences are when they are written in the active voice:

The principal will appoint the committee.

We have received reports . . .

The manager will make provisions in case of a subway strike.

Avoid Using the Passive Voice

The passive voice always takes more words to say what could be said just as well (and probably better) in the active voice. In the passive voice, the subject also becomes less personal and may seem less important, and the motion of the sentence grinds to a halt.

There are times, of course, when the passive voice is useful and justified—as when the person or thing doing the action is unknown or unimportant.

When we use the lifeless passive voice indiscriminately, we make our writing weak, ineffective, and dull. Remember that the normal English word order is subject-verb-object. There may be occasions in your writing when you feel that the passive voice is preferable. But should such an occasion arise, think twice before you write; the passive voice rarely improves your style. Before using a passive construction, make certain that you have a specific reason. After using it, check to see that your sentence is not misleading.

Take a Direct Approach

Closely related to passive voice construction is indirect phrasing.

It is requested . . .

It is recommended . . .

It has been brought to the attention of . . .

It is the opinion of . . .

Again this is so familiar to us that we don't even question it. But *who* requested? *Who* recommended? *Who* knows? *Who* believes? No one knows from reading such sentences!

This indirect way of writing, this use of the passive voice and the indirect phrase, is perhaps the most characteristic feature of the formal style of the past. There are many explanations for it. A psychiatrist might say the writer was afraid to take the responsibility for what he or she is writing or merely passing the buck. The writer may unjustifiably believe this style makes him or her anonymous or makes him or her sound less dogmatic and authoritarian.

Express your ideas immediately and directly. Unnecessary expressions like *it is, there is,* and *there are* weaken sentences and delay comprehension. They also tend to place part of the sentence in the passive voice.

It is the recommendation of the sales manager that the report be forwarded immediately.

is more directly expressed as

The sales manager recommends that we send the report immediately.

Change Long Modifiers

Dr. Barnes, who is president of the board, will preside.

Vehicles that are defective are . . .

They gave us a month for accomplishment of the task.

. . . to Shorter Ones

Dr. Barnes, the board president, will preside.

Defective vehicles are . . .

They gave us a month to do the job.

Break Long Sentences . . .

There is not enough time available for the average executive to do everything that might be done and so it is necessary for him to determine wisely the essentials and do them first, then spend the remaining time on things that are "nice to do."

. . . into Shorter Ones

The average executive lacks time to do everything that might be done. Consequently, he must decide what is essential and do it first. Then he can spend the remaining time on things that are "nice to do."

4. Make Every Word Count

Don't cheat your readers. They are looking for ideas—for meaning—when they read your letter, report, or directive. If they have to read several words that have little to do with the real meaning of a sentence or if they have to read a number of sentences to get just a little meaning, you are cheating them. Much of their time and effort is wasted because they aren't getting full benefit. They expected something that you didn't deliver.

Make Each Word Advance Your Thought

Each word in a sentence should advance the thought of that sentence. To leave a word out would destroy the meaning you are trying to convey.

"Naturally," you might say. "Of course!" But reread the last school essay you wrote. Are some of your sentences rather wordy? Could you have said the same thing in fewer words? And finally, how many times did you use a whole phrase to say what could have been said in one word, or a whole clause for what could have been expressed in a brief phrase? In short, try tightening up a sentence like this:

The reason that prices rose was that the demand was increasing at the same time that the production was decreasing.

Rewritten:

Prices rose because the demand increased while production decreased.

Doesn't our rewrite say the same thing as the original? Yet we have saved the reader some effort by squeezing the unnecessary words out of a wordy sentence.

Now try this one:

Wordy:　The following statistics serve to give a good idea of the cost of production.

Improved:　The following statistics give a good idea of the production costs.

　　　　or

　　　　These statistics show production costs.

And this one:

Wordy:　I have a production supervisor who likes to talk a great deal.

Improved:　I have a talkative production supervisor.

In all of those rewritten sentences we have saved our reader some time. The same thing has been said in fewer words.

Of course you can be *too* concise. If your writing is too brief or terse, it may "sound" rude and abrupt, and you may lose more than you gain. You need, then, to be politely concise. What you are writing, what you are writing about and whom you are writing for will help you decide just where to draw the line. However, the general rule, make every word count, still stands. Say what you have to say in as few words as clarity *and tact* will allow.

Consolidate Ideas

A second way to save the reader's effort is to consolidate ideas whenever possible. Pack as much meaning as possible into each sentence *without making the sentence structure too complicated.*

Each sentence is by definition an idea, a unit of thought. Each time your readers read one of these units, they should get as much meaning as possible. It takes just about as much effort to read a sentence with a simple thought as it does to read one with a strong idea or with two or three strong ideas.

There are several things we can do to pack meaning into a sentence. In general, they all have to do with summarizing, combining, and consolidating ideas.

Some people write sentences that are weak and insignificant, in both structure and thought. Ordinarily several such sentences can be summarized and the thought put into one good, mature sentence. For example:

We left Wisconsin the next morning. I remember watching three aircraft. They were F-4s. They were flying very low. I felt sure they were going to crash over a half a dozen times. The F-4 is new to me. I hadn't seen one before.

Rewritten:

When we left Wisconsin the next morning, I remember watching three F-4s, a type of aircraft I had never seen before. They were flying so low that over a half-dozen times I felt sure they were going to crash.

When summarizing like this, be sure to emphasize the main action. Notice in the next example how we have kept the main action as our verb and made the other actions subordinate by changing them to verbals.

Poor:　It was in 2010 that he *retired* from teaching and he *devoted* his time to *writing* his autobiography. (three verbs, one verbal)

Improved:　In 2010 he *retired* from teaching to *devote* his time to *writing* his autobiography. (one verb, two verbals)

Here is an example similar to ones we might find in a directive:

Poor:　The evaluation forms will be picked up from your respective personnel offices. You should have these completed by 1700 hours, 18 May. They will be delivered immediately to the security section.

Notice that in the instructions above all of the actions are to be performed by the reader or "you." Now let's put these into one sentence, placing the things to be done in a series and using a single subject.

Improved:　Pick up the evaluation forms from your personnel office; complete and deliver them to the security section by 1700 hours, 18 May. (The subject [you] is understood.)

The same thing can be done with subjects or predicates:

Poor:　Horror stories shown on television appear to contribute to juvenile delinquency. Comic books with their horror stories seem to have the same effect. Even the reports of criminal activities which appear in our newspapers seem to contribute to juvenile delinquency.

Improved:　Television, comic books, and newspapers seem to contribute to juvenile delinquency by emphasizing stories of horror and crime.

There is one more thing we can do to make our sentences better. We can vary their length and complexity. The following paragraphs suggest ways to do this.

5. Vary Your Sentence Patterns

We should, as a general rule, write predominantly short sentences. Similarly, we should keep our sentences simple enough for our readers to understand them easily and quickly.

But most people soon get tired of reading nothing but simple, straightforward sentences. So, give your reader an occasional change of pace. Vary both the length and the construction of your sentences.

Vary Sentence Length

Some writers use nothing but short, choppy sentences ("The road ended in a wrecked village. The lines were up beyond. There was much artillery around."). In the hands of Hemingway, from whom this example is taken, short sentences can give an effect of purity and simplicity; in the hands of a less skillful writer, choppy sentences are usually only monotonous.

The other extreme, of course, is just as bad. The writer who always writes heavy sentences of 20 to 30 words soon loses the reader. Some great writers use long sentences effectively, but most writers do not.

The readability experts suggest that, for the most effective *communication*, a sentence should rarely exceed 20 words. Their suggestion is a good rule of thumb, but sentence length should vary. And an occasional long sentence is not hard to read if it is followed by shorter ones. A fair goal for most letter writers is an average of 21 words per sentence. For longer types of writing, such as regulations and manuals, sentences should average 15 words or fewer. The sentences in opening paragraphs and in short letters may run a little longer than the average.

Vary Sentence Construction

Just as important as varied sentence length is variety of construction. Four common sentence categories are simple, compound, complex, and compound-complex.

A *simple sentence* consists of only one main (independent) clause:

Rain came down in torrents.

Rain and hail started falling. (Simple sentence with compound subject)

The storm began and soon grew in intensity. (Simple sentence with compound predicate)

A *compound sentence* has two or more main clauses:

Rain started falling, and all work stopped.

The storm began; all work stopped.

The storm began, the workers found shelter, and all work stopped.

A *complex sentence* has one main clause and at least one subordinate (dependent) clause. (Subordinate clauses are underlined in the following sentences.)

They were just starting their work <u>when the rain started.</u>

<u>Before they had made any progress,</u> the rain started falling.

The storm, <u>which grew rapidly in intensity,</u> stopped all work.

A *compound-complex sentence* has two or more main clauses and at least one subordinate clause. (Subordinate clauses are underlined in the following sentences.)

Rain started falling, and all work stopped <u>before they had made any progress.</u>

<u>Although the workers were eager to finish the job,</u> the storm forced them to stop, and they quickly found shelter.

They had made some progress <u>before the storm began,</u> but <u>when it started,</u> all work stopped.

The names of the categories are really not important except to remind you to vary your sentence structure when you write. But remember that sentence variety is not just a mechanical chore to perform after your draft is complete. Good sentence variety comes naturally as the result of proper coordination and subordination when you write.

For example, if two or more short sentences have the same subject, combine them into one simple sentence with a compound verb:

The NASCAR drivers were hot. They were tired, too. They were also angry.

The NASCAR drivers were hot and tired and angry.

If you have two ideas of equal weight or parallel thought, write them as two clauses in a compound sentence:

The day was hot and humid. The NASCAR drivers had worked hard.

The NASCAR drivers had worked hard, and the day was hot and humid.

The day was hot and humid, but the NASCAR drivers had worked hard.

If one idea is more important than others, put it in the main clause of a complex sentence:

Poor: The NASCAR drivers were tired, and they had worked hard, and the day was hot.

Better: The NASCAR drivers were tired because they had worked hard on a hot day.

or

Although the day was hot and the NASCAR drivers were tired, they worked hard.

If the adverbial modifier is the least important part of a complex sentence, put it first and keep the end position for the more important main clause:

Poor: The NASCAR drivers finished the job in record time, even though the day was hot and humid and they were tired.

Better: Even though the day was hot and humid and the NASCAR drivers were tired, they finished the job in record time.

But be careful about having long, involved subordinate clauses come before the main clause. The reader may get lost or confused before getting to your main point or give up before getting to it. Also beware of letting too many modifying words, phrases, or clauses come between the subject and the verb. This is torture for the reader. The subject and the verb are usually the most important elements of a sentence; keep them close together whenever possible.

ESSAY PROMPTS AND PERSPECTIVES

For You to Practice Your Essay Writing

Essay Prompt 1

Given the importance of human creativity, one would think that it should have a high priority in modern society. But if we look at reality, we see a different picture. Basic scientific research is minimized in favor of immediate practical applications. The arts are increasingly seen as dispensable luxuries. Yet as competition heats up around the globe, exactly the opposite strategy is needed. In your opinion, is creativity needed more than ever in the world today?

Carefully read the following perspectives, which describe the importance and effects of creativity in society and importance and the effects of not having creativity in society.

Perspective One

Encouraging creativity in our society may lead to breakthroughs such as a cure for cancer. Creativity inspires new ideas and can result in a more efficient lifestyle in the long run.

Perspective Two

Discouraging creativity in our society will result in the achievement of more practical goals. There is no real need for the development of the arts or the esoteric sciences because no one can use these to enhance daily life.

Perspective Three

The encouragement of creativity may not appear relevant to daily life but may, in fact, have unforeseen practical applications in the long term. A musical piece or poem may inspire a scientific breakthrough partially because it inspires a new way of thinking or a new way of expressing a concept.

Essay Directions

Write a meaningful and logical essay in which you describe and evaluate multiple perspectives on advantages of creativity as compared to just having practical applications. You may refer to creativity as related to various subjects such as science, art, music, and practical applications such as communication, living, health care. In your essay, make sure that you

- clearly state and analyze your own perspective in relation to at least one other perspective
- support your statements with clear reasoning and specific examples
- organize your material logically
- communicate effectively using standard written English

Note that your perspective may be completely in agreement with any of the others, may be partially in agreement, or may be in complete disagreement. In any case, you must support your essay with logic, making detailed references to the passages and using specific examples to support your points.

Note on Planning the Essay

Develop ideas and plan your essay using the space below. Your notes will not be scored. Consider the following points as you critically think about what you are going to write.

Strengths and weaknesses related to the three perspective presented:

- What insights can be found in these perspectives and what insights do they fail to show?
- Why is each perspective persuasive or not persuasive?

Your personal experience, knowledge and values:

- What is your own perspective on this issue and what are your perspective's strengths and weaknesses?
- How will you support your perspective in your essay?

Use this page for a practice essay that responds to Essay Prompt 1.

Essay Prompt 2

Some people claim that each individual is solely responsible for what happens to him or her. That is, external circumstances do not play a significant role. The claim that we ought to take absolute responsibility for the kinds of people we are and the kinds of lives we lead suggests that we have complete control over our lives. We may not. The circumstances of our lives can make it more or less impossible to make certain kinds of choices. In your opinion, are we free to make our own decisions or are we limited in the choices we can make?

Carefully read the following perspectives, which describe the question of whether or not we are free or limited in making our own decisions.

Perspective One

Because there are so many variables controlling what happens to us, we cannot control our destiny. We may be able to relieve the intensity of some occurrence but we cannot control the occurrence or the effects of the occurrence itself.

Perspective Two

For any situation that happens we can make the best of it and even perhaps turn it around so that it is it favorable for us. We can protect ourselves from negative situations by taking active and not passive approaches.

Perspective Three

By not allowing ourselves to get involved with situations we might not otherwise be able to control, we can control our lives. By immunizing ourselves we can avoid disease. By eating properly we can prolong our lifespan, etc.

Essay Directions

Write a meaningful and logical essay in which you describe and evaluate multiple perspectives on the extent to which the choices you make in response to a situation will ensure your control over its effect on your life. In your essay, make sure that you

- clearly state and analyze your own perspective in relation to at least one other perspective
- support your statements with clear reasoning and specific examples
- organize your material logically
- communicate effectively using standard written English

Note that your perspective may be completely in agreement with any of the others, may be partially in agreement, or may be in complete disagreement. In any case, you must support your essay with logic, making detailed references to the passages and using specific examples to support your points.

Note on Planning the Essay

Develop ideas and plan your essay using the space below. Your notes will not be scored. Consider the following points as you critically think about what you are going to write.

Strengths and weaknesses related to the three perspective presented:

- What insights can be found in these perspectives and what insights do they fail to show?
- Why is each perspective persuasive or not persuasive?

Your personal experience, knowledge and values:

- What is your own perspective on this issue and what are your perspective's strengths and weaknesses?
- How will you support your perspective in your essay?

Use this page for a practice essay that responds to Essay Prompt 2.

PART 10

Three
ACT Practice Tests

5 IMPORTANT REASONS

FOR TAKING THESE PRACTICE TESTS

Each of the three Practice ACT tests in the final part of this book is modeled very closely after the actual ACT. You will find that each of these Practice Tests has

(a) the same level of difficulty as the actual ACT

and

(b) the same question formats as the actual ACT questions.

Note: On the actual ACT exam, the question choices use an alternating series of letters: A, B, C, D, followed by F, G, H, J, then returning to A, B, C, D. (For the five-choice Math Test, it's A, B, C, D, and E, followed by F, G, H, J, and K.) This system is replicated in the three Practice Tests that follow.

Taking each of the following tests is like taking the actual ACT. There are five important reasons for taking each of these Practice ACT tests:

1. To find out which areas of the ACT you still need to work on.

2. To know just where to concentrate your efforts to eliminate weaknesses.

3. To reinforce the Critical-Thinking Skills—19 Math Strategies and 9 Reading Strategies—that you learned in Part 3 of this book, the Strategy Section. As we advised you at the beginning of Part 3, diligent study of these strategies will result in a sharp rise in your ACT Math and Reading scores.

4. To strengthen your basic Math skills that might still be a bit rusty. We hope that Part 6, the Complete ACT Math Refresher, helped you to polish your skills.

5. To strengthen your grammar and writing skills. To review these skills, look at Part 9, the ACT Writing Test, and Part 8, The Complete ACT Grammar and Usage Refresher.

These five reasons for taking the three Practice Tests in this section of the book tie in closely with a very important educational principle:

WE LEARN BY DOING!

9 TIPS

FOR TAKING THESE PRACTICE TESTS

1. Observe the time limits exactly as given.

2. Allow no interruptions.

3. Permit no talking by anyone in the "test area."

4. Use the answer sheets provided at the beginning of each Practice Test. Don't make extra marks. Two answers for one question constitute an omitted question.

5. Use scratch paper to figure things out. (On your actual ACT, you are permitted to use only the test booklet for scratchwork.)

6. Skip a question when you start "struggling" with it. Go back to that question later if you have time to do so.

7. Don't get upset if you can't answer several of the questions. You can still get a high score on the test. Even if only 55 percent of the questions you answer are correct, you will get an average or above-average score.

8. You get the same credit for answering an easy question correctly as you do for answering a tough question correctly.

9. It is advisable to guess if you are not sure of the answer. There is no penalty for a wrong answer.

ACT PRACTICE TEST 1

TO SEE HOW YOU WOULD DO ON AN ACT AND WHAT YOU SHOULD DO TO IMPROVE

This ACT test is very much like the actual ACT. It follows the genuine ACT very closely. Taking this test is like taking the actual ACT. The following is the purpose of taking this test:

1. To find out what you are *weak* in and what you are *strong* in.
2. To learn where to concentrate your efforts in order to be fully prepared for the actual test.

Taking this test will prove to be a very valuable *timesaver* for you. Why waste time studying what you already know? Spend your time profitably by studying what you *don't* know. That is what this test will tell you.

In this book, we do not waste precious pages. We get right down to the business of helping you to increase your ACT scores.

Other ACT preparation books place their emphasis on drill, drill, drill. We do not believe that drill work is of primary importance in preparing for the ACT exam. Drill work has its place. In fact, this book contains a great variety of drill materials, practically all of which have explanatory answers also keyed to basic skills and strategies. Our drill work is coordinated with learning Critical-Thinking Skills. These skills will help you to think clearly and critically so that you will be able to answer many more ACT questions correctly.

Ready? Start taking the test. It's just like the real thing.

ANSWER SHEET

It is recommended that you use a No. 2 pencil. It is very important that you fill in the entire circle darkly and completely. If you change your response, erase as completely as possible. Incomplete marks or erasures may affect your score.

Complete Mark ●   **Examples of Incomplete Marks** ◐ ⊗ ⊖ ◌ ⊘ ◓ ◑ ◍ ◐

SECTION 1: ENGLISH TEST

	A B C D		F G H J		A B C D		F G H J		A B C D
1	○ ○ ○ ○	16	○ ○ ○ ○	31	○ ○ ○ ○	46	○ ○ ○ ○	61	○ ○ ○ ○
2	○ ○ ○ ○	17	○ ○ ○ ○	32	○ ○ ○ ○	47	○ ○ ○ ○	62	○ ○ ○ ○
3	○ ○ ○ ○	18	○ ○ ○ ○	33	○ ○ ○ ○	48	○ ○ ○ ○	63	○ ○ ○ ○
4	○ ○ ○ ○	19	○ ○ ○ ○	34	○ ○ ○ ○	49	○ ○ ○ ○	64	○ ○ ○ ○
5	○ ○ ○ ○	20	○ ○ ○ ○	35	○ ○ ○ ○	50	○ ○ ○ ○	65	○ ○ ○ ○
6	○ ○ ○ ○	21	○ ○ ○ ○	36	○ ○ ○ ○	51	○ ○ ○ ○	66	○ ○ ○ ○
7	○ ○ ○ ○	22	○ ○ ○ ○	37	○ ○ ○ ○	52	○ ○ ○ ○	67	○ ○ ○ ○
8	○ ○ ○ ○	23	○ ○ ○ ○	38	○ ○ ○ ○	53	○ ○ ○ ○	68	○ ○ ○ ○
9	○ ○ ○ ○	24	○ ○ ○ ○	39	○ ○ ○ ○	54	○ ○ ○ ○	69	○ ○ ○ ○
10	○ ○ ○ ○	25	○ ○ ○ ○	40	○ ○ ○ ○	55	○ ○ ○ ○	70	○ ○ ○ ○
11	○ ○ ○ ○	26	○ ○ ○ ○	41	○ ○ ○ ○	56	○ ○ ○ ○	71	○ ○ ○ ○
12	○ ○ ○ ○	27	○ ○ ○ ○	42	○ ○ ○ ○	57	○ ○ ○ ○	72	○ ○ ○ ○
13	○ ○ ○ ○	28	○ ○ ○ ○	43	○ ○ ○ ○	58	○ ○ ○ ○	73	○ ○ ○ ○
14	○ ○ ○ ○	29	○ ○ ○ ○	44	○ ○ ○ ○	59	○ ○ ○ ○	74	○ ○ ○ ○
15	○ ○ ○ ○	30	○ ○ ○ ○	45	○ ○ ○ ○	60	○ ○ ○ ○	75	○ ○ ○ ○

Complete Mark ● **Examples of Incomplete Marks** ◐ ⊗ ⊖ ○ ◑ ◓ ◕ ○

SECTION 2: MATHEMATICS TEST

	A B C D E		A B C D E		A B C D E		A B C D E		A B C D E
1	○ ○ ○ ○ ○	13	○ ○ ○ ○ ○	25	○ ○ ○ ○ ○	37	○ ○ ○ ○ ○	49	○ ○ ○ ○ ○
	F G H J K		F G H J K		F G H J K		F G H J K		F G H J K
2	○ ○ ○ ○ ○	14	○ ○ ○ ○ ○	26	○ ○ ○ ○ ○	38	○ ○ ○ ○ ○	50	○ ○ ○ ○ ○
	A B C D E		A B C D E		A B C D E		A B C D E		A B C D E
3	○ ○ ○ ○ ○	15	○ ○ ○ ○ ○	27	○ ○ ○ ○ ○	39	○ ○ ○ ○ ○	51	○ ○ ○ ○ ○
	F G H J K		F G H J K		F G H J K		F G H J K		F G H J K
4	○ ○ ○ ○ ○	16	○ ○ ○ ○ ○	28	○ ○ ○ ○ ○	40	○ ○ ○ ○ ○	52	○ ○ ○ ○ ○
	A B C D E		A B C D E		A B C D E		A B C D E		A B C D E
5	○ ○ ○ ○ ○	17	○ ○ ○ ○ ○	29	○ ○ ○ ○ ○	41	○ ○ ○ ○ ○	53	○ ○ ○ ○ ○
	F G H J K		F G H J K		F G H J K		F G H J K		F G H J K
6	○ ○ ○ ○ ○	18	○ ○ ○ ○ ○	30	○ ○ ○ ○ ○	42	○ ○ ○ ○ ○	54	○ ○ ○ ○ ○
	A B C D E		A B C D E		A B C D E		A B C D E		A B C D E
7	○ ○ ○ ○ ○	19	○ ○ ○ ○ ○	31	○ ○ ○ ○ ○	43	○ ○ ○ ○ ○	55	○ ○ ○ ○ ○
	F G H J K		F G H J K		F G H J K		F G H J K		F G H J K
8	○ ○ ○ ○ ○	20	○ ○ ○ ○ ○	32	○ ○ ○ ○ ○	44	○ ○ ○ ○ ○	56	○ ○ ○ ○ ○
	A B C D E		A B C D E		A B C D E		A B C D E		A B C D E
9	○ ○ ○ ○ ○	21	○ ○ ○ ○ ○	33	○ ○ ○ ○ ○	45	○ ○ ○ ○ ○	57	○ ○ ○ ○ ○
	F G H J K		F G H J K		F G H J K		F G H J K		F G H J K
10	○ ○ ○ ○ ○	22	○ ○ ○ ○ ○	34	○ ○ ○ ○ ○	46	○ ○ ○ ○ ○	58	○ ○ ○ ○ ○
	A B C D E		A B C D E		A B C D E		A B C D E		A B C D E
11	○ ○ ○ ○ ○	23	○ ○ ○ ○ ○	35	○ ○ ○ ○ ○	47	○ ○ ○ ○ ○	59	○ ○ ○ ○ ○
	F G H J K		F G H J K		F G H J K		F G H J K		F G H J K
12	○ ○ ○ ○ ○	24	○ ○ ○ ○ ○	36	○ ○ ○ ○ ○	48	○ ○ ○ ○ ○	60	○ ○ ○ ○ ○

Complete Mark ●   **Examples of Incomplete Marks** ◐ ⊗ ⊖ ○ ◔ ◠ ◕ ◑

SECTION 3: READING TEST

	A B C D		A B C D		A B C D		A B C D		A B C D
1	○ ○ ○ ○	9	○ ○ ○ ○	17	○ ○ ○ ○	25	○ ○ ○ ○	33	○ ○ ○ ○
	F G H J		F G H J		F G H J		F G H J		F G H J
2	○ ○ ○ ○	10	○ ○ ○ ○	18	○ ○ ○ ○	26	○ ○ ○ ○	34	○ ○ ○ ○
	A B C D		A B C D		A B C D		A B C D		A B C D
3	○ ○ ○ ○	11	○ ○ ○ ○	19	○ ○ ○ ○	27	○ ○ ○ ○	35	○ ○ ○ ○
	F G H J		F G H J		F G H J		F G H J		F G H J
4	○ ○ ○ ○	12	○ ○ ○ ○	20	○ ○ ○ ○	28	○ ○ ○ ○	36	○ ○ ○ ○
	A B C D		A B C D		A B C D		A B C D		A B C D
5	○ ○ ○ ○	13	○ ○ ○ ○	21	○ ○ ○ ○	29	○ ○ ○ ○	37	○ ○ ○ ○
	F G H J		F G H J		F G H J		F G H J		F G H J
6	○ ○ ○ ○	14	○ ○ ○ ○	22	○ ○ ○ ○	30	○ ○ ○ ○	38	○ ○ ○ ○
	A B C D		A B C D		A B C D		A B C D		A B C D
7	○ ○ ○ ○	15	○ ○ ○ ○	23	○ ○ ○ ○	31	○ ○ ○ ○	39	○ ○ ○ ○
	F G H J		F G H J		AF G H J		F G H J		F G H J
8	○ ○ ○ ○	16	○ ○ ○ ○	24	○ ○ ○ ○	32	○ ○ ○ ○	40	○ ○ ○ ○

SECTION 4: SCIENCE TEST

	A B C D		A B C D		A B C D		A B C D		A B C D
1	○ ○ ○ ○	9	○ ○ ○ ○	17	○ ○ ○ ○	25	○ ○ ○ ○	33	○ ○ ○ ○
	F G H J		F G H J		F G H J		F G H J		F G H J
2	○ ○ ○ ○	10	○ ○ ○ ○	18	○ ○ ○ ○	26	○ ○ ○ ○	34	○ ○ ○ ○
	A B C D		A B C D		A B C D		A B C D		A B C D
3	○ ○ ○ ○	11	○ ○ ○ ○	19	○ ○ ○ ○	27	○ ○ ○ ○	35	○ ○ ○ ○
	F G H J		F G H J		F G H J		F G H J		F G H J
4	○ ○ ○ ○	12	○ ○ ○ ○	20	○ ○ ○ ○	28	○ ○ ○ ○	36	○ ○ ○ ○
	A B C D		A B C D		A B C D		A B C D		A B C D
5	○ ○ ○ ○	13	○ ○ ○ ○	21	○ ○ ○ ○	29	○ ○ ○ ○	37	○ ○ ○ ○
	F G H J		F G H J		F G H J		F G H J		F G H J
6	○ ○ ○ ○	14	○ ○ ○ ○	22	○ ○ ○ ○	30	⊗ ⊖ ○ ○	38	○ ○ ○ ○
	A B C D		A B C D		A B C D		A B C D		A B C D
7	○ ○ ○ ○	15	○ ○ ○ ○	23	○ ○ ○ ○	31	○ ○ ○ ○	39	○ ○ ○ ○
	F G H J		F G H J		F G H J		F G H J		F G H J
8	○ ○ ○ ○	16	○ ○ ○ ○	24	○ ○ ○ ○	32	○ ○ ○ ○	40	○ ○ ○ ○

SECTION 1: ENGLISH TEST

45 Minutes, 75 Questions

Turn to Section 1 of your answer sheet (page 395) to answer the questions in this section.

Directions

Each passage below is accompanied by a number of questions. For some questions, you will consider how the passage might be revised to improve the expression of ideas. For other questions, you will consider how the passage might be edited to correct errors in sentence structure, usage, or punctuation.

Some questions will direct you to an underlined portion of a passage. Other questions will direct you to a location in a passage or ask you to think about the passage as a whole.

After reading each passage, choose the answer to each question that most effectively improves the quality of writing in the passage or that makes the passage conform to the conventions of standard written English. Many questions include a "NO CHANGE" option. Choose that option if you think the best choice is to leave the relevant portion of the passage as it is.

Questions 1–15 are based on the following passage, *Dolphin Ingenuity*.

Most of the intelligent land animals have (1) grasping organs for (2) an exploration of their environment— hands in man and his anthropoid relatives, the sensitive, inquiring trunk (3) in the elephant makeup.

One of the surprising things about the dolphin is (4) because his superior brain is unaccompanied by any type of manipulative organ. He has, however, a remarkable (5) ability for range finding involving some sort of echo sounding.

Perhaps this acute sense—(6) far more accurate (7) then any man has been able to devise (8) artificially brings him greater knowledge of his watery surroundings than might at first seem possible. Human beings think of intelligence as geared to things. The hand and the tool are (9) to us unconscious symbols of our intellectual attainment.

It is difficult for us to visualize another kind of lonely, almost disembodied intelligence floating in the wavering green fairyland of the sea—an intelligence (10) possible near or comparable to our own but without hands to build, (11) transmit knowledge (12) with writing, or to alter by one hair's breadth the planet's surface. Yet at the same time (13) they're indications that the dolphin's intelligence is a warm, friendly, and eager intelligence, quite capable of coming to the assistance of injured companions and striving to rescue them from drowning. (14)

Dolphin Ingenuity Questions

1. (A) NO CHANGE
   (B) organs to do grasping
   (C) grasp-organs
   (D) grasp-like organs

2. (F) NO CHANGE
   (G) to explore
   (H) exploration into
   (J) exploring

3. (A) NO CHANGE
   (B) that the elephant has
   (C) in the elephant
   (D) as in the elephant

4. (F) NO CHANGE
   (G) that
   (H) as
   (J) why

Go on to the next page. ⇨

5. Which of the following alternatives to the underlined portion would NOT be acceptable?

(A) range-finding ability involving

(B) ability that lets him find his range and involves

(C) range finding ability involving

(D) ability to find his range involving

6. (F) NO CHANGE

(G) far accurate

(H) far accurater

(J) more accurate by a long shot

7. (A) NO CHANGE

(B) than any

(C) any

(D) as any

8. (F) NO CHANGE

(G) artificially, brings

(H) artificially—brings

(J) artificially, bringing

9. All of the following would be acceptable placements for the underlined portion EXCEPT

(A) where it is now

(B) after the word *unconscious*

(C) at the beginning of the sentence (revising capitalization accordingly)

(D) after the word *tool*

10. (F) NO CHANGE

(G) possibly near to that or comparable to

(H) possibly near or comparable to

(J) possible nearly or comparable to

11. (A) NO CHANGE

(B) to transmit

(C) transmitting

(D) or to transmit

12. (F) NO CHANGE

(G) to write

(H) by the written word

(J) of writing

13. (A) NO CHANGE

(B) there is

(C) their are

(D) there are

14. The writer is considering adding the following true statement.

> In Monterey, California, dolphins encircled and saved a surfer being attacked by a great white shark after the shark had bitten the man three times.

Should the writer make this addition here?

(F) Yes, because the sentence adds an interesting supporting example of dolphins' unique abilities.

(G) Yes, because the sentence exemplifies dolphins' warm, friendly nature.

(H) No, because the sentence strays from the paragraph's focus on the nature of dolphin intelligence.

(J) No, because information about a dolphin confronting a shark contradicts the point that dolphins are friendly creatures.

Question 15 asks about the previous passage as a whole.

15. Upon reviewing the essay and finding that some information has been left out, the writer composes the following sentence:

> Although dolphins lack such an external symbol of intellect, researchers have discovered that they can use tools to solve problems and invent novel behaviors.

This sentence would most logically be placed after sentence

(A) 1 in paragraph 1

(B) 1 in paragraph 3

(C) 3 in paragraph 3

(D) 1 in paragraph 4

Go on to the next page. ⇨

Questions 16–30 are based on the following passage, *Breeding Rumors*.

Repeating rumors is the (16) most crudest way of spreading stories—by passing them on from mouth to mouth. (17) But in civilized countries in normal times have better sources of news than rumor. (18) It has radio, television, and newspapers. In times of stress and (19) confusion; however, rumor emerges and becomes rife. At such times (20) these different kind of news media are in (21) competition; the press, television, and radio versus the grapevine.

Rumors are especially likely to spread when war requires censorship on many important matters. The customary news sources no longer give out enough information. (22) Although the people, cannot learn (23) all that they are anxious to know through legitimate channels, they pick up "news" wherever they (24) can, and rumor thrives.

Rumors are often repeated even (25) by people which do not (26) believe the stories. There is a fascination (27) about them. (28) The reason is that the cleverly designed rumor gives expression to something deep in the hearts of the tellers—the fears, suspicions, forbidden hopes, or daydreams that they hesitate to have voiced directly. (29) Pessimistic rumors about defeat and disasters show that the people who repeat these rumors are worried and anxious. Optimistic rumors about record production or peace to come soon point to complacency or confidence—(30) and often to overconfidence.

Breeding Rumors Questions

16. (F) NO CHANGE
    (G) way most crude
    (H) more crude way
    (J) crudest way

17. (A) NO CHANGE
    (B) But countries, that are civilized,
    (C) But civilized countries
    (D) But countries with civilization

18. (F) NO CHANGE
    (G) Countries have
    (H) They have
    (J) Such as

19. (A) NO CHANGE
    (B) confusion however,
    (C) confusion, however,
    (D) confusion, however

20. (F) NO CHANGE
    (G) this different kinds
    (H) these different kinds
    (J) all these different kind

21. (A) NO CHANGE
    (B) competition: the
    (C) competition. The
    (D) competition, the

22. (F) NO CHANGE
    (G) Since the people
    (H) Consequently, the people who
    (J) The people, if they

23. (A) NO CHANGE
    (B) through legitimate channels in all that they are anxious to know,
    (C) what they are anxious to know through legitimate channels,
    (D) through legitimate channels all that they are anxious to know,

24. (F) NO CHANGE
    (G) can, and rumor has thrived.
    (H) can, rumor thrives.
    (J) can, rumor thriving.

25. (A) NO CHANGE
    (B) by them as
    (C) by they who
    (D) by people who

26. (F) NO CHANGE
    (G) have belief of
    (H) dig
    (J) give credibility to

27. (A) NO CHANGE
    (B) with
    (C) over
    (D) because of

Go on to the next page. ⇨

28. Upon reviewing the paragraph, the writer considers deleting this sentence. If the writer were to delete the sentence, the paragraph would lose primarily

    (F) an argument that spreading rumors is dangerous to national security
    (G) a defense of rumors as an inevitable part of human nature
    (H) an example of mass media's justification for repeating rumors
    (J) a generalization introducing examples of the root cause of people's participation in rumors

29. Which choice would best fit the paragraph's key point about why rumors spread?

    (A) NO CHANGE
    (B) Pessimistic rumors about defeat and disasters never fail to illustrate the gullibility of the public.
    (C) Pessimistic rumors about defeat and disasters are evidence that mass media can play a major role in manipulating human behavior.
    (D) Pessimistic rumors about defeat and disasters have often shaped the outcome of war and other crisis situations.

30. If the writer were to delete the underlined phrase, the sentence would lose primarily

    (F) a sarcastic edge
    (G) a tone of disdain for people who spread rumors
    (H) the implication that people who spread false information are themselves misled
    (J) a concrete example of a rumor that was eventually proved false

Questions 31–45 are based on the following passage, *There Is No Open-and-Shut Case.*

Average citizens today are knowledgeable about "landmark" court decisions (31) as racial segregation, legislative apportionment, prayers in the public schools, or (32) that the defendant in a criminal prosecution has the right to have counsel. Too often, however, they think that (33) this settles matters once and for all. Actually, of course, these well-publicized court decisions are merely guideposts (34) that have the effect of pointing toward a virtually endless series of vexing legal questions (35). A person (36) whom the decisions

(37) affects must often still endure lengthy court cases before his fate is decided. It is often more difficult to determine how far the courts should travel along a road (38) than deciding (39) whatever road should be taken.

(40) Illustrations of this difficulty exist in all areas of the law, especially in those with which the lay public is most familiar. For example, in the recent past, this nation could hardly have failed to agree that (41) state compelled racial segregation in the public schools (42) will be a denial of the equal protection of the laws guaranteed by the 14th Amendment. The real difficulty (43) lied in determining how desegregation (44) shall be accomplished and how to solve the problem of de facto school segregation, perpetuated by the practical if unfortunate realities of residential patterns.

There Is No Open-and-Shut Case Questions

31. (A) NO CHANGE
    (B) such as
    (C) like
    (D) concerning such questions as

32. (F) NO CHANGE
    (G) the right of the defendant to counsel in criminal prosecution.
    (H) the right in criminal prosecution to counsel of the defendant.
    (J) the defendant has a right to counsel in criminal prosecution.

33. (A) NO CHANGE
    (B) these decisions settle
    (C) these settle
    (D) those settle

34. (F) NO CHANGE
    (G) with the purpose of pointing
    (H) pointing
    (J) that are pointing

35. Which phrase when added to the end of the preceding sentence best clarifies the phrase "vexing legal questions"?

    (A) in the form of appeals and unanticipated social consequences.
    (B) that make agreement impossible.
    (C) that may never be answered.
    (D) that are argued in the media.

Go on to the next page.

36. (F) NO CHANGE
    (G) who
    (H) which
    (J) as to whom

37. (A) NO CHANGE
    (B) effect
    (C) effects
    (D) affect

38. (F) NO CHANGE
    (G) than
    (H) than it is to decide
    (J) than to decide

39. (A) NO CHANGE
    (B) as to whose
    (C) what
    (D) whichever

40. Which choice would most effectively open this paragraph and introduce the supporting examples?
    (F) NO CHANGE
    (G) You are no doubt familiar with many highly publicized court cases.
    (H) Several examples show how difficult it is for a high court to reach consensus.
    (J) Many high-profile court decisions have caused unforeseen problems down the road.

41. (A) NO CHANGE
    (B) state-compelled racial-segregation
    (C) state compelled racial-segregation
    (D) state-compelled racial segregation

42. (F) NO CHANGE
    (G) will have been
    (H) is
    (J) had been

43. (A) NO CHANGE
    (B) lay
    (C) laid
    (D) was lying

44. (F) NO CHANGE
    (G) will be accomplished
    (H) was to be accomplished
    (J) were to be accomplished

Question 45 asks about the previous passage as a whole.

45. Suppose the writer had been asked to write a persuasive essay urging public support for laws with broad social significance once they are passed. Would this essay fulfill that assignment?
    (A) Yes, because the essay describes how challenging it is for a judge to reach these decisions.
    (B) Yes, because the essay clearly spells out the consequences of public polarization on legal issues of national significance.
    (C) No, because the essay provides examples of decisions that turned out to have negative outcomes.
    (D) No, because the essay's purpose is to describe a common public misperception about how historically significant court cases are resolved.

Questions 46–60 are based on the following passage, *The Highest Form of Education.*

The man who reads well is the man who thinks well, (46) he has a background for opinions and a touchstone for judgment. He may be a Lincoln (47) who derives wisdom from a few books or a Roosevelt who reads everything from Icelandic sagas to *Penrod*. But reading makes (48) his a full man, and out of his fullness (49) to draw that example and precept which (50) has stood him in good stead when confronted with problems (51) which beset a chaotic universe. Mere reading, of course, is nothing. (52) It is also the veneer of education. But wise reading is a help to action. (53) American versatility is too frequently dilettantism, but reinforced by knowledge, versatility becomes motive power. (54) "Learning" as James L. Mursell says, "cashes the (55) blank check of native versatility." (56) Ones learning is a process not to be concluded with the formal teaching of school days or (57) only to be enriched by the active experience of later years, but to be broadened and deepened by persistent and judicious reading. (58) "The true University of these days is a Collection of Books,"

Go on to the next page. ⇨

said Carlyle. If that is not the whole of the truth, it is enough of the truth for every young person to hug to their breasts. Whoever follows this advice (59) <u>will become a truly educated person.</u>

The Highest Form of Education Questions

46. (F) NO CHANGE
    (G) who
    (H) and
    (J) whom

47. (A) NO CHANGE
    (B) , deriving wisdom
    (C) , a deriver of wisdom
    (D) , wisdom deriving

48. (F) NO CHANGE
    (G) he
    (H) him
    (J) himself

49. (A) NO CHANGE
    (B) draws
    (C) drawing
    (D) he draws

50. (F) NO CHANGE
    (G) stands
    (H) stood
    (J) stand

51. Which of the following alternatives to the underlined portion would NOT be acceptable?

    (A) besetting
    (B) , that beset
    (C) that beset
    (D) that have always beset

52. (F) NO CHANGE
    (G) It is but the veneer
    (H) It is the veneer only
    (J) The veneer is

53. If the writer were to delete the sentence "American versatility . . ." the essay would lose primarily

    (A) an effective transitional statement between two different ideas
    (B) use of repetition to reinforce an argumentative point

(C) an expansion and clarification of the distinction between reading and learning
(D) a digression with no relationship to the essay's main point

54. (F) NO CHANGE
    (G) "Learning,"
    (H) "Learning,
    (J) "Learning"—

55. (A) NO CHANGE
    (B) blanked check
    (C) check that is blank
    (D) blanked out check

56. (F) NO CHANGE
    (G) One
    (H) One's
    (J) Ones'

57. (A) NO CHANGE
    (B) to be enriched only
    (C) to be only enriched
    (D) to only be enriched

58. If the writer were to delete the underlined quote, the paragraph would lose primarily

    (F) consideration of a viewpoint opposing the essay's central argument
    (G) a concrete example of the rich knowledge one can acquire from books
    (H) a comment by a well-known thinker that encapsulates the essay's point about reading and learning
    (J) an argument for pursuing a college education

59. (A) NO CHANGE
    (B) will be able to read even the most challenging material.
    (C) will love learning for the rest of his life.
    (D) will truly be ready to advance to university education.

Go on to the next page. ⇨

Question 60 asks about the previous passage as a whole.

60. Suppose the writer had been asked to write an essay arguing the superiority of informal education to formal study. Would this essay fulfill that assignment?

(F) Yes, because it argues that reading is the best substitute for an expensive education.

(G) Yes, because the essay suggests that formal education is too restrictive and passive, while reading leads to activism.

(H) No, because the essay points out that formal higher education is required in complex, chaotic times.

(J) No, because the essay illustrates how formal education and informal learning complement and enrich each other.

Questions 61–75 are based on the following passage, *No Time to Lose.*

We streamlined our leisure hours for higher production, lived by the clock even when time did not matter, standardized and mechanized our homes, and (61) <u>have sped</u> the machinery of living so that we (62) <u>can go</u> to the most places and do the most things in the (63) <u>shorter</u> period of time possible. We tried to eat, sleep, and (64) <u>loaf efficiently.</u> (65) <u>Even on holidays and Sundays, the efficient person relaxed on schedule with one eye on the clock and the other on an appointment sheet.</u>

(66) <u>To have squeezed</u> the most out of each shining hour, we streamlined the opera, condensed the classics, (67) <u>energize pellets,</u> and culture into pocket-sized packages. We made the busy bee look like an (68) <u>idler, the ant like a sluggard.</u> We lived sixty miles a minute and the great god (69) <u>efficiency</u> smiled. (70) <u>We wished we could have returned</u> to that pleasant day when we (71) <u>considered</u> time a friend instead of a competitor, when we had done things (72) <u>spontaneously</u> and because we had wanted to do them rather than (73) <u>on account of</u> our schedule had called for it. But (74) <u>that,</u> of course, had not been efficient; and every single one of us Americans (75) <u>are expected</u> to be efficient.

No Time to Lose Questions

61. (A) NO CHANGE
    (B) speed
    (C) speeding
    (D) sped

62. (F) NO CHANGE
    (G) could go
    (H) are able to go
    (J) go

63. (A) NO CHANGE
    (B) shortest
    (C) short
    (D) most short

64. (F) NO CHANGE
    (G) to loaf efficiently.
    (H) loaf efficient.
    (J) to loaf efficient.

65. Which sentence best emphasizes the paragraph's point about the American lifestyle?

    (A) NO CHANGE
    (B) Relaxation was so important to us, we scheduled it into our lives every day.
    (C) Being on time for scheduled appointments has been a hallmark of our efficiency.
    (D) Holidays and Sundays have traditionally been the days reserved for leisure.

66. (F) NO CHANGE
    (G) In order for squeezing
    (H) In order for having squeezed
    (J) To squeeze

67. (A) NO CHANGE
    (B) gave pellets energy,
    (C) energy into pellets,
    (D) and put energy into pellets

68. (F) NO CHANGE
    (G) idler, the ant as a sluggard.
    (H) idler. The ant like a sluggard.
    (J) idler; the ant as a sluggard.

69. (A) NO CHANGE
    (B) , efficiency,
    (C) Efficiency
    (D) , Efficiency,

Go on to the next page.

70. (F) NO CHANGE
    (G) (DO NOT begin a new paragraph) We wished we could have returned,
    (H) (Begin a new paragraph) We wished we could have returned
    (J) (Begin a new paragraph) We wished, we could have returned

71. (A) NO CHANGE
    (B) had considered
    (C) consider
    (D) will consider

72. (F) NO CHANGE
    (G) with spontaneity
    (H) in a spontaneous manner
    (J) spontaneous

73. (A) NO CHANGE
    (B) because
    (C) when
    (D) OMIT

74. Given that all are true, which choice most clearly conveys the writer's message about American efficiency?
    (F) NO CHANGE
    (G) wasting time
    (H) wishing to live at a more relaxed pace
    (J) ignoring our responsibilities

75. (A) NO CHANGE
    (B) are to be expected
    (C) expect
    (D) is expected

STOP!

If you finish before time is called, you may check your work on this section only.
Do not turn to any other section in the test.

SECTION 2: MATHEMATICS TEST

60 Minutes, 60 Questions

Turn to Section 2 of your answer sheet (page 396) to answer the questions in this section. You may use the bottom of each page for figuring.

Directions

Solve each problem, choose the correct answer, and then fill in the corresponding circle on your answer sheet.

Do not linger over problems that take too much time. Solve as many as you can; then return to the others in the time you have left for this test.

You are permitted to use a calculator on this test. You may use your calculator for any problems you choose, but some of the problems may best be done without using a calculator.

Note: Unless otherwise stated, all of the following should be assumed.

1. Figures are NOT necessarily drawn to scale.
2. Geometric figures lie in a plane.
3. The word *line* indicates a straight line.
4. The word *average* indicates arithmetic mean.

1. A band wants to produce CDs from their music. They have an original CD but need to duplicate the CD to sell to the public. The band buys a CD burning machine for $169.99. Each blank CD they use will cost $1.50. What is the total production cost for making x CDs from their original CD?

   (A) $168.49
   (B) $169.99 + $1.50x$
   (C) $169.99x + 1.50
   (D) $171.49
   (E) $1.50x$

2. List all the positive factors of 16.

   (F) 1, 8
   (G) 2, 4, 8
   (H) 2, 4, 8, 16
   (J) 1, 2, 4, 8, 16
   (K) 1, 2, 4, 8, 12, 16

3. Which of the following is equal to $(3x^3)^3$?

   (A) $9x^6$
   (B) $9x^9$
   (C) $27x^6$
   (D) $27x^9$
   (E) $3x^9$

Go on to the next page. ⇨

4. What is the value of the expression $(a - b)^2$ when $a = 3$ and $b = -2$?

   (F) 1
   (G) 5
   (H) 25
   (J) 50
   (K) 100

5. The figure below shows a triangle ABC where A, E, C, and D are collinear. What is the measure of $\angle ABE$ if $\angle BAE = 70°$, $\angle CBE = 40°$, and $\angle BCD = 140°$?

   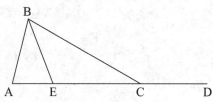

   (A) 30°
   (B) 35°
   (C) 40°
   (D) 45°
   (E) 50°

6. What is the slope of a line passing through coordinates $(-3,1)$ and $(4,5)$ in the (x,y) coordinate plane?

   (F) $\dfrac{4}{7}$
   (G) $-\dfrac{4}{7}$
   (H) 1
   (J) -4
   (K) 4

7. In a store, DVDs were marked down 25% from the list price. If I want to write a program for the marked price in the store of any DVD that carries a list price of x, what would the expression be for the discounted price of the DVD?

   (A) $x - \dfrac{x}{4}$
   (B) $x - 25x$
   (C) $x - \dfrac{1}{4}$
   (D) $\left(\dfrac{1}{4}\right)x$
   (E) $25x$

8. Which of the following expressions is the same as the expression $3(5y + 8) - 4(2y - 6)$?

   (F) $7y$
   (G) $7y + 48$
   (H) $2y$
   (J) $2y + 48$
   (K) $3y + 2$

9. For all values of x, what is the expression $(2x + 9)^2$ equivalent to?

   (A) $4x + 18$
   (B) $4x^2 + 18$
   (C) $4x^2 + 81$
   (D) $4x^2 + 18x + 81$
   (E) $4x^2 + 36x + 81$

Go on to the next page. ⇨

10. 180 tennis players are competing in a tournament. The tennis players are separated into three levels of ability: **A** (high), **B** (middle), and **C** (low), with the number of players in each category shown in the table below.

Level	Number of Players
A	30
B	60
C	90

The tennis committee has 54 prizes and will award them proportionately to the number of players at each level. How many prizes will be awarded to players in level A?

(F) 5
(G) 6
(H) 7
(J) 8
(K) 9

11. In the following figure, adjacent sides meet at right angles. What is the perimeter of the figure?

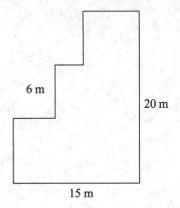

6 m

20 m

15 m

(A) 35 m
(B) 70 m
(C) 140 m
(D) 160 m
(E) 180 m

12. There are five boxes placed around a circle, as shown below. If a straight line is used to connect two of the boxes, what is the maximum number of connections that can be made without repeating?

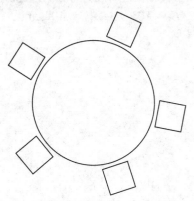

(F) 7
(G) 8
(H) 9
(J) 10
(K) 11

13. Which of the following is equivalent to $6x^2 - 9x - 6$?

(A) $(x - 2)(6x + 3)$
(B) $(x - 2)(6x - 3)$
(C) $(x + 2)(6x + 3)$
(D) $(3x + 2)(2x - 3)$
(E) $(3x - 2)(2x + 3)$

14. In the figure below, the perpendicular bisectors of AB and AE meet at point H. A circle with center H and radius AH must pass through which of the following points?

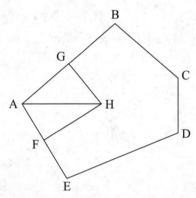

(F) A only
(G) A and E only
(H) A and B only
(J) A, B, and E only
(K) A, B, D, and E only

15. A circle in the xy plane is represented by the equation:

$$x^2 + y^2 - 8y + 4 = 0$$

What is the radius of the circle?

(A) $\sqrt{10}$
(B) $2\sqrt{3}$
(C) $\sqrt{14}$
(D) 4
(E) $3\sqrt{2}$

16. $\dfrac{32}{18 - \dfrac{5}{0.5}} =$

(F) 4
(G) $\dfrac{16}{5}$
(H) $\dfrac{5}{16}$
(J) $\dfrac{32}{5}$
(K) 8

17. If $f(y) - 2^{y+4}$ for all y, real, then $f(0) =$

(A) 4
(B) 8
(C) 12
(D) 16
(E) 20

18. The graph below shows the highest temperature recorded on the given day. What is the highest temperature recorded on October 21?

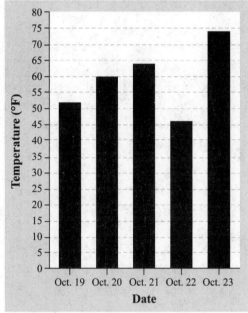

(F) 60°
(G) 64°
(H) 72°
(J) 54°
(K) 66°

Go on to the next page. ⇨

19. If $i^2 = -1$, what does $(3 + 4i)(6i - 1)$ equal?

    (A) $14i - 27$
    (B) $14i + 27$
    (C) $42i - 3$
    (D) $14i - 21$
    (E) $14i + 21$

20. The value of x in the equation $\log_3 36 - \log_3 4 = \log_4 x$ is

    (F) 2
    (G) 4
    (H) 8
    (J) 16
    (K) 32

21. A ladder is set up against the wall as shown below. The bottom of the ladder is 5 feet from the wall. Which is true of the angle the ladder makes with the ground if the ladder is 8 feet in length?

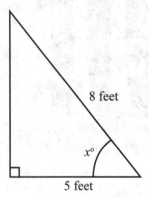

    8 feet

    $x°$

    5 feet

    (A) $\sin x° = \dfrac{5}{8}$

    (B) $\cos x° = \dfrac{8}{5}$

    (C) $\cot x° = \dfrac{5}{8}$

    (D) $\tan x° = \dfrac{5}{8}$

    (E) $\sec x° = \dfrac{8}{5}$

22. Which of the following is correct, according to the diagram of the rectangle below?

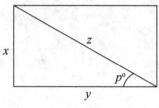

    (F) $\cos p° = \dfrac{x}{z}$

    (G) $\sin p° = \dfrac{y}{z}$

    (H) $\tan p° = \dfrac{y}{x}$

    (J) $\sec p° = \dfrac{z}{y}$

    (K) $\cot p° = \dfrac{x}{y}$

23. The chickens on a certain farm consumed 600 pounds of feed in half a year. During that time, the total number of eggs laid was 5,000. If the feed cost $1.25 per pound, then the feed cost per egg was

    (A) $0.0750
    (B) $0.1250
    (C) $0.15
    (D) $0.25
    (E) $0.3333

Go on to the next page. ⇨

24. If X is the set of negative numbers and Y is the set of positive numbers, then the union of X and Y and 0 is the set of

(F) all real numbers
(G) all integers
(H) all rational numbers
(J) all irrational numbers
(K) all odd integers

25. In the figure below, there are three circles, A, B, and C. The area of A is three times that of B, and the area of B is three times that of C. If the area of B is 1, find the sum of the areas of A, B, and C.

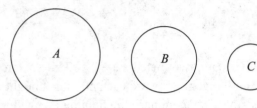

(A) 3
(B) $3\frac{1}{3}$
(C) $4\frac{1}{3}$
(D) 5
(E) $6\frac{1}{3}$

26. In the figure below, two concentric circles with center P are shown. PQR, a radius of the larger circle, equals 9. PQ, a radius of the smaller circle, equals 4. If a circle L (not shown) is drawn with center at R and Q on its circumference, find the radius of circle L.

(F) 13
(G) 5
(H) 4
(J) 2
(K) It cannot be determined from the information given.

27. Which equation or equations would be represented by the graph below?

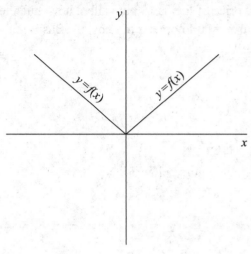

(A) $y = x$
(B) $y = |x|$
(C) $y = x^2$
(D) $y = x, x > 0$
    $y = 0, x = 0$
    $y = -|x|, x < 0$
(E) $y = -x$

28. What is the slope of line l in the figure below?

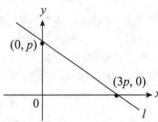

(F) -3
(G) $-\frac{1}{3}$
(H) 0
(J) $\frac{1}{3}$
(K) 3

Go on to the next page. ⟹

29. Bus A averages 40 kilometers per gallon of fuel. Bus B averages 50 kilometers per gallon of fuel. If the price of fuel is $3 per gallon, how much less would an 800-kilometer trip cost for Bus B than for Bus A?

    (A) $18
    (B) $16
    (C) $14
    (D) $12
    (E) $10

30. $m \| n$ in the figure below. Find y.

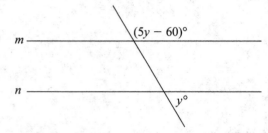

    (F) 10
    (G) 20
    (H) 40
    (J) 65
    (K) 175

31. If an ant runs randomly through an enclosed circular field of radius 2 feet with an inner circle of radius 1 foot, what is the probability that the ant will be in the inner circle at any one time?

    (A) $\dfrac{1}{8}$

    (B) $\dfrac{1}{6}$

    (C) $\dfrac{1}{4}$

    (D) $\dfrac{1}{2}$

    (E) 1

32. The length and width of a rectangle are $3w$ and w, respectively. The length of the hypotenuse of a right triangle, one of whose acute angles is 30°, is $2w$. What is the ratio of the area of the rectangle to that of the triangle?

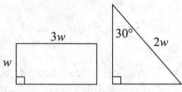

    (F) $2\sqrt{3} : 1$
    (G) $\sqrt{3} : 1$
    (H) $1 : \sqrt{3}$
    (J) $1 : 2\sqrt{3}$
    (K) $1 : 6$

33. At one instant, two meteors are 2,500 kilometers apart and traveling toward each other in straight paths along the imaginary line joining them. One meteor has a velocity of 300 meters per second while the other travels at 700 meters per second. Assuming that their velocities are constant and that they continue along the same paths, how many seconds elapse from the first instant to the time of their collision? (1 kilometer = 1,000 meters)

    (A) 250
    (B) 500
    (C) 1,250
    (D) 2,500
    (E) 5,000

34. Given that the volume of a cube is 8 cubic meters, find the distance from any vertex to the center point inside the cube.

    (F) 1 m
    (G) $\sqrt{2}$ m
    (H) $2\sqrt{2}$ m
    (J) $2\sqrt{3}$ m
    (K) $\sqrt{3}$ m

Go on to the next page. ⇨

35. The sum of a number of consecutive positive integers will always be divisible by 2 if the numbe of integers is a multiple of

  (A) 6
  (B) 5
  (C) 4
  (D) 3
  (E) 2

36. If $\dfrac{a}{b} = \dfrac{1}{4}$, where a is a positive integer, which of the following is a possible value of $\dfrac{a^2}{b}$?

  I. $\dfrac{1}{4}$

  II. $\dfrac{1}{2}$

  III. 1

  (F) None
  (G) I only
  (H) I and II only
  (J) I and III only
  (K) I, II, and III

37. A plane left airport A and has traveled x kilometers per hour for y hours. In terms of x and y, how many kilometers from airport A had the plane traveled $\dfrac{2}{3}y$ hours ago?

  (A) $\dfrac{xy}{6}$

  (B) $\dfrac{xy}{3}$

  (C) xy

  (D) $\dfrac{3xy}{2}$

  (E) $\dfrac{xy}{12}$

38. The average (arithmetic mean) of k scores is 20. The average of 10 of these scores is 15. Find the average of the remaining scores in terms of k.

  (F) $\dfrac{20k + 150}{10}$

  (G) $\dfrac{20k - 150}{10}$

  (H) $\dfrac{150 - 20k}{10}$

  (J) $\dfrac{150 - 20k}{k - 10}$

  (K) $\dfrac{20k - 150}{k - 10}$

39. Using the formula $C = \dfrac{5}{9}(F - 32)$, if the Celsius (C) temperature increased 35°, by how many degrees would the Fahrenheit (F) temperature be increased?

  (A) $19\dfrac{4}{9}°$

  (B) 31°

  (C) 51°

  (D) 63°

  (E) 82°

40. In the figure below, one side of a triangle has been extended. What is the value of $w + x + y$?

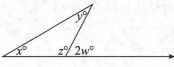

  (F) $3w$
  (G) $3z$
  (H) $2x + y$
  (J) $2x + 2y$
  (K) $2w + z$

Go on to the next page. ⇨

Questions 41–42 refer to the following game.

A computer generates numbers. Points are assigned as described in the following table each time any of the four number pairs given appears in a number. As an example, the number 4,347 is assigned 4 points for "43" and 6 points more for "34," giving a total of 10 points.

Number Pair	Number of Points
"33"	11
"34"	6
"43"	4
"44"	3

41. Which of the following numbers would be assigned the most points?

(A) 934,432
(B) 464,457
(C) 834,415
(D) 437,934
(E) 336,283

42. If a certain number has 13 points assigned to it, which of the following statements must be true?

I. 33 is not in the number.
II. 34 and 43 are both in the number.
III. 43 is in the number.

(F) I only
(G) II only
(H) III only
(J) I and III only
(K) I, II, and III

43. The square in the figure below has two sides tangent to the circle. If the area of the circle is $9a^2\pi^2$, find the area of the square in terms of a and π.

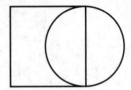

(A) $12a^2\pi^2$
(B) $36a^2\pi$
(C) $36a^2\pi^2$
(D) $18a^4\pi^2$
(E) $9a^4\pi^2$

44. Equilateral polygon *ABCDEF* is inscribed in the circle. If the length of arc *BAF* is 14π, find the length of the diameter of the circle.

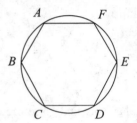

(F) 7
(G) 14
(H) 7π
(J) 21
(K) 42

45. If $f(x) = a^x$, then

(A) $f(x + y) = f(x) + f(y)$
(B) $f(x + y) = f(x)f(y)$
(C) $f(x - y) = f(x) - f(y)$
(D) $f(xy) = f(x)f(y)$
(E) $f\left(\dfrac{x}{y}\right) = \dfrac{f(x)}{f(y)}$

Go on to the next page. ⇨

46. Container A holds twice as much as container B, and container C holds as much as A and B put together. If we start with A and B full, and C empty, and pour half the contents of A and a third of the contents of B into container C, what fraction of C's capacity will be filled?

(F) $\dfrac{5}{6}$

(G) $\dfrac{4}{9}$

(H) $\dfrac{5}{12}$

(J) $\dfrac{7}{12}$

(K) $\dfrac{7}{18}$

47. What is the diameter of a wheel which, when rotating at a speed of 10 revolutions per minute, takes 12 seconds to travel 16 feet? (Assume no slippage.)

(A) 4π feet

(B) $\dfrac{\pi}{4}$ feet

(C) 8π feet

(D) $\dfrac{8}{\pi}$ feet

(E) $\dfrac{16}{\pi}$ feet

48. In the figure below, the sides of rectangle $ABCD$ are parallel to the y-axis and x-axis, as shown. If the rectangle is rotated clockwise about the origin through $90°$, what are the new coordinates of B?

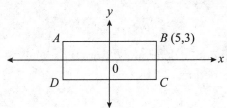

(F) $(3,-5)$
(G) $(-3,5)$
(H) $(-3,-5)$
(J) $(5,-3)$
(K) $(-5,3)$

49. The half-life of a certain radioactive substance is 6 hours. In other words, if you start with 8 grams of the substance, 6 hours later you will have 4 grams. If a sample of this substance contains x grams, how many grams remain after 24 hours?

(A) $\dfrac{x}{32}$

(B) $\dfrac{x}{16}$

(C) $\dfrac{x}{8}$

(D) $2x$

(E) $4x$

50. Box A contains 3 cards, numbered 3, 4, and 5. Box B contains 3 cards, numbered 6, 7, and 8. If one card is drawn from each box and the sum of the two cards is calculated, how many different numerical results are possible?

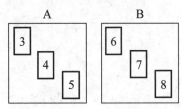

(F) eight
(G) seven
(H) six
(J) five
(K) four

51. If $\dfrac{\pi}{2} > x > 0$,

$$\sin x\sqrt{1 - \sin^2 x} + \cos x\sqrt{1 - \cos^2 x} =$$

(A) 1
(B) 2
(C) $\sin 2x$
(D) $\cos 2x$
(E) $\tan x$

Go on to the next page. ⇨

52. Which of the following equations could not represent any of the graphs shown?

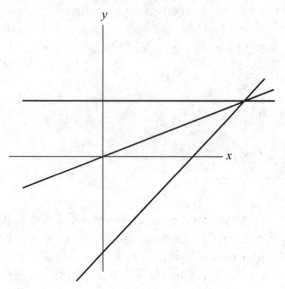

(F) $2y = x$
(G) $y = 2$
(H) $y = 2x - 6$
(J) $y = 2x + 4$
(K) $y = 4$

53. If $f(x) = |x| - x$, which of the following is true?

(A) $f(x) = f(-x)$
(B) $f(2x) = 2f(x)$
(C) $f(x + y) = f(x) + f(y)$
(D) $f(x) = -f(-x)$
(E) $f(x - y) = 0$

54. A projector emits light onto a 10-foot screen, as shown below. The projection covers the full 10 feet exactly. The screen is directly in front of the projector, as shown. If you wanted to calculate the distance in feet from the projector to the screen, you would use which of the following expressions?

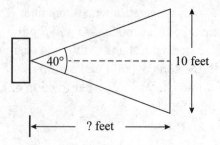

(F) $\dfrac{5}{\tan 20°}$

(G) $\dfrac{5}{\tan 40°}$

(H) $5 \tan 20°$

(J) $5 \tan 40°$

(K) $10 \tan 20°$

55. In the figure below, two bicycles are being pedaled in opposite directions around a circular racetrack of circumference = 120 feet. Bicycle A is traveling at 5 feet/second in the counterclockwise direction, and Bicycle B is traveling at 8 feet/second in the clockwise direction. When Bicycle B has completed exactly 600 revolutions, how many complete revolutions will Bicycle A have made?

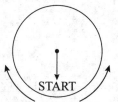

Bicycle B Bicycle A

(A) 180
(B) 375
(C) 475
(D) 960
(E) It cannot be determined from the given information.

Go on to the next page. ⇨

56. A square of side x is inscribed inside an equilateral triangle of area $x^2\sqrt{3}$. If a rectangle with width x has the same area as the shaded region shown in the figure below, what is the length of the rectangle in terms of x?

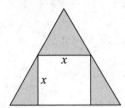

   (F) $\sqrt{3}x - 1$
   (G) $x\sqrt{3}$
   (H) $\sqrt{3} - x$
   (J) $x(\sqrt{3} - 1)$
   (K) $x^2(\sqrt{3} - x^2)$

57. At a certain college, the number of freshmen is three times the number of seniors. If $\frac{1}{4}$ of the freshmen and $\frac{1}{3}$ of the seniors attend a football game, what fraction of the total number of freshmen and seniors attend the game?

   (A) $\dfrac{5}{24}$

   (B) $\dfrac{13}{48}$

   (C) $\dfrac{17}{48}$

   (D) $\dfrac{11}{24}$

   (E) $\dfrac{23}{48}$

58. At Jones College, there are a total of 100 students. If 30 of the students have cars on campus, 50 have bicycles, and 20 have both cars and bicycles, then how many students have neither a car nor a bicycle on campus?

   (F) 80
   (G) 60
   (H) 40
   (J) 20
   (K) 0

59. An odd function is defined by the following: $f(x)$ is an odd function if and only if, for every value of x, $f(-x) = -f(x)$. Which of the following graphs represents an odd function in the xy plane?

   (A)

   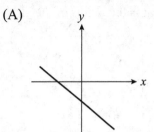

   (B)

   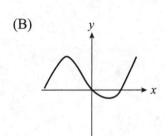

   (C)

   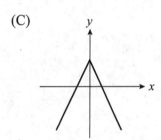

   (D)

   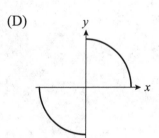

   (E)

   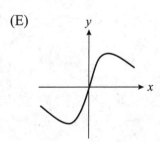

Go on to the next page. ⇨

60. In a woodworking class, John cuts a circular piece of wood from a square piece of wood, as shown below. The side of the square is 3 inches. If the area of the circle cutout is equal to the area of the remaining wood, what is the radius of the circle in inches?

3 inches

(F) $\dfrac{3}{\sqrt{2\pi}}$

(G) $\dfrac{9}{\sqrt{2\pi}}$

(H) $\dfrac{3}{\sqrt{\pi}}$

(J) $\dfrac{9}{\sqrt{\pi}}$

(K) $\dfrac{3}{2\pi}$

STOP!

If you finish before time is called, you may check your work on this section only.
Do not turn to any other section in the test.

SECTION 3: READING TEST

35 Minutes, 40 Questions

Turn to Section 3 of your answer sheet (page 397) to answer the questions in this section.

Directions

There are four passages in this test. Each passage is followed by several questions. After reading a passage, choose the best answer to each question and fill in the corresponding circle on your answer sheet. You may refer to the passages as often as necessary.

Passage I: Prose Fiction

The first part of this passage, here titled "Oliver," is from Charles Dickens's novel Oliver Twist *(1838). The second part, "Nat," is from Louisa May Alcott's novel* Little Men *(1871). The passages describe life for two orphaned boys in two very different situations.*

Oliver

The room in which the boys were fed, was a large stone hall, with a copper at one end: out of which the master, dressed in an apron for the purpose, and assisted by one or two women, ladled the gruel at mealtimes. Of this
5 festive composition each boy had one porringer, and no more—except on occasions of great public rejoicing, when he had two ounces and a quarter of bread besides.

The evening arrived; the boys took their places. The master, in his cook's uniform, stationed himself at the
10 copper; his pauper assistants ranged themselves behind him; the gruel was served out; and a long grace was said over the short commons. The gruel disappeared; the boys whispered each to other, and winked at Oliver; while his next neighbors nudged him. Child as he was,
15 he was desperate with hunger, and reckless with misery. He rose from the table; and advancing to the master, basin and spoon in hand, said, somewhat alarmed at his own temerity:

"Please, sir, I want some more."

20 The master was a fat, healthy man; but he turned very pale. He gazed in stupefied astonishment on the small rebel for some seconds, and then clung for support to the copper. The assistants were paralyzed with wonder; the boys with fear. . . .

25 "For more!" said Mr. Limbkins. . . . "Do I understand that he asked for more, after he had eaten the supper allotted by the dietary?"

"He did, sir," replied Bumble.

"That boy will be hung," said the gentleman in the
30 white waistcoat. "I know that boy will be hung."

Nobody controverted the prophetic gentleman's opinion. An animated discussion took place. Oliver was ordered into instant confinement; and a bill was next morning pasted on the outside of the gate, offering
35 a reward of five pounds to anybody who would take Oliver Twist off the hands of the parish. In other words, five pounds and Oliver Twist were offered to any man or woman who wanted an apprentice to any trade, business, or calling.

Nat

40 When Nat went into school on Monday morning, he quaked inwardly, for now he thought he should have to display his ignorance before them all. But Mr. Bhaer gave him a seat in the deep window, where he could turn his back on the others, and Franz heard him say his
45 lessons there, so no one could hear his blunders or see how he blotted his copybook. He was truly grateful for this, and toiled away so diligently that Mr. Bhaer said, smiling, when he saw his hot face and inky fingers:

"Don't work so hard, my boy; you will tire yourself
50 out, and there is time enough."

"But I must work hard, or I can't catch up with the others. They know heaps, and I don't know anything," said Nat, who had been reduced to a state of despair by hearing the boys recite their grammar, history, and
55 geography with what he thought amazing ease and accuracy.

"You know a good many things which they don't," said Mr. Bhaer, sitting down beside him, while Franz led a class of small students through the intricacies of
60 the multiplication table.

"Do I?" and Nat looked utterly incredulous.

"Yes; for one thing, you can keep your temper, and Jack, who is quick at numbers, cannot; that is an excellent lesson, and I think you have learned it well. Then,
65 you can play the violin, and not one of the lads can, though they want to do it very much. But, best of all, Nat, you really care to learn something, and that is half the battle. It seems hard at first, and you will feel discouraged, but plod away, and things will get easier and
70 easier as you go on." . . .

Thinking that a lesson in learning to help one another was better than arithmetic just then, Mr. Bhaer told them about Nat, making such an interesting and touching little story out of it that the good-hearted lads
75 all promised to lend him a hand, and felt quite honored to be called upon to impart their stores of wisdom to the chap who fiddled so capitally. This appeal established the right feeling among them, and Nat had few hindrances to struggle against, for every one was glad
80 to give him a "boost" up the ladder of learning.

Passage I Questions

1. In the "Oliver" passage (lines 20–39), the adults' attitude toward the boys is one of:

   (A) fear
   (B) paternalism
   (C) tolerance
   (D) contempt

2. Which of the following is the most appropriate title for lines 1–39?

   (F) A Workhouse Education
   (G) Hunger at the Orphanage
   (H) The Orphans' Revolt
   (J) Proper Discipline for Children

3. The author's reference to "this festive composition" (lines 4–5) is intended to be understood as

   (A) ironic
   (B) literal
   (C) facetious
   (D) understated

4. The author states or implies in the "Oliver" passage that the orphans were treated

   (F) according to accepted standards of the time
   (G) as trade apprentices being prepared for adulthood
   (H) as children in need of compassion
   (J) as inmates in a prison

5. Which of these contrasting moods best characterizes the boys in "Oliver" versus the boys in "Nat"?

   (A) apathetic vs. mischievous
   (B) angry vs. content
   (C) fearful vs. supportive
   (D) combative vs. compliant

6. It can be inferred from the "Nat" passage that Mr. Bhaer believes that

   (F) discipline is most important when raising boys
   (G) children should be motivated by competition
   (H) academic studies are more important than moral lessons
   (J) the students should help and support one another

7. Which statement best summarizes the contrasting views presented in the "Oliver" and "Nat" passages?

   (A) "Oliver" presents the boys as burdensome, while "Nat" presents the boys as children to be nurtured.
   (B) The boy Oliver is worthy of scorn, while Nat is worthy of admiration.
   (C) The author of "Oliver" believes that children should be exploited, whereas the author of "Nat" believes they should be raised as Christians.
   (D) In the world of "Oliver" children are inherently bad, while in the world of "Nat" they are inherently good.

8. Which view do both authors most likely hold in common?

   (F) Boys should be supported and not mistreated.
   (G) Boys will be boys and will get into trouble.
   (H) Boys are naturally aggressive and need discipline.
   (J) Boys who are abused will revert to their animal instincts.

Go on to the next page. ⇨

9. We can infer from the passage that
   (A) the "Oliver" author believes most boys are bad
   (B) the "Nat" author believes that most boys are good
   (C) the "Oliver" author believes that children have a strong survival instinct
   (D) both authors believe that schools should focus on morality before academics

10. Which situation or condition is described or mentioned in one section but not in the other?
    I.   The sociable and friendly nature of the people
    II. The positive effects of the environment
    III. The impact of the boys on one another

    (F) I and III only
    (G) I and II only
    (H) II and III only
    (J) III only

Passage II: Social Science

This passage, adapted from "An Enduring Empire," is about the Chinese Empire, the forces that kept the Empire together, its culture, and its philosophy.

First of all, it is important to note that the old China was an empire rather than a state. To the Chinese and their rulers, the word *China* did not exist and to them it would have been meaningless. They sometimes used
5 a term which we translate "the Middle Kingdom." To them there could be only one legitimate ruler for all civilized mankind. All others were rightly subordinate to him and should acknowledge his suzerainty. From this standpoint, there could not, as in Europe, be dip-
10 lomatic relations between equal states, each of them sovereign. When, in the nineteenth century, Europeans insisted upon intercourse with China on the basis of equality, the Chinese were at first amused and then scandalized and indignant. Centuries of training had
15 bred in them the conviction that all other rulers should be tributary to the Son of Heaven.

The tie which bound this world-embracing empire together, so the Chinese were taught to believe, was as much cultural as political. As there could be only one
20 legitimate ruler to whom all mankind must be subject, so there could be only one culture that fully deserved to be called civilized. Other cultures might have worth,

but ultimately they were more or less barbarous. There could be only one civilization, and that was the civiliza-
25 tion of the Middle Kingdom. Beginning with the Han, the ideal of civilization was held to be Confucian. The Confucian interpretation of civilization was adopted and inculcated as the norm. Others might be tolerated, but if they seriously threatened the Confucian institu-
30 tions and foundations of society they were to be curbed and, perhaps, exterminated as a threat to the highest values.

Since the bond of the Empire was cultural and since the Empire should include all civilized mankind, racial
35 distinctions were not so marked as in most other parts of the world. The Chinese did not have so strong a sense of being of different blood from non-Chinese as twentieth-century conceptions of race and nation later led them to develop. They were proud of being "the
40 sons of Han" or "the men of Tang," but if a people fully adopted Chinese culture no great distinction was perceived between them and those who earlier had been governed by that culture.

This helps to account for the comparative content-
45 ment of Chinese under alien rulers. If, as was usually the case, these invading conquerors adopted the culture of their subjects and governed through the accustomed machinery and by traditional Confucian principles, they were accepted as legitimate Emperors. Few of the non-
50 Chinese dynasties completely made this identification. This probably in part accounts for such restiveness as the Chinese showed under their rule. For instance, so long as they were dominant, the Manchus, while they accepted much of the Chinese culture and prided them-
55 selves on being experts in it and posed as its patrons, never completely abandoned their distinctive ancestral ways.

The fact that the tie was cultural rather than racial helps to account for the remarkable homogeneity of
60 the Chinese. Many different ethnic strains have gone to make up the people whom we call the Chinese. Presumably in the Chou and probably, earlier, in the Shang, the bearers of Chinese culture were not a single race. As Chinese culture moved southward it encoun-
65 tered differing cultures and, almost certainly, divergent stocks. The many invaders from the north and west brought in more variety. In contrast with India, where caste and religion have tended to keep apart the racial strata, in China assimilation made great progress. That

Go on to the next page. ⇨

70 assimilation has not been complete. Today the discern-
ing observer can notice differences even among those
who are Chinese in language and customs, and in many
parts of China Proper there are groups who preserve
not only their racial but also their linguistic and cultural
75 identities. Still, nowhere else on the globe is there so
numerous a people who are so nearly homogeneous as
are the Chinese.

This homogeneity is due not merely to a common
cultural tie, but also to the particular kind of culture
80 which constitutes that tie. Something in the Chinese
tradition recognized as civilized those who conformed
to certain ethical standards and social customs. It was
the fitting into Confucian patterns of conduct and of
family and community life rather than blood kinship or
85 ancestry which labeled one as civilized and as Chinese.

Passage II Questions

11. The force that kept the Chinese Empire together
    was largely

    (A) military
    (B) economic
    (C) a fear of invasion from the north and west
    (D) the combination of a political and a cultural
        bond

12. The reason China resisted having diplomatic rela-
    tions with European nations was that

    (F) for centuries the Chinese had believed that
        their nation must be supreme among all other
        countries
    (G) the Chinese saw nothing of value in European
        culture
    (H) China was afraid of European military power
    (J) the danger of disease was ever present when
        foreigners arrived

13. Confucianism stresses, above all,

    (A) recognition of moral values
    (B) division of church and state
    (C) acceptance of foreigners
    (D) separation of social classes

14. Han and Tang were Chinese

    (F) philosophers
    (G) holidays
    (H) dynasties
    (J) generals

15. If the unifying force in the Chinese empire had
    been racial, it is likely that

    (A) China would be engaged in constant warfare
    (B) China would have become a highly industrial-
        ized nation
    (C) there would have been increasing discontent
        under foreign rulers
    (D) China would have greatly expanded its
        influence

16. A problem of contemporary India that does not
    trouble China is

    (F) the persistence of the caste system
    (G) a lack of modern industrial development
    (H) a scarcity of universities
    (J) a low standard of living

17. The Manchus encountered some dissatisfaction
    within the empire because

    (A) of their tyrannical rule
    (B) they retained some of their original cultural
        practices
    (C) of the heavy taxes they levied
    (D) they rejected totally Chinese culture

18. The Chinese are basically a homogeneous people
    because

    (F) different races were able to assimilate to a
        great degree
    (G) there has always been only one race in China
    (H) the other races came to look like the Chinese
        because of geographical factors
    (J) all other races were forcibly kept out of China

19. The author uses the word *restiveness* in line 51 to
    mean

    (A) authority
    (B) happiness
    (C) impatience
    (D) quietude

20. The perception of the Chinese that other cultures
    were *barbarous* (line 23) most nearly meant that

    (F) they threatened the Middle Kingdom with
        invasion
    (G) the Chinese considered themselves more
        cosmopolitan than other cultures
    (H) other cultures were racially inferior
    (J) other cultures lacked Chinese traditions,
        values, and Confucian philosophy

Go on to the next page.

Passage III: Humanities

The following passage is adapted from Christopher Lehmann-Haupt's "Books of the Times," appearing in The New York Times *on May 29, 1974. In it he discusses the pros and cons of B. F. Skinner's work on behaviorism.*

In his compact and modestly titled book *About Behaviorism*, Dr. B. F. Skinner, the noted behavioral psychologist, lists the 20 most salient objections to "behaviorism or the science of behavior," and he has
5 gone on to answer them both implicitly and explicitly. He has answers and explanations for everyone.

For instance, to those who object that behaviorists "deny the existence of feelings, sensations, ideas, and other features of mental life," Dr. Skinner concedes that
10 "a good deal of clarification" is in order. What such people are really decrying is "methodological behaviorism," an earlier stage of the science whose goal was precisely to close off mentalistic explanations of behavior, if only to counteract the 2,500-year-old influence of mental-
15 ism. But Dr. Skinner is a "radical behaviorist." "Radical behaviorism . . . takes a different line. It does not deny the possibility of self-observation or self-knowledge or its possible usefulness. . . . It restores introspection. . . ."

For instance, to those who object that behaviorism
20 "neglects innate endowment and argues that all behavior is acquired during the lifetime of the individual," Dr. Skinner expresses puzzlement. Granted, "A few behaviorists . . . have minimized if not denied a genetic contribution, and in their enthusiasm for what may be done
25 through the environment, others have no doubt acted as if a genetic endowment were unimportant, but few would contend that behavior is 'endlessly malleable.'" And Dr. Skinner himself, sounding as often as not like some latter-day Social Darwinist, gives as much weight
30 to the "contingencies of survival" in the evolution of the human species as to the "contingencies of reinforcement" in the lifetime of the individual.

For instance, to those who claim that behaviorism "cannot explain creative achievements—in art, for
35 example, or in music, literature, science, or mathematics"—Dr. Skinner provides an intriguing ellipsis. "Contingencies of reinforcement also resemble contingencies of survival in the production of novelty. . . . In both natural selection and operant conditioning the appearance
40 of 'mutations' is crucial. Until recently, species evolved because of random changes in genes or chromosomes, but the geneticist may arrange conditions under which mutations are particularly likely to occur. We can also discover some of the sources of new forms of behavior
45 which undergo selection by prevailing contingencies or reinforcement, and fortunately the creative artist or thinker has other ways of introducing novelties."

And so go Dr. Skinner's answers to the 20 questions he poses—questions that range all the way from
50 asking if behaviorism fails "to account for cognitive processes" to wondering if behaviorism "is indifferent to the warmth and richness of human life, and . . . is incompatible with the . . . enjoyment of art, music, and literature and with love for one's fellow men."
55 But will it wash? Will it serve to silence those critics who have characterized B. F. Skinner variously as a mad, manipulative doctor, as a naïve 19th-century positivist, as an unscientific technician, and as an arrogant social engineer? There is no gainsaying that *About Behavior-*
60 *ism* is an unusually compact summary of both the history and "the philosophy of the science of human behavior" (as Dr. Skinner insists on defining behaviorism). It is a veritable artwork of organization. And anyone who reads it will never again be able to think of behaviorism as a
65 simplistic philosophy that reduces human beings to black boxes responding robotlike to external stimuli.

Still, there are certain quandaries that *About Behaviorism* does not quite dispel. For one thing, though Dr. Skinner makes countless references to the advances in
70 experiments with human beings that behaviorism has made since it first began running rats through mazes many decades ago, he fails to provide a single illustration of these advances. And though it may be true, as Dr. Skinner argues, that one can extrapolate from pigeons to
75 people, it would be reassuring to be shown precisely how.

More importantly, he has not satisfactorily rebutted the basic criticism that behaviorism "is scientistic rather than scientific. It merely emulates the sciences." A true science doesn't predict what it will accomplish when
80 it is firmly established as a science, not even when it is posing as "the philosophy of that science." A true science simply advances rules for testing hypotheses.

But Dr. Skinner predicts that behaviorism will produce the means to save human society from impending
85 disaster. Two key concepts that keep accreting to that prediction are "manipulation" and "control." And so, while he reassures us quite persuasively that his science would practice those concepts benignly, one can't shake off the suspicion that he was advancing a science
90 just in order to save society by means of "manipulation" and "control." And that is not so reassuring.

Go on to the next page. ⇨

Passage III Questions

21. According to the passage, Skinner would be most likely to agree that

    (A) studies of animal behavior are applicable to human behavior
    (B) introspection should be used widely to analyze conscious experience
    (C) behaviorism is basically scientistic
    (D) behavioristic principles and techniques will be of no use in preventing widespread disaster

22. The reader may infer that

    (F) Skinner's philosophy is completely democratic in its methodology
    (G) behaviorism, in its early form, and mentalism were essentially the same
    (H) methodological behaviorism preceded both mentalism and radical behaviorism
    (J) the author of the article has found glaring weaknesses in Skinner's defense of behaviorism

23. When Skinner speaks of "contingencies of survival" (line 30) and "contingencies of reinforcement" (lines 31–32), the word *contingency* most accurately means

    (A) frequency of occurrence
    (B) something incidental
    (C) a quota
    (D) dependence on chance

24. The author of the article says that Skinner sounds "like some latter-day Social Darwinist" (lines 28–29) most probably because Skinner

    (F) is a radical behaviorist who has differed from methodological behaviorists
    (G) has predicted that human society faces disaster
    (H) has been characterized as a 19th-century positivist
    (J) has studied animal behavior as applicable to human behavior

25. It can be inferred from the passage that "extrapolate" (line 74) means

    (A) to gather unknown information by extending known information
    (B) to determine how one organism may be used to advantage by another organism
    (C) to insert or introduce between other things or parts

    (D) to change the form or the behavior of one thing to match the form or behavior of another thing

26. One *cannot* conclude from the passage that

    (F) Skinner is a radical behaviorist but not a methodological behaviorist
    (G) *About Behavior* does not show how behaviorists have improved in experimentation with human beings
    (H) only human beings are used in experiments conducted by behaviorists
    (J) methodological behaviorism rejects the introspective approach

27. In Skinner's statement that "few would contend that behavior is 'endlessly malleable'" (line 27), he means that

    (A) genetic influences are of primary importance in shaping human behavior
    (B) environmental influences may be frequently supplemented by genetic influences
    (C) self-examination is the most effective way of improving a behavior pattern
    (D) the learning process continues throughout life

28. According to the author, which of the following are true concerning *scientistic* and *scientific* disciplines?

    I. The scientific one develops the rules for testing the theory; the scientistic one does not.
    II. There is no element of prediction in scientistic disciplines.
    III. Science never assumes a philosophical nature.

    (F) I only
    (G) I and III only
    (H) I and II only
    (J) II and III only

29. The word *veritable* (line 63) means

    (A) careful
    (B) political
    (C) true
    (D) believable

30. Regarding the essay's final paragraph, which statement best summarizes the author's attitude toward Skinner's prediction?

    (F) The consistency of Skinner's arguments lends credibility to the idea that behaviorism can save society.

Go on to the next page.

(G) "Manipulation" and "control" are the only weak lines in an otherwise solid theory.

(H) Skinner's prediction lacks credibility because it relies on repetition of the slogan "manipulation and control" without supporting evidence.

(J) The full extent of Skinner's true agenda is unknown, which raises troubling questions about how the techniques of manipulation and control might be applied in the future.

Passage IV: Natural Science

This passage, adapted from the article "Ingredients of Scientific Genius," explains the scientific process.

The discoveries made by scientific geniuses, from Archimedes through Einstein, have repeatedly revolutionized both our world and the way we see it. Yet no one really knows how the mind of a scientific genius
5 works. Most people think that a very high IQ sets the great scientist apart. They assume that flashes of profound insight like Einstein's are the product of mental processes so arcane that they must be inaccessible to more ordinary minds.
10 But a growing number of researchers in psychology, psychiatry, and the history of science are investigating the way scientific geniuses think. The researchers are beginning to give us tantalizing glimpses of the mental universe that can produce the discoveries of an
15 Einstein, an Edison, a Da Vinci—or any Nobel Prize winner.

Surprisingly, most researchers agree that the important variable in scientific genius is not the IQ but creativity. Testers start with 135 as the beginning of the
20 "genius" category, but the researchers seem to feel that, while an IQ above a certain point—about 120—is very helpful for a scientist, having an IQ that goes much higher is not crucial for producing a work of genius. All human beings have at least four types of intelligence.
25 The great scientist possesses the ability to move back and forth among them— the logical-mathematical; the spatial, which includes visual perception; the linguistic; and the bodily kinesthetic.

Some corroboration of these categories comes from
30 the reports of scientists who describe thought processes centered around images, sensations, or words. Einstein reported a special "feeling at the tips of the fingers" that told him which path to take through a problem.

The idea for a self-starting electric motor came to
35 Nikola Tesla one evening as he was reciting a poem by Goethe and watching a sunset. Suddenly he imagined a magnetic field rapidly rotating inside a circle of electromagnets.

Some IQ tests predict fairly accurately how well
40 a person will do in school and how quickly he or she will master knowledge, but genius involves more than knowledge. The genius has the capacity to leap significantly beyond his present knowledge and produce something new. To do this, he sees the relationship
45 between facts or pieces of information in a new or unusual way.

The scientist solves a problem by shifting from one intelligence to another, although the logical-mathematical intelligence is dominant. Creative individuals seem to
50 be marked by a special fluidity of mind. They may be able to think of a problem verbally, logically, and also spatially.

Paradoxically, fluid thinking may be connected to another generally agreed-upon trait of the scientific
55 genius—persistence, or unusually strong motivation to work on a problem. Persistence kept Einstein looking for the solution to the question of the relationship between the law of gravity and his special theory of relativity. Yet surely creative fluidity enabled him to
60 come up with a whole new field that included both special relativity and gravitation.

Many scientists have the ability to stick with a problem even when they appear not to be working on it. Werner Heisenberg discovered quantum mechanics one
65 night during a vacation he had taken to recuperate from the mental jumble he had fallen into trying to solve the atomic-spectra problem.

Passage IV Questions

31. Which statement is true, according to the passage?

(A) The law of gravity followed the publication of Einstein's theory of relativity.

(B) Nikola Tesla learned about magnets from his research on the works of Goethe.

(C) Archimedes and Einstein lived in the same century.

(D) We ought to refer to intelligences rather than to intelligence.

Go on to the next page. ⇨

32. The author believes that, among the four intelligences he cites, the most important one for the scientist is

    (F) spatial
    (G) linguistic
    (H) logical-mathematical
    (J) not singled out

33. The author focuses on the circumstances surrounding the work of great scientists in order to show that

    (A) scientific geniuses are usually eccentric in their behavior
    (B) the various types of intelligence have come into play during their work
    (C) scientists often give the impression that they are relaxing when they are really working on a problem
    (D) great scientific discoveries are almost always accidental

34. The passage can best be described as

    (F) an account of the unexpected things that led to great discoveries by scientists
    (G) an explanation of the way scientific geniuses really think
    (H) a criticism of intelligence tests as they are given today
    (J) a lesson clarifying scientific concepts such as quantum mechanics and relativity

35. The passage suggests that a college football star who is majoring in literature is quite likely to have which intelligences to a high degree?

    I. logical-mathematical
    II. spatial
    III. linguistic
    IV. bodily kinesthetic

    (A) I only
    (B) II only
    (C) I, II, and III only
    (D) II, III, and IV only

36. Which statement would the author most likely not agree with?

    (F) Most people believe that IQ is what makes the scientist brilliant.
    (G) Some scientists may come up with a solution to a problem when they are working on something else.
    (H) Creativity is much more important than basic intelligence in scientific discovery.
    (J) Scientists usually get the answer to a problem fairly quickly, and if they get stuck they usually go on to another problem.

37. As used in the passage, *fluidity* (line 59) can best be defined as

    (A) persistence when faced with a problem
    (B) having a flighty attitude in dealing with scientific problems
    (C) being able to move from one scientific area to another
    (D) having an open mind in dealing with scientific phenomena

38. The word *paradoxically* in line 53 is used to mean

    (F) ironically
    (G) seemingly contradictorily
    (H) in a manner of speaking
    (J) conditionally

39. The author's attitude toward scientists in this passage can be seen as one of

    (A) objective intrigue
    (B) grudging admiration
    (C) subtle jealousy
    (D) boundless enthusiasm

40. According to the passage, the best way to understand genius is as a combination of

    (F) very high IQ, content knowledge, and ability to multitask
    (G) creativity, persistence, and mental flexibility
    (H) relativity, creativity, and knowledge of quantum physics
    (J) revolutionary outlook, sensitivity, and desire for variety

STOP!

If you finish before time is called, you may check your work on this section only.
Do not turn to any other section in the test.

SECTION 4: SCIENCE TEST

35 Minutes, 40 Questions

Turn to Section 4 of your answer sheet (page 397) to answer the questions in this section.

Directions

There are several passages in this test. Each passage is followed by several questions. After reading a passage, choose the best answer to each question and fill in the corresponding circle on your answer document. You may refer to the passages as often as necessary.

You are NOT permitted to use a calculator on this test.

Passage I

Tables 1 and 2 and Figure 1 provide information about the energy, vitamin, and mineral contents of several foods. After examining the tables and graphs, choose the best answer for each of the questions that follow. Fill in the corresponding circle on your answer sheet.

Table 1: Nutritional values per serving for selected foods

Food	Serving Size	Vitamin B$_1$	Niacin	Potassium	Calcium	Vitamin C	Calories
Asparagus	1 cup	.15 mg	1.5 mg	404 mg	28 mg	44 mg	30
Lobster	3 oz	.368 mg	1.23 mg	236 mg	26 mg	0 mg	77
Cucumber	1 cup	.032 mg	.321 mg	156 mg	14 mg	4.8 mg	14
Broccoli	1 cup	.058 mg	.56 mg	286 mg	42 mg	82 mg	24

Figure 1: Percent daily values of nutrients in avocado

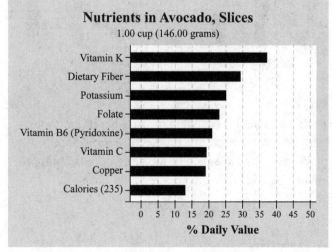

Nutrients in Avocado, Slices
1.00 cup (146.00 grams)

Table 2: Minimum required daily values of several nutrients

Nutrient	Daily Value (mg)
Vitamin C	60
Calcium	1,000
Niacin	20
Potassium	3,500
Iron	18

From www.whfoods.org

Go on to the next page. ⇨

Passage I Questions

1. Scurvy is a disease that is caused by a lack of vitamin C in one's diet. Based on Table 1, one might best prevent scurvy by eating which of the following?

   (A) 9 oz of lobster per day
   (B) 2 cups of asparagus per day
   (C) 1 cup of broccoli per day
   (D) 3 cups of cucumber per day

2. According to Figure 1, one can obtain about 40% of the daily value of copper by eating

   (F) 1 cup of avocado
   (G) 2 cups of avocado
   (H) 3 cups of avocado
   (J) 4 cups of avocado

3. Given the information in Tables 1 and 2, which of the following conclusions is correct?

   (A) Humans require more calcium in their diets than any other nutrient.
   (B) Niacin is not required every day.
   (C) Eating 1 cup of broccoli will provide enough vitamin C for one day.
   (D) Eating 4 cups of cucumber will provide enough potassium for one day.

4. According to Table 1, which of the following is true?

   (F) A single serving of broccoli provides more vitamin C, but less potassium, than a single serving of asparagus.
   (G) Of the listed foods, cucumber is the best source of calcium.
   (H) Lobster provides more niacin per serving than the other three foods.
   (J) Broccoli provides more energy in calories per serving than does lobster.

5. According to Figure 1, one would need to eat how many cups of avocado in order to obtain enough potassium for the day?

   (A) 1 cup
   (B) 2 cups
   (C) 3 cups
   (D) 4 cups

Passage II

The following two graphs provide information about the evolutionary relationship between several organisms and populations.

Figure 1: Phylogenetic tree for several organisms showing eras and historical time

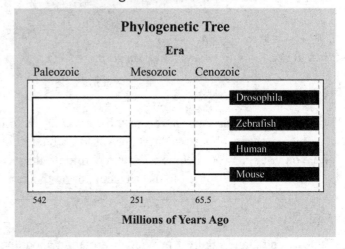

Figure 2: Selective pressure in a population of peppered moths

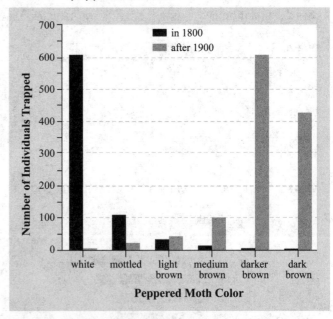

Each set of data is based on the number of individuals trapped and released in a one-week period. Moths were marked on the underside of the wing after counting to ensure individuals were counted only once.

Go on to the next page. ⇨

Passage II Questions

6. Based on the information in Figure 1, the closest evolutionary relationship is between

   (F) zebrafish and Drosophila
   (G) zebrafish and human
   (H) mouse and human
   (J) human and Drosophila

7. According to Figure 1, the mouse and zebrafish last shared a common ancestor

   (A) more than 542 million years ago
   (B) 542 million years ago
   (C) 251 million years ago
   (D) 65.5 million years ago

8. Given the information in Figure 2, which of the following conclusions can be drawn concerning the evolution of peppered moths?

   (F) After 1900, the moth population tended toward more lightly colored individuals.
   (G) After 1900, the moth population tended toward more darkly colored individuals.
   (H) After 1900, the moth population tended toward more medium-colored individuals.
   (J) There was no apparent effect on the color of individuals in the moth population during the period from 1800 to 1900.

9. According to Figure 2, after 1900, the majority of individuals in the moth population were

   (A) white   (C) light brown
   (B) mottled   (D) darker brown

10. If a scientist wanted to test the effects of tree color on the survival of a population of moths, the best experiment would be to

    (F) place 50 light-colored moths on light-colored trees and count the number of light and dark moths after a few weeks
    (G) place 50 dark-colored moths on light-colored trees and count the number of light and dark moths after a few weeks
    (H) place 50 light-colored moths and 50 dark-colored moths on light-colored trees and count the number of light and dark moths after a few weeks
    (J) place 50 light-colored moths on light-colored trees and 50 light-colored moths on dark-colored trees and count the number of individuals in each population after a few weeks

Passage III

The relationship between the temperature and volume of a gas was studied while the pressure remained constant. A sample of helium gas was placed in a balloon, which provided an approximately constant pressure, and the volume of the gas could be measured by calculating the volume of the balloon. Several experiments were performed.

Experiment 1

In the first experiment, the sample was held at a constant pressure of 1 atmosphere, while the temperature was raised in 10-Kelvin intervals. The volume was measured after seven minutes of equilibrium time to allow the sample to reach a steady temperature.

Temperature (Kelvin)	Volume (mL)
300	100.0
310	103.3
320	106.6
330	110.0
340	113.3

Experiment 2

The first experiment was repeated, but this time the sample of helium was held at a constant pressure of 2 atmospheres.

Temperature (Kelvin)	Volume (mL)
300	50.0
310	51.6
320	53.5
330	55.0
340	56.6

Passage III Questions

11. How is the design of Experiment 2 different from Experiment 1?

    (A) The initial pressure of the gas in Experiment 1 is double that of Experiment 2.
    (B) The initial pressure of the gas in Experiment 2 is double that of Experiment 1.

Go on to the next page.

(C) The gas used in Experiment 2 was different from the gas used in Experiment 1.

(D) The container used in Experiment 1 is different from the one used in Experiment 2.

12. Two nineteenth-century scientists named Jacques Charles and Joseph Louis Gay-Lussac discovered that as the temperature of any confined gas increases (with the number of molecules and pressure held constant), the volume increases. The best way to verify these results would be to repeat Experiment 1 using

(F) a hard, insulated container
(G) an identical volume of water
(H) an unsealed container
(J) several different gases with an equal number of molecules

13. If Experiment 1 is continued and the temperature is raised to 360 Kelvin, the gas would be expected to occupy a volume of approximately

(A) 116.6 mL
(B) 120 mL
(C) 123.3 mL
(D) 126.6 mL

14. If Experiment 2 had started with a volume of 25 mL of helium when the temperature was 300 Kelvin, what volume would be recorded when the temperature reached 340 Kelvin?

(F) 28.3 mL
(G) 29.2 mL
(H) 31.3 mL
(J) 34.4 mL

15. Which of the following statements best explains why the volume of the gas increases when the temperature is raised from 300 Kelvin to 340 Kelvin in Experiment 2?

(A) As the temperature goes up, the number of molecules in the sample increases, leading the gas field to increase in volume.

(B) As the temperature goes up, heat flows from the surroundings into the gas, causing the molecules to move faster and the gas field to increase in volume.

(C) As the temperature goes up, heat flows from the gas into the surroundings, causing the gas molecules to move faster and the gas field to increase in volume.

(D) As the temperature goes up, the pressure decreases, causing the molecules to increase in volume.

16. Suppose that Experiment 1 was repeated with a starting temperature of 600 Kelvin. What would you expect to happen to the initial volume of the sample?

(F) The initial volume of the sample would be about one-third the initial volume of Experiment 1.

(G) The initial volume of the sample would be about one-half the initial volume of Experiment 1.

(H) The initial volume of the sample would be about double the initial volume of Experiment 1.

(J) The initial volume of the sample would be about triple the initial volume of Experiment 1.

Passage IV

A group of scientists studied potential water pollution in a river located next to a chemical plant. They conducted the following river studies.

Study 1

Samples of water from a river located next to a chemical plant were collected at various times of day. Samples were taken upstream of the plant and downstream of the plant on a clear winter day. The temperature and pH of the water, and the concentration of several ions and molecules, were measured. The following tables provide the data from the experiment.

Study 2

Samples of water from a river located next to the chemical plant were collected again at various times of day from the same locations on a clear, late spring day. The temperature, the acidity as represented by pH, and the concentration of several ions and molecules were measured. The following tables provide the data from the experiment.

Go on to the next page. ⟹

Study 1 Table 1: Upstream data

Time of Day	Temperature (°C)	pH	Concentration (ppm)			
			SO_4^{2-}	NO_3^{2-}	Fe^{3+}	O_2
6 a.m.	5	7.0	7.0	5.2	4.0	2.2
12 p.m.	6	7.0	6.9	5.0	4.0	2.1
3 p.m.	6	7.0	6.9	4.9	4.0	2.1
6 p.m.	5	7.0	6.9	4.9	4.0	1.6

Study 1 Table 2: Downstream data

Time of Day	Temperature (°C)	pH	Concentration (ppm)			
			SO_4^{2-}	NO_3^{2-}	Fe^{3+}	O_2
6 a.m.	5	7.0	7.0	5.2	4.0	2.2
12 p.m.	9	7.3	7.4	5.0	4.0	1.7
3 p.m.	12	7.4	7.6	4.9	4.0	1.5
6 p.m.	11	7.4	7.7	4.9	4.0	1.6

Study 2 Table 1: Upstream data

Time of Day	Temperature (°C)	pH	Concentration (ppm)			
			SO_4^{2-}	NO_3^{2-}	Fe^{3+}	O_2
6 a.m.	18	7.0	7.0	4.6	3.7	1.7
12 p.m.	19	7.0	6.9	4.3	3.7	1.8
3 p.m.	19	7.0	6.9	4.1	3.7	1.9
6 p.m.	19	7.0	6.9	4.0	3.7	1.9

Study 2 Table 2: Downstream data

Time of Day	Temperature (°C)	pH	Concentration (ppm)			
			SO_4^{2-}	NO_3^{2-}	Fe^{3+}	O_2
6 a.m.	24	7.0	7.0	5.0	4.0	1.2
12 p.m.	25	7.3	7.4	4.9	4.0	1.1
3 p.m.	26	7.4	7.7	4.8	4.0	1.1
6 p.m.	27	7.4	7.8	4.7	4.0	1.0

Go on to the next page. ⇨

Passage IV Questions

17. The difference between the designs of Study 1 and Study 2 was that

    (A) the locations used in Study 2 were farther downstream than those used in Study 1
    (B) the scientists added Fe^{3+} to the water in Study 2
    (C) the times of day of sampling were later in Study 1 than in Study 2
    (D) the time of year was different in Study 2 and in Study 1

18. The scientists concluded that some ions were affected by the presence of the chemical plant. What is the most accurate conclusion they might draw?

    (F) The presence of the chemical plant decreased the concentration of NO_3^{2-} in water upstream from the plant.
    (G) The presence of the chemical plant increased the concentration of SO_4^{2-} in water downstream from the plant.
    (H) The presence of the chemical plant decreased the concentration of SO_4^{2-} in water downstream from the plant.
    (J) The presence of the chemical plant increased the concentration of Fe^{3+} upstream from the plant.

19. The scientists hypothesized that the highest downstream pH would be recorded at plant closing time (6 p.m.) every day. The best way to test this hypothesis would be to repeat Study 1 but

    (A) test downstream samples at the same four times of day every day for a month
    (B) test upstream samples at the same four times of day every day for a year
    (C) test upstream and downstream samples at 6 p.m. every day for a year
    (D) test upstream and downstream samples on another day

20. The scientists noted that the concentration of Fe^{3+} was different in upstream samples in Study 2. They concluded, however, that the chemical plant was not directly affecting the concentration of Fe^{3+}. The evidence that best supports this conclusion is that

    (F) the concentration of Fe^{3+} is higher downstream in Study 2
    (G) the concentration of Fe^{3+} is constant in upstream and downstream samples in Study 1
    (H) the concentration of Fe^{3+} is constant in upstream and downstream samples in Study 2
    (J) the concentration of Fe^{3+} changes at various times of day

21. A possible explanation for the increased difference in upstream and downstream data for O_2 between the winter and spring data is that

    (A) the lower Fe^{3+} concentration lowers the O_2 concentration
    (B) more O_2 is able to dissolve in water when the temperature is high
    (C) increased plant growth in spring decreases O_2 concentration
    (D) more O_2 is able to dissolve in water when the temperature is low

22. The graph below best represents the relationship between time of day and concentration for which ion in Study 2?

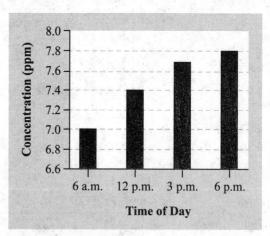

    (F) SO_4^{2-} downstream
    (G) SO_4^{2-} upstream
    (H) NO_3^{2-} downstream
    (J) NO_3^{2-} upstream

Go on to the next page. ⇨

Passage V

The following table and graph provide information about seismic movement and earthquake data.

Table 1: Understanding the Richter Scale

Richter Magnitude	Comparable Effect in TNT (Dynamite) Explosion at Earthquake Focus	Extra Information
0–1	6 oz to 30 lbs of dynamite	We cannot feel these.
2	1 ton of dynamite	Smallest quake people can normally feel.
3	29 tons of dynamite	People near the epicenter feel this quake.
4	1,000 tons of dynamite	Will cause damage around the epicenter. Comparable to a small fission bomb.
5	32,000 tons of dynamite	Damage done to weak buildings in the area of the epicenter.
6	1 million tons of dynamite	Can cause great damage around the epicenter.
7	32 million tons of dynamite	Creates enough energy to heat New York City for a year. Can be detected all over the world. Causes serious damage.
8	1 billion tons of dynamite	Causes death and major destruction. Destroyed San Francisco in 1906.
9	32 billion tons of dynamite	Rare; causes extreme, widespread damage and devastation.

Figure 1: Annual average number of earthquakes

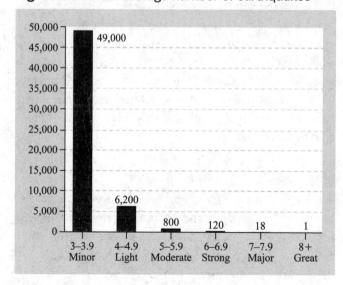

Passage V Questions

23. Based on Table 1, the increase in strength of an earthquake for each unit on the Richter Scale after magnitude 2 is closest to

    (A) 60 times
    (B) 30 times
    (C) 10 times
    (D) 5 times

24. Earthquakes that can be felt in areas significantly distant from the epicenter are

    (F) magnitude 6 and higher
    (G) magnitude 7 and higher
    (H) magnitude 7 and 8 only
    (J) magnitude 3 to 6 only

Go on to the next page. ⇨

25. Based on Figure 1, one can expect an average of more than one earthquake per day in which of the following categories?

    (A) Great
    (B) Strong
    (C) Minor and Light
    (D) Minor, Light, and Moderate

26. According to Table 1, the clearest pattern emerges for which range of magnitude on the Richter Scale?

    (F) 0–3
    (G) 2–4
    (H) 4–9
    (J) 2–9

27. Based on the trends in Figure 1, one might expect the average annual number of earthquakes in the 0–2 range on the Richter Scale to be

    (A) less than 1
    (B) between 800 and 6,200
    (C) between 6,200 and 49,000
    (D) greater than 49,000

Passage VI

Enzymes are biological catalysts made of protein. Each reaction in the human body is carried out with the assistance of an enzyme. The structure of each enzyme is specified in DNA, and with the help of RNA and ribosomes, many enzyme molecules can be synthesized. Studies of the function of several enzymes on their specific substrates (the reactants of the reaction) have led to the development of two different models that attempt to explain how enzymes are able to catalyze biological reactions.

When an enzyme, such as peroxidase, is added to its substrate, in this case hydrogen peroxide, the rate of reaction increases. However, if peroxidase is boiled for several minutes, then added to the reactant, the reaction occurs as slowly as it would were the catalyst never added. Crystallization of enzymes, with and without their substrates, demonstrates that enzymes are generally globular in shape and are formed by the folding of a long chain of amino acids into a specific shape. A specific part of the enzyme, called the *active site*, provides the place for the substrate to bind.

Figure 1: Energy diagram for an enzyme-catalyzed reaction compared to an uncatalyzed reaction

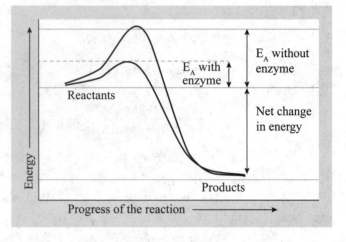

Model 1: The Lock-and-Key Model

In 1894, Emil Fischer suggested that the active site of an enzyme and its substrate are complementary in shape. He suggested that the substrate fits perfectly and somewhat rigidly into the active site of its enzyme, much as a key fits into a lock. The amino acid side chains on the enzyme create an environment where the substrate bounces in, with product released immediately. The enzyme is left unchanged and can be reused over and over again as more substrate (the key) enters the active site (the keyhole), is changed chemically, and is expelled as product.

According to Fischer's model, hydrogen peroxide would hit the active site of peroxidase, fit perfectly in that site because of its shape and the shape and type of amino acids in that part of the enzyme, and be expelled as the two products of the reaction, water and oxygen gas. Because the shape of the active site is perfect for hydrogen peroxide, peroxidase is prevented from doing other reactions in the cell, and this shape provides the enzyme's specificity.

Model 2: The Induced-Fit Model

The induced-fit model of enzyme function was proposed by Daniel Koshland Jr. in 1958. Biologists had noted that enzymes and substrates do not immediately attach and bounce apart as product but rather that a short-term complex of enzyme with substrate is formed before substrate is converted into product. Further, some enzymes are not as specific as others.

Go on to the next page. ⇨

Figure 2: Example of induced-fit model

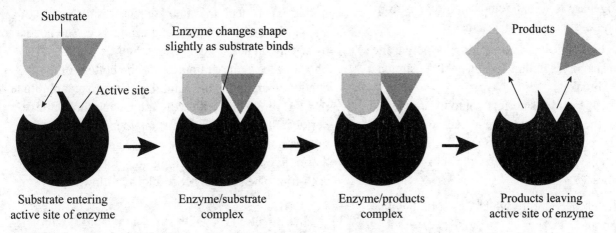

Substrate entering active site of enzyme → Enzyme/substrate complex → Enzyme/products complex → Products leaving active site of enzyme

Some classes of kinase, an enzyme that adds phosphate groups onto molecules, are able to add phosphate onto more than one similar molecule.

Because of these inconsistencies, and because proteins are somewhat less rigid in their structure than the lock-and-key model implies, Koshland proposed that the bonding of the substrate, which fits well but not perfectly into the environment created by the amino acid side chains at the active site, actually alters the enzyme's shape slightly. This temporary bond between the enzyme and the substrate creates a complex that changes the shape of both the enzyme and the substrate slightly. The change of shape in the substrate stretches bonds within the substrate, allowing the enzyme to lower the activation energy of the reaction. Product is then released from the active site, and without the substrate bonded, the enzyme returns to its previous shape, or conformation, allowing it to once again attach to the substrate.

Passage VI Questions

28. Which of the following assumptions is implicit in the lock-and-key model?

   (F) Many substrates can fit in one enzyme.
   (G) Enzymes break down after bonding with substrates.
   (H) Enzymes form a short-term complex with substrates.
   (J) Only one substrate fits into each enzyme's active site.

29. The induced-fit model could best be tested by

   (A) adding a substrate to its enzyme and measuring the amount of product produced over time
   (B) heating the enzyme and substrate and measuring the amount of product produced
   (C) crystallizing the enzyme by itself and examining its structure with an electron microscope
   (D) crystallizing an enzyme by itself and an enzyme with substrate and comparing the shapes and structures

30. The lock-and-key model of enzymes accounts best for which of the following observations about enzyme function?

   (F) Enzymes form temporary complexes with substrates.
   (G) Some enzymes can catalyze more than one reaction with more than one substrate.
   (H) Most enzymes are specific for one substrate.
   (J) Proteins are somewhat flexible in their shape.

31. The induced-fit model best accounts for which of the following observations that the lock-and-key model does not?

   (A) Molecules with a shape that is complementary to those of the substrate are sometimes able to react in the active site of an enzyme.
   (B) Most enzymes are specific for only one substrate.
   (C) Enzymes catalyze all reactions in a cell.
   (D) When boiled, an enzyme loses its shape.

Go on to the next page. ⇨

32. According to the induced-fit model, succinic acid dehydrogenase is able to remove hydrogens from its substrate, succinic acid, because

   (F) the binding of succinic acid to the active site causes bonds within succinic acid to stretch and break
   (G) succinic acid fits perfectly into the active site and the hydrogens are removed
   (H) it is specific for succinic acid
   (J) the enzyme heats the succinic acid, causing it to break

33. Both models account for which of the following observations?

   (A) Most enzymes are specific for the substrates that they catalyze.
   (B) Enzymes are flexible.
   (C) Enzymes can be broken down by their substrates.
   (D) Enzymes form temporary complexes with substrates that cannot be isolated and viewed.

34. Biologists have noted that the enzyme RuBisCO, which fixes carbon dioxide in the beginning of the light-dependent reactions of photosynthesis, is unable to distinguish between carbon dioxide gas and oxygen gas. As a result, some product of this reaction can be wasted when a 5-carbon molecule is produced instead of the intended 6-carbon molecule. Which of the following models is supported by this observation?

   (F) the lock-and-key model, because RuBisCO is able to fix carbon dioxide
   (G) the lock-and-key model, because RuBisCO is able to fix oxygen gas
   (H) the induced-fit model, because RuBisCO is able to fix carbon dioxide
   (J) the induced-fit model, because RuBisCO is able to fix oxygen gas

Passage VII

A physics student is studying the movement of pendulums. She sets up a basic pendulum by hanging a string from a fixed object and attaching a weight to the bottom of the string. After a brief review of terms, she discovers that the *period* of a pendulum is the time that it takes for the pendulum to swing from one side to the other and then back again to its starting point. She carries out the following experiments to help her understand how a pendulum works.

Experiment 1

In this experiment, the student measures the period of a pendulum with various weights attached. She begins by setting up her string at a length of 24 centimeters. She attaches a one-gram mass to the bottom of the pendulum and pulls the pendulum back to an amplitude (height) of 6 inches, allowing it to swing through five periods. She records the time and then divides by five to obtain the length of one period. She retests the pendulum five more times, adding one gram of weight for each trial. She records her results as follows.

Mass (grams)	Time of One Period (seconds)
1	1.0
2	1.0
3	1.0
4	1.0
5	1.0
6	1.0

Experiment 2

In this experiment, the student again measures the effects of mass on her pendulum. She again sets up a pendulum but this time measures out a string length of 99 centimeters. She again attaches a one-gram mass, then carries out five additional trials, increasing the weight by one gram for each trial. Her results are as follows.

Mass (grams)	Time of One Period (seconds)
1	1.9
2	2.0
3	1.9
4	1.9
5	2.0
6	2.0

Experiment 3

In her final experiment, the student sets up a 24-centimeter pendulum with her six weights. This time, she pulls the pendulum back to an amplitude of 12 inches before releasing, and then she times the length of five periods of the pendulum.

Go on to the next page. ⇨

Mass (grams)	Time of One Period (seconds)
1	0.9
2	1.0
3	1.0
4	0.9
5	1.0
6	1.0

Passage VII Questions

35. What is the difference between Experiment 1 and Experiment 3?

(A) The student attaches heavier weights to the pendulum in Experiment 1.

(B) The student uses a string of quadruple length to assemble the pendulum in Experiment 3.

(C) The student doubles the amplitude of the pendulum in Experiment 3.

(D) The student triples the amplitude of the pendulum in Experiment 1.

36. Which of the following was the same in Experiment 2 and Experiment 3?

(F) the length of the pendulum

(G) the amplitude of the pendulum

(H) the weights used in all six trials

(J) the time of one period

37. If Experiment 2 were repeated with a string length of 200 centimeters, how would this affect the time of one period?

(A) The 200-cm string would have a shorter period than the 24-cm string.

(B) The 200-cm string would have a longer period than the 99-cm string.

(C) The 200-cm string would have the same period as the 99-cm string.

(D) The 200-cm string would have the same period as the 24-cm string.

38. Which of the following statements is best supported by the data from Experiment 1?

(F) The amount of weight on the pendulum does not affect the period of the pendulum.

(G) The amount of weight on the pendulum does not affect the amplitude of the pendulum.

(H) The length of the pendulum does not affect the period of the pendulum.

(J) The weight and length of the pendulum do not affect the period of the pendulum.

39. Comparing data from Experiment 1 and Experiment 2 allows the student to draw conclusions about which of the following features of the experiments?

(A) the effect of weight on the amplitude of the pendulum

(B) the effect of amplitude on the period of the pendulum

(C) the effect of period on the weight of the pendulum

(D) the effect of length of the pendulum on the period

40. Based on all three experiments, which of the following best describes the conclusions that the student could draw about the function of pendulums?

(F) The weight and amplitude of a pendulum do not affect its period, but the length of the pendulum does.

(G) The weight and length of a pendulum do not affect its period, but the amplitude does.

(H) The amplitude and length of a pendulum do not affect its period, but the weight does.

(J) The amplitude, length, and weight of a pendulum do not affect its period.

Note:

If you plan to take the ACT Plus Writing, take a five-minute break and then continue with the Writing Test on page 438.

If you do not plan to take the ACT Plus Writing, turn to page 444 for instructions on scoring your multiple-choice tests.

STOP!
If you finish before time is called, you may check your work on this section only.
Do not turn to any other section in the test.

SECTION 5: WRITING TEST (OPTIONAL)

40 Minutes

Turn to the sheets on pages 440–443 to write your essay.

Directions

You may use the unlined pages in this test booklet to plan your essay. These pages will not be scored. **You must write your essay in pencil on the lined pages in the answer folder.** Your writing on those lined pages will be scored. You may not need all the lined pages, but to ensure you have enough room to finish, do NOT skip lines. You may write corrections or additions neatly between the lines of your essay, but do NOT write in the margins of the lined pages. **Illegible essays cannot be scored, so you must write (or print) clearly.**

If you finish before time is called, you may review your work. Lay your pencil down immediately when time is called.

When the supervisor announces that 40 minutes have passed, you must stop writing the essay. Do not go on to any other section in the test.

You may make notes on this page, but you must write your essay on the answer sheet.

Writing Prompt

One of the main purposes of education is to get students excited about the "process" behind problem solving instead of rushing into an answer and just concentrating on the final result. Often students can extract something from a problem that leads to an answer. Students can relax and think more clearly when they concentrate on the wonderful process or the game,

if you will, of thinking. In many cases, the problem solver is concerned just about getting the answer, and not about the "process" of how answers are discovered. By not having faith in the process, he or she often does not arrive at the solution. However, many people believe that focusing on getting an answer and not so much being concerned about the process is key to getting a result.

Carefully read the following perspectives, which describe the question of the importance of "process" in solving problems as opposed to just fixating on the correct answer to the problem.

Perspective One

If you want to solve a problem or have a task to do, it is much better to get involved with the process than to fixate only on getting a bottom-line answer. The answer will come as a result of the process.

Perspective Two

One should not be so concerned about the "process" but rather focus on getting some result or answer in solving a problem. Concentrating on the "process" distracts one from getting the necessary result.

Perspective Three

In solving a problem or performing a task, one should always keep in mind what form the answer or goal should take while utilizing what one has previously learned and how it can be used to get closer to the answer or final result.

Go on to the next page.

Essay Directions

Write a meaningful and logical essay in which you describe and evaluate multiple perspectives on the importance of concentrating on the "process" in solving a problem in contrast to fixating on the answer only. In your essay, make sure that you

- clearly state and analyze your own perspective in relation to at least one other perspective
- support your statements with clear reasoning and specific examples
- organize your material logically
- communicate effectively using standard written English

Note that your perspective may be completely in agreement with any of the others, may be partially in agreement, or may be in complete disagreement. In any case, you must support your essay with logic, making detailed references and providing specific examples.

Note on Planning the Essay

Plan your essay using the space here. These pages will not be scored.

Develop ideas and plan your essay using the space below. Consider the following points as you critically think about what you are going to write.

Strengths and weaknesses related to the three perspective presented:

- What insights can be found in them and what insights do they fail to show?
- Why might they be persuasive to others or why might they not be persuasive?

Your personal experiences, knowledge, and values:

- What is your own perspective on this issue, and what are the strengths and weaknesses of that perspective?
- How will you support your perspective in your essay?

SECTION 5: WRITING TEST *(OPTIONAL)*

Begin your essay on this page. If you need more space, continue on the next page. Do not write outside of the essay box.

Continue on the next page if necessary.

Continuation of essay from previous page. Write below only if you need more space.

Continue on the next page if necessary.

Continuation of essay from previous page. Write below only if you need more space.

Continue on the next page if necessary.

Continuation of essay from previous page. Write below only if you need more space.

HOW DID YOU DO ON THIS TEST?

Pages 446–452 will show you how to calculate
your scores on this test. Explanatory answers
with strategies and basic skills follow.

THERE'S ALWAYS ROOM
FOR IMPROVEMENT!

ANSWER KEY

Section 1: English Test Answers

1. A	20. H	39. C	58. H
2. J	21. B	40. F	59. A
3. C	22. G	41. D	60. J
4. G	23. D	42. H	61. D
5. C	24. F	43. B	62. G
6. F	25. D	44. H	63. B
7. B	26. F	45. D	64. F
8. H	27. B	46. G	65. A
9. B	28. J	47. A	66. J
10. H	29. A	48. H	67. D
11. B	30. H	49. D	68. F
12. F	31. D	50. J	69. C
13. D	32. G	51. B	70. H
14. H	33. B	52. G	71. B
15. C	34. H	53. C	72. F
16. J	35. A	54. G	73. B
17. C	36. F	55. A	74. H
18. H	37. D	56. H	75. D
19. C	38. J	57. B	

English Test Raw Score
(number of correct answers) _____

Section 2: Mathematics Test Answers

1. B	16. F	31. C	46. G
2. J	17. D	32. F	47. D
3. D	18. G	33. D	48. F
4. H	19. A	34. K	49. B
5. A	20. J	35. C	50. J
6. F	21. E	36. K	51. C
7. A	22. J	37. B	52. J
8. G	23. C	38. K	53. B
9. E	24. F	39. D	54. F
10. K	25. C	40. F	55. B
11. B	26. G	41. A	56. J
12. J	27. B	42. J	57. B
13. A	28. G	43. B	58. H
14. J	29. D	44. K	59. E
15. B	30. H	45. B	60. F

Mathematics Test Raw Score
(number of correct answers) _____

Section 3: Reading Test Answers

1. D	11. D	21. A	31. D
2. G	12. F	22. J	32. H
3. A	13. A	23. D	33. B
4. J	14. H	24. J	34. G
5. C	15. C	25. A	35. D
6. J	16. F	26. H	36. J
7. A	17. B	27. B	37. C
8. F	18. F	28. F	38. G
9. C	19. C	29. C	39. A
10. F	20. J	30. J	40. G

Reading Test Raw Score
(number of correct answers) _____

Section 4: Science Test Answers

1. B	11. B	21. D	31. A
2. G	12. J	22. F	32. F
3. C	13. B	23. B	33. A
4. F	14. F	24. G	34. J
5. D	15. C	25. D	35. C
6. H	16. H	26. H	36. H
7. C	17. D	27. D	37. B
8. G	18. G	28. J	38. F
9. D	19. A	29. D	39. D
10. J	20. H	30. H	40. F

Science Test Raw Score
(number of correct answers) _____

TABLE FOR CONVERTING
RAW SCORES TO SCALE SCORES

Raw Scores *(number of correct answers)*				Scale Score
Test 1 **English**	Test 2 **Mathematics**	Test 3 **Reading**	Test 4 **Science**	
75	60	40	40	**36**
72–74	58–59	39	39	**35**
71	57	38	38	**34**
70	55–56	37	37	**33**
68–69	54	35–36	—	**32**
67	52–53	34	36	**31**
66	50–51	33	35	**30**
65	48–49	32	34	**29**
63–64	45–47	31	33	**28**
62	43–44	30	32	**27**
60–61	40–42	29	30–31	**26**
58–59	38–39	28	28–29	**25**
56–57	36–37	27	26–27	**24**
53–55	34–35	25–26	24–25	**23**
51–52	32–33	24	22–23	**22**
48–50	30–31	22–23	21	**21**
45–47	29	21	19–20	**20**
43–44	27–28	19–20	17–18	**19**
41–42	24–26	18	16	**18**
39–40	21–23	17	14–15	**17**
36–38	17–20	15–16	13	**16**
32–35	13–16	14	12	**15**
29–31	11–12	12–13	11	**14**
27–28	8–10	11	10	**13**
25–26	7	9–10	9	**12**
23–24	5–6	8	8	**11**
20–22	4	6–7	7	**10**
18–19	—	—	5–6	**9**
15–17	3	5	—	**8**
12–14	—	4	4	**7**
10–11	2	3	3	**6**
8–9	—	—	2	**5**
6–7	1	2	—	**4**
4–5	—	—	1	**3**
2–3	—	1	—	**2**
0–1	0	0	0	**1**

Your Scale Score

English Test _____

Mathematics Test _____

Reading Test _____

Science Test _____

_____

Sum of scores _____

Composite score _____
(sum ÷ 4)

NORMS TABLES

Use the tables on page 448.

	Your Estimated Percent at or below on Practice Test
English	_____
Mathematics	_____
Reading	_____
Science	_____
Composite	_____
Combined English/Writing	_____
Writing	_____

National Distributions of Cumulative Percents for ACT Test Scores
ACT-Tested High School Graduates from Recent Years

Score	English	Mathematics	Reading	Science	Composite	Score
36	99	99	99	99	99	36
35	99	99	99	99	99	35
34	99	99	99	99	99	34
33	98	99	97	99	99	33
32	97	98	95	98	99	32
31	96	97	94	98	98	31
30	94	96	91	97	97	30
29	92	94	89	96	95	29
28	90	92	86	94	92	28
27	87	89	82	92	89	27
26	84	85	78	90	85	26
25	80	80	74	85	81	25
24	74	75	70	79	75	24
23	69	69	64	73	69	23
22	64	63	58	65	63	22
21	58	58	53	57	56	21
20	51	53	48	48	48	20
19	43	47	41	38	40	19
18	36	41	34	29	33	18
17	31	33	30	21	26	17
16	26	24	24	16	19	16
15	21	14	19	12	13	15
14	15	07	15	08	08	14
13	11	02	09	06	05	13
12	09	01	06	04	02	12
11	06	01	03	02	01	11
10	04	01	01	01	01	10
09	03	01	01	01	01	09
08	02	01	01	01	01	08
07	01	01	01	01	01	07
06	01	01	01	01	01	06
05	01	01	01	01	01	05
04	01	01	01	01	01	04
03	01	01	01	01	01	03
02	01	01	01	01	01	02
01	01	01	01	01	01	01
Mean	20.6	20.8	21.4	20.9	21.1	
S.D.	5.9	5.1	6.1	4.7	4.9	

ACT Writing Test Norms

Score	Combined English/Writing	Writing	Score
36	99		36
35	99		35
34	99		34
33	99		33
32	99		32
31	97		31
30	95		30
29	93		29
28	90		28
27	86		27
26	82		26
25	77		25
24	72		24
23	66		23
22	57		22
21	51		21
20	42		20
19	35		19
18	29		18
17	23		17
16	19		16
15	14		15
14	10		14
13	7		13
12	5	99	12
11	4	99	11
10	2	98	10
09	1	89	09
08	1	77	08
07	1	44	07
06	1	29	06
05	1	9	05
04	1	5	04
03	1	1	03
02	1	1	02
01	1		01
Mean	21.4	7.5	
S.D.	5.4	1.7	

6-POINT HOLISTIC SCORING RUBRIC
FOR THE ACT WRITING TEST

It is recommended that you approach two adults who you know are well qualified to judge basic grammar and composition as your two scorers for your practice Writing Test—perhaps an English teacher, a college-age student majoring in English or journalism, a parent, etc. Have those two adults read through this scoring rubric and refer to it when they score your practice test.

A Few Words about Scoring the Essay

Even with some errors in spelling, punctuation, and grammar, a student can get a top score on the essay. The highly trained high school and college composition teachers who score the essays will follow a rubric that focuses upon content, organization, and language usage and sentence structure. Each essay will be independently scored on a 1–6 scale by two such readers in *four* domains: Ideas and Analysis, Development and Support, Organization, and Language Use. If the readers' scores differ by more than two points, the test will be evaluated by a third reader. Fewer than 2 percent of all scored essays require a third reader.

Some general points about the scoring rubrics are summarized here. For full descriptions of the criteria for each of the four domains, refer to "Preparing for the ACT Test" at https://www.act.org/content/dam/act/unsecured/documents/Preparing-for-the-ACT.pdf. Essays at each level will exhibit all or most of the characteristics described below.

Score = 6

Essays at this score point demonstrate effective skill in responding to the task.

The essay shows a clear understanding of the task. The essay takes a position on the issue and may offer a critical context for discussion. The essay addresses complexity by examining different perspectives presented on the issue, by evaluating the implications and/or complications of the issue, and/or by fully responding to counterarguments to the writer's position. Development of ideas is ample, specific, and logical. Most ideas are fully elaborated. A clear focus on the specific issue in the prompt is maintained. The organization of the essay is clear: the organization may be somewhat predictable or it may grow from the writer's purpose. Ideas are logically sequenced. Most transitions reflect the writer's logic and are usually integrated into the essay. The introduction and conclusion are effective, clear, and well developed. The essay shows a good command of language. Sentences are varied and word choice is varied and precise. There are few, if any, errors to distract the reader.

Score = 5

Essays at this score point demonstrate well-developed skill in responding to the task.

The essay shows a clear understanding of the task. The essay takes a position on the issue and may offer a broad context for discussion. The essay shows recognition of complexity by partially evaluating the implications and/or complications of the given perspectives, and by responding to counterarguments to the writer's position. Development of ideas is specific and logical. Most ideas are elaborated, with clear movement between general statements and specific reasons, examples, and details. Focus on the specific issue in the prompt is maintained. The organization of the essay is clear, although it may be predictable. Ideas are logically sequenced, although simple and obvious transitions may be used. The introduction and conclusion are clear and generally well developed. Language is competent. Sentences are somewhat varied and word choice is somewhat varied and precise. There may be a few errors, but they are rarely distracting.

Score = 4

Essays at this score point demonstrate adequate skill in responding to the task.

The essay shows an understanding of the task. The essay takes a position on the issue and may offer some context for discussion based on the given perspectives. The essay may show some recognition of complexity by providing some response to counterarguments to the writer's position. Development of ideas is adequate, with some movement between general statements and specific reasons, examples, and details. Focus on the specific issue in the prompt is maintained throughout most of the essay. The organization of the essay is apparent but predictable. Some evidence of logical sequencing of ideas is apparent, although most transitions are simple and obvious. The introduction and conclusion are clear and somewhat developed. Language is adequate, with some sentence variety and appropriate word choice. There may be some distracting errors, but they do not impede understanding.

Score = 3

Essays at this score point demonstrate some developing skill in responding to the task.

The essay shows some understanding of the task. The essay takes a position on the issue but does not offer a context for discussion. The essay may acknowledge a counterargument to the writer's position, but its development is brief or unclear. Development of ideas is limited and may be repetitious, with little, if any, movement between general statements and specific reasons, examples, and details. Focus on the general topic is maintained, but focus on the specific issue in the prompt may not be maintained. The organization of the essay is simple. Ideas are logically grouped within parts of the essay, but there is little or no evidence of logical sequencing of ideas. Transitions, if used, are simple and obvious. An introduction and conclusion are clearly discernible but underdeveloped. Language shows a basic control. Sentences show a little variety and word choice is appropriate. Errors may be distracting and may occasionally impede understanding.

Score = 2

Essays at this score point demonstrate inconsistent or weak skill in responding to the task.

The essay shows a weak understanding of the task. The essay may not take a position on the issue, or the essay may take a position but fail to convey reasons to support that position, or the essay may take a position but fail to maintain a stance. There is little to no recognition of a counterargument to the author's position. The essay is thinly developed. If examples are given, they are general and may not be clearly relevant. The essay may include extensive repetition of the writer's ideas or of ideas in the prompt. Focus on the general topic is maintained, but focus on the specific issue in the prompt may not be maintained. There is some indication of an organizational structure, and some logical grouping of ideas within parts of the essay is apparent. Transitions, if used, are simple and obvious, and they may be inappropriate or misleading. An introduction and conclusion are discernible but minimal. Sentence structure and word choice are usually simple. Errors may be frequently distracting and may sometimes impede understanding.

Score = 1

Essays at this score point show little or no skill in responding to the task.

The essay shows little or no understanding of the task. If the essay takes a position, it fails to convey reasons to support that position. The essay is minimally developed. The essay may include excessive repetition of the writer's ideas or of ideas in the prompt. Focus on the general topic is usually maintained, but focus on the specific issue in the prompt may not be maintained. There is little or no evidence of an organizational structure or of the logical grouping of ideas. Transitions are rarely used. If present, an introduction and conclusion are minimal. Sentence structure and word choice are simple. Errors may be frequently distracting and may significantly impede understanding.

CALCULATING YOUR COMBINED ENGLISH/WRITING SCORE

1. Find your English Test scale score on page 446. Enter it here: _____.

2. Enter your Writing Test score (1–6) here: _____; double it to get your Writing subscore (2–12): _____. (If two people read and scored your Writing Test, add those two scores to get your Writing subscore.)

3. Use the table on page 452 to find your Combined English/Writing score.

   ■ First, circle your ACT English Test score in the left column.
   ■ Second, circle your ACT Writing subscore at the top of the table.
   ■ Finally, follow the English Test score row across and the Writing subscore column down until the two meet. Circle the Combined English/Writing score where the row and column meet. (For example, for an English Test score of 19 and a Writing subscore of 6, the Combined English/Writing score is 18.)

4. Using the number you circled, write your Combined English/Writing score here: _____. (The highest possible Combined English/Writing score is 36, and the lowest possible score is 1.)

   ACT English Test score   _____

   Writing subscore   _____

   Combined English/Writing Score   _____
   (from table on page 452)

COMBINED ENGLISH/WRITING SCALE SCORES

English Test Score	Writing Subscore										
	2	3	4	5	6	7	8	9	10	11	12
1	1	2	3	4	5	6	7	8	9	10	11
2	2	3	4	5	6	6	7	8	9	10	11
3	2	3	4	5	6	7	8	9	10	11	12
4	3	4	5	6	7	8	9	10	11	12	13
5	4	5	6	7	8	9	10	11	12	12	13
6	5	6	7	7	8	9	10	11	12	13	14
7	5	6	7	8	9	10	11	12	13	14	15
8	6	7	8	9	10	11	12	13	14	15	16
9	7	8	9	10	11	12	13	13	14	15	16
10	8	9	9	10	11	12	13	14	15	16	17
11	8	9	10	11	12	13	14	15	16	17	18
12	9	10	11	12	13	14	15	16	17	18	19
13	10	11	12	13	14	14	15	16	17	18	19
14	10	11	12	13	14	15	16	17	18	19	20
15	11	12	13	14	15	16	17	18	19	20	21
16	12	13	14	15	16	17	18	19	20	20	21
17	13	14	15	16	16	17	18	19	20	21	22
18	13	14	15	16	17	18	19	20	21	22	23
19	14	15	16	17	18	19	20	21	22	23	24
20	15	16	17	18	19	20	21	21	22	23	24
21	16	17	17	18	19	20	21	22	23	24	25
22	16	17	18	19	20	21	22	23	24	25	26
23	17	18	19	20	21	22	23	24	25	26	27
24	18	19	20	21	22	23	23	24	25	26	27
25	18	19	20	21	22	23	24	25	26	27	28
26	19	20	21	22	23	24	25	26	27	28	29
27	20	21	22	23	24	25	26	27	28	28	29
28	21	22	23	24	24	25	26	27	28	29	30
29	21	22	23	24	25	26	27	28	29	30	31
30	22	23	24	25	26	27	28	29	30	31	32
31	23	24	25	26	27	28	29	30	30	31	32
32	24	25	25	26	27	28	29	30	31	32	33
33	24	25	26	27	28	29	30	31	32	33	34
34	25	26	27	28	29	30	31	32	33	34	35
35	26	27	28	29	30	31	31	32	33	34	35
36	26	27	28	29	30	31	32	33	34	35	36

EXPLANATORY ANSWERS

Section 1: English Test

1. Choice A is correct. Choice B is incorrect because it is wordy. Choice C ("grasp-organs") does not sound as effective as Choice A ("grasping organs"). Choice D does not convey the meaning intended.

2. Choice J is correct. Choice F is incorrect because it is wordy. Choice G is incorrect because, in modern idiomatic English, an infinitive is not used to complete a prepositional phrase. Choice H is incorrect because "exploration into" is unidiomatic.

3. Choice C is correct. The two phrases after the dash must be in parallel construction. Therefore, Choices A and B are incorrect. Choice D includes an unneeded "as."

4. Choice G is correct. You don't use the word "because" here: you are already stating a reason so "because" would be redundant. Use the subordinating conjunction "that" instead.

5. Choice C is correct. Choice A is acceptable because it correctly hyphenates the compound adjective "range-finding ability." Choice B is acceptable because it uses correct parallel structure. Choice C is the unacceptable choice because it omits the hyphen in the compound adjective "range finding." The hyphen is necessary when the compound adjective precedes the noun it describes, "ability" in this case. Choice D unnecessarily invents an awkward compound verb, "range-find."

6. Choice F is correct. Choice G is incorrect because it omits the comparative "more." Choice H is incorrect because it gives a nonexistent form. Choice J is incorrect because it is unnecessarily lengthy.

7. Choice B is correct. The comparative "more" is completed with "than." "Then" (Choice A) means "at that time." Choice C is incorrect because it omits "than." Choice D is incorrect because it substitutes "as" for "than."

8. Choice H is correct. The clause that begins after the dash ends with the word *artificially*, so the word should be followed by a dash. Dashes can be used to set off long parenthetical remarks, but they are used in pairs.

9. Choice B is correct. Choices A, C, and D are all acceptable placements of the phrase. Choice B is the unacceptable placement because it creates a misplaced modifier ("to us symbols") and an ambiguous meaning.

10. Choice H is correct. Choice F is incorrect because "possible" should be the adverb form, "possibly," to modify the adjectives "near" and "comparable." Choice G is incorrect because "that" is not needed. Choice J is incorrect because of "nearly."

11. Choice B is correct. Choice A is incorrect because, although "to" as the infinitive sign is often omitted in series, the third member of the series includes "to": "to alter." Therefore, "to" is needed with "transmit" for parallelism. Choices C and D are also incorrect because they destroy the parallel construction needed.

12. Choice F is correct. Choice G is unidiomatic. Choice H is wordy. Choice J distorts the meaning.

13. Choice D is correct. Choice A is incorrect because "they're" is a contraction for "they are," which does not fit here. Choice B is incorrect because the subject of the verb is "indications," which is plural. Choice C is incorrect because "their" is a possessive pronoun, which is out of place here.

14. Choice H is correct. Choices F and G are not appropriate reasons to add the sentence in the given location because they do not accurately reflect the essay's focus. Choice H correctly identifies the essay's focus and rejects the addition of the new sentence. Choice J is correct in rejecting the new sentence but misidentifies the essay's focus.

15. Choice C is correct. Choice A is incorrect because the essay has not yet introduced the subject of dolphins, the essay's focus. Choice B is incorrect because "such an external symbol of intellect" refers indirectly to a phrase ("symbols of our intellectual attainment") not used until a later sentence. Choice C is correct because the new sentence contains transitional phrases linking it directly back to sentence 3 in paragraph 3. Choice D is incorrect because the essay has transitioned to a new phase of discussion, away from the idea of intellectual "tools."

16. Choice J is correct. Choice F is incorrect because it has a double superlative. Either "the most crude way" or "the crudest way" would be correct. Choice G is awkward. Choice H is the comparative degree, whereas the superlative degree is called for.

17. Choice C is correct. "Civilized countries" is the subject of the sentence. Choice A is incorrect because it makes "civilized countries" the object of the preposition "in," thus depriving the sentence of a subject. Choice B makes "that are civilized" nonrestrictive, but the phrase should be restrictive. Choice D is indirect.

18. Choice H is correct. Choice F is incorrect because a plural subject is required, since the antecedent is plural ("countries"). Choice G is too general. Not all countries have radio, television, and newspapers. Choice J creates a sentence fragment.

19. Choice C is correct. Used parenthetically, "however" should be set off by commas. Only Choice C sets "however" off in this way.

20. Choice H is correct. The demonstrative adjectives "this" and "these" must agree in number with the word being modified. Only Choice H contains the required agreement.

21. Choice B is correct. "The press, television, and radio . . . the grapevine" are examples of news media; therefore, a colon is the correct punctuation after "competition."

22. Choice G is correct. Choice F is incorrect because the complete dependent clause ends with "channels." Choice F separates a subject ("people") from its verb ("cannot") with a comma. Choice H is incorrect because "who" makes "cannot . . . channels" a subordinate clause and at the same time makes "the people . . . they" redundant. The same is true of Choice J; in this case "if they . . . channels" is the subordinate clause that makes "the people . . . they" redundant.

23. Choice D is correct. "Through legitimate channels" modifies "learn," not "know," so the phrase should be placed close to "learn." Therefore, Choices A and C are incorrect. Choice B is incorrect because the preposition "in" is not to be used here.

24. Choice F is correct. Choice G is incorrect because the present ("thrives")—not the present perfect ("has thrived")—is the right tense here. Choice H is incorrect because it presents a run-on sentence. Choice J is incorrect because "rumor thriving" does not modify anything.

25. Choice D is correct. Choice A is incorrect because "which" cannot be used as a relative pronoun to refer to people. Choice B is bad usage. Choice C is incorrect—"by those who" would be correct.

26. Choice F is correct. Choices G and J are unnecessarily formal. Choice H is slang.

27. Choice B is correct. Choice A is incorrect because "fascination about" is not correct wording of the common idiom "fascination *with*." In addition, *about* used in this way is ambiguous, meaning either *regarding* or *near*. Choice B uses the correct preposition to create the two-word idiom. Choices C and D are nonstandard variations.

28. Choice J is correct. Choice F is incorrect because the essay refers to national crises such as war as a cause of rumors but makes no claims about the effect of rumors on national events. Choice G is incorrect because, while the essay does connect

rumors with universal human conditions such as fear, it is not primarily a defensive argument. Choice H is incorrect because while the essay mentions media's role, it does not provide any examples of media perspective on the issue. Choice J best summarizes the essay's explanatory purpose.

29. Choice A is correct. Choice A is correct because the existing sentence is most consistent with the essay's tone and central point. Choice B is incorrect because the essay explains the public's participation in believing and spreading rumors but avoids explicitly judging those behaviors. Choice C is incorrect because while media is mentioned, focus remains on the general public's role. Choice D is incorrect because the essay makes no claims about the *effect* of rumors.

30. Choice H is correct. Choices F and G are incorrect because they inaccurately represent the essay's tone and attitude toward its subject. Choice H is correct because the sentence implies that some types of rumors spring from people's false sense of confidence, thus that the people are misled. Choice J is incorrect because the essay includes no specific examples of popular rumors that were demonstrated to be false information.

31. Choice D is correct. Choices A, B, and C are incorrect because the decisions were not "segregation," etc., but were "about" or "concerning" these topics.

32. Choice G is correct. Choices F and J are not in parallel construction with the other elements of the series. Choice H is awkward because the prepositional phrase "of the defendant" is too far away from "the right," which the prepositional phrase modifies.

33. Choice B is correct. Choices A, C, and D are all incorrect because there is no definite antecedent for the pronouns "this," "these," and "those."

34. Choice H is correct. Although all the choices are grammatically correct, Choice H is best because it is most economical in the use of words.

35. Choice A is correct. Choice A is correct because it accurately summarizes and introduces the upcoming examples of situations that prevent full resolution of legal issues even after court cases are closed. Choice B is incorrect because the essay never claims that agreement is impossible, only that decisions can be complex and lengthy. Choice C overstates the essay's point. Choice D is incorrect because the idea is never stated or implied in the essay.

36. Choice F is correct. Choice G is incorrect because the relative pronoun is the object of the verb "affect" (see question 37), so the objective case must be used (Choice F). Choice H is incorrect because "which" is not used with people. Choice J is incorrect because it is awkward.

37. Choice D is correct. *To affect* means "to influence" or "to produce a change in." *To effect* means "to bring about." Here, "affect" is appropriate, so Choices B and C are incorrect. Choice A is incorrect because the subject of the verb is "decisions," a plural that demands a plural verb.

38. Choice J is correct. The words that follow a comparative adjective and "than" must be in parallel construction. Here the comparative adjective is "more difficult." An infinitive follows "more difficult," so an infinitive must follow "than." Therefore, Choice J is correct and the other choices are incorrect.

39. Choice C is correct. Here "what" is a relative adjective modifying "road." Choices A and D are incorrect because "whatever" and "whichever" indicate that any of a number of choices is acceptable. That meaning is not appropriate here. Choice B is incorrect because it is vague in meaning.

40. Choice F is correct. Choice G is incorrect because it uses second-person perspective inappropriately in a topic-focused essay. Choice H is incorrect because the essay does not specifically focus on high court decisions requiring consensus. Choice J is incorrect because the upcoming example does not illustrate problems *caused* by a legal decision but instead describes a decision that did not resolve a problem that already existed.

41. Choice D is correct. When two words jointly modify another, the two are often hyphenated for clarity. Here "state" and "compelled" jointly modify "segregation," so "state" and "compelled" should

be hyphenated. There is no reason to hyphenate "racial" and "segregation." "Racial" is an adjective modifying "segregation"; the two words do not modify any other.

42. Choice H is correct. The present tense is used to state a lasting or universal truth. That "segregation . . . is a denial" is such a truth, so the present tense is needed.

43. Choice B is correct. We are dealing here with the verb "to lie," meaning "to rest." The past tense is "lay."

44. Choice H is correct. Since we have a past tense ("lay") in the main clause, sequence of tenses requires that we have a past tense ("was") with a future implication in the form of the infinitive ("to be accomplished") in the subordinate clause.

45. Choice D is correct. Choice A is incorrect because the essay alludes to challenges surrounding legal decisions but does not deal not specifically with the judge's role. Choice B is incorrect because public polarization is not discussed directly or even alluded to in the essay. Choice C is incorrect because it focuses on the difficulties of reaching closure on a legal decision, not the consequences *resulting from* legal decisions. Choice D correctly summarizes the essay's purpose.

46. Choice G is correct. Choice F is incorrect because it forms a run-on sentence. Choice G is correct because it creates a parallel construction with the previous "who" clause. Choice H is incorrect because it starts a clause that is not a logical follow-up of what precedes. Choice J is incorrect because "whom" is an object pronoun. A subject pronoun ("who") is needed here.

47. Choice A is correct. Choice A is the only choice that provides the parallelism required in this sentence. Any of the other choices would throw the style of the sentence out of balance.

48. Choice H is correct. The pronoun is the object of "makes." The only object pronoun given is "him," Choice H. Choice F is the possessive adjective or pronoun, Choice G the subject pronoun, and Choice J the reflexive pronoun.

49. Choice D is correct. The comma and "and" after "man" together indicate a compound sentence. A subject and verb for the second independent clause is therefore needed. Choice A is an infinitive. Choice B is a verb without the subject "he." The specific subject is necessary because the understood subject of "draws" would be "reading." Choice C is a participle, so it is incorrect. Choice D has a subject and a verb and is correct.

50. Choice J is correct. Choice F is incorrect because the antecedent of "which" is "example and precept," making "which" plural. Therefore, the verb "has stood" should be plural. Choice G is incorrect for the same reason: "stands" is singular. Choice H is incorrect because the past tense is not logical, since the rest of the sentence is in the present tense.

51. Choice B is correct. Choice A is incorrect because it is an acceptable use of a present participle to modify a noun (*problems*). Choice B is correct because it is unacceptable to place a comma before the restrictive relative pronoun *that*. Choice C is incorrect because it is an acceptable use of the restrictive relative pronoun *that*. Choice D is incorrect because it is an acceptable use of the restrictive relative pronoun and present perfect verb tense.

52. Choice G is correct. The meaning intended is best expressed by Choice G.

53. Choice C is correct. Choice A is incorrect because the writer is elaborating on an idea, not transitioning to a new one. Choice B is incorrect because the sentence adds a new dimension to the distinctions the writer is trying to make between reading and learning (a substantive and meaningful outcome of reading) by comparing dilettantism (superficial interest in art, culture, and so on) and versatility that is substantive and motivates people to act on their interests. Choice C is correct in identifying the sentence as an expansion and clarification of a point. Choice D is incorrect because, while the point may not be obvious, it is relevant as explained in Choice C.

54. Choice G is correct. The correct way to punctuate the first part of a broken quotation is quotation mark, comma, quotation mark.

55. Choice A is correct. The accepted term for a bank check bearing a signature but no stated amount is "blank check." The idea here is that "Learning" is the signature required so that "native versatility" will be of worth.

56. Choice H is correct. "Learning" is a gerund here, so it takes a possessive pronoun. Therefore, Choices F and G are incorrect. Choice J is incorrect because it gives the plural possessive, but the singular "one" is used as an impersonal pronoun, not the plural.

57. Choice B is correct. "Only" modifies "by the active experience . . ." so "only" should be placed after that phrase. Choices A, C, and D are therefore incorrect.

58. Choice H is correct. Choice F is incorrect because the quote supports rather than contradicts the essay's argument about the value of reading widely. Choice G is incorrect because the essay focuses on the general value of reading with no limiting specifics. Choice H correctly identifies the function of the quote by Thomas Carlyle, an influential Victorian-era essayist and historian. Choice J is incorrect because the essay's main focus is on reading to learn, a process that complements a formal education. According to the essay, formal schooling alone is not sufficient to make someone a truly educated person.

59. Choice A is correct. Choice A is correct because it provides closure for the essay while reinforcing the essay's definition of an educated person. Choice B is incorrect because the essay's focus is not on how to read but on how reading becomes learning. Choice C is incorrect because it digresses somewhat from the essay's focus on the *nature* of learning and education. Choice D is incorrect because the sentence would contradict the essay's advice that formal education alone is insufficient to create well-rounded, educated individuals.

60. Choice J is correct. Choice F is incorrect because while the essay argues the importance of learning through books, it does not argue against formal schooling in general or criticize formal schooling on any specific basis such as cost. Choice G is incorrect because the essay does suggest that what one learns through reading can support action, but it does not state or imply that formal education restricts or discourages action. Choice H is incorrect because the essay emphasizes reading as the most important factor in shaping people's ability to exercise critical thinking and sound judgment when the times most demand them. Choice J is correct because it best summarizes the essay's stance on the relationship between the two forms of education.

61. Choice D is correct. Choice A is incorrect because it is not parallel to the other verbs in the series: e.g., "streamlined," "mechanized." Choice B is incorrect because it is the present tense and a past tense is needed. Choice C is incorrect because it is a participle, but a verb is needed.

62. Choice G is correct. The past tense ("could go") is required in the subordinate clause since the verb of the main clause is in the past tense.

63. Choice B is correct. The superlative form of the adjective is needed here, as indicated by the word *possible*. Choice A is the comparative, Choice C the positive degree. Choice D is incorrect because it is an awkward form of the superlative.

64. Choice F is correct. In a series, the infinitive sign "to" is often omitted in all but the first infinitive. That is the case here, so Choices G and J are incorrect. Choices H and J are incorrect because they contain the adjective form "efficient" instead of the adverb form "efficiently."

65. Choice A is correct. Choice A is correct because it best fits the theme that Americans do not relax even in their leisure time. Choice B is incorrect because it misrepresents the situation and loses the irony of the idea that we "relax on schedule." Choice C is incorrect because it changes the tone of the writer's remarks about American scheduling and time-consciousness. Choice D is incorrect for the same reason.

66. Choice J is correct. The present tense is required in this verbal construction to indicate a time that is the same as that of "streamlined." Therefore, Choices F and H are incorrect. The gerund construction of Choice G is awkward. The present infinitive construction of Choice J is correct.

67. Choice D is correct. Choice A is incorrect because "energize" is in the present tense, but a past tense is needed. Choice B does not sound right because it personalizes "pellets" unnecessarily. Choice C is incorrect because it does not supply a verb for either "energy into pellets" or "culture . . . packages."

68. Choice F is correct. "The ant like a sluggard" is elliptical—that is, some of its parts seem to be missing. Without ellipsis, this sentence would read: "We made the ant look like a sluggard." Since this form is the same as that of the first clause, ellipsis is acceptable; the parts left out are exactly the same and are used in exactly the same way as they are in the first clause. The correct punctuation in a case like this is a comma, so Choices H and J are incorrect. Choice G is incorrect because "as" is substituted for "like."

69. Choice C is correct. Choice C is correct because the concept of efficiency has here been personified. When a common noun is personified, the practice is to make it a proper noun by capitalizing it. Therefore, Choices A and B are incorrect. The noun here is not to be set off by commas since it has a restrictive function in this sentence. Therefore, Choices B (again) and D are incorrect.

70. Choice H is correct. Choice F is incorrect because the tone and topic shift, and therefore a new paragraph is called for. Choice G is incorrect because it fails to begin a new paragraph and adds an unnecessary comma. Choice H is correct because it begins a new paragraph and leaves punctuation as is. Choice J is incorrect because it adds an unnecessary comma between the subject and predicate.

71. Choice B is correct. Since "considering time a friend" preceded the "wishing," "had considered," the past perfect, is the correct answer. Another reason the past perfect tense is correct is that "had done," which is in parallel construction with "had considered," is in the past perfect.

72. Choice F is correct. There is no reason to use two words (Choice G) or four words (Choice H) when one word (Choice F) expresses the thought clearly. The adjective (Choice J) is incorrect. The adverb ("spontaneously") is required to modify the verb ("had done").

73. Choice B is correct. The prepositional phrase ("on account of") is incorrect. The conjunction "because" should be used to introduce the subordinate clause. Therefore, Choice A is wrong and Choice B is right. The conjunction "when" (Choice C) does not give the thought intended. The conjunction "because" (Choice B) is necessary. Therefore, Choice D is incorrect.

74. Choice H is correct. Choice F is incorrect because the antecedent of that in the long preceding sentence is unclear. Choice G is incorrect as a replacement for *that* because the preceding sentence is not intended to be interpreted literally as wasting time. The writer is using sarcasm to point out that this wishful, nostalgic thinking would be taken as inefficient in our time-conscious culture. Choice H correctly restates the specific antecedent of *that*. Choice J is incorrect because, similar to Choice G, it is not consistent with the writer's point.

75. Choice D is correct. Since the subject of the clause is "one," we must have a singular verb ("is expected"). Therefore, Choice D is correct and all the other choices are incorrect.

EXPLANATORY ANSWERS

Section 2: Mathematics Test

As you read these solutions, you are advised to do two things if you answered the Math question incorrectly:

1. *When a specific Math Strategy is referred to in the solution, study that strategy, which you will find in the "19 Math Strategies" (beginning on page 44).*

2. *When the solution directs you to the "Complete ACT Math Refresher" (beginning on page 147)—for example, Math Refresher #305—study the math principle to get a clear idea of the math operation you needed to know in order to answer the question correctly.*

1. Choice B is correct.

   (Use Strategy 2: Translate words into mathematical expressions.)

   The total cost of production equals the cost of the machine ($169.99) plus the cost of the CDs: (cost of 1 CD) × (number of CDs produced). Since we know that 1 CD costs $1.50 and we're producing x CDs, the total cost is

   $$\$169.99 + \$1.50x$$

   (Math Refresher #200)

2. Choice J is correct. 16 can be divided evenly by 1, 2, 4, 8, and 16.

   (Math Refresher #607)

3. Choice D is correct.

   $$(3x^3)^3 = (3)^3(x^3)^3$$
   $$3^3 = 3 \times 3 \times 3 = 27$$
   $$(x^3)^3 = x^{3 \times 3} = x^9$$
   $$(3x^3)^3 = 27x^9$$

   (Math Refresher #429)

4. Choice H is correct.

   Substitute $a = 3$ and $b = -2$ in the expression:

   $$[3 - (-2)]^2 = (3 + 2)^2 = 5^2 = 25$$

   (Math Refresher #405a)

5. Choice A is correct.

   (Use Strategy 14: Label angles.)

   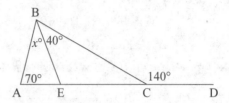

   First label the angles as above.

   (Use Strategy 18: Know facts about triangles.)

   Now use the fact that an exterior angle of a triangle is equal to the sum of the remote interior angles. Thus

   $$140 = 70 + (x + 40) = 110 + x$$
   $$x = 30°$$

   (Math Refresher #505)

6. Choice F is correct. The slope of a line passing through coordinates (x_1, y_1) and (x_2, y_2) is

   $$\frac{(y_2 - y_1)}{(x_2 - x_1)}$$

   Here $x_1 = -3$, $y_1 = 1$, $x_2 = 4$, and $y_2 = 5$.

   $$\frac{(y_2 - y_1)}{(x_2 - x_1)} = \frac{5 - 1}{4 - (-3)} = \frac{4}{7}$$

   (Math Refresher #416)

7. Choice A is correct.

   (Use Strategy 2: Translate words into mathematical expressions.)

   The discount price equals list price (x) minus the discount (25% of the list price). Since x is the list price, we get

   $$x - 25\%x$$
   $$= x - \left(\frac{1}{4}\right)x$$
   $$= x - \frac{x}{4}$$

   (Math Refresher #405a)

8. Choice G is correct.

$$3(5y + 8) = 3(5y) + 3(8) = 15y + 24$$
$$-4(2y - 6) = -4(2y) - 4(-6) = -8y + 24$$
$$3(5y + 8) - 4(2y - 6) = 15y - 8y + 24 + 24$$
$$= 7y + 48$$

(Math Refresher #406)

9. Choice E is correct.

(Use Strategy 4: Know classic forms.)

$$(a + b)^2 = a^2 + 2ab + b^2$$

Here $a = 2x$ and $b = 9$, so

$$(2x + 9)^2 = (2x)^2 + 2(2x)(9) + (9)^2$$
$$= 4x^2 + 36x + 81$$

(Math Refresher #409)

10. Choice K is correct.

(Use Strategy 17: Use given information effectively.)

The phrase "proportionately…in each category" means that

$$\frac{\text{number of tennis players in Category A}}{\text{total number of tennis players}}$$
$$= \frac{\text{number of prizes awarded in Category A}}{\text{total number of prizes}}$$

So, where x is the number of prizes awarded in Category A:

$$\frac{30}{180} = \frac{x}{54}$$
$$\frac{1}{6} = \frac{x}{54}$$
$$x = \frac{54}{6} = 9$$

(Math Refresher #120)

11. Choice B is correct.

(Use Strategy 14: Label sides.)

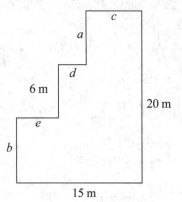

Label the sides of the figure, adding variables where no number is given. You can see that for the vertical sides of the figure

$$a + 6\,m + b = 20\,m$$

while for the horizontal sides

$$c + d + e = 15\,m$$

The perimeter

$$= b + e + 6\,m + d + a + c + 20\,m + 15\,m$$
$$= (a + 6\,m + b) + (c + d + e) + 20\,m + 15\,m$$
$$= (20\,m) + (15\,m) + 20\,m + 15\,m = 70\,m$$

(Math Refresher #530)

12. Choice J is correct.

(Use Strategy 14: Label the boxes.)

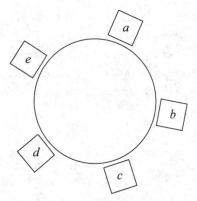

If a straight line connects two of the boxes, the maximum number of connections equals five combinations taken two at a time: $ab, ac, ad, ae,$ bc, etc.

$$_xC_y = \frac{x!}{y!(x - y)!}$$
$$_5C_2 = \frac{5!}{2!(5 - 2)!}$$
$$= \frac{5 \times 4 \times 3 \times 2 \times 1}{2 \times 1(3 \times 2 \times 1)}$$
$$= \frac{5 \times 4}{2 \times 1} = 10$$

(Math Refresher #613)

13. Choice A is correct.

(Use Strategy 7: Use specific numerical examples to prove your guess.)

When $x = 1$:

$$6x^2 - 9x - 6 = 6(1)^2 - 9(1) - 6 = -9$$

A: $(x - 2)(6x + 3) = (1 - 2)(6 + 3) = -9$
B: $(x - 2)(6x - 3) = (1 - 2)(6 - 3) = -3$
C: $(x + 2)(6x + 3) = (1 + 2)(6 + 3) = 27$

D: $(3x + 2)(2x - 3) = (3 + 2)(2 - 3) = -5$

E: $(3x - 2)(2x + 3) = (3 - 2)(2 + 3) = 5$

(Math Refresher #409)

14. Choice J is correct.

(Use Strategy 14: Draw lines.)

Draw BH and HE.

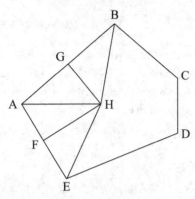

Since GH is the perpendicular bisector of AB, triangles AHG and BHG are congruent (side-angle-side). Therefore, $AH = BH$ and BH is the radius of the circle.

Since AHF and EHF are also congruent, $AH = EH$ and EH is the radius of the circle.

If the hypotenuse of a right triangle equals the radius of the circle, then the length of either of its sides (GH or FH) is less than the radius; therefore F and G are not on the circle. Since the location of points C and D are not specified, the circle does not necessarily pass through points C or D.

(Math Refreshers #511 and #524)

15. Choice B is correct.

(Use Strategy 17: Use given information effectively.)

Any circle with radius r in the xy plane whose center is (a,b) can be represented as

$$(x - a)^2 + (y - b)^2 = r^2$$

$x^2 + y^2 - 8y + 4 = 0$ can be factored:

$$(x - 0)^2 + (y - 4)^2 = 12$$

Thus $a = 0, b = 4$, and $r^2 = 12$

$$r = \sqrt{12} = \sqrt{4 \times 3} = 2\sqrt{3}$$

(Math Refreshers #410b and #524)

16. Choice F is correct.

$$\frac{32}{18 - \dfrac{5}{0.5}} = \frac{32}{18 - \dfrac{50}{5}} = \frac{32}{18 - 10} = \frac{32}{8} = 4$$

(Math Refreshers #101, #102, #111, and #112)

17. Choice D is correct.

$$f(0) = 2^{0 + 4}$$
$$= 2^4$$
$$= 16$$

(Math Refreshers #616 and #429)

18. Choice G is correct.

(Use Strategy 17: Use given information effectively.)

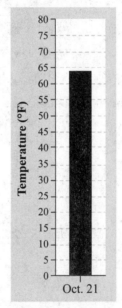

To interpret this bar graph, one must first locate the bar corresponding to October 21. Then follow the bar until it reaches its furthest extremity, slightly below the 65° line. This means that for temperature x, $60 < x < 65$.

(Math Refresher #704)

19. Choice A is correct.

$(3 + 4i)(6i - 1) = 3(6i) + 4i(6i) + 3(-1) + 4i(-1)$
$= 18i + 24i^2 - 3 - 4i$
$= 24i^2 + 14i - 3$

Since $i^2 = -1$:

$(3 + 4i)(6i - 1) = 24(-1) + 14i - 3 = 14i - 27$

(Math Refresher #618)

20. Choice J is correct.

$$\log_3 36 - \log_3 4 = \log_3 \frac{36}{4} = \log_3 9 = 2$$

$$\log_4 x = 2$$

$$x = 4^2 = 16$$

(Math Refresher #617)

21. Choice E is correct.

(Use Strategy 17: Use given information effectively.)

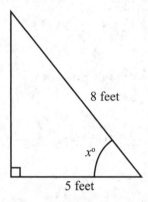

8 feet

$x°$

5 feet

Since you've been given the lengths of the adjacent side and the hypotenuse, first check the functions that involve those two values.

$$\cos x° = \frac{\text{adjacent}}{\text{hypotenuse}} = \frac{5}{8}$$

$$\sec x° = \frac{1}{\cos x°} = \frac{8}{5}$$

(Math Refresher #901)

22. Choice J is correct.

(Use Strategy 17: Use given information effectively.)

$$\sec p° = \frac{1}{\cos p°} = \frac{z}{y}$$

(Math Refresher #901)

23. Choice C is correct.

(Use Strategy 2: Translate words into algebra.)

In $\frac{1}{2}$ year, 600 pounds of feed were used at a rate of $1.25 per pound. Thus (600 pounds) × ($1.25 per pound), or $750, was spent. Hence,

$$\text{Feed cost per egg} = \frac{\text{total cost for feed}}{\text{number of eggs}}$$

$$= \frac{\$750}{5,000 \text{ eggs}}$$

(Use Strategy 19: Factor and reduce.)

$$= \frac{\$75 \times 10}{500 \times 10 \text{ eggs}}$$

$$= \frac{\$25 \times 3}{25 \times 20 \text{ eggs}}$$

$$= \frac{\$3}{20} \text{ per egg}$$

$$= \$0.15 \text{ per egg}$$

(Math Refresher #200)

24. Choice F is correct. The union of X and Y and 0 is the set of all the elements of X and Y and 0. The elements of all *negative*, *0*, and *positive* numbers is the set of all *real* numbers.

(Math Refresher #802)

25. Choice C is correct.

(Use Strategy 2: Translate words into algebra.)

Given: Area B = 1	1
Area A = 3(Area B)	2
Area B = 3(Area C)	3

Substitute 1 into 2. We get

Area A = 3(1) = 3	4

Substitute 1 into 3. We get

1 = 3(Area C)

$\frac{1}{3}$ = Area C	5

Using 1, 4 and 5, we have

$$\text{Sum of areas A, B, and C} = 3 + 1 + \frac{1}{3}$$

$$\text{Sum of areas A, B, and C} = 4\frac{1}{3}$$

(Math Refresher #200)

26. Choice G is correct.

(Use Strategy 3: The whole equals the sum of its parts.)

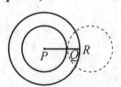

Given: PQR = 9	1
PQ = 4	2

From the diagram, we see that

PQR = PQ + QR	3

Substitute 1 and 2 into 3. We get

$$9 = 4 + QR$$
$$5 = QR$$

QR is the radius of a circle with center R and Q on its circumference. (See dotted circle in diagram.)

(Math Refresher #524)

27. Choice B is correct.

(Use Strategy 15: Know how to eliminate certain choices.)

$y = f(x)$ is positive or 0 for all x, so only Choices B and C are appropriate. Since $y = f(x)$ represents straight lines, then Choice B is appropriate, while Choice C is eliminated.

(Math Refreshers #616 and #615)

28. Choice G is correct.

(Use Strategy 17: Use the given information effectively.)

Slope is defined as

$$\frac{y_2 - y_1}{x_2 - x_1}$$

where (x_1, y_1) is a point on the line and (x_2, y_2) is another point on the line. We are given that one point is $(0, p)$ and the other point is $(3p, 0)$, so

$$\frac{y_2 - y_1}{x_2 - x_1} = \frac{p - 0}{0 - 3p} = \frac{p}{-3p} = -\frac{1}{3}$$

(Math Refresher #416)

29. Choice D is correct.

Given: Bus A averages $\dfrac{40 \text{ km}}{\text{gallon}}$ 1

Bus B averages $\dfrac{50 \text{ km}}{\text{gallon}}$ 2

Trip distance = 800 km   3

Fuel cost = $\dfrac{\$3}{\text{gallon}}$ 4

(Use Strategy 10: Know how to use units.)

Divide 3 by 1. We get

$$\frac{800 \text{ km}}{40 \dfrac{\text{km}}{\text{gallon}}} = \frac{800 \text{ gallons}}{40}$$

$$= 20 \text{ gallons used by Bus A} \quad 5$$

Divide 3 by 2. We get

$$\frac{800 \text{ km}}{50 \dfrac{\text{km}}{\text{gallon}}} = \frac{800 \text{ gallons}}{50}$$

$$= 16 \text{ gallons used by Bus B} \quad 6$$

Multiply 5 by 4. We get

$$20 \text{ gallons} \times \frac{\$3}{\text{gallon}} = \$60 \text{ cost for fuel for Bus A}$$
7

Multiply 6 by 4. We get

$$16 \text{ gallons} \times \frac{\$3}{\text{gallon}} = \$48 \text{ cost for fuel for Bus B}$$
8

(Use Strategy 13: Find unknowns by subtracting.)

Subtract 8 from 7. We get $\$60 - \$48 = \$12$ difference in the fuel costs between Bus A and Bus B for an 800 km trip.

(Math Refresher #202)

30. Choice H is correct.

(Use Strategy 17: Use the given information effectively.)

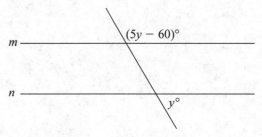

Given: $m \| n$ 1

From 1 we know that the two angles are supplementary. Therefore,

$$(5y - 60)° + y° = 180°$$
$$6y - 60 = 180°$$
$$6y = 240°$$
$$y = 40°$$

(Math Refresher #504)

31. Choice C is correct. The probability is the number of favorable ways divided by the number of total ways. The total ways is the number of points in the large circle of radius 2 feet. We can look at that as the area of the large circle, which is

$$\pi r^2 = 2 \times 2\pi = 4\pi$$

The favorable ways are the number of points in the inner circle, which we can look at as the area of that circle, which is

$$\pi r^2 = 1 \times 1\pi = 1\pi$$

Thus the probability is $\dfrac{1\pi}{4\pi} = \dfrac{1}{4}$.

(Math Refresher #614)

32. **Choice F is correct.**

    (Use Strategy 18: Remember special right triangles.)

    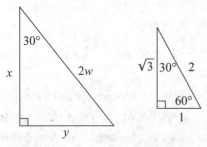

    The triangle at left (given) is similar to the triangle at right, which is one of the standard triangles. Corresponding sides of similar triangles are proportional. Therefore,

    $$\frac{2w}{2} = \frac{y}{1} \quad \text{and} \quad \frac{2w}{2} = \frac{x}{\sqrt{3}}$$

    $$\text{or} \quad y = w \quad \text{and} \quad x = w\sqrt{3}$$

    $$\text{Area of triangle} = \frac{1}{2}(\text{base})(\text{height})$$

    $$= \frac{1}{2}(y)(x)$$

    $$= \frac{1}{2}(w)(w\sqrt{3})$$

    $$\text{Area of triangle} = \frac{\sqrt{3}}{2}w^2 \qquad \boxed{1}$$

    $$\text{Area of rectangle} = (3w)(w) = 3w^2 \qquad \boxed{2}$$

    Using $\boxed{1}$ and $\boxed{2}$, we have

    $$\frac{\text{Area of rectangle}}{\text{Area of triangle}} = \frac{3w^2}{\frac{\sqrt{3}}{2}w^2}$$

    $$= \frac{3}{\frac{\sqrt{3}}{2}} = 3 \times \frac{2}{\sqrt{3}}$$

    $$= \frac{6}{\sqrt{3}} = \frac{6\sqrt{3}}{3} = 2\sqrt{3}$$

    $$= 2\sqrt{3} : 1$$

    (Math Refreshers #510, #509, #306, and #304)

33. **Choice D is correct.**

    (Use Strategy 9: Know rate, time, and distance relationships.)

    Given:

Meteor 1 travels at 300 meters/second	$\boxed{1}$
Meteor 2 travels at 700 meters/second	$\boxed{2}$

    Draw a diagram:

    ⊢——— 2,500 km ———⊣

    |300 m/sec   700 m/sec|

    Let t be the time it takes meteors to meet. Call x the distance Meteor 1 travels. Then $2,500 - x$ is the distance Meteor 2 travels.

    $$\text{Rate} \times \text{Time} = \text{Distance}$$

300 m/sec $\times\ t = x$	$\boxed{3}$
700 m/sec $\times\ t = 2,500 - x$	$\boxed{4}$

    (Use Strategy 13: Find unknowns by addition.)

    Add $\boxed{3}$ and $\boxed{4}$

    $$(300 \text{ m/sec })t + (700 \text{ m/sec })t = 2,500 \text{ km}$$

    $$(1,000 \text{ m /sec })t = 2,500 \text{ km} \qquad \boxed{5}$$

    (Use Strategy 10: Know how to use units.)

    $$1 \text{ km} = 1,000 \text{ m} \qquad \boxed{6}$$

    Substitute $\boxed{6}$ in $\boxed{5}$:

    $$(1,000 \text{ m/sec})t = 2,500(1,000) \text{ m} \qquad \boxed{7}$$

    Divide $\boxed{7}$ by 1,000 m:

    $$t/\text{sec} = 2,500$$

    $$t \quad\ = 2,500 \text{ sec}$$

    (Math Refreshers #121, #201, and #202)

34. **Choice K is correct.**

    (Use Strategy 17: Use the given information effectively.)

    The center point inside a cube is the midpoint of an inner diagonal of the cube. Thus, the distance from any vertex to this center point is $\frac{1}{2}$ the length of the inner diagonal.

    We know the length of the inner diagonal of a cube

    $$= \sqrt{(\text{edge})^2 + (\text{edge})^2 + (\text{edge})^2}$$

inner diagonal $= \sqrt{3(\text{edge})^2}$	$\boxed{1}$
inner diagonal $= \text{edge }\sqrt{3}$	$\boxed{2}$
Given: Volume = 8 cubic meters	$\boxed{3}$

    We know volume of a cube $= (\text{edge})^3 \qquad \boxed{4}$

    Substituting $\boxed{3}$ into $\boxed{4}$, we get

    $$8 \text{ cubic meters} = (\text{edge})^3$$

    $$\sqrt[3]{8 \text{ cubic meters}} = \sqrt[3]{(\text{edge})^3}$$

    $$2 \text{ meters} = \text{edge} \qquad \boxed{5}$$

    Substituting $\boxed{5}$ into $\boxed{2}$, we get

    $$\text{inner diagonal} = 2\sqrt{3} \text{ meters} \qquad \boxed{6}$$

    Using $\boxed{1}$ and $\boxed{6}$, we find

    $$\text{distance we need} = \frac{1}{2}(\text{ inner diagonal})$$

    $$= \frac{1}{2}(2\sqrt{3} \text{ meters})$$

    $$= \sqrt{3} \text{ meters}$$

    $$\text{Distance we need} = \sqrt{3} \text{ m}$$

    (Math Refreshers #313, #429, #430, and #406)

35. Choice C is correct.

    (Use Strategy 2: Translate from words into algebra.)

    Let a = a positive integer
    Then $a + 1$, $a + 2$, $a + 3$, $a + 4$, etc., are the next positive integers.

    (Use Strategy 13: Find unknowns by addition.)

    Add the first two positive integers. We get

    Sum of first 2 positive integers
    $$= a + a + 1 = 2a + 1 \qquad \boxed{1}$$

    $\boxed{1}$ is not divisible by 2.

    Now add the third positive integer, $a + 2$, to $\boxed{1}$. We get

    Sum of first 3 positive integers
    $$= 2a + 1 + a + 2 = 3a + 3 \qquad \boxed{2}$$

    $\boxed{2}$ is not divisible by 2.

    Now add the fourth positive integer, $a + 3$, to $\boxed{2}$. We have

    Sum of first 4 positive integers
    $$= 3a + 3 + a + 3$$
    $$= 4a + 6 \qquad \boxed{3}$$

    Since $\boxed{3}$ can be written as $2(2a + 3)$, it is divisible by 2.

    Therefore, if the number of integers is a multiple of 4, the sum of the consecutive positive integers will be divisible by 2.

    (Math Refreshers #200 and #607)

36. Choice K is correct.

    (Use Strategy 13: Find unknowns by multiplying.)

    $$Given: \frac{a}{b} = \frac{1}{4} \qquad \boxed{1}$$

    Cross-multiply $\boxed{1}$. We have
    $$4a = b \qquad \boxed{2}$$

    Substituting $4a = b$ in the given $\dfrac{a^2}{b}$, we get
    $$\frac{a^2}{b} = \frac{a^2}{4a} = \frac{a}{4} \qquad \boxed{3}$$

    (Use Strategy 7: Use numerics to help find the answer.)

    If $a = 1$ is substituted into $\boxed{3}$ we have
    $$\frac{a^2}{b} = \frac{a}{4} = \frac{1}{4}$$

    Thus, Choice I is satisfied. If $a = 2$ is substituted into $\boxed{3}$, we get
    $$\frac{a^2}{b} = \frac{a}{4} = \frac{2}{4} = \frac{1}{2}$$

    Thus, Choice II is satisfied. If $a = 4$ is substituted into $\boxed{3}$, we have
    $$\frac{a^2}{b} = \frac{a}{4} = \frac{4}{4} = 1$$

    Thus Choice III is satisfied.

    (Math Refreshers #111 and #112)

37. Choice B is correct.

    (Use Strategy 2: Translate from words into algebra.)

    $$Given: \text{Rate of plane} = x\,\frac{\text{km}}{\text{hour}} \qquad \boxed{1}$$
    $$\text{Time of flight} = y \text{ hours} \qquad \boxed{2}$$

    Need: Distance plane had flown $\frac{2}{3}y$ hours ago $\qquad \boxed{3}$

    Subtracting $\boxed{3}$ from $\boxed{2}$, we get

    Time plane had flown $\frac{2}{3}y$ hours ago $= y - \frac{2}{3}y$

    Time plane had flown $\frac{2}{3}y$ hours ago $= \frac{1}{3}y$ hours $\boxed{4}$

    (Use Strategy 9: Know the rate, time, and distance relationship.)

    We know: Rate $\times$ Time = Distance $\qquad \boxed{5}$

    Substitute $\boxed{1}$ and $\boxed{4}$ into $\boxed{5}$. We get
    $$x\,\frac{\text{km}}{\text{hour}} \times \frac{1}{3}y \text{ hours} = \text{distance}$$
    $$\frac{xy}{3} = \text{distance plane had flown } \frac{2}{3}y \text{ hours ago}$$

    (Math Refreshers #201 and #202)

38. Choice K is correct.

    (Use Strategy 5: Average =
    $$\frac{sum\ of\ values}{total\ number\ of\ values})$$

    We know that Average =
    $$\frac{\text{sum of values}}{\text{total number of values}} \qquad \boxed{1}$$

    Given: Average of k scores is 20 $\qquad \boxed{2}$

    Substitute $\boxed{2}$ into $\boxed{1}$. We get
    $$20 = \frac{\text{sum of } k \text{ scores}}{k}$$
    $$20k = \text{sum of } k \text{ scores} \qquad \boxed{3}$$

    Given: Average of 10 of these scores is 15. $\qquad \boxed{4}$

    Substitute $\boxed{4}$ into $\boxed{1}$. We have
    $$15 = \frac{\text{sum of 10 scores}}{10}$$
    $$150 = \text{sum of 10 scores} \qquad \boxed{5}$$

    There are $k - 10$ scores remaining. $\qquad \boxed{6}$

(Use Strategy 3: The whole equals the sum of its parts.)

We know: sum of 10 scores + sum of remaining scores

$$= \text{sum of } k \text{ scores} \qquad \boxed{7}$$

Substituting $\boxed{3}$ and $\boxed{5}$ into $\boxed{7}$, we get

$$150 + \text{sum of remaining scores} = 20k$$
$$\text{sum of remaining scores} = 20k - 150 \qquad \boxed{8}$$

Substituting $\boxed{6}$ and $\boxed{8}$ into $\boxed{1}$, we get

$$\text{average of remaining scores} = \frac{20k - 150}{k - 10}$$

(Math Refresher #601)

39. Choice D is correct.

Given: $C = \dfrac{5}{9}(F - 32)$

Call the number of degrees that the Fahrenheit temperature (F°) increases, x.

(Now use Strategy 17: Use the given information effectively.)

The Celsius temperature (C°) is given as

$$C = \frac{5}{9}(F - 32)$$

This can be rewritten as:

$$C = \frac{5}{9}F - \frac{5}{9}(32) \qquad \boxed{1}$$

When the Celsius temperature increases by 35°, the Fahrenheit temperature increases by x°, so we get:

$$C + 35 = \frac{5}{9}[(F + x) - 32]$$
$$C + 35 = \frac{5}{9}F + \frac{5}{9}x - \frac{5}{9}(32) \qquad \boxed{2}$$

(Now use Strategy 13: Find unknowns by subtraction.)

Subtract $\boxed{1}$ from $\boxed{2}$:

$$C + 35 = \frac{5}{9}F + \frac{5}{9}x - \frac{5}{9}(32) \qquad \boxed{2}$$
$$- \quad C = \frac{5}{9}F \qquad - \frac{5}{9}(32) \qquad \boxed{1}$$
$$\overline{\qquad 35 = \qquad \frac{5}{9}x \qquad} \qquad \boxed{3}$$

Multiply $\boxed{3}$ by 9:

$$35 \times 9 = 5x \qquad \boxed{4}$$

(Use Strategy 19: Don't multiply when reducing can be done first.)

Divide $\boxed{4}$ by 5:

$$\frac{35 \times 9}{5} = x \qquad \boxed{4}$$

Now reduce $\dfrac{35}{5}$ to get 7 and we get for $\boxed{5}$

$$7 \times 9 = x$$
$$63 = x$$

(Math Refresher #406)

40. Choice F is correct.

(Use Strategy 3: The whole equals the sum of its parts.)

From the given diagram, it is clear that

$$z + 2w = 180 \qquad \boxed{1}$$

Since the sum of the measures of the angles of a triangle is 180, then

$$x + y + z = 180 \qquad \boxed{2}$$

(Use Strategy 13: Find unknowns by subtracting equations.)

Subtracting $\boxed{2}$ from $\boxed{1}$,

$$2w - (x + y) = 0$$
$$\text{or} \quad 2w = x + y \qquad \boxed{3}$$

Using $\boxed{3}$, we calculate the unknown expression,

$$w + x + y = w + 2w$$
$$= 3w$$

(Math Refreshers #501, #505, and #406)

41. Choice A is correct.

(Use Strategy 11: Use new definitions carefully.)

All choices must be evaluated using the definition.

Choice A, 934,432, would be assigned $6 + 3 + 4 = 13$ points, while the other choices all receive fewer than 13 points.

(Math Refresher #702)

42. Choice J is correct.

Number Pair	Number of Points
"33"	11
"34"	6
"43"	4
"44"	3

Given: A certain number has 13 points.

(Use Strategy 11: Use new definitions carefully.)

From the chart, the only ways to accumulate 13 points are:

$$6 + 4 + 3 \qquad \boxed{1}$$
$$3 + 3 + 3 + 4 \qquad \boxed{2}$$

I. 33 is not in the number is always true.

II. 34 and 43 are both in the number is *not* true in $\boxed{2}$

III. 43 is in the number is always true.

Thus, I and III are always true.

(Math Refresher #702)

43. Choice B is correct.

(Use Strategy 17: Use the given information effectively.)

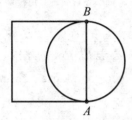

Given: Area of circle $= 9a^2\pi^2$ $\boxed{1}$

Two sides of the square are tangent to the circle $\boxed{2}$

We know that the area of a circle $= \pi r^2$ where r is the radius. $\boxed{3}$

Substituting $\boxed{1}$ into $\boxed{3}$, we have
$$9a^2\pi^2 = \pi r^2 \qquad \boxed{4}$$

Dividing by π, we get
$$9a^2\pi = r^2 \qquad \boxed{5}$$

Since $2r$ is the side of the square, the area of the square is
$$(2r)^2 = 4r^2$$

From $\boxed{5}$, multiplying both sides of the equation by 4, we get
$$4(9a^2\pi) = 4r^2$$

Thus $36a^2\pi = 4r^2 =$ area of square

(Math Refreshers #303, #310, and #406)

44. Choice K is correct.

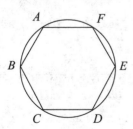

Given: $\widehat{BAF} = 14\pi$ $\boxed{1}$

$ABCDEF$ is equilateral $\boxed{2}$

From $\boxed{2}$ we know that all 6 sides are equal. $\boxed{3}$

From $\boxed{3}$ we know that all 6 arcs are equal. $\boxed{4}$

From $\boxed{1}$ and $\boxed{4}$ and noting that $\widehat{AB} = \frac{1}{2}\widehat{BAF}$, we find
$$\widehat{AB} = \widehat{BC} = \widehat{CD} = \widehat{DE} = \widehat{EF} = \widehat{FA} = 7\pi \qquad \boxed{5}$$

(Use Strategy 3: The whole equals the sum of its parts.)

Circumference of circle $=$
$$6 \times 7\pi \text{ (since there are 6 arcs)} \qquad \boxed{6}$$

We know circumference $= 2\pi r$ $\boxed{7}$

Using $\boxed{6}$ and $\boxed{7}$, we get
$$2\pi r = 6 \times 7\pi$$
$$2\pi r = 42\pi$$
$$2r = 42 \qquad \boxed{8}$$

We know diameter $= 2 \times$ radius $\boxed{9}$

So diameter $= 42$

(Math Refreshers #310 and #524)

45. Choice B is correct.
$$f(x) = a^x$$
$$\text{so} \quad f(x + y) = a^{x+y}$$
$$a^{x+y} = a^x a^y = f(x)f(y)$$

Choice A is incorrect:
$$f(x + y) = a^{x+y} = a^x a^y = f(x)f(y)$$

Choice C is incorrect:
$$f(x - y) = a^{x-y} = \frac{a^x}{a^y} = \frac{f(x)}{f(y)}$$

Choice D is incorrect:
$$f(xy) = a^{xy} = (a^x)^y = [f(x)]^y$$

Choice E is incorrect:
$$f\left(\frac{x}{y}\right) = a^{\frac{x}{y}} = (a^x)^{\frac{1}{y}} = [f(x)]^{\frac{1}{y}}$$

(Math Refreshers #616 and #429)

46. Choice G is correct.

(Use Strategy 2: Translate from words into algebra.)

Let the capacity of container B be x. Then the capacity of container A will be $2x$, and that of container C will be $3x$. The amount poured into container C is equal to half of $2x$ plus one-third of x, or $\frac{2x}{2} + \frac{x}{3} = x + \frac{x}{3} = \frac{4x}{3}$. Dividing this amount by the total capacity of container C, we find the fraction that was filled:
$$\frac{\left(\frac{4x}{3}\right)}{3x} = \frac{4}{9}$$

(Math Refresher #406)

47. Choice D is correct.

(Use Strategy 17: Use the given information effectively.)

In 12 seconds, the wheel travels through 2 revolutions (since 12 seconds is $\frac{1}{5}$ of the minute it would take for ten revolutions). Since this distance is equal to 16 feet, the wheel travels 8 feet per revolution; therefore, 8 feet must be the circumference of the wheel. To find the diameter, we divide this figure by π (because the circumference of a circle is π times its diameter). Therefore, the diameter is $\frac{8}{\pi}$ feet.

(Math Refresher #310)

48. Choice F is correct.

(Use Strategy 14: Draw lines to help solve the problem.)

Before the rotation, we have

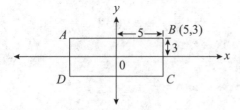

After the rotation, we have

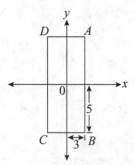

Note that the new y-coordinate of B is negative because B is below the x-axis. Since B is to the right of the y-axis, its x-coordinate is positive. By looking at the second diagram, we see that the coordinates of B are:

$$(3, -5)$$

(Math Refresher #410b)

49. Choice B is correct.

(Use Strategy 11: Use new definitions carefully.)

After 6 hours, $\frac{x}{2}$ grams remain.

After 12 hours, $\frac{1}{2}\left(\frac{x}{2}\right)$ grams remain.

After 18 hours, $\frac{1}{2}\left(\frac{1}{2}\right)\left(\frac{x}{2}\right)$ grams remain.

After 24 hours, $\frac{1}{2}\left(\frac{1}{2}\right)\left(\frac{1}{2}\right)\left(\frac{x}{2}\right) = \frac{x}{16}$ grams remain.

(Math Refresher #431)

50. Choice J is correct.

(Use Strategy 11: Use new definitions carefully.)

The smallest sum occurs when we choose 3 from A and 6 from B.

Therefore, the minimum sum = $3 + 6 = 9$

The largest sum occurs when we choose 5 from A and 8 from B.

Therefore, the maximum sum = $5 + 8 = 13$

All numbers from 9 to 13 inclusive can be sums.

Therefore, there are 5 different sums possible.

(Math Refresher #431)

51. Choice C is correct.

(Use Strategy 17: Use the given information effectively.)

Since $\sin^2 x + \cos^2 x = 1$,
$1 - \sin^2 x = \cos^2 x$
$1 - \cos^2 x = \sin^2 x$
$\sin x\sqrt{1 - \sin^2 x} + \cos x\sqrt{1 - \cos^2 x}$
$= \sin x\sqrt{\cos^2 x} + \cos x\sqrt{\sin^2 x}$
$= \sin x(\cos x) + \cos x(\sin x)$
$= 2\sin x(\cos x)$

Since $\sin 2x = 2\sin x(\cos x)$:
$\sin x\sqrt{1 - \sin^2 x} + \cos x\sqrt{1 - \cos^2 x} = \sin 2x$.

(Math Refresher #901)

52. Choice J is correct.

(Use Strategy 8: When all choices must be tested, start with the last choice and work backward.)

The equation that does not represent any of the illustrated graphs is $y = 2x + 4$ because none of the illustrated graphs has a slope of 2 and crosses the y-axis ($x = 0$) at $y = 4$.

(Math Refreshers #416 and #414)

53. Choice B is correct.

$$f(2x) = |2x| - 2x = 2|x| - 2x = 2f(x)$$

Choice A is incorrect:

$$f(x) = |x| - x$$
$$f(-x) = |-x| - (-x) = |x| + x$$
$$|x| - x \neq |x| + x$$

Choice C is incorrect:

$$f(x + y) = |x + y| - (x + y)$$
$$f(x) = |x| - x$$
$$f(y) = |y| - y$$
$$f(x + y) = |x + y| - (x + y) \neq |x| - x + |y| - y$$

This is because

$$|x + y| \neq |x| + |y|$$

Example: Suppose $x = 2$ and $y = -2$. Then

$$0 = |2 - 2| \neq |2| + |-2| = 4$$

Choice D is incorrect.

$$-f(-x) = -|-x| - (-x)$$
$$= -|-x| + x$$
$$f(x) = |x| - x \neq -|-x| + x$$

For example if $x = -1$, then

$$f(x) = |-1| - (-1) = 2 \neq -|-(-1)| + (-1)$$
$$= -1 - 1 = -2$$

Choice E is incorrect:

$$f(x - y) = |x - y| - (x - y)$$

If $x = -1$ and $y = 0$, then

$$f(x - y) = |-1 - 0| - (-1 - 0) = 1 + 1$$
$$= 2 \neq 0.$$

(Math Refreshers #616 and #615)

54. Choice F is correct.

(Use Strategy 14: Label sides.)

Draw a right triangle depicting half of the projection, with the distance from projector to screen as x.

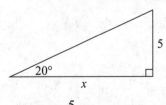

$$\tan 20° = \frac{5}{x}$$

$$x = \frac{5}{\tan 20°}$$

(Math Refresher #901)

55. Choice B is correct.

(Use Strategy 9: Use R × T = D formula.)

Distance for Bicycles A and B = Revolutions × Circumference of Track

Distance A = $x(120)$

Distance B = $600(120)$

(Use Strategy 17: Use given information effectively.)

Note that both riders stop (having traveled different distances) at the *same time* (t).

So, for Bicycle A: (5 ft/s)$t = x(120)$

For Bicycle B: (8 ft/s)$t = 600(120)$

(Use Strategy 13: Find unknowns by dividing.)

Divide Equation A by Equation B:

$$= \frac{5t}{8t} = \frac{x(120)}{600(120)}$$

$$= \frac{5}{8} = \frac{x}{600}$$

$$8x = 5(600)$$

$$x = \frac{3,000}{8} = 375$$

(Math Refreshers #200, #201, and #202)

56. Choice J is correct. The key to this problem is to find the area of the shaded region in terms of known quantities.

(Use Strategy 3: The whole equals the sum of its parts.)

Area of shaded region and also the area of the rectangle

$$= \text{area of triangle} - \text{area of square}$$
$$= x^2\sqrt{3} - x^2$$
$$= x^2(\sqrt{3} - 1)$$

We are given that an unknown rectangle has

width = x 1

and area = $x^2(\sqrt{3} - 1)$ 2

Since length × width = area,

length = area ÷ width   3

Substituting 1 and 2 into 3, we have

$$\text{length of rectangle} = \frac{x^2(\sqrt{3} - 1)}{x}$$

$$\text{length of rectangle} = x(\sqrt{3} - 1)$$

(Math Refreshers #303, #304, and #306)

57. Choice B is correct.

    (Use Strategy 2: Translate from words into algebra.)

    Let f = number of freshmen

    s = number of seniors

    We are given $f = 3s$ **1**

    $\frac{1}{4}$ of the freshmen $= \frac{1}{4}f$ **2**

    $\frac{1}{3}$ of the seniors $= \frac{1}{3}s$ **3**

    Total number of freshmen and seniors $= f + s$ **4**

    (Use Strategy 17: Use the given information effectively.)

    The desired fraction uses **2**, **3**, and **4** as follows:

    $$\frac{\frac{1}{4}f + \frac{1}{3}s}{f + s} \quad \mathbf{5}$$

    Substituting **1** in **5**, we get

    $$\frac{\frac{1}{4}(3s) + \frac{1}{3}s}{3s + s} = \frac{\frac{3}{4}s + \frac{1}{3}s}{4s} \quad \mathbf{6}$$

    Multiplying **6**, numerator and denominator, by 12 we get:

    $$\left(\frac{12}{12}\right)\frac{\frac{3}{4}s + \frac{1}{3}s}{4s}$$

    $$= \frac{9s + 4s}{48s}$$

    $$= \frac{13s}{48s}$$

    $$= \frac{13}{48}$$

    (Math Refreshers #200 and #402)

58. Choice H is correct.

    (Use Strategy 2: Translate from words into algebra.)

    Set up a Venn diagram:

    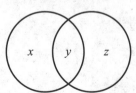

    x = number of students with *only* a car

    z = number of students with *only* a bicycle

    y = number of students having a car and a bicycle

Total students $= 100$ **1**

We are given: $x + y = 30$ **2**

$z + y = 50$ **3**

$y = 20$ **4**

Substituting **4** into **2** and into **3**, we get

$x = 10, z = 30$ **5**

Using **4** and **5**, we have:

The sum of $x + y + z =$

$10 + 20 + 30 = 60$ **6**

This is the number of students who have either a car, a bicycle, or both.

Using **1** and **6**, we get $100 - 60 = 40$ as the number who have neither a car nor a bicycle nor both.

(Math Refreshers #200 and #406)

59. Choice E is correct.

    $f(-x) = -f(x)$ means that for every positive value of x, the y-coordinate is minus the y-coordinate for the corresponding negative value of x.

    (Use Strategy 8: Start with the last choice.)

    Start with Choice E. You can see that these conditions are met on the graph.

    (Math Refresher #616)

60. Choice F is correct.

    (Use Strategy 3: Subtract knowns from knowns to get unknowns.)

    $$\text{area}_{\text{square}} - \text{area}_{\text{circle}} = \text{area}_{\text{remains}}$$

    So where r is the radius of the circle:

    $$3^2 - \pi r^2 = \text{area}_{\text{remains}}$$

    But the area of the remaining piece equals the area of the circle, so:

    $$3^2 - \pi r^2 = \pi r^2$$

    $$9 = 2\pi r^2$$

    $$\frac{9}{2\pi} = r^2$$

    $$\sqrt{\frac{9}{2\pi}} = r$$

    $$\frac{3}{\sqrt{2\pi}} = r$$

    (Math Refreshers #303 and #310)

EXPLANATORY ANSWERS

Section 3: Reading Test

As you read these explanatory answers, you are advised to refer to the "9 Reading Comprehension Strategies" (beginning on page 102) whenever a specific strategy is referred to in the answer. Of particular importance is the Reading Comprehension Strategy 2 (page 105).

Note: *All Reading questions use Reading Strategies 1, 2, and 3 (pages 102–108) as well as other strategies indicated.*

1. Choice D is correct. When Oliver requests more gruel, the master (Mr. Bumble) responds with "stupefied astonishment" (line 21), and Mr. Limbkins regards the request as a near-criminal act, predicting "That boy will be hung." The request earns Oliver "instant confinement" (line 33) and, the next day, 5 pounds to "any man or woman who wanted an apprentice to any trade, business, or calling" (lines 37–39). Of the choices offered, "contempt" comes closest to the attitude that results in this treatment.

2. Choice G is correct. The "Oliver" passage takes place during, and discusses the events surrounding, mealtimes at the workhouse. The nourishment is emphasized: ". . . each boy had one porringer, and no more—except on occasions of great public rejoicing, when he had two ounces and a quarter of bread besides" (lines 5–7). After the meal Oliver remains "desperate with hunger" (line 15).

3. Choice A is correct. "This festive composition" (lines 4–5) refers directly back to the gruel ladled out at mealtimes. Gruel is very thin, watery porridge; the word *gruel* is related to the word *grueling*, meaning "harsh." The single "porringer" each boy received (line 5) refers to the small, shallow dish in which the gruel is served. This meal is the opposite of "festive" both in the sense of its thinness and due to the fact that not enough is served to satisfy the hungry children, as Oliver

makes clear when he requests more (line 19). One form of irony is to use terms—here "festive"—to mean the opposite.

4. Choice J is correct. The institution overseen by Master Bumble is described in terms that resemble a prison, with the "large stone hall" (lines 1–2) where the boys take their meals, the boys whispering to each other rather than speaking in full voices (line 13), the obviously inadequate food, and the boys paralyzed with fear (line 24) after Oliver asks for a second helping. Choice F is incorrect because the passage does not indicate anything about what the "standards of the time" might have been. Choice G is incorrect because there is no indication that the children are subjected to any training. Choice H is incorrect because the children are starved and treated harshly, not with compassion.

5. Choice C is correct. The boys in the "Oliver" passage are described as reacting with "fear" (line 24) when Oliver requests more food. In the "Nat" passage, "the good-hearted lads all promised to lend him a hand" (lines 74–75). The characterizations in the other choices are not supported by the passage.

6. Choice J is correct. See lines 71–73: "Thinking that a lesson in learning to help one another was better than arithmetic just then, Mr. Bhaer told them about Nat. . . ."

7. Choice A is correct. In the "Nat" passage, the reaction of both the teacher, Mr. Bhaer, and the other boys in the school is consistently positive: Mr. Bhaer expresses his concern for Nat and his sensitivity to his nervousness as a new student by giving him a seat near the window (lines 42–43), and soothes his fear of not being as good as the other boys: "Nat, you really care to learn something. . . ." (line 67). In response to this leadership, the other boys are supportive: ". . . for every one was glad to

give him a 'boost' up the ladder of learning" (lines 79–80). By contrast, the boys in the "Oliver" passage are fearful and underfed. The minute Oliver has the "temerity" (line 18) to request an additional portion of food, he is offloaded to the first party that will take him off the hands of the parish (lines 35–36).

8. Choice F is correct. The author (Dickens) is showing through this mistreatment, through the negative depiction of the adults who run the institution, and through his use of irony (lines 4–7) that this should not be happening. The author of "Nat" (Alcott) presents her scenario as a positive example of the way children should be treated.

9. Choice C is correct. Although "alarmed at his own temerity" (lines 17–18), Oliver requests more food: "Child as he was, he was desperate with hunger, and reckless with misery" (lines 14–16).

10. Choice F is correct. The "Nat" passage illustrates the sociable and friendly nature of both teacher and students (condition I); it also describes the impact of the boys on Nat (condition III) by describing Nat's concern about how well he is performing as well as the boys' willingness to help Nat. The "Oliver" passage makes reference to neither condition I nor condition III.

11. Choice D is correct. See lines 17–19: "The tie which bound this world-embracing empire together . . . was as much cultural as political."

12. Choice F is correct. See lines 14–16: "Centuries of training had bred in them the conviction that all other rulers should be tributary to the Son of Heaven."

13. Choice A is correct. See the last paragraph about the close relationship between "ethical standards" and "Confucian patterns."

14. Choice H is correct. The reader should infer from paragraphs 3 and 4 that Han and Tang were dynasties—just as there was a Manchu dynasty.

15. Choice C is correct. The passage points out that since more emphasis was placed on being members of the same culture rather than on being members of the same race, there was a "comparative contentment of Chinese under alien rulers" (lines 44–45).

16. Choice F is correct. See lines 67–69: "In contrast with India, where caste and religion have tended to keep apart the racial strata, in China assimilation made great progress."

17. Choice B is correct. Lines 52–57 point out that the Manchus never gave up some of their ancestral ways, and this disturbed segments of the population.

18. Choice F is correct. The passage states that assimilation made great progress in China. (See the answer to question 16.)

19. Choice C is correct. From the context of the sentence and the sentence before and after it, it can be seen that "restiveness" must mean impatience or restlessness. See also **Reading Comprehension Strategy 5**.

20. Choice J is correct because the Chinese understanding of "civilized" vs. "barbarous" was based on the content of the cultures, not, as the incorrect Choice F suggests, perceived threats from those classified as barbarous. See lines 22–23. Choice G is incorrect because the Chinese did not consider cosmopolitanism desirable, as evidenced by the perception that communication with other cultures as equals was pointless, even "scandalous" (lines 12–14). Choice H is incorrect because racial identity was not the basis for China's assessment of Chinese or foreign cultures (lines 34–36).

21. Choice A is correct. See lines 73–75: ". . . as Dr. Skinner argues, that one can extrapolate from pigeons to people. . . ." Choice B is incorrect because, though Skinner agrees that introspection may be of some use (line 18), nowhere does the article indicate that he suggests wide use of the introspective method. Choice C is incorrect since Skinner, so the author says (lines 77–79), "has not satisfactorily rebutted the basic criticism that behaviorism 'is scientistic rather than scientific.'" Choice D is incorrect because lines 83–85 state that "Skinner predicts . . . impending disaster."

22. Choice J is correct. Choice F is incorrect. See lines 85–91: "Two key concepts . . . not so reassuring." Choice G is incorrect. See lines 12–15: ". . . an earlier stage of . . . influence of mentalism." Choice H is incorrect since mentalism evolved before methodological and radical behaviorism. See lines 10–18: "What such people . . . its possible usefulness." Choice J is correct. The passage, from line 67 to the end, brings out weaknesses in Skinner's presentation.

23. Choice D is correct. Skinner, in lines 26–27, says ". . . few would contend that behavior is 'endlessly malleable.' " Also see lines 36–43: "Contingencies of reinforcement . . . likely to occur." In effect, Skinner is saying that behavior cannot always, by plan or design, be altered or influenced; behavior must depend, to some extent, on the element of chance.

24. Choice J is correct. Skinner is known for his experiments with pigeons. Also, behaviorists have frequently used rats in experimentation. See lines 67–75. In addition, see lines 38–40: "In both natural . . . is crucial." The other choices are not relevant to Darwin or his work.

25. Choice A is correct. From the context in the rest of the sentence where "extrapolate" appears, Choice A fits best. Note: The word "extrapolate" is derived from the Latin "extra" (outside) and "polire" (to polish). See also **Reading Comprehension Strategy 5**.

26. Choice H is correct. Choice F is incorrect because Choice F is true according to lines 11–15. Choice G is incorrect because Choice G is true according to lines 68–73. Choice H is correct because Choice H is *not* true according to lines 67–73. Choice J is incorrect because Choice J is true according to lines 11–15.

27. Choice B is correct. Choice A is incorrect. See lines 19–22: ". . . to those who object . . . Skinner expresses puzzlement." Choice B is correct because Skinner, a radical behaviorist, though believing that environmental influences are highly important in shaping human behavior, nevertheless states in lines 36–40: "Contingencies of reinforcement . . . is crucial." Operant conditioning is, according to behaviorists, a vital aspect of learning.

Choice C is incorrect. Although Skinner accepts introspection (lines 16–18) as part of his system, nowhere does he place primary importance on introspection. Choice D is incorrect. Though Skinner may agree with this choice, nowhere in the passage does he state or imply this opinion. Note: The word "malleable" means "capable of being shaped or formed"—from the Latin "malleare," meaning "to hammer." The quote in the stem of the question says, in effect, that few people would say that behavior can always be shaped.

28. Choice F is correct. I is correct; see lines 81–82. II is incorrect; don't be fooled by what is in lines 78–81. It does not refer to *scientistic* areas. III is incorrect; see lines 78–81.

29. Choice C is correct. Given the context of the sentence and the sentences preceding and succeeding it, "veritable" means "true." One may also note the "ver" in "veritable" and may associate that with the word "verify," which means "to prove to be true." This is the association strategy, which can be used to figure out clues to meanings of words. See also **Reading Comprehension Strategy 5**.

30. Choice J is correct because of the sentence "while he reassures us" about science practicing the concepts "benignly" (meaning in a harmless fashion), "one can't shake off the suspicion. . . ." Choice F is incorrect; the author points out Skinner's repetition of the manipulation and control concepts, but not to assess the effect on his credibility. Choices G and H are incorrect because neither of these ideas is stated or implied in the paragraph.

31. Choice D is correct. See lines 23–24: "All human beings have at least four types of intelligence." Choice A is incorrect. See lines 56–59: "Persistence kept Einstein looking for the solution to the question of the relationship between the law of gravity and his special theory of relativity." Isaac Newton (1642–1727) formulated the law of gravitation. Choice B is incorrect. The passage simply states: "The idea for a self-starting electric motor came to Nikola Tesla one evening as he was reciting a poem by Goethe and watching a sunset" (lines 34–36). Choice C is incorrect. The author indicates a span of time when he states: "The discoveries made by scientific geniuses, from

Archimedes through Einstein . . ." (lines 1–2). Archimedes was an ancient Greek mathematician, physicist, and inventor (287–212 BC), whereas Einstein was, of course, a modern scientist (1879–1955).

32. Choice H is correct. See lines 47–49: "The scientist solves a problem by shifting from one intelligence to another, although the logical-mathematical intelligence is dominant." Accordingly, Choices F, G, and J are incorrect.

33. Choice B is correct. When the author describes the work experiences of Einstein and Tesla, he refers to their use of one or more of the four types of intelligence. Moreover, lines 29–31 state: "Some corroboration of these [four intelligence] categories comes from the reports of scientists who describe thought processes centered around images, sensations, or words." Choices A, C, and D are incorrect because the author does not refer to these choices in the passage.

34. Choice G is correct. The author indicates that great scientists use to advantage four intelligences—logical-mathematical, spatial, linguistic, and bodilykinesthetic. See lines 25–28: "The great scientist possesses the ability to move back and forth among them—the logical-mathematical; the spatial, which includes visual perception; the linguistic; and the bodily kinesthetic." Choices F and H are brought out in the passage, but not at any length. Therefore, Choices F and H are incorrect. Choice J is incorrect because though the concepts are mentioned, they are certainly not clarified in the passage.

35. Choice D is correct. As a football star, he would certainly have to have a high level of (a) spatial intelligence (II), which involves space sensitivity as well as visual perception, and (b) bodily kinesthetic intelligence (IV), which involves the movement of muscles, tendons, and joints. As a literature major, he would certainly have to have a high level of linguistic intelligence (III), which involves the ability to read, write, speak, and listen. Whether he would have logical-mathematical intelligence to a high degree is questionable. It follows that Choices A, B, and C are incorrect.

36. Choice J is correct. According to what is stated in lines 53–59, persistence is an important characteristic of the scientist. Thus the author would probably not agree with the statement in Choice J. The author would agree with the statement in Choice F: See lines 5–6. Note that although the author may not agree that IQ is what makes the scientist brilliant, he believes that *most* people feel that way. The author would agree with the statement in Choice G. See lines 34–36 and lines 62–68. The author would agree with the statement in Choice H. See lines 17–19 in the context of the rest of the passage.

37. Choice C is correct. See lines 59–61. Note that although persistence is mentioned in lines 53–59, the passage states that fluid thinking may be connected to persistence, not defined as persistence. Thus Choice A is incorrect. See also **Reading Comprehension Strategy 5**.

38. Choice G is correct. Given the context in lines 53–61, the word "paradoxically" means "seemingly contradictorily." See also **Reading Comprehension Strategy 5**.

39. Choice A is correct. It can be seen in the passage that the author is intrigued by and interested in the way the scientist thinks but at the same time feels that the scientist reports the findings very objectively.

40. Choice G is correct. See lines 18–19, 62, 56, 50, and 59. Choice F is incorrect because the author notes that an IQ above a certain point does not contribute to the productivity of a genius (lines 22–23) and that content knowledge alone is not sufficient; the key is how the genius connects pieces of information (lines 44–46). Choice H is incorrect because the theory of relativity is mentioned as one of Einstein's most noteworthy contributions, not as a quality of genius, and similarly, quantum physics is a specific form of content knowledge. Choice J is incorrect because none of the examples of geniuses had an explicit "revolutionary" agenda and in fact made discoveries sometimes by accident. Neither of the other traits is mentioned in regard to commonalities among geniuses.

EXPLANATORY ANSWERS

Section 4: Science Test

1. Choice B is correct. If you compare the data from the serving size column with the vitamin C column, you'll see that asparagus has 44 mg/cup, lobster has 0 mg/oz, cucumber has 4.8 mg/cup, and broccoli has 82 mg/cup. Therefore, 9 oz of lobster has 0 mg, 2 cups of asparagus have 88 mg, 1 cup of broccoli has 82 mg, and 3 cups of cucumber have 14.4 mg.

2. Choice G is correct. If you look at the copper column, you'll see that avocado provides ~20% of your daily copper value *per serving*. The top of the chart reveals that a serving size is 1.00 cup. Therefore, 40% of your daily value of copper can come from 2 cups of avocado slices.

3. Choice C is correct. From Figure 3, we see that the recommended daily amount of vitamin C is 60 mg. From Figure 1, we see that 1 cup of broccoli provides 82 mg of vitamin C, more than enough to meet the daily recommendation.

4. Choice F is correct. Comparing values in the vitamin C and potassium columns reveals that broccoli has more vitamin C but asparagus has more potassium per serving.

5. Choice D is correct. Since the chart shows that ~25% is provided per cup, 4 cups would be needed to meet the recommended daily amount.

6. Choice H is correct. Figure 1 shows the mouse and human chains split most recently, 65.5 million years ago. Before that, they had a common ancestor who was not as closely related to the zebrafish or Drosophila.

7. Choice C is correct. The split between mouse and zebrafish occurs at the 251 mark on the chart.

8. Choice G is correct. The 1800 data set clearly favors whiter moths, while the "after 1900" set reveals a high concentration of dark-colored moths. It can be reasonably concluded that the population tended to get darker over this time period.

9. Choice D is correct. The greatest value in the "after 1900" data set is for darker brown moths.

10. Choice J is correct. Since tree color is the independent variable in this experiment, the scientist must test multiple colors of trees. All of the other experiments only test light-colored trees.

11. Choice B is correct. The experiment descriptions reveal that Experiment 2 sets the helium pressure at 2 atmospheres, while Experiment 1 is conducted at 1 atmosphere.

12. Choice J is correct. Experiment 1 verified this conclusion for only one gas sample (helium). Testing other gases will best help us to determine if the conclusion is true for "any confined gas." Choice F would not allow for changes in volume, Choice G tests a liquid instead of a gas, and Choice H would not allow us to maintain constant pressure.

13. Choice B is correct. Examining the data from Experiment 1, we see that the volume increases ~3.3 mL for every 10 Kelvin; since we are increasing the sample temperature 20 Kelvin higher than the last recorded test, we can expect the result to be 6.6 mL greater than the results of the last test: $113.3 + 6.6 = 119.9$, or ~120 mL.

14. Choice F is correct. If the new experiment uses an initial volume $\frac{1}{2}$ the size of that used in Experiment 2, we can expect the results at 340 Kelvin to be $\frac{1}{2}$ the size of the results at 340 Kelvin in Experiment 2: $\frac{56.6}{2} = 28.3$ mL.

15. Choice B is correct. As the temperature goes up, the molecules gain energy, move faster, and spread out, increasing the volume. Choice A assumes that molecules spontaneously generate in a closed space, Choice C assumes that the helium molecules *lose* energy, and Choice D assumes a change in pressure (the experiment description notes that the pressure is constant).

16. Choice H is correct. Taking the information from Question 12, we know that volume increases proportionally to temperature. Therefore, doubling the temperature (from 300 to 600 Kelvin) should double the volume.

17. Choice D is correct. The only variable that changed for Experiment 2 is that it took place in spring.

18. Choice G is correct. SO_4^{2-} is more prominent in each downstream sample than in the corresponding upstream samples.

19. Choice A is correct. Since this question is inquiring about the downstream pH only, you would need to test only the downstream pH. To determine the time of day that the pH is highest would require testing the downstream pH multiple times each day for a large number of days. Only Choice A provides testing of downstream pH multiple times per day for many days. Choice B is incorrect because it suggests testing only upstream pH. Choice C suggests testing at only one time of day. And Choice D suggests only one day of testing.

20. Choice G is correct. If the plant were changing the concentration of Fe^{3+}, the effect should have been seen in the winter samples as well.

21. Choice D is correct. For Choice A to be true, there would need to be a lower concentration of Fe^{3+} both upstream and downstream; Choice B is inconsistent with the temperature data recorded; Choice C is false because plants produce *increased* O_2 levels via photosynthesis.

22. Choice F is correct. This question tests your ability to match data from a graph with data from a table. The *y*-values are identical to the SO_4^{2-} column from Table 2 (downstream).

23. Choice B is correct. Taking any value from column 2, we can see that it is about 29–32 times as large as the previous value, making 30 the best estimate.

24. Choice G is correct. Read the third column of Figure 1; earthquakes at magnitude 6 or lower are felt at the epicenter (if at all).

25. Choice D is correct. Since there are approximately 365 days in a year, you're looking for values of at least 366—so Minor (49,000), Light (6,200), and Moderate (800) qualify, while Strong (120) and greater do not.

26. Choice H is correct. From magnitude 4–9, the comparable effect in TNT rises at a constant rate of ~32 per level of magnitude: 1,000–32,000–1,000,000–32,000,000–1,000,000,000–32,000,000.

27. Choice D is correct. Figure 2 suggests that the lower the magnitude of an earthquake, the more frequently they occur. If earthquakes at magnitude 0–2 are therefore more common than earthquakes at magnitude 3–3.9, their average annual value will be greater than 49,000.

28. Choice J is correct. The statement that "only one substrate fits into each enzyme's active site" assumes the *specificity* of the shapes, a central idea of the lock-and-key model.

29. Choice D is correct. The induced-fit model claims that the enzyme shifts slightly as the substrate bonds, changing its shape. By comparing the lone enzyme with the enzyme/substrate complex, you could observe whether or not a change of shape occurred.

30. Choice H is correct. The lock-and-key model best accounts for the specificity of enzymes. Choices F, G, and J do not apply to the lock-and-key model.

31. Choice A is correct. Because the induced-fit model proposes that the enzyme changes shape to fit the substrate, it is a better model than lock-and-key to explain unintentional reactions.

32. Choice F is correct. When the enzyme bonds to the substrate, it changes shape, allowing bonds within the substrate to break more easily.

33. Choice A is correct. While the lock-and-key model addresses specificity more directly, both models indicate that the shape of both enzyme and substrate are important for bonding.

34. Choice J is correct. The reaction is supposed to take place using carbon dioxide; when it uses oxygen instead (because of its similar shape), this example supports the induced-fit model.

35. Choice C is correct. In Experiment 1, the amplitude is 6 inches; in Experiment 3, the amplitude is 12 inches.

36. Choice H is correct. The mass of each weight (1 g, 2 g, 3 g, etc.) is the same in both experiments.

37. Choice B is correct. When the length of string increased (99 cm > 24 cm), the period also increased (1.99 s > 1.0 s). It is safe to assume that if the string is even longer (200 cm > 99 cm), the time of one period will be longer than it was with the 99-cm string.

38. Choice F is correct. Experiment 1 varies the mass with each trial yet records no change in the length of the period.

39. Choice D is correct. Weight and amplitude were unchanged between experiments; the only altered variable was the length of the pendulum.

40. Choice F is correct. Comparing Experiments 1 and 3 reveals a negligible difference in times of period, despite an amplitude that is twice as long. We've already seen how weight does not alter the period, while length of the pendulum clearly does.

WHAT YOU MUST DO NOW TO RAISE YOUR ACT SCORE

1. Follow the directions on pages 444–452 to find your scale score for the ACT Test you've just taken. These results will give you a good idea about how hard you'll need to study in order to achieve a certain score on the actual ACT.

   Using your scale score count as a basis, indicate for yourself your areas of strength and weakness as revealed by the Norms Tables on pages 447–448.

2. Eliminate your weaknesses in each of the ACT Test areas by taking the following Giant Steps toward ACT success:

Reading Part

Giant Step 1

Take advantage of the Reading Strategies that begin on page 102. Read again the explanatory answer for each of the Reading questions that you got wrong. Refer to the Reading Strategy that applies to each of your incorrect answers. Learn each of these Reading Strategies thoroughly. These strategies are crucial if you want to raise your ACT score substantially.

Giant Step 2

You can improve your vocabulary by doing the following:

1. Read as widely as possible—not only novels. Nonfiction is important too—and don't forget to read newspapers and magazines.

2. Listen to people who speak well. Tune in to worthwhile TV programs.

3. Use the dictionary frequently and extensively—at home, on the bus, at work, etc.

4. Review the Hot Prefixes and Roots beginning on page 128.

Math Part

Giant Step 3

Make good use of the 19 Math Strategies that begin on page 44. Read again the solutions for each Math question that you answered incorrectly. Refer to the Math Strategy that applies to each of your incorrect answers. Learn each of these Math Strategies thoroughly. We repeat that these strategies are crucial if you want to raise your ACT Math score substantially.

Giant Step 4

You may want to take the 101 Most Important Math Questions You Need to Know How to Solve test beginning on page 13 and follow the directions after the test for a basic Math skills diagnosis.

For each Math question that you got wrong on the test, note the reference to the Complete ACT Math Refresher section beginning on page 147. This reference will explain clearly the mathematical principle involved in the solution of the question you answered incorrectly. Learn that particular mathematical principle thoroughly.

For Both the Math and Reading Parts

Giant Step 5

You may want to take the World's Shortest Practice Test for the ACT Exam beginning on page 1 to assess whether you're using the best strategies for the questions.

For the English Test and Writing Part

Giant Step 6

Take a look at Part 9, the ACT Writing Test, which describes the Writing Section. For the English Test, make use of Part 7, A Brief Review of English Grammar, and Part 8, the Complete ACT Grammar and Usage Refresher.

After you have done some of the tasks you have been advised to do in the suggestions above, proceed to ACT Practice Test 2, beginning on page 481.

After taking ACT Practice Test 2, concentrate on the weaknesses that still remain.

If you do the job *right* and follow the steps listed above, you are likely to raise your ACT score significantly.

Remember:

I am the master of my fate:
I am the captain of my soul.

—From the poem "Invictus"
by William Ernest Henley

ACT PRACTICE TEST 2

ANSWER SHEET

It is recommended that you use a No. 2 pencil. It is very important that you fill in the entire circle darkly and completely. If you change your response, erase as completely as possible. Incomplete marks or erasures may affect your score.

Complete Mark ● **Examples of Incomplete Marks** ◉ ⊗ ⊖ ◐ ◑ ◓ ◔ ◯

SECTION 1: ENGLISH TEST

	A B C D		F G H J		A B C D		F G H J		A B C D
1	○○○○	16	○○○○	31	○○○○	46	○○○○	61	○○○○
2	F G H J ○○○○	17	A B C D ○○○○	32	F G H J ○○○○	47	A B C D ○○○○	62	F G H J ○○○○
3	A B C D ○○○○	18	F G H J ○○○○	33	A B C D ○○○○	48	F G H J ○○○○	63	A B C D ○○○○
4	F G H J ○○○○	19	A B C D ○○○○	34	F G H J ○○○○	49	A B C D ○○○○	64	F G H J ○○○○
5	A B C D ○○○○	20	F G H J ○○○○	35	A B C D ○○○○	50	F G H J ○○○○	65	A B C D ○○○○
6	F G H J ○○○○	21	A B C D ○○○○	36	F G H J ○○○○	51	A B C D ○○○○	66	F G H J ○○○○
7	A B C D ○○○○	22	F G H J ○○○○	37	A B C D ○○○○	52	F G H J ○○○○	67	A B C D ○○○○
8	F G H J ○○○○	23	A B C D ○○○○	38	F G H J ○○○○	53	A B C D ○○○○	68	F G H J ○○○○
9	A B C D ○○○○	24	F G H J ○○○○	39	A B C D ○○○○	54	F G H J ○○○○	69	A B C D ○○○○
10	F G H J ○○○○	25	A B C D ○○○○	40	F G H J ○○○○	55	A B C D ○○○○	70	F G H J ○○○○
11	A B C D ○○○○	26	F G H J ○○○○	41	A B C D ○○○○	56	F G H J ○○○○	71	A B C D ○○○○
12	F G H J ○○○○	27	A B C D ○○○○	42	F G H J ○○○○	57	A B C D ○○○○	72	F G H J ○○○○
13	A B C D ○○○○	28	F G H J ○○○○	43	A B C D ○○○○	58	F G H J ○○○○	73	A B C D ○○○○
14	F G H J ○○○○	29	A B C D ○○○○	44	F G H J ○○○○	59	A B C D ○○○○	74	F G H J ○○○○
15	A B C D ○○○○	30	F G H J ○○○○	45	A B C D ○○○○	60	F G H J ○○○○	75	A B C D ○○○○

Complete Mark ●   **Examples of Incomplete Marks** ⦿ ⊗ ⊖ ◐ ◑ ◖ ◖ ◑

SECTION 2: MATHEMATICS TEST

	A B C D E		A B C D E		A B C D E		A B C D E		A B C D E
1	○ ○ ○ ○ ○	13	○ ○ ○ ○ ○	25	○ ○ ○ ○ ○	37	○ ○ ○ ○ ○	49	○ ○ ○ ○ ○
	F G H J K		F G H J K		F G H J K		F G H J K		F G H J K
2	○ ○ ○ ○ ○	14	○ ○ ○ ○ ○	26	○ ○ ○ ○ ○	38	○ ○ ○ ○ ○	50	○ ○ ○ ○ ○
	A B C D E		A B C D E		A B C D E		A B C D E		A B C D E
3	○ ○ ○ ○ ○	15	○ ○ ○ ○ ○	27	○ ○ ○ ○ ○	39	○ ○ ○ ○ ○	51	○ ○ ○ ○ ○
	F G H J K		F G H J K		F G H J K		F G H J K		F G H J K
4	○ ○ ○ ○ ○	16	○ ○ ○ ○ ○	28	○ ○ ○ ○ ○	40	○ ○ ○ ○ ○	52	○ ○ ○ ○ ○
	A B C D E		A B C D E		A B C D E		A B C D E		A B C D E
5	○ ○ ○ ○ ○	17	○ ○ ○ ○ ○	29	○ ○ ○ ○ ○	41	○ ○ ○ ○ ○	53	○ ○ ○ ○ ○
	F G H J K		F G H J K		F G H J K		F G H J K		F G H J K
6	○ ○ ○ ○ ○	18	○ ○ ○ ○ ○	30	○ ○ ○ ○ ○	42	○ ○ ○ ○ ○	54	○ ○ ○ ○ ○
	A B C D E		A B C D E		A B C D E		A B C D E		A B C D E
7	○ ○ ○ ○ ○	19	○ ○ ○ ○ ○	31	○ ○ ○ ○ ○	43	○ ○ ○ ○ ○	55	○ ○ ○ ○ ○
	F G H J K		F G H J K		F G H J K		F G H J K		F G H J K
8	○ ○ ○ ○ ○	20	○ ○ ○ ○ ○	32	○ ○ ○ ○ ○	44	○ ○ ○ ○ ○	56	○ ○ ○ ○ ○
	A B C D E		A B C D E		A B C D E		A B C D E		A B C D E
9	○ ○ ○ ○ ○	21	○ ○ ○ ○ ○	33	○ ○ ○ ○ ○	45	○ ○ ○ ○ ○	57	○ ○ ○ ○ ○
	F G H J K		F G H J K		F G H J K		F G H J K		F G H J K
10	○ ○ ○ ○ ○	22	○ ○ ○ ○ ○	34	○ ○ ○ ○ ○	46	○ ○ ○ ○ ○	58	○ ○ ○ ○ ○
	A B C D E		A B C D E		A B C D E		A B C D E		A B C D E
11	○ ○ ○ ○ ○	23	○ ○ ○ ○ ○	35	○ ○ ○ ○ ○	47	○ ○ ○ ○ ○	59	○ ○ ○ ○ ○
	F G H J K		F G H J K		F G H J K		F G H J K		F G H J K
12	○ ○ ○ ○ ○	24	○ ○ ○ ○ ○	36	○ ○ ○ ○ ○	48	○ ○ ○ ○ ○	60	○ ○ ○ ○ ○

Complete Mark ● **Examples of Incomplete Marks** ◍ ⊗ ⊖ ◌ ⊘ ◌ ◍ ◍

SECTION 3: READING TEST

	A B C D		A B C D		A B C D		A B C D		A B C D
1	○ ○ ○ ○	9	○ ○ ○ ○	17	○ ○ ○ ○	25	○ ○ ○ ○	33	○ ○ ○ ○
	F G H J		F G H J		F G H J		F G H J		F G H J
2	○ ○ ○ ○	10	○ ○ ○ ○	18	○ ○ ○ ○	26	○ ○ ○ ○	34	○ ○ ○ ○
	A B C D		A B C D		A B C D		A B C D		A B C D
3	○ ○ ○ ○	11	○ ○ ○ ○	19	○ ○ ○ ○	27	○ ○ ○ ○	35	○ ○ ○ ○
	F G H J		F G H J		F G H J		F G H J		F G H J
4	○ ○ ○ ○	12	○ ○ ○ ○	20	○ ○ ○ ○	28	○ ○ ○ ○	36	○ ○ ○ ○
	A B C D		A B C D		A B C D		A B C D		A B C D
5	○ ○ ○ ○	13	○ ○ ○ ○	21	○ ○ ○ ○	29	○ ○ ○ ○	37	○ ○ ○ ○
	F G H J		F G H J		F G H J		F G H J		F G H J
6	○ ○ ○ ○	14	○ ○ ○ ○	22	○ ○ ○ ○	30	○ ○ ○ ○	38	○ ○ ○ ○
	A B C D		A B C D		A B C D		A B C D		A B C D
7	○ ○ ○ ○	15	○ ○ ○ ○	23	○ ○ ○ ○	31	○ ○ ○ ○	39	○ ○ ○ ○
	F G H J		F G H J		AF G H J		F G H J		F G H J
8	○ ○ ○ ○	16	○ ○ ○ ○	24	○ ○ ○ ○	32	○ ○ ○ ○	40	○ ○ ○ ○

SECTION 4: SCIENCE TEST

	A B C D		A B C D		A B C D		A B C D		A B C D
1	○ ○ ○ ○	9	○ ○ ○ ○	17	○ ○ ○ ○	25	○ ○ ○ ○	33	○ ○ ○ ○
	F G H J		F G H J		F G H J		F G H J		F G H J
2	○ ○ ○ ○	10	○ ○ ○ ○	18	○ ○ ○ ○	26	○ ○ ○ ○	34	○ ○ ○ ○
	A B C D		A B C D		A B C D		A B C D		A B C D
3	○ ○ ○ ○	11	○ ○ ○ ○	19	○ ○ ○ ○	27	○ ○ ○ ○	35	○ ○ ○ ○
	F G H J		F G H J		F G H J		F G H J		F G H J
4	○ ○ ○ ○	12	○ ○ ○ ○	20	○ ○ ○ ○	28	○ ○ ○ ○	36	○ ○ ○ ○
	A B C D		A B C D		A B C D		A B C D		A B C D
5	○ ○ ○ ○	13	○ ○ ○ ○	21	○ ○ ○ ○	29	○ ○ ○ ○	37	○ ○ ○ ○
	F G H J		F G H J		F G H J		F G H J		F G H J
6	○ ○ ○ ○	14	○ ○ ○ ○	22	○ ○ ○ ○	30	⊗ ⊖ ○ ○	38	⊗ ○ ○ ○
	A B C D		A B C D		A B C D		A B C D		A B C D
7	○ ○ ○ ○	15	○ ○ ○ ○	23	○ ○ ○ ○	31	○ ○ ○ ○	39	○ ○ ○ ○
	F G H J		F G H J		F G H J		F G H J		F G H J
8	○ ○ ○ ○	16	○ ○ ○ ○	24	○ ○ ○ ○	32	○ ○ ○ ○	40	○ ○ ○ ○

SECTION 1: ENGLISH TEST

45 Minutes, 75 Questions

Turn to Section 1 of your answer sheet (page 481) to answer the questions in this section.

Directions

Each passage below is accompanied by a number of questions. For some questions, you will consider how the passage might be revised to improve the expression of ideas. For other questions, you will consider how the passage might be edited to correct errors in sentence structure, usage, or punctuation.

Some questions will direct you to an underlined portion of a passage. Other questions will direct you to a location in a passage or ask you to think about the passage as a whole.

After reading each passage, choose the answer to each question that most effectively improves the quality of writing in the passage or that makes the passage conform to the conventions of standard written English. Many questions include a "NO CHANGE" option. Choose that option if you think the best choice is to leave the relevant portion of the passage as it is.

Questions 1–15 are based on the following passage, *The Money behind Movie Musicals.*

Since (1) the origination of movies, (2) there had always been people interested (3) in being financially involved in films. Nowadays, these people are called backers. A backer is (4) someone who the director or the producer has chosen. But (5) between you and myself, when the money (6) he or she has paid mounts up to the staggering sums required to produce a movie musical, he or she becomes as important to the film (7) as any person involved. (8)

Why back a movie (9) which cost millions to shoot? How do backers recoup their investment in a project that looks and feels like a stage production people may

have already seen? (10) Mostly to the point, why (11) except the arbitrary confines of the theater proscenium? Because the music and story are usually already well known and beloved by Broadway audiences, it pays to stay as faithful as possible to the original version. In doing so, however, producers can use the camera to open up a world of fantasy and fun to larger audiences. Being faithful to the original story while *looking* original is only part of the (12) story, and not scarcely the most important part. To produce (13) any kind of stage presentation for film is purely handyman's work, a matter of picking the pieces and pasting them together. A truly successful adaptation from stage to screen, on the other hand, (14) will have called for imagination, finesse, and creativity. (15) Perhaps that is why it is so rare.

The Money behind Movie Musicals Questions

Which of the following alternatives to the underlined portion would NOT be acceptable?

1. (A) movies were invented,
   (B) the movies' invention,
   (C) the invention of movies,
   (D) having invented movies,

2. (F) NO CHANGE
   (G) there have always been
   (H) there were always
   (J) there will always be

3. (A) NO CHANGE
   (B) to finance
   (C) in financing
   (D) in finance

4. (F) NO CHANGE
   (G) someone who is the one
   (H) someone whom
   (J) someone, whomever

Go on to the next page.

5. (A) NO CHANGE
   (B) you and me
   (C) you and I
   (D) you and also me

6. (F) NO CHANGE
   (G) they have paid
   (H) the backer has paid
   (J) the backer had paid

7. (A) NO CHANGE
   (B) as any other one
   (C) as anyone
   (D) as anyone else

8. The writer is considering adding the following true statement:

   > Consider the fact that in 1978, the total budget for *Grease* was $6 million, whereas in 2007, *Hairspray* cost approximately $75 million, a relatively low budget by Hollywood standards.

   Should the writer make this addition here?

   (F) Yes, because the sentence supports the importance of the financial backer with a concrete example of increasing costs.
   (G) Yes, because the example of successful movie musicals supports the writer's argument that movie financiers should see musicals as a good investment.
   (H) No, because the sentence neglects to identify the backers of these films.
   (J) No, because the sentence is irrelevant to the essay's focus on the producer's role.

9. (A) NO CHANGE
   (B) who costs
   (C) that costs
   (D) that costed

10. (F) NO CHANGE
    (G) Even better to the point,
    (H) Even more to the point,
    (J) More to the point is,

11. (A) NO CHANGE
    (B) accept
    (C) excepting
    (D) accepting

12. (F) NO CHANGE
    (G) story. And scarcely
    (H) story. Scarcely
    (J) story—and scarcely

13. (A) NO CHANGE
    (B) these kind of stage presentation
    (C) any of those kinds of stage presentation
    (D) some of these kinds of stage presentation

14. (F) NO CHANGE
    (G) called for
    (H) had called for
    (J) calls for

15. Given that all of the choices are true, which one is most relevant to the focus of this essay?

    (A) NO CHANGE
    (B) These qualities are rare among musical screenwriters.
    (C) One of the finest examples of an artful adaptation is the movie version of *Chicago*.
    (D) These qualities are rare, but they are often a hallmark of musical adaptations that do well at the box office and return their backers' investment.

Questions 16–30 are based on the following passage, *Diving Dangers*.

(16) Despite patience is the most important quality a treasure hunter can have, (17) the hunting about for treasure demands a certain amount of courage too. I have my share of guts but make no boast (18) in regards to ignoring the hazards of diving. (19) All good divers know, the business of plunging into an alien world with an artificial air supply as your only link to the world above (20) this occupation can be (21) more dangerous as stepping into a den of lions. Most of the danger rests within the diver himself. (22)

The (23) devil-may-care diver who shows great bravado underwater is the worst risk of all. He may lose his bearings in the glimmering dim light (24) that penetrates the sea and (25) become separate from his diving companions. He may dive too deep, too long, and suffer painful, sometimes fatal, bends.

Once, (26) when I was salvaging brass from the sunken hulk of an old steel ship, I brushed lightly

Go on to the next page. ⇨

against a huge engine cylinder that looked (27) <u>like it was</u> as solid as it was on the day the ship was launched. Although the pressure of my touch was hardly enough to topple a toy soldier, the heavy mass of cast iron collapsed, (28) <u>having caused</u> a chain reaction in which the rest of the old engine crumbled. Tons of iron dropped all around me. (29) <u>Sheer luck saved me from being crushed.</u> I (30) <u>was</u> wary of swimming around steel shipwrecks ever since.

Diving Dangers **Questions**

16. (F) NO CHANGE
    (G) Although
    (H) However
    (J) Because

17. (A) NO CHANGE
    (B) this
    (C) treasure hunting
    (D) it

18. (F) NO CHANGE
    (G) concerning ignorance of
    (H) to ignore
    (J) about ignoring

19. (A) NO CHANGE
    (B) As all good divers know,
    (C) Like all good divers know,
    (D) As all good divers are knowing,

20. (F) NO CHANGE
    (G) this can
    (H) can
    (J) doing this can

21. (A) NO CHANGE
    (B) as dangerous as
    (C) dangerous as
    (D) so dangerous as

22. Upon reviewing the essay's first paragraph, the writer considers deleting the preceding sentence. If the writer were to delete the sentence, the paragraph would primarily lose:
    (F) an emotional appeal designed to inspire sympathy for divers
    (G) the element of suspense
    (H) a focusing statement suggesting a cause/effect relationship
    (J) a first-person perspective on treasure hunting

23. If the writer were to delete the underlined phrase, the paragraph would primarily lose:
    (A) the connection the writer wants to make between the fate of the diver and spiritual questions
    (B) an essential part of the writer's classification of different types of divers
    (C) a visual image that helps the reader picture the diver
    (D) a vivid adjective reinforcing the writer's point about divers' responsibility for their own fate

24. (F) NO CHANGE
    (G) that is penetrating
    (H) that penetrated
    (J) that has penetrated

25. (A) NO CHANGE
    (B) became separated
    (C) become separated
    (D) became separate

26. (F) NO CHANGE
    (G) during salvaging
    (H) while salvaging
    (J) during the time that I was salvaging

27. (A) NO CHANGE
    (B) as if it was
    (C) as if it were
    (D) DELETE the underlined portion

28. (F) NO CHANGE
    (G) to cause
    (H) caused
    (J) causing

29. Which choice would most clearly communicate the precariousness of the diver's situation?
    (A) NO CHANGE
    (B) Good thing I didn't give the engine cylinder a stronger shove.
    (C) Another day, another near-death experience!
    (D) My experience saw me through yet again.

30. (F) NO CHANGE
    (G) am
    (H) had been
    (J) have been

Go on to the next page.

Questions 31–45 are based on the following passage, *Who Makes the Music?*

This passage is adapted from Aaron Copland, What to Listen for in Music, *1939.*

Most people want to know (31) how are things made? They frankly (32) admit; however, that they feel completely at sea when it comes to understanding (33) how the making of a piece of music is done. Where the composer begins, how he or she manages to (34) keep going, how and where the composer learns the trade—(35) all is shrouded in impenetrable darkness. The composer, (36) fortunately, is a person of mystery and (37) the composers workshop an unapproachable ivory tower.

(38) One of the first things the layperson wants to hear the story of is the part inspiration plays in composing. He or she finds it difficult to believe that composers (39) are not much preoccupied with that question, that composing is as natural for the composer (40) as him or her eating or sleeping. Composing is something that the composer happens (41) to be born to do, and because of that, (42) lost the character of a special virtue in the composer's eyes.

The composer, therefore, does not say: "Do I feel inspired?" He or she says: "Do I feel like composing today?" And if the composer feels like composing, he or she composes. It is more or less (43) like saying to himself or to herself: "Do I feel sleepy?" If you feel sleepy, you go to sleep. If you don't feel sleepy, you stay up. If the composer doesn't feel like composing, (44) he or she doesn't. It's as simple as that.

Who Makes the Music? Questions

31. (A) NO CHANGE
    (B) how are things made.
    (C) how things are made.
    (D) how things are made?

32. (F) NO CHANGE
    (G) admit however
    (H) admit, however,
    (J) admit; however

33. (A) NO CHANGE
    (B) how to make a piece of music.
    (C) how making a piece of music is done.
    (D) how a piece of music is made.

34. Which choice would best clarify the underlined phrase as it is used in this sentence?
    (F) NO CHANGE
    (G) get through the day
    (H) stay in this competitive business
    (J) withstand the pressure

35. (A) NO CHANGE
    (B) all are
    (C) all this is
    (D) all them are

36. (F) NO CHANGE
    (G) nevertheless,
    (H) thereby,
    (J) in short,

37. (A) NO CHANGE
    (B) the composers' workshop
    (C) the composer's workshop
    (D) the workshop of the composer

38. Which choice would most effectively introduce the main idea of this paragraph?
    (F) NO CHANGE
    (G) The layperson doesn't understand the composer's methods.
    (H) Many would-be composers find it frustrating that the process seems to require inborn talent rather than skill that can be taught.
    (J) Laypeople and composers often disagree about the best approach to musical composition.

39. (A) NO CHANGE
    (B) are preoccupied not too much with
    (C) are not preoccupied very with
    (D) are not too very preoccupied with

40. (F) NO CHANGE
    (G) as his or her eating or sleeping.
    (H) as that he or she eats or sleeps.
    (J) as that he or she is eating or sleeping.

41. (A) NO CHANGE
    (B) to have been born
    (C) to having been born
    (D) to be being born

Go on to the next page.

42. (F) NO CHANGE
    (G) it lost
    (H) loses
    (J) it loses

43. (A) NO CHANGE
    (B) as if he or she says to him or to her:
    (C) like saying to his or to her own self:
    (D) like saying to he himself or to she herself:

44. (F) NO CHANGE
    (G) he or she doesn't do it.
    (H) he or she doesn't compose.
    (J) he or she doesn't do any composing.

Question 45 asks about the preceding passage as a whole.

45. Suppose the writer had been asked to write a personal narrative describing his insights into the composer's creative process. Would this essay fulfill that goal?

    (A) Yes, because the writer shares his frustrations that the composer's talent is misunderstood.
    (B) Yes, because the writer includes first-person questions he asks himself in order to begin the creative process.
    (C) No, because the essay is a third-person, objective definition of "composer."
    (D) No, because the essay is a third-person exploration of what the writer knows about composers and what is unknown.

Questions 46–60 are based on the following passage, *A New View of Man*.

(46) The American museum of natural history (47) had long portrayed various aspects of man. Primitive cultures have been shown (48) kind of through habitat groups and displays of man's tools, utensils, and art. In more recent years, (49) there has been a tendency to delineate man's place in nature, displaying his destructive and constructive activities on the earth he inhabits.

(50) For the first time, now, the museum has taken man apart, enlarged the delicate mechanisms that make him run, and examined him as a biological phenomenon. (51) In the new Hall of the Biology of Man, museum technicians have created a series of (52) displays that is instructive to a degree (53) never achieved in an exhibit hall. Using new techniques and new

materials, (54) movement has been produced as well as form and color. It is a human belief (55) that beauty is skin deep only. (56) But nature has proved to be a master designer, not only in the matter of man's bilateral symmetry (57) as well as in the marvelous packaging job that has arranged all man's organs and systems (58) inside his skin covered-case. When these are taken out of the case, greatly enlarged, and given color, they reveal form and design that give the lie to that old saying. (59) Visitors will surprise to discover that man's insides, too, are beautiful.

A New View of Man Questions

46. (F) NO CHANGE
    (G) The American Museum of Natural History
    (H) The American Museum of natural history
    (J) The American museum of Natural History

47. (A) NO CHANGE
    (B) portrayed for a long time
    (C) has long portrayed
    (D) portrays for a long time

48. (F) NO CHANGE
    (G) not only through
    (H) through
    (J) throughout

49. (A) NO CHANGE
    (B) it has been a tendency
    (C) a tendency being
    (D) a tendency is

50. (F) NO CHANGE
    (G) Now for the first time
    (H) Now, for the first time
    (J) Now, for the first time,

51. If the writer were to delete the opening sentence of this paragraph (so the paragraph would begin "In the new Hall of the Biology of Man"), the paragraph would primarily lose:

    (A) a process analysis of the technology that makes the exhibit run
    (B) a transition introducing the theme and significance of the new exhibit
    (C) an argument for the museum's importance and relevance
    (D) a contrast between the American Museum of Natural History and other museums of its kind

Go on to the next page.

52. (F) NO CHANGE
    (G) displays, which are instructive,
    (H) displays that are instructive
    (J) displays as are instructive

53. (A) NO CHANGE
    (B) never before achieved
    (C) never to be achieved
    (D) not never before achieved

54. (F) NO CHANGE
    (G) they have been able to produce movement
    (H) it has been possible to produce movement
    (J) the possibility of producing movement has been realized

55. (A) NO CHANGE
    (B) that only beauty is skin deep.
    (C) only that beauty is skin deep.
    (D) that beauty is only skin deep.

56. If the writer were to delete the preceding sentence, the paragraph would primarily lose:
    (F) a concrete example of a theme brought to life in the museum exhibit
    (G) a sentence setting up the writer's interpretation of the exhibit's meaning
    (H) a comment on the human condition
    (J) part of the writer's critique of the exhibit

57. (A) NO CHANGE
    (B) but also the marvelous
    (C) and in the marvelous
    (D) but also in the marvelous

58. (F) NO CHANGE
    (G) in his skin-covered case.
    (H) within his skin-covered case.
    (J) with his skin covered case.

59. Which choice would best tie the conclusion of the essay to its opening sentence?
    (A) NO CHANGE
    (B) Visitors may be upset by the unusually graphic nature of the display.
    (C) Thanks to the American Museum of Natural History, visitors will be surprised to discover that man's insides, too, are beautiful.
    (D) More visitors than ever will flock to American museums to see groundbreaking exhibits.

Question 60 refers to the preceding passage as a whole.

60. Suppose the writer had been asked to write an essay that compares and contrasts representations of man in art and natural history museums. Would this essay fulfill that assignment?
    (F) Yes, because the essay describes use of form and color as well as other artistic choices in the exhibit.
    (G) Yes, because the essay implies that visiting the Museum of Natural History is a more instructive experience than visiting an art museum.
    (H) No, because the essay focuses on the purpose of all museums, to show the beauty of its subjects.
    (J) No, because the writer's analysis of the natural history exhibit as art is only implied.

Questions 61–75 are based on the following passage, *Modigliani's Art.*

The futurists (61) had broken passionately with Renaissance art. (62) Gone was its single center of interest, its naturalistic color, and its emphasis on humanism. (63) A year only or two later, however, Modigliani (64) is to turn back to (65) one of his ancestors, Botticelli, and, in a most daring union, attempt to join (66) this artists sinuous elegance to the primitive power of (67) newly discovering African American art. (68) Himself limited almost solely to the portraits,(69) to juxtapose Botticelli's fluent line and urbane individualism with tribal memories of Africa, miraculously inventing a language of his own as authentic as those he combined. Wistful, lost in reverie and loneliness, (70) he transcends the stylized conventions that produced his figures. (71) In other hands, these elongated necks, ovoid heads, and flattened noses might seem contrived, even "modernistic." With Modigliani they are not clever technical (72) exercises, they are engrossing human documents touched by humor, pathos, sensuality, and compassion. (73) Because his methods were easily imitated but his content unexpectedly evasive, he established no school. His was a brush as personal as those of the Renaissance masters he admired. A symbol of (74) our 20th century, Modigliani was in love with primitive art while remaining faithful to his own heritage. The transformation (75) he must of affected was not due to a gentle refurbishing of the past but to a new image forged from two alien cultures.

Go on to the next page. ⇨

Modigliani's Art Questions

61. (A) NO CHANGE
    (B) were broke
    (C) broke
    (D) did break

62. (F) NO CHANGE
    (G) Far gone was
    (H) Gone were
    (J) Gone away were

63. (A) NO CHANGE
    (B) Only a year or two later,
    (C) A year or only two later,
    (D) A year or two later only,

64. (F) NO CHANGE
    (G) is to have turned
    (H) was to have turned
    (J) was to turn

65. (A) NO CHANGE
    (B) his ancestor, Botticelli,
    (C) Botticelli, his ancestor,
    (D) Botticelli his ancestor,

66. (F) NO CHANGE
    (G) this artist's
    (H) this artists'
    (J) this artist

67. (A) NO CHANGE
    (B) new discovered
    (C) new discovering
    (D) newly discovered

68. (F) NO CHANGE
    (G) Limiting he
    (H) Limiting him
    (J) Limiting himself

69. (A) NO CHANGE
    (B) juxtaposing
    (C) he juxtaposed
    (D) to have juxtaposed

70. (F) NO CHANGE
    (G) the stylized conventions that produced his figures are transcended.
    (H) transcending the stylized conventions that produced his figures.
    (J) his figures transcend the stylized conventions that produced them.

71. (A) NO CHANGE
    (B) (DO NOT begin a new paragraph) In other hands these elongated necks,
    (C) (Begin new paragraph) In other hands these elongated necks,
    (D) (Begin new paragraph) In other hands, these elongated necks,

72. (F) NO CHANGE
    (G) exercises; they
    (H) exercises and they
    (J) exercises: they

73. Which sentence would best express the writer's assessment of Modigliani's legacy in the art world?

    (A) NO CHANGE
    (B) Modigliani's works were often copied, but Modigliani himself has largely been forgotten.
    (C) Few artists study Modigliani's techniques because they are so difficult to understand.
    (D) Modigliani resisted teaching art because he did not want his techniques to be copied.

74. Which choice would most logically specify the writer's interpretation of Modigliani as a symbol in the essay's closing lines?

    (F) NO CHANGE
    (G) the art-obsessed 20th century
    (H) the abstract 20th-century style
    (J) both 20th-century innovation and embrace of folk traditions,

75. (A) NO CHANGE
    (B) he affected
    (C) he must of effected
    (D) he effected

STOP!

If you finish before time is called, you may check your work on this section only.
Do not turn to any other section in the test.

SECTION 2: MATHEMATICS TEST

60 Minutes, 60 Questions

Turn to Section 2 of your answer sheet (page 482) to answer the questions in this section. You may use the bottom of each page for figuring.

Directions

Solve each problem, choose the correct answer, and then fill in the corresponding oval on your answer sheet.

Do not linger over problems that take too much time. Solve as many as you can; then return to the others in the time you have left for this test.

You are permitted to use a calculator on this test. You may use your calculator for any problems you choose, but some of the problems may best be done without using a calculator.

Note: Unless otherwise stated, all of the following should be assumed.

1. Figures are NOT necessarily drawn to scale.

2. Geometric figures lie in a plane.

3. The word *line* indicates a straight line.

4. The word *average* indicates arithmetic mean.

1. Tommy and Bobby like to watch their school's baseball team play. Tommy watched $\frac{2}{3}$ of all the games the team played last season. Bobby watched 28 games. If Tommy watched more games than Bobby did last season, which of the following could be the number of games the team played last season?

   (A) 33
   (B) 36
   (C) 39
   (D) 42
   (E) 45

2. If 8 people share a winning lottery ticket and divide the cash prize equally, what percent of the prize do 2 of them together receive?

   (F) 8%
   (G) 10%
   (H) 20%
   (J) 25%
   (K) 40%

3. Find the value of $x + x^3 + x^5 + x^6$ if $x = -1$.

   (A) −4
   (B) −2
   (C) 1
   (D) 2
   (E) 4

Go on to the next page. ➡

4. Simplify:

$(4a) + (-6a) - (3a + a)$

(F) $10a$

(G) $4a$

(H) $-4a$

(J) $-6a$

(K) $6a$

5. At 8:00 a.m. the outside temperature was $-15°F$. At 11:00 a.m. the temperature was $0°F$. If the temperature continues to rise at the same uniform rate, what will the temperature be at 5:00 p.m. on the same day?

(A) $-15°$

(B) $-5°$

(C) $0°$

(D) $15°$

(E) $30°$

6. Which of the following is the closest approximation of the lowest cost per shirt, when a box of shirts is purchased?

Number of Shirts	Total Price
1	$12.00
Box of 3	$22.50
Box of 6	$43.40

(F) $7.10

(G) $7.20

(H) $7.30

(J) $7.40

(K) $7.50

7. If $5x^2 - 15x = 0$ and $x \neq 0$, find the value of x.

(A) -10

(B) -3

(C) 10

(D) 5

(E) 3

8. Which inequality is equivalent to the inequality $2(x + 3) > 3(x - 4)$?

(F) $x < 18$

(G) $x < 16$

(H) $x < 14$

(J) $x < 12$

(K) $x < 10$

9. Where $x \neq 1$, the expression $\dfrac{x - 1}{x^3 - x} =$

(A) $\dfrac{1}{x^2} + \dfrac{1}{x}$

(B) $\dfrac{1}{x^3} + \dfrac{1}{x}$

(C) $\dfrac{1}{x^2 - 1}$

(D) $\dfrac{1}{x^2 + x}$

(E) $\dfrac{1}{x^2 - x}$

10. If $a - 3 = 7$, then $2a - 14 =$

(F) -6

(G) -4

(H) 2

(J) 4

(K) 6

Go on to the next page. ⇨

11. $\dfrac{7}{10} + \dfrac{7}{100} + \dfrac{77}{1,000} =$

    (A) 0.0091

    (B) 0.7777

    (C) 0.784

    (D) 0.847

    (E) 0.854

12. Parallel lines m and n are intersected by line l, as shown. Find the value of $x + y$.

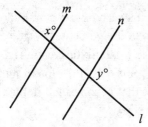

    (F) 180

    (G) 150

    (H) 120

    (J) 90

    (K) It cannot be determined from the information given.

13. If $\dfrac{3x}{4} = 9$, find $6x$.

    (A) 12

    (B) 18

    (C) 27

    (D) 36

    (E) 72

14. In the figure below, each pair of intersecting segments is perpendicular with lengths as shown. Find the length of the dashed line segment.

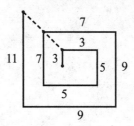

    (F) 7

    (G) $6\sqrt{3}$

    (H) $4\sqrt{2}$

    (J) $\sqrt{46}$

    (K) $\sqrt{59}$

15. If $\sqrt{x}$ is an odd integer, which of the following *MUST* be even?

    (A) x

    (B) $3\sqrt{x}$

    (C) $\sqrt{2x}$

    (D) $2\sqrt{x}$

    (E) x^2

16. If a rectangle is drawn on the grid below with $\overline{MN}$ as one of its diagonals, which of the following could be the coordinates of another vertex of the rectangle?

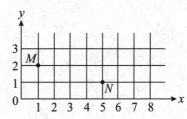

    (F) (1,0)

    (G) (2,0)

    (H) (3,3)

    (J) (4,3)

    (K) (5,2)

Go on to the next page. ⇨

17. According to the table, for what value of x does $f(x) = x + 2$?

x	$f(x)$
0	3
1	4
2	2
3	5
4	8

(A) 0
(B) 1
(C) 2
(D) 3
(E) 4

18. Which equation could represent the graph below?

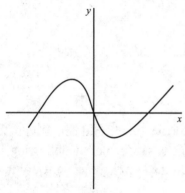

(F) $y = x^3 + 2$
(G) $y = x^3 + 2x + 4$
(H) $y = x^2$
(J) $y = x^3 - x$
(K) $y = x^3 + x^2 - x - 1$

19. The degree measures of the four angles of a quadrilateral are w, x, y, and z, respectively. If w is the average (arithmetic mean) of x, y, and z, then $x + y + z =$

(A) 45°
(B) 90°
(C) 120°
(D) 180°
(E) 270°

20. A certain mixture contains carbon, oxygen, hydrogen, and other elements in the percentages shown in the graph below. If the total mixture weighs 24 pounds, which number represents the closest number of pounds of carbon that is contained in the mixture?

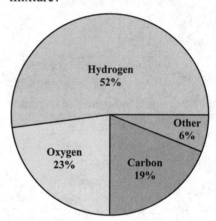

(F) 5.2
(G) 4.6
(H) 2.1
(J) 1.2
(K) 0.5

Go on to the next page. ⇨

21. An athlete runs 90 laps in 6 hours. This is the same as how many laps per minute?

    (A) $\frac{1}{15}$

    (B) $\frac{1}{9}$

    (C) $\frac{1}{4}$

    (D) $\frac{1}{2}$

    (E) 1

22. If $x = 16$, then $x^{-\frac{3}{4}} =$

    (F) $\frac{1}{2}$

    (G) $\frac{1}{4}$

    (H) $\frac{1}{8}$

    (J) $\frac{1}{16}$

    (K) $\frac{1}{32}$

23. Which of the following is a graph of $y = 2x - 4$?

    (A)

    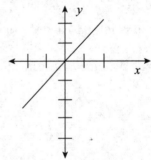

    (B)

    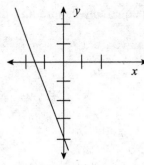

    (C)

    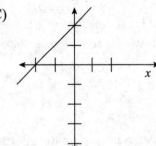

    (D)

    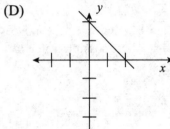

    (E)

    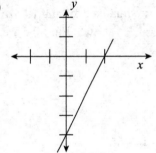

Go on to the next page. ⇨

24. Given that $\left(\frac{3}{10}\right)^2$ is equal to p hundredths, find the value of p.

    (F) 5
    (G) 6
    (H) 9
    (J) 12
    (K) 32

25. Paul's average (arithmetic mean) for 3 tests was 85. The average of his scores for the first 2 tests was also 85. What was his score for the third test?

    (A) 80
    (B) 85
    (C) 90
    (D) 95
    (E) It cannot be determined from the information given.

26. The positive integer x is a multiple of 9 and also a multiple of 12. The smallest possible value of x is

    (F) 3
    (G) 12
    (H) 21
    (J) 36
    (K) 72

27. In the figure below, squares I, II, and III are situated along the x-axis as shown. Find the area of square II

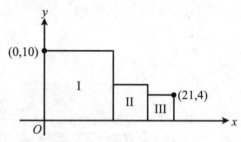

    (A) 16
    (B) 25
    (C) 49
    (D) 100
    (E) 121

28. A certain cup holds 100 grams of butter. If a cake requires 75 grams of butter and a pie requires 225 grams of butter, then 4 cups of butter is *not* enough for any of the following *except*

    (F) 6 cakes
    (G) 2 pies
    (H) 3 cakes and 1 pie
    (J) 2 cakes and 2 pies
    (K) 2 cakes and 1 pie

29. In the rectangular coordinate system below, which of the following is true about line l?

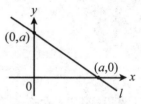

    I.   The slope is -1.
    II. The distance of point $(0,a)$ to point $(a,0)$ is equal to $a\sqrt{2}$.
    III. The acute angle that line l makes with the x-axis is 45°.

    (A) I only
    (B) II only
    (C) III only
    (D) II and III only
    (E) I, II, and III

Go on to the next page. ⇨

30. In the number line below, *a*, *b*, and *c* are real numbers. Which is true?

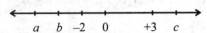

a   b   –2   0   +3   c

(F) $b > -1$
(G) $|b| < 2$
(H) $-|c| = c$
(J) $|b| > |a|$
(K) $|a| > |b|$

31. If the sum of the four terms in each of the diagonal rows is the same, then $A =$

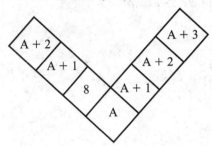

(A) 4
(B) 5
(C) 6
(D) 7
(E) 8

32. The two dials shown below operate simultaneously in the following manner. The hand in A turns *counterclockwise* while the hand in B turns *clockwise*. In the first move, the hand of A moves to 9 at exactly the same moment that the hand of B moves to 3. In the second move, the hand of A moves to 6 at exactly the same moment that the hand of B moves to 6, and so on. If each hand starts at 12, where will each hand be at the end of 17 moves?

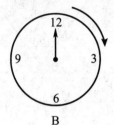

(F) Both at 12
(G) Both at 9
(H) A at 3 and B at 12
(J) A at 3 and B at 9
(K) A at 9 and B at 3

33. A painter earns $10 an hour for all hours spent on a job. For a certain job, he worked from 7:00 a.m. until 5:00 p.m. on Monday, Tuesday, and Thursday, and from 1:00 p.m. until 7:00 p.m. on Wednesday, Friday, and Saturday. How much did he earn for the entire job?

(A) $420
(B) $450
(C) $480
(D) $510
(E) $540

Go on to the next page. ⇨

34. Given △RST below, what is the value of b?

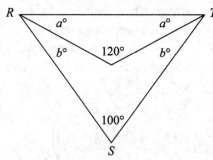

(F) 50°
(G) 40°
(H) 30°
(J) 20°
(K) 10°

35. John works for five days. His daily earnings are displayed on the graph below. If John earned $35 on the sixth day, what would be the difference between the median and the mode of the wages for the six days?

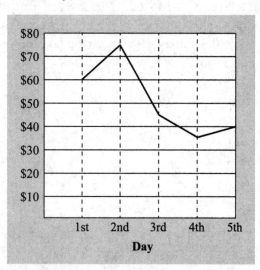

(A) $5.50
(B) $6.50
(C) $7.50
(D) $8.50
(E) $9.50

36. If $@ⓑ = \dfrac{a+1}{b-1}$, where a and b are positive integers and $b > 1$, which of the following is largest?

(F) ②③
(G) ③③
(H) ③⑤
(J) ④⑤
(K) ⑤③

37. In △RST below, RS and ST have lengths equal to the same integer. All of the following could be the area of triangle RST except

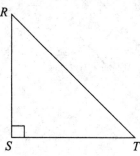

(A) $\dfrac{1}{2}$

(B) 2

(C) $4\dfrac{1}{2}$

(D) $12\dfrac{1}{2}$

(E) 20

38. A rectangular solid has dimensions of 2 feet × 2 feet × 1 foot. If it is sliced in small cubes, each with an edge of length 0.1 foot, what is the maximum number of such cubes that can be formed?

(F) 40
(G) 500
(H) 1,000
(J) 2,000
(K) 4,000

Go on to the next page. ⇨

39. A circle is inscribed in a square. If the perimeter of the square is 40, what is the area of the circle?

   (A) 100π
   (B) 50π
   (C) 40π
   (D) 25π
   (E) 5π

40. Where $i = \sqrt{-1}$, $(4 + 3i)(3 + 4i) =$

   (F) $16 + 25i$
   (G) $12 + 12i$
   (H) 12
   (J) $25i$
   (K) none of the above

41. If $\log_{10}5 = a$, then $\log_{10}2 =$

   (A) $\dfrac{1}{a}$
   (B) $\dfrac{2}{5}a$
   (C) $10 - a$
   (D) $1 - a$
   (E) $a + 3$

42. If $0 \le x° \le 90°$ and $\sin^2 x° = \dfrac{3}{4}$, then $x° =$

   (F) 0
   (G) 30
   (H) 45
   (J) 60
   (K) 90

43. If $f(x) = 2x + 3^x$, what is the value of $f(2)$?

   (A) 9
   (B) 10
   (C) 11
   (D) 12
   (E) 13

44. The graphs of $y = x + 2$ and $y = x^2 + 4x + 4$ intersect at

   (F) $x = 2, x = -1$
   (G) $x = -2$ only
   (H) $x = -1$ only
   (J) $x = -1, x = -2$
   (K) $x = 2, x = 1$

45. In the figure below, AC is a straight line segment. Line segments are drawn from B to D, E, F, G, H, I, J, and K, respectively. Which of the following angles has a degree measure that can be found?

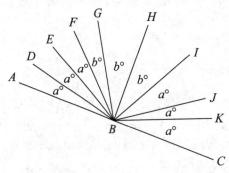

   (A) $\angle FBG$
   (B) $\angle EBG$
   (D) $\angle DBG$
   (D) $\angle GBI$
   (D) $\angle GBJ$

Go on to the next page. ⇨

46. In the figure below, cos θ =

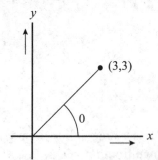

(F) $\dfrac{1}{2}$

(G) $\dfrac{\sqrt{2}}{2}$

(H) $\dfrac{\sqrt{3}}{2}$

(J) 1

(K) $\sqrt{2}$

47. If points (1,2) and (x,y) are on the line represented in the diagram, which of the following could represent the value of x and y?

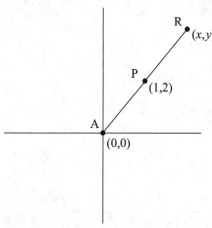

(A) $x = 3, y = 5$

(B) $x = 4, y = 8$

(C) $x = 5, y = 11$

(D) $x = 6, y = 15$

(E) $x = 7, y = 17$

48. According to the table below, of Harry's total collection, U.S. air mail stamps make up

Distribution of Stamps in Harry's Collection	
English	22%
French	18%
South American	25%
U.S.	35%

Distribution of U.S. Stamps in Harry's Collection	
Commemoratives	52%
Special delivery	10%
Postage due	15%
Air mail	23%

(F) 4.00%

(G) 8.05%

(H) 15.50%

(J) 16.00%

(K) 21.35%

49. In order to obtain admission into a special school program, all applicants must take an exam, which is passed by three out of every five applicants. Of those who pass the exam, one-fourth are finally accepted. What is the percentage of all applicants who *fail* to gain admission into the program?

(A) 55

(B) 60

(C) 75

(D) 85

(E) 90

Go on to the next page. ⇨

50. If $\dfrac{\sin \theta}{\tan \theta} = x$, then which of the following is equal to x?

   (F) $\cos \theta$

   (G) $\sin \theta$

   (H) $\dfrac{1}{\cos \theta}$

   (J) $\dfrac{1}{\sin \theta}$

   (K) $\dfrac{\cos^2 \theta}{\sin^2 \theta}$

51. Which of the following represents a possible length of the hypotenuse of a triangle whose perpendicular sides are both integers?

   (A) $\sqrt{44}$

   (B) $\sqrt{45}$

   (C) $\sqrt{46}$

   (D) $\sqrt{47}$

   (E) $\sqrt{48}$

52. At the Bates School, special programs in French and Spanish are available. If there are N students enrolled in the French program and M students enrolled in the Spanish program, including P students enrolled in both programs, how many students are taking only one (but not both) of the language programs?

   (F) $N + M$

   (G) $N + M - P$

   (H) $N + M + P$

   (J) $N + M - 2P$

   (K) $N + M + 2P$

53. Lines l and n are parallel to each other, but line m is parallel to neither of the other two. Find $\dfrac{p}{q}$ if $p + q = 13$.

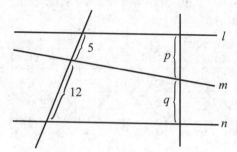

   (A) $\dfrac{13}{5}$

   (B) $\dfrac{12}{5}$

   (C) $\dfrac{7}{6}$

   (D) $\dfrac{1}{5}$

   (E) The answer cannot be determined from the information given.

54. Ross wants to make up three-letter combinations. He wants each combination to have exactly 3 of the following letters: A, B, C, and D. No letter can be used more than once. For example, "AAB" is not acceptable. What is the maximum number of such triplets that Ross can make? (The order of the letters must be considered. Example: "ABC" and "CBA" are acceptable triplets.)

   (F) 6

   (G) 9

   (H) 24

   (J) 27

   (K) 64

Go on to the next page. ⟹

55. The tables below show the number of uniforms ordered at two schools and the cost of the types of uniforms ordered in child and adult sizes. Find the total cost of all the uniforms in child sizes ordered at School B.

Number of Child Uniforms Ordered			
	Type A	Type B	Type C
School A	20	50	40
School B	30	60	50

Cost of Uniforms		
	Child	Adult
Type A	$9	$12
Type B	$10	$14
Type C	$11	$16

(A) $30
(B) $140
(C) $1,420
(D) $1,480
(E) $1,490

56. In the right triangle below, the lengths of the sides are 5 feet and 2 feet. Which of the following is equal to cos $a°$?

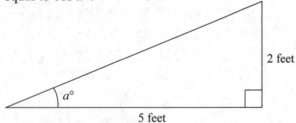

57. The figure below is a piece of fish net. Which of the following statements must be true about an ant crawling on the net from Point A to Point B?

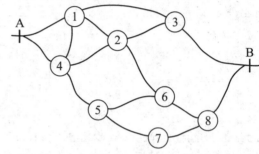

(A) If it goes through 2, it must go through 7.
(B) If it goes through 3, it must go through 1.
(C) Its route must go through either 2 or 7.
(D) If it goes through 4, it must go through 3 or 5.
(E) If it goes through 8, it must go through 2 or 5.

58. A sequence of integers is defined as follows: The first term is 2, and every additional term is obtained by subtracting 2 from the previous term and tripling the resulting difference. For example, the second term would be 0. Which of the following is a true statement about this sequence?

(F) The terms behave as follows: even, even, odd, odd, even, even, odd, odd, . . .
(G) The terms behave as follows: even, odd, even, odd, even, odd, . . .

(F) $\dfrac{2}{\sqrt{29}}$

(G) $\dfrac{5}{\sqrt{29}}$

(H) $\dfrac{2}{5}$

(J) $\dfrac{5}{2}$

(K) $\dfrac{5}{7}$

Go on to the next page. ⇨

(H) The terms behave as follows: even, even, even, odd, odd, odd, even, even, even, . . .

(J) All of the terms, except for the first one, are odd.

(K) All of the terms are even.

59. If n is a member of both the sets A and B below, which of the following must be true?

$$A = \left\{\frac{3}{8}, 2, \frac{3}{2}, 6, \frac{13}{2}, 8\right\}$$

$$B = \left\{\frac{3}{8}, \frac{8}{3}, 6, 8\right\}$$

  I. n is an integer

 II. $8n$ is an integer

III. $n = 6$

(A) None

(B) I only

(C) II only

(D) III only

(E) I and II only

60. If the segments shown in the diagram have the indicated lengths, find the value of x.

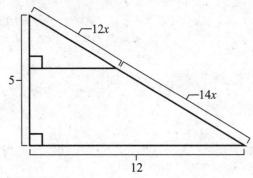

(F) 13

(G) 12

(H) 5

(J) 2

(K) $\frac{1}{2}$

STOP!

If you finish before time is called, you may check your work on this section only.

Do not turn to any other section in the test.

SECTION 3: READING TEST

35 Minutes, 40 Questions

Turn to Section 3 of your answer sheet (page 483) to answer the questions in this section.

Directions

There are four passages in this test. Each passage is followed by several questions. After reading a passage, choose the best answer to each question and fill in the corresponding circle on your answer sheet. You may refer to the passages as often as necessary.

Passage I: Prose Fiction

This passage is adapted from Elizabeth Taylor's 1957 novel Angel, *set in early twentieth-century England.*

"I never thought I would live in such a beautiful place," Mrs. Deverell told Angel when they first moved in. But nowadays she often suffered from the lowering pain of believing herself happy when she was not. "Who could
5 be miserable in such a place?" she asked. Yet, on misty October evenings or on Sundays, when the church bells began, sensations she had never known before came over her.

She sometimes felt better when she went back to
10 see her friends on Volunteer Street; but it was a long way to go. Angel discouraged the visits, and her friends seemed to have changed. Either they put out their best china and thought twice before they said anything, or they were defiantly informal—"You'll have to take us
15 as you find us"—and would persist in making remarks like "Pardon the apron, but there's no servants here to polish the grate." In each case, they were watching her for signs of grandeur or condescension. She fell into little traps they laid and then they were able to report to
20 the neighbors. "It hasn't taken *her* long to start putting on airs." She had to be especially careful to recognize everyone she met, and walked up the street with an expression of anxiety which was misinterpreted as disdain.

25 The name "Deverell Family Grocer" stayed for a long time over the shop, and she was pleased that it should, although Angel frowned with annoyance when she heard of it. Then one day the faded name was scraped and burnt away, and on her next visit to
30 Volunteer Street, she saw that "Cubbage's Stores" was painted there instead. She felt an unaccountable panic and dismay at the sight of this and at the strange idea of other people and furniture in those familiar rooms. "Very nice folk," she was told. "She's so
35 friendly. Always the same. And such lovely kiddies." Mrs. Deverell felt slighted and wounded; going home she was so preoccupied that she passed the wife of the landlord of The Volunteer without seeing her. "I wouldn't expect Alderhurst people to speak to a bar-
40 keep's wife," the woman told everyone in the saloon bar. "Even though it was our Gran who laid her husband out when he died." All of their kindnesses were remembered and brooded over, any past kindness Mrs. Deverell had done—and they were many—only served
45 to underline the change which had come over her.

At a time of her life when she needed the security of familiar things, these were put beyond her reach. It seemed to her that she had wasted her years acquiring skills which in the end were to be of no use to her:
50 her weather-eye for a good drying day; her careful ear for judging the gentle singing sound of meat roasting in the oven; her touch for the freshness of meat; and how, by smelling a cake, she could tell if it were baked. These arts, which had taken so long to perfect, fell
55 now into disuse. She would never again, she grieved, gather up a great fragrant line of washing in her arms to carry indoors. One day when they had first come to the new house, she had passed through the courtyard where sheets were hanging out: she had taken them in
60 her hands and, finding them just at the right stage of drying, had begun to unpeg them. They were looped all about her shoulders when Angel caught her. "Please

Go on to the next page. ⇨

leave work to the people who should do it," she had
said. "You will only give offense." She tried hard not to
65 give offense, but it was difficult. The smell of ironing
being done or the sound of eggs being whisked set up a
restlessness which she could scarcely control.

The relationship of mother and daughter seemed to
have been reversed, and Angel, now in her early twen-
70 ties, was the authoritative one; since girlhood she had
been taking on one responsibility after another, until
she had left her mother with nothing to perplex her
but how to while away the hours when the servants
were busy and her daughter was at work. Fretfully, she
75 would wander around the house, bored, but afraid to
interrupt; she was like an intimidated child.

Passage I Questions

1. The "Deverell Family Grocer" sign (line 25) seems
to represent what to Mrs. Deverell?

   (A) an embarrassing symbol of the family's low-
   status past
   (B) a cause for envy when it's replaced with the
   more modern "Cubbage's Stores" sign
   (C) a cherished symbol of familiarity and comfort
   (D) a cause for sadness at the changing face of the
   old neighborhood

2. In noting that Mrs. Deverell fell into the "little
traps they laid" (line 19), the author means that her
former friends

   (F) were testing her to see how much Mrs.
   Deverell really knew about high society
   (G) interpreted her every action as proof that Mrs.
   Deverell had changed and now saw herself as
   superior
   (H) were insecure about their place in Mrs.
   Deverell's new life
   (J) were gossips intent on getting information they
   could pass on to the curious neighborhood

3. The author suggests that the signs of condescension Mrs. Deverell's friends attribute to her are in
actuality

   (A) self-consciousness and fear of offending her
   friends
   (B) absentmindedness
   (C) a haughty sense of pride
   (D) depression

4. Angel's interactions with her mother suggest a
pattern of

   (F) status consciousness
   (G) disobedience to parental authority
   (H) artistic free spirit
   (J) aversion to doing manual labor

5. By the end of the passage, the reader can reasonably conclude that Mrs. Deverell

   (A) will find comfort in simple household objects
   and tasks
   (B) will reach out to her old friends for comfort
   and companionship
   (C) will become more and more desperate in trying to convince her friends of her worth
   (D) will become increasingly bored and anxious
   as she feels less and less like herself

6. "Nothing to *perplex* her" in line 72 refers to

   (F) how easily Mrs. Deverell is confused by her
   new role and responsibilities
   (G) Angel's efforts to make her mother's life easy
   and comfortable
   (H) Mrs. Deverell's attempts to figure out her old
   friends' attitude toward her
   (J) the lack of things to occupy Mrs. Deverell's
   hands and mind

7. The author's primary purpose in including the
scene in which Mrs. Deverell passes sheets drying
on the line (lines 57–61) is to show

   (A) how far she has come since she did this kind
   of work on a daily basis
   (B) how she used her daughter's resources to
   escape household chores
   (C) her natural gravitation toward, and enjoyment
   of, housekeeping tasks
   (D) the difference in socioeconomic status
   between Mrs. Deverell and her old neighbors

8. What possible significance might the author have
intended in naming the street on which Mrs.
Deverell used to live "Volunteer Street" (line 10)?

   (F) to emphasize how active Mrs. Deverell had
   once been in doing charitable work
   (G) to contrast the work ethic of people in the old
   neighborhood with Mrs. Deverell's new life of
   leisure

Go on to the next page. ⇨

(H) to underscore the fact that many men in the old neighborhood had served in the military

(J) to underscore Mrs. Deverell's attachment to the old neighborhood and the life she would freely choose if she could

9. The primary difference between the attitudes of Mrs. Deverell and her daughter toward housekeeping can best be summarized as

(A) a clash between neatness and untidiness

(B) a clash between belief in self-reliance and a sense of entitlement to household help

(C) a perception of household chores as a pleasant sensory experience versus a perception of household chores as drudgery beneath a wealthy person

(D) a difference of opinion about technique

10. Mrs. Deverell's character can best be expressed as

(F) rigid and resistant to change

(G) limited in intelligence and imagination

(H) willing to sacrifice herself in order to please others

(J) frustrated by modernization

Passage II: Social Science

This passage is adapted from "Strongholds of the Aristocracy," an article about the importance of castles in medieval Europe and how they affected the society at that time.

Medieval Europe abounded in castles. Germany alone had ten thousand and more, most of them now vanished; all that a summer journey in the Rhineland and the southwest now can show are a handful of ruins

5 and a few nineteenth-century restorations. Nevertheless, anyone journeying from Spain to the Dvina, from Calabria to Wales, will find castles rearing up again and again to dominate the open landscape. There they still stand, in desolate and uninhabited districts where the

10 only visible forms of life are herdsmen and their flocks, with hawks circling the battlements, far from the traffic and comfortably distant even from the nearest small town: these were the strongholds of the European aristocracy.

15 The weight of aristocratic dominance was felt in Europe until well after the French Revolution; political and social structure, the Church, the general tenor

of thought and feeling were all influenced by it. Over the centuries, consciously or unconsciously, the other

20 classes of this older European society—the clergy, the bourgeoisie and the "common people"—adopted many of the outward characteristics of the aristocracy, who became their model, their standard, their ideal. Aristocratic values and ambitions were adopted along-

25 side aristocratic manners and fashions of dress. Yet the aristocracy were the object of much contentious criticism and complaint; from the thirteenth century onwards their military value and their political importance were both called in question. Nevertheless, their

30 opponents continued to be their principal imitators. In the eleventh and twelfth centuries, the reforming Papacy and its clerical supporters, although opposed to the excessively aristocratic control of the Church (as is shown by the Investiture Contest), nevertheless them-

35 selves first adopted and then strengthened the forms of this control. Noblemen who became bishops or who founded new Orders helped to implant aristocratic principles and forms of government deep within the structure and spiritual life of the Church. Again, in the

40 twelfth and thirteenth centuries the urban bourgeoisie, made prosperous and even rich by trade and industry, were rising to political power as the servants and legal proteges of monarchy. These "patricians" were critical of the aristocracy and hostile towards it. Yet they also

45 imitated the aristocracy, and tried to gain admittance to the closed circle and to achieve equality of status. Even the unarmed peasantry, who usually had to suffer more from the unrelieved weight of aristocratic dominance, long remained tenaciously loyal to their lords, held to

50 their allegiance by that combination of love and fear, *amor et timor*, which was so characteristic of the medieval relationship between lord and servant, between God and man.

The castles and strongholds of the aristocracy

55 remind us of the reality of their power and superiority. Through the long warring centuries when men went defenseless and insecure, the "house," the lord's fortified dwelling, promised protection, security and peace to all whom it sheltered. From the ninth to the eleventh

60 centuries, if not later, Europe was in many ways all too open. Attack came from the sea, in the Mediterranean from Saracens and Vikings, the latter usually in their swift, dragon-prowed, easily maneuvered longboats, manned by some sixteen pairs of oarsmen and with a

Go on to the next page. ⇨

65 full complement of perhaps sixty men. There were periods when the British Isles and the French coasts were being raided every year by Vikings and in the heart of the continent marauding Magyar armies met invading bands of Saracens. The name of Pontresina, near
70 St. Moritz in Switzerland, is a memento of the stormy tenth century; it means *pons Saracenorum*, the "fortified Saracen bridge," the place where plundering expeditions halted on their way up from the Mediterranean.

It was recognized in theory that the Church and the
75 monarchy were the principal powers and that they were bound by the nature of their office to ensure peace and security and to do justice; but at this period they were too weak, too torn by internal conflicts to fulfill their obligations. Thus more and more power passed into
80 the hands of warriors invested by the monarchy and the Church with lands and rights of jurisdiction, who in return undertook to support their overlords and to protect the unarmed peasantry.

Their first concern, however, was self-protection.
85 It is almost impossible for us to realize how primitive the great majority of these early medieval "castles" really were. Until about 1150 the fortified houses of the Anglo-Norman nobility were simple dwellings surrounded by a mound of earth and a wooden stockade.
90 These were the motte and bailey castles: the motte was the mound and its stockade, the bailey an open court lying below and also stockaded. Both were protected, where possible, by yet another ditch filled with water, the moat. In the middle of the motte there was a
95 wooden tower, the keep or *donjon*, which only became a genuine stronghold at a later date and in places where stone was readily available. The stone castles of the French and German nobility usually had only a single communal room in which all activities took place.
100 In such straitened surroundings, where warmth, light and comfort were lacking, there was no way of creating an air of privacy. It is easy enough to understand why the life of the landed nobility was often so unrestrained, so filled with harshness, cruelty and brutality, even in
105 later, more "chivalrous" periods. The barons' daily life was bare and uneventful, punctuated by war, hunting (a rehearsal for war), and feasting. Boys were trained to fight from the age of seven or eight, and their education in arms continued until they were twenty-one,
110 although in some cases they started to fight as early as fifteen. The peasants of the surrounding countryside,

bound to their lords by a great variety of ties, produced the sparse fare which was all that the undeveloped agriculture of the early medieval period could sustain.
115 Hunting was a constant necessity, to make up for the lack of butcher's meat, and in England and Germany in the eleventh and twelfth centuries even the kings had to progress from one crown estate to another, from one bishop's palace to the next, to maintain themselves and
120 their retinue.

Passage II Questions

11. According to the passage, class conflict in the Middle Ages was kept in check by

    (A) the fact that most people belonged to the same class
    (B) tyrannical suppressions of rebellions by powerful monarchs
    (C) the fact that all other classes admired and attempted to emulate the aristocracy
    (D) the fear that a relatively minor conflict would lead to a general revolution

12. According to the author, the urban bourgeoisie were hostile to the aristocracy because

    (F) the bourgeoisie were prevented by the aristocracy from seeking an alliance with the kings
    (G) aristocrats often confiscated the wealth of the bourgeoisie
    (H) the bourgeoisie saw the aristocracy as their rivals
    (J) the aristocrats often deliberately antagonized the bourgeoisie

13. According to the passage, castles were originally built

    (A) as status symbols
    (B) as strongholds against invaders
    (C) as simple places to live in
    (D) as luxurious chateaux

14. One of the groups that invaded central Europe during the Middle Ages from the ninth century on was the

    (F) Magyars
    (G) Franks
    (H) Celts
    (J) Welsh

Go on to the next page. ⇨

15. It can be seen from the passage that the aristocracy originally included

    (A) the great landowners
    (B) the king's warriors
    (C) merchants who became wealthy
    (D) slaves who had rebelled

16. The reform popes eventually produced an aristocratic church because

    (F) they depended on the aristocracy for money
    (G) they themselves were more interested in money than in religion
    (H) they were defeated by aristocrats
    (J) many aristocrats entered the structure of the church and impressed their values on it

17. According to the passage, hunting served the dual purpose of

    (A) preparing for war and getting meat
    (B) learning how to ride and how to shoot
    (C) testing horses and men
    (D) getting furs and ridding the land of excess animals

18. The phrase "*amor et timor*" in line 51 is used to describe

    (F) the rivalry between the bourgeoisie and the aristocracy
    (G) the Church's view of man and his relationship to God
    (H) the peasant's loyalty to the aristocracy
    (J) the adaptation of aristocratic manners and dress

19. The passage indicates that protection of the peasantry was implemented by

    (A) the king's warriors
    (B) the Magyar mercenaries
    (C) the replacement of wood towers by stone donjons
    (D) the ruling monarchy

20. The interiors of the castles within which the nobility lived can be generally characterized as offering

    (F) a haven for the pursuit of individual interests
    (G) a center for schooling boys in the liberal arts
    (H) a secure but uncomfortable environment
    (J) a space for gluttonous celebrations

Passage III: Humanities

This passage is adapted from the essay "Self-Reliance" by the American writer Ralph Waldo Emerson.

Infancy conforms to nobody: all conform to it, so that one babe commonly makes four or five out of the adults who prattle and play to it. So God has armed youth and puberty and manhood no less with its own piquancy
5 and charm, and made it enviable and gracious and its claims not to be put by, if it will stand by itself. Do not think the youth has no force, because he cannot speak to you and me. Hark! in the next room his voice is sufficiently clear and emphatic. It seems he knows how to
10 speak to his contemporaries. Bashful or bold, then, he will know how to make us seniors very unnecessary.

    The nonchalance of boys who are sure of a dinner, and would disdain as much as a lord to do or say aught to conciliate one, is the healthy attitude of
15 human nature. A boy is in the parlor what the pit is in the playhouse; independent, irresponsible, looking out from his corner on such people and facts as pass by, he tries and sentences them on their merits, in the swift, summary way of boys, as good, bad, interesting, silly,
20 eloquent, troublesome. He lumbers himself never about consequences, about interests; he gives an independent, genuine verdict. You must court him: he does not court you. But the man is, as it were, clapped into jail by his consciousness. As soon as he has once acted or spoken
25 with eclat, he is a committed person, watched by the sympathy or the hatred of hundreds, whose affections must now enter into his account. There is no Lethe for this. Ah, that he could pass again into his neutrality.

    These are the voices which we hear in solitude,
30 but they grow faint and inaudible as we enter into the world. Society everywhere is in conspiracy against the manhood of every one of its members. Society is a joint-stock company, in which the members agree, for the better securing of his bread to each shareholder, to
35 surrender the liberty and culture of the eater. The virtue in most request is conformity. Self-reliance is its aversion. It loves not realities and creators, but names and customs.

    Whoso would be a man must be a nonconformist. He
40 who would gather immortal palms must not be hindered by the name of goodness, but must explore if it be goodness. Nothing is at last sacred but the integrity of your own mind.

Go on to the next page. ⇨

No law can be sacred to me but that of my nature.
45 Good and bad are but names very readily transferable to
that or this; the only right is what is after my constitution, the only wrong what is against it. A man is to carry
himself in the presence of all opposition as if every
thing were titular and ephemeral but he. I am ashamed
50 to think how easily we capitulate to badges and names,
to large societies and dead institutions. Every decent and
well-spoken individual affects and sways me more than
is right. I ought to go upright and vital, and speak the
rude truth in all ways.
55   I shun father and mother and wife and brother, when
my genius calls me. I would write on the lintels of
the doorpost, *Whim*. I hope it is somewhat better than
whim at last, but we cannot spend the day in explanation. Expect me not to show cause why I seek or why I
60 exclude company. Then, again, do not tell me, as a good
man did to-day, of my obligation to put all poor men
in good situations. Are they *my* poor? I tell thee, thou
foolish philanthropist, that I grudge the dollar, the dime,
the cent, I give to such men as do not belong to me and
65 to whom I do not belong. There is a class of persons to
whom by all spiritual affinity I am bought and sold; for
them I will go to prison, if need be; but your miscel-
laneous popular charities; the education at college of
fools; the building of meetinghouses to the vain end to
70 which many now stand; alms to sots; and the thousand-
fold Relief Societies;—though I confess with shame I
sometimes succumb and give the dollar, it is a wicked
dollar which by and by I shall have the manhood to
withhold.
75   For nonconformity the world whips you with its
displeasure. And therefore a man must know how to
estimate a sour face. The by-standers look askance on
him in the public street or in the friend's parlor. If this
aversion had its origin in contempt and resistance like
80 his own, he might well go home with a sad countenance;
but the sour faces of the multitude, like their sweet
faces, have no deep cause, but are put on and off as the
wind blows and a newspaper directs. Yet is the discon-
tent of the multitude more formidable than that of the
85 senate and the college.
     The other terror that scares us from self-trust is
our consistency; a reverence for our past act or word,
because the eyes of others have no other data for computing our orbit than our past acts, and we are loath to
90 disappoint them.

But why should you keep your head over your shoulder? Why drag about this corpse of your memory, lest
you contradict somewhat you have stated in this or that
public place? Suppose you should contradict yourself;
95 what then?
     A foolish consistency is the hobgoblin of little minds,
adored by little statesmen and philosophers and divines.
With consistency a great soul has simply nothing to do.
He may as well concern himself with his shadow on
100 the wall. Speak what you think now in hard words, and
to-morrow speak what to-morrow thinks in hard words
again, though it contradict everything you said to-day.—
"Ah, so you shall be sure to be misunderstood."—Is
it so bad, then, to be misunderstood? Pythagoras was
105 misunderstood, and Socrates, and Jesus, and Luther, and
Copernicus, and Galileo, and Newton, and every pure
and wise spirit that ever took flesh. To be great is to be
misunderstood.

Passage III Questions

21. The main theme of the selection is best expressed
    as follows:

    (A) "A foolish consistency is the hobgoblin of
        little minds."
    (B) "Eternal youth means eternal independence."
    (C) "Whoso would be a man must be a noncon-
        formist."
    (D) "Colleges are designed to educate fools."

22. We are most nonconformist during our period of

    (F) infancy
    (G) puberty
    (H) youth
    (J) old age

23. According to the author, "To be great is to be mis-
    understood" means that

    (A) one should never say exactly what one means
    (B) to be misunderstood is to be great
    (C) all great men have always been misunder-
        stood
    (D) a man should not hesitate to change his mind
        if he sees the need to, even at the risk of being
        considered inconsistent

Go on to the next page. ⇨

24. The refusal of young people to cater to accepted public opinion is, according to the author,

    (F) characteristic of the rebelliousness of youth
    (G) a healthy attitude of human nature
    (H) a manifestation of deep-seated immaturity
    (J) simply bad manners

25. From the selection, one may infer that the "pit in the playhouse" was

    (A) a section containing the best seats in the theater
    (B) favored by independent, outspoken, unselfconscious playgoers
    (C) an underground theater
    (D) a generally staid, quiet section of the theater, favored by young people only

26. "Society is a joint-stock company" (lines 32–33) is one way in which the author shows

    (F) that the public is anti-culture
    (G) that society is highly organized and structured
    (H) how society rejects self-reliance
    (J) that there is no room for solitude in our world

27. The word "eclat" (line 25), as used in this selection, means

    (A) violence and force
    (B) disrespect and resistance
    (C) reason and logic
    (D) spirit and enthusiasm

28. "I would write on the lintels of the doorpost, *Whim*." By this, the author means

    (F) that one should renounce his immediate family
    (G) that signposts have an important educational function in our society
    (H) that an impulsive action may have a subsequent rational explanation
    (J) that one must never be held responsible for what one says and does

29. The statement that best sums up the spirit and sense of this selection is

    (A) "Nothing is at last sacred but the integrity of your own mind."
    (B) "With consistency a great soul has simply nothing to do."

    (C) "Do not think the youth has no force, because he cannot speak to you and me."
    (D) "The virtue in most request is conformity."

30. The author suggests that people can resist the pressure to conform if they remember

    (F) that society reacts negatively to ideas that violate their deeply held values and beliefs
    (G) that people's public demeanor oftentimes differs from their private behavior
    (H) that "sour" faces are like public opinion, fickle and based on shallow beliefs
    (J) that society is easily bored and is always seeking novelty

Passage IV: Natural Science

This passage is adapted from the article "The Bleeding Disease."

Queen Victoria ruled the British Empire for more than 63 years—the longest reign in England's history. During her lifetime, England was more prosperous than it had ever been before.

5   But if England prospered under her rule, Queen Victoria's own family did not. For in her genes—the coded chemical units that pass on characteristics from one generation to another—she carried an often fatal genetic defect. She was a carrier of hemophilia (heem-
10 oh-FEEL-ee-uh), a disease in which the blood clots, or coagulates, very slowly.

    Strangely, only Victoria's male descendants became "bleeders." All of her daughters and granddaughters were apparently healthy. Yet many later gave birth to
15 hemophiliac sons.

    The genes—including defective ones—are strung like beads on objects known as chromosomes. These are found within every human cell. Each normal human cell carries 46 chromosomes—two sets of 23. One set
20 of 23 chromosomes originally comes from the mother's ovum—the egg cell. The other set of 23 comes from one of the father's sperm cells. Each set carries a complete "blueprint" for the "design" of a human being.

    When the egg is fertilized by the sperm, both sets
25 of chromosomes come together within the egg. But they do not necessarily produce a "blend" of characteristics.Why? Because some genes can control their "matching" gene (say, eye-color gene) from the other

Go on to the next page. ⇨

parent. These "controller" genes are called dominants.
30 The genes that can be controlled are called recessives. Whenever a dominant gene and a recessive gene are paired, the individual always develops the characteristic of the dominant gene.

The gene that causes hemophilia is recessive. If it
35 is paired with a "healthy" gene, the individual does not develop the symptoms of hemophilia. But even so, the gene is still present. It can be passed along to the next generation.

This explains why not all of Victoria's children actu-
40 ally suffered from hemophilia. But why should Victoria's daughters *never* get the disease?

One particular set of chromosomes that we inherit are known as X and Y chromosomes.

Egg cells contain only X chromosomes. A female
45 thus always passes along X chromosomes. But sperm cells contain either an X or a Y chromosome. A male can pass along one or the other.

The gene that causes hemophilia is always linked to the X chromosome. It is a sex-linked gene (just like
50 color-blindness).

As you recall, each normal cell contains 46 chromosomes—23 donated by the mother and 23 donated by the father. In a female—such as Queen Victoria—such cells hold two X chromosomes. And, in Victoria, only
55 one of these chromosomes held the defective gene. Since a female's egg cells hold only one X chromosome, there was a 50 percent chance of any of Victoria's children inheriting the defective gene.

What's more, since the gene is also recessive, a
60 female will not show the symptoms of the disease if she has one non-hemophilic X in her cells. (Victoria's daughters had one non-hemophilic X in their cells.)

But the male has only one X that he inherits from his mother. Without an "opposite" X, the defective
65 X becomes dominant. Thus, Victoria's sons would become hemophiliacs if they inherited her defective X chromosome.

Queen Victoria probably never knew that she carried the defective hemophilia gene. Her doctors could
70 not explain the disease or even treat it.

But today, medical scientists not only know the genetic basis of the disease, but how to control it as well. Hemophilia is caused by the lack of a protein—one of the building blocks of tissue—in the blood. This
75 protein is called Factor VIII or AHF—antihemophilic

factor. Without this protein, the blood of hemophiliacs clots extremely slowly.

One important method of treating hemophiliacs is to concentrate AHF extracted from the plasma of donated
80 blood. Plasma is the thin, watery part of the blood that contains many blood proteins. When the AHF is injected into a hemophiliac, the blood begins to clot normally.

Passage IV Questions

31. A female descendant of Queen Victoria would probably not be the victim of hemophilia due to the fact that

    (A) both of her genes are always recessive and so she will never contract the disease
    (B) she has two X chromosomes, and one counteracts the other
    (C) she contains only Y chromosomes, which never carry the gene for hemophilia
    (D) she has neither an X nor a Y chromosome

32. A characteristic very similar to hemophilia is

    (F) hair color
    (G) Rh blood factor
    (H) skin pigmentation
    (J) color-blindness

33. The determining factors of the hereditary characteristics of an individual are known as

    (A) genes
    (B) chromosomes
    (C) amino acids
    (D) blood cells

34. The human sperm cell contains

    (F) 44 chromosomes and 2 X chromosomes
    (G) 46 chromosomes
    (H) 23 chromosomes
    (J) 23 chromosomes, and 1 X and 1 Y chromosome

35. The protein needed by a hemophiliac can be found in and obtained from

    (A) tissues of the body
    (B) human gametes
    (C) egg cells
    (D) blood plasma

Go on to the next page. ⇨

36. The primary problem associated with hemophilia is that the hemophiliac

    (F) has blood that circulates too slowly
    (G) develops blood clots easily
    (H) tends to bleed excessively
    (J) is hypersensitive to proteins in the blood

37. The most accurate statement about the process that contributes to the formation of the genetic blueprint is

    (A) male and female chromosomes create an equal blend of genetic traits
    (B) the male chromosome always determines the dominant genes
    (C) the female chromosome always determines the dominant genes
    (D) gender does not always determine which genes act as dominants and recessives

38. The *antihemophilic factor* referred to in lines 75–76 is

    (F) a set of precautions taken to avoid passing the disease on through the generations
    (G) a new testing procedure that allows parents to determine if their children will inherit the disease

    (H) an injectable substance that can counteract the effects of hemophilia
    (J) a high-protein diet regimen that can counteract the effects of hemophilia

39. A sex-linked gene (line 49) is one that

    (A) is always linked to either the X or Y chromosome but not both
    (B) determines gender in humans
    (C) is linked only to the X chromosome
    (D) is linked only to the Y chromosome

40. As an illustration of how a genetic defect may work in lines 63–67, Queen Victoria's sons

    (F) never got hemophilia
    (G) always got hemophilia
    (H) got hemophilia if they had two X chromosomes
    (J) got hemophilia if their sole X chromosome was defective

STOP!

If you finish before time is called, you may check your work on this section only.
Do not turn to any other section in the test.

SECTION 4: SCIENCE TEST

35 Minutes, 40 Questions

Turn to Section 4 of your answer sheet (page 483) to answer the questions in this section.

Directions

There are several passages in this test. Each passage is followed by several questions. After reading a passage, choose the best answer to each question and fill in the corresponding oval on your answer sheet. You may refer to the passages as often as necessary.

You are NOT permitted to use a calculator on this test.

Passage I
Study 1

A man develops a bacterial infection and feels ill. On day 4 of his infection he feels terrible, so he visits the doctor's office. The doctor does a bacterial culture and prescribes penicillin, an antibiotic, to treat the bacterial infection. The prescription is for 10 days. The man begins taking the prescription on day 4, but he is feeling better by day 8. Disregarding the doctor's instructions, he stops taking the penicillin on day 8. He returns to the doctor on day 13 when he feels ill again.

Figure 1: Bacterial load in the lungs of an individual with pneumonia

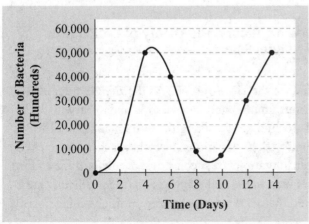

Study 2

Additionally, a town in Finland was studied over a span of several years. Researchers collected data on the number of times that antibiotics were used to treat middle ear infections in children. Bacteria from these infections were cultured and studied, and the percent of strains that were resistant to one or more antibiotics was tracked over the same time period. The following graphs present these data.

Figure 2: Annual use of antibiotics for middle ear infections in a single town

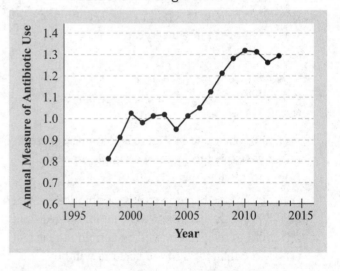

Figure 3: Annual percent of resistant bacteria from middle ear infections in a single town

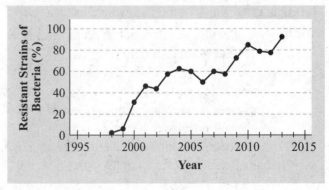

Go on to the next page. ⇨

Passage I Questions

1. Based on the information in Figure 1, after 4 days of antibiotics, approximately how many bacteria (in hundreds) were in the man's lungs?

   (A) about 50,000
   (B) about 25,000
   (C) about 10,000
   (D) about 5,000

2. According to the information in Figure 1, what might the man most correctly conclude happened when he stopped taking the antibiotics?

   (F) He developed a new infection of different bacteria that made him sick.
   (G) The antibiotics made him more ill than the initial bacterial infection.
   (H) The infection could not be successfully treated by the antibiotic.
   (J) The bacteria that remained after he stopped treatment with the antibiotic reproduced, causing further infection.

3. Based on the data given in Figure 2, antibiotic use was at its lowest in which year?

   (A) 1998
   (B) 2005
   (C) 2008
   (D) 2014

4. Assuming the trend in Figure 3 continues, what might we expect to find if we sample a population from this town in the year 2020?

   (F) 50% of the bacteria will be antibiotic-resistant.
   (G) 80% of the bacteria will be antibiotic-resistant.
   (H) 90% of the bacteria will be antibiotic-resistant.
   (J) More than 90% of the bacteria will be antibiotic-resistant.

5. Scientists examining the data from Figures 2 and 3 might draw which of the following conclusions?

   (A) Use of antibiotics does not affect the presence of resistant strains of bacteria.
   (B) Increases in use of antibiotics coincide with increases in resistant bacteria.
   (C) Decreases in use of antibiotics coincide with decreases in resistant bacteria.
   (D) Antibiotic-resistant bacteria are unaffected by human activities.

Passage II

In the history of biology, several scientists developed theories for the process by which evolution of organisms occurs. Two such theories were developed by Jean-Baptiste Lamarck and Charles Darwin.

Lamarck's Theory: The Theory of Inheritance by Acquired Characteristics

In the early 1800s, Lamarck developed his theory of the process by which evolution happens. He had noted that an animal's environment seems to lead to change in the animal's body structure; for instance, blindness in moles, which live underground in tunnels where sight would be useless. Lamarck's theory was based on commonly held beliefs of his time and his observations of animals in their environments. First, Lamarck noted that, over time, animals developed from simple organisms into complex organisms. Therefore, single-celled organisms predated mammals. Simple organisms never disappeared, he thought, because they were able to spontaneously generate.

Second, Lamarck noted that organisms seem to match their environments in many ways, and the offspring of organisms tend to be similar to their parents. Lamarck postulated that organisms adapt to their environments based on use and disuse of characteristics. For instance, if an organism similar to a giraffe, but with a short neck, lived in an environment where the only food available was the leaves on the trees, the environment would provide a driving force for the "giraffe" to reach higher and higher to gather food. As the giraffe used its neck more by stretching, the neck would grow longer. Over time, an organism with a very long neck would emerge. When that long-necked individual reproduced, its offspring would have the long neck it acquired through use.

Darwin's Theory: The Theory of Evolution by Natural Selection

In the early 1830s, Charles Darwin was the ship naturalist for the HMS *Beagle*. As the *Beagle* traveled to various uninhabited lands and islands, Darwin's job was to study and catalog the animal and plant life found in these locations. Darwin noted what he called "transmutation" of species of a particular type of bird, the finch, in the Galapagos Islands. Specifically, he noted that while all the species of finch on the nearby

Go on to the next page. ⇨

islands shared many common features, the differences in the beaks, and in the ways of life, among these birds were often great.

Darwin's theory was based on his understanding of population sizes and dynamics. Others had already demonstrated that while organisms reproduce at an exponential rate, the environment has a limiting amount of resources. He had also noted great variety even within species (for instance, though all humans share many traits, some traits, like eye color, have great variety). This variety exists at birth, based on traits given by the parents. Because of the overly large number of individuals produced, and because of the variety in those individuals, the individuals with traits that make them in some way better able to function in their environment tend to survive and thereby reproduce. These individuals are then more likely to pass on the traits that have made them successful. Over time, Darwin hypothesized, the population develops into a new species with traits that have been "selected" by the demands of the environment.

Passage II Questions

6. A key feature of Lamarck's theory is that

    (F) variety is inborn in organisms
    (G) organisms reproduce uncontrollably
    (H) use of characteristics leads to their further development
    (J) organisms are unaffected by their environment

7. If you were to fray (tear) the wings of a butterfly and continue this practice on the offspring for the next 20 generations, according to Lamarck's theory of evolution, the latest offspring might

    (A) be born with frayed wings
    (B) have normal wings
    (C) have normal wings but higher susceptibility to frayed wings during normal use
    (D) be expected to give rise to normal-winged offspring

8. Which of the following assumptions is implicit in Darwin's theory of evolution by natural selection?

    (F) Many organisms do not survive to reproduce.
    (G) The environment is not a major factor in the features of organisms.
    (H) All organisms in a given population are the same.
    (J) New species appear quickly.

9. According to Darwin's theory of evolution, giraffes have long necks because

    (A) they were able to stretch their shorter necks to reach the trees for food
    (B) no food was available on the ground
    (C) the giraffes with the longest necks were able to survive and reproduce
    (D) the giraffes with the shortest necks had an advantage

10. A large island is devastated by a volcanic eruption. Most of the horses die except for the heaviest males and heaviest females of the group. They survive, reproduce, and perpetuate the population. The offspring of the next generation are on average heavier than every previous generation of horses. Which of the following theories is supported by these observations?

    (F) Lamarck's theory, because the horses are heavier.
    (G) Lamarck's theory, because the lighter horses died.
    (H) Darwin's theory, because the offspring of the next generation are heavier.
    (J) Darwin's theory, because the horses survived.

11. According to Lamarck's theory, simple organisms exist because

    (A) they are able to survive in many environments
    (B) they develop traits through use of features that allow them to survive
    (C) they are regenerated by spontaneous generation
    (D) they develop from more complex organisms

12. Darwin's finches provided the best evidence for his theory because

    (F) they had many different beaks
    (G) they lived on many different islands
    (H) there was variety in their population
    (J) their beaks allowed them to survive in a specific environment

Go on to the next page.

Passage III

Isotopes are versions of atoms of a given element that have either a higher or a lower mass than a typical atom of that element. Isotopes differ in the number of neutrons they contain. Atoms consist of three types of particles: protons, neutrons, and electrons. Table 1 provides information about each of these particles.

Protons determine the identity of an atom; that is to say, an atom with eight protons is, by definition, oxygen. Since virtually all of the mass of an atom comes from its protons and neutrons, the difference between isotopes of one type of atom is determined by the number of neutrons present in the nucleus. Table 2 provides information about three known isotopes of carbon.

Table 3 provides information about naturally occurring radioactive isotopes and their abundance relative to other isotopes of that element.

Table 1

Particle	Location in the Atom	Charge of Particle	Mass of Particle
Proton	Nucleus	+1	1 atomic mass unit
Neutron	Nucleus	Neutral	1 atomic mass unit
Electron	Outside of nucleus	−1	5.44×10^{-4} atomic mass units

Table 2

Name	Total Protons (Atomic #)	Total Neutrons	Total Protons and Neutrons (Mass #)	Total Electrons
Carbon-12	6	6	12	6
Carbon-13	6	7	13	6
Carbon-14	6	8	14	6

Passage III Questions

13. According to the information in Table 1, the majority of the mass of an atom is located where?

    (A) in the nucleus
    (B) outside the nucleus
    (C) distributed evenly throughout the atom
    (D) in the protons

14. According to Table 2, all of the isotopes of carbon share which features in common?

    (F) the number of protons only
    (G) the number of neutrons only
    (H) the number of neutrons and protons
    (J) the number of protons and electrons

15. Biologists have used carbon-14 as a radioactive isotope for following the movement of carbon in biochemical processes. For instance, carbon dioxide containing carbon-14 can be provided to plants, and, due to the radioactive qualities of carbon-14, we can see how the carbon dioxide is used in photosynthesis. According to Table 3, carbon-14 can easily be used for this purpose because

    (A) it is very abundant, so biologists can obtain a lot of carbon-14
    (B) it is very rare, so it is unlikely that the plant would naturally have any carbon-14 in it
    (C) it is very radioactive, so it is easy to see
    (D) it glows because of its radioactivity

Table 3

Isotope	Abundance (%)
Hydrogen-3	0.00013
Carbon-14	Trace
Potassium-40	0.0012
Rubidium-87	27.8
Indium-115	95.8
Rhenium-187	62.9
Platinum-190	0.012

Go on to the next page. ⇨

16. According to Table 3, some elements are more common in their radioactive isotopes than they are in other forms. Some examples of these elements include

(F) hydrogen-3 and rhenium-187

(G) rubidium-87, rhenium-187, and indium-115

(H) rhenium-187 and indium-115

(J) potassium-40

17. According to Table 1, the major difference between protons and neutrons is

(A) their charge

(B) their mass

(C) their location

(D) There is no difference.

Passage IV

In addition to studying the products of chemical reactions and processes, chemists often study the energy used and produced in chemical reactions. Figures 1 and 2 provide potential energy diagrams for endothermic reactions, such as the reaction that occurs in a chemical cold pack, and exothermic reactions, such as combustion. Figure 3 provides the energy diagram for a reaction in which a catalyst speeds the process.

Figure 1: Endothermic reaction

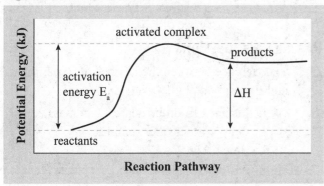

Figure 2: Exothermic reaction

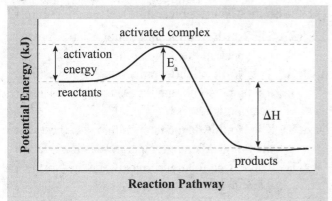

Figure 3: Catalyzed exothermic reaction

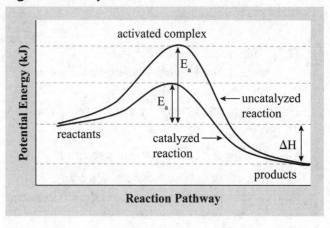

Passage IV Questions

18. Based on Figure 1, which of the following statements is most correct?

(F) The reactants in an endothermic reaction have more potential energy than do products.

(G) The reactants in an endothermic reaction have less potential energy than do products.

(H) The reactants in an endothermic reaction have the same potential energy as the products.

(J) The reactants in an endothermic reaction spontaneously convert into product.

19. Based on Figure 2, activation energy is

(A) the energy released when reactants are converted into product

(B) the energy used when reactants are converted into product

(C) the energy used to start the reaction to make product

(D) the same as the reactant

20. Photosynthesis is a process in which plants take low-energy molecules of carbon dioxide and, using energy from the sun, make high-energy glucose molecules for later use. This process would best be classified as

(F) endothermic, because there is more energy in the reactant than there is in the product

(G) endothermic, because there is more energy in the product than there is in the reactant

(H) exothermic, because there is more energy in the reactant than there is in the product

(J) exothermic, because there is more energy in the product than there is in the reactant

Go on to the next page. ⇒

21. Based on Figure 3, the difference between a catalyzed reaction and an uncatalyzed reaction is that

(A) different reactants are used
(B) different products are made
(C) there is more potential energy during a cata-
lyzed reaction
(D) there is less potential energy during a cata-
lyzed reaction

22. Based on Figure 2, an exothermic reaction

(F) releases energy into the environment
(G) takes in and uses energy from the environment
(H) has no overall change in energy
(J) does not produce any product

Passage V

Sunspots are areas of magnetic disturbance on the sun's
surface. Sunspots can change from day to day and
month to month. A scientist hypothesized that since the
sun provides the majority of Earth's energy, the presence of sunspots might affect the energy of the planet.
He decided to collect data to determine if sunspots do
indeed affect the energy of the planet, as measured by
temperature of the ocean.

Experiment 1

The number of sunspots on the sun's surface was
recorded monthly, and the temperature of the surface
of the ocean was measured monthly at approximately
the same point about 3 miles away from the nearest
landmass in the North Atlantic.

Experiment 2

The number of sunspots on the sun's surface was
recorded monthly, and the temperature of the surface
of the ocean was measured monthly at approximately
the same point about 3 miles away from the nearest
landmass in the South Atlantic.

Experiment 3

The number of sunspots on the sun's surface was
recorded monthly, and the temperature of the surface
of the ocean was measured monthly at approximately
the same point about 3 miles away from the nearest
landmass in the tropics.

    The data from all three experiments were combined
to create the following charts.

Figure 1: Ocean surface temperatures recorded in
Experiments 1–3

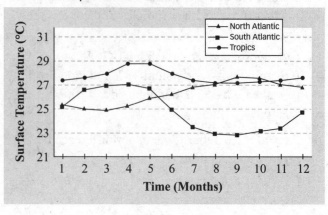

Figure 2: Mean number of sunspots per month

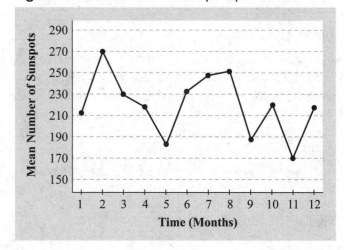

Passage V Questions

23. The difference between the designs of Experiment
1 and Experiment 2 is

(A) the distance from the nearest landmass
(B) the depth of the water sample
(C) the time of day
(D) the latitude of the test site

24. Which of the following best describes the relationship between the North Atlantic temperatures and
the South Atlantic temperatures as seen in Figure 1?

(F) The North Atlantic and South Atlantic data
both peak in the same months.
(G) The North Atlantic temperature is lowest in
the same month that the South Atlantic temperature is lowest.
(H) The North Atlantic temperature is highest when
the South Atlantic temperature is lowest.
(J) There is no relationship between the North
Atlantic and South Atlantic data.

Go on to the next page.

25. The researcher observed that water temperature in the tropics varies less than either the North Atlantic or the South Atlantic water temperature. The best explanation for this observation is that

   (A) the South Atlantic receives more sunlight than the tropics
   (B) the North Atlantic receives more sunlight than the tropics
   (C) the tropics receive a more consistent amount of sunlight than the North or South Atlantic
   (D) the water contains more salt in the tropics

26. Based on Figure 1, the temperature we would expect for the South Atlantic in the next month (13) would be

   (F) 22–23°C
   (G) 23–24°C
   (H) 24–25°C
   (J) 25–26°C

27. The best conclusion about the relationship between ocean surface temperature and sunspots is that

   (A) there is no relationship between ocean surface temperature and sunspots
   (B) the number of sunspots is high when the water temperature is low
   (C) the number of sunspots is high when the water temperature is high
   (D) the temperature in the tropics determines the number of sunspots

28. The scientist proposes that perhaps the number of sunspots does not affect water temperature because of water's high specific heat and resistance to change in temperature. He wonders if air temperature is related to the number of sunspots. The best way to test this hypothesis would be to

   (F) redo Experiment 1, taking air temperature readings in the same spot 25 feet above the ocean's surface
   (G) redo all three experiments, taking air temperature readings in all three spots 25 feet above the surface of the water
   (H) take the temperature every day for one week in New York City
   (J) redo Experiment 2, taking air temperature readings in the same spot 25 feet above the ocean's surface

Passage VI

A physics student performed experiments to study the effects of several factors on the falling time of an object.

Experiment 1

An apparatus with a long, marked vacuum tube and a dispenser on a pulley system was set up. The dispenser dropped small metal balls of equal mass (2 grams) from heights that increased by 3 meters in each trial, and the student recorded the time each ball took to reach the ground. Air resistance was minimized by the presence of the vacuum tube.

Table 1: Height versus drop time with 2-gram balls

Height of Drop (m)	Drop Time (s)
6	1.2
9	1.4
12	1.6
15	1.8
18	1.9
21	2.1
24	2.2
27	2.3
30	2.5

Experiment 2

The student repeated the first experiment using the same apparatus. However, this time she used metal balls with equal mass of 10 grams. The time of the drop was again recorded.

Table 2: Height versus drop time with 10-gram balls

Height of Drop (m)	Drop Time (s)
6	1.2
9	1.4
12	1.6
15	1.8
18	1.9
21	2.1
24	2.2
27	2.3
30	2.5

Go on to the next page. ⇨

Passage VI Questions

29. Which of the following was the independent variable (the variable that can be manipulated) in each experiment?

(A) drop time
(B) height of drop
(C) mass of balls
(D) type of ball

30. Experiments 1 and 2 were repeated, this time outside of the vacuum tube using a 10-gram ball and a 2-gram cube of the exact same metal. The 10-gram mass landed before the 2-gram mass in each trial. What is the best explanation for this phenomenon?

(F) The larger mass dropped faster because it was more affected by air resistance than the smaller mass.
(G) The larger mass dropped faster because it was less affected by air resistance than the smaller mass.
(H) The smaller mass dropped more slowly because it was less affected by air resistance than the larger mass.
(J) The larger mass dropped faster because it was heavier than the smaller mass.

31. Which of the following graphs best represents the relationship between height of drop and drop time in Experiment 1?

(A)

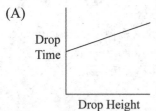

(B)

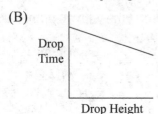

(C)

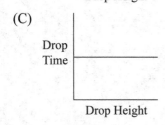

(D)

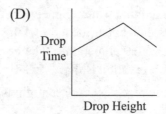

32. If Experiment 2 were continued and the 10-gram mass were dropped from a height of 36 m in a vacuum, what drop time would you expect?

(F) 2.5 to 2.7 seconds
(G) 2.7 to 2.9 seconds
(H) 2.9 to 3.1 seconds
(J) 3.1 to 3.3 seconds

33. Perhaps the *most* striking thing that Experiments 1 and 2 show is which of the following?

(A) The time it takes for a ball to drop is related to the height it drops.
(B) The height that a ball drops is related to the time it needs to drop.
(C) The time that it takes a ball to drop a certain height is independent of the mass of the ball.
(D) The height that a ball drops is based on multiples of 3.

34. The dependent variable in Experiment 2 is

(F) drop height
(G) drop time
(H) the mass of the ball
(J) the type of metal used

Passage VII

Scientists have puzzled over the origins and development of life. In the 18th and 19th centuries, several scientists conducted experiments to determine whether life comes only from life or if life can be spontaneously generated from inanimate matter.

Experiment 1

In 1745, John Needham conducted a simple experiment based on the observation that boiling of liquids kills the microorganism that spoil foods. Needham boiled a sample of chicken broth, then poured the broth into a flask, which he sealed completely. After a few days, he noted the growth of microorganisms in the broth.

Go on to the next page. ⇨

Experiment 2

Twenty years later, an Italian biologist named Lazzaro Spallanzani performed a variation on Needham's experiment. Spallanzani placed samples of chicken broth in three sets of flasks. The broth in the first set of flasks was boiled for one hour; then air was drawn out of the flasks and the flasks were sealed completely by melting the mouths of the flasks closed. The second set of flasks was assembled and sealed in the same manner, but the broth was boiled only a few minutes before sealing. The third batch was assembled and boiled in the same manner as the first set but was sealed with corks that could allow air in.

Spallanzani noted no growth in the set of flasks that had been boiled for one hour and sealed. The flasks that were sealed after a few minutes of boiling and the flasks that were sealed with cork both showed signs of microorganism growth within a few days.

Experiment 3

In 1859, Louis Pasteur conducted an experiment to determine once and for all whether microorganisms spontaneously generate or whether they are present in the air. Pasteur used three sets of flasks. All flasks were filled with meat broth. The first set of flasks was boiled and was then left open to the air. The second set of flasks were special in their design; after the meat broth was boiled, Pasteur melted the neck of these flasks into an S shape to allow air in but prevent dust and particles from making their way into the broth. The final set of flasks was boiled and sealed with cotton; this would again allow air into the flask but prevent entry of dust and particles.

Figure 1: Diagram of Pasteur's S-necked flask

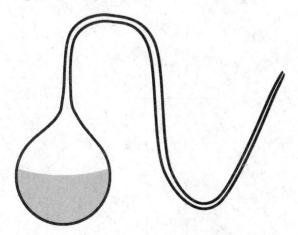

After several days, Pasteur noted that the first set of flasks contained microorganisms that caused cloudiness and rotting of the meat broth. The second and third sets of flasks were both free from microorganism growth. Further, if Pasteur tilted the flask with the S-shaped neck to allow the broth to touch the bottom of the S, then allowed the flask to sit, microorganisms grew. S-shaped flasks that were not subjected to this treatment remained free of microorganisms.

Passage VII Questions

35. The major difference between the flasks from Experiment 1 and Experiment 2 was that

    (A) the flasks in Experiment 2 were sealed, while the flasks in Experiment 1 were not

    (B) the flasks in Experiment 1 were sealed completely, while the flasks in Experiment 2 were not

    (C) the broth in Experiment 1 was boiled, while the broth in Experiment 2 was not

    (D) the broth in Experiment 1 was boiled in a separate container, while the broth in Experiment 2 was boiled in the flasks

36. One example of a control group in Experiment 3 was

    (F) the flasks that were boiled and left open to the air

    (G) the flasks that were boiled and then sealed with an S-shaped neck

    (H) the flasks that were boiled and then sealed with cotton balls

    (J) there was no control group in Experiment 3

37. Needham concluded from Experiment 1 that microorganisms are able to spontaneously generate from a "life force" left after boiling. The problem with Needham's conclusion, based on the design of his experiment, is that

    (A) microorganisms are not able to grow in chicken broth

    (B) the broth was poured after boiling into a flask that had already been exposed to air and dust

    (C) the broth was poured before boiling into a flask that had already been exposed to air and dust

    (D) the broth was boiled in the same flask that he sealed

Go on to the next page. ⇨

38. After Spallanzani's experiment, Needham argued that Spallanzani had not disproved spontaneous generation. Rather, he said, Spallanzani had destroyed the "life force" of the broth in the first set of flasks by boiling for too long and by not allowing access to any air, which would replenish the "life force." The flasks in Pasteur's experiment (Experiment 3), which were designed to test Needham's assertions about the "life force," were

    (F) only the flasks that were boiled and left completely open at the top
    (G) only the flasks that were boiled and sealed into an S
    (H) only the flasks that were boiled and sealed with cotton
    (J) both the flasks that were sealed into an S and the flasks that were sealed with cotton

39. The most likely reason that microorganisms grew in S-shaped flasks after Pasteur tipped them was that

    (A) the "life force" from the air was allowed to enter the broth
    (B) the dust and particles from the air contained microorganisms that had settled into the bottom of the S
    (C) the broth was already contaminated
    (D) he had not boiled the flask for long enough

40. In 1936, Alexander Oparin published *The Origin of Life*, in which he detailed the conditions under which he believed the first life developed on Earth. Many scientists were reluctant to believe his conclusions because of Pasteur's experiment. More recently, scientists have accepted that spontaneous generation could have occurred under the conditions Oparin specified because

    (F) Pasteur's experiment was invalid because he did not have any control groups
    (G) Pasteur's experiment was invalid because he did not have enough control groups
    (H) Pasteur's experiment was valid but had only proven that life could not spontaneously generate under one specific set of conditions
    (J) Needham's experiment was valid; Pasteur's was not

Note:

If you plan to take the ACT Plus Writing, take a five-minute break and then continue with the Writing Test on page 523.

If you do not plan to take the ACT Plus Writing, turn to page 529 for instructions on scoring your multiple-choice tests.

STOP!

If you finish before time is called, you may check your work on this section only.
Do not turn to any other section in the test.

SECTION 5: WRITING TEST (OPTIONAL)

40 Minutes

Turn to the sheets on pages 525–528 to write your essay.

Directions

You may use the unlined pages in this test booklet to plan your essay. These pages will not be scored. **You must write your essay in pencil on the lined pages in the answer folder.** Your writing on those lined pages will be scored. You may not need all the lined pages, but to ensure you have enough room to finish, do NOT skip lines. You may write corrections or additions neatly between the lines of your essay, but do NOT write in the margins of the lined pages. **Illegible essays cannot be scored, so you must write (or print) clearly.**

If you finish before time is called, you may review your work. Lay your pencil down immediately when time is called.

When the supervisor announces that 40 minutes have passed, you must stop writing the essay. Do not go on to any other section in the test.

You may make notes on this page, but you must write your essay on the answer sheet.

Writing Prompt

It has often been said that rapid technological change requires us to change our morals, customs, and institutions. This observation is believable only if we assume that humanity was made for the machine, not the machine for humanity. If anything, technological progress makes our sense of tradition more necessary than ever.

Maintaining traditions is not (or need not be) merely a resistance to change, but a positive attachment to some particular way of life and the community that embodies it. However, many people still insist that technological advances still affect traditions and compromise morals, customs, and institutions.

Carefully read the following perspectives, which describe the effect of technological advances on traditions concerning morals, customs, and institutions.

Perspective One

Technological progress, with all its innovation and scientific developments, can enforce traditional modes in all areas, including morals, customs, and institutions.

Perspective Two

Technological advances compromise long-held traditions in light of the radical effects they have on our lifestyle, communication, and other aspects of living and working. Technological advances also make us change our way of thinking.

Perspective Three

Technological advances can reinforce traditions depending on how they are used. It is up to the individual to utilize new technologies to their best advantage and to maintain morals and customs so that technology and traditions do not conflict.

Essay Directions

Write a meaningful and logical essay in which you describe and evaluate multiple perspectives on the effect of technological advances on traditions concerning morals, customs, and institutions. In your essay, make sure that you

- clearly state and analyze your own perspective in relation to at least one other perspective
- support your statements with clear reasoning and specific examples
- organize your material logically
- communicate effectively using standard written English

Go on to the next page.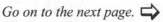

Note that your perspective may be completely in agreement with any of the others, may be partially in agreement, or may be in complete disagreement. In any case, you must support your essay with logic, making detailed references and providing specific examples.

Note on Planning the Essay

Plan your essay using the space here. These pages will not be scored.

Develop ideas and plan your essay using the space below. Consider the following points as you critically think about what you are going to write.

Strengths and weaknesses related to the three perspective presented:

- What insights can be found in them and what insights do they fail to show?
- Why might they be persuasive to others or why might they not be persuasive?

Your personal experiences, knowledge, and values:

- What is your own perspective on this issue, and what are the strengths and weaknesses of that perspective?
- How will you support your perspective in your essay?

SECTION 5: WRITING TEST (OPTIONAL)

Begin your essay on this page. If you need more space, continue on the next page. Do not write outside of the essay box.

Continue on the next page if necessary.

Continuation of essay from previous page. Write below only if you need more space.

Continue on the next page if necessary.

Continuation of essay from previous page. Write below only if you need more space.

Continue on the next page if necessary.

Continuation of essay from previous page. Write below only if you need more space.

HOW DID YOU DO ON THIS TEST?

Pages 531–537 will show you how to calculate
your scores on this test. Explanatory answers
with strategies and basic skills follow.

THERE'S ALWAYS ROOM
FOR IMPROVEMENT!

ANSWER KEY

Section 1: English Test Answers

1. D	20. H	39. A	58. H
2. G	21. B	40. G	59. C
3. C	22. H	41. B	60. J
4. H	23. D	42. J	61. C
5. B	24. F	43. A	62. H
6. H	25. C	44. H	63. B
7. D	26. H	45. D	64. J
8. F	27. C	46. G	65. A
9. C	28. J	47. C	66. G
10. H	29. A	48. H	67. D
11. B	30. J	49. A	68. J
12. J	31. C	50. J	69. C
13. A	32. H	51. B	70. J
14. J	33. D	52. H	71. D
15. D	34. F	53. B	72. G
16. G	35. B	54. G	73. A
17. C	36. J	55. D	74. J
18. J	37. C	56. G	75. D
19. B	38. F	57. D	

English Test Raw Score
(number of correct answers) _____

Section 2: Mathematics Test Answers

1. E	16. K	31. B	46. G
2. J	17. D	32. K	47. B
3. B	18. J	33. C	48. G
4. J	19. E	34. K	49. D
5. E	20. G	35. C	50. F
6. G	21. C	36. K	51. B
7. E	22. H	37. E	52. J
8. F	23. E	38. K	53. E
9. D	24. H	39. D	54. H
10. K	25. B	40. J	55. C
11. D	26. J	41. D	56. G
12. F	27. C	42. J	57. E
13. E	28. K	43. E	58. K
14. H	29. E	44. J	59. C
15. D	30. K	45. C	60. K

Mathematics Test Raw Score
(number of correct answers) _____

Section 3: Reading Test Answers

1. C	11. C	21. C	31. B
2. G	12. H	22. F	32. J
3. A	13. B	23. D	33. A
4. F	14. F	24. G	34. H
5. D	15. B	25. B	35. D
6. J	16. J	26. H	36. H
7. C	17. A	27. D	37. D
8. J	18. H	28. H	38. H
9. C	19. A	29. A	39. A
10. H	20. H	30. H	40. J

Reading Test Raw Score
(number of correct answers) _____

Section 4: Science Test Answers

1. C	11. C	21. D	31. A
2. J	12. J	22. F	32. G
3. A	13. A	23. D	33. C
4. J	14. J	24. H	34. G
5. B	15. B	25. C	35. D
6. H	16. H	26. J	36. F
7. A	17. A	27. A	37. B
8. F	18. G	28. G	38. J
9. C	19. C	29. B	39. B
10. H	20. G	30. G	40. H

Science Test Raw Score
(number of correct answers) _____

TABLE FOR CONVERTING
RAW SCORES TO SCALE SCORES

| Raw Scores (number of correct answers) | | | | | | Your Scale Score |
Test 1 English	Test 2 Mathematics	Test 3 Reading	Test 4 Science	Scale Score		
75	60	40	40	36	English Test	_____
72–74	58–59	39	39	35	Mathematics Test	_____
71	57	38	38	34	Reading Test	_____
70	55–56	37	37	33	Science Test	_____
68–69	54	35–36	—	32		
67	52–53	34	36	31		
66	50–51	33	35	30	Sum of scores	_____
65	48–49	32	34	29		
63–64	45–47	31	33	28	Composite score	_____
62	43–44	30	32	27	(sum ÷ 4)	
60–61	40–42	29	30–31	26		
58–59	38–39	28	28–29	25		
56–57	36–37	27	26–27	24		
53–55	34–35	25–26	24–25	23		
51–52	32–33	24	22–23	22		
48–50	30–31	22–23	21	21		
45–47	29	21	19–20	20		
43–44	27–28	19–20	17–18	19		
41–42	24–26	18	16	18		
39–40	21–23	17	14–15	17		
36–38	17–20	15–16	13	16		
32–35	13–16	14	12	15		
29–31	11–12	12–13	11	14		
27–28	8–10	11	10	13		
25–26	7	9–10	9	12		
23–24	5–6	8	8	11		
20–22	4	6–7	7	10		
18–19	—	—	5–6	9		
15–17	3	5	—	8		
12–14	—	4	4	7		
10–11	2	3	3	6		
8–9	—	—	2	5		
6–7	1	2	—	4		
4–5	—	—	1	3		
2–3	—	1	—	2		
0–1	0	0	0	1		

NORMS TABLES

Use the tables on page 533.

	Your Estimated Percent at or below on Practice Test
English	_____
Mathematics	_____
Reading	_____
Science	_____
Composite	_____
Combined English/Writing	_____
Writing	_____

National Distributions of Cumulative Percents for ACT Test Scores
ACT-Tested High School Graduates from Recent Years

Score	English	Mathematics	Reading	Science	Composite	Score
36	99	99	99	99	99	36
35	99	99	99	99	99	35
34	99	99	99	99	99	34
33	98	99	97	99	99	33
32	97	98	95	98	99	32
31	96	97	94	98	98	31
30	94	96	91	97	97	30
29	92	94	89	96	95	29
28	90	92	86	94	92	28
27	87	89	82	92	89	27
26	84	85	78	90	85	26
25	80	80	74	85	81	25
24	74	75	70	79	75	24
23	69	69	64	73	69	23
22	64	63	58	65	63	22
21	58	58	53	57	56	21
20	51	53	48	48	48	20
19	43	47	41	38	40	19
18	36	41	34	29	33	18
17	31	33	30	21	26	17
16	26	24	24	16	19	16
15	21	14	19	12	13	15
14	15	07	15	08	08	14
13	11	02	09	06	05	13
12	09	01	06	04	02	12
11	06	01	03	02	01	11
10	04	01	01	01	01	10
09	03	01	01	01	01	09
08	02	01	01	01	01	08
07	01	01	01	01	01	07
06	01	01	01	01	01	06
05	01	01	01	01	01	05
04	01	01	01	01	01	04
03	01	01	01	01	01	03
02	01	01	01	01	01	02
01	01	01	01	01	01	01
Mean	20.6	20.8	21.4	20.9	21.1	
S.D.	5.9	5.1	6.1	4.7	4.9	

ACT Writing Test Norms

Score	Combined English/Writing	Writing	Score
36	99		36
35	99		35
34	99		34
33	99		33
32	99		32
31	97		31
30	95		30
29	93		29
28	90		28
27	86		27
26	82		26
25	77		25
24	72		24
23	66		23
22	57		22
21	51		21
20	42		20
19	35		19
18	29		18
17	23		17
16	19		16
15	14		15
14	10		14
13	7		13
12	5	99	12
11	4	99	11
10	2	98	10
09	1	89	09
08	1	77	08
07	1	44	07
06	1	29	06
05	1	9	05
04	1	5	04
03	1	1	03
02	1	1	02
01	1		01
Mean	21.4	7.5	
S.D.	5.4	1.7	

6-POINT HOLISTIC SCORING RUBRIC
FOR THE ACT WRITING TEST

It is recommended that you approach two adults who you know are well qualified to judge basic grammar and composition as your two scorers for your practice Writing Test—perhaps an English teacher, a college-age student majoring in English or journalism, a parent, etc. Have those two adults read through this scoring rubric and refer to it when they score your practice test.

A Few Words about Scoring the Essay

Even with some errors in spelling, punctuation, and grammar, a student can get a top score on the essay. The highly trained high school and college composition teachers who score the essays will follow a rubric that focuses upon content, organization, and language usage and sentence structure. Each essay will be independently scored on a 1–6 scale by two such readers in *four* domains: Ideas and Analysis, Development and Support, Organization, and Language Use. If the readers' scores differ by more than two points, the test will be evaluated by a third reader. Fewer than 2 percent of all scored essays require a third reader.

Some general points about the scoring rubrics are summarized here. For full descriptions of the criteria for each of the four domains, refer to "Preparing for the ACT Test" at https://www.act.org/content/dam/act/unsecured/documents/Preparing-for-the-ACT.pdf. Essays at each level will exhibit all or most of the characteristics described below.

Score = 6

Essays at this score point demonstrate effective skill in responding to the task.

The essay shows a clear understanding of the task. The essay takes a position on the issue and may offer a critical context for discussion. The essay addresses complexity by examining different perspectives presented on the issue, and by evaluating the implications and/or complications of the issue, and/or by fully responding to counterarguments to the writer's position. Development of ideas is ample, specific, and logical. Most ideas are fully elaborated. A clear focus on the specific issue in the prompt is maintained. The organization of the essay is clear: the organization may be somewhat predictable or it may grow from the writer's purpose. Ideas are logically sequenced. Most transitions reflect the writer's logic and are usually integrated into the essay. The introduction and conclusion are effective, clear, and well developed. The essay shows a good command of language. Sentences are varied and word choice is varied and precise. There are few, if any, errors to distract the reader.

Score = 5

Essays at this score point demonstrate well-developed skill in responding to the task.

The essay shows a clear understanding of the task. The essay takes a position on the issue and may offer a broad context for discussion. The essay shows recognition of complexity by partially evaluating the implications and/or complications of the given perspectives, and by responding to counterarguments to the writer's position. Development of ideas is specific and logical. Most ideas are elaborated, with clear movement between general statements and specific reasons, examples, and details. Focus on the specific issue in the prompt is maintained. The organization of the essay is clear, although it may be predictable. Ideas are logically sequenced, although simple and obvious transitions may be used. The introduction and conclusion are clear and generally well developed. Language is competent. Sentences are somewhat varied and word choice is somewhat varied and precise. There may be a few errors, but they are rarely distracting.

Score = 4

Essays at this score point demonstrate adequate skill in responding to the task.

The essay shows an understanding of the task. The essay takes a position on the issue and may offer some context for discussion based on the given perspectives. The essay may show some recognition of complexity by providing some response to counterarguments to the writer's position. Development of ideas is adequate, with some movement between general statements and specific reasons, examples, and details. Focus on the specific issue in the prompt is maintained throughout most of the essay. The organization of the essay is apparent but predictable. Some evidence of logical sequencing of ideas is apparent, although most transitions are simple and obvious. The introduction and conclusion are clear and somewhat developed. Language is adequate, with some sentence variety and appropriate word choice. There may be some distracting errors, but they do not impede understanding.

Score = 3

Essays at this score point demonstrate some developing skill in responding to the task.

The essay shows some understanding of the task. The essay takes a position on the issue but does not offer a context for discussion. The essay may acknowledge a counterargument to the writer's position, but its development is brief or unclear. Development of ideas is limited and may be repetitious, with little, if any, movement between general statements and specific reasons, examples, and details. Focus on the general topic is maintained, but focus on the specific issue in the prompt may not be maintained. The organization of the essay is simple. Ideas are logically grouped within parts of the essay, but there is little or no evidence of logical sequencing of ideas. Transitions, if used, are simple and obvious. An introduction and conclusion are clearly discernible but underdeveloped. Language shows a basic control. Sentences show a little variety and word choice is appropriate. Errors may be distracting and may occasionally impede understanding.

Score = 2

Essays at this score point demonstrate inconsistent or weak skill in responding to the task.

The essay shows a weak understanding of the task. The essay may not take a position on the issue, or the essay may take a position but fail to convey reasons to support that position, or the essay may take a position but fail to maintain a stance. There is little to no recognition of a counterargument to the author's position. The essay is thinly developed. If examples are given, they are general and may not be clearly relevant. The essay may include extensive repetition of the writer's ideas or of ideas in the prompt. Focus on the general topic is maintained, but focus on the specific issue in the prompt may not be maintained. There is some indication of an organizational structure, and some logical grouping of ideas within parts of the essay is apparent. Transitions, if used, are simple and obvious, and they may be inappropriate or misleading. An introduction and conclusion are discernible but minimal. Sentence structure and word choice are usually simple. Errors may be frequently distracting and may sometimes impede understanding.

Score = 1

Essays at this score point show little or no skill in responding to the task.

The essay shows little or no understanding of the task. If the essay takes a position, it fails to convey reasons to support that position. The essay is minimally developed. The essay may include excessive repetition of the writer's ideas or of ideas in the prompt. Focus on the general topic is usually maintained, but focus on the specific issue in the prompt may not be maintained. There is little or no evidence of an organizational structure or of the logical grouping of ideas. Transitions are rarely used. If present, an introduction and conclusion are minimal. Sentence structure and word choice are simple. Errors may be frequently distracting and may significantly impede understanding.

CALCULATING YOUR COMBINED ENGLISH/WRITING SCORE

1. Find your English Test scale score on page 531. Enter it here: _____.

2. Enter your Writing Test score (1–6) here: _____; double it to get your Writing subscore (2–12): _____. (If two people read and scored your Writing Test, add those two scores to get your Writing subscore.)

3. Use the table on page 537 to find your Combined English/Writing score.

   - First, circle your ACT English Test score in the left column.
   - Second, circle your ACT Writing subscore at the top of the table.
   - Finally, follow the English Test score row across and the Writing subscore column down until the two meet. Circle the Combined English/Writing score where the row and column meet. (For example, for an English Test score of 19 and a Writing subscore of 6, the Combined English/Writing score is 18.)

4. Using the number you circled, write your Combined English/Writing score here: _____. (The highest possible Combined English/Writing score is 36, and the lowest possible score is 1.)

ACT English Test score _____

Writing subscore _____

Combined English/Writing Score _____
(from table on page 537)

COMBINED ENGLISH/WRITING SCALE SCORES

English Test Score	Writing Subscore										
	2	3	4	5	6	7	8	9	10	11	12
1	1	2	3	4	5	6	7	8	9	10	11
2	2	3	4	5	6	6	7	8	9	10	11
3	2	3	4	5	6	7	8	9	10	11	12
4	3	4	5	6	7	8	9	10	11	12	13
5	4	5	6	7	8	9	10	11	12	12	13
6	5	6	7	7	8	9	10	11	12	13	14
7	5	6	7	8	9	10	11	12	13	14	15
8	6	7	8	9	10	11	12	13	14	15	16
9	7	8	9	10	11	12	13	13	14	15	16
10	8	9	9	10	11	12	13	14	15	16	17
11	8	9	10	11	12	13	14	15	16	17	18
12	9	10	11	12	13	14	15	16	17	18	19
13	10	11	12	13	14	14	15	16	17	18	19
14	10	11	12	13	14	15	16	17	18	19	20
15	11	12	13	14	15	16	17	18	19	20	21
16	12	13	14	15	16	17	18	19	20	20	21
17	13	14	15	16	16	17	18	19	20	21	22
18	13	14	15	16	17	18	19	20	21	22	23
19	14	15	16	17	18	19	20	21	22	23	24
20	15	16	17	18	19	20	21	21	22	23	24
21	16	17	17	18	19	20	21	22	23	24	25
22	16	17	18	19	20	21	22	23	24	25	26
23	17	18	19	20	21	22	23	24	25	26	27
24	18	19	20	21	22	23	23	24	25	26	27
25	18	19	20	21	22	23	24	25	26	27	28
26	19	20	21	22	23	24	25	26	27	28	29
27	20	21	22	23	24	25	26	27	28	28	29
28	21	22	23	24	24	25	26	27	28	29	30
29	21	22	23	24	25	26	27	28	29	30	31
30	22	23	24	25	26	27	28	29	30	31	32
31	23	24	25	26	27	28	29	30	30	31	32
32	24	25	25	26	27	28	29	30	31	32	33
33	24	25	26	27	28	29	30	31	32	33	34
34	25	26	27	28	29	30	31	32	33	34	35
35	26	27	28	29	30	31	31	32	33	34	35
36	26	27	28	29	30	31	32	33	34	35	36

EXPLANATORY ANSWERS

Section 1: English Test

1. Choice D is correct. Choice A is incorrect because it is an acceptable use of past tense. Choice B is incorrect because it is an acceptable use of a possessive. Choice C is incorrect because it is an acceptable use of a prepositional phrase. Choice D is the correct answer because it is an unacceptable use of a passive adverb clause and is a dangling modifier (there is no subject for "having invented").

2. Choice G is correct. Choice F is incorrect because it uses the past perfect tense, whereas the present perfect tense is required (Choice G). Choices H and J also give the wrong tenses: Choice H, simple past; Choice J, simple future.

3. Choice C is correct. Choice A is wordy. Choice B is incorrect because the gerund "financing," not the infinitive, should be used in this construction. Choice D says that people have always been interested in films about finance; this statement does not make sense here.

4. Choice H is correct. Choice F is incorrect because "who" should be "whom" (Choice H), as the object of "has chosen." Choice G is wordy. Choice J makes "whomever . . . has chosen" a nonrestrictive clause, but it is actually restrictive.

5. Choice B is correct. The object pronoun is used after prepositions, so Choices A and C are incorrect. Choice D is incorrect because "also" is unnecessary and awkward.

6. Choice H is correct. Choice F is incorrect because there are three possible antecedents for "he or she": "backer," "director," and "producer." Choice G is incorrect because the antecedent of "they" is unclear and because the singular, referring to "backer," is needed logically. Choice J is incorrect

because the present perfect tense is needed; the action of paying began in the past and continues in the present ("mounts up").

7. Choice D is correct. Choices A and C are incorrect because they omit "else" or "other," needed because the backer is himself involved in the film. Choice B is awkward.

8. Choice F is correct. Choice F is correct because by providing an example of the increasing cost of movie musicals, the sentence supports the essay's thesis that the financial backer is an important part of the films' production. Choice G is incorrect because the essay's purpose is primarily explanatory for a general audience, not argumentative or directed at an audience of financial backers. Choice H is incorrect because it suggests that the sentence should not be added unless irrelevant information (names of backers) is included. Choice J is incorrect because it misidentifies the essay's focus and rejects the new sentence.

9. Choice C is correct. Choice A is incorrect because the present tense "costs" is needed. Choice B is incorrect because "who" refers to people, not things. Choice D is incorrect for two reasons: (1) "costed" is not a word; (2) the past tense would be wrong.

10. Choice H is correct. Choices F and G are unidiomatic. Choice H is the idiomatic phrase. Choice J is incorrect because of the lack of subordination of the phrase "more to the point." Also, "More to the point is, why accept" is awkward.

11. Choice B is correct. Choices A and C wrongly substitute "except" for "accept." *To accept* means "to receive" or "to accommodate oneself to"; *to except* means "to exclude." Choice D is incorrect because a verb, not a verbal, is needed as the main verb of the sentence.

12. Choice J is correct. Choice F has a double negative: "not scarcely." Choices G and H produce sentence fragments: "And . . . way" and "Scarcely . . . way." Choice J gives an acceptable use of the dash—that is, to set up a parenthetical comment. (Note: Dashes are used in pairs; only one dash appears here because the sentence ends at the end of the comment.)

13. Choice A is correct. Choice B is ungrammatical because *this–these* and *kind–kinds* must both be either singular or plural. Choices C and D are awkward.

14. Choice J is correct. Choice F contains the future perfect tense. Choice G contains the simple past tense. Choice H contains the past perfect tense. These are incorrect because the simple present tense (Choice J) is used to state a universal or lasting truth.

15. Choice D is correct. Choice A is incorrect because the sentence focuses on one of the essay's subtopics, adaptation, not the main topic of financial backers. Choice B is incorrect because it focuses on the screenwriter's, not the backer's, role. Choice C is incorrect because it causes the essay to digress toward the subject of successful/unsuccessful adaptation and away from the backer's role. Choice D is correct because it ties the essay's final sentence back to the essay's primary focus, the backer, and how the backer makes money on the investment.

16. Choice G is correct. Choice F is incorrect because "despite" is a preposition and cannot introduce a clause. Choice H is incorrect because "however" (an adverb) does not make sense here. Choice J is incorrect because "because" gives the opposite meaning of that intended.

17. Choice C is correct. Choice A is too wordy. Choices B and D are incorrect because there is no logical antecedent for "this" or "it." The noun that precedes is "hunter," which does not make sense as the antecedent. Choice C is clear and correct.

18. Choice J is correct. Choice F is incorrect because "in regards to" is unidiomatic ("in regard to" and "as regards" are acceptable). Choice G is incorrect because it is wordy and because "ignorance" does not have the desired meaning of "not paying attention to." Choice H is incorrect because it beclouds the meaning intended.

19. Choice B is correct. Choice A is incorrect. It would be correct without the comma after "know" or without the comma and with *that* after "know." Choice C is incorrect because "like" cannot be used with clauses. Choice D is incorrect because the progressive present ("are knowing") is incorrect here.

20. Choice H is correct. The subject of this sentence is "the business," so any other noun or pronoun with a similar or the same meaning before the verb is redundant. Therefore, Choices F ("this occupation can"), G ("this can"), and J ("doing this can") are incorrect.

21. Choice B is correct. The construction for comparison is "as . . . as." The construction "so . . . as" is a formal construction that may be used to replace "as . . . as" in negative constructions— e.g., "it is not so dangerous as. . . ." Choice A is unidiomatic. Choice C is incorrect because it omits the first "as." Choice D is incorrect because it uses "so . . . as" in a positive construction.

22. Choice H is correct. Choice F is incorrect because it is a declarative sentence placing responsibility on divers, not eliciting emotional reaction in divers' favor. Choice G is incorrect because it states a point explicitly and uses no suspense-building devices. Choice H is correct because it implies that the *cause* of a particular effect, diving hazards, is most often the actions of the diver. Choice J is incorrect because the sentence is not written from a first-person perspective.

23. Choice D is correct. Choice A is incorrect because "devil-may-care" has nothing to do with the Devil, and there is no pattern of spiritual references in the essay. Choice B is incorrect because the essay's focus is on the hazards of diving, not on classifying types of divers. Choice C is incorrect because the sentence is a third-person reference to divers of a particular type. Choice D is correct because "devil-may-care" is a way of restating the writer's point that divers themselves are responsible for the risks they take.

24. Choice F is correct. The penetration of the sea by the light is a constant truth, so the simple present is correct. Choice G is the present progressive. Choice H is the simple past. Choice J is the present perfect.

25. Choice C is correct. Parallel structure is required here. "He may lose . . ." balances with ". . . may become." Therefore Choices A and D are incorrect because "separate" does not make sense. The diver is always separate—that is, a separate person from his group. The danger is that he will become "separated" from his group. Choice B is incorrect. You wouldn't say, "became separated" because you are talking about a future situation.

26. Choice H is correct. Choices F and J are incorrect because they are too wordy. Choice G is incorrect because "during salvaging" is awkward.

27. Choice C is correct. Choice A is incorrect because "like" cannot be used with clauses. Choice B is incorrect because the "contrary to fact" subjunctive *were* is needed. (Choice A has this error also.) Choice D is incorrect because, if this clause were omitted, the construction would be incomplete.

28. Choice J is correct. Choice F is incorrect because the "causing" cannot logically precede in time the collapse of the heavy mass, so the past participle is incorrect. Choice G is incorrect because the infinitive is not idiomatic here. Choice H is incorrect because there is no coordinating conjunction to join "collapsed" and "caused." Choice J is correct because the present participle indicates an action that occurs at the same time as the action of the main verb.

29. Choice A is correct. Choice A is correct because this sentence emphasizes both the diver's lack of control after he touches the cylinder and the potential danger of being crushed. Choice B is incorrect because in its tone and in the information left out, the sentence doesn't communicate the possible consequences of touching the cylinder. Choice C is incorrect because it is too flippant to match the writer's serious point. Choice D is incorrect because the self-congratulatory content and first-person wording do not fit the writer's thesis.

30. Choice J is correct. The present perfect tense ("I have been") indicates action that began in the past but still continues in the present. This is the tense required in this sentence, so Choice J is correct and the other choices are incorrect. Choice F is the simple past. Choice G is the simple present. Choice H is the past perfect.

31. Choice C is correct. Choice A is incorrect because for a direct question, the clause should be preceded by a comma and the first word should be capitalized. Choice B is incorrect for the same reason. (The direct question is indicated in these two choices by the inverted word order: "are things.") Choice C is correct; it is an indirect question. Choice D is incorrect because indirect questions do not take question marks.

32. Choice H is correct. In this sentence, "however" is a parenthetic word—not a conjunctive adverb. Therefore, it should be preceded and followed by a comma only, not preceded by a semicolon. Therefore, Choices F and J are incorrect, and Choice H is correct. Choice G is incorrect because it lacks commas.

33. Choice D is correct. Choices A and C are too wordy. Choice B implies that "people," not the composer, are going "to make" the piece of music. The passive voice, as in Choice D, is preferable.

34. Choice F is correct. Choice F is correct in the context of the sentence, and "keeps going" is a logical progression from "where the composer begins." Choice G is incorrect because it is inappropriately general. Choice H is incorrect because it refers to the business aspect of composing in a sentence focusing on the artistic process. Choice J is incorrect because it implies something about the process (that it is a high-pressure endeavor) not supported within the sentence or the essay.

35. Choice B is correct. Choice A is incorrect because the "all" are those things described in the preceding three adverbial clauses, so "all" is plural, as in Choice B. Choice C is incorrect for the same reason; adding "this" does not help. Choice D is incorrect because "them" is an object pronoun, whereas a subject pronoun is needed (e.g., "all *these*," "*they* all").

36. Choice J is correct. Nothing in the passage suggests that it is good that composers and composing are difficult to understand, so Choice A does not make sense. The sentence containing question 36 says the same thing that the preceding sentences say, so "nevertheless," Choice G, does not make sense. The sentences preceding the one in question do not prove what is said in this sentence, so "thereby," Choice H, does not make sense. This sentence does, however, sum up what came before, so "in short," Choice J, does make sense and is correct.

37. Choice C is correct. What is needed here is the singular possessive. Choice A has no possessive. Choice B is the plural possessive. Choice D is a roundabout way to give the singular possessive; here, this method is not needed.

38. Choice F is correct. Choice F is correct and is the best topic sentence because the paragraph focuses on the role of inspiration in composing. Choice G is incorrect because although it reflects one implication in the paragraph, it is not specific enough to serve as the topic sentence. Choice H is incorrect because the idea of frustrated composers is never mentioned in the paragraph. Choice J is incorrect because the paragraph does address a misunderstanding about the process of composition, but it does not describe a disagreement about technique.

39. Choice A is correct. Choice B is incorrect because "not too much" should precede "preoccupied." Choice C is incorrect because "very" should precede "preoccupied." Choice D is incorrect because "too" and "very" are both intensifiers and have similar meanings, so including them both is redundant.

40. Choice G is correct. Choice F is incorrect because "eating" and "sleeping" are gerunds, so a possessive pronoun is needed: "his or her." Choices H and J are incorrect because only the gerunds are needed to complete the construction, not clauses. In addition, both choices are awkward.

41. Choice B is correct. Choice A is incorrect because the past infinitive (Choice B) is needed; being born preceded in time the composing. Choice C is incorrect because it is not an infinitive form. Choice D is incorrect because the progressive sense of "being" is inappropriate; the composer is completely born before he becomes a composer.

42. Choice J is correct. Choices F and H are incorrect because they omit the pronoun "it." This pronoun is needed as the subject of the second independent clause (semicolons join independent clauses). Choice G (and Choice F also) is incorrect because the present tense is needed, since the passage is in the present tense.

43. Choice A is correct. Choice B is incorrect because the reflexive "himself or herself" is needed. Choice C is incorrect because "his or her own self" is not acceptable English. Choice D is incorrect because "he or she" is not needed; moreover, the objective pronoun, not the subjective, must be used after a preposition ("to").

44. Choice H is correct. Choice F is incorrect because it is vague: the composer doesn't "feel like composing" or doesn't "compose"? Choice G is awkward. Choice J is too wordy.

45. Choice D is correct. Choice A is incorrect because the essay's purpose is expository; it is not a personal essay or argumentative piece. Choice B is incorrect because the writer uses a third-person, not a first-person, perspective. Choice C is incorrect because while the essay's perspective is third-person, defining "composer" is not its primary purpose. Choice D is correct because it accurately summarizes the essay's content and point of view.

46. Choice G is correct. The full name of the museum is the American Museum of Natural History. Each important word must be capitalized. ("The" is capitalized only because it is the first word in the sentence.) Therefore, Choices F, H, and J are incorrect.

47. Choice C is correct. The act of portraying began in the past and continues in the present. The present perfect tense is used to indicate this type of action. Choice A is the past perfect (used to show action that began in the past and ended before some other action in the past). Choice B uses the simple past tense (which indicates an action that began and ended in the past). Choice D uses the simple present tense.

48. Choice H is correct. Choice F is incorrect because "kind of through" is not an acceptable expression. Choice G is incorrect because "not only" works as a partner of "but also," and there is no "but also" in this sentence. Choice J is incorrect because "throughout" means "everywhere in," which does not make sense here.

49. Choice A is correct. Choice B is incorrect because the antecedent of "it" is unclear. Choice C is incorrect because the lack of a verb ("being" is a verbal) creates a fragmentary sentence. Choice D is incorrect because the tendency is not confined to the present—it has been going on for some years. Choice A is correct.

50. Choice J is correct. The complete clause is "Now the museum has taken man apart." "For the first time" is parenthetical. Therefore, "for the first time" must be set off by commas and Choices G and H are incorrect. Choice F is incorrect because it is awkward.

51. Choice B is correct. Choice A is incorrect because the sentence does not describe the workings of any mechanism or process in step-by-step order. Choice B is correct because the sentence transitions into the specific aspect of the museum that will be discussed and begins describing its uniqueness. Choice C is incorrect because the sentence is primarily descriptive, not argumentative. Choice D is incorrect because the sentence makes no direct comparison with any other museums.

52. Choice H is correct. It is the displays that are instructive, not the series, so the singular verb is incorrect (Choice F). The clause "which are instructive" is restrictive, so it should not be set off by commas (Choice G). Choice J is incorrect because "as" should not be used to mean "that."

53. Choice B is correct. Choice A is illogical: the degree of instructiveness has been achieved in this museum, so it has not "never" been achieved. Choice B is correct because it says that this feat has never been achieved "before." Choice C is incorrect because it omits "before" and because the infinitive indicates that this feat will not be achieved in the present or in the future. This

statement does not make sense since the feat has already been achieved. Choice D contains a double negative.

54. Choice G is correct. It is "they" (the technicians) who are "using," so "they" must be the subject of the sentence. Choices F, H, and J make "using new techniques and new materials" a dangling participial phrase. Choice J is also wordy.

55. Choice D is correct. In speech the placement of "only" is very loose, but in writing "only" should be placed as close as possible to the words it modifies. In this sentence "only" modifies "skin deep," so Choices B and C are incorrect. Choice A is incorrect because it is awkward.

56. Choice G is correct. Choice F is incorrect because the sentence cites a common belief without reference to any specific museum example. Choice G is correct because the common belief is referenced in order to contrast it with the idea the writer takes from the exhibit. Choice H is incorrect because the writer expresses no opinion about the human condition. Choice J is incorrect because the writer does not offer any criticism of the exhibit in the essay.

57. Choice D is correct. "Not only" works with "but also," so Choices A and C are incorrect. Choice B is incorrect because it is not in parallel construction with the "not only" phrase. The preposition "in" is needed: "not only in . . . but also in. . . ."

58. Choice H is correct. When two words work together to modify another word, they are often hyphenated for the sake of clarity. In this sentence "skin" and "covered" work together to modify "case," so "skin-covered" should be hyphenated. Choices F and J are therefore incorrect. Choice J is further incorrect and Choice G is incorrect because a preposition that indicates "in the interior part" is needed. Neither "with" nor "in" so indicates.

59. Choice C is correct. Choice A is incorrect because the sentence as it is written does relate to the idea of beauty explored in the final paragraph, but it does not connect back to the first paragraph's focus on the museum. Choice B is incorrect because the writer describes the graphic display as beautiful, not shocking. Choice C is correct because it adds

a reference to the museum, better reflecting the whole essay as opposed to the beauty of man's insides alone. Choice D is incorrect because neither the opening line nor the essay as a whole draws any conclusions about visitor reaction or how museums in general may benefit.

60. Choice J is correct. Choice F is incorrect because the essay does describe the exhibit from an artistic perspective, but it does not make any direct comparisons or contrasts with art museums. Choice G is incorrect because the essay does not compare the experiences of spectators at different types of museums. Choice H is incorrect because the essay does not state an opinion about what the purpose of this or any museum should be. Choice J is correct because it accurately summarizes how the writer handles the topic of art (only indirectly).

61. Choice C is correct. Choice C (the simple past tense) is correct here. Choice A is the past perfect tense. Choice B is incorrect because "were broke" means "had no money" and makes no sense here. Choice D is incorrect because the emphatic "did break" is not necessary; nothing is being emphasized.

62. Choice H is correct. Choice F is incorrect because the verb should be plural ("were"): the subject is "center, . . . color, and . . . emphasis." Choice G is incorrect because "far gone" (meaning "nearly exhausted") is not what is meant here. Moreover, the verb should be plural. Choice H is correct because the verb is plural. Choice J is incorrect because the adverb "away" is unnecessary.

63. Choice B is correct. "Only" modifies the whole phrase, so the word should not be in such a position that it modifies "a year" (Choice A) or "two" (Choice C). Choice D is awkward.

64. Choice J is correct. Choice F is incorrect because the main verb should be in the past tense, as is the rest of the passage. Choice G is incorrect for the same reason. Choice H is incorrect because the past infinitive ("to have turned") indicates that the turning occurred at some prior time, whereas "only a year or two later" indicates that the turning occurred at a later time. This is indicated by the present infinitive, as in Choice J.

65. Choice A is correct. Choice A is correct because "Botticelli" is in apposition to "one of his ancestors" and is therefore set off by commas. Choice B is incorrect because the apposition implies that Botticelli was Modigliani's only ancestor; this implication does not make sense. Choice C is incorrect because "his ancestor" is not set off by commas; moreover, "his" has an indefinite antecedent: both "Botticelli" and "Modigliani" precede the singular third-person masculine pronoun "his." Choice D is incorrect because "his" has an indefinite antecedent and because "his ancestor" is not set off by commas.

66. Choice G is correct. The singular possessive is needed. Choice F contains no possessive. Choice H contains the plural possessive. Choice J contains no possessive.

67. Choice D is correct. The past participle ("discovered") acts as an adjective, so an adverb is needed as modifier. Therefore, Choices B and C are incorrect. Choice A is incorrect because the past participle is needed since African art was already discovered before Modigliani drew from it.

68. Choice J is correct. Choice F is incorrect because "himself limited" means that Modigliani was limited by nature, not that he consciously limited himself, as the passage indicates. Choices G and H are incorrect because the reflexive "himself" (Choice J) is needed. The person doing the limiting and the person limited are the same; this relationship is indicated by the reflexive pronoun.

69. Choice C is correct. A main verb is needed for the sentence. Only Choice C supplies a main verb. Choice A gives the infinitive. Choice B gives the present participle. Choice D gives the past infinitive.

70. Choice J is correct. Choices F and G make the introductory phrase a dangling construction. "His figures" are what are "wistful" etc., so "his figures" must be the subject of the sentence. Choice H creates a sentence fragment; there is no main verb given.

71. Choice D is correct. Choice A is incorrect because this sentence should begin a new paragraph. Choice B is incorrect because the sentence should begin a new paragraph and because the comma after the introductory phrase "In other hands" is incorrectly omitted. Choice C is incorrect because, although the sentence correctly begins a new paragraph, the comma after the introductory phrase "In other hands" is incorrectly omitted. Choice D is correct because the sentence correctly begins a new paragraph and commas are correctly placed after the introductory phrase and the first item in a series ("elongated necks").

72. Choice G is correct. Choice F presents a run-on sentence. Choice G is correct; a semicolon joins independent clauses. Choice H is incorrect because, if we do use a conjunction here, it should be "but"—not "and." Choice J is incorrect because the second clause does not exemplify the first, as is indicated by the use of a colon.

73. Choice A is correct. Choice A is correct because the sentence offers two examples to explain a specific result, "he established no school." Choice B is incorrect because establishing no "school" of artistic style is not equivalent to being forgotten. The essay implies that Modigliani has not been forgotten. Choice C is incorrect because it makes two points not supported anywhere else in the essay (that few artists study Modigliani and that his techniques are impossible to understand). Choice D is incorrect because it makes assertions not supported elsewhere in the essay.

74. Choice J is correct. Choice F is incorrect because it is too vague to be meaningful. Choice G is incorrect because it does not connect to or receive support from any other part of the essay. Choice H is incorrect because it only partially reflects the upcoming examples. Choice J is correct because it is the best synthesis of the upcoming examples and is therefore the best phrasing.

75. Choice D is correct. *To affect* means "to influence." *To effect* means "to bring about." In this case "to effect" has the logical meaning, so Choices A and B are incorrect. "Must of" is an illiteracy for "must have," so Choices A and C are incorrect. Choice D contains neither error and is correct.

EXPLANATORY ANSWERS

Section 2: Mathematics Test

As you read these solutions, you are advised to do two things if you answered the Math question incorrectly:

1. *When a specific Math Strategy is referred to in the solution, study that strategy, which you will find in the "19 Math Strategies" (beginning on page 44).*

2. *When the solution directs you to the "Complete ACT Math Refresher" (beginning on page 147)—for example, Math Refresher #305—study the math principle to get a clear idea of the math operation you needed to know in order to answer the question correctly.*

1. Choice E is correct.

   (Use Strategy 2: Translate from words into algebra.)

   Let g = number of games the team played
   28 = number of games Bobby watched
   $\frac{2}{3}g$ = number of games Tommy watched

   We are given

   $$\frac{2}{3}g > 28 \qquad 1$$

   Multiplying $\boxed{1}$ by $\frac{3}{2}$, we get

   $$\left(\frac{3}{2}\right)\frac{2}{3}g > 28\left(\frac{3}{2}\right)$$
   $$g > 42$$

   Only Choice E satisfies this relationship.

   (Math Refreshers #200, #422, and #426)

2. Choice J is correct.

   (Use Strategy 2: Translate from words into algebra.)

   Given: 8 people divide a cash prize equally $\qquad 1$

   From $\boxed{1}$ we get:

   Each person receives $\frac{1}{8}$ of the total prize $\qquad 2$

   Two people receive $\frac{2}{8} = \frac{1}{4}$ of the prize $\qquad 3$

   To change $\boxed{3}$ to a percent, we multiply by 100.

   $$100\left(\frac{1}{4}\right) = \frac{100}{4}$$
   $$= 25\%$$

   (Math Refreshers #200 and #106)

3. Choice B is correct.

   Given: $x + x^3 + x^5 + x^6$ $\qquad 1$

   $\qquad\quad x = -1$ $\qquad\qquad\qquad\qquad\quad 2$

   Substitute $\boxed{2}$ into $\boxed{1}$. We get

   $$-1 + (-1)^3 + (-1)^5 + (-1)^6 =$$
   $$-1 - 1 - 1 + 1 = -2$$

   (Math Refreshers #431 and #429)

4. Choice J is correct.

   Break the equation in two, simplify each half, then put them together.

   $$(4a) + (-6a) = 4a - 6a = -2a$$
   $$-(3a + a) = -(4a) = -4a$$
   $$-2a - 4a = -6a$$

   (Math Refresher #405a)

5. Choice E is correct.

   Given: Temperature at 11:00 a.m. = 0°F $\qquad 1$
   $\qquad\qquad$ Temperature at 8:00 a.m. = -15°F $\qquad 2$
   Let x = temperature at 5:00 p.m. $\qquad\qquad 3$
   $\qquad y$ = temperature rise $\qquad\qquad\qquad\quad 4$

   (Use Strategy 13: Find unknowns by subtracting.)

   Subtract $\boxed{2}$ from $\boxed{1}$. We get

   $\qquad$ Temperature rise in 3 hours = 15°F $\qquad 5$

   Subtract the times in $\boxed{1}$ and $\boxed{3}$. We get

   $\qquad\qquad$ time change = 6 hours $\qquad\qquad 6$

   Use $\boxed{4}$, $\boxed{5}$, and $\boxed{6}$ to find temperature rise from 11:00 a.m. to 5:00 p.m. We get

   $$\frac{3 \text{ hours}}{6 \text{ hours}} = \frac{15°F}{y}$$
   $$3y = 6 \times 15°F$$
   $$y = 30°F \qquad 7$$

Use 1, 3, and 7 to find the final temperature.

$$x = 0°F + 30°F$$
$$x = 30°F$$

(Math Refresher #120)

6. Choice G is correct.

Number of Shirts	Total Price
1	$12.00
Box of 3	$22.50
Box of 6	$43.40

From the chart above, we know

$$6 \text{ shirts} = \$43.40 \quad \boxed{1}$$

(Use Strategy 13: Find unknowns by division.)

Dividing 1 by 6, we get

$$\frac{6 \text{ shirts}}{6} = \frac{\$43.40}{6}$$
$$1 \text{ shirt} = \$7.23\overline{3}$$
$$\text{Cost per shirt} \approx \$7.20$$

(Math Refresher #406)

7. Choice E is correct.

$$\text{Given: } 5x^2 - 15x = 0 \quad \boxed{1}$$
$$x \neq 0 \quad \boxed{2}$$

(Use Strategy 12: Try not to make tedious calculations.)

Factoring 1, we get

$$5x(x - 3) = 0$$
$$5x = 0 \quad \text{or} \quad x - 3 = 0$$
$$x = 0 \quad \text{or} \quad x = 3 \quad \boxed{3}$$

Applying 2 to 3, we get

$$x = 3$$

(Math Refresher #409)

8. Choice F is correct.

(Use Strategy 6: Know how to manipulate inequalities.)

$$2(x + 3) = 2x + 6$$
$$3(x - 4) = 3x - 12$$

So we get:

$$2x + 6 > 3x - 12$$
$$(2x + 6) - 2x > (3x - 12) - 2x$$
$$6 > x - 12$$
$$(6) + 12 > (x - 12) + 12$$
$$18 > x$$
$$x < 18$$

(Math Refresher #420)

9. Choice D is correct.

(Use Strategy 12: Factor to make simpler.)

Factor $x^3 - x$:

$$x(x^2 - 1)$$

(Use Strategy 4: Remember classic expressions.)

$$x^2 - 1 = (x + 1)(x - 1)$$

So $\quad x^3 - x = x(x^2 - 1) = x(x + 1)(x - 1)$

Plug in to the original expression:

$$\frac{x - 1}{x^3 - 1} = \frac{x - 1}{x(x + 1)(x - 1)}$$
$$= \frac{1}{x(x + 1)}$$
$$= \frac{1}{x^2 + x}$$

(Math Refresher #409)

10. Choice K is correct.

$$\text{Given: } a - 3 = 7 \quad \boxed{1}$$

(Use Strategy 13: Find unknowns by addition, subtraction, and multiplication.)

Fast Method: From 1, we can subtract 7 from both sides, and then add 3 to both sides to get

$$a - 7 = 3 \quad \boxed{2}$$

Multiplying 2 by 2, we get

$$2a - 14 = 6$$

Slow Method: Solve 1 to get

$$a = 10 \quad \boxed{3}$$

Now substitute 3:

$$2a - 14 = 2(10) - 14 = 6$$

(Math Refreshers #406 and #431)

11. Choice D is correct.

(Use Strategy 17: Use the given information effectively.)

Change all fractions to decimal form:

$$\frac{7}{10} = 0.7$$
$$\frac{7}{100} = 0.07$$
$$\frac{77}{1,000} = 0.077$$

Adding these, we get 0.847

(Math Refresher #104)

12. Choice F is correct.

    (Use Strategy 14: Label unknown quantities to help solve the problem.)

    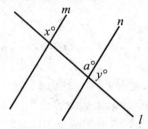

    Know the properties of parallel lines. If 2 parallel lines are crossed by a transversal, the pairs of corresponding angles are equal. Thus,

    $$x = a \qquad \boxed{1}$$

    From the diagram, $a + y = 180$ $\qquad \boxed{2}$

    Substituting $\boxed{1}$ into $\boxed{2}$, we get

    $$x + y = 180$$

    (Math Refresher #504)

13. Choice E is correct.

    Given: $\dfrac{3x}{4} = 9$ $\qquad \boxed{1}$

    (Use Strategy 13: Find unknowns by multiplying.)

    Multiplying $\boxed{1}$ by 4, we get

    $$4\left(\frac{3x}{4}\right) = (9)4$$
    $$3x = 36 \qquad \boxed{2}$$

    Multiply $\boxed{2}$ by 2. We have

    $$2(3x) = 2(36)$$
    $$6x = 72$$

    (Math Refresher #406)

14. Choice H is correct.

    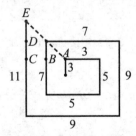

    From the diagram we find that

    $$AB = 2 \qquad \boxed{1}$$
    $$BC = 2 \qquad \boxed{2}$$
    $$CD = 2 \qquad \boxed{3}$$
    $$DE = 2 \qquad \boxed{4}$$

    (Use Strategy 3: The whole equals the sum of its parts.)

    We know $AB + BC = AC$ $\qquad \boxed{5}$

    Substituting $\boxed{1}$ and $\boxed{2}$ into $\boxed{5}$, we get

    $$2 + 2 = AC$$
    $$4 = AC \qquad \boxed{6}$$

    We know $CD + DE = CE$ $\qquad \boxed{7}$

    Substituting $\boxed{3}$ and $\boxed{4}$ into $\boxed{7}$, we get

    $$2 + 2 = CE$$
    $$4 = CE \qquad \boxed{8}$$

    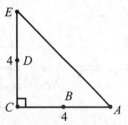

    Filling $\boxed{6}$ and $\boxed{8}$ into the diagram and using the fact that all the segments drawn were perpendicular, we have $\triangle ECA$ is an isosceles right triangle.

    (Use Strategy 18: Know and use facts about triangles.)

    In the isosceles right triangle, the

    $$\text{hypotenuse} = \text{leg}(\sqrt{2}) \qquad \boxed{9}$$

    Substituting $\boxed{6}$ or $\boxed{8}$ into $\boxed{9}$, we get

    $$EA = 4\sqrt{2}$$

    (Math Refreshers #507 and #509)

15. Choice D is correct.

    Method I:

    (Use Strategy 8: When all choices must be tested, start with the last choice and work backward.)

    Since $\sqrt{x}$ is odd, then x is odd. $\qquad \boxed{1}$

    Let us start with solution E.

    Choice E: If x is odd (from $\boxed{1}$), then x^2 is odd.

    Choice D: If $\sqrt{x}$ is odd, $2\sqrt{x}$ is *even*, and the solution is found.

    Method II:

    (Use Strategy 7: Use numerics to help you get the answer.)

    Choose an odd number for $\sqrt{x}$—for example,

    $$\sqrt{x} = 3$$
    $$\text{Then } x = 9$$

    Choice E $\quad x^2 = 81$ (odd)

    Choice D $\quad 2\sqrt{x} = 2\sqrt{9} = 2(3) = 6$ (even)

    The answer is clearly Choice D.

    (Math Refreshers #430 and #431, and #603)

16. Choice K is correct.

    (Use Strategy 8: When all choices must be tested, start with the last choice and work backward.)

    Since we must check all the choices, we should start with Choice K. Clearly, if x is the point whose coordinates are (5,2), then $m\angle MXN = 90°$ and Choice K must be correct.

    (Math Refresher #410b)

17. Choice D is correct.

    You want to find a value of x such that $f(x) = x + 2$, so you look for a value of x in the x-column that makes $f(x)$ in the $f(x)$ column, $x + 2$. You can see that $x = 3$ corresponds to $f(x) = 5$, which is just $x + 2$ (or $3 + 2$).

    (Math Refreshers #616 and #702)

18. Choice J is correct.

    (Use Strategy 15: Know how to eliminate certain choices.)

    Since (according to the graph), $y = 0$ when $x = 0$, Choices F, G, and K are incorrect. Choice H is incorrect, since the graph is not a parabola. The only feasible choice is Choice J.

    (Math Refresher #410b)

19. Choice E is correct.

    (Use Strategy 2: Translate from words into algebra.)

    The sum of the degree measures of the 4 angles of any quadrilateral is always 360. Therefore,

    $$w + x + y + z = 360° \qquad \boxed{1}$$

    (Use Strategy 5:
    $$Average = \frac{sum\ of\ values}{total\ number\ of\ values})$$

    If w is the average (arithmetic mean) of x, y, and z, then

    $$w = \frac{x + y + z}{3}$$

    Multiplying both sides of the above equation by 3, we have

    $$3w = x + y + z \qquad \boxed{2}$$

    Substituting equation $\boxed{2}$ into equation $\boxed{1}$, we get

    $$w + 3w = 360°$$
    $$4w = 360°$$
    $$w = 90°$$

From equation $\boxed{2}$, we conclude that
$$x + y + z = 3w = 3(90) = 270°$$

(Math Refreshers #521, #601, and #406)

20. Choice G is correct.

    (Use Strategy 17: Use the given information effectively.)

    The circle graph tells you that 19% of this mixture is carbon. Since the total mixture weighs 24 pounds, 19% of that will be the amount of carbon in the mixture (in pounds). We would multiply 24 lbs × .19. But since the choices are not that close and since we are looking for the *closest* number of pounds, make the problem simpler by multiplying 24 × .20 = 4.8, which is close to 4.6.

    (Math Refresher #705)

21. Choice C is correct.

    (Use Strategy 10: Know how to use units.)

    We are given his rate is $\dfrac{90\ laps}{6\ hours}$

    $$\frac{90\ laps}{6\ \cancel{hours}} = \frac{1\ \cancel{hour}}{60\ minutes}$$

    $$= \frac{1}{4}\ lap\ per\ minute$$

    (Math Refresher #121)

22. Choice H is correct.

    $$x^{-\frac{3}{4}} = \frac{1}{x^{\frac{3}{4}}} = \frac{1}{\left(\sqrt[4]{x}\right)^3}$$

    $$x^{-\frac{3}{4}} = \frac{1}{\left(\sqrt[4]{16}\right)^3}$$

    $$= \frac{1}{(2)^3}$$

    $$= \frac{1}{8}$$

    (Math Refresher #901)

23. Choice E is correct.

    (Use Strategy 15: Know how to eliminate certain choices.)

    The graph $y = 2x - 4$ is a straight line such that when $x = 0$, $y = -4$, and when $y = 0$, $2x - 4 = 0$ and thus $x = 2$. So we look for a line that cuts the y-axis (vertical axis where $x = 0$) at $y = -4$, and cuts the x-axis (horizontal axis where $y = 0$) at $x = 2$.

    (Math Refresher #413)

24. Choice H is correct.

    (Use Strategy 17: Use the given information effectively.)

    $$\left(\frac{3}{10}\right)^2 = \frac{9}{100} = \frac{p}{100}$$

    Thus $p = 9$

    (Math Refresher #429)

25. Choice B is correct.

    Given: Paul's average on 3 tests $= 85$ ☐1

    Paul's average on first 2 tests $= 85$ ☐2

    (Use Strategy 5:

    $$Average = \frac{sum\ of\ values}{total\ number\ of\ values}\Big)$$

    We know Average $= \dfrac{\text{sum of values}}{\text{total number of values}}$ ☐3

    Let x be the first test score ☐4

    y be the second test score ☐5

    z be the third test score ☐6

    Substituting ☐1, ☐4, ☐5, and ☐6 into ☐3, we have

    $$85 = \frac{x + y + z}{3}$$ ☐7

    (Use Strategy 13: Find unknowns by multiplying.)

    Multiply ☐7 by 3. We get

    $$3(85) = \left(\frac{x + y + z}{3}\right)3$$

    $$255 = x + y + z$$ ☐8

    Substituting ☐2, ☐4, and ☐5 into ☐3, we have

    $$85 = \frac{x + y}{2}$$ ☐9

    Multiplying ☐9 by 2, we get

    $$2(85) = \left(\frac{x + y}{2}\right)2$$

    $$170 = x + y$$ ☐10

    Substituting ☐10 into ☐8, we get

    $$225 = 170 + z$$

    $$85 = z$$

    (Math Refreshers #601, #431, and #406)

26. Choice J is correct.

    (Use Strategy 2: Translate from words into algebra.)

    x is a multiple of 9, gives

    $x : \{9, 18, 27, 36, 45, 54, \ldots\ldots\}$ ☐1

    x is a multiple of 12, gives

    $x : \{12, 24, 36, 48, 60, 72, \ldots\ldots\}$ ☐2

    The smallest value that appears in both sets ☐1 and ☐2 is 36.

    (Math Refreshers #801 and #803)

27. Choice C is correct.

    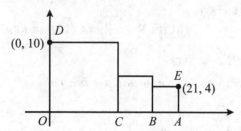

    We want to find the area of the middle square, which is $(CB)^2$.

    (Use Strategy 3: The whole equals the sum of its parts.)

    $$OA = OC + CB + BA$$ ☐1

    From the diagram, we get

    $$OA = 21$$ ☐2

    $$AE = 4$$ ☐3

    $$OD = 10$$ ☐4

    Since each figure is a square, we get

    $$BA = AE$$ ☐5

    $$OC = OD$$ ☐6

    Substituting ☐5 into ☐3, we get

    $$AE = BA = 4$$ ☐7

    Substituting ☐6 into ☐4, we get

    $$OD = OC = 10$$ ☐8

    Substituting ☐2, ☐7, and ☐8 into ☐1, we get

    $$21 = 10 + CB + 4$$

    $$21 = 14 + CB$$

    $$7 = CB$$ ☐9

    Area of square II $= (CB)^2$

    Area of square II $= 7^2$ (from ☐9)

    Area of square II $= 49$

    (Math Refreshers #410 and #303)

28. Choice K is correct.

    Given: 1 cup $= 100$ grams ☐1

    1 cake $= 75$ grams ☐2

    1 pie $= 225$ grams ☐3

    Using ☐1, we get

    $$4 \text{ cups} = 4(100 \text{ grams})$$

    $$4 \text{ cups} = 400 \text{ grams}$$ ☐4

    (Using Strategy 8: When all choices must be tested, start with the last choice and work backward.)

    2 cakes and 1 pie is Choice K. ☐5

    Substituting ☐2 and ☐3 in ☐5, we get

    $$2(75 \text{ grams}) + 225 \text{ grams}$$

    $$= 150 \text{ grams} + 225 \text{ grams}$$

    $$= 375 \text{ grams}$$ ☐6

Since 6 is less than 4, there is *enough* in 4 cups. So Choice K is correct.

(Math Refreshers #121 and #431)

29. Choice E is correct.

(Use Strategy 18: Know and use facts about triangles.)

I. Slope is defined as $\dfrac{y_2 - y_1}{x_2 - x_1}$ where (x_1, y_1) and (x_2, y_2) are points on the line. Thus here, $0 = x_1$, $a = y_1$, $a = x_2$, and $0 = y_2$.

Thus $\dfrac{y_2 - y_1}{x_2 - x_1} = \dfrac{0 - a}{a - 0} = -1$: I is therefore true.

II. The triangle created is an isosceles right triangle with sides a, a, $a\sqrt{2}$. Thus II is true.

III. In an isosceles right triangle, the interior angles of the triangle are 90–45–45 degrees. Thus III is true.

(Math Refreshers #416, #411, and #509)

30. Choice K is correct.

(Use Strategy 8: When all choices must be tested, start with the last choice and work backward.)

Choice F is incorrect: On the number line, b is to the left of -2 so this implies that b is less than -2 (written as $b < -2$). Since $b < -2$, b is certainly less than -1 (written as $b < -1$). Thus Choice F is incorrect. Choice G is false because if $b < -2$, the absolute value of b (denoted as $|b|$) must be greater than 2. Choice H is false: c is positive ($c > +3 > 0$) so $c \neq -|c|$, since $-|c|$ is negative. Choice J is false: Since a and b are negative numbers and since $a < b$, $|a| > |b|$, Choice K is correct and Choice J is incorrect.

(Math Refreshers #419, #615, and #410a)

31. Choice B is correct.

(Use Strategy 2: Translate from words into algebra.)

We are told:

$$A + 8 + A + 1 + A + 2$$
$$= A + A + 1 + A + 2 + A + 3 \qquad \boxed{1}$$

(Use Strategy 1: Cancel expressions that appear on both sides of an equation.)

Each side contains an A, $A + 1$, and $A + 2$. Canceling each of these from each side, we get,

$$\cancel{A} + 8 + \cancel{A+1} + \cancel{A+2}$$
$$= \cancel{A} + \cancel{A+1} + \cancel{A+2} + A + 3$$

Thus, $8 = A + 3$

$$5 = A$$

(Math Refresher #406)

32. Choice K is correct.

(Use Strategy 11: Use new definitions carefully.)

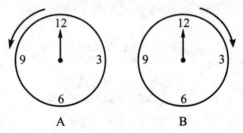

By the definition of a move, every 4 moves brings each hand back to 12.

Thus, after 4, 8, 12, and 16 moves, respectively, each hand is at 12.

Hand A, moving counterclockwise, moves to 9 on its 17th move.

Hand B, moving clockwise, moves to 3 on its 17th move.

33. Choice C is correct.

(Use Strategy 2: Translate from words into algebra.)

The number of hours from 7:00 a.m. to 5:00 p.m. is 10.

The number of hours from 1:00 p.m. to 7:00 p.m. is 6.

He worked 10 hours for 3 days and 6 hours for 3 days. Thus,

Total hours $= 3(10) + 3(6)$

$\qquad\qquad = 30 + 18$

Total hours $= 48$ ⬛1

Total earnings $=$ hours worked $\times$ hourly rate ⬛2

Given: He earns \$10 per hour ⬛3

Substituting ⬛1 and ⬛3 into ⬛2, we get

Total earnings $= 48 \times \$10$

Total earnings $= \$480$

(Math Refreshers #200 and #406)

34. Choice K is correct.

(Use Strategy 3: The whole equals the sum of its parts.)

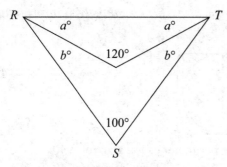

The sum of the angles in a $\Delta = 180$. For the small triangle we have

$$120 + a + a = 180$$
$$120 + 2a = 180$$
$$2a = \quad 60$$
$$a = \quad 30 \qquad \boxed{1}$$

For ΔRST, we have

$$100 + m\angle SRT + m\angle STR = 180 \qquad \boxed{2}$$

From the diagram, we get

$$m\angle SRT = a + b \qquad \boxed{3}$$
$$m\angle STR = a + b \qquad \boxed{4}$$

Substituting $\boxed{3}$ and $\boxed{4}$ into $\boxed{2}$, we get

$$100 + a + b + a + b = 180$$
$$100 + 2a + 2b = 180$$
$$2a + 2b = \quad 80 \qquad \boxed{5}$$

Substituting $\boxed{1}$ into $\boxed{5}$, we get

$$2(30) + 2b = 80$$
$$60 + 2b = 80$$
$$2b = 20$$
$$b = 10$$

(Math Refreshers #505 and #406)

35. Choice C is correct.

(Use Strategy 14: Draw lines and label unknown quantities to help find the answer.)

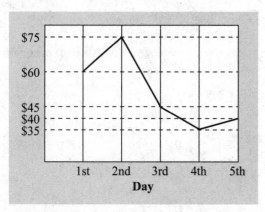

In ascending order, the wages for the six days are:

$35
$35
$40
$45
$60
$75

The median is the middle number. But wait! There is no middle number. So we average the two middle numbers, 40 and 45, to get 42.5.

The mode is the number appearing most frequently, that is, 35. So $42.50 - 35 = 7.50$.

(Math Refreshers #200 and #607)

36. Choice K is correct.

(Use Strategy 11: Use new definitions carefully.)

(Using Strategy 8: When all choices must be tested, start with the last choice and work backward.)

Given: $ⓐⓑ = \dfrac{a + 1}{b - 1}$

Choice K: $⑤③ = \dfrac{5 + 1}{3 - 1} = \dfrac{6}{2} = 3$

Choice K is the only choice with $a > b$.

Therefore, it must be the largest.

The remaining choices are shown below.

Choice J: $④⑤ = \dfrac{4 + 1}{5 - 1} = \dfrac{5}{4} = 1\dfrac{1}{4}$

Choice H: $③⑤ = \dfrac{3 + 1}{5 - 1} = \dfrac{4}{4} = 1$

Choice G: $③③ = \dfrac{3 + 1}{3 - 1} = \dfrac{4}{2} = 2$

Choice F: $②③ = \dfrac{2 + 1}{3 - 1} = \dfrac{3}{2} = 1\dfrac{1}{2}$

(Math Refresher #431)

37. Choice E is correct.

(Use Strategy 17: Use the given information effectively.)

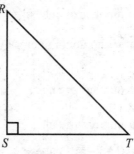

We know that the area of $\Delta = \dfrac{1}{2} \times$ base $\times$ height $\qquad \boxed{1}$

We are given that $RS = ST =$ an integer　　2

Substituting 2 into 1, we get

Area $\triangle RST = \frac{1}{2} \times$ (an integer) $=$ (same integer)

Area $\triangle RST = \frac{1}{2} \times$ (an integer)^2　　3

Multiplying 3 by 2, we have

2(area $\triangle RST$) $=$ (an integer)^2　　4

(Use Strategy 8: When each choice must be tested, start with the last choice and work backward.)

Substituting Choice E, 20, into 4 , we get

$2(20) =$ (an integer)^2

$40 =$ (an integer)^2　　5

5 is *not* possible, since 40 isn't the square of an integer.

(Math Refreshers #307, #406, and #431)

38. Choice K is correct.

(Use Strategy 17: Use the given information effectively.)

Volume of rectangular solid $= l \times w \times h$　　1

Substituting the given dimensions into 1, we get

Volume of solid $= 2$ feet $\times 2$ feet $\times 1$ foot

Volume of solid $= 4$ cubic feet　　2

Volume of cube $=$ (edge)^3　　3

Substituting edge $= 0.1$ foot into 3, we get

Volume of cube $= (0.1$ foot$)^3$

Volume of cube $= 0.001$ cubic feet　　4

(Use Strategy 3: The whole equals the sum of its parts.)

Since the volume of the rectangular solid must equal the sum of the small cubes, we need to know

$\dfrac{\text{volume of rectangular solid}}{\text{volume of cube}} =$ number of cubes　　5

Substituting 2 and 4 into 5, we get

$\dfrac{4 \text{ cubic feet}}{0.001 \text{ cubic feet}} =$ number of cubes

$\dfrac{4}{0.001} =$ number of cubes

Multiplying the numerator and denominator by 1,000, we get

$\dfrac{4}{0.001} \times \dfrac{1,000}{1,000} =$ number of cubes

$\dfrac{4,000}{1} =$ number of cubes

$4,000 =$ number of cubes

(Math Refreshers #312 and #313)

39. Choice D is correct.

(Use Strategy 2: Translate from words into algebra.)

(Now use Strategy 17: Use the given information effectively.)

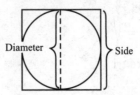

Given the perimeter of the square $= 40$

Thus, 4(side) $= 40$

side $= 10$　　1

A side of the square $=$ length of diameter of circle.

Thus, diameter $= 10$ from 1

Since diameter $= 2$(radius)

$10 = 2$(radius)

$5 =$ radius　　2

Area of a circle $= \pi r^2$　　3

Substituting 2 into 3, we have

Area of circle $= \pi 5^2$

Area of circle $= 25\pi$

(Math Refreshers #303 and #310)

40. Choice J is correct.

$(4 + 3i)(3 + 4i)$

$= 12 + 9i + 16i + 12i^2$

$= 12 + 25i + 12i^2$

Since $i^2 = -1$

$12 + 25i + 12i^2 = 12 + 25i - 12 = 25i$

(Math Refresher #618)

41. Choice D is correct.

$\log_{10} 2 = \log_{10} \dfrac{10}{5}$

$= \log_{10} 10 - \log_{10} 5$

$= 1 - \log_{10} 5$

Since $\log_{10} 5 = a$

$\log_{10} 2 = 1 - a$

(Math Refresher #617)

42. **Choice J is correct.**

    (Use Strategy 18: Know and use facts about triangles.)

    Take the square root of the equation:

    $$\sqrt{\sin^2 x°} = \sqrt{\frac{3}{4}}$$

    $$\sin x° = \sqrt{\frac{3}{2}}$$

    This is one of the standard triangles:

    $$\sin 60° = \sqrt{\frac{3}{2}}$$

    $$x = 60$$

    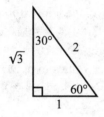

    (Math Refresher #901)

43. **Choice E is correct.**

    We substitute $x = 2$. So

    $$f(2) = 2(2) + 3^2 = 4 + 9 = 13$$

    (Math Refresher #616)

44. **Choice J is correct.**

    (Use Strategy 17: Use the given information effectively.)

    We set $x + 2 = x^2 + 4x + 4$.

    Since $x^2 + 4x + 4 = (x + 2)(x + 2)$,
    we have $x + 2 = (x + 2)(x + 2)$.
    Thus $x = -2$, or $1 = x + 2$.
    Therefore $x = -2$ or $x = -1$

    (Math Refresher #417)

45. **Choice C is correct.**

    (Use Strategy 3: The whole equals the sum of its parts.)

    The whole straight angle ABC is equal to the sum of the individual angles.

    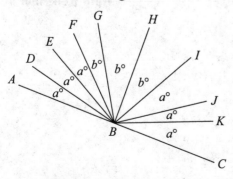

Thus,

$$m\angle ABC = a + a + a + b + b + b + a + a + a$$

$$m\angle ABC = 6a + 3b \qquad \boxed{1}$$

We know $m\angle ABC = 180°$ $\qquad \boxed{2}$

Substituting $\boxed{2}$ into $\boxed{1}$, we get

$$180° = 6a + 3b \qquad \boxed{3}$$

(Use Strategy 13: Find an unknown expression by dividing.)

Dividing both sides of $\boxed{3}$ by 3, we have

$$60° = 2a + b \qquad \boxed{4}$$

Choice C, $m\angle DBG = 2a + b$, so its measure can be determined. It is 60° (from $\boxed{4}$).

(Math Refreshers #501 and #406)

46. **Choice G is correct.**

    (Use Strategy 14: Draw lines and label unknown quantities to help find the answer.)

    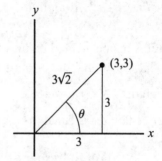

    From the diagram above, we have a 3–3–3 $\sqrt{2}$ right triangle.

    $$\cos \theta = \frac{3}{3\sqrt{2}} = \frac{1}{\sqrt{2}}$$

    Multiplying the numerator and denominator by $\frac{\sqrt{2}}{2}$ (known as "rationalizing"), we get:

    $$\cos \theta = \frac{1}{\sqrt{2}} \left(\frac{\sqrt{2}}{\sqrt{2}} \right) = \frac{\sqrt{2}}{2}$$

    (Math Refreshers #307, #410b, #411, #509, and #901)

47. **Choice B is correct.**

    (Use Strategy 17: Use the given information effectively.)

    Since the slope of the line is constant, the *ratio* of the *difference* in y-coordinates to the difference in x-coordinates must be constant for any two points on the line. For points P and A, this ratio is

    $$\frac{2 - 1}{1 - 0} = 2$$

The only choice of x and y, which gives the ratio 2 for point R and point A, is Choice B, since if $x = 4$ and $y = 8$,

$$\frac{8 - 0}{4 - 0} = 2$$

All the other choices give a different ratio from 2.

(Math Refresher #416)

48. Choice G is correct.

(Use Strategy 2: Translate words into numbers.)

35% of all of Harry's stamps are American, and 23% of these are air mail. 23% of 35% equals

$$\frac{23}{100} \times \frac{35}{100} = \frac{805}{10,000} = \frac{8.05}{100}$$

which equals 8.05%.

(Math Refresher #702)

49. Choice D is correct.

(Use Strategy 17: Use the given information effectively.)

Two-fifths, or 40%, of the applicants fail on the examination. Of the 60% remaining, three-fourths fail to get into the program. $\frac{3}{4} \times 60\% = 45\%$.

Thus, the total number of failures is equal to 40% + 45%, or 85%.

(Math Refresher #106)

50. Choice F is correct.

(Use Strategy 14: Draw lines, label sides and angles.)

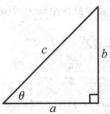

According to the triangle above, $\sin \theta = \frac{b}{c}$ and $\tan \theta = \frac{b}{a}$

So $\dfrac{\sin \theta}{\tan \theta} = \dfrac{\left(\frac{b}{c}\right)}{\left(\frac{b}{a}\right)} = \left(\frac{b}{c}\right)\left(\frac{a}{b}\right) = \frac{a}{c}$

$\cos \theta = \dfrac{a}{c}$

$x = \cos \theta$

(Math Refresher #901)

51. Choice B is correct.

(Use Strategy 18: Know and use facts about triangles.)

Let the two perpendicular sides equal a and b, and the hypotenuse be c. By the Pythagorean theorem, $a^2 + b^2 = c^2$. Thus, c^2 must be the sum of two square numbers; but our only possible choices for c^2 are 44, 45, 46, 47, and 48. Listing the square numbers which do not exceed these, we find 1, 4, 9, 16, 25, and 36. The only choice that can be broken down into the sum of two of these squares is 45, which equals 36 + 9. (To show that we cannot so break down the others, we need only notice that 36 + 16 = 52 is too large, 36 + 4 = 40 is too small; 25 + 25 = 50 is too large, 25 + 16 = 41 is too small; and there are no other values in between, so 36 + 9 = 45 is the only choice.) Since $c^2 = 45$, c must equal $\sqrt{45}$.

(Math Refreshers #509, #307, and #430)

52. Choice J is correct.

(Use Strategy 17: Use the given information effectively.)

Of the N French students, P are in both programs, so only $(N - P)$ are in the French program alone; similarly, $(M - P)$ students are in the Spanish program alone. Thus, the number of students in only one language program is equal to $(N - P) + (M - P)$, which equals $N + M - 2P$.

Note: The following diagram may help you to visualize the answer better.

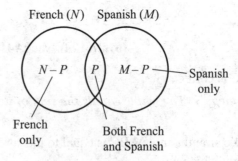

(Math Refresher #613)

53. Choice E is correct.

(Use Strategy 17: Use the given information effectively.)

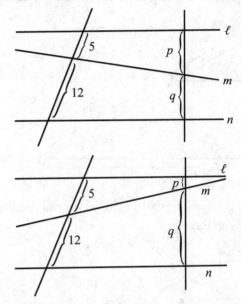

Since we know only that m is not parallel to either ℓ or n, both of the situations depicted in these diagrams could be true.

Note: $p + q = 13$ is still true in both cases in the drawings above.

Clearly, the value of $\frac{p}{q}$ is different for each case.

Hence, $\frac{p}{q}$ cannot be determined unless we know more about m.

54. Choice H is correct.

(Use Strategy 17: Use the given information effectively.)

There are 4 choices for the first letter of the 3-letter combinations. Since each letter cannot be used more than once in a combination, there are only 3 choices for the second letter and only 2 choices for the third letter. Therefore, the maximum number of 3-letter combinations that Ross can make up is

$$= 4 \cdot 3 \cdot 2$$
$$= 24$$

(Math Refresher #613a)

55. Choice C is correct.

(Use Strategy 17: Use the given information effectively and ignore irrelevant information.)

To find the total cost of all uniforms in *child* sizes at *School B*, we would multiply the number of uniforms at School B of Type A with the Child's Type A cost, multiply the number of uniforms at School B of Type B with the Child's Type B cost, and multiply the number of uniforms at School B of Type C with the Child's Type C cost and add those three quantities. That is: $30 \times \$9 + 60 \times \$10 + 50 \times \$11 = \$1,420$.

(Math Refresher #702)

56. Choice G is correct.

(Use Strategy 18: Know and use facts about triangles.)

Let the hypotenuse be x. According to the Pythagorean theorem:
$$2^2 + 5^2 = x^2$$
$$4 + 25 = x^2$$
$$29 = x^2$$
$$x = \sqrt{29}$$
$$\cos a = \frac{5}{\sqrt{29}}$$

(Math Refreshers #307, #509, and #901)

57. Choice E is correct.

(Use Strategy 8: When each choice must be tested, start with the last choice and work backward.)

The only way to solve this question is to test the choices one by one. We start with Choice E, and it is correct. You can see that if the ant goes through 8, it must go from 5 to 6 to 8 or from 5 to 7 to 8 or from 2 to 6 to 8.

58. Choice K is correct.

(Use Strategy 11: Use new definitions carefully. These problems are generally easy.)

The first few terms of the sequence are found as follows:

Given: Term 1 = 2

By definition, Term 2 = (Term 1 − 2)3

$$= (2 - 2)3$$
$$= (0)3$$
$$\text{Term 2} = 0$$
$$\text{Term 3} = (\text{Term 2} - 2)3$$
$$= (0 - 2)3$$
$$= (-2)3$$
$$= -6$$
$$\text{Term 4} = (\text{Term 3} - 2)3$$
$$= (-6 - 2)3$$
$$= (-8)3$$
$$= -24$$

and so on.

2, 0, −6, and −24 are all even, so Choices F, G, H, and J can be eliminated.

(Math Refresher #431)

59. Choice C is correct.

(Use Strategy 11: Use new definitions carefully.)

$n = \frac{3}{8}$ is a member of both sets. Note that n is not an integer in this case, and certainly in this case n is not equal to 6. Thus I and III are not true for this case. Members of both sets are $\frac{3}{8}$, 6, and 8. So for any of these members, $8n$ is an integer. Thus II is always true.

(Math Refresher #801)

60. Choice K is correct.

Method I:

(Use Strategy 18: Remember right triangle facts.)

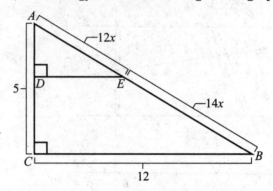

Triangle *BCA* is a right triangle, so we can use the Pythagorean theorem:

$$(AB)^2 = (AC)^2 + (BC)^2$$
$$(12x + 14x)^2 = 5^2 + 12^2$$
$$(26x)^2 = 25 + 144$$
$$676x^2 = 169$$
$$x^2 = \frac{169}{676}$$

(Use Strategy 19: Factor and reduce.)

$$x^2 = \frac{\cancel{13} \times \cancel{13}}{\cancel{13} \times \cancel{13} \times 4} = \frac{1}{4}$$
$$x = \frac{1}{2}$$

Method II:

(Use Strategy 18: Remember right triangles.)

Triangle *BCA* is a right triangle with legs 5 and 12. 5, 12, 13 is a special right triangle. Thus, *AB* must = 13.

$$\text{Therefore } 12x + 14x = 13$$
$$26x = 13$$
$$x = \frac{13}{36}$$
$$x = \frac{1}{2}$$

(Math Refreshers #509 and #406)

EXPLANATORY ANSWERS

Section 3: Reading Test

As you read these explanatory answers, you are advised to refer to the "9 Reading Comprehension Strategies" (beginning on page 102) whenever a specific strategy is referred to in the answer. Of particular importance is the Reading Comprehension Strategy 2 (page 105).

Note: *All Reading questions use Reading Strategies 1, 2, and 3 (pages 102–108) as well as other strategies indicated.*

1. Choice C is correct. The presence of the sign gave Mrs. Deverell pleasure, and its replacement was a cause for "panic and dismay." Choices A and B are incorrect in their implication that Mrs. Deverell views the old sign negatively. Choice D is incorrect because Mrs. Deverell's emotions are personal in rather than generalized feelings about changes in the neighborhood.

2. Choice G is correct (see lines 43–45). The examples given indicate that Mrs. Deverell's old friends assume that she will judge their speech and manners, they watch her for "signs of grandeur or condescension," and whatever she does is taken as verification of these. Choice F is incorrect because there is no indication that Mrs. Deverell's former friends were testing her to see how much she really knew about high society. Choices H and J may also be implied in their behavior, but because they are motives one might only surmise from the story, they do not represent the best answer.

3. Choice A is correct, as suggested most clearly in lines 21–24. Choices B, C, and D are not supported in the story.

4. Choice F is correct, based upon Angel's attempts to get her mother to cut her ties to the old neighborhood and to leave all manual work to "the people who should do it" (line 63). Choice G is incorrect because, although lines 68–70 point out the reversal in the relationship between mother and daughter, the reversal is based on the daughter's new authority over her mother rather than rejection of authority. Choice H could be assumed based on Angel's career as a novelist, but it is not described in the passage. Choice J may be assumed, but the issue of manual labor is mentioned only as it relates to what Angel thinks her mother's activities should be.

5. Choice D is correct, an interpretation implied strongly in Mrs. Deverell's yearning for familiarity and, in the final two paragraphs, her "restlessness" (line 67), her fretful wandering (lines 74–75), her boredom (line 75), and her playing the unaccustomed role of "intimidated child" (line 76). Choices A, B, and C are incorrect because these interpretations would contradict Mrs. Deverell's pattern of obeying her daughter's wishes and dealing with her hurt feelings passively.

6. Choice J is correct, reflecting a somewhat archaic meaning of *perplex*, meaning to involve or occupy, rather than the more current connotation, to confuse. Choices F, G, and H, then, are all incorrect..

7. Choice C is correct. Mrs. Deverell's instinctive reaction is to finish the work. In addition, she associates these sorts of tasks with pleasant sensory experiences and artistic skill. Choices A, B, and D are incorrect in implying that she had wished to escape household chores or associated them negatively with low socioeconomic status.

8. Choice J is correct as the answer most consistently supported in the story. The conduct of Mrs. Deverell's new life is dictated primarily by her daughter and prescribed social roles, while her old life is the source of all her genuine emotional attachments and pleasures. Choices F, G, and H are not supported by any description or comment in the story.

9. Choice C is correct as the most accurate summary of the difference. Choices A and D are not supported in the story and are incorrect, and Choice B may be a reasonable surmise but is not addressed directly in the story.

10. Choice H is correct. Most of Mrs. Deverell's actions are based on avoidance of offense and therefore suppression of her true desires. Incorrect answers F, G, and J are not supported in the story.

11. Choice C is correct. The second paragraph states that "the other classes . . . adopted many of the outward characteristics of the aristocracy."

12. Choice H is correct. The second paragraph implies that the bourgeoisie was "rising to political power" and rivaling the power of the aristocracy.

13. Choice B is correct. The third and fifth paragraphs describe the castles as "strongholds" and "fortified houses."

14. Choice F is correct. This information is given in paragraph 3, where it states that "the Magyar armies" harried central Europe.

15. Choice B is correct. The fourth paragraph relates how "power passed into the hands of warriors invested by the monarchy and the Church with lands."

16. Choice J is correct. Paragraph 2 states, "Noblemen who became bishops or who founded new Orders helped to implant aristocratic principles . . . deep within . . . the Church."

17. Choice A is correct. The last paragraph states that hunting was a rehearsal for war and it made up "for the lack of butcher's meat."

18. Choice H is correct. See paragraph 2: "Even the unarmed peasantry . . . long remained tenaciously loyal to their lords, held to their allegiance by that combination of love and fear, *amor et timor*. . . ."

19. Choice A is correct. See paragraph 4: ". . . warriors . . . undertook . . . to protect the unarmed peasantry."

20. Choice H is correct. Although well-fortified (lines 84–99), castles are described as lacking warmth, light, and comfort, and life is filled with "harshness" (lines 100–105). Choice F is incorrect, the author making the point that privacy was lacking (lines 101–102). Choice G is incorrect; the article mentions schooling only in warfare (lines 107–111). Choice J is incorrect; *gluttonous* refers to the excessive consumption of food, but the author points out that agriculture was underdeveloped and foodstuffs in short supply (lines 111–114).

21. Choice C is correct. The theme of this essay is expressed in various other ways. For example: in referring to the independence of opinion that one loses with one's loss of early youth; in condemning our surrender of the freedom of solitude to the group actions of society at large; and in encouraging us not to fear the consequences of being inconsistent and misunderstood.

22. Choice F is correct. The infant can be, and is expected to be, completely irresponsible. "Infancy conforms to nobody: all conform to it, so that one babe commonly makes four or five out of the adults who prattle and play to it."

23. Choice D is correct. "Speak what you think now in hard words, and to-morrow speak what to-morrow thinks in hard words again, though it contradict everything you said to-day." The misunderstanding will occur because what you say may be the opposite of conventional opinion, or may be ahead of its time. But the risk is worth it.

24. Choice G is correct. It is a natural prerogative of youth to give "an independent, genuine verdict." He naturally cares very little about what older people may think because "It seems he knows how to speak to his contemporaries. Bashful or bold, then, he will know how to make us seniors very unnecessary."

25. Choice B is correct. The "pit" or gallery in a theater usually contains the least expensive seats. Consequently, it is favored by those less economically endowed, and, according to the author, less committed to conventional manners and highly dignified behavior. In effect, these are the people who go to the theater to see, rather than to be seen.

26. Choice H is correct. When people desert solitude (or individual action) to join society (group action), they surrender a large part of individual freedom in exchange for a livelihood. They thus become more reliant and dependent on others than on themselves. The metaphor of the jointstock company is a good one because such a company is faceless and without identity. No one member stands out above any other member.

27. Choice D is correct. "Spirit and enthusiasm" are something individualistic and definite. To be spirited and enthusiastic is to be spontaneous, natural, and uninhibited. One must (according to the author) be committed and courageous "As soon as he has once acted or spoken with eclat. . . ." See also **Reading Comprehension Strategy 5**.

28. Choice H is correct. To act out of whim is to act impulsively and in an unpremeditated, spontaneous (and generally sincere) manner. The author, however, is not endorsing *whimsical* action simply because it is uninhibited ("I hope it is somewhat better than whim at last, but we cannot spend the day in explanation") but because it is a way of speaking freely, and usually with complete honesty.

29. Choice A is correct. The essence of true self-reliance and genuine nonconformity is, as Shakespeare put it, "To thine own self be true." If one is dishonest with oneself, one will be dishonest with others; if one is honest with oneself, one will be honest with others.

30. Choice H is correct. See lines 81–83. Choice F is incorrect because of the author's emphasis on the idea that people's beliefs are based on their desire to conform, not on sincerely held values. Choices G and J are incorrect because these ideas are not stated or implied.

31. Choice B is correct. Line 44 states that egg cells contain only X chromosomes. Lines 63–67 say that a male lacks the "opposite" X chromosome, and the hemophilia gene becomes dominant in him. In the female this never happens.

32. Choice J is correct. See lines 48–50. Both hemophilia and color-blindness are known to be sex-linked characteristics, being carried on the sex chromosomes and identifiable with one sex.

33. Choice A is correct. Lines 6–8 state this to be the function of genes.

34. Choice H is correct. Lines 18–22 tell us that a human cell has 46 chromosomes, with two sets of 23 each contributed by the two human gametes.

35. Choice D is correct. The last paragraph tells us that blood plasma contains AHF, the protein that causes blood to clot.

36. Choice H is correct. As the second paragraph explains, the blood of hemophiliacs, or "bleeders" (third paragraph), clots too slowly. Thus we can infer, although it is not explicitly stated, that excessive bleeding is the risk for people with this condition.

37. Choice D is correct. See the fifth paragraph, as well as paragraph ten on sex-linked genes. The key point is that an *equal* blend of chromosomes is not possible because some genes are dominant and will control others, and gender only sometimes determines the dominance of genes.

38. Choice H is correct. *Antihemophilic factor* (AHF), a protein, is italicized in the next to the last paragraph and is further defined in the final paragraph, which mentions injecting the substance into the person with hemophilia.

39. Choice A is correct. Sex-linked genes are first mentioned in paragraph 10 and explained through the example of Queen Victoria's children in the following three paragraphs.

40. Choice J is correct. The answer is explained in paragraph 13. This paragraph explains the sons' greater probability of inheriting the disease due to males' single X chromosome, which if defective has no chance to play the recessive role to a second healthy, dominant X.

EXPLANATORY ANSWERS

Section 4: Science Test

1. Choice C is correct. According to the passage, "the man begins taking the prescription on day 4," so to determine his bacteria count *after* 4 days of medication, look at the value for day 8: about 10,000 (hundreds of bacteria).

2. Choice J is correct. You can see in Figure 1 that the bacteria count never reaches 0 between days 8 and 10. The same infection remains, only to reproduce at an exponential rate. Choices G and H are disproved by the sharp rate of decline in his bacterial count while on the medication (days 4–7).

3. Choice A is correct. The lowest value on the chart is for 1998.

4. Choice J is correct. Antibiotic resistance rates have increased fairly steadily since 1998 and the value for 2013 is already 90%; assuming rates continue to rise, by 2020 more than 90% of the bacteria will be antibiotic-resistant.

5. Choice B is correct. Figure 2 shows a trend of increased antibiotic use; Figure 3 shows a rising rate of antibiotic-resistant bacteria over the same time period. The data does not necessarily support the reverse trend (Choice C).

6. Choice H is correct. The second paragraph states: "Lamarck postulated that organisms adapt to their environments based on use and disuse of characteristics."

7. Choice A is correct. Lamarck theorized that an organism that acquired a trait over the course of its lifetime would then pass on that trait to its offspring.

8. Choice F is correct. Darwin's theory that "the individuals with traits that made them in some way better able to function in their environment tend to survive and thereby reproduce" assumes that not all individuals survive long enough to reproduce.

9. Choice C is correct. The fourth paragraph states, "the individuals with traits that made them in some way better able to function in their environment tend to survive and thereby reproduce." Since suitable food (foliage) is accessible only by those individuals with the more favorable trait (longer necks), the presence of that trait allows the individuals to survive and reproduce, passing on the same trait to the next generation.

10. Choice H is correct. Darwin's theory supports the *passing on* of traits that best suit the individual for survival.

11. Choice C is correct. From the first paragraph: "Simple organisms never disappeared, he thought, because they were able to spontaneously generate."

12. Choice J is correct. Choices F, G, and H merely note the existence of variety; Choice J indicates how the variety of traits best suits individuals for survival in a variety of settings.

13. Choice A is correct. The fourth column reveals that protons and neutrons have equal mass and are much greater than electrons. Since the heaviest particles all reside in the nucleus (column 2), the majority of the mass should be located there.

14. Choice J is correct. All of the carbon isotopes contain 6 protons (column 2) and 6 electrons (column 5), while the neutron count varies (column 3).

15. Choice B is correct. Table 3 shows the abundance of the radioactive isotopes, so the answer will involve the quantity of the isotope in nature, eliminating Choices C and D. Since carbon-14 is *not* abundant in nature, that leaves us with Choice B.

16. Choice H is correct. In order for an isotope to be "more common" than the other forms, it needs to have an abundance of greater than 50.0% (column 2). Only rhenium-187 and indium-115 meet this criterion.

17. Choice A is correct. Values for protons and neutrons are equal in columns 2 (location) and 4 (mass) but differ in column 3 (charge).

18. Choice G is correct. Potential energy is the vertical component of the graph; reactants are lower on the graph than products, meaning they contain *less* potential energy.

19. Choice C is correct. You can see on the chart that activation energy is the energy required to make a reactant an activated complex (to start the reaction). The difference between reaction and product in an exothermic reaction is a loss of *heat* (Choices A and B).

20. Choice G is correct. In photosynthesis, the reactant (carbon dioxide) has low potential energy, while the product (glucose) has high potential energy. You can see the same condition in Figure 1 (an endothermic reaction).

21. Choice D is correct. The same reactants and products are involved, eliminating Choices A and B. You can see from the graphs that the potential energy is always greater for the uncatalyzed reaction than for the catalyzed reaction.

22. Choice F is correct. The products in an exothermic reaction have less potential energy than the reactants; the extra energy is released into the environment as heat.

23. Choice D is correct. According to the design, Experiment 1 measures in the *North* Atlantic, while Experiment 2 measures in the *South* Atlantic.

24. Choice H is correct. The graphs are roughly mirror images of each other, warmest in the North Atlantic when it's coldest in the South Atlantic (month 9).

25. Choice C is correct. Because the tropics are nearest to the equator, they receive more consistent sunlight, which in turn leads to more consistent temperatures.

26. Choice J is correct. Remember that we're graphing months; month 13 would be month 1 of a new year, so expect the data to mimic month 1 of the first year: between 25 and 26 degrees.

27. Choice A is correct. The number of sunspots varies unpredictably from month to month according to Figure 2, while the ocean temperatures vary based on location and time of year. Given only this data, there appears to be no relationship between sunspots and ocean surface temperature.

28. Choice G is correct. Taking temperatures at all three locations will provide more samples and allow the scientist to draw better conclusions from the data.

29. Choice B is correct. The student is manipulating the height at which she drops the ball in order to chart the difference in drop time (the dependent variable).

30. Choice G is correct. Choices F and H are false because *more* air resistance would make the ball fall more slowly, while less air resistance would make the ball fall faster. Choice J is incorrect because the experiments demonstrated that mass is not a factor in the speed of the fall. The surface area of a sphere (or ball) is less than that of a cube, meaning the 10-gram mass fell faster.

31. Choice A is correct. The drop times increase as the drop heights increase in an almost constant manner, so look for the graph with a positive, linear slope (Choice A).

32. Choice G is correct. The drop time seems to increase 0.1 s or 0.2 s for every 3 m of height added; since the change in height from the last test would be an additional 6 m, the change in drop time should be an additional 0.2 s to 0.4 s. Minimum: 2.5 + 0.2 + 2.7 s. Maximum: 2.5 + 0.4 = 2.9 s.

33. Choice C is correct. According to Experiments 1 and 2, a change in mass has no impact on the drop time of the ball in a vacuum tube. Choices A and B do not factor in the changing variable between the two experiments (mass of the ball).

34. Choice G is correct. Drop time is affected by the drop height (independent variable). Mass and type of metal are not affected by the independent variable.

35. Choice D is correct. According to the passage, Needham poured his boiled broth into a separate flask.

36. Choice F is correct. Pasteur's experiment was designed to measure the impact of exposure to air and particulates; the flasks left to the open air represent *normal*, uninhibited exposure (a positive control group).

37. Choice B is correct. Once Needham poured the broth into a separate flask, it became impossible to tell whether any new life came from the "life force" in the boiled broth or from the contaminated glass.

38. Choice J is correct. The second flask was boiled thoroughly while the third flask was not, to disprove Needham's claim of overboiling. Both flasks were designed to allow air (for any potential growth) but keep out dust and particles that could include new life from outside the sample.

39. Choice B is correct. Because of gravity, dust and particles had settled at the bottom of the S. When Pasteur tipped the flask to allow the uncontaminated broth to pour into the bottom of the S, microorganisms from the dust began to repopulate, fed by the broth.

40. Choice H is correct. Pasteur's experiment was designed to disprove Needham's conclusions in the flask experiment only. It was not designed to make a conclusive statement about the possibility of spontaneous generation under other conditions.

WHAT YOU MUST DO NOW TO RAISE YOUR ACT SCORE

1. Follow the directions on pages 529–537 to find your scale score for the ACT Test you've just taken. These results will give you a good idea about how hard you'll need to study in order to achieve a certain score on the actual ACT.

   Using your scale score count as a basis, indicate for yourself your areas of strength and weakness as revealed by the Norms Tables on pages 532–533.

2. Eliminate your weaknesses in each of the ACT Test areas by taking the following Giant Steps toward ACT success:

Reading Part

Giant Step 1

Take advantage of the Reading Strategies that begin on page 102. Read again the explanatory answer for each of the Reading questions that you got wrong. Refer to the Reading Strategy that applies to each of your incorrect answers. Learn each of these Reading Strategies thoroughly. These strategies are crucial if you want to raise your ACT score substantially.

Giant Step 2

You can improve your vocabulary by doing the following:

1. Read as widely as possible—not only novels. Non-fiction is important too—and don't forget to read newspapers and magazines.

2. Listen to people who speak well. Tune in to worthwhile TV programs.

3. Use the dictionary frequently and extensively—at home, on the bus, at work, etc.

4. Review the Hot Prefixes and Roots beginning on page 128.

Math Part

Giant Step 3

Make good use of the 19 Math Strategies that begin on page 44. Read again the solutions for each Math question that you answered incorrectly. Refer to the Math Strategy that applies to each of your incorrect answers. Learn each of these Math Strategies thoroughly. We repeat that these strategies are crucial if you want to raise your ACT Math score substantially.

Giant Step 4

You may want to take the 101 Most Important Math Questions You Need to Know How to Solve test beginning on page 13 and follow the directions after the test for a basic Math skills diagnosis.

For each Math question that you got wrong on the test, note the reference to the Complete ACT Math Refresher section beginning on page 147. This reference will explain clearly the mathematical principle involved in the solution of the question you answered incorrectly. Learn that particular mathematical principle thoroughly.

For Both the Math and Reading Parts

Giant Step 5

You may want to take the World's Shortest Practice Test for the ACT Exam beginning on page 1 to assess whether you're using the best strategies for the questions.

For the English Test and Writing Part

Giant Step 6

Take a look at Part 9, the ACT Writing Test, which describes the Writing Section. For the English Test, make use of Part 7, A Brief Review of English Grammar, and Part 8, the Complete ACT Grammar and Usage Refresher.

After you have done some of the tasks you have been advised to do in the suggestions above, proceed to ACT Practice Test 3, beginning on page 565.

After taking ACT Practice Test 3, concentrate on the weaknesses that still remain.

If you do the job *right* and follow the steps listed above, you are likely to raise your ACT score significantly.

Remember:

I am the master of my fate:
I am the captain of my soul.

—From the poem "Invictus"
by William Ernest Henley

ACT PRACTICE TEST 3

ANSWER SHEET

It is recommended that you use a No. 2 pencil. It is very important that you fill in the entire circle darkly and completely. If you change your response, erase as completely as possible. Incomplete marks or erasures may affect your score.

Complete Mark ● **Examples of Incomplete Marks** ◓ ⊗ ⊖ ◐ ◑ ◔ ◕ ◒

SECTION 1: ENGLISH TEST

	A B C D		F G H J		A B C D		F G H J		A B C D
1	○○○○	16	○○○○	31	○○○○	46	○○○○	61	○○○○
2	F G H J ○○○○	17	A B C D ○○○○	32	F G H J ○○○○	47	A B C D ○○○○	62	F G H J ○○○○
3	A B C D ○○○○	18	F G H J ○○○○	33	A B C D ○○○○	48	F G H J ○○○○	63	A B C D ○○○○
4	F G H J ○○○○	19	A B C D ○○○○	34	F G H J ○○○○	49	A B C D ○○○○	64	F G H J ○○○○
5	A B C D ○○○○	20	F G H J ○○○○	35	A B C D ○○○○	50	F G H J ○○○○	65	A B C D ○○○○
6	F G H J ○○○○	21	A B C D ○○○○	36	F G H J ○○○○	51	A B C D ○○○○	66	F G H J ○○○○
7	A B C D ○○○○	22	F G H J ○○○○	37	A B C D ○○○○	52	F G H J ○○○○	67	A B C D ○○○○
8	F G H J ○○○○	23	A B C D ○○○○	38	F G H J ○○○○	53	A B C D ○○○○	68	F G H J ○○○○
9	A B C D ○○○○	24	F G H J ○○○○	39	A B C D ○○○○	54	F G H J ○○○○	69	A B C D ○○○○
10	F G H J ○○○○	25	A B C D ○○○○	40	F G H J ○○○○	55	A B C D ○○○○	70	F G H J ○○○○
11	A B C D ○○○○	26	F G H J ○○○○	41	A B C D ○○○○	56	F G H J ○○○○	71	A B C D ○○○○
12	F G H J ○○○○	27	A B C D ○○○○	42	F G H J ○○○○	57	A B C D ○○○○	72	F G H J ○○○○
13	A B C D ○○○○	28	F G H J ○○○○	43	A B C D ○○○○	58	F G H J ○○○○	73	A B C D ○○○○
14	F G H J ○○○○	29	A B C D ○○○○	44	F G H J ○○○○	59	A B C D ○○○○	74	F G H J ○○○○
15	A B C D ○○○○	30	F G H J ○○○○	45	A B C D ○○○○	60	F G H J ○○○○	75	A B C D ○○○○

Complete Mark ●   **Examples of Incomplete Marks** ⊙ ⊗ ⊖ ◯ ◯ ◌ ◉ ⬤

SECTION 2: MATHEMATICS TEST

	A B C D E		A B C D E		A B C D E		A B C D E		A B C D E
1	◯ ◯ ◯ ◯ ◯	13	◯ ◯ ◯ ◯ ◯	25	◯ ◯ ◯ ◯ ◯	37	◯ ◯ ◯ ◯ ◯	49	◯ ◯ ◯ ◯ ◯
	F G H J K		F G H J K		F G H J K		F G H J K		F G H J K
2	◯ ◯ ◯ ◯ ◯	14	◯ ◯ ◯ ◯ ◯	26	◯ ◯ ◯ ◯ ◯	38	◯ ◯ ◯ ◯ ◯	50	◯ ◯ ◯ ◯ ◯
	A B C D E		A B C D E		A B C D E		A B C D E		A B C D E
3	◯ ◯ ◯ ◯ ◯	15	◯ ◯ ◯ ◯ ◯	27	◯ ◯ ◯ ◯ ◯	39	◯ ◯ ◯ ◯ ◯	51	◯ ◯ ◯ ◯ ◯
	F G H J K		F G H J K		F G H J K		F G H J K		F G H J K
4	◯ ◯ ◯ ◯ ◯	16	◯ ◯ ◯ ◯ ◯	28	◯ ◯ ◯ ◯ ◯	40	◯ ◯ ◯ ◯ ◯	52	◯ ◯ ◯ ◯ ◯
	A B C D E		A B C D E		A B C D E		A B C D E		A B C D E
5	◯ ◯ ◯ ◯ ◯	17	◯ ◯ ◯ ◯ ◯	29	◯ ◯ ◯ ◯ ◯	41	◯ ◯ ◯ ◯ ◯	53	◯ ◯ ◯ ◯ ◯
	F G H J K		F G H J K		F G H J K		F G H J K		F G H J K
6	◯ ◯ ◯ ◯ ◯	18	◯ ◯ ◯ ◯ ◯	30	◯ ◯ ◯ ◯ ◯	42	◯ ◯ ◯ ◯ ◯	54	◯ ◯ ◯ ◯ ◯
	A B C D E		A B C D E		A B C D E		A B C D E		A B C D E
7	◯ ◯ ◯ ◯ ◯	19	◯ ◯ ◯ ◯ ◯	31	◯ ◯ ◯ ◯ ◯	43	◯ ◯ ◯ ◯ ◯	55	◯ ◯ ◯ ◯ ◯
	F G H J K		F G H J K		F G H J K		F G H J K		F G H J K
8	◯ ◯ ◯ ◯ ◯	20	◯ ◯ ◯ ◯ ◯	32	◯ ◯ ◯ ◯ ◯	44	◯ ◯ ◯ ◯ ◯	56	◯ ◯ ◯ ◯ ◯
	A B C D E		A B C D E		A B C D E		A B C D E		A B C D E
9	◯ ◯ ◯ ◯ ◯	21	◯ ◯ ◯ ◯ ◯	33	◯ ◯ ◯ ◯ ◯	45	◯ ◯ ◯ ◯ ◯	57	◯ ◯ ◯ ◯ ◯
	F G H J K		F G H J K		F G H J K		F G H J K		F G H J K
10	◯ ◯ ◯ ◯ ◯	22	◯ ◯ ◯ ◯ ◯	34	◯ ◯ ◯ ◯ ◯	46	◯ ◯ ◯ ◯ ◯	58	◯ ◯ ◯ ◯ ◯
	A B C D E		A B C D E		A B C D E		A B C D E		A B C D E
11	◯ ◯ ◯ ◯ ◯	23	◯ ◯ ◯ ◯ ◯	35	◯ ◯ ◯ ◯ ◯	47	◯ ◯ ◯ ◯ ◯	59	◯ ◯ ◯ ◯ ◯
	F G H J K		F G H J K		F G H J K		F G H J K		F G H J K
12	◯ ◯ ◯ ◯ ◯	24	◯ ◯ ◯ ◯ ◯	36	◯ ◯ ◯ ◯ ◯	48	◯ ◯ ◯ ◯ ◯	60	◯ ◯ ◯ ◯ ◯

Complete Mark ● **Examples of Incomplete Marks** ⦿ ⊗ ⊖ ⦸ ⦸ ◔ ◉ ◉

SECTION 3: READING TEST

	A B C D		A B C D		A B C D		A B C D		A B C D
1	○ ○ ○ ○	9	○ ○ ○ ○	17	○ ○ ○ ○	25	○ ○ ○ ○	33	○ ○ ○ ○
	F G H J		F G H J		F G H J		F G H J		F G H J
2	○ ○ ○ ○	10	○ ○ ○ ○	18	○ ○ ○ ○	26	○ ○ ○ ○	34	○ ○ ○ ○
	A B C D		A B C D		A B C D		A B C D		A B C D
3	○ ○ ○ ○	11	○ ○ ○ ○	19	○ ○ ○ ○	27	○ ○ ○ ○	35	○ ○ ○ ○
	F G H J		F G H J		F G H J		F G H J		F G H J
4	○ ○ ○ ○	12	○ ○ ○ ○	20	○ ○ ○ ○	28	○ ○ ○ ○	36	○ ○ ○ ○
	A B C D		A B C D		A B C D		A B C D		A B C D
5	○ ○ ○ ○	13	○ ○ ○ ○	21	○ ○ ○ ○	29	○ ○ ○ ○	37	○ ○ ○ ○
	F G H J		F G H J		F G H J		F G H J		F G H J
6	○ ○ ○ ○	14	○ ○ ○ ○	22	○ ○ ○ ○	30	○ ○ ○ ○	38	○ ○ ○ ○
	A B C D		A B C D		A B C D		A B C D		A B C D
7	○ ○ ○ ○	15	○ ○ ○ ○	23	○ ○ ○ ○	31	○ ○ ○ ○	39	○ ○ ○ ○
	F G H J		F G H J	AF	G H J		F G H J		F G H J
8	○ ○ ○ ○	16	○ ○ ○ ○	24	○ ○ ○ ○	32	○ ○ ○ ○	40	○ ○ ○ ○

SECTION 4: SCIENCE TEST

	A B C D		A B C D		A B C D		A B C D		A B C D
1	○ ○ ○ ○	9	○ ○ ○ ○	17	○ ○ ○ ○	25	○ ○ ○ ○	33	○ ○ ○ ○
	F G H J		F G H J		F G H J		F G H J		F G H J
2	○ ○ ○ ○	10	○ ○ ○ ○	18	○ ○ ○ ○	26	○ ○ ○ ○	34	○ ○ ○ ○
	A B C D		A B C D		A B C D		A B C D		A B C D
3	○ ○ ○ ○	11	○ ○ ○ ○	19	○ ○ ○ ○	27	○ ○ ○ ○	35	○ ○ ○ ○
	F G H J		F G H J		F G H J		F G H J		F G H J
4	○ ○ ○ ○	12	○ ○ ○ ○	20	○ ○ ○ ○	28	○ ○ ○ ○	36	○ ○ ○ ○
	A B C D		A B C D		A B C D		A B C D		A B C D
5	○ ○ ○ ○	13	○ ○ ○ ○	21	○ ○ ○ ○	29	○ ○ ○ ○	37	○ ○ ○ ○
	F G H J		F G H J		F G H J		F G H J		F G H J
6	● ○ ○ ○	14	○ ○ ○ ○	22	○ ○ ○ ○	30	⊗ ⊖ ○ ○	38	○ ○ ○ ○
	A B C D		A B C D		A B C D		A B C D		A B C D
7	○ ○ ○ ○	15	○ ○ ○ ○	23	○ ○ ○ ○	31	○ ○ ○ ○	39	○ ○ ○ ○
	F G H J		F G H J		F G H J		F G H J		F G H J
8	○ ○ ○ ○	16	○ ○ ○ ○	24	○ ○ ○ ○	32	○ ○ ○ ○	40	○ ○ ○ ○

SECTION 1: ENGLISH TEST

45 Minutes, 75 Questions

Turn to Section 1 of your answer sheet (page 565) to answer the questions in this section.

Directions

Each passage below is accompanied by a number of questions. For some questions, you will consider how the passage might be revised to improve the expression of ideas. For other questions, you will consider how the passage might be edited to correct errors in sentence structure, usage, or punctuation.

Some questions will direct you to an underlined portion of a passage. Other questions will direct you to a location in a passage or ask you to think about the passage as a whole.

After reading each passage, choose the answer to each question that most effectively improves the quality of writing in the passage or that makes the passage conform to the conventions of standard written English. Many questions include a "NO CHANGE" option. Choose that option if you think the best choice is to leave the relevant portion of the passage as it is.

Questions 1–15 are based on the following passage, *Interpreting the Middle Ages*.

The Middle Ages (c. A.D. 400–1500) have long been called (1) The Dark Ages because (2) then science and scientific thought (3) had hardly existed. Anyone who dared to seek scientific knowledge, (4) as some did, opened himself to persecution and prosecution (5) both by civil and religious authorities. In many cases these two types of authorities were one and the same because Europe was Catholic, the Reformation (6) had not begun until 1517, when Luther wrote his Ninety-Five Theses. (7)

Recently, however, (8) perhaps because of a renewed interest in things spiritual, this period of history has come to be called an age of faith. It (9) cannot be disputed that during medieval times the Church played an enormous role in the day-to-day lives of the (10) people. Moreover life was so hard that many people went on living only in the hope (11) that by leading Christian lives they would be rewarded after death. (12) Promising eternal life in heaven, many men and women turned to the Church totally and became priests, brothers, or nuns.

(13) Other future generations will, of course, decide for themselves what to call the Middle Ages. It may be safely assumed that a scientific society (14) would be likely to see the Middle Ages as dark, whereas a more spiritual or religious society will see those historical times as enlightened by faith. Historians, looking back on twentieth-century America, will know that about midway through the twentieth century America started to shift from a generally scientific to a more spiritual view of life. (15)

Interpreting the Middle Ages Questions

1. (A) NO CHANGE
   (B) the Dark Ages
   (C) the dark ages
   (D) dark ages

2. (F) NO CHANGE
   (G) at the time
   (H) during that time
   (J) during those days then

3. Which of the following alternatives to the underlined portion would NOT be acceptable?
   (A) were scarce
   (B) were virtually nonexistent
   (C) hardly even existed
   (D) were totally unknown

4. (F) NO CHANGE
   (G) such as some people,
   (H) like some did,
   (J) for instance, some people,

Go on to the next page.

5. (A) NO CHANGE
   (B) by both civil and religious authorities.
   (C) by both civil and by religious authorities.
   (D) by authorities both civil and religious.

6. (F) NO CHANGE
   (G) not beginning
   (H) not having begun
   (J) beginning not

7. The writer is considering adding the following true statement:

   > The Ninety-Five Theses argued against corrupt Church practices and rituals people believed would guarantee them salvation.

   Should the writer make the addition here?

   (A) Yes, because the sentence explains what the Reformation was.
   (B) Yes, because the sentence adds an example of someone who risked prosecution by questioning authority.
   (C) No, because the sentence elaborates on Luther's Theses, not the perception of the Middle Ages described in the paragraph.
   (D) No, because the sentence contradicts the idea of the Middle Ages as the Dark Ages.

8. Given that all of the choices are true, which wording serves as the best introduction for this paragraph?

   (F) NO CHANGE
   (G) perhaps because of the comparative ease of living today,
   (H) perhaps because of our more optimistic outlook,
   (J) perhaps because of the Church's efforts to improve its reputation,

9. (A) NO CHANGE
   (B) cannot hardly be disputed that
   (C) cannot be disputed except that
   (D) cannot be a dispute that

10. (F) NO CHANGE
    (G) people, moreover life
    (H) people; moreover, life
    (J) people, moreover, life

11. (A) NO CHANGE
    (B) that leading Christian lives they will be rewarded

    (C) of being rewarded for leading Christian lives
    (D) that having led Christian lives they will be rewarded

12. (F) NO CHANGE
    (G) Due to the promise of
    (H) From the promise of
    (J) Because of the promise of

13. (A) NO CHANGE
    (B) Future generations that will follow this one
    (C) Future generations
    (D) Generations, in the future,

14. (F) NO CHANGE
    (G) is
    (H) will have been
    (J) will be

15. Which of the following sequences places the sentences in paragraph 3 in the most logical order?
    (A) NO CHANGE
    (B) 3, 1, 2
    (C) 1, 3, 2
    (D) 2, 3, 1

Questions 16–30 are based on the following passage, *Protecting the Environment.*

The Environmental Protection Agency was created (16) in the beginning part of the 1970s, (17) in part in reaction to the demands of environmentalist groups. Although some of (18) these type groups have been in existence for many years, e.g., the Sierra (19) Club, whereas others are newly formed, (20) e.g. the Environmental Defense Fund. (21) Some are called (22) conservationist or preservationist. The main difference (23) between the first type and the second is that the former (24) wants to use the nation's and world's resources in such a way that they will not run out, while the latter does not want those resources used at all. An example of the difference between the two philosophies (25) is the lumber industry. Conservationists would approve selective cutting, but preservationists (26) would only approve leaving the forest alone entirely.

One aspect of the EPA's program that both groups think is important is the demand for environmental-impact statements. These statements are filed by the government agency responsible for granting a permit for a particular project, such as a new (27) dam a water-treatment plant, or an electricity-generating plant. The

Go on to the next page. ⇨

environmental-impact statement must include positive and negative effects that the project will have on the (28) immediate and far-flung environment—including water supplies, landmasses, animals, plants, and humans. By examining these statements, the EPA can determine whether a project is safe or its positive impact will outweigh (29) it's negative. Only if one of these two circumstances obtains does EPA grant permission for the (30) project being carried out.

Protecting the Environment Questions

16. (F) NO CHANGE
    (G) in the first few years of the 1970s
    (H) in the early 1970s
    (J) in the first division of the 1970s

17. (A) NO CHANGE
    (B) somewhat in reaction to
    (C) in a way in reaction to
    (D) as a consequence of the reaction to

18. (F) NO CHANGE
    (G) this type of groups
    (H) these types of group
    (J) these groups

19. (A) NO CHANGE
    (B) Club; whereas
    (C) club,
    (D) Club,

20. (F) NO CHANGE
    (G) eg.,
    (H) e.g.;
    (J) e.g.,

21. Upon reviewing this essay, the writer considers deleting the preceding sentence. If the writer were to delete the sentence, the paragraph would lose primarily:

    (A) a comparison between more and less powerful environmental groups
    (B) background information setting up a contrast between types of environmental groups
    (C) concrete examples of the groups' missions
    (D) well-known names readers can identify with

22. (F) NO CHANGE
    (G) conservationist. Some
    (H) conservationist; some
    (J) conservationist, some

23. (A) NO CHANGE
    (B) among
    (C) with
    (D) in

24. Which choice most clearly communicates the difference between the two types of groups?
    (F) NO CHANGE
    (G) wants to conserve resources, while the latter wants to preserve them.
    (H) uses resources for selfish purposes, while the latter protects resources for all.
    (J) has a relationship with industry that is different from that of the latter.

25. (A) NO CHANGE
    (B) can be found in lumber.
    (C) can be found in the lumber industry.
    (D) is in the industry of lumber.

26. (F) NO CHANGE
    (G) would approve only leaving
    (H) approve only leaving
    (J) only approve of leaving

27. (A) NO CHANGE
    (B) dam, a water-treatment plant,
    (C) dam, or a water-treatment plant,
    (D) dam, a water treatment plant,

28. If the writer were to delete the adjectives "immediate" and "far-flung" from the sentence, the sentence would lose primarily:

    (F) the emotional impact of an appeal for environmental protection
    (G) a contrast between the specialization areas of the two environmental groups
    (H) context specifying the scope of environmental impact statements
    (J) unnecessary redundancy

29. (A) NO CHANGE
    (B) its negative.
    (C) it's negative impact.
    (D) its negative impact.

30. (F) NO CHANGE
    (G) project to be carried out.
    (H) project to be done.
    (J) carrying out of the project.

Go on to the next page.

Questions 31–45 are based on the following passage, *The Disappearance of the Classics*.

Classical and biblical (31) illusions are virtually non-existent in present-day literature. The reason for this paucity (32) is not so much on account of today's readers would not know (33) what the references are being made as (34) today's writers are not familiar enough with the Bible and with classical literature to refer to them in the first place. Not so very long ago, (35) anyone who had been sufficiently educated to write a book, whether fiction or nonfiction, had been steeped in the classics as a student. (36) Latin and Greek was studied in the schools of Europe, the United States, and Great Britain from the early grades onward. Now the belief that these languages and their literatures (37) will have been necessary for producing an educated person has all but disappeared, replaced by a growing desire for relevance and utility in school courses at all levels.

One wonders if this trend is positive or negative. Certainly, (38) the sciences constitute one subject that are important to the maintenance of today's technical society. On the other hand, (39) must computer languages totally replace Greek? Must the theory of relativity usurp the traditional place of Plutarch's *Lives* in the curriculum? Alas, (40) this seems to have occurred already.

(41) Naturally, society cannot go back to what it was a hundred or more years ago. Not many would make such a suggestion, this writer included. No one wants to return to the great class distinctions of past centuries or to stop upward mobility in social or professional areas, but (42) must it all be lost? Why not enjoy both cultures— (43) scientific and humanism? Why not educate people in such a way that they can read both Homer and (44) B. F. Skinner (the twentieth-century psychologist.) But perhaps, after all, this task is impossible. Perhaps it is like reaching for the stars.

The Disappearance of the Classics Questions

31. (A) NO CHANGE
    (B) referrals
    (C) allusions
    (D) affinities

32. (F) NO CHANGE
    (G) is not so much that
    (H) is not that
    (J) is not just that

33. (A) NO CHANGE
    (B) to what the allusions are being made
    (C) that the allusions are being made
    (D) that to which the allusions are being made

34. (F) NO CHANGE
    (G) because today's writers
    (H) the fact that today's writers
    (J) that todays writers

35. (A) NO CHANGE
    (B) anyone, who was sufficiently educated,
    (C) anyone who was educated
    (D) anyone who was sufficiently educated

36. (F) NO CHANGE
    (G) Latin, along with Greek, were
    (H) Latin, besides Greek, were
    (J) Latin, as well as Greek, was

37. (A) NO CHANGE
    (B) is
    (C) are
    (D) would be

38. (F) NO CHANGE
    (G) the sciences is
    (H) science is one subject that is
    (J) science is one type subject that is

39. Which replacement for the underlined phrase would best specify the contrast between ancient and modern languages?

    (A) Dell and Apple
    (B) slang
    (C) email and text messaging
    (D) surfing the Internet

40. (F) NO CHANGE
    (G) it seems that this has
    (H) these changes seem to have
    (J) this change seems to have

41. Which of the choices provides the best introductory sentence for the essay's concluding paragraph?

    (A) NO CHANGE
    (B) Those who ignore the humanities do so at their own risk.
    (C) Science can never teach us about ourselves like classical literature can.
    (D) It's never too late to turn a trend around.

Go on to the next page. ⇨

42. (F) NO CHANGE
    (G) must all classical learning be lost?
    (H) should all be lost?
    (J) must it all be lost.

43. (A) NO CHANGE
    (B) science and humanism.
    (C) scientific and humanitarian?
    (D) the scientific and the humanistic?

44. (F) NO CHANGE
    (G) B. F. Skinner a twentieth-century psychologist?
    (H) psychologist B. F. Skinner of the twentieth-century?
    (J) B. F. Skinner, a twentieth-century psychologist?

Question 45 refers to the preceding passage as a whole.

45. Suppose the writer had been asked to write a persuasive essay urging students to study the classics. Would this essay fulfill that assignment?

    (A) Yes, because the writer mentions several writers of classical Greece and Rome who were especially meaningful to him/her.
    (B) Yes, because the writer argues that classical learning is superior preparation for life.
    (C) No, because the writer implies that neither type of education is effective.
    (D) No, because the writer uses third-person perspective to weigh the general importance of both.

Questions 46–60 are based on the following passage, *Rain Forest Acrobats*.

In the South American rain forest (46) abides the greatest acrobats on earth. The monkeys of the Old World, (47) in spite of agility, cannot hang by their tails. It is only the monkeys of North and South America that possess this skill. They are called ceboids, and their unique group includes marmosets, owl monkeys, sakis, spider monkeys, squirrel monkeys, and howlers.

(48) Regarding these, the star gymnast is the skinny, intelligent spider monkey. Hanging head down (49) as a trapeze artist from the loop of a (50) liana, (a climbing plant), he may suddenly give a short swing, (51) launch him into space and, (52) soaring outward and downward across a 50-foot void of air, lightly catch a bough on which he (53) had spied a shining berry. (54)

No owl monkey can match this leap, for (55) their arms are shorter and their (56) tail untalented. The marmosets, smallest of the tribe, (57) tough noisy hoodlums that travel in gangs, are also capable of leaps into space, but their landings are (58) rough: smack against a tree trunk with arms and legs spread wide. (59)

Rain Forest Acrobats Questions

46. (F) NO CHANGE
    (G) abide
    (H) do abide
    (J) can abide

47. (A) NO CHANGE
    (B) with the agility they have,
    (C) agile as they are,
    (D) even with agility,

48. (F) NO CHANGE
    (G) Between these,
    (H) In these,
    (J) Among these,

49. (A) NO CHANGE
    (B) like a trapeze artist
    (C) imitating a trapeze artist
    (D) following a trapeze artist

50. (F) NO CHANGE
    (G) liana (a climbing plant),
    (H) liana, (a climbing plant)
    (J) liana (a climbing plant)

51. (A) NO CHANGE
    (B) launch himself
    (C) launch itself
    (D) launch it

52. (F) NO CHANGE
    (G) soar
    (H) to soar
    (J) soared

53. (A) NO CHANGE
    (B) will spy
    (C) is spying
    (D) has spied

Go on to the next page. ⟹

54. If the writer were to delete the opening sentence of this paragraph, the paragraph would lose primarily:

    (F) an amusing personification of one member of the ceboid family

    (G) a topic sentence introducing the paragraph on spider monkeys

    (H) the contrast between the spider monkey and the less agile ceboids

    (J) an anecdote illustrating the spider monkey's intelligence

55. (A) NO CHANGE

    (B) his arms are shorter and his

    (C) his arms are shorter and

    (D) their arms are shorter and

56. (F) NO CHANGE

    (G) tails are untalented.

    (H) tail is untalented.

    (J) tails untalented.

57. If the writer were to delete the underlined phrase, the sentence would lose primarily:

    (A) an important part of a metaphor the writer is using to personify the marmoset

    (B) descriptive detail meant to caution readers who might encounter marmosets in the wild

    (C) detail used to contrast the personality of marmosets with the more gentle spider monkeys

    (D) a reason for marmosets' inability to coexist with other species in the wild

58. Which of the following alternatives to the underlined portion would NOT be acceptable?

    (F) rough. They smack

    (G) rough, smacking

    (H) rough, the marmosets smacking

    (J) rough as they smack

59. Which choice would best tie the conclusion of this essay to its opening sentence?

    (A) NO CHANGE

    (B) Every acrobat has a rough landing sometimes.

    (C) The marmoset, then, really can't compete with other rain forest acrobats.

    (D) It's a good thing marmosets have the ceboid tail.

Question 60 refers to the preceding passage as a whole.

60. Suppose the writer had been asked to write a brief expository essay focusing on one unique aspect of a single group of rain forest animals. Would this essay fulfill that assignment?

    (F) Yes, because the essay focuses on the acrobatic prowess of the ceboid group.

    (G) Yes, because the essay personifies the monkeys to argue against the destruction of the rain forest and its endangered species.

    (H) No, because the writer uses examples of several different animals rather than focusing on one.

    (J) No, because the writer is primarily critiquing the abilities of various monkeys.

Questions 61–75 are based on the following passage, *College Enrollment Trends*.

(61) Recently as the 1950s, colleges in the United States had far more applicants (62) than they had enough space for. In the early 1970s, however, this picture changed. Many colleges even began to recruit students, sending them and their parents letters (63) inviting them to consider enrollment. One may well (64) ask why did this happen? There were many reasons, as there usually are when human decisions are involved. (65) One reason was that the coming-of-age in the 1960s of the babies of the 1940s baby boom spurred colleges to expand. Unfortunately, the subsequent decline in the birthrate was not considered. (66) In short, expansion of college facilities and expansion of college-age population were not in step with each other.

    Another reason that colleges (67) would have begun to cultivate potential students instead of vice versa was the end of the military draft. Some young men who years (68) ago would have enrolled in college to avoid the draft were free to go to work (69) without the fear of being inducted into the armed forces. Yet another reason was the economic situation of the country during the early 1970s. Money was (70) tight; and many parents could not afford to send all, or in some cases any, of their children to college. These young people

Go on to the next page. ⇨

often went to a junior college, (71) <u>were in attendance at a trade or secretarial school,</u> or joined a technical training program such as (72) <u>medical technician.</u>

    All in all, these circumstances (73) <u>made the picture brighter for those who did want to go to college.</u> Fewer applicants meant not only that prospective college students (74) <u>have more choice,</u> (75) <u>and those who did apply</u> had a better chance of being accepted.

College Enrollment Trends Questions

61. (A) NO CHANGE
    (B) As recent as
    (C) As recently as
    (D) Recently,

62. (F) NO CHANGE
    (G) than they had space.
    (H) and far less space.
    (J) than space.

63. (A) NO CHANGE
    (B) inviting the students to consider
    (C) that invite them to consider
    (D) inviting considering

64. (F) NO CHANGE
    (G) ask "Why did this happen?"
    (H) ask, "Why did this happen?"
    (J) ask why this happened?

65. (A) NO CHANGE
    (B) (Do NOT begin a new paragraph) One reason was, that the coming-of-age
    (C) (Begin new paragraph) One reason was that the coming-of-age
    (D) (Begin new paragraph) One reason was, that the coming-of-age

66. Which sentence best summarizes the information in the paragraph?
    (F) NO CHANGE
    (G) College recruiting, therefore, is a relatively recent phenomenon.
    (H) Expanding colleges during times of lower enrollment has never made sense.
    (J) These are just a few of the ways in which colleges have ended up in financial difficulty.

67. (A) NO CHANGE
    (B) had begun
    (C) have begun
    (D) began

68. (F) NO CHANGE
    (G) since
    (H) before
    (J) past

69. (A) NO CHANGE
    (B) absent the fear
    (C) less the fear
    (D) minus the fear

70. (F) NO CHANGE
    (G) tight. And
    (H) tight, and
    (J) tight,

71. (A) NO CHANGE
    (B) trade or secretarial schools,
    (C) attended trade or secretarial schools,
    (D) trade, or secretarial, schools.

72. (F) NO CHANGE
    (G) medical technology.
    (H) in the medical field.
    (J) for medical technician.

73. Which phrasing would most clearly describe the outlook for prospective college students during the era the essay describes?
    (A) NO CHANGE
    (B) were confusing for students interested in going to college
    (C) favored a select few
    (D) created a boom for junior and technical colleges

74. (F) NO CHANGE
    (G) will have more choice,
    (H) had more choice
    (J) will be having more choice,

75. (A) NO CHANGE
    (B) but also
    (C) but those who did apply
    (D) but also that those who did apply

STOP!

If you finish before time is called, you may check your work on this section only.
Do not turn to any other section in the test.

SECTION 2: MATHEMATICS TEST

60 Minutes, 60 Questions

Turn to Section 2 of your answer sheet (page 566) to answer the questions in this section. You may use the bottom of each page for figuring.

Directions

Solve each problem, choose the correct answer, and then fill in the corresponding oval on your answer sheet.

Do not linger over problems that take too much time. Solve as many as you can; then return to the others in the time you have left for this test.

You are permitted to use a calculator on this test. You may use your calculator for any problems you choose, but some of the problems may best be done without using a calculator.

Note: Unless otherwise stated, all of the following should be assumed.

1. Figures are NOT necessarily drawn to scale.

2. Geometric figures lie in a plane.

3. The word *line* indicates a straight line.

4. The word *average* indicates arithmetic mean.

1. Given that $500w = 3 \times 700$, find the value of w.

   (A) $\dfrac{5}{21}$

   (B) 2

   (C) $\dfrac{11}{5}$

   (D) $\dfrac{21}{5}$

   (E) 7

2. If $\dfrac{3 + y}{y} = 7$, then $y =$

   (F) 4

   (G) 3

   (H) 2

   (J) 1

   (K) $\dfrac{1}{2}$

3. $-2m(4n - 2m) + 2 =$

   (A) $-8mn + 4m^2 - 4m$

   (B) $-8mn + 2m + 2$

   (C) $-8mn - 4m^2 + 2$

   (D) $-6m + 4m^2 + 2$

   (E) $-8mn + 4m^2 + 2$

4. If the perimeter of a square is 20 meters, how many square meters are contained in its area?

   (F) 100

   (G) 25

   (H) 20

   (J) 10

   (K) 5

Go on to the next page. ⇨

5. Given that $80 + a = -32 + b$, find the value of $b - a$.

   (A) -112
   (B) -48
   (C) 2.5
   (D) 48
   (E) 112

6. If x is a positive integer, which of the following must be an even integer?

   (F) $x + 2$
   (G) $2x + 1$
   (H) $3x + 1$
   (J) $x^2 + x + 1$
   (K) $x^2 + x + 2$

7. Given that $\frac{3}{4} < x < \frac{4}{5}$, which of the following is a possible value of x?

   (A) $\frac{7}{16}$
   (B) $\frac{13}{20}$
   (C) $\frac{31}{40}$
   (D) $\frac{16}{20}$
   (E) $\frac{6}{7}$

8. $2 \times 10^{-5} \times 8 \times 10^2 \times 5 \times 10^2 =$

   (F) $.00008$
   (G) $.008$
   (H) $.08$
   (J) 8
   (K) 800

9. If John buys a 2 lb. apple pie with ingredients distributed as shown, how much of his pie is water?

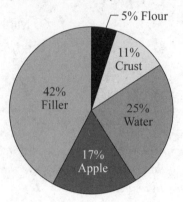

   (A) $\frac{1}{4}$ lb.
   (B) $\frac{1}{2}$ lb.
   (C) $\frac{3}{4}$ lb.
   (D) 1 lb.
   (E) $1\frac{1}{4}$ lb.

10. In the figure below, S is a point (not shown) such that segment RS divides the area of circle O into two equal parts. What are the coordinates of S?

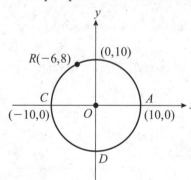

   (F) $(6,-8)$
   (G) $(6,8)$
   (H) $(8,-6)$
   (J) $(-6,-8)$
   (K) $(8,6)$

11. The table below is a partially filled-in score card for a video game contest. Isaac, Arisa, and Dylan each played in all of the three games, There were no ties. What is the *minimum* possible score for Dylan in this tournament?

	First Place (6 points)	Second Place (4 points)	Third Place (2 points)
Game 1			
Game 2		Arisa	
Game 3			Arisa

(A) 2
(B) 6
(C) 8
(D) 12
(E) The answer cannot be determined from the information given.

12. In the figure below, if line k has a slope of -1, what is the y-intercept of k?

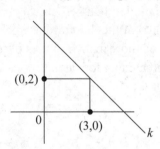

(F) 4
(G) 5
(H) 6
(J) 7
(K) 8

13. Over the first few weeks of the baseball season, the league's five leading pitchers had the following won–lost records. (All games ended in a win or loss for that pitcher.)

	Won	Lost
Pitcher A	4	2
Pitcher B	3	2
Pitcher C	4	1
Pitcher D	2	2
Pitcher E	3	1

At the time these statistics were compiled, which pitcher was leading the league in winning percentage? (That is, which pitcher had won the greatest percentage of his games?)

(A) Pitcher A
(B) Pitcher B
(C) Pitcher C
(D) Pitcher D
(E) Pitcher E

14. In the watch shown below, the normal numbers 1, 2, 3, . . . , 12 have been replaced by the letters A, B, C, . . . , L. In terms of these letters, a correct reading of the time shown would be

(F) I minutes after L
(G) 3E minutes before A
(H) 5C minutes after L
(J) I minutes before A
(K) none of the above

Go on to the next page. ⇨

15. 27 equal cubes, each with a side of length r, are arranged so as to form a single larger cube with a volume of 81. If the larger cube has a side of length s, then r divided by s equals

(A) $\dfrac{1}{3}$

(B) $\dfrac{\sqrt{3}}{3}$

(C) $\dfrac{1}{2}$

(D) $\dfrac{1}{8}$

(E) $\dfrac{1}{27}$

16. A piece of rope is lying on a number line. One of its ends is at coordinate -4, and the other is at coordinate 7. What is the length of the rope?

(F) 3

(G) 5

(H) 7

(J) 9

(K) 11

17. A long jumper has jumps of 8.4 meters, 8.1 meters, and 9.3 meters. What is the average (arithmetic mean) of these jumps?

(A) 8.5

(B) 8.6

(C) 8.7

(D) 8.8

(E) 8.9

18. Jayden deposited $50 in a savings bank at the beginning of the year. Jayden's money earns him interest at the rate of 8 percent of the amount deposited, for each year that Jayden leaves his money in the bank. If Jayden leaves his $50 in the bank for exactly one year and then decides to withdraw all of his money, how much money (including interest) can he withdraw? (The interest is not compounded.)

(F) $50.04

(G) $50.08

(H) $54.00

(J) $54.08

(K) $58.00

19. If $(x + 6)^2 = 12x + 72$, then $x =$

(A) 0

(B) ± 1

(C) ± 3

(D) ± 6

(E) ± 12

20. A child threatens his mother that he will watch television every minute of the day for one week. To the nearest hundred, how many minutes of television is the child threatening to watch?

(F) 1,000

(G) 1,100

(H) 10,000

(J) 10,100

(K) 11,000

Go on to the next page. ⇨

21. If $\boxed{\nabla x}$ is defined by the equation $\boxed{\nabla x} = \dfrac{x^3}{4}$ for real numbers x, which of the following equals 16?

(A) $\boxed{\nabla 2}$

(B) $\boxed{\nabla 4}$

(C) $\boxed{\nabla 8}$

(D) $\boxed{\nabla 16}$

(E) $\boxed{\nabla 64}$

22. 200 pieces of candy have been randomly put into five jars. The number of pieces of candy in three of the five jars is shown in the figure. What is the maximum possible value of x? (x is the number of pieces of candy in the fourth jar.)

(F) 69

(G) 75

(H) 102

(J) 144

(K) 200

23. There are 16 pages in a booklet. Last night, Ron read $\dfrac{1}{4}$ of the booklet. This morning, Ron read $\dfrac{1}{4}$ of the remaining pages. How many pages does Ron still have left to read?

(A) 7

(B) 8

(C) 9

(D) 10

(E) 11

24. A motorist is traveling 180 miles on a highway. The speed limit is 60 miles per hour. While risking a speeding ticket, how much time would the motorist save by going 10 miles over the speed limit, as opposed to following the limit?

(F) $\dfrac{1}{10}$ hr

(G) $\dfrac{1}{3}$ hr

(H) $\dfrac{3}{7}$ hr

(J) $\dfrac{1}{2}$ hr

(K) $\dfrac{4}{7}$ hr

25. The figure below is an equilateral triangle. What is its perimeter?

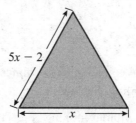

(A) $\dfrac{1}{4}$

(B) $\dfrac{1}{2}$

(C) $1\dfrac{1}{2}$

(D) $3\dfrac{1}{2}$

(E) The answer cannot be determined from the information given.

Go on to the next page. ⇨

26. In the chart below, the amount represented by each shaded triangle is three times that represented by each unshaded triangle. What fraction of the total production represented by the chart was produced in Alaska?

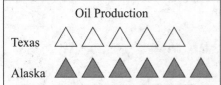

(F) $\dfrac{6}{11}$

(G) $\dfrac{18}{5}$

(H) $\dfrac{18}{23}$

(J) $\dfrac{12}{17}$

(K) $\dfrac{23}{17}$

27. A box contains exactly 24 coins—nickels, dimes, and quarters. The probability of selecting a nickel by reaching into the box without looking is $\dfrac{3}{8}$. The probability of selecting a dime by reaching into the box without looking is $\dfrac{1}{8}$. How many quarters are in the box?

(A) 6

(B) 8

(C) 12

(D) 14

(E) 16

28. What is the area of quadrilateral $ABCO$ in the figure below?

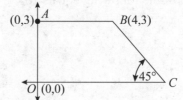

(F) 10.5

(G) 14.5

(H) 16.5

(J) 21.0

(K) The answer cannot be determined from the information given.

29. In the figure below, $ABCDEFGHIJKL$ is a regular dodecagon (a regular twelve-sided polygon). The curved path is made up of 12 semicircles, each of whose diameter is a side of the dodecagon. If the perimeter of the dodecagon is 24, find the area of the shaded region.

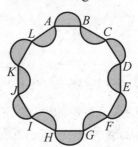

(A) 6π

(B) 12π

(C) 24π

(D) 36π

(E) 48π

Go on to the next page. ⇨

30. Find the solution to the equations
$$4x + 3y = 0$$
$$8x - 3y = 10$$

(F) $x = -\dfrac{5}{6}, y = \dfrac{1}{9}$

(G) $x = \dfrac{5}{6}, y = -\dfrac{10}{9}$

(H) $x = 2, y = 1$

(J) $x = 1, y = 2$

(K) $x = \dfrac{5}{6}, y = -\dfrac{1}{6}$

31. If $f(x) = x^2 + 2x + 1$, then $f(x - 1) =$

(A) $x^2 + 2x$

(B) 0

(C) 1

(D) x^2

(E) $2x + 1$

32. In the figure below, $AB = BC$ and $AC = CD$. How many of the angles have a measure of 45 degrees?

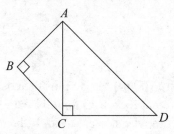

(F) none

(G) two

(H) three

(J) four

(K) five

33. Which of the rectangles below has a length of $\dfrac{4}{3}$, if each has an area of 4?

(A)   Length
$\dfrac{3}{4}$

(B)   Length
3

(C)   Length
4

(D)   Length
$\dfrac{4}{3}$

(E)   Length
$\dfrac{1}{4}$

34. O is the center of a circle of diameter 20 and $\angle AOC = 108°$. Find the sum of the lengths of minor arcs $\overparen{AC}$ and $\overparen{DB}$.

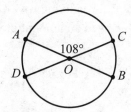

(F) 5π

(G) 8π

(H) 10π

(J) 12π

(K) 15π

Go on to the next page. ⇨

35. Which is true of the graphs $y = 2x^2$ and $y = -2x^2$?

   I. They have only one point in common.

   II. The shapes of both are the same but one is right-side up and the other is upside down.

   III. They both represent linear functions.

   (A) I only

   (B) II only

   (C) III only

   (D) I and II only

   (E) I, II, and III

36. A box of candy contains 0.6 of a pound of caramels and 3.6 pounds of coconut. What percent of the contents of the box, by weight, consists of caramels?

   (F) 6%

   (G) $14\frac{2}{7}\%$

   (H) $16\frac{2}{3}\%$

   (J) 25%

   (K) $33\frac{1}{3}\%$

37. The circle graph describes the distribution of $100,000 to five high schools for land improvement. Which high school received an amount closest to $25,000?

Distribution of $100,000 Land Improvement
Funds to Five High Schools

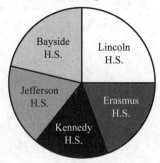

(A) Bayside H.S.

(B) Lincoln H.S.

(C) Erasmus H.S.

(D) Kennedy H.S.

(E) Jefferson H.S.

38. Which of the following is true if the three polygons below have equal perimeters?

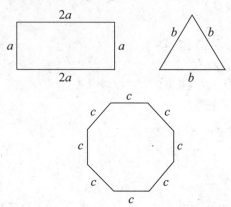

(F) $b < a < c$

(G) $a < c < b$

(H) $a < b < c$

(J) $c < b < a$

(K) $c < a < b$

39. Skiing lessons cost $100 per lesson plus the cost of ski rental. The rental fee varies directly with the square root of the time the skis are used. If the total cost of a 25-minute lesson is $200, what is the total cost of a 64-minute lesson?

(A) $160

(B) $240

(C) $260

(D) $300

(E) $360

Go on to the next page. ⇨

40. In the *xy*-coordinate system below, the lines *q* and *p* are perpendicular. The point (3,*a*) is on line *p*. What is the value of *a*?

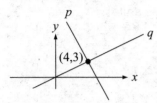

(F) 3

(G) 4

(H) $4\frac{1}{3}$

(J) $4\frac{2}{3}$

(K) $5\frac{1}{3}$

41. A sphere is inscribed in a cube whose volume is 64. What is the diameter of the sphere?

(A) 2

(B) $2\sqrt{2}$

(C) 8

(D) $4\sqrt{2}$

(E) 4

42. $\log_a b =$

(F) $-\log_b a$

(G) $\log_{10} b + \log_{10} a$

(H) $\log_{10} b - \log_{10} a$

(J) $\dfrac{1}{\log_b a}$

(K) $a + b$

43. Arc *BE* is a quarter circle with radius 6, and *C*, which is not shown, is an arbitrary point on arc *BE*. If $AB = BD = AD = 6$, then all of the possible values of the perimeter *P* of the quadrilateral *ABCD* are

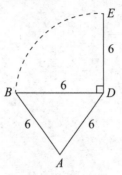

(A) $P = 18$

(B) $12 < P \le 18$

(C) $18 < P \le 24$

(D) $18 < P \le 18 + 6\sqrt{2}$

(E) $18 < P \le 30$

44. Which of the following is equal to $\left|\dfrac{x}{y}\right|$ for all real numbers *x* and *y*?

(F) $\dfrac{x}{y}$

(G) $\dfrac{|x|}{y}$

(H) $\dfrac{x}{|y|}$

(J) $\dfrac{|x|}{|y|}$

(K) $-\left|\dfrac{x}{y}\right|$

Go on to the next page. ⇨

45. If $3AC = BC$ in the figure below, what are the coordinates of B?

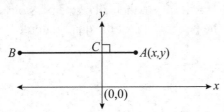

(A) $(x,3y)$
(B) $(-x,3y)$
(D) $(3x,y)$
(D) $(-3x,y)$
(D) $(-3x,+3y)$

46. In the figure below, $m\angle ACB = 110°$ and $AC = CD$. What is the value of $2y$?

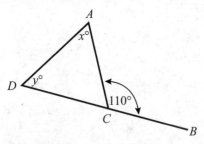

(F) 45
(G) 70
(H) 90
(J) 110
(K) 140

47. On a unit circle with center O, the figure below shows two points, A and B, on the circle. If the angle $AOB = a$, the distance from A to B as expressed in coordinate units is:

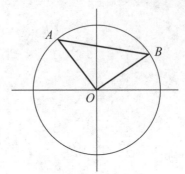

(A) $2\sqrt{\dfrac{1 - \cos a}{2}}$

(B) $2\sqrt{\dfrac{1 + \cos a}{2}}$

(C) $2\sqrt{\dfrac{1 - \sin a}{2}}$

(D) $2\sqrt{\dfrac{1 + \sin a}{2}}$

(E) $2 \sin a \cos a$

48. If each of the 3 distinct points A, B, and C are the same distance from point D, which of the following could be true?

  I. A, B, C, and D are the four vertices of a square.
  II. A, B, C, and D lie on the circumference of a circle.
  III. A, B, and C lie on the circumference of the circle whose center is D.

(F) I only
(G) II only
(H) III only
(J) II and III only
(K) I, II, and III

Go on to the next page. ⇨

49. Of the following five diagrams, which diagram describes the dark region as the set of elements that belongs to all of the sets A, B, and C?

(A)

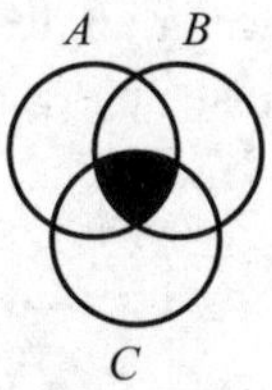

(B)

(C)

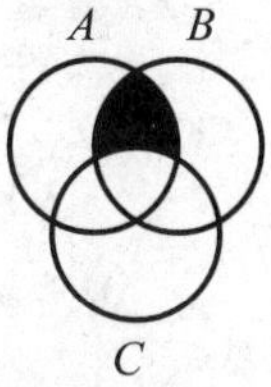

(D)

(E)

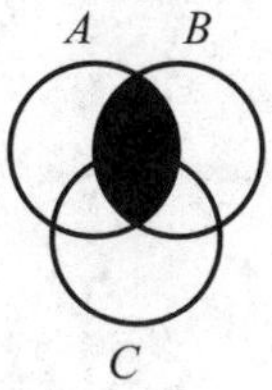

50. If the points $(1,3)$, $(3,5)$, and $(6,y)$ all lie on the same line, what is the value of y?

(F) 8

(G) 7

(H) 6

(J) 5

(K) 4

51. In Merriville, p gallons of gasoline are needed per month for each car in town. At this rate, if there are r cars in town, how long, in months, will q gallons last?

(A) $\dfrac{pq}{r}$

(B) $\dfrac{qr}{p}$

(C) $\dfrac{r}{pq}$

(D) $\dfrac{q}{pr}$

(E) pqr

52. If θ is the angle that the line $y = 2x + 3$ makes with the x-axis, then what is the value of $\sin \theta$?

(F) $\dfrac{1}{\sqrt{5}}$

(G) $\dfrac{2}{\sqrt{5}}$

(H) $\dfrac{3}{\sqrt{5}}$

(J) $\dfrac{4}{\sqrt{5}}$

(K) $\dfrac{5}{\sqrt{5}}$

Go on to the next page. ⇨

53. If the area of the square is twice the area of the triangle and $bc = 100$, then find a^2.

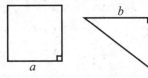

(A) 400
(B) 200
(C) 100
(D) 50
(E) 25

54. The figure above shows water in a tank whose base is 2 feet by 6 feet. If a rectangular solid whose dimensions are 1 foot by 1 foot by 2 feet is totally immersed in the water, how many *inches* will the water rise?

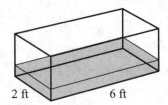

(F) $\dfrac{1}{6}$
(G) 1
(H) 2
(J) 3
(K) 12

55. In the triangle shown below, $\angle B = 26°$, $\angle C = 45°$, and $AB = 20$ units. What is the length of BC?

Note: According to the law of sines, in any triangle the ratios of the sines of the interior angles to the lengths of the sides opposite those angles are equal.

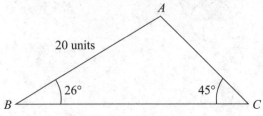

(A) $20\left(\dfrac{\sin 109°}{\sin 45°}\right)$

(B) $20\left(\dfrac{\sin 109°}{\sin 26°}\right)$

(C) $20\left(\dfrac{\sin 71°}{\sin 26°}\right)$

(D) $20\left(\dfrac{\sin 45°}{\sin 109°}\right)$

(E) $20\left(\dfrac{\sin 45°}{\sin 71°}\right)$

56. In the figure below, the area of the square is equal to $\dfrac{1}{5}$ the area of the triangle. Find the value of y, the side of the square.

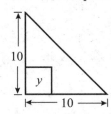

(F) 2
(G) 4
(H) 5
(J) $2\sqrt{5}$
(K) $\sqrt{10}$

Go on to the next page. ⇨

57. The x-coordinate of point B is

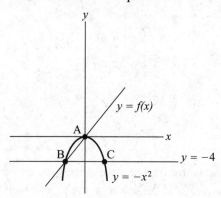

(A) −2
(B) −3
(C) −4
(D) −5
(E) −6

58. The cost, C, of a business trip is represented by the equation below, where m is a constant, d is the number of days of the complete trip, and t is the cost of transportation, which does not change. If the business trip was increased by 5 days, how much more did the business trip cost than the originally planned trip?

$$C = md + t$$

(F) $5d$
(G) $5m$
(H) $5t$
(J) $d(m − 3)$
(K) $m(d − 3)$

59. At how many points does the graph of the equation $y = x^4 + x^3$ intersect the x-axis?

(A) 0
(B) 1
(C) 2
(D) 3
(E) 4

60. Six containers, whose capacities in cubic centimeters are shown, appear in the figure above. The 25-cubic-centimeter container is filled with flour, and the rest are empty. The contents of the 25-cubic-centimeter container are used to fill the 16-cubic-centimeter container, and the excess is dumped into the 50-cubic-centimeter container. Then the 16-cubic-centimeter container is used to fill the 9-cubic-centimeter container, and the excess is dumped into the 50-cubic-centimeter container. The process is repeated until all containers, except the 1-cubic-centimeter and the 50-cubic-centimeter containers, are empty. What percent of the 50-cubic-centimeter container is empty?

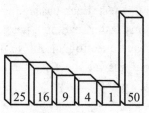

(F) 24%
(G) 48%
(H) 50%
(J) 52%
(K) 76%

STOP!

If you finish before time is called, you may check your work on this section only.
Do not turn to any other section in the test.

SECTION 3: READING TEST

35 Minutes, 40 Questions

Turn to Section 3 of your answer sheet (page 567) to answer the questions in this section.

Directions

There are four passages in this test. Each passage is followed by several questions. After reading a passage, choose the best answer to each question and fill in the corresponding circle on your answer sheet. You may refer to the passages as often as necessary.

Passage I: Prose Fiction

This passage is adapted from Anne Tyler's novel Searching for Caleb *(1975), which is set in Baltimore in 1952.*

Something came over Duncan that year. No one could quite put a finger on it. He had what he wanted, didn't he? He was studying science, wasn't he? Yet it seemed sometimes that he was more dissatisfied than ever,
5 almost as if he regretted winning the scholarship. He complained about living at home, which he had to do because college was so expensive. He said the expense was an excuse; this was just the family's way of punishing him. Punishing! To live at home with your own
10 close family? He was morose and difficult to talk to. He did not appear to have any friends at all, at least none that he would introduce. Well, of course he had always been somewhat of a problem. Surely this was just another of his stages, the aunts told his mother.
15 But then he started reading Dostoevsky.*
Naturally they had all read Dostoevsky—or at least the uncles had, in college. Or his *Crime and Punishment*, at any rate. At least in the abridged edition. But this was different. Duncan didn't just *read* Dostoevsky;
20 he sank in, he buried himself in Dostoevsky, he stopped attending classes entirely and stayed in his room devouring obscure novels and diaries none of the rest

of the family had heard of. On a soft spring evening, in the midst of a peaceful discussion on the merits of buy-
25 ing a home freezer, Uncle Two's branch of the family might be startled by the crash of enormous footsteps down the stairs and Duncan's wild, wiry figure explod-ing into the living room to wave a book at them. "Lis-ten! Listen!" and he would read out some passage too
30 loudly and too quickly for them to follow—a jumble of extravagant Russian prose, where emotions were stated outright in a surprising way and a great many extreme adjectives were used and feverish fancies kept darting and flashing. Paragraphs were layered and dense and
35 complicated like chunks of mica. "Did you *hear*?" he shouted. His parents nodded and smiled, their embar-rassed expressions giving them the look of sleepers dazzled by bright light. "*Well* then!" he would say, and off he spun, up the stairs. His parents stared at each
40 other. His father went to talk to the grandfather, who understood it no better. "But I thought he was scien-tific!" he said. "What is he reading for?" And then, "Ah well, never mind. At least it's the classics, they surely can't hurt him."
45   But that was before Easter Sunday. On Easter Sun-day, at the dinner table, the aunts were discussing Mrs. Norman Worth's extensive collection of eggshell min-iatures. The lawyer uncles were arguing the details of a hypothetical legal problem: If a farmer, while turning
50 on the water to irrigate the fields, accidentally startled another farmer's mule, which, in turn, kicked down the fence enclosing a prize-winning Angus bull, who there-upon . . .
"Neither of these subjects is fit table conversation,"
55 Duncan said.
Everybody thought about that for a minute.
"But what's wrong with them, dear?" his mother said finally.
"They're not real."
60   Great-Grandma, who had lived longest and was hardest to shock, poured more ice water into her

---

* Russian novelist (1821–1881) whose works combine religious mysticism with profound psychological insight.

Go on to the next page. ⇨

tumbler. "To you they may *not* be," she said, "but I myself find eggshell miniatures fascinating and if I didn't have this tremor I would take them up myself."

65 "You owe us an apology, Duncan boy," said Uncle Two.

"You owe *me* an apology," said Duncan, "I've spent eighteen years here growing deader and deader, listening to you skate across the surface. Watching

70 you dodge around what matters like painting blue sea around boats, with spaces left for safety's sake—"

"*What?*"

"Can't you say something that *means* something?" Duncan asked.

75 "About what?" said his mother.

"I don't care. Anything. Anything but featherstitch and the statute of limitations. Don't you want to get to the bottom of things? Talk about whether there's a God or not."

80 "But we already know," said his mother.

What was so terrible about that? None of them could see it. But Duncan stood up, as wild-eyed as any character in a Dostoevsky story, and said, "I'm leaving. I'm going for good."

85 He slammed out of the dining room. Cousin Justine jumped up to follow him, but then she stopped in the doorway, undecided. "*He'll* be back," Uncle Two said comfortably. "It's only growing pains. Ten years from now he'll talk the same as all the rest of us."

Passage I Questions

1. The "something" that came over Duncan in this passage (line 1) can best be described as

   (A) extreme alienation from human society

   (B) retribution for abuse at the hands of family members

   (C) frustration with the intellectually stifling atmosphere in the family home

   (D) delusional immersion in fictional works

2. Lines 10–14 are intended to paraphrase

   (F) Duncan's unspoken feelings about attending college

   (G) the narrator's disapproval of Duncan's lack of gratitude

   (H) the content of Duncan's typical arguments with his family

   (J) his family's interpretation of his surprising behavior

3. Duncan's interest in Dostoevsky illustrates

   (A) his deep emotional identification with the ideas in the novels

   (B) his search for entertainment to help him escape from boredom at home

   (C) his tendency to substitute books for social relationships

   (D) his absorption in his college course work

4. Outbursts of reading Dostoevsky aloud (lines 29–36) are probably motivated by

   (F) Duncan's desire to embarrass his family by reading out loud from passages they consider inappropriate

   (G) Duncan's increasing disconnection from reality and growing incognizance of his family's feelings

   (H) Duncan's pleasure in reminding his family of his intellectual superiority

   (J) Duncan's absorption in ideas he considers important

5. Duncan's remark about "fit table conversation" (line 54) reflects a turning point in the story in that

   (A) it reveals the extent to which Duncan is disturbed by his family's lack of manners

   (B) it represents the first time Duncan overtly criticizes his family

   (C) it demonstrates Duncan's readiness to assume a leadership role in his family

   (D) it forces into the open Duncan's and his family's repressed frustrations with each other

6. Upon reading the complete passage, the reader can logically surmise

   (F) that Duncan is more excited by philosophical questions than scientific ones

   (G) that Duncan will leave home to devote his life to science

   (H) that Duncan will withdraw from college because the pressures of living up to the conditions of his scholarship are too great

   (J) that Duncan will withdraw from college in rebellion against his family's wishes

7. Duncan's greatest frustration with the family appears to be

   (A) their lack of formal education

   (B) their excessive consumerism

Go on to the next page.

    (C) their inability to understand who he really is

    (D) their lack of interest in philosophical and spiritual matters

8. The author's selection of Dostoevsky as the author Duncan connects with is meaningful in that

    (F) it serves as the perfect counterpoint to reading material his family considers morally acceptable

    (G) the complex, emotional style underscores and gives expression to Duncan's own personality

    (H) because the novels are classics that members of the family have also read, they contrast the two generations' responses to the books

    (J) it illustrates the potential of college assignments to mold the minds of young people

9. In dealing with Duncan, the family in the passage shows a pattern that can best be characterized as

    (A) authoritarian and unforgiving

    (B) amused and overindulgent

    (C) shocked and offended

    (D) misunderstanding and underestimating

10. The presence of extended family throughout the passage is a significant story element in that

    (F) it illustrates the impact the absence of one or more parent(s) can have on a young person

    (G) it represents several family traditions, such as pursuing the legal profession, among which Duncan must choose

    (H) it suggests the pervasiveness of passivity and routine across generations that makes Duncan's rebellion stand out more powerfully

    (J) it creates opportunities for dialogue that reveal a variety of differences in the family members' worldview

Passage II: Social Science

This passage is from "Of Our Spiritual Strivings," the first chapter of W.E.B. Dubois's The Souls of Black Folk, *1903. In it Dubois introduced some of his most famous concepts of race relations and describes the experience of African Americans living in a white-dominated America during the early years of the twentieth century.*

Between me and the other world there is ever an unasked question: unasked by some through feelings of delicacy; by others through the difficulty of rightly framing it. All, nevertheless, flutter round it. They
5 approach me in a half-hesitant sort of way, eye me curiously or compassionately, and then, instead of saying directly, How does it feel to be a problem? they say, I know an excellent colored man in my town; or, I fought at Mechanicsville; or, Do not these Southern outrages
10 make your blood boil? At these I smile, or am interested, or reduce the boiling to a simmer, as the occasion may require. To the real question, How does it feel to be a problem? I answer seldom a word.

    And yet, being a problem is a strange experience—
15 peculiar even for one who has never been anything else, save perhaps in babyhood and in Europe. It is in the early days of rollicking boyhood that the revelation first bursts upon one, all in a day, as it were. I remember well when the shadow swept across me. I was a
20 little thing, away up in the hills of New England. . . . In a wee wooden schoolhouse, something put it into the boys' and girls' heads to buy gorgeous visiting-cards— ten cents a package—and exchange. The exchange was merry, till one girl, a tall newcomer, refused my card—
25 refused it peremptorily, with a glance. Then it dawned upon me with a certain suddenness that I was different from the others; or like, mayhap, in heart and life and longing, but shut out from their world by a vast veil. I had thereafter no desire to tear down that veil, to creep
30 through; I held all beyond it in common contempt, and lived above it in a region of blue sky and great wandering shadows. That sky was bluest when I could beat my mates at examination-time, or beat them at a foot-race, or even beat their stringy heads. Alas, with the years
35 all this fine contempt began to fade; for the words I longed for, and all their dazzling opportunities, were theirs, not mine. . . . With other black boys the strife was not so fiercely sunny: their youth shrunk into tasteless sycophancy, or into silent hatred of the pale world
40 about them and mocking distrust of everything white; or wasted itself in a bitter cry, Why did God make me an outcast and a stranger in mine own house? The shades of the prison-house closed round about us all: walls strait and stubborn to the whitest, but relentlessly
45 narrow, tall, and unscalable to sons of night who must plod darkly on in resignation, or beat unavailing palms against the stone, or steadily, half hopelessly, watch the streak of blue above.

    After the Egyptian and Indian, the Greek and
50 Roman, the Teuton and Mongolian, the Negro is a sort of seventh son, born with a veil, and gifted with second-sight in this American world—a world which

Go on to the next page. ⇨

yields him no true self-consciousness, but only lets him
see himself through the revelation of the other world.
55 It is a peculiar sensation, this double-consciousness,
this sense of always looking at one's self through the
eyes of others, of measuring one's soul by the tape of a
world that looks on in amused contempt and pity. One
ever feels his twoness—an American, a Negro; two
60 souls, two thoughts, two unreconciled strivings; two
warring ideals in one dark body, whose dogged strength
alone keeps it from being torn asunder.

The history of the American Negro is the history of
this strife—this longing to attain self-conscious man-
65 hood, to merge his double self into a better and truer
self. In this merging he wishes neither of the older
selves to be lost. He would not Africanize America, for
America has too much to teach the world and Africa.
He would not bleach his Negro soul in a flood of white
70 Americanism, for he knows that Negro blood has a
message for the world. He simply wishes to make it
possible for a man to be both a Negro and an American, without being cursed and spit upon by his fellows,
without having the doors of Opportunity closed roughly
75 in his face.

Passage II Questions

11. It can be inferred from this passage that the
author is

(A) Native American
(B) black
(C) white
(D) a child

12. What is the "other world" mentioned in the first
line of the passage?

(F) the world of black people
(G) the world of white people
(H) the post–Civil War era
(J) the world of the wealthy

13. The question "How does it feel to be a problem?"
can be interpreted as coded language for

(A) How does it feel to be poor?
(B) How does it feel to be a slave?
(C) How does it feel to be a liberal?
(D) How does it feel to be black?

14. In paragraph 2, white people's comments to the
author can be characterized as

I. patronizing
II. condescending
III. hostile

(F) I and II only
(G) I only
(H) II only
(J) III only

15. The use of the word "shadow" in line 19 refers to

(A) fury
(B) elation
(C) sadness
(D) empathy

16. When does the author first become aware of racial
prejudice?

(F) when a white person tells him about knowing
an "excellent colored man"
(G) when he beats a classmate in a foot-race
(H) when the new girl at school refuses to accept
his visiting-card
(J) when he is traveling in Europe

17. The metaphor of the veil introduced in line 28
represents

I. the barrier between the races
II. racial differences in human values
III. opportunities withheld from blacks

(A) II only
(B) I and II only
(C) I and III only
(D) I, II, and III

18. Initially the author's response to "the veil" leads
him to regard whites with

(F) pity
(G) superiority
(H) sycophancy
(J) contempt

Go on to the next page. ⇨

19. What does the author mean by "double-consciousness"?

    (A) the ability to see two viewpoints at once

    (B) a heightened empathy for others

    (C) a tendency toward mental illness

    (D) a constant awareness of himself as whites see him

20. According to the author, African Americans long to

    (F) Africanize America

    (G) improve their social status

    (H) be fully accepted as both black and American

    (J) become more like whites

Passage III: Humanities

By the time President Abraham Lincoln delivered his Second Inaugural Address on March 4, 1865, Union victory was all but assured. In this speech he looks back at four years of civil war and forward toward its conclusion, which was officially announced on May 9. Shortly after delivering this speech, on April 15, Lincoln died at the hands of an assassin.

Fellow-countrymen: At this second appearing to take the oath of the presidential office, there is less occasion for an extended address than there was at the first. Then a statement, somewhat in detail, of a course to be

5 pursued, seemed fitting and proper. Now, at the expiration of four years, during which public declarations have been constantly called forth on every point and phase of the great contest which still absorbs the attention and engrosses the energies of the nation, little that

10 is new could be presented. The progress of our arms, upon which all else chiefly depends, is as well known to the public as to myself; and it is, I trust, reasonably satisfactory and encouraging to all. With high hope for the future, no prediction in regard to it is ventured.

15 On the occasion corresponding to this four years ago, all thoughts were anxiously directed to an impending civil war. All dreaded it—all sought to avert it. While the inaugural address was being delivered from this place, devoted altogether to saving the Union

20 without war, insurgent agents were in the city seeking to destroy it without war—seeking to dissolve the Union, and divide effects, by negotiation. Both parties

deprecated war; but one of them would make war rather than let the nation survive; and the other would

25 accept war rather than let it perish. And the war came.

One-eighth of the whole population were colored slaves, not distributed generally over the Union, but localized in the Southern part of it. These slaves constituted a peculiar and powerful interest. All knew

30 that this interest was, somehow, the cause of the war. To strengthen, perpetuate, and extend this interest was the object for which the insurgents would rend the Union, even by war; while the government claimed no right to do more than to restrict the territorial

35 enlargement of it.

Neither party expected for the war the magnitude or the duration which it has already attained. Neither anticipated that the cause of the conflict might cease with, or even before, the conflict itself should cease.

40 Each looked for an easier triumph, and a result less fundamental and astounding. Both read the same Bible, and pray to the same God; and each invokes his aid against the other. It may seem strange that any men should dare to ask a just God's assistance in wringing

45 their bread from the sweat of other men's faces; but let us judge not, that we be not judged. The prayers of both could not be answered—that of neither has been answered fully.

The Almighty has his own purposes. . . . Fondly

50 do we hope—fervently do we pray—that this mighty scourge of war may speedily pass away. Yet, if God wills that it continue until all the wealth piled by the bondman's two hundred and fifty years of unrequited toil shall be sunk, and until every drop of blood drawn

55 with the lash shall be paid by another drawn with the sword, as was said three thousand years ago, so still it must be said, "The judgments of the Lord are true and righteous altogether."

With malice toward none; with charity for all; with

60 firmness in the right, as God gives us to see the right, let us strive on to finish the work we are in; to bind up the nation's wounds; to care for him who shall have borne the battle, and for his widow, and his orphan—to do all which may achieve and cherish a just and lasting

65 peace among ourselves, and with all nations.

Go on to the next page. ⟹

Passage III Questions

21. What is the "great contest" to which Lincoln refers in line 8?

  (A) the question of slavery
  (B) the Civil War
  (C) the recent presidential campaign
  (D) relations between blacks and whites

22. Lincoln's expectations for the war's outcome can be characterized as

  I. hopeful
  II. guarded
  III. despairing

  (F) I only
  (G) II only
  (H) III only
  (J) I and II only

23. According to Lincoln, how did the North and South approach the war?

  (A) They were eager to engage in it.
  (B) They were resigned to the necessity of it.
  (C) They were well prepared for it.
  (D) They attempted to avoid it.

24. The speech indicates that the war was caused by

  I. slavery
  II. economic interests
  III. the wish to preserve national unity

  (F) I, II, and III
  (G) I and II only
  (H) I and III only
  (J) II and III only

25. It can be inferred that Lincoln believes that

  (A) the North was more responsible for starting war
  (B) the North and South were equally responsible
  (C) the South was more responsible
  (D) each side worked equally hard to avoid war

26. Where were most slaves located before the war?

  (F) the North
  (G) the South
  (H) the new territories
  (J) all over the nation

27. What is Lincoln referring to (lines 38–39) when he says that the war's *cause* ceased before the conflict itself ended?

  (A) Stockpiles of Southern cotton had been destroyed.
  (B) So many soldiers had died that few fighting forces were left.
  (C) The nation's appetite for war had waned but the fighting continued.
  (D) The Emancipation Proclamation had freed Southern slaves.

28. How long had American slavery existed when Lincoln delivered this speech?

  (F) two hundred fifty years
  (G) four years
  (H) for the war's duration
  (J) since the beginning of civilization

29. According to Lincoln, the war's outcome will be determined by

  (A) the Confederacy
  (B) the Union
  (C) Almighty God
  (D) the side with the stronger military

30. The overall tone of the speech is

  (F) fiery and preaching
  (G) pleading and desperate
  (H) somber and conciliatory
  (J) condemnatory and bombastic

Go on to the next page. ⇨

Passage IV: Natural Science

This passage is adapted from "The Chemistry of Glassmaking."

Glass is considered to be a state of matter, rather than a particular substance. It has been defined by G. W. Morey as "an inorganic substance in a condition which is continuous with, and analogous to, the liquid state
5 of that substance, but which, as a result of a reversible change in viscosity during cooling, has attained so high a degree of viscosity as to be for all practical purposes rigid."

Man-made siliceous glass is a mixture of ingredi-
10 ents rather than a chemical compound. Therefore it has no formula, and the proportions of its ingredients may vary. Nevertheless, there are some differences in the chief reasons for presence of ingredients, and this principle allows the ingredients of glass to be divided
15 into the following three main classes.

First there are the basic, or constitutional, ingredients. These are

   (a) silica (SiO_2). In a conventional soda-lime glass, silica may form about 60% of the glass by
20   weight. This is obtained from siliceous rock or sand.

   (b) an ingredient which lowers the temperature of fusion of the silica. One or both of the alkalis sodium oxide or potassium oxide, obtained
25   from soda or potash respectively, serve this purpose. Lead oxide can also serve this purpose.

   (c) other ingredients. Some provide chemical stability or act as a flux, such as calcium oxide (lime) or aluminum oxide. Some, often iron,
30   may be considered impurities.

The most commonly encountered glass composition is the soda-lime glass, which conventionally contains 60% silica, 15% sodium oxide, and 5% calcium oxide. Another commonly encountered composition is
35 the potassium glass, characterized by 15% potassium oxide rather than sodium oxide. Although one does not often see the term "potassium-lime" glass, it is usual for potassium glasses to contain 5–20% calcium oxide. Soda-lime glasses are typical of the ancient Near East,
40 the ancient Occident, the medieval Near East, and the modern world. Only medieval Europe is a well-known exception: here the potassium glass is typical.

The second main class of ingredients is made up of the glassmakers' additives. These are added for
45 an artistic or technical purpose, such as to color, to decolorize, to opacify, or to clarify.

Up until the nineteenth and twentieth centuries the conventional means of coloring glasses were few. Opaque red and blue-green could both be created with
50 copper. Green could be created with copper or iron or both. Manganese yielded purple, cobalt gave royal blue, and black usually consisted of either exceedingly dark green, purple, or royal blue. Opaque yellow and orange were created from undissolved compounds of
55 antimony and lead or of tin and lead, with the presence of zinc pushing the color towards orange.

The last main class is formed by the trace elements, or impurities. They are the elements present in low concentration over which presumably the glassmakers
60 exerted no control.

Some scrap glass, or cullet, was and is almost always included in glass batches in order to aid vitrification.

The chemical ingredients of a glass sample need have no recognizable relation to the geographical
65 region in which the glass factory lies. This is mainly because ideal ingredients are not universally distributed, and therefore the glass is often made by mixing ingredients from different geographical regions. The written history of glass contains numerous notices of an
70 international commerce in silica, alkalis, cullet or other scavenged material, colorants, and even possible glass ingots and similar material. Indeed in some respects glassmakers participated in something like an international cult. They visited and copied one another; there
75 are frequent accounts of rather large-scale migrations of glassmakers and their families; and to a large extent the occupation itself spread along family lines. It has been remarked that it is easier to judge the date of an ancient artifact than its place of manufacture.
80 Another reason for the difficulty in tracing glass to a region of manufacture may be that glassmakers of the past did not see their ingredients with a modern chemical perspective. They were aiming at a result, not a chemical composition intelligible to posterity. It should
85 not be thought that glassmakers used pure elements to make the glass. The fact that alkalis could be divided into two types, soda and potash, was not clearly understood until the eighteenth century. It is said that many glassmakers were not aware that lime is desirable for
90 stability, but their ingredients were so impure that they put in sufficient lime unawares. One must remember that modern chemistry itself did not exist before the

Go on to the next page. ⇨

eighteenth century. Past glassmaking was a craft carried out according to a good deal of unwritten lore.
95 Alchemists and glassmakers had much in common, and
even today not every glassmaker's trick is understood
according to modern chemical precepts.

Passage IV Questions

31. The chemical formula for glass is

    (A) 60% silica, 15% sodium oxide, and 5%
        calcium oxide
    (B) dependent upon whether sodium oxide or
        potassium oxide is used
    (C) divided into three classes
    (D) not determinable

32. The alkalis commonly used in glass are

    (F) sodium oxide and potassium oxide
    (G) soda obtained from potash
    (H) sodium oxide, potassium oxide, and lead
        oxide
    (J) calcium oxide and aluminum oxide

33. The original glass windows of the medieval
    European cathedrals were probably

    (A) all broken after placement on account of
        chemical instability
    (B) exceptional for their transparency due to the
        absence of undissolved compounds
    (C) made of potassium glass
    (D) made from scavenged ancient material

34. According to the article, the three main classes of
    glass ingredients are

    (F) silica, alkali, and other ingredients which
        provide stability or act as a flux
    (G) major ingredients, minor ingredients, and
        trace elements
    (H) basic ingredients, glassmakers' additives, and
        trace elements
    (J) silica, glassmakers' additives, and an alkali

35. The chemical ingredients of a glass can

    (A) reveal its probable place of manufacture
    (B) provide knowledge of the trace elements in
        common use
    (C) show that glassmakers and alchemists
        belonged to similar cult-like organizations
    (D) come from places that are far apart

36. Glassmakers of the past

    (F) came from a very few closely related families
    (G) contributed to the ultimate invention of mod-
        ern chemistry
    (H) used an unwritten lore enabling them to
        obtain a purity of ingredients otherwise only
        available to alchemists
    (J) showed a practical craftsmanship that compen-
        sated for ignorance about their raw materials
        that today might be considered a defect

37. Copper, manganese, and iron were all substances
    traditionally added to glass for the purpose of

    (A) increasing the rigidity and durability of glass
    (B) coloring glass
    (C) increasing the purity of the chemical composi-
        tion of glass
    (D) creating a geographical "signature" to make
        the glass a unique regional composition

38. Glasses from different periods and regions of the
    world are distinguished primarily by

    (F) color
    (G) proportion of natural substances such as
        potassium and silica
    (H) records of glassmakers' family lineage
    (J) purity of the elements used to make the glass

39. Which of the following is NOT a true statement?

    (A) Glassmaking as an occupation spread mainly
        along family lines.
    (B) Glassmakers sometimes developed a cult-like
        following.
    (C) Dating glass is easier than pinpointing the
        location of its making.
    (D) Scrap glass cannot be used in making new
        glass.

40. Glassmakers' additives were used for all of these
    purposes EXCEPT

    (F) opacifying
    (G) liquefying
    (H) decolorizing
    (J) clarifying

STOP!

If you finish before time is called, you may check your work on this section only.
Do not turn to any other section in the test.

SECTION 4: SCIENCE TEST

35 Minutes, 40 Questions

Turn to Section 4 of your answer sheet (page 567) to answer the questions in this section.

Directions

There are several passages in this test. Each passage is followed by several questions. After reading a passage, choose the best answer to each question and fill in the corresponding circle on your answer sheet. You may refer to the passages as often as necessary.

You are NOT permitted to use a calculator on this test.

Passage I

The final velocity, v_f, of an object in feet per second (ft/s) after it slides down a frictionless inclined plane is

$$v_f = \sqrt{64h + v_0^2}$$

where v_0 is the initial velocity in ft/s of the object and h is the height of the inclined plane.

Experiment 1

Students used a timepiece (accurate to 0.01 second) to measure the times required for a 500-g wooden block and a 500-g glass block to slide down an inclined plane lubricated with the same amount of antifriction spray for each trial. The blocks had the same dimensions. The length of the incline was known in all cases. Students first determined the time interval for each block and then the final velocity.

The students measured the time required for each block to slide down an inclined plane with a height of 4 feet.

The expected outcome, according to the formula above, was a time interval of 0.5 s and a v_f of 16 ft/s. The actual results are recorded in Table 1.

Table 1

Trial	Time of Slide(s)	
	Wooden Block	*Glass Block*
1	0.82	0.61
2	0.78	0.60
3	0.77	0.58
4	0.80	0.59
5	0.83	0.62

The average time for the wooden block was 0.80 s; the average time for the glass block was 0.60 s. Using these average times, the students calculated v_f for each block, deriving 10.10 ft/s for the wooden block and 13.40 ft/s for the glass block.

Experiment 2

The students repeated Experiment 1 using the same inclined plane, but now with a height of 6 feet.

The expected outcome, according to the formula, was a time interval of 0.41 s and a v_f of 22.63 ft/s. The actual results are recorded in Table 2.

Table 2

Trial	Time of Slide(s)	
	Wooden Block	*Glass Block*
1	0.68	0.52
2	0.69	0.50
3	0.73	0.48
4	0.72	0.51
5	0.71	0.48

The average time for the wooden block was 0.71 s; the average time for the glass block was 0.50 s. Using these average times, the students calculated v_f for each block, deriving 12.99 ft/s for the wooden block and 18.44 ft/s for the glass block.

Go on to the next page. ⇨

Experiment 3

The students attempted to correct for human error in the following fashion. Using a light that was known to blink every 1.00 s, the students measured the time interval between flashes of light. The results are given in Table 3.

Table 3

Trial	Time(s)
1	1.08
2	1.06
3	1.07
4	1.08
5	1.11

The average time recorded was 1.08 s.

Passage I Questions

1. In Experiment 1, if an additional trial were conducted using the wooden block, the time interval measured would most likely be nearest

   (A) 0.60 s
   (B) 0.71 s
   (C) 0.75 s
   (D) 0.80 s

2. The students most likely used both wooden and glass blocks in Experiments 1 and 2 in order to determine whether the block's final velocity was affected by

   (F) surface area
   (G) mass
   (H) material composition
   (J) volume

3. The best evidence that, despite the antifriction spray, friction still played a role in the discrepancy between expected and observed results in both Experiments 1 and 2 was that the expected velocity was

   (A) greater than that of the wooden block but less than that of the glass block
   (B) greater than that of the glass block but less than that of the wooden block
   (C) greater than that of either block
   (D) less than that of either block

4. Based on the passage, if the glass block was placed on the inclined plane for which $h = 8$, then the average observed time interval would most likely be

   (F) less than that of the glass block in Experiment 2 and less than that of a wood block placed on the inclined plane for which $h = 8$
   (G) greater than that of the glass block in Experiment 2 and greater than that of a wood block placed on the inclined plane for which $h = 8$
   (H) greater than that of the glass block in Experiment 2 and less than that of a wood block placed on the inclined plane for which $h = 8$
   (J) less than that of the glass block in Experiment 2 and greater than that of a wood block placed on the inclined plane for which $h = 8$

5. Given that Experiment 3 showed that students were consistently overestimating the time intervals in their measurements in Experiments 1 and 2, which of the following is most likely?

   (A) The final velocities calculated for each block are lower than the actual velocities.
   (B) The final velocities calculated for each block are higher than they should be.
   (C) The final velocities calculated for the wooden blocks, but not for the glass blocks, are lower than they should be.
   (D) The final velocities calculated for the wooden blocks, but not for the glass blocks, are higher than they should be.

6. Given the discrepancy between the final velocities of the wooden and glass blocks in Experiments 1 and 2, which of the following is the most likely explanation?

   (F) Final velocity is the same for all materials but is always more than the expected value.
   (G) Final velocity is the same for all materials but is always less than the expected value.
   (H) Final velocity differs depending on the material but is always more than the expected value.
   (J) Final velocity differs depending on the material but is always less than the expected value.

Go on to the next page.

Passage II

Table 1

Chicken	Order of Introduction into Pen	Mass (kg)	Age (years)	Sex	Position in Pecking Order
A	1st	4.3	6.4	Male	1st
B	2nd	6.2	2.8	Male	6th
C	3rd	5.1	4.4	Female	3rd
D	4th	3.9	3.0	Female	5th
E	5th	7.0	4.5	Male	4th
F	6th	5.5	6.3	Female	2nd

When chickens from different flocks are exposed to each other, they spontaneously organize themselves into a *pecking order*. The most dominant chicken, by definition, can peck at all other chickens; the next chicken down the pecking order can peck at all chickens except the top chicken, and so on. Between any two chickens, the dominant chicken forces the submissive chicken to retreat during a confrontation. A biologist determined the pecking order among six chickens by placing them in an enclosed pen and observing and recording their interactions. Chickens were ranked according to their position in the pecking order that spontaneously arose from their interactions, with the most dominant chicken taking the first position in the pecking order and the least dominant chicken taking the sixth position in the pecking order. The results are shown in Table 1.

Passage II Questions

7. Which of the following generalizations about the relationship between a chicken's rank in the pecking order and its mass is consistent with the data in Table 1?

    (A) The largest chicken will be at the top of the pecking order.
    (B) The smallest chicken will be at the top of the pecking order.
    (C) The smallest chicken will be at the bottom of the pecking order.
    (D) A chicken's mass has no relation to its position in the pecking order.

8. From the results, one would conclude that a male chicken with an age of 5.5 years and a mass of 4.9 kilograms would most likely take a position in

the pecking order between which of the following chickens?

    (F) A and F
    (G) F and C
    (H) C and E
    (J) E and D

9. Which of the following graphs best represents the relationship between a chicken's age and its position in the pecking order?

(A)

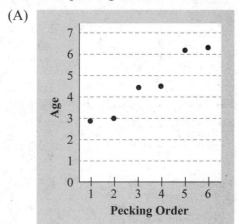

(B)

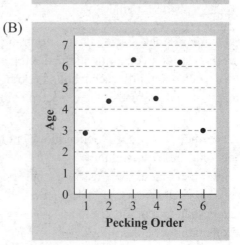

Go on to the next page. ⟹

(C)

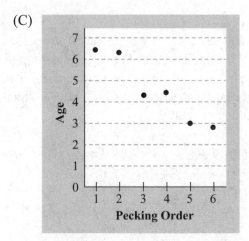

(D)

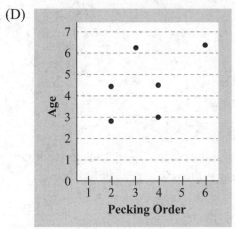

10. Based on the data, which of the following is the most correct?

    (F) The sex of a chicken determines its position in the pecking order.

    (G) The mass of a chicken determines its position in the pecking order.

    (H) The age of a chicken determines its position in the pecking order.

    (J) Sex, mass, and age do not seem to affect a chicken's position in the pecking order.

11. The scientist breeds the male and female who were highest in the pecking order (chickens A and F). The new chicks are placed in the pen with the other six chickens. Where will they rank in the pecking order?

    (A) Since their parents were dominant, the chicks will also be dominant and rise near the top of the pecking order, just below their parents.

    (B) Since their parents were both dominant, the chicks will be more dominant than the previous generation and rise to the very top of the pecking order.

    (C) Since they aren't as massive as the original six chickens, they will be dominated and fall to the bottom of the pecking order.

    (D) Since they are younger than the others, the chicks will begin at the bottom of the pecking order.

12. When Individual A is removed from the pen, Individual E takes over the top of the pecking order, with F, C, D, and B following as 2 through 5. What is the most likely explanation for this phenomenon?

    (F) The second chicken in the pecking order will become first when the individual who was formerly first is removed.

    (G) A female is usually at the top of a pecking order in a flock.

    (H) A male is usually at the top of a pecking order in a flock.

    (J) When one individual is removed, the pecking order changes completely.

Go on to the next page. ⇨

Passage III

Experiment 1

A chemistry student is conducting an experiment on the relationship between mass and volume of various metal samples. For this experiment, she takes four samples of copper foil and measures the mass of each sample. She then uses water displacement in a graduated cylinder to measure the volume of each sample in mL. She plots her data in Figure 1. Using the data, she then calculates an approximate density for copper of 8.9 g/mL.

Figure 1: Mass vs. volume of copper samples

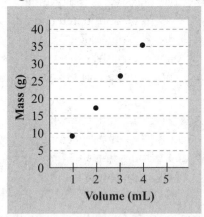

Experiment 2

The student again measures the mass and volume of various samples using a balance and water displacement. In this experiment, she takes the measures of four samples of zinc shot and plots her data in Figure 2. Using the data, she then calculates an approximate density for zinc of approximately 7.0 g/mL.

Figure 2: Mass vs. volume of zinc samples

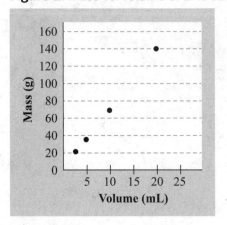

Experiment 3

The student gathers four United States pennies from the year 1973 and four United States pennies from the year 1995. She measures the mass and volume of each penny and calculates a density for each penny, with the results recorded in Table 1.

Table 1: Density of U.S. pennies from 1973 and 1995

Year of Penny	Penny Number	Density (g/mL)
1973	1	8.9
1973	2	8.8
1973	3	8.9
1973	4	8.8
1995	1	7.4
1995	2	7.5
1995	3	7.4
1995	4	7.4

She conducts some research and finds the following information about measured densities of several known metals.

Table 2: Density of known metals

Metal	Density (g/mL)
Aluminum	2.7
Copper	8.9
Lead	7.9
Tin	7.3
Zinc	7.0

Passage III Questions

13. What was the difference between Experiment 1 and Experiment 2?

    (A) The student measured volume using water displacement in the first experiment but not in the second.

    (B) The student used zinc in the second experiment.

    (C) The student used more samples of metal in the first experiment.

    (D) The student measured density in different units in the second experiment.

Go on to the next page. ⇨

14. After examining data from Experiment 3, which is the most likely conclusion the student might have drawn?

    (F) Both the 1973 and the 1995 pennies were made almost entirely from copper.
    (G) Both the 1973 and the 1995 pennies were made almost entirely from zinc.
    (H) While the 1973 pennies were made mostly from zinc, the 1995 pennies were made mostly from copper.
    (J) While the 1973 pennies were made mostly from copper, the 1995 pennies were made mostly from zinc.

15. Using her graphs from Experiments 1 and 2, the student was able to determine the density of each of the metal samples because

    (A) the density of a metal is equal to its volume
    (B) the density of a metal is equal to its mass
    (C) the density of a metal is equal to the slope of the graph
    (D) density is the same for both metals

16. The student is given a sample of an unknown metal. After measuring its mass and volume, she calculates a density of 7.0 g/mL. The best conclusion from these data would be that

    (F) the sample is most likely copper
    (G) the sample is most likely zinc
    (H) the sample is most likely a mixture of zinc and copper
    (J) the sample could be zinc, but further testing would be needed to ensure that it is not an alloy or another metal

17. According to Table 2, for the same volume, which would represent the correct order of mass for the five metals, the first being greatest, the last being least?

    (A) lead, copper, tin, zinc, aluminum
    (B) aluminum, zinc, tin, lead, copper
    (C) copper, lead, tin, zinc, aluminum
    (D) This cannot be determined unless the volume is known for each of the metals.

18. The student is given samples of a third pure metal, and once again she conducts an experiment in which she measures the mass and volume of each sample. She obtains the following data:

Mass (g)	Volume (mL)
27.0	10.0
53.0	19.5
81.0	30.0
108.0	39.5

Given these data and the information in Table 2, the metal is most likely

    (F) aluminum
    (G) tin
    (H) lead
    (J) copper

Go on to the next page. ⇨

Passage IV

A researcher obtains human population data for two countries (the United Kingdom and Bangladesh) in the year 2000. He also gathers estimates for the population trends in the United Kingdom and overall world population data. He develops several graphs of the information obtained, allowing him to examine trends in human population in the world, together with trends in a developed country (the United Kingdom) and a developing country (Bangladesh).

Passage IV Questions

19. According to Figure 1, the greatest number of females in the United Kingdom in 2000 were in which age range?

(A) 15–19
(B) 20–24
(C) 30–34
(D) 35–39

Figure 1: Male and female population data (in millions) for the United Kingdom in 2000

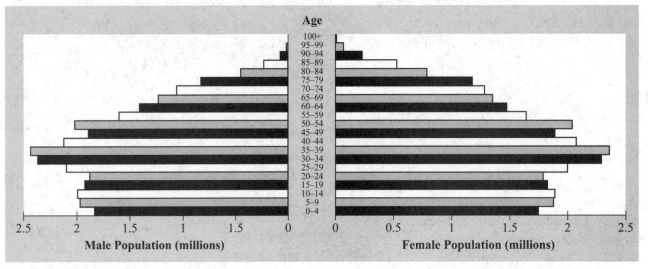

Source: U.S. Census Bureau International Data Base

Figure 2: Projected male and female population data (in millions) for the United Kingdom in 2025

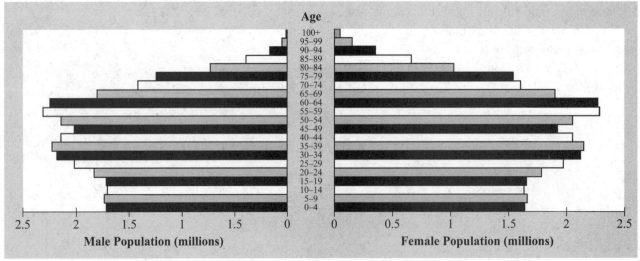

Source: U.S. Census Bureau International Data Base

Go on to the next page. ⟹

Figure 3: Male and female population data (in millions) for Bangladesh in 2000

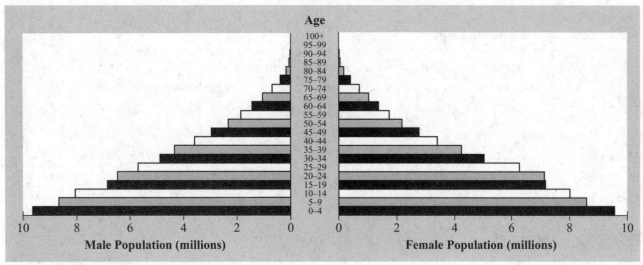

Source: U.S. Census Bureau International Data Base

20. According to Figure 4, the expected world population in 2050 will likely be

(F) 8.5 billion
(G) 9.0 billion
(H) 9.5 billion
(J) 10.0 billion

21. Based on information presented in Figures 1 and 2:

(A) The birthrate in the United Kingdom is on the rise between the years 2000 and 2025.
(B) The death rate in the United Kingdom is on the rise between the years 2000 and 2025.
(C) More individuals will be in the 60–64 age range in the United Kingdom in 2025 than there were in 2000.
(D) Fewer individuals will be in the 60–64 age range in the United Kingdom in 2025 than there were in 2000.

22. Which of the following is a possible reason for the differences in population distribution in Figures 1 and 3?

(F) The two graphs include estimated population data from different years.
(G) The two graphs are based on population predictions rather than actual measured data.
(H) Individuals in the United Kingdom are less likely to live as long as those in Bangladesh because of differences in health care.
(J) Individuals in the United Kingdom are more likely to live longer than those in Bangladesh because of differences in health care.

Figure 4: World population, 1950–2050

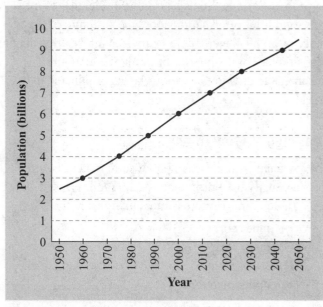

Source: U.S. Census Bureau International Data Base, June 2009 Update

23. Based on the data in Figure 4, the world population has grown by about 1 billion people approximately every

(A) 5–7 years
(B) 7–9 years
(C) 9–11 years
(D) 11–15 years

Go on to the next page. ⇨

Passage V

Table 1: Composition and layers of Earth

Layer	Density (g/cm³)	Temperature (°F)	State of Matter	Minerals and Elements Present
Inner core	12	8,600	Solid	Iron, nickel, sulfur
Outer core	10.0–12.1	7,000	Liquid	Iron, nickel, sulfur
Lower mantle	3.3–5.7	2,700–5,400	Solid	Iron, magnesium oxides, silicates
Upper mantle	3.3	2,300–2,700	Plastic, mobile	Iron, magnesium oxides, silicates
Crust (oceanic)	2.9–3.1	0–100s	Solid	Silicon, aluminum, potassium, magnesium, iron oxides, silicates
Crust (continental)	2.7	0–100s	Solid	Silicon, aluminum, potassium, magnesium, iron oxides, silicates

The use of rock-sampling techniques and seismographic data from various events has allowed scientists to measure and infer information about the structure of the interior of the planet. Table 1 provides information about the structure of the interior of Earth, while Figure 1 is a schematic drawing of various layers of mineral and rock.

Figure 1: Schematic of the layers of Earth

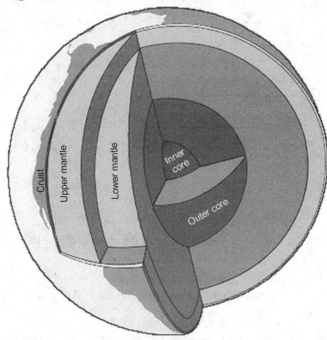

Source: U.S. Geological Survey

Passage V Questions

24. A scientist finds a sample of solid material with a density of approximately 12.0 g/cm³. Based on Table 1, this sample is most likely from the

    (F) inner core
    (G) outer core
    (H) lower mantle
    (J) upper mantle

25. According to Table 1, the major difference between the oceanic and continental crusts is that

    (A) the oceanic crust is liquid, while the continental crust is solid
    (B) the oceanic crust is solid, while the continental crust is liquid
    (C) the oceanic crust has a generally lower density than the continental crust
    (D) the oceanic crust has a generally higher density than the continental crust

26. Based on information in both the table and the figure, which of the following is true about the trends in density and temperature in the layers of Earth?

    (F) The inner layers of Earth generally have a higher density and a higher temperature than the outer layers.
    (G) The outer layers of Earth generally have a higher density and a higher temperature than the inner layers.

Go on to the next page. ⇨

(H) The inner layers of Earth generally have a higher density but a lower temperature than the outer layers.

(J) The inner layers of Earth generally have a lower density but a higher temperature than the outer layers.

27. The majority of information about the inner layers of Earth is measured and inferred indirectly through the use of seismic and earthquake data. Seismic data seem to indicate that the inner core is solid crystal while the outer core is liquid. Why is this most likely possible?

(A) The inner core is made of elements that are different from those that form the outer core.

(B) The outer core has a higher temperature than the inner core, causing the outer core to melt into a liquid.

(C) The inner core has a lower temperature than the outer core, causing the inner core to melt into a liquid.

(D) The inner core has a higher temperature than the outer core but also is under higher pressure, allowing it to remain solid.

28. Based on the information in both the table and the figure, what is the most likely explanation for the existence of earthquakes?

(F) The movement of plates of crust above the plastic upper mantle leads to interactions between areas of rock.

(G) The movement of plates of crust above the plastic lower mantle leads to interactions between areas of rock.

(H) The movement of the liquid outer core leads to eruption of lava and movement of rock.

(J) The movement of plastic oceanic crusts causes shifts in the solid continental crusts.

Go on to the next page. ⇨

Passage VI

Students in a biology class are studying producer-consumer relationships in a temperate deciduous forest. They obtain information about the eating and predatory patterns of various organisms, along with the movement of energy within that ecosystem.

Figure 1: Representative food web for the temperate deciduous forest

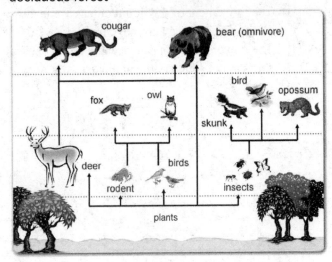

Source: Parenting the Next Generation

Figure 2: Representative energy pyramid for the temperate deciduous forest

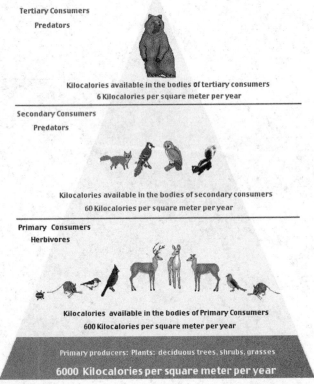

Source: California State University, Los Angeles

Passage VI Questions

29. Based on information in Figure 1, which of the following is the most likely relationship in a deciduous forest?

    (A) A cougar eats a rodent.
    (B) A deer eats a bear.
    (C) An owl eats grass.
    (D) A bird eats insects.

30. Rodents are eaten by owls. Examining Figure 1, what does the direction of each arrow in the food web most likely indicate?

    (F) The arrow points to the animal that is being eaten.
    (G) The arrow points in the direction of energy flow.
    (H) The arrow points away from the direction of energy flow.
    (J) The arrow indicates that photosynthesis is occurring.

31. Based on the information in Figure 2, if a fourth level of organism were eating the tertiary consumers, we would expect those organisms to have available in their bodies

    (A) no energy from the tertiary consumers
    (B) all of the energy from the tertiary consumers
    (C) 1 kilocalorie per square meter per year
    (D) 0.6 kilocalorie per square meter per year

32. What is the advantage to using a food web such as that in Figure 1, rather than an energy pyramid, to represent producer–consumer relationships in an ecosystem?

    (F) Food webs are able to show the amount of energy being passed from one level of ecosystem to another.
    (G) Food webs are able to show that some organisms eat more than one type of organism.
    (H) Food webs are able to show producers, while energy pyramids are not.
    (J) Food webs are able to show every level of consumer, while energy pyramids are not.

Go on to the next page. ⇨

33. A food chain is a simplified way to show the relationships between organisms in an ecosystem. In a food chain, only one organism is represented at each energy level. Based on Figure 1, a correct food chain for the deciduous forest is

   (A) plants → insects → skunk
   (B) plants → bear → cougar
   (C) plants → owl → cougar
   (D) cougar → bird → plants

Passage VII

Static Theory of Gases

Sir Isaac Newton and other scientists of his time viewed the behavior of gases as very similar to the behavior of atoms and molecules in a solid. It was widely accepted that atoms in a given sample are able to interact with each other in various ways, and some of these forces cause atoms to bond more closely to each other. However, gases, unlike liquids and solids, are infinitely expandable; that is, a sample of gas expands to take up all available space.

Because of this difference between the behaviors of solids and gases, Newton proposed that perhaps the individual atoms in a sample of gas are in fact arranged in a static lattice, like those in a solid. However, the atoms within a sample of gas, rather than being attracted to each other, are instead subject to a repulsive force. The atoms, surrounded by a form of heat referred to as *calorics*, repel each other. As more heat is added, more calorics arrange themselves between atoms, causing the distance between these individual atoms to increase. As distance increases because of the presence of these calorics, the repulsive forces decrease, and atoms spread into a wider lattice.

As the volume of a sample of gas decreases, the atoms and calorics are pushed closer together. Newton showed that this would lead to the characteristic increase in pressure noted when the volume of a gas is decreased.

Kinetic Molecular Theory of Gases

The work of Robert Boyle and Daniel Bernoulli led to a new theory to explain the behavior of gases. Initially, Boyle hypothesized that, unlike in the static theory, the atoms in a gas are in fact in motion. He suggested that

this motion occurred within a fluid substance. Bernoulli later postulated that while the atoms were in fact moving, they were moving in a void. Heat, according to Bernoulli, was nothing more than the motion of these atoms. Atoms with more heat moved more quickly.

According to the kinetic molecular theory of gases, the atoms in a sample of gas neither attract nor repel each other. Rather, the atoms in a gas are moving around so quickly and are not close enough together (as in a solid or liquid) to be able to interact with each other, except when, through the random motion of the atoms, they collide with each other. While the sample may take up a significant amount of space, the majority of that volume consists of nothing; rather, the motion of the atoms causes their spread. Finally, as individual molecules bounce off of each other, energy is conserved, and they move away from each other with the same energy.

Passage VII Questions

34. A key feature of the static theory is that

   (F) heat leads to the increased motion of atoms
   (G) atoms move quickly in a sample of gas
   (H) gases may not expand when heated
   (J) the atoms in a sample of gas are arranged in a lattice

35. The idea of collision is important to
   (A) the static theory, because it accounts for the increase in calorics in a sample of gas
   (B) the static theory, because it causes the atoms in a sample of gas to spread out
   (C) the kinetic molecular theory, because it accounts for the increase in calorics in a sample of gas
   (D) the kinetic molecular theory, because it causes the atoms in a sample of gas to spread out

36. Which of the following assumptions is implicit in kinetic molecular theory?

   (F) Atoms with more heat will tend to spread out.
   (G) Atoms with less heat will tend to spread out to avoid collision.
   (H) Heat does not affect the movement of atoms.
   (J) Heat is a physical entity that separates atoms in a sample of gas.

Go on to the next page. ⇨

37. According to the kinetic molecular theory of gases, in a closed container, the pressure of a sample of gas should increase when

   (A) the heat of the sample of gas increases
   (B) the heat of the sample of gas decreases
   (C) the volume of the sample of gas increases
   (D) the atoms interact with each other

38. Samples of two different gases are heated in a container that is able to measure pressure changes. The first container holds one mole of water vapor, while the second container holds one mole of carbon dioxide gas. Data indicate that when either gas is heated to a common temperature with the volume held constant, the pressure increases equally. Which of the following theories is supported by these observations?

   (F) Static theory, because the repulsions between different gases are different, leading to different pressures.
   (G) Kinetic molecular theory, because the repulsions between different gases are different, leading to different pressures.
   (H) Static theory, because the repulsions between different gases are same, leading to equal pressures.
   (J) Kinetic molecular theory, because the interactions between molecules are unimportant; so long as the number of molecules, temperature, and volume are constant, the pressure of any gas will be the same.

39. Why does kinetic molecular theory apply only to gases (and not to solids or liquids)?

   (A) Solids and liquids are subject to the forces of calorics.
   (B) Atoms in a solid or liquid bounce off of each other with no loss of energy.

   (C) The atoms in a solid or liquid are much closer together, which results in interactions.
   (D) The atoms in a gas are not moving as rapidly and therefore are subject to interactions between atoms.

40. What is the major philosophical difference between kinetic molecular theory and static theory?

   (F) In kinetic molecular theory, the molecules are in motion, while in static theory they are not.
   (G) In static theory, the molecules are in motion, while in kinetic molecular theory they are not.
   (H) In kinetic molecular theory, heat affects the volume of a sample of gas, while in static theory it does not.
   (J) In static theory, heat affects the volume of a sample of gas, while in kinetic molecular theory it does not.

Note:

If you plan to take the ACT Plus Writing, take a five-minute break and then continue with the Writing Test on page 609.

If you do not plan to take the ACT Plus Writing, turn to page 615 for instructions on scoring your multiple-choice tests.

STOP!
If you finish before time is called, you may check your work on this section only.
Do not turn to any other section in the test.

SECTION 5: WRITING TEST *(OPTIONAL)*

40 Minutes

Turn to the sheets on pages 611–614 to write your essay.

Directions

You may use the unlined pages in this test booklet to plan your essay. These pages will not be scored. **You must write your essay in pencil on the lined pages in the answer folder.** Your writing on those lined pages will be scored. You may not need all the lined pages, but to ensure you have enough room to finish, do NOT skip lines. You may write corrections or additions neatly between the lines of your essay, but do NOT write in the margins of the lined pages. **Illegible essays cannot be scored, so you must write (or print) clearly.**

If you finish before time is called, you may review your work. Lay your pencil down immediately when time is called.

When the supervisor announces that 40 minutes have passed, you must stop writing the essay. Do not go on to any other section in the test.

You may make notes on this page, but you must write your essay on the answer sheet.

Writing Prompt

The well-known proverb "Ignorance is bliss" suggests that people with knowledge of the world's complexities and its limitations are often unhappy, while their less knowledgeable counterparts remain contented. But how accurate is this folk wisdom? A recent study showed that well-informed people were more likely to report feelings of well-being. In fact, more knowledge leads people to feel better about themselves and more satisfied with their lives. Does more knowledge make you happier?

Carefully read the following perspectives, which describe the effect of increased knowledge on happiness. Does more knowledge make you happier or not?

Perspective One

More knowledge enables you to pursue more interests and do more things with your life. By opening yourself to new ideas and developments, you can enhance your life by using that knowledge in many areas of work and pleasure.

Perspective Two

More knowledge may expose you to the negative aspects of life. There is an old saying, "What you don't know won't hurt you." Having more knowledge will expose you to the injustices and tragedies of life that you may not have been exposed to before. More knowledge will, as they say, "upset the apple cart."

Perspective Three

Using specific knowledge that will enhance your life and discounting or not accepting knowledge that will degrade your life will make you happier. For example, if you like a piece of music, you may not want to find that it may have been written by a terrible person. If you have been content using a typewriter, you might find a computer to be far more efficient.

Essay Directions

Write a meaningful and logical essay in which you describe and evaluate multiple perspectives on the effect of increased knowledge on happiness. In your essay, make sure that you

■ clearly state and analyze your own perspective in relation to at least one other perspective

■ support your statements with clear reasoning and specific examples

- organize your material logically
- communicate effectively using standard written English

Note that your perspective may be completely in agreement with any of the others, may be partially in agreement, or may be in complete disagreement. In any case, you must support your essay with logic, making detailed references and providing specific examples.

Note on Planning the Essay

Plan your essay using the space here. These pages will not be scored.

Develop ideas and plan your essay using the space below. Consider the following points as you critically think about what you are going to write.

Strengths and weaknesses related to the three perspective presented:

- What insights can be found in them and what insights do they fail to show?
- Why might they be persuasive to others or why might they not be persuasive?

Your personal experience, knowledge, and values:

- What is your own perspective on this issue, and what are the strengths and weaknesses of that perspective?
- How will you support your perspective in your essay?

SECTION 5: WRITING TEST *(OPTIONAL)*

Begin your essay on this page. If you need more space, continue on the next page. Do not write outside of the essay box.

Continue on the next page if necessary.

Continuation of essay from previous page. Write below only if you need more space.

Continue on the next page if necessary.

Continuation of essay from previous page. Write below only if you need more space.

Continue on the next page if necessary.

Continuation of essay from previous page. Write below only if you need more space.

HOW DID YOU DO ON THIS TEST?

Pages 617–623 will show you how to calculate
your scores on this test. Explanatory answers
with strategies and basic skills follow.

THERE'S ALWAYS ROOM
FOR IMPROVEMENT!

ANSWER KEY

Section 1: English Test Answers

1. B	20. J	39. C	58. G
2. H	21. B	40. H	59. B
3. D	22. J	41. A	60. F
4. F	23. A	42. G	61. C
5. B	24. F	43. D	62. J
6. H	25. C	44. J	63. B
7. C	26. G	45. D	64. H
8. F	27. B	46. G	65. A
9. A	28. H	47. C	66. F
10. H	29. D	48. J	67. D
11. A	30. G	49. B	68. H
12. J	31. C	50. G	69. A
13. C	32. G	51. B	70. H
14. J	33. B	52. F	71. C
15. D	34. H	53. D	72. G
16. H	35. D	54. G	73. A
17. A	36. J	55. B	74. H
18. J	37. C	56. H	75. D
19. D	38. H	57. A	

English Test Raw Score
(number of correct answers) _____

Section 2: Mathematics Test Answers

1. D	16. K	31. D	46. J
2. K	17. B	32. J	47. A
3. E	18. H	33. B	48. H
4. G	19. D	34. J	49. A
5. E	20. J	35. D	50. F
6. K	21. B	36. G	51. D
7. C	22. G	37. B	52. G
8. J	23. C	38. K	53. C
9. B	24. H	39. C	54. H
10. F	25. C	40. H	55. A
11. C	26. H	41. E	56. K
12. G	27. C	42. J	57. A
13. C	28. H	43. D	58. G
14. G	29. A	44. J	59. C
15. A	30. G	45. D	60. J

Mathematics Test Raw Score
(number of correct answers) _____

Section 3: Reading Test Answers

1. C	11. B	21. B	31. D
2. J	12. G	22. J	32. F
3. A	13. D	23. D	33. C
4. J	14. F	24. F	34. H
5. B	15. C	25. C	35. D
6. F	16. H	26. G	36. J
7. D	17. C	27. D	37. B
8. G	18. J	28. F	38. G
9. D	19. D	29. C	39. D
10. H	20. H	30. H	40. G

Reading Test Raw Score
(number of correct answers) _____

Section 4: Science Test Answers

1. D	11. D	21. C	31. D
2. H	12. H	22. J	32. G
3. C	13. B	23. D	33. A
4. F	14. J	24. F	34. J
5. A	15. C	25. D	35. D
6. J	16. J	26. F	36. F
7. D	17. C	27. D	37. A
8. G	18. F	28. F	38. J
9. C	19. D	29. D	39. C
10. H	20. H	30. G	40. F

Science Test Raw Score
(number of correct answers) _____

TABLE FOR CONVERTING
RAW SCORES TO SCALE SCORES

Raw Scores (number of correct answers)						Your Scale Score
Test 1 English	Test 2 Mathematics	Test 3 Reading	Test 4 Science	Scale Score		
75	60	40	40	36	English Test	_____
72–74	58–59	39	39	35	Mathematics Test	_____
71	57	38	38	34	Reading Test	_____
70	55–56	37	37	33	Science Test	_____
68–69	54	35–36	—	32		
67	52–53	34	36	31		
66	50–51	33	35	30	Sum of scores	_____
65	48–49	32	34	29		
63–64	45–47	31	33	28	Composite score	_____
62	43–44	30	32	27	(sum ÷ 4)	
60–61	40–42	29	30–31	26		
58–59	38–39	28	28–29	25		
56–57	36–37	27	26–27	24		
53–55	34–35	25–26	24–25	23		
51–52	32–33	24	22–23	22		
48–50	30–31	22–23	21	21		
45–47	29	21	19–20	20		
43–44	27–28	19–20	17–18	19		
41–42	24–26	18	16	18		
39–40	21–23	17	14–15	17		
36–38	17–20	15–16	13	16		
32–35	13–16	14	12	15		
29–31	11–12	12–13	11	14		
27–28	8–10	11	10	13		
25–26	7	9–10	9	12		
23–24	5–6	8	8	11		
20–22	4	6–7	7	10		
18–19	—	—	5–6	9		
15–17	3	5	—	8		
12–14	—	4	4	7		
10–11	2	3	3	6		
8–9	—	—	2	5		
6–7	1	2	—	4		
4–5	—	—	1	3		
2–3	—	1	—	2		
0–1	0	0	0	1		

NORMS TABLES

Use the tables on page 619.

	Your Estimated Percent at or below on Practice Test
English	_____
Mathematics	_____
Reading	_____
Science	_____
Composite	_____
Combined English/Writing	_____
Writing	_____

National Distributions of Cumulative Percents for ACT Test Scores
ACT-Tested High School Graduates from Recent Years

Score	English	Mathematics	Reading	Science	Composite	Score
36	99	99	99	99	99	36
35	99	99	99	99	99	35
34	99	99	99	99	99	34
33	98	99	97	99	99	33
32	97	98	95	98	99	32
31	96	97	94	98	98	31
30	94	96	91	97	97	30
29	92	94	89	96	95	29
28	90	92	86	94	92	28
27	87	89	82	92	89	27
26	84	85	78	90	85	26
25	80	80	74	85	81	25
24	74	75	70	79	75	24
23	69	69	64	73	69	23
22	64	63	58	65	63	22
21	58	58	53	57	56	21
20	51	53	48	48	48	20
19	43	47	41	38	40	19
18	36	41	34	29	33	18
17	31	33	30	21	26	17
16	26	24	24	16	19	16
15	21	14	19	12	13	15
14	15	07	15	08	08	14
13	11	02	09	06	05	13
12	09	01	06	04	02	12
11	06	01	03	02	01	11
10	04	01	01	01	01	10
09	03	01	01	01	01	09
08	02	01	01	01	01	08
07	01	01	01	01	01	07
06	01	01	01	01	01	06
05	01	01	01	01	01	05
04	01	01	01	01	01	04
03	01	01	01	01	01	03
02	01	01	01	01	01	02
01	01	01	01	01	01	01
Mean	20.6	20.8	21.4	20.9	21.1	
S.D.	5.9	5.1	6.1	4.7	4.9	

ACT Writing Test Norms

Score	Combined English/Writing	Writing	Score
36	99		36
35	99		35
34	99		34
33	99		33
32	99		32
31	97		31
30	95		30
29	93		29
28	90		28
27	86		27
26	82		26
25	77		25
24	72		24
23	66		23
22	57		22
21	51		21
20	42		20
19	35		19
18	29		18
17	23		17
16	19		16
15	14		15
14	10		14
13	7		13
12	5	99	12
11	4	99	11
10	2	98	10
09	1	89	09
08	1	77	08
07	1	44	07
06	1	29	06
05	1	9	05
04	1	5	04
03	1	1	03
02	1	1	02
01	1		01
Mean	21.4	7.5	
S.D.	5.4	1.7	

6-POINT HOLISTIC SCORING RUBRIC FOR THE ACT WRITING TEST

It is recommended that you approach two adults who you know are well qualified to judge basic grammar and composition as your two scorers for your practice Writing Test—perhaps an English teacher, a college-age student majoring in English or journalism, a parent, etc. Have those two adults read through this scoring rubric and refer to it when they score your practice test.

A Few Words about Scoring the Essay

Even with some errors in spelling, punctuation, and grammar, a student can get a top score on the essay. The highly trained high school and college composition teachers who score the essays will follow a rubric that focuses upon content, organization, and language usage and sentence structure. Each essay will be independently scored on a 1–6 scale by two such readers in *four* domains: Ideas and Analysis, Development and Support, Organization, and Language Use. If the readers' scores differ by more than two points, the test will be evaluated by a third reader. Fewer than 2 percent of all scored essays require a third reader.

Some general points about the scoring rubrics are summarized here. For full descriptions of the criteria for each of the four domains, refer to "Preparing for the ACT Test" at https://www.act.org/content/dam/act/unsecured/documents/Preparing-for-the-ACT.pdf. Essays at each level will exhibit all or most of the characteristics described below.

Score = 6

Essays at this score point demonstrate effective skill in responding to the task.

The essay shows a clear understanding of the task. The essay takes a position on the issue and may offer a critical context for discussion. The essay addresses complexity by examining different perspectives presented on the issue, and by evaluating the implications and/or complications of the issue, and/or by fully responding to counterarguments to the writer's position. Development of ideas is ample, specific, and logical. Most ideas are fully elaborated. A clear focus on the specific issue in the prompt is maintained. The organization of the essay is clear: the organization may be somewhat predictable or it may grow from the writer's purpose. Ideas are logically sequenced. Most transitions reflect the writer's logic and are usually integrated into the essay. The introduction and conclusion are effective, clear, and well developed. The essay shows a good command of language. Sentences are varied and word choice is varied and precise. There are few, if any, errors to distract the reader.

Score = 5

Essays at this score point demonstrate well-developed skill in responding to the task.

The essay shows a clear understanding of the task. The essay takes a position on the issue and may offer a broad context for discussion. The essay shows recognition of complexity by partially evaluating the implications and/or complications of the given perspectives, and by responding to counterarguments to the writer's position. Development of ideas is specific and logical. Most ideas are elaborated, with clear movement between general statements and specific reasons, examples, and details. Focus on the specific issue in the prompt is maintained. The organization of the essay is clear, although it may be predictable. Ideas are logically sequenced, although simple and obvious transitions may be used. The introduction and conclusion are clear and generally well developed. Language is competent. Sentences are somewhat varied and word choice is somewhat varied and precise. There may be a few errors, but they are rarely distracting.

Score = 4

Essays at this score point demonstrate adequate skill in responding to the task.

The essay shows an understanding of the task. The essay takes a position on the issue and may offer some context for discussion based on the given perspectives. The essay may show some recognition of complexity by providing some response to counterarguments to the writer's position. Development of ideas is adequate, with some movement between general statements and specific reasons, examples, and details. Focus on the specific issue in the prompt is maintained throughout most of the essay. The organization of the essay is apparent but predictable. Some evidence of logical sequencing of ideas is apparent, although most transitions are simple and obvious. The introduction and conclusion are clear and somewhat developed. Language is adequate, with some sentence variety and appropriate word choice. There may be some distracting errors, but they do not impede understanding.

Score = 3

Essays at this score point demonstrate some developing skill in responding to the task.

The essay shows some understanding of the task. The essay takes a position on the issue but does not offer a context for discussion. The essay may acknowledge a counterargument to the writer's position, but its development is brief or unclear. Development of ideas is limited and may be repetitious, with little, if any, movement between general statements and specific reasons, examples, and details. Focus on the general topic is maintained, but focus on the specific issue in the prompt may not be maintained. The organization of the essay is simple. Ideas are logically grouped within parts of the essay, but there is little or no evidence of logical sequencing of ideas. Transitions, if used, are simple and obvious. An introduction and conclusion are clearly discernible but underdeveloped. Language shows a basic control. Sentences show a little variety and word choice is appropriate. Errors may be distracting and may occasionally impede understanding.

Score = 2

Essays at this score point demonstrate inconsistent or weak skill in responding to the task.

The essay shows a weak understanding of the task. The essay may not take a position on the issue, or the essay may take a position but fail to convey reasons to support that position, or the essay may take a position but fail to maintain a stance. There is little to no recognition of a counterargument to the author's position. The essay is thinly developed. If examples are given, they are general and may not be clearly relevant. The essay may include extensive repetition of the writer's ideas or of ideas in the prompt. Focus on the general topic is maintained, but focus on the specific issue in the prompt may not be maintained. There is some indication of an organizational structure, and some logical grouping of ideas within parts of the essay is apparent. Transitions, if used, are simple and obvious, and they may be inappropriate or misleading. An introduction and conclusion are discernible but minimal. Sentence structure and word choice are usually simple. Errors may be frequently distracting and may sometimes impede understanding.

Score = 1

Essays at this score point show little or no skill in responding to the task.

The essay shows little or no understanding of the task. If the essay takes a position, it fails to convey reasons to support that position. The essay is minimally developed. The essay may include excessive repetition of the writer's ideas or of ideas in the prompt. Focus on the general topic is usually maintained, but focus on the specific issue in the prompt may not be maintained. There is little or no evidence of an organizational structure or of the logical grouping of ideas. Transitions are rarely used. If present, an introduction and conclusion are minimal. Sentence structure and word choice are simple. Errors may be frequently distracting and may significantly impede understanding.

CALCULATING YOUR COMBINED ENGLISH/WRITING SCORE

1. Find your English Test scale score on page 617. Enter it here: _____.

2. Enter your Writing Test score (1–6) here: _____; double it to get your Writing subscore (2–12): _____. (If two people read and scored your Writing Test, add those two scores to get your Writing subscore.)

3. Use the table on page 623 to find your Combined English/Writing score.

   ■ First, circle your ACT English Test score in the left column.
   ■ Second, circle your ACT Writing subscore at the top of the table.
   ■ Finally, follow the English Test score row across and the Writing subscore column down until the two meet. Circle the Combined English/Writing score where the row and column meet. (For example, for an English Test score of 19 and a Writing subscore of 6, the Combined English/Writing score is 18.)

4. Using the number you circled in the table below, write your Combined English/Writing score here: _____. (The highest possible Combined English/Writing score is 36, and the lowest possible score is 1.)

ACT English Test score   _____

Writing subscore   _____

_____

Combined English/Writing Score   _____
(from table on page 623)

COMBINED ENGLISH/WRITING SCALE SCORES

English Test Score	Writing Subscore										
	2	3	4	5	6	7	8	9	10	11	12
1	1	2	3	4	5	6	7	8	9	10	11
2	2	3	4	5	6	6	7	8	9	10	11
3	2	3	4	5	6	7	8	9	10	11	12
4	3	4	5	6	7	8	9	10	11	12	13
5	4	5	6	7	8	9	10	11	12	12	13
6	5	6	7	7	8	9	10	11	12	13	14
7	5	6	7	8	9	10	11	12	13	14	15
8	6	7	8	9	10	11	12	13	14	15	16
9	7	8	9	10	11	12	13	13	14	15	16
10	8	9	9	10	11	12	13	14	15	16	17
11	8	9	10	11	12	13	14	15	16	17	18
12	9	10	11	12	13	14	15	16	17	18	19
13	10	11	12	13	14	14	15	16	17	18	19
14	10	11	12	13	14	15	16	17	18	19	20
15	11	12	13	14	15	16	17	18	19	20	21
16	12	13	14	15	16	17	18	19	20	20	21
17	13	14	15	16	16	17	18	19	20	21	22
18	13	14	15	16	17	18	19	20	21	22	23
19	14	15	16	17	18	19	20	21	22	23	24
20	15	16	17	18	19	20	21	21	22	23	24
21	16	17	17	18	19	20	21	22	23	24	25
22	16	17	18	19	20	21	22	23	24	25	26
23	17	18	19	20	21	22	23	24	25	26	27
24	18	19	20	21	22	23	23	24	25	26	27
25	18	19	20	21	22	23	24	25	26	27	28
26	19	20	21	22	23	24	25	26	27	28	29
27	20	21	22	23	24	25	26	27	28	28	29
28	21	22	23	24	24	25	26	27	28	29	30
29	21	22	23	24	25	26	27	28	29	30	31
30	22	23	24	25	26	27	28	29	30	31	32
31	23	24	25	26	27	28	29	30	30	31	32
32	24	25	25	26	27	28	29	30	31	32	33
33	24	25	26	27	28	29	30	31	32	33	34
34	25	26	27	28	29	30	31	32	33	34	35
35	26	27	28	29	30	31	31	32	33	34	35
36	26	27	28	29	30	31	32	33	34	35	36

EXPLANATORY ANSWERS

Section 1: English Test

1. Choice B is correct. Generally speaking, "the" is not included in the proper name of an era, so Choice A is incorrect. Since the Dark Ages is a particular time in history, the term "Dark Ages" is a proper noun and should therefore be capitalized, so Choice C is incorrect. The general description given in Choice D is unclear, so this choice is incorrect. Choice B is correct.

2. Choice H is correct. Choice F is incorrect because "then" is inexact in this sentence. Choice G is incorrect because "at the time" is much too narrow to cover a period of 1,100 years (A.D. 400–1500) Choice H is correct because it uses "that" to refer to the era (Dark Ages) previously mentioned. Choice J is incorrect because it is redundant.

3. Choice D is correct. Choice A is incorrect because it is an acceptable use of past tense and subject/verb agreement. Choice B is incorrect because it is also an acceptable use of past tense and subject/verb agreement. Choice C is incorrect because it is an acceptable use of past tense and subject/verb agreement. Choice D is correct because although subject/verb agreement is correct, it is an overstatement and the language is too informal.

4. Choice F is correct. The parenthetical phrase ("as some did") must be in the same form as the part of the sentence it is explaining. That part has a subject and a verb, so the phrase must also. Choice G incorrectly introduces "such" and lacks a verb. Choice J also lacks a verb and is awkward. Choice H is incorrect because the preposition "like" cannot introduce a clause.

5. Choice B is correct. When using "both," one must be careful to maintain parallel construction. Only Choice B contains a parallel construction.

6. Choice H is correct. Choice F is incorrect because it produces a run-on sentence. Choice G is incorrect because the present participle indicates two actions taking place at the same time; these two actions are not concurrent. Choice H is correct because it is part of the nominative absolute construction ("the Reformation not having begun"). Choice J is incorrect because it contains the present participle and because the word order is faulty.

7. Choice C is correct. Choice A is incorrect because the essay's focus is the period between A.D. 400 and the period just before the Reformation. In addition, the added sentence does not define the Reformation itself; it mentions an event that helped give rise to the Reformation movement. Choice B is incorrect because it strays too far from the essay's focus on interpretations of the era preceding the Reformation when challenges to authority were rare. Choice C is correct because it rejects the new sentence due to its lack of relevance to the essay's focus. Choice D is incorrect because it does reject the new sentence, but misinterprets its function.

8. Choice F is correct because the sentence in its current form is most consistent with the discussion that follows. Choice G is incorrect because it relates only indirectly to *one* of the paragraph's examples about the influence of the Church. Choice H is incorrect because it is not supported by any information in the paragraph or the essay's other paragraphs. Choice J is incorrect because it too is unsupported by anything else in the essay.

9. Choice A is correct. Choice B is incorrect because "cannot hardly" creates a double negative. Choice C is incorrect because the "except" thought gives us a meaning opposite to what the writer means to bring out. Choice D is awkward. Choice A is correct.

10. Choice H is correct. "Moreover" is a conjunctive adverb. As such it has the power to join independent clauses. A conjunctive adverb must be preceded by a semicolon and followed by a comma. Choice F is, thus, incorrect. Choices G and J present run-on sentences because they ignore the conjunctive function of "moreover."

11. Choice A is correct. The problems in this question are tense sequence and logic. The sentence is in the past tense; the participle must be a present participle, showing action concurrent with the time of the sentence, but the "reward" is in the future. To show this relationship, the future conditional of the verb "to be" must be used. This is "would be." Therefore, Choices B and D are incorrect. Choice C has two problems: first, "leading" should be "having led," since the "leading" precedes the "reward"; second, this sentence would say that they led Christian lives "after death"—an impossible feat.

12. Choice J is correct. Choice F presents a dangling participle. Choice G is incorrect because it uses "due to" to mean "because of." Choice H is incorrect because it is not idiomatic English.

13. Choice C is correct. Choice A is incorrect because only one set of future generations is mentioned; therefore, "other" is incorrect and should be omitted. Choice B is incorrect because it is too wordy: "future generations" will logically "follow this one," so the phrase should be omitted. Choice D is incorrect because it is unnecessarily complicated in that it uses a prepositional phrase when an appropriate adjective exists. Choice C is correct.

14. Choice J is correct. Choice F is incorrect because it is not parallel with "will see" in the second half of the sentence. ("Would be" would have been correct if the second clause contained "would see.") Choice G also lacks parallel construction. Choice H not only lacks parallel construction, but also is illogical; the future perfect is used to indicate an action that will be completed in the future before some other action is completed. Here, there is no second action.

15. Choice D is correct. Choice A is incorrect because the first sentence points toward the future prematurely (this is usually the function of a concluding sentence), and sentence 3 causes the essay to end with a specific detail it's too late to explain. Choice B is incorrect because beginning the paragraph with sentence 3 creates an awkward transition between this paragraph and the previous one. Choice C is incorrect because it too would begin the paragraph with a sentence more appropriate for a conclusion. Choice D is correct because sentence 2 serves as the most effective transition from the previous paragraph and brings together the two major ideas about the Middle Ages as the essay nears a conclusion. Sentence 3 expands on sentence 2 by providing an example of a society perceiving the Middle Ages in different ways depending on its own spiritual climate. Sentence 1 effectively concludes the essay by reflecting back on the essay's point and looking toward the future.

16. Choice H is correct. Choices F, G, and J are incorrect because they are unnecessarily wordy.

17. Choice A is correct. Choices B, C, and D are incorrect because they are not direct in conveying the necessary information.

18. Choice J is correct. Choice F is both awkward and ungrammatical. Choices G and H are too wordy.

19. Choice D is correct. Choice A is incorrect for the following reason: Since the first clause begins with "although," it is a dependent clause. Accordingly, the second clause must be independent. The subordinate conjunction "whereas" makes the second clause dependent, so the inclusion of "whereas" makes the choice incorrect. Choice B is further incorrect because of the semicolon, which joins a dependent clause to an independent clause. Semicolons join only two independent clauses. Choice C is incorrect because "Club" is part of the name of the group and should therefore be capitalized.

20. Choice J is correct. The abbreviation "e.g." is Latin for *exempli gratia*, meaning "for the sake of example." The only correct punctuation for its use is the letter "e" followed by a period, the letter "g" followed by a period, then a comma. Therefore, Choice J is the correct choice.

21. Choice B is correct. Choice A is incorrect because the writer draws no conclusions about the relative influence of the two groups, making the point

that both groups influenced the EPA's creation. Choice B is correct because the sentence provides examples of environmental groups and begins to make the point that there are important differences between them. Choice C is incorrect because the sentence offers broad definition, not concrete examples. Choice D is incorrect because although the Sierra Club is one of the best-known environmental groups, the Environmental Defense Fund may be unknown to many readers, and the familiarity of the names is not the writer's primary reason for including them.

22. Choice J is correct. Choice F implies incorrectly that the terms "conservationist" and "preservationist" are interchangeable. Choice G presents "Some preservationist" as a sentence, but it is not. Choice H also indicates that "some preservationist" is an independent clause, which it is not, having no verb. Choice J is correct because in this elliptical construction a comma is the correct punctuation.

23. Choice A is correct because it is the appropriate preposition to use when referring to two subjects. Choice B is incorrect because *among* is the preposition to use when referring to *more* than two subjects. Choice C is incorrect because it creates a nonstandard phrasing of a prepositional phrase. Choice D is incorrect because it is nonstandard phrasing of a prepositional phrase.

24. Choice F is correct because it is most specific in identifying the different philosophies of the two groups regarding use of natural resources. Choice G is incorrect because it only repeats in slightly different wording the "conservationist/preservationist" labels without explaining them. Choice H is incorrect because it is a judgment of the group's actions rather than an explanation and therefore does not fit the essay's overall tone and purpose. Choice J is incorrect because, while the sentence *may* be true (as implied by one upcoming example), it is not explicitly supported and the sentence fails to define the terms *conservationist* and *preservationist*.

25. Choice C is correct. Choice A is illogical. The lumber industry is not itself the example. Choice B is also illogical since the example is in the industry, not in the wood. Choice D is unnecessarily inverted; this inversion makes it wordy and awkward.

26. Choice G is correct. The placement of "only" is very loose in speech (as Choice F illustrates), but in written material this adverb should be placed closest to the word it modifies. In this case, "only" should modify "leaving . . . alone." Choices H and J contain another error as well: the lack of parallel construction. "Would approve" should be used, as it is in the first clause.

27. Choice B is correct. Choice A is incorrect because it omits a comma after "dam." This comma is needed because a series of items is given. (The comma after "plant" is disappearing in common usage, but it is still considered necessary according to most style manuals.) Choice C is incorrect because a comma followed by "or" in the middle of a series indicates apposition. (At the end of a series, if we wish to connect the last two items in the series, we use "or" to indicate a choice among the members of the series.) Choice D is incorrect because it omits the hyphen in "water-treatment plant." The hyphen is needed because "water" and "treatment" act jointly as an adjective modifying "plant."

28. Choice H is correct. Choice F is incorrect because the sentence and essay focus on objective definition and explanation, not argumentation. The writer uses no emotional appeals. Choice G is incorrect because the sentence is describing an EPA function the groups both support (the environmental impact statement), not the groups themselves. Choice H is correct because it describes the scope of the statements. Choice J is incorrect because the information is not redundant.

29. Choice D is correct. The two problems in this question are the difference between "its" and "it's" and the use of ellipsis. "Its" is a possessive pronoun; "it's" is a contraction of "it is." In this sentence "its" is needed, modifying "negative impact." Therefore, Choices A and C are incorrect. Choice B is incorrect (as is A) because of the omission of "impact." In this case ellipsis makes the sentence unclear because "negative" can be a noun as well as an adjective.

30. Choice G is correct. Choice F is incorrect because the permission is being granted for the carrying out of the project; thus, "project" should be possessive. Choice G is correct because no possessive is used

with an infinitive phrase. Choice H is incorrect because "done" is an imprecise verb. It should not be used when a more exact verb exists. Choice J is incorrect because it makes the sentence awkward.

31. Choice C is correct. Choice A is incorrect because "illusions" are "fantasies." Choice B is incorrect because the form of "refer" that is appropriate here is "references." Choice D is incorrect because "affinities" are "attractions."

32. Choice G is correct. Choice F is incorrect because the prepositional construction "on account of" must be replaced by a subordinate conjunction ("that"). Choices H and J are incorrect because they lack "so much," which is needed to go with "as" in the next clause.

33. Choice B is correct. Choice A is incorrect because the preposition "to" is omitted. One "refers to" something. Choice C does not make sense in the sentence. Choice D is incorrect because it unnecessarily includes the lengthy "that to which".

34. Choice H is correct. Choice F is incorrect because it omits "the fact that." Choice G is incorrect because it uses "because" instead of "the fact that." Choice J is incorrect because it neglects to make "today" possessive.

35. Choice D is correct. Choice A is incorrect because of the verb tense. The simple past is required ("was")—not the past perfect ("had been"). Choice B is incorrect because the clause "who was . . . book" is restrictive and should not be set off by commas. Choice C is incorrect because by omitting "sufficiently" the meaning of the sentence is changed. It sounds as if these people were educated solely to enable them to write books.

36. Choice J is correct. Choice F is incorrect because "Latin and Greek" require the plural verb "were." Choice G and H are incorrect because "Latin" is the singular subject requiring the verb "was." The prepositional phrases "along with Greek" and "besides Greek" are not part of the subject.

37. Choice C is correct. The present tense, plural number, is needed here. Choice B is incorrect, although in the present tense, because it is singular when a plural is needed.

38. Choice H is correct. Choice F is incorrect because the singular construction "that is" must be used since the antecedent of "that" ("subject") is singular. Choice G is incorrect because "sciences" requires the plural verb "are." Choice J is incorrect because "type" cannot be used as an adjective.

39. Choice C is correct. Choice A is incorrect because computer makers are not parallel with a language, so this choice would create an illogical comparison. Choice B is incorrect because although slang is parallel with Greek as a form of language, the choice does not closely approximate the writer's original idea, *computer languages*. Choice C is correct because although email and text messaging are not languages themselves, they are ways of using language unique to computers and other electronic devices. Choice D is incorrect because *surfing the Internet*, a gerund, is not grammatically parallel with *Greek*, a noun, nor is the idea parallel with the Greek language.

40. Choice H is correct. It is incorrect to use "this" and "that" loosely—that is, without a definite antecedent. Choices F and G contain this error. Choice J is incorrect because the singular is given when the plural is required.

41. Choice A is correct because it serves as an effective transition from the paragraphs reflecting on the loss of tradition, while introducing the writer's resolution of the problem. Choice B is incorrect because its ominous tone is inconsistent with the writer's reflective purpose and voice. Choice C is incorrect because the writer has not argued against science itself, only the displacement of humanism in favor of science. In addition, the writer has not specifically addressed either form of education as a way of gaining self-knowledge. Choice D is incorrect because the writer is not so much suggesting the need to stop the trend toward science and technology as to enrich it with an equal part of humanities. In addition, the sentence's certainty contradicts the writer's uncertainty in the essay's closing lines.

42. Choice G is correct. The problem here is the indefinite antecedent. Choice F is incorrect because "it" does not have an antecedent. Choice G is correct because "classical learning" is a good general term for what has been discussed in the passage. Choice

H is incorrect because "all" has no antecedent. Choice J is additionally incorrect because it omits the question mark.

43. Choice D is correct. A parallel construction is needed to complete this sentence. Choice A gives an adjective and a noun. Choice B gives two nouns but omits a needed question mark. Choice C gives two adjectives, but "humanitarian" is the wrong word here.

44. Choice J is correct. Choice F is incorrect because of the end punctuation. The words inside the parentheses do not form a sentence, so they should not carry a period. Moreover, the sentence is a question. Choice G is incorrect because "a twentieth-century psychologist" is in apposition to "B. F. Skinner" and should therefore be set off by a comma. Choice H is awkward. Choice J is correct. The comma after "Skinner" shows that the phrase that follows is in apposition to the name.

45. Choice D is correct. Choice A is incorrect because the authors mentioned are third-person examples with no personal narrative. Choice B is incorrect because the writer is not arguing a particular basis for valuing humanist education, and in fact mentions the utility and professional practicality of science-based education. Choice C is incorrect because the writer implies that both types of education are valuable in different ways. Choice D is correct because the writer's conclusion is that both educational cultures can be valued and enjoyed.

46. Choice G is correct. The subject of the sentence is "acrobats," a plural noun. Therefore, the singular "abides" is incorrect (Choice F), and the plural "abide" is correct (Choice G). The sentence is making a simple statement, so the emphatic verb form "do abide" (Choice H) is unnecessary. Choice J does not make sense. The monkeys actually do live there, so that the fact that they are able to do so ("can abide") is already indicated.

47. Choice C is correct. The clause "agile as they are" is most economical without omitting any needed words. Choice A and D would be improved by adding "their": "their agility." Choice B does not make sense; it is *despite* their agility, not *with* their agility.

48. Choice J is correct. When more than two things are being discussed, "among," not "between," should be used. Therefore, Choice G is incorrect and Choice J is correct. Choice F is incorrect because "regarding" does not point out one among many items. The same is true of Choice H.

49. Choice B is correct. The use of "like" in prepositional phrase "like a trapeze artist" correctly compares two things (the spider monkey and a trapeze artist); "as" would be used to compare actions (or verbs), which is not being done here and which in any case would require the addition of the word "does" ("as a trapeze artist *does*"). Therefore, Choice A is incorrect and Choice B is correct. Choice C is incorrect because it implies that the monkey knows that he looks like a trapeze artist; it is highly unlikely that he does know. Choice D is incorrect because "following" in the sense of *imitating* does not make sense.

50. Choice G is correct. The words in parentheses explain "liana," so any punctuation that would follow "liana" without the parentheses now follows the parentheses. In other words, the comma follows the parentheses. Choice G is correct, and the other choices are incorrect.

51. Choice B is correct. The reflexive pronoun, "himself," not the object pronoun "him," is correct, because the action is performed by and upon the same subject—i.e., the monkey. "Himself " rather than "itself " is correct because throughout the passage the personal *he/him* has been used, not the impersonal *it*.

52. Choice F is correct. This is a compound-complex sentence. The compound verbs are "may give," "may launch," and "may catch." The participial construction ("soaring outward . . . air") is correct here. Choice G is incorrect because it makes "soar" one of the main verbs. Choice H is incorrect because the participle, not the infinitive, is needed. Choice J is incorrect because it makes "soar" a main verb, which, moreover, is in the wrong tense (past instead of present).

53. Choice D is correct. The spying of the berry must logically have preceded in time all the other action of the sentence; when, exactly, the monkey spied

the berry is not specified, but the close connection between the monkey's present action and the earlier spying suggests that the spying has immediately preceded the monkey's soaring toward the berry—hence the use of the present perfect tense, "has spied." The tenses used in Choices A, B, and C are incorrect.

54. Choice G is correct. Choice F is incorrect because the sentence is an example of personification, but personifying the monkey is not the sentence's primary function. Choice G is correct because the sentence introduces the paragraph's main idea. Choice H is incorrect because although comparisons with other members of the ceboid family are implied later, none occur here. Choice J is incorrect because the monkey's intelligence is mentioned, but with no supporting anecdote.

55. Choice B is correct. The antecedent is "monkey," a singular. Therefore, the possessive pronoun must be singular and Choices A and D are incorrect. Choice C is incorrect because it omits the second "his," the use of which is preferable idiomatically.

56. Choice H is correct. Since it is one monkey that is being spoken of, only one "tail" is involved, and Choices G and J are incorrect. Choice F is incorrect because the ellipsis (implying "are") is faulty. The singular verb "is" is needed with the singular "tail."

57. Choice A is correct. Choice A is correct because the sentence does use personification to characterize marmoset behavior. Choice B is incorrect because the sentence and essay describe the animals' behavior only with others of their kind, with no reference to humans. Choice C is incorrect because the writer compares the marmosets with the other ceboid monkeys on the basis of size only. Choice D is incorrect because the writer makes no reference to the ceboids' relationship with other species.

58. Choice G is correct. Choice F is incorrect because two complete sentences are appropriately separated with a period. Choice G is the correct answer, the unacceptable version, because it is an unacceptable use of an -ing participle (smacking), which creates a dangling modifier. Smacking appears to modify landings, rather than describing the marmosets. The other choices are acceptable and therefore

incorrect: Choice H is incorrect because the sentence clearly identifies marmosets as the subject of the verb *smacking*. Choice J is incorrect because it includes a clear subject, *they*, to refer to the marmosets, and a verb.

59. Choice B is correct. Choice A is incorrect because the sentence is a specific detail without repetition or connection to the essay's opening sentence. Choice B is correct because the sentence concludes the description of the marmosets' rough landings with a reference back to the opening image of the monkeys as acrobats. Choice C is incorrect because it places inappropriate emphasis on just one of the monkeys and a judgment that is inconsistent with the content or tone of the essay. Choice D is incorrect because reference to the tail is too specific to synthesize the essay or connect it to the opening.

60. Choice F is correct because the essay is limited according to the general guidelines for the assignment. Choice G is incorrect because personification is used, but not for an argumentative purpose or with any reference to rain forest destruction. Choice H is incorrect because the writer has limited the essay to one family of monkeys with several distinct members. Choice J is incorrect because although the essay sometimes implies a mock critique ("their landings are rough"), the writer's purpose in describing the monkey's athleticism is primarily informative.

61. Choice C is correct. The comparison needed is indicated by "as . . . as." Omitting either "as" is incorrect, so Choices A and D are incorrect. Choice B is incorrect because it contains the adjective "recent" instead of the adverb "recently." Choice D is additionally incorrect because the adverb alone does not make sense.

62. Choice J is correct. The construction "more . . . than" t akes parallel construction. Since "more" is followed by "applicants" (a noun), "than" should be followed only by "space" (also a noun). Therefore, only Choice J is correct.

63. Choice B is correct. The reason Choices A and C are incorrect is that they contain a "them" that does not have a definite antecedent. Logically, "them" should refer to "students," but two other third-person plural

nouns appear between "students" and "them"; the two are "parents" and "letters." Choice D is incorrect because, although it avoids the "them" problem, it contains an unidiomatic construction.

64. Choice H is correct. If the question is going to be given as a question, it must be treated as a direct quotation—that is, it must be set off by a comma and the first word must be capitalized. Only Choice H does this. (Choice J would be correct if it ended in a period instead of a question mark.)

65. Choice A is correct because the sentence is not the topic sentence of a new paragraph but a supporting example for an existing paragraph. Choice B is incorrect because a comma interrupts the subject of the sentence and the verb. Choice C is incorrect because the sentence should not begin a new paragraph. Choice D is incorrect because the sentence should not begin a new paragraph and a comma interrupts the subject of the sentence and the verb.

66. Choice F is correct because it is the best synthesis of the trends described in the paragraph. Choice G is incorrect because the sentence does not offer an explanation for the *need* to recruit in keeping with the essay's purpose. Choice H is incorrect because its explicit commentary is inconsistent with the essay's expository tone and because the reader expects a reason colleges began to recruit rather than commentary. Choice J is incorrect for the same reasons as Choice H.

67. Choice D is correct. The simple past tense is correct. The action is in the past and is complete. Choice A implies that the colleges did not begin to cultivate students, although that this did occur is stated in the passage.

68. Choice H is correct. Since the sentence is in the past tense, "before" must be used to show that the action would have occurred before the time of the sentence. "Ago" is used in the present tense to mean the same thing, but from whatever the present time is, not a past point in time. "Since" and "past" are not correctly used here, so Choices G and J are incorrect.

69. Choice A is correct. "Without" is the idiomatic preposition, and the word "without" makes grammatical sense in the sentence.

70. Choice H is correct. Both clauses of this compound sentence take place "during the early 1970s." They are therefore closely related. In addition, they are simple clauses. Therefore, a comma followed by "and" is the best connective between these clauses.

71. Choice C is correct. A is incorrect because "were in attendance" is too wordy—the verb "attended" is better. Therefore Choice C is correct. Choice B is incorrect because it does not contain a verb, which is needed for parallel construction with the clauses that precede and follow this clause. Choice D is incorrect because it does not contain a verb and because by setting "or secretarial" off with commas, apposition between "secretarial" and "trade" schools is incorrectly indicated.

72. Choice G is correct. A type of training program must be given after "such as." Choice F gives a profession. Choice G is correct because it gives a type of program. Choices H and J are awkward.

73. Choice A is correct because it follows logically from the preceding information and is supported in the essay's final sentence. Choice B is incorrect because it is not supported anywhere else in the essay. Choice C is incorrect because it contradicts the point that colleges were recruiting and accepting more students. Choice D is incorrect because junior and technical colleges are mentioned only for having traditionally served as an option for students who couldn't afford a four-year college.

74. Choice H is correct. The simple past tense is correct. The action took place, and was completed, in the past.

75. Choice D is correct. The construction "not only . . . but also" demands parallelism. "Not only" must also be followed by a full *that*-clause. Choice A omits the "but also" completely. Choice B omits "that" and a subject. Choice C omits "that."

EXPLANATORY ANSWERS

Section 2: Mathematics Test

As you read these solutions, you are advised to do two things if you answered the Math question incorrectly:

1. *When a specific Math Strategy is referred to in the solution, study that strategy, which you will find in the "19 Math Strategies" (beginning on page 44).*

2. *When the solution directs you to the "Complete ACT Math Refresher" (beginning on page 147)—for example, Math Refresher #305—study the math principle to get a clear idea of the math operation you needed to know in order to answer the question correctly.*

1. Choice D is correct.

   (Use Strategy 13: Find an unknown by dividing.)

   Given that $500w = 3 \times 700$ 1

   Divide 1 by 500, giving

   $$\frac{\cancel{500}w}{\cancel{500}} = \frac{3 \times 700}{500}$$

   (Use Strategy 19: Factor and reduce first. Then multiply.)

   $$w = \frac{3 \times 7 \times \cancel{100}}{5 \times \cancel{100}}$$

   $$w = \frac{21}{5}$$

   (Math Refresher #406)

2. Choice K is correct.

   (Use Strategy 13: Find an unknown by multiplying.)

   Given: $\dfrac{3 + y}{y} = 7$ 1

Multiply 1 by y, to get:

$$y\left(\frac{3 + y}{\cancel{y}}\right) = (7)y$$

$$3 + y = 7y$$

$$3 = 6y$$

$$\frac{3}{6} = y$$

$$\frac{1}{2} = y$$

(Math Refresher #406)

3. Choice E is correct.

   $-2m(4n - 2m) + 2$
   $= -2m(4n) - 2m(-2m) + 2$
   $= -8mn + 4m^2 + 2$

   (Math Refresher #405a)

4. Choice G is correct.

   (Use Strategy 2: Translate from words into algebra.)

   Perimeter of a square $= 4 \times$ side   1
   We are given that perimeter $= 20$ meters   2

   Substituting 2 into 1, we get

   20 meters $= 4 \times$ side
   5 meters $=$ side   3
   Area of square $=$ (side)^2 4

   Substituting 3 into 4, we get

   Area of square $=$ (5 meters)^2
   Area of square $= 25$ square meters

   (Math Refresher #303)

5. Choice E is correct.

(Use Strategy 17: Use the given information effectively.)

$$\text{Given: } 80 + a = -32 + b \qquad \boxed{1}$$

Subtract a from both sides, getting

$$
\begin{array}{rl}
80 + a & = -32 + b \\
\underline{ -a \quad\quad\quad -a} \\
80 & = -32 + b - a
\end{array}
$$

Add 32 to both sides, giving

$$
\begin{array}{rl}
80 & = -32 + b - a \\
\underline{+32 \quad\quad +32} \\
112 = & \quad b - a
\end{array}
$$

(Math Refresher #406)

6. Choice K is correct.

(Use Strategy 8: When all choices must be tested, start with the last choice and work backward.)

Choice K is $x^2 + x + 2$

(Use Strategy 7: Use specific number examples.)

Let $x = 3$ (an odd positive integer)

Then $x^2 + x + 2 =$
$$3^2 + 3 + 2 =$$
$$9 + 3 + 2 =$$
$$14 = \text{(an even result)}$$

Now let $x = 2$ (an even positive integer)

Then $x^2 + x + 2 =$
$$2^2 + 2 + 2 =$$
$$4 + 2 + 2 =$$
$$8 = \text{(an even result)}$$

Whether x is odd or even, Choice K is even.

(Math Refresher #431)

More sophisticated solution:

(Use Strategy 8: When all choices must be tested, start with the last choice and work backward.)

Choice K is $x^2 + x + 2$

Now factor: $x^2 + x + 2 = x(x + 1) + 2$.

Note that since x is an integer, $x(x + 1)$ is always the product of an even integer multiplied by an odd integer. So $x(x + 1)$ is even and thus 2 times an integer. $+2$ is even so $x(x + 1) + 2$ is even. And since $x(x + 1) + 2 = x^2 + x + 2$, then $x^2 + x + 2$ is even.

(Math Refresher #409)

7. Choice C is correct.

(Use Strategy 17: Use the given information effectively.)

$$\text{Given: } \frac{3}{4} < x < \frac{4}{5}$$

Change both fractions to fractions with the same denominator. Thus,

$$\frac{3}{4} < x < \frac{4}{5}$$

becomes

$$\frac{15}{20} < x < \frac{16}{20}$$

(Use Strategy 15: Certain choices may be easily eliminated.)

Choice B $= \dfrac{13}{20}$ can be instantly eliminated.

Choice D $= \dfrac{16}{20}$ can be instantly eliminated.

Change both fractions to 40ths to compare Choice C. Thus,

$$\frac{30}{40} < x < \frac{32}{40}$$

Choice C $= \dfrac{31}{40}$ is a possible value of x.

(Math Refreshers #108 and #419)

8. Choice J is correct.

(Use Strategy 17: Use the given information effectively.)

$$
\begin{aligned}
& 2 \times 10^{-5} \times 8 \times 10^2 \times 5 \times 10^2 \\
= &\ 8 \times 2 \times 5 \times 10^{-5} \times 10^2 \times 10^2 \\
= &\ 8 \times 10^0 \\
= &\ 8 \times 1 \\
= &\ 8
\end{aligned}
$$

(Math Refresher #429)

9. Choice B is correct.

(Use Strategy 2: Translate from words into math.)

From the diagram we can see that 25% is water, so

0.25×2 lb. $= \dfrac{1}{2}$ lb. is water.

(Math Refresher #705)

10. Choice F is correct.

(Use Strategy 17: Use the given information effectively.)

A segment that divides the area of a circle into two equal parts must be a diameter. Thus, segment RS must go through point O.

Since *ROS* is a diameter, then *RO* = *OS*, each segment being a radius.

Since *R* is in the 2nd quadrant, *S* must be in the 4th quadrant.

You can see that the *x*-coordinate of *S* must be positive and the *y*-coordinate of *S* must be negative.

$$S = [-1(-6), -1(8)]$$
$$S = (6, -8)$$

(Math Refreshers #524 and #410b)

11. Choice C is correct.

    (Use Strategy 17: Use the given information effectively.)

	First Place (6 points)	Second Place (4 points)	Third Place (2 points)
Game 1			
Game 2		Arisa	
Game 3			Arisa

    Dylan can attain the *minimum* possible score by placing third in Game 1 and Game 2 and second in Game 3.

    From the chart he would have 2, 2, and 4 points for each of these finishes.

    Thus, minimum score = 2 + 2 + 4

    minimum score = 8 points

    (Math Refreshers #701 and #702)

12. Choice G is correct.

    (Use Strategy 17: Use the given information effectively.)

    Use $y = mx + b$ for representation of line *k*. *m* is the slope of the line and *b* is the *y*-intercept (that is, the value of *y* when *x* = 0). You can see that a point on the graph is at $x = 3$ and $y = 2$ from the points (0,2) and (3,0). Thus, substituting $x = 3$ and $y = 2$ into $y = mx + b$, we get $2 = m(3) + b$. Since *m* is the slope of the graph and is equal to -1, we get

    $$2 = (-1)(3) + b$$
    $$2 = -3 + b$$
    and so $5 = b$

    (Math Refreshers #415 and #416)

13. Choice C is correct.

    (Use Strategy 2: Remember how to calculate percent.)

    Winning percentage =
    $$\frac{\text{\# of games won}}{\text{total \# of games played}} \times 100$$

    For example,

    Winning % for pitcher A

    $$= \frac{4}{4+2} \times 100 = \frac{4}{6} \times 100$$
    $$= \frac{\cancel{2} \times 2}{\cancel{2} \times 3} \times 100$$
    $$= \frac{200}{3} = 66\frac{2}{3}\%$$

    For each pitcher, we have

Pitcher	Winning Percentage
A	$66\frac{2}{3}\%$
B	60%
C	80%
D	50%
E	75%

    Pitcher C has the highest winning percentage.

    (Math Refresher #106)

14. Choice G is correct.

    (Use Strategy 11: Use new definitions carefully.)

    Given: A, B, C, . . . , L =

    1, 2, 3, . . . , 12 (respectively)　　　1

    The time on the watch is 15 minutes before 1.　　2

    From 1, we know that

    E = 5 and A = 1　　　3

    Substituting 3 into 2, we have

    3E minutes before A.

    (Math Refresher #431)

15. Choice A is correct.

    Volume of cube = (side)³

    Thus, volume of each small cube = r^3　　1

    volume of larger cube = s^3　　2

    and sum of the volumes of the 27 cubes = $27r^3$　　3

    (Use Strategy 3: The whole equals the sum of its parts.)

We are told that the sum of the volumes of the 27 cubes = the volume of the larger cube

$$= 81 \qquad \boxed{4}$$

From $\boxed{2}$, $\boxed{3}$, and $\boxed{4}$ together, we have

$$27r^3 = 81 \qquad \boxed{5}$$
$$s^3 = 81 \qquad \boxed{6}$$

(Use Strategy 13: Find unknown expressions by division.)

Dividing $\boxed{5}$ by $\boxed{6}$, we get

$$27\frac{r^3}{s^3} = 1 \qquad \boxed{7}$$

Multiplying $\boxed{7}$ by $\frac{1}{27}$, we get

$$\frac{r^3}{s^3} = \frac{1}{27}$$

or $\frac{r}{s} = \frac{1}{3}$

(Math Refreshers #313 and #429)

16. Choice K is correct.

The distance between points on a number line is found by:

$$|a - b| = |-4 - (7)| =$$
$$|-4 - 7| = |-11| = 11$$

(Math Refresher #410a)

17. Choice B is correct.

(Use Strategy 5:

$$Average = \frac{total\ of\ values}{total\ number\ of\ values}\Big)$$

The average is found by $\frac{8.4 + 8.1 + 9.3}{3} =$

$$\frac{25.8}{3} = 8.6$$

(Math Refresher #601)

18. Choice H is correct.

(Use Strategy 10: Know how to use units.)

Interest = rate $\times$ time $\times$ amount deposited

$$= \frac{8\%}{year} \times 1\ year \times \$50$$
$$= .08 \times 1 \times \$50$$
$$= \$4$$

(Use Strategy 3: The whole equals the sum of its parts.)

Total amount = deposit + interest
$$= \$50 + \$4$$
$$= \$54$$

(Math Refreshers ##113, #114, and #121)

19. Choice D is correct.

Given: $(x + 6)^2 = 12x + 72$ $\qquad \boxed{1}$

(Use Strategy 17: Use the given information effectively.)

Complete the squaring operation on the left side of the equation:

$$(x + 6)^2 = x^2 + 12x + 36$$

Continue the equation with $\boxed{1}$

$$x^2 + 12x + 36 = 12x + 72 \qquad \boxed{1}$$

(Use Strategy 1: Cancel numbers and expressions that appear on both sides of an equation.)

We get therefore, $x^2 + 36 = 72$

$$x^2 = 36$$
$$x = \pm 6$$

(Math Refresher #409)

20. Choice J is correct.

(Use Strategy 10: Know how to use units.)

Since 60 min = 1 hour, 24 hours = 1 day, and 7 days = 1 week, we have

$$\left(\frac{60\ min}{\cancel{hour}}\right)\left(\frac{24\ \cancel{hours}}{day}\right)\left(\frac{7\ \cancel{days}}{week}\right) = 10.080$$

or 1 week = 10,080 minutes. To the nearest hundred, 1 week $\approx$ 10,100 minutes.

(Math Refresher #121)

21. Choice B is correct.

(Use Strategy 11: Use new definitions carefully.)

Method I:

By definition $\nabla x = \frac{x^3}{4}$

We are looking for

$$\frac{x^3}{4} = 16 \qquad \boxed{1}$$

(Use Strategy 13: Find unknowns by multiplication.)

Multiplying $\boxed{1}$ by 4, we have

$$x^3 = 64$$
$$x = 4$$

Method II:

Calculate each of the choices, A through E, until you find the one whose value is 16.

(Math Refreshers #429 and #431)

22. Choice G is correct.

    (Use Strategy 2: Translate from words into math.)

    We are given:

    $$42 + 27 + 56 + x + y = 200$$
    $$\text{or} \quad 125 + x + y = 200$$
    $$\text{or} \quad x + y = 75$$
    $$\text{or} \quad x = 75 - y \qquad \boxed{1}$$

    (Use Strategy 17: Use the given information effectively.)

    From $\boxed{1}$, it is clear that x is a maximum when y is a minimum. Since y is the number of pieces of candy in a jar, its minimum value is

    $$y = 0 \qquad \boxed{2}$$

    Substituting $\boxed{2}$ into $\boxed{1}$,

    $$x = 75$$

    (Math Refreshers #200, #426, and #431)

23. Choice C is correct.

    (Use Strategy 2: Translate from words into algebra.)

    Number of pages Ron read last night

    $$= \frac{1}{4} \times 16 = 4$$

    (Use Strategy 3: The whole equals the sum of its parts.)

    Number of pages remaining immediately after Ron finished reading last night $= 16 - 4 = 12$

    Number of pages read this morning $= \frac{1}{4} \times 12 = 3$

    Pages still not read
    $= $ remaining pages $-$ pages read this morning
    $= 12 - 3$
    Pages still not read $= 9$

    (Math Refresher #200)

24. Choice H is correct.

    (Use Strategy 9: Use $R \times T = D$ formula.)

    Let t_1 be the time spent traveling at 60 mph. Let t_2 stand for the time spent traveling 70 mph.
    Using $R \times T = D$,

    $$60t_1 = 180$$
    $$70t_2 = 180$$
    $$t_1 = \frac{180}{60}$$
    $$t_2 = \frac{180}{70}$$

So the time saved (the difference of t_2 from t_1) is

$$\frac{180}{60} - \frac{180}{70} = 180\left(\frac{1}{60} - \frac{1}{70}\right)$$
$$= 180\left(\frac{70 - 60}{60 \times 70}\right)$$
$$= \frac{180}{60} \times \frac{1}{7}$$
$$= 3 \times \frac{1}{7}$$
$$= \frac{3}{7}$$

(Math Refreshers #110 and #409)

25. Choice C is correct.

    (Use Strategy 17: Use the given information effectively.)

    Since the triangle is equilateral, all of its sides are equal. Thus,

    $$5x - 2 = x$$
    $$4x = 2$$
    $$x = \frac{1}{2}$$

    Perimeter $= $ sum of 3 sides $= \frac{1}{2} + \frac{1}{2} + \frac{1}{2}$
    $$= 1\frac{1}{2}$$

    (Math Refreshers #508 and #406)

26. Choice H is correct.

    (Use Strategy 2: Translate from words into algebra.)

    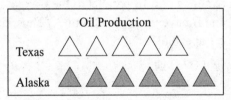

    We are told $\blacktriangle = 3\triangle$

    (Use Strategy 17: Use the given information effectively.)

    Texas total $= 5$
    Alaska total $= 3(6) = 18$

    (Use Strategy 3: Know how to find unknown quantities from known quantities.)

    $$\frac{\text{Alaska production}}{\text{total production}} = \frac{18}{5 + 18}$$
    $$= \frac{18}{23}$$
    $$= \text{required ratio}$$

    (Math Refreshers #200 and #431)

27. Choice C is correct.

Probability is defined as

$$\frac{\text{number of favorable ways (coins)}}{\text{total number of ways (coins)}} = \frac{F}{N}$$

If the probability of selecting a nickel is $\frac{3}{8}$, then for nickels, $\frac{F}{N} = \frac{3}{8}$. But N (the total number of ways, or coins) is 24.

So $\frac{F}{N} = \frac{3}{8} = \frac{F}{24}$; $F = 9$ (nickels)

The probability of selecting a dime is $\frac{1}{8}$, so for a dime, $\frac{F}{N} = \frac{1}{8} = \frac{F}{24}$; $F = 3$ (dimes)

(Use Strategy 3: Subtract whole from parts.)

Since there are 24 coins and there are 9 nickels and 3 dimes, $24 - 3 - 9 = 12$ quarters.

(Math Refresher #614)

28. Choice H is correct.

Method I:

(Use Strategy 17: Use the given information effectively.)

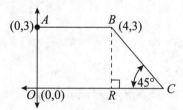

The figure above has AB parallel to the x-axis. (Both A and B have y-coordinates of 3.) Thus, the figure is a trapezoid.

Its height (OA) is 3. [1]
Its top base is 4. [2]

(Use Strategy 14: Draw lines when appropriate.)

Draw BR perpendicular to the x-axis.
$$BR = OA = 3 \text{ and } AB = OR = 4$$

(Use Strategy 18: Remember isosceles triangle facts.)

Triangle BRC is an isosceles right triangle.
Thus, $RB = RC = 3$
The bottom base of the trapezoid
$$= OC = OR + RC = 4 + 3 = 7$$ [3]
The area of a trapezoid
$$= \frac{1}{2}h(\text{base 1} + \text{base 2})$$ [4]

Substituting [1], [2], and [3] into [4], we have
$$\text{Area of trapezoid} = \frac{1}{2}(3)(4 + 7) = \frac{1}{2}(3)(11)$$
$$= 16.5$$

Method II:

(Use Strategy 14: Draw lines when appropriate.)

Draw BR perpendicular to the x-axis.

$ABRO$ is a rectangle and BRC is an isosceles triangle.

$$\text{Area } ABRO = \text{base} \times \text{height}$$
$$= 4 \times 3$$
$$= 12$$ [1]

$$\text{Area } BRC = \frac{1}{2} \times \text{base} \times \text{height}$$
$$= \frac{1}{2} \times 3 \times 3$$
$$= 4.5$$ [2]

(Use Strategy 3: The whole equals the sum of its parts.)

Using [1] and [2], the total area of figure $ABCO$
$$= \text{area of } ABRO + \text{area of } BRC$$
$$= 12 + 4.5$$
$$= 16.5$$

(Math Refreshers #410, #304, #306, #309, and #431)

29. Choice A is correct.

(Use Strategy 3: The whole equals the sum of its parts.)

The area between the curved path and the dodecagon is simply the sum of the areas of the 12 semi-circles.

Since area of circle $= \pi r^2$

then area of semicircle $= \frac{1}{2}\pi r^2$

where r is the radius of the circle.

Thus, the area of the shaded region $= 12\left(\frac{1}{2}\pi r^2\right)$
$$= 6\pi r^2$$ [1]

We are told that the diameter of a semicircle = the side of the dodecagon. [2]

Since each side of a regular dodecagon has the same length, then

length of a side of dodecagon
$$= \frac{\text{perimeter of dodecagon}}{12}$$
$$= \frac{24}{12}$$
$$= 2$$

From 2 , we know that diameter of semicircle = 2

Thus, radius of semicircle = 1　　　　　3

Substituting 3 into 1 , area of shaded region = 6π

(Math Refreshers #310, #311, and #522)

30. Choice G is correct.

(Use Strategy 13: Add equations.)

Adding both sides of the equations we get

$$4x + 8x + 3y - 3y = 0 + 10$$

Simplifying, we obtain

$$12x = 10$$
$$x = \frac{10}{12}$$
$$= \frac{5}{6}$$

We now substitute $x = \frac{5}{6}$ into one of the original equations:

$$4\left(\frac{5}{6}\right) + 3y = 0$$
$$4\left(\frac{5}{6}\right) = -3y$$
$$-\frac{10}{9} = y$$

Thus $x = \frac{5}{6}$ and $y = -\frac{10}{9}$

(Math Refresher #407)

31. Choice D is correct.

$$f(x - 1) = (x - 1)^2 + 2(x - 1) + 1$$
$$= x^2 - 2x + 1 + 2x - 2 + 1$$
$$= x^2$$

(Math Refreshers #616 and #409)

32. Choice J is correct.

(Use Strategy 18: Remember the isosceles right triangle.)

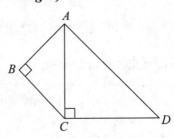

Given: $AB = BC$　　　　　1

$AC = CD$　　　　　2

From 1 we get that $\triangle ABC$ is an isosceles right triangle. Therefore, $\angle BAC$ and $\angle BCA$ are each 45-degree angles.

From 2 we get that $\triangle ACD$ is an isosceles right triangle. Therefore, $\angle CAD$ and $\angle CDA$ are each 45-degree angles.

Thus, there are four 45-degree angles.

(Math Refreshers #505 and #509)

33. Choice B is correct.

(Use Strategy 2: Translate from words into algebra.)

We know that:

area of rectangle = length × width　　　1

We are given: area = 4　　　　　2

length = $\frac{4}{3}$　　　　　3

Substituting 2 and 3 into 1 , we get

$$4 = \frac{4}{3} \times \text{width}$$　　　4

(Use Strategy 13: Find unknowns by multiplication.)

Multiply 4 by $\frac{3}{4}$. We get

$$\frac{3}{4}(4) = \frac{\cancel{3}}{\cancel{4}}\left(\frac{\cancel{4}}{\cancel{3}} \times \text{width}\right)$$
$$3 = \text{width}$$

(Math Refreshers #304 and #406)

34. Choice J is correct.

Since vertical angles are equal, then

$$m\angle AOC = m\angle DOB = 108$$　　　1

Thus, from 1 , we get length of

minor $\overset{\frown}{AC}$ = length of minor $\overset{\frown}{DB}$　　　2

From geometry we know length of

minor $\overset{\frown}{AC} = \frac{108}{360} \times$ circumference of circle

$$= \frac{108}{360} \times \pi(\text{diameter})$$
$$= \frac{108}{360} \times \pi(20)$$

(Use Strategy 19: Factor and reduce.)

length of minor $\overset{\frown}{AC} = \frac{\cancel{18} \times 6}{\cancel{18} \times \cancel{20}} \times \pi(\cancel{20})$

length of minor $\overset{\frown}{AC} = 6\pi$　　　3

Length $\overset{\frown}{AC}$ + length $\overset{\frown}{DB}$ can be found using 2 and 3

length $\overset{\frown}{AC}$ + length $\overset{\frown}{DB} = 6\pi + 6\pi$

length $\overset{\frown}{AC}$ + length $\overset{\frown}{DB} = 12\pi$

(Math Refreshers #503 and #310)

35. Choice D is correct.

The graphs are represented as follows:

Plot $x = 0, y = 0$.

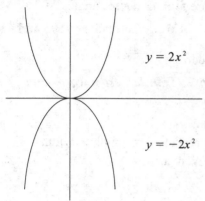

For $y = 2x^2$, when $x = \pm 1, y = 2$;
 when $x = \pm 2, y = 8$

For $y = -2x^2$, when $x = \pm 1, y = -2$;
 when $x = \pm 2, y = -8$

Thus, I and II are true. III is false. A linear function is of the form $y = mx + b$.

(Math Refresher #410b)

36. Choice G is correct.

(Use Strategy 2: Know the definition of percent.)

Percent of caramels =

$$\frac{\text{weight of caramels}}{\text{total weight}} \times 100 \qquad \boxed{1}$$

 Given:
  Weight of caramels = 0.6 pound $\boxed{2}$
  Weight of coconuts = 3.6 pounds $\boxed{3}$

Adding $\boxed{2}$ and $\boxed{3}$, we get
  Total weight = 0.6 pounds + 3.6 pounds
  Total weight = 4.2 pounds $\boxed{4}$

Substituting $\boxed{2}$ and $\boxed{4}$ into $\boxed{1}$, we have

$$\text{Percent of caramels} = \frac{0.6 \text{ pounds}}{4.2 \text{ pounds}} \times 100$$

$$= \frac{0.6}{4.2} \times 100$$

$$= \frac{6}{42} \times 100$$

$$= \frac{600}{42}$$

$$= \frac{300}{21}$$

$$\text{Percent of caramels} = 14\frac{2}{7}$$

(Math Refreshers #106 and #107)

37. Choice B is correct.

(Use Strategy 17: Use the given information effectively.)

Notice that $25,000 is one-fourth of $100,000 (the total funds).

That is, $\dfrac{25,000}{100,000} = \dfrac{1}{4}$.

So look for the piece or part of the circle that is closest to $\dfrac{1}{4}$ of the whole circle. $\dfrac{1}{4}$ of the whole circle (360°) is 90°. Lincoln H.S. represents about $\dfrac{1}{4}$ of the whole circle, or 90°.

(Math Refresher #705)

38. Choice K is correct.

(Use Strategy 2: Translate from words into algebra.)

 Given: The 3 polygons have equal perimeters, which gives us

$$6a = 3b \qquad \boxed{1}$$
$$8c = 6a \qquad \boxed{2}$$

Dividing $\boxed{1}$ by 6, we get

$$a = \frac{3}{6}b = \frac{1}{2}b \qquad \boxed{3}$$

Thus, a < b.

Dividing $\boxed{2}$ by 8, we get

$$c = \frac{6}{8}a = \frac{3}{4}a \qquad \boxed{4}$$

Thus, c < a.

(Use Strategy 6: Know how to use inequalities.)

Using the Transitive Property of Inequalities with $\boxed{3}$ and $\boxed{4}$, we have $c < a < b$.

(Math Refreshers #304, #306 and #406)

39. Choice C is correct.

(Now use Strategy 17: Use the given information effectively.)

The total cost would be the cost of the lesson ($100) + the cost of the rental of the skis ($r). Now since the cost of the skis varies directly with the square root of the time the skis are used, by calling the time of use t and the cost of ski rental r we get

$$\frac{r}{\sqrt{t}} = k \quad \text{or} \quad r = k\sqrt{t}, \text{where } k \text{ is constant}$$

The total cost is $100 + $k\sqrt{t}$

If, as stated, a 25-minute lesson costs $200, we can solve for k.

$$100 + k\sqrt{25} = 200$$
$$k\sqrt{25} = 200$$
$$5k = 100$$
$$k = 20$$

So then, for a 64-minute lesson, the cost C is represented by

$$C = 100 + k\sqrt{64}$$
$$C = 100 + 20\sqrt{64}$$
$$C = 100 + (20 \times 8)$$
$$C = \$260$$

(Math Refreshers #122 and #406)

40. **Choice H is correct.**

For line q, $y = mx + b_1$. Since the line q crosses the origin, where $x = 0$ and $y = 0$, b_1 must $= 0$. Thus for line q, $y = mx$. Now since $(4,3)$ is on line q, this means when $x = 4$, $y = 3$, so if $y = mx$, $3 = m(4)$ and $m = \frac{3}{4}$. Now let's look at line p. For this line, $y = Mx + b$. Since the lines p and q are perpendicular, the slope of one is the *negative reciprocal* of the other. Thus $m = -\frac{1}{M}$. Since $m = \frac{3}{4}$, $\frac{3}{4} = -\frac{1}{M}$ and so $M = -\frac{4}{3}$. Thus for line p, $y = -\left(\frac{4}{3}\right)x + b$. The point $(4,3)$ is also on line p, so substituting $x = 4$ and $y = 3$ in the equation $y = -\left(\frac{4}{3}\right)x + b$, we get $3 = -\left(\frac{4}{3}\right)(4) + b$.

We get $3 = -\frac{16}{3} + b$, and thus $3 + \frac{16}{3} = b$ and $b = \frac{25}{3}$. Thus for line p, $y = -\left(\frac{4}{3}\right)x + \frac{25}{3}$. If $(3,a)$ is on line p, then substituting $x = 3$ and $y = a$, we get

$$a = -\left(\frac{4}{3}\right)3 + \frac{25}{3} = -4 + \frac{25}{3} = \frac{13}{3} = 4\frac{1}{3}.$$

(Math Refresher #414)

41. **Choice E is correct.**

(Use Strategy 17: Use the given information effectively.)

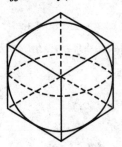

Clearly, we can see from the picture above that the diameter of the sphere has the same length as a side of the cube. We know

Volume of cube = (length of side)³ **1**

We are given

Volume of cube = 64 **2**

Substituting **2** into **1**, 64 = (length of side)³

Thus, length of side = 4 = diameter of sphere

(Math Refreshers #313 and #315)

42. **Choice J is correct.**

Let $\log_a b = x$

$$a^x = b$$ **1**

Take logs of both sides of **1** as follows:

$$\log_b a^x = \log_b b$$ **2**

Then from **2**, $x\log_b a = 1$

And we get

$$\log_b a = \frac{1}{x}$$

So $\log_a b = x = \dfrac{1}{\log_b a}$

(Math Refresher #617)

43. **Choice D is correct.**

(Use Strategy 14: Draw lines where appropriate.)

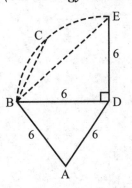

Given: $AB = BD = AD = 6$ **1**

C can be any point on arc *BE*, not just where it appears in the drawing above. For any point *C* on arc *BE*

$$CD = 6 \qquad \boxed{2}$$

because *CD* = radius of the circular arc.

(Use Strategy 3: The whole equals the sum of its parts.)

We want to find *P* = perimeter of

$$ABCD = AB + BC + CD + AD \qquad \boxed{3}$$

Substituting $\boxed{2}$ and $\boxed{1}$ into $\boxed{3}$,

$$P = 18 + BC \qquad \boxed{4}$$

We cannot find *BC*, but we can find the highest and lowest possible values for *BC*. Clearly, since *BC* is a side of a quadrilateral,

$$BC > 0 \qquad \boxed{5}$$

By looking at the diagram, we see that the highest possible value of *BC* occurs when *C* coincides with E.

$$BC \le BE \qquad \boxed{6}$$

must be true. *BE* can easily be found. Δ*EDB* is similar to one of the standard triangles discussed before.

(Use Strategy 18: Remember special right triangles.)

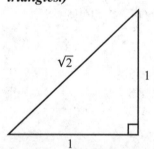

Corresponding sides of similar triangles are proportional, so that

$$\frac{\sqrt{2}}{1} = \frac{BE}{6}$$

$$\text{or} \quad BE = 6\sqrt{2} \qquad \boxed{7}$$

Substituting $\boxed{7}$ into $\boxed{6}$,

$$BC \le 6\sqrt{2} \qquad \boxed{8}$$

Comparing $\boxed{4}$ and $\boxed{8}$,

$$P = 18 + BC \le 18 + 6\sqrt{2} \qquad \boxed{9}$$

Comparing $\boxed{4}$ and $\boxed{5}$,

$$P = 18 + BC > 18 \qquad \boxed{10}$$

From $\boxed{9}$ and $\boxed{10}$ together,

$$18 < P \le 18 + 6\sqrt{2}$$

(Math Refreshers #431, #507, #509, and #510)

44. Choice J is correct.

(Use Strategy 7: Use numerics to help find the answer.)

You can show that

$$\left|\frac{x}{y}\right| = \frac{|x|}{|y|}$$

For example: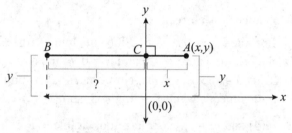

(Math Refresher #615)

45. Choice D is correct.

(Use Strategy 14: Label unknown quantities to help find the answer.)

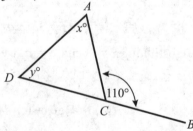

As shown in the diagram above, the *y*-coordinates of *A* and *B* must be the same because they both lie along the same horizontal line. Since *B* lies to the left of the *y*-axis, its *x*-coordinate must be negative. Since $3AC = BC$, then the *x*-coordinate of *B* is $-3x$, and we already know that the *y*-coordinate is *y*.

Thus, $(-3x, y)$ is the answer.

(Math Refresher #410b)

46. Choice J is correct.

(Use Strategy 18: Remember isosceles triangle facts.)

Since $AC = CD$, we know that

$$x = y \qquad \boxed{1}$$

We also know that

$$m\angle ACB = m\angle D + m\angle A \qquad \boxed{2}$$

Substituting the given into $\boxed{2}$, we have

$$110 = y + x \qquad \boxed{3}$$

Substituting 1 into 3, we get
$$110 = y + y$$
$$110 = 2y$$

(Math Refreshers #507 and #406)

47. Choice A is correct.

    (Use Strategy 14: Draw lines and label sides.)

    Draw the triangle separate from the circle and let side $AB = x$

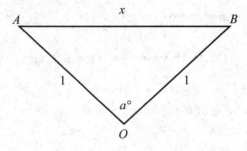

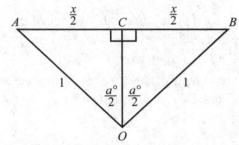

Now draw a perpendicular, OC. Side $AC = \dfrac{x}{2}$ and $\angle AOC = \dfrac{a}{2}$ (see above).

$$\sin\frac{a}{2} = \frac{\frac{x}{2}}{1} = \frac{x}{2}$$

$$x = 2\left(\sin\frac{a}{2}\right)$$

Remember that $\sin\dfrac{a}{2} = \sqrt{\dfrac{1 - \cos a}{2}}$;

therefore $x = 2\sqrt{\dfrac{1 - \cos a}{2}}$;

(Math Refresher #901)

48. Choice H is correct.

    (Use Strategy 17: Use the given information effectively.)

    For I, we have:

Clearly $DB < DA$. So I could not be true.

For II, we have:

Clearly D can be the same distance from 2 points (A and B), but not from 3, so II does not apply.

Only Choice C, III only, is now possible. Choice III is demonstrated below, although it was not necessary for us to examine it.

By definition, all points on the circle are the same distance from the center. So $DA = DB = DC$.

(Math Refreshers #303 and #310)

49. Choice A is correct.

    It can be seen that the dark region in Choice A is common to sets A, B, and C. Thus the diagram in Choice A describes the dark region as the set of elements that belongs to all of the sets A, B, and C.

    (Math Refresher #803)

50. Choice F is correct.

    (Use Strategy 17: Use the given information effectively.)

    Since the slope of a line is constant, the *ratio* of the *difference* in y-coordinates to the *difference* in x-coordinates must be constant for any two points on the line. For points $(1,3)$ and $(3,5)$ this ratio is

    $$\frac{5 - 3}{3 - 1} = 1$$

    Thus, for points $(6,y)$ and $(3,5)$ we must have

    $$\frac{y - 5}{6 - 3} = 1$$

    Therefore,

    $$y - 5 = 3$$
    $$\text{and } y = 8.$$

    (Math Refresher #416)

51. Choice D is correct.

    (Use Strategy 10: Know how to use units.)

    $\left(\dfrac{p \text{ gallons}}{\text{cars}}\right) \times (r \text{ cars}) = pr$ gallons for each month

    $\dfrac{q \text{ gallons}}{pr \dfrac{\text{gallons}}{\text{months}}} = \dfrac{q}{pr}$ months

    (Math Refresher #121)

52. Choice G is correct.

    (Use Strategy 18: Know and use facts about triangles.)

    The graph of $y = 2x + 3$ forms a right triangle with the x-axis and the y-axis. When $x = 0, y = 3$, and when $y = 0, x = \dfrac{-3}{2}$.

    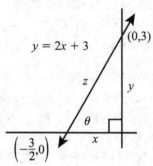

    By the Pythagorean theorem, $x^2 + y^2 = z^2$, so with

    $$x = \frac{3}{2} \text{ and } y = 3,$$

    $$\left(\frac{3}{2}\right)^2 + 3^2 = z^2$$

    $$\frac{9}{4} + 9 = z^2$$

    $$9\left(\frac{1}{4} + 1\right) = z^2$$

    $$9\left(\frac{5}{4}\right) = z^2$$

    $$\sqrt{\frac{9 \times 5}{4}} = z$$

    $$\frac{3\sqrt{5}}{2} = z$$

    $$\sin \theta = \frac{y}{z} = \frac{3}{\dfrac{3\sqrt{5}}{2}} = \frac{2}{\sqrt{5}}$$

    (Math Refreshers #414, #415, and #901)

53. Choice C is correct.

    (Use Strategy 2: Translate from words into algebra.)

    We are told that the area of the square is twice the area of the triangle. This translates into:

    $$a^2 = 2\left(\frac{1}{2}b \times c\right)$$
    $$a^2 = bc \qquad \boxed{1}$$

    We are given that $bc = 100$ $\qquad \boxed{2}$

    Substituting $\boxed{2}$ into $\boxed{1}$, we get
    $$a^2 = 100$$

    (Math Refreshers #200, #303, and #306)

54. Choice H is correct.

    The volume of the rectangular solid to be immersed is:

    $$V = (1 \text{ ft})(1 \text{ ft})(2 \text{ ft}) = 2 \text{ cu ft} \qquad \boxed{1}$$

    When the solid is immersed, the volume of the displaced water will be:

    $$(2 \text{ ft})(6 \text{ ft})(x \text{ ft}) = 12x \text{ cu ft} \qquad \boxed{2}$$

    where x represents the height of the displaced water. $\boxed{1}$ and $\boxed{1}$ must be equal. So

    $$2 \text{ cu ft} = 12x \text{ cu ft}$$
    $$\frac{1}{6} \text{ ft} = x$$

    (Use Strategy 10: Know how to use units.)

    $$\left(\frac{1}{6} \text{ ft}\right)\left(\frac{12 \text{ inches}}{\text{foot}}\right)$$

    $$= \frac{12}{6} \text{ inches}$$

    $= 2$ inches that the displaced water will rise.

    (Math Refreshers #312 and #121)

55. Choice A is correct.

    (Use Strategy 14: Label sides and angles.)

    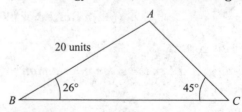

    Let side $BC = x$ and find angle A (sum of angles in a triangle $= 180°$; $A = 180 - 45 - 26 = 109°$).

From the law of sines:

$$\frac{\sin 45°}{20} = \frac{\sin 109°}{x}$$
$$x(\sin 45°) = 20(\sin 109°)$$
$$x = 20\left(\frac{\sin 109°}{\sin 45°}\right)$$

(Math Refresher #901)

56. Choice K is correct.

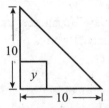

We know that the area of a triangle =

$$\frac{1}{2} \times \text{base} \times \text{height} \qquad \boxed{1}$$

Using the diagram and substituting into $\boxed{1}$, we get

$$\text{Area of triangle} = \frac{1}{2} \times 10 \times 10$$
$$= 50 \qquad \boxed{2}$$

(Use Strategy 2: Translate from words into algebra.)

We are told:

$$\text{area of square} = \frac{1}{5} \times \text{area of triangle} \qquad \boxed{3}$$

We know that

$$\text{area of a square} = (\text{side})^2 \qquad \boxed{4}$$

Using the diagram and substituting into $\boxed{4}$, we get

$$\text{area of square} = y^2 \qquad \boxed{5}$$

Substituting $\boxed{2}$ and $\boxed{5}$ into $\boxed{3}$, we have

$$y^2 = \frac{1}{5} \times 50$$
$$y^2 = 10 \qquad \boxed{6}$$

Take the square root of both sides of $\boxed{6}$. We get

$$y = \sqrt{10}$$

(Math Refreshers #200, #303, #307, and #430)

57. Choice A is correct.

(Use Strategy 17: Use the given information effectively.)

$y = -x^2 = -4$. $x = 2$ or $x = -2$. Since point B lies on the left side of the y-axis, $x = -2$.

(Math Refresher #410b)

58. Choice G is correct.

(Use Strategy 13: Subtract equations.)

Using $C = md + t$, if the business trip were increased by 5 days, $C' = m(d + 5) + t$. Subtracting equations, $C' - C = m(d + 5) + t - (md + t) = md + 5m + t - md - t = 5m$.

(Math Refresher #122)

59. Choice C is correct.

Where the graph intersects the x-axis, $y = 0$. Thus we set $y = 0 = x^4 + x^3$

We can write this as

$$x^3(x + 1) = 0$$

Thus $x = 0$ and $x = -1$.

The graph therefore intersects the x-axis at two points.

(Math Refresher #415)

60. Choice J is correct.

The procedure, as described, can be summarized in the following table:

Given Container	−	Receiving Container	=	Excess to 50 cm³ Container
25 cm³	−	16 cm³	=	9 cm³
16 cm³	−	9 cm³	=	7 cm³
9 cm³	−	4 cm³	=	5 cm³
4 cm³	−	1 cm³	=	3 cm³
		Total	=	24 cm³

(Use Strategy 2: Remember the definition of percent.)

Thus, $\frac{24 \text{ cm}^3}{50 \text{ cm}^3} \times 100 = 48\%$ of the 50 cm³ container is full.

(Use Strategy 3: The whole equals the sum of its parts.)

So, $100\% - 48\% = 52\%$ of the 50 cm³ container is empty.

(Math Refresher #107)

EXPLANATORY ANSWERS

Section 3: Reading Test

As you read these explanatory answers, you are advised to refer to the "9 Reading Comprehension Strategies" (beginning on page 102) whenever a specific strategy is referred to in the answer. Of particular importance is the Reading Comprehension Strategy 2 (page 105).

Note: *All Reading questions use Reading Strategies 1, 2, and 3 (pages 102–108) as well as other strategies indicated.*

1. Choice C is correct, and this frustration culminates in the questions Duncan asks and his pronouncement that he is leaving for good in lines 83–84. There are elements of rage in his behavior and he apparently has few friends (line 11), but Choice A is incorrect because it does not reflect the most significant contributing factor. Choice B is incorrect because there is no evidence of abuse other than boring conversation, and Choice D is incorrect because Duncan's immersion in novels is not portrayed as delusional.

2. Choice J is correct. These lines indirectly summarize what family members are saying to themselves (and perhaps to each other) about Duncan's dissatisfaction and unpleasant mood; in fact, the paragraph culminates in a diagnosis attributed to the aunts (lines 12–14). Choices F, G, and H are unsupported and are therefore incorrect.

3. Choice A is correct. It is the best answer because it is not the style or plot that moves Duncan to confront his family, but the questions about life in which he apparently takes a passionate interest. Choice B is incorrect because the novels clearly represent more than entertainment to Duncan. Choice C is incorrect; lines 11–12 point out that Duncan has never brought friends home, but we don't know anything about Duncan's life outside of his family home. Choice D is incorrect; he

is studying something he displays no interest in throughout the passage, and line 21 points out that he has stopped attending classes.

4. Choice J is correct. Choice F is incorrect because when Duncan "explodes into the living room" waving books at the family, he appears to be in the grip of passion, not engaging in calculated behavior or necessarily cognizant of his family's reaction. Choice G is incorrect because there is no evidence that Duncan is losing touch with reality; in fact, he believes it is his family who is out of touch with reality (line 59). Choice H is incorrect because Duncan may well believe himself to be intellectually superior, but this is not a claim he makes explicitly as Choice H indicates.

5. Choice B is correct because up to this point, he has expressed himself, it is implied, only in angry moods and reading out loud from novels. Choices A and C are not supported and are incorrect. Choice D is incorrect because while Duncan explicitly makes known his frustrations with his family, they are largely puzzled and attribute his behavior to "growing pains" (line 88). Uncle Two's request for an apology relates only to the remark about table conversation, not Duncan's behavior prior to this incident.

6. Choice F is correct and best reflects Duncan's character throughout the passage. Choice G reflects what his family believed his purpose to be, but not Duncan's actual inclination. Choices H and J do not reflect motives for dropping out of school supported in the story and are incorrect.

7. Choice D is correct, as his family's total lack of interest in "getting to the bottom of things" (lines 77–78), for example exploring the existence of God, moves the story to its climax, Duncan's

decision to leave. We could surmise that there is some truth in Choices A, B, and C, but these answers are not the best choices; they are incorrect.

8. Choice G is correct. The description of the novel's style in lines 30–35 very much echoes the descriptions of Duncan as wild and emotional, as does the complexity Duncan craves in conversation. Choices F and H are incorrect; no mention is made of the family's reaction on moral grounds, or their reactions at all, except to point out that the uncles have skimmed the abridged version of *Crime and Punishment*. Choice J is incorrect because, apparently, the novels consume Duncan's time instead of college.

9. Choice D is correct. From the first paragraph on, all the family members tend to underestimate the extent of Duncan's dissatisfaction and its root cause. They do not believe Duncan is serious when he announces his departure in the final paragraph and assume he will eventually "talk the same as all the rest of us." None of the other choices accurately describes the family's reaction, so A, B, and C are all incorrect.

10. Choice H is correct. Choice F is incorrect; "his parents" (lines 36–37) are mentioned collectively, and both his mother and father singly. Choice G is incorrect, because choosing to follow in any of his family members' footsteps is never an issue in the story. Choice J is incorrect because the dialogue among the family is too limited to make this point.

11. Choice B is correct. See lines 1–10: The comments of people from the "other world" refer to the Civil War, Southern "outrages," and most tellingly an "excellent colored man."

12. Choice G is correct. See lines 1–13: The author is black; the "other world" is the world of whites.

13. Choice D is correct. See lines 1–13. Choices A and C are incorrect; the passage does not refer to being poor or liberal. Choice B is incorrect; the reference to the Civil War battle at Mechanicsville is in the past tense, telling us that the context is after the Civil War and thus after slavery.

14. Choice F is crrect. The comments are both patronizing and condescending—e.g., "I know an excellent colored man" (lines 7–8). The white

people making these comments are hesitant, curious, and compassionate (lines 5–6), but they are not characterized as hostile.

15. Choice C is correct. See lines 23–24: The author was "merry" until rejected by his new classmate. The shadow signifies sadness.

16. Choice H is correct. See lines 25–26: When the new girl rejects his card, "it dawned on me . . . that I was different. . . ."

17. Choice C is correct. The metaphor of a veil describes both the barrier between the races and opportunities unavailable to blacks (lines 35–37). The veil also refers to what it means to be black in a racially divided world (lines 37–40). By contrast, human values are held in common by both races: ". . . like, mayhap, in heart and life and longing. . . ." (lines 27–28).

18. Choice J is correct. See line 30: Initially the author "held all beyond [the veil] in common contempt."

19. Choice D is correct. See lines 55–58: ". . . this double-consciousness, this sense of always looking at one's self through the eyes of others, of measuring one's soul by the tape of a world that looks on in amused contempt and pity."

20. Choice H is correct. See the last paragraph: "He simply wishes to make it possible for a man to be both a Negro and an American. . . ." Choices F and J are things the black man does *not* wish to do (lines 67–71). Choice G is incorrect because there is no reference to social status.

21. Choice B is correct. Although in the first paragraph Lincoln refers to the "great contest" only obliquely—e.g., "progress of our arms"—the first sentence of paragraph 2 explicitly refers to the "civil war."

22. Choice J is correct. Lincoln states that he is hopeful (line 13), but he is also guarded: He sees the "progress of our arms" as "reasonably" encouraging but also makes "no prediction in regard to [the war]" (lines 13–14).

23. Choice D is correct. Paragraph 2 makes it clear that both sides dreaded and sought to avert war (line 17). Thus neither side was eager (Choice A)

or resigned (Choice B) to war. Choice C is incorrect; there is no mention of war preparations; in addition, "Neither party expected for the war the magnitude or the duration which it has already attained" (lines 36–37).

24. Choice F is correct. The speech points to all three reasons for the war: slavery (lines 28–30), the "peculiar and powerful" economic interests of slave labor (line 29), and the North's determination to "accept war rather than let [the nation] perish" (line 25).

25. Choice C is correct. Lincoln emphasizes that both the North and South sought to avoid war, but he tips the scale of responsibility toward the South: ". . . one of them [the South] would make war rather than let the nation survive; and the other [the North] would accept war rather than let [the nation] perish" (lines 23–25). Lincoln sees the South as the primary aggressor: ". . . the government claimed no right to do more than to restrict the territorial enlargement of [slavery]" (lines 33–35).

26. Choice G is correct. See lines 26–28: "One-eighth of the whole population were colored slaves . . . localized in the Southern part of [the nation]."

27. Choice D is correct. See lines 28–30, where Lincoln names slavery as the cause of the war: "These slaves constituted a peculiar and powerful interest. All knew that this interest was, somehow, the cause of the war." Choice D, the Emancipation Proclamation, is the only choice that ended slavery.

28. Choice F is correct: "the bondman's two hundred and fifty years of unrequited toil" (lines 53–54).

29. Choice C is correct. Lincoln expresses hope for a quick end to the war, but he acknowledges that if God wills it, the war may "continue until all the wealth piled by the bondman's two hundred and fifty years of unrequited toil shall be sunk" (lines 51–54).

30. Choice H is correct. Lincoln's tone is somber, resigned, and conciliatory. He expresses the war-weariness of the nation but accepts that divine will directs the outcome (lines 49–58). He also prepares us for the possibility of reconciliation between North and South when he refers to what Northerners and Southerners have in common: "Both read

the same Bible. . . " (lines 41–42). The last paragraph, especially, stresses the need to "bind up the nation's wounds," "with malice toward none; with charity toward all."

31. Choice D is correct. See lines 10–11: "Therefore it has no formula. . . ."

32. Choice F is correct. See lines 23–24 and 86–88, indicating that there were two alkali substances, sodium oxide and potassium oxide.

33. Choice C is correct. See lines 41–42 stating that potassium glass was typical of medieval Europe.

34. Choice H is correct. Lines 12–15 explain the basis for classification, and the classification is explicitly pointed out in lines 16 ("First there are . . ."), 43 ("The second main class . . ."), and 57 ("The last main class . . .").

35. Choice D is correct. See lines 67–68: "glass is often made by mixing ingredients from different geographical regions."

36. Choice J is correct. See the last paragraph, especially lines 81–83, indicating that glassmakers were ignorant of chemistry by modern standards, and lines 95–97, indicating that the glass craftsman's tricks need not be based on a modern knowledge of chemistry in order to succeed.

37. Choice B is correct. See lines 50–51. Glass was colored in this manner until new techniques were developed in the nineteenth century and beyond, as explained throughout paragraph 6.

38. Choice G is correct. Lines 39–42 describe common compositions of glass and the general regions of the world where each composition was likely to be encountered.

39. Choice D is correct. Lines 61–62 mention that scrap glass was and still is a component of the glassmaking process.

40. Choice G is correct. See line 44. The functions of additives are summarized in the fifth paragraph. Liquefying is not one of them because at this stage, the idea is that glass, which began in a liquid state, is becoming rigid matter (see the introduction to this passage, too).

EXPLANATORY ANSWERS

Section 4: Science Test

1. Choice D is correct. The average observed time in the previous trials was 0.80 s.

2. Choice H is correct. In the experimental design, it states that the masses are equal (500 g) and that "the blocks had the same dimensions," meaning there is no difference in volume or surface area.

3. Choice C is correct. As reported in the third paragraph of Experiment 1, the expected v_f for this test was 16 ft/s; neither block reached this velocity. In Experiment 2, the expected v_f was 22.63 ft/s; again, neither block reached this velocity. If none of the blocks reached their expected velocity, they must have experienced drag (in this case, friction).

4. Choice F is correct. Because the incline is greater than in Experiment 2, the block will move faster, resulting in *less* observed time. Experiments 1 and 2 have shown that a glass block travels faster than an equal-size wooden block, so we can expect the same to occur at $h = 8$.

5. Choice A is correct. If the actual time of travel (over the same distance) is less than the data recorded, the blocks are traveling at a higher velocity than calculated.

6. Choice J is correct. In any real-world test, friction will cause the final velocities to be lower; different materials (even with identical surface areas) are subject to different amounts of friction.

7. Choice D is correct. The most massive chicken is neither at the top nor at the bottom of the pecking order; there appears to be no relationship between mass and rank.

8. Choice G is correct. The chicken's mass is irrelevant. Age appears to be a primary factor determining rank in the pecking order; since this chicken is the third oldest, he should take a position between hens F (second) and C (formerly third).

9. Choice C is correct. The oldest chickens are at the top of the pecking order (1 and 2), while the youngest chickens are at the bottom (5 and 6).

10. Choice H is correct. While not the only factor for determining rank (see chickens C and E), age is the factor that most closely correlates.

11. Choice D is correct. Age is a greater determining factor than mass, size, or heredity.

12. Choice H is correct. Table 1 shows that chicken E is the oldest male in the pen once chicken A is removed. Apart from his promotion, the pecking order remains unchanged.

13. Choice B is correct. Copper was used for the first experiment, while zinc was used for the second experiment.

14. Choice J is correct. The 1973 pennies have the same density as copper, while the 1995 pennies have a density closer in value to that of zinc.

15. Choice C is correct. The slope of the graph equals mass (*y*-value) divided by volume (*x*-value), which is also how density is calculated.

16. Choice J is correct. You have been given only the densities of a small number of metals. While the sample could be zinc, there are not enough data for a solid conclusion.

17. Choice C is correct. For the same volume (mL), greater density (g/mL) equals greater mass (g), regardless of the exact value of the volume (therefore, Choice D is incorrect). From Table 2, we see that the densest metal is copper (8.9 g/mL), followed by lead (7.9 g/mL), tin (7.3 g/mL), zinc (7.0 g/mL), and aluminum (2.7 g/mL).

18. Choice F is correct. Examining the first row of the table, we see that the mystery metal has a density (mass/volume) of 27.0 g/10.0 mL or 2.7 g/mL. Since Table 2 indicates that aluminum also has a density of about 2.7 g/mL, and we know from the question that this is a pure metal, they are most likely the same.

19. Choice D is correct. The largest value on the female half of Figure 1 belongs to the 35–39 age range.

20. Choice H is correct. The trend line intersects the 2050 vertical roughly halfway between 9 and 10 billion.

21. Choice C is correct. In Figure 1 (2000), the values for both males and females in the 60–64 age range are near 1.5 million. In Figure 2 (2025), the values for both males and females in the 60–64 age range are greater than 2 million.

22. Choice J is correct. Figures 1 and 3 both feature actual population data from 2000 (eliminating Choices F and G). The population distribution of Bangladesh goes from large to small as age increases, while the UK features a swell at middle age, meaning the average individual in the UK has a longer life expectancy than the average individual in Bangladesh (eliminating Choice H).

23. Choice D is correct. The 6 billion mark is left of (before) the 2000 mark and 7 billion occurs right of (after) the 2010 mark, meaning there are more than 10 years between each billion (eliminating Choices A and B). The distance between 8 and 9 billion (or 3 and 4 billion) appears to be even greater than the distance between 6 and 7 billion, suggesting a range of 11–15 years.

24. Choice F is correct. First, compare the densities (column 2): only the inner core or outer core contain samples of density 12.0 g/cm³. Additionally, the sample is solid; since the outer core is in a liquid state (column 4), the sample must come from the inner core.

25. Choice D is correct. Looking at column 2, the density of oceanic crust (2.9–3.1) is greater than the density of continental crust (2.7). Both crusts are solid, not liquid.

26. Choice F is correct. Based on Figure 1, we know that the rows in Table 1 are ordered from innermost layer to outermost layer. So, if density (column 2) and temperature (column 3) both decrease as you read down the columns, then the innermost layers of Earth have a higher density and a higher temperature than the outermost layers.

27. Choice D is correct. Choice A is disproved by column 5 (Minerals and Elements Present) of Table 1, while Choices B and C are disproved by column 3 (Temperature). Because of extreme high pressure, the higher-temperature inner core remains a solid.

28. Choice F is correct. The upper mantle is plastic, while the lower mantle and oceanic crust are both solid (eliminating Choices G and J). Earthquakes are caused by interactions of solid plates, not the movement of liquid.

29. Choice D is correct. Birds are shown eating insects (on the right side of Figure 1). Cougars and rodents are not in the same web, bears eat deer (not the other way around), and owls do not eat plants.

30. Choice G is correct. When the owl eats the rodents, it gains energy (as all creatures do when they eat food); the arrow therefore points in the direction of energy flow.

31. Choice D is correct. In Figure 2, about 10% of the energy from the previous level is passed on (6000–600–60–6); 6 kilocalories at the tertiary level would yield only 0.6 kilocalories per square meter per year for the consumer.

32. Choice G is correct. The correct answer is G. Food webs (unlike energy pyramids) are able to show an organism eating multiple food sources.

33. Choice A is correct. The arrow indicates which direction the energy is traveling (identifies the eater, not the eaten). Plants are eaten by insects, which are eaten by skunks. According to Figure 1, cougars do not eat bears, owls do not eat plants, and birds do not eat cougars, so none of the other choices is correct.

34. Choice J is correct. From the passage: "Newton proposed that perhaps the individual atoms in a sample of gas are in fact arranged in a static lattice."

35. Choice D is correct. The static theory assumes that atoms in a gas are both static (not moving) and in a state of mutual repulsion. Collision of atoms in such a state would be impossible, leaving us with kinetic molecular theory as an explanation. "Calorics" are an element of static theory, so Choice C is incorrect.

36. Choice F is correct. As noted in the passage, "Heat . . . was nothing more than the motion of these atoms," and "the motion of the atoms causes their spread." Therefore, more heat equals more motion, which poses a greater risk for collision. In order to minimize the risk, atoms in a gas spread out, according to kinetic molecular theory.

37. Choice A is correct. Increased heat means increased motion; if the atoms are not allowed to spread out (i.e., if the volume of the gas is kept constant), tremendous amounts of pressure will build up until the gas forcefully expels heat or increases in volume: an explosion.

38. Choice J is correct. Since the molecules of a gas do not interact in kinetic molecular theory, the pressure of the gas is not dependent on its chemical makeup.

39. Choice C is correct. As the kinetic molecular theory of gases states, the atoms in a gas are moving around so quickly and are not close enough together (as in a solid or liquid) to be able to interact with each other, except when, through the random motion of atoms, they collide with each other.

40. Choice F is correct. Heat affects the volume of a gas in both theories, although in different ways; this means Choices H and J are incorrect. Molecules do not move in static theory, while they move at high speeds in kinetic molecular theory.

WHAT YOU MUST DO
NOW TO RAISE YOUR ACT SCORE

1. Follow the directions on pages 615–623 to find your scale score for the ACT Test you've just taken. These results will give you a good idea about how hard you'll need to study in order to achieve a certain score on the actual ACT.

   Using your scale score count as a basis, indicate for yourself your areas of strength and weakness as revealed by the Norms Tables on pages 618–619.

2. Eliminate your weaknesses in each of the ACT Test areas by taking the following Giant Steps toward ACT success:

Reading Part

Giant Step 1

Take advantage of the Reading Strategies that begin on page 102. Read again the explanatory answer for each of the Reading questions that you got wrong. Refer to the Reading Strategy that applies to each of your incorrect answers. Learn each of these Reading Strategies thoroughly. These strategies are crucial if you want to raise your ACT score substantially.

Giant Step 2

You can improve your vocabulary by doing the following:

1. Read as widely as possible—not only novels. Non-fiction is important too—and don't forget to read newspapers and magazines.

2. Listen to people who speak well. Tune in to worth-while TV programs.

3. Use the dictionary frequently and extensively—at home, on the bus, at work, etc.

4. Review the Hot Prefixes and Roots beginning on page 128.

Math Part

Giant Step 3

Make good use of the 19 Math Strategies that begin on page 44. Read again the solutions for each Math question that you answered incorrectly. Refer to the Math Strategy that applies to each of your incorrect answers. Learn each of these Math Strategies thoroughly. We repeat that these strategies are crucial if you want to raise your ACT Math score substantially.

Giant Step 4

You may want to take the 101 Most Important Math Questions You Need to Know How to Solve test beginning on page 13 and follow the directions after the test for a basic Math skills diagnosis.

For each Math question that you got wrong on the test, note the reference to the Complete ACT Math Refresher section beginning on page 147. This reference will explain clearly the mathematical principle involved in the solution of the question you answered incorrectly. Learn that particular mathematical principle thoroughly.

For Both the Math and Reading Parts

Giant Step 5

You may want to take the World's Shortest Practice Test for the ACT Exam beginning on page 1 to assess whether you're using the best strategies for the questions.

For the English Test and Writing Part

Giant Step 6

Take a look at Part 9, the ACT Writing Test, which describes the Writing Section. For the English Test, make use of Part 7, A Brief Review of English Grammar, and Part 8, the Complete ACT Grammar and Usage Refresher.

If you do the job *right* and follow the steps listed above, you are likely to raise your ACT score significantly.

Remember:

I am the master of my fate:
I am the captain of my soul.

—From the poem "Invictus"
by William Ernest Henley

NOTES